An Introduction to the Biology of Marine Life

An Introduction to the

Biology of Marine Life

Second Edition

James L. Sumich
Grossmont College

Wm. C. Brown Company Publishers
Dubuque, Iowa

wcb

Wm. C. Brown
Chairman of the Board

Larry W. Brown
President, WCB Group

Book Team

Louise Barrett Welp/
John Stout
Editors

Marilyn A. Phelps
Designer

Lynne M. Meyers
Production Editor

Faye M. Huseman
Visual Research

Wm. C. Brown Company Publishers, College Division

Lawrence E. Cremer
President

Raymond C. Deveaux
Vice President/Product Development

David Wm. Smith
Assistant Vice President/National Sales Manager

Matt Coghlan
National Marketing Manager

David A. Corona
Director of Production Development and Design

William A. Moss
Production Editorial Manager

Marilyn Phelps
Manager of Design

Mary M. Heller
Visual Research Manager

Cover photo/Bud Higdon
Biological illustrations/Stephen R. Haney
Charts, graphs and maps/Sandra G. Sumich
Color photographs/Dr. Hans Bertsch and Michael Weeks

Library of Congress Catalog Card Number 79-52783

ISBN 0-697-04574-9

Printed in the United States of America

Contents

Preface

An Introduction to the Biology of Marine Life was written to satisfy the growing need for an introductory college-level text dealing with the biology of marine plants and animals. Developments in the field of marine biology during the past decade have shown that courses in this subject provide an exciting and effective framework for presenting basic biological principles. As a result, marine biology courses for the nonmajor or premajor student have become increasingly popular.

It is for the introductory marine biology student that this text is written. No previous knowledge of marine biology is assumed. However, some general exposure to the basic concepts of biology would be helpful. I have, by intent, used selected groups of marine plants and animals to develop an understanding of biological principles and processes that are basic to all forms of life in the sea. To build on these basics, additional information dealing with several aspects of marine ecology and physiology is presented. Students are also encouraged, through supplementary reading lists at the end of each chapter, to go beyond the confines of the text for further information. Additional references are listed at the end of the text. These will normally be useful only for the more advanced students who have the enthusiasm and communication skills necessary to cope with the challenges of reading the original literature.

Within the broad scope of "marine biology," I have exercised some license in topic selection and organization. This text includes somewhat more material than the average student can assimilate in a single semester. Instructors have the option to select and mold the material to match their teaching styles and time limitations. Suggestions also are provided in the accompanying instructor's manual for using this test for a two-quarter or two-semester course with judicious use of outside supplementary readings.

The first two chapters consist of a general introduction to the marine environment, its inhabitants, and how the two have evolved together to the present. Chapter 3 is a cursory survey of marine animal groups, included here to avoid cumbersome definitions and descriptions in later discussions. Chapters 4, 6, and 9 emphasize the roles that marine plants and animals assume in their respective environmental situations. In chapters 5, 7, and 8, the structural and physiological adaptations necessary to adequately fill those roles are examined in more detail. In the final chapter, I have attempted to develop a perspective for understanding the effects of human intervention into marine ecosystems, such as food-gathering and pollution. Each chapter contains numerous illustrations, graphs, and charts to assist students in visualizing the concepts presented. End-of-chapter summaries and questions for discussion are designed to further encourage exploration of the topics covered.

I have avoided regional limitations where practical. This text is therefore of little use as a detailed field guide for local marine plants and animals. A companion text, *Laboratory and Field Investigations in Marine Biology,* by J. L. Sumich and G. H. Dudley, is available for courses emphasizing field or laboratory experiences.

The widespread and positive reception of the first edition of this text has been very encouraging. This edition is not a radical revision of the first, but rather a restrained attempt to better meet the needs of its users. The many suggestions and comments from readers of the first edition have been considered in the modifications that were made. The chapter order has been rearranged to follow a more logical topic sequence by placing the discussion of the benthos before the chapters on marine plants and plant productivity. In addition, the sections on estuaries and deep-sea benthos have been expanded, and a new section on the feeding habits and distribution of zooplankton has been added to chapter 7.

It is impossible to properly credit all the individuals involved in the development of this text. Useful comments and criticisms of the first edition were offered by the many students and instructors who have used the text during the course of several semesters. I thank my instructors of the past and colleagues of the present for their contributions to my education and to this book. Special thanks also go to the individuals and institutions that graciously supplied many of the photographs. Michael Weeks and Dr. Hans Bertsch, Curator of Marine Invertebrates of the San Diego Natural History Museum, provided the photographs for the color plates. Dr. Bertsch acknowledges the assistance of Earthwatch research grants, which enabled him to obtain several of the photographs published here. Most of the biological illustrations are the work of a fine artist, Steve Haney. Figures 3.12 and 7.2 were drawn by Eva Oemick. Most of all, I thank my patient wife, Sandy, who has encouraged and helped me with this endeavor from conception to completion. Without her efforts as typist, critic, draftsperson, and friend, this text would not have been written.

James L. Sumich

An Introduction to the Biology of Marine Life

Earth from space. Courtesy National Aeronautics and Space Administration.

The Ocean as a Habitat

1

The World Ocean
Properties of Seawater
The Ocean in Motion
Classification of the Marine Environment

The ocean environment is home for a tremendous variety of plants and animals that are uniquely adapted to the special conditions of the sea. To a large extent, the general features of these organisms and the variety of marine life itself are products of the many properties of the ocean habitat. The first section of this chapter is, therefore, a brief survey of the geography of the ocean basins, and is followed by a discussion of some properties of seawater. Finally, mechanisms and patterns of ocean circulation are presented.

The World Ocean

The world ocean covers approximately 70% of the earth's surface with an average depth of about 3,700 m. This may seem like a lot of water, but when compared to the earth's diameter of 13,250 km, the ocean is actually a very thin film of water covering the earth's crust. On a globe scaled down to the size of a basketball, the depth of the oceans could be represented by the water left after wiping the globe with a wet cloth. Conventionally, the world ocean has been separated into four major ocean basins: the **Atlantic, Pacific, Indian,** and **Arctic** oceans. A more realistic but less workable approach is to view the marine environment as one large interconnected ocean system. This can best be visualized from a South Polar view of the earth (fig. 1.1). The Antarctic

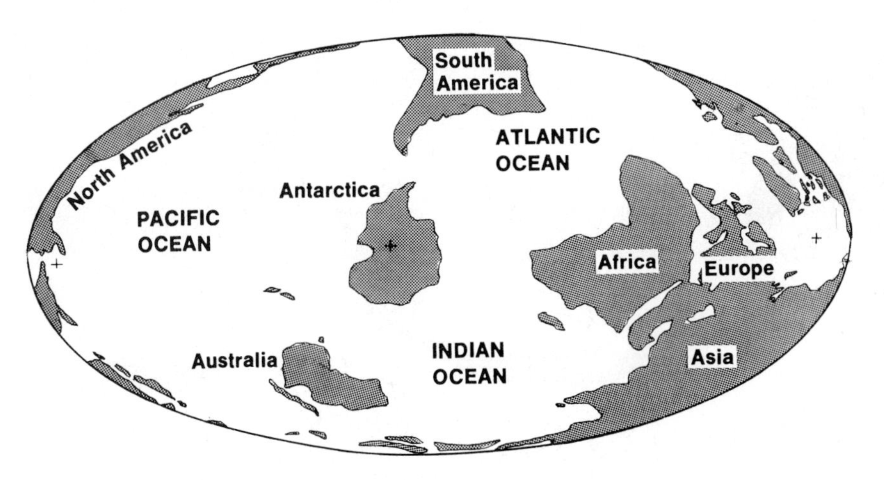

Fig. 1.1 South Polar view of the world ocean, showing the extensive oceanic connections between major ocean basins. (+) indicates the positions of the North and South Poles.

continent is surrounded by an "Antarctic Ocean," which has three large embayments extending northward. These three oceanic extensions, partially separated by continental barriers, are the Atlantic, Pacific, and Indian oceans. Other smaller oceans and seas, such as the Arctic Ocean and the Mediterranean Sea, project from the margins of the larger ocean basins. Connections between the major ocean basins permit exchange of seawater and marine organisms.

Figure 1.2 presents a more conventional view of the world ocean. Note that this type of map does not emphasize the extensive southern connections that are apparent in figure 1.1. The format of figure 1.2 is more useful because interest in the marine environment has been centered in the temperate and tropical regions of the earth. In addition, the equator is a very real physical boundary between the northern and southern halves of the large ocean basins. The curvature of the earth's surface causes areas near the equator to receive more radiant energy from the sun than equal-sized areas in polar regions. The resultant heat gradient from tropical to polar regions establishes the basic pattern of atmospheric and oceanic circulation. Surface ocean current patterns display a mirror-image symmetry in the northern and southern halves of the Pacific and Atlantic oceans. This hemispheric symmetry establishes the equator as a natural focus for the graphic representation of these features.

The distribution of continents and oceans over the earth's surface does not follow a regular pattern. Nearly two-thirds of the land area is located in the Northern Hemisphere. The Southern Hemisphere is an oceanic hemisphere, with 80% of its surface covered by water. The Pacific Ocean alone

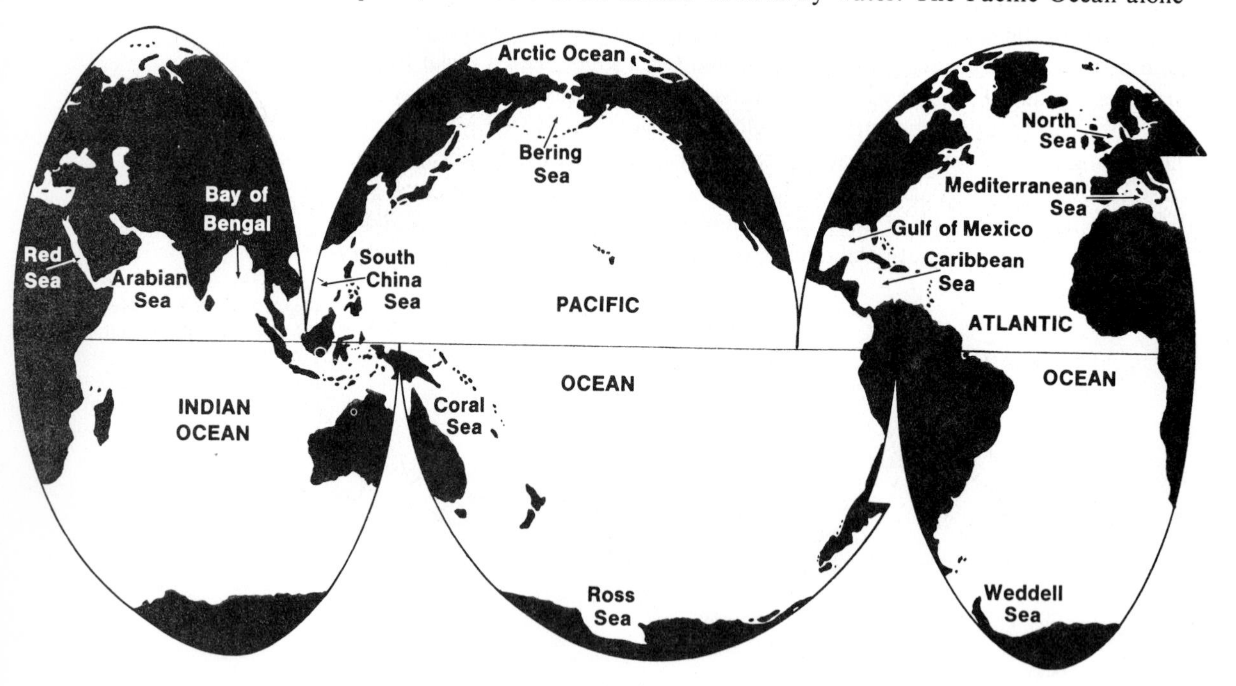

Fig. 1.2 An equatorial view of the world ocean.

Table 1.1. *Some Comparative Features of the Major Ocean Basins.*

Ocean	Area	Volume	Average Depth	Maximum Depth
	x10⁶km²	*x10⁶km³*	*m*	*m*
Pacific	165.2	707.6	4,282	11,022
Atlantic	82.4	323.6	3,926	9,200
Indian	73.4	291.0	3,963	7,460
Arctic	14.1	17.0	1,205	4,300
Caribbean	4.3	9.6	2,216	7,200
Mediterranean	3.0	4.2	1,429	4,600
Other	18.7	17.3		
Total	361.1	1,370.3	3,795	

accounts for nearly one-half of the total ocean area. Some statistics for the six largest ocean basins are listed in table 1.1.

Oceanic depths extend to over 11,000 m, but most of the ocean bottom lies between 3,000 and 6,000 m. An idealized cross section of an ocean basin (fig. 1.3) indicates the large-scale features of the ocean bottom.

The **continental shelf,** an underwater extension of the continent, is a structural part of the continental landmass, and would not be considered an oceanic feature if sea level were lowered by as little as 5% of its present average depth. In fact, much of what is now continental shelf was exposed as recently as 10,000 to 15,000 years ago during the last "Ice Age." The width of the continental shelves varies from almost nothing off Miami, Florida, to over 800 km north of Siberia in the Arctic Ocean. The continental shelves account for only about 8% of the ocean's surface area. However, this is equivalent to nearly one-sixth of the earth's total land area. Most continental shelves are relatively smooth and slope gently seaward. The outer edge of the shelf, sometimes called the **shelf break,** is a vaguely defined feature that usually occurs at depths of 120 to 200 m. Beyond the shelf break, the bottom steepens to become the **continental slope.** The slope is the boundary between the continental mass and the true ocean basin. The continental slope is steep, dropping rapidly to depths of 3,000 to 4,000 m.

A large portion of the deep ocean basin consists of flat, sediment-covered areas called **abyssal plains.** Most abyssal plains are situated near the margins

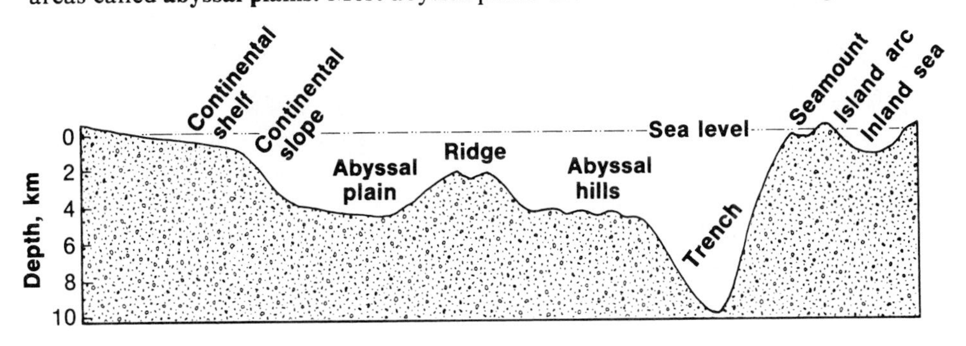

Fig. 1.3 An idealized cross section of the ocean bottom. The vertical scale is greatly exaggerated.

of the ocean basins at depths between 3,000 and 5,000 m. **Oceanic ridge** and **rise systems,** such as the Mid-Atlantic Ridge and East Pacific Rise, occupy over 30% of the ocean basin area. The ridge and rise systems are rugged linear features that form a continuous underwater mountain chain encircling the earth. Isolated peaks of these mountain systems occasionally extend above sea level to form **islands** such as Iceland and Ascension Island in the Atlantic Ocean. **Trenches** are distinctive ocean-floor features, generally deeper than 6,000 m. Most trenches, including the five deepest, are located along the margins of the Pacific Ocean. The Challenger Deep, in the Marianas Trench of the western North Pacific, extends to 11,022 m, the greatest depth found anywhere in the oceans. Trenches account for less than 2% of the ocean bottom area, but they are significant because of the rigorous temperature and pressure regimes imposed on their inhabitants.

Most oceanic islands and **seamounts** have been formed by volcanic action. Islands are volcanic features that extend above sea level; seamounts are those that do not. The majority of these features are located in the Pacific Ocean. Islands located in tropical areas are often capped by coral **atolls** or fringed by coral **reefs.**

Properties of Seawater

Many properties of seawater are crucial to the survival and well-being of the ocean's inhabitants. Water provides buoyancy and body support for swimming and floating organisms, thereby reducing the need for heavy skeletal structures. Water accounts for about 80–90% of the bulk of most marine organisms. Water is also the medium for most chemical reactions needed to sustain life. The life processes of marine organisms in turn alter many of the fundamental physical and chemical properties of seawater, including its transparency and chemical makeup. As a result, marine plants and animals are an integral part of the total marine environment. Understanding the interactions between these organisms and their environment requires a brief study of some of the significant physical and chemical attributes of seawater. The characteristics of pure water and seawater differ in some respects and are similar in others. For this reason it is helpful to consider first the basic properties of pure water, then to study the effects of dissolved substances on these properties.

Pure Water

Water is a very common substance on the earth's surface. It is abundant in its liquid form, while large quantities also exist as a gas in the atmosphere and as a solid in the form of ice and snow. The water molecule has a simple structure, yet its properties are very complex. It is composed of one atom of oxygen (O) and two atoms of hydrogen (H), which together form water (H_2O). The many unique properties of water stem from its unusual molecular shape. The two hydrogen atoms form an angle of about 105° with the oxygen atom (fig. 1.4). This configuration produces an **asymmetry** of the water molecule, with the oxygen atom dominating one end of the molecule and the hydrogen atoms dominating the other end. The bonds between the hydrogen atoms and the oxygen atom are formed by the sharing of two negatively charged electrons between each H—O association. The larger oxygen atom dominates the H—O association and attracts the electron pair. With an excess of electrons, the oxygen end of the water molecule assumes a slight negative charge. The hydrogen end of the molecule, by giving up part of its electron complement, is left with a small positive charge. The resultant electrical charge separation causes each water molecule to behave like a miniature magnet, one end with a positive charge and the other with a negative charge. Each end of one water molecule attracts the oppositely charged end of other water molecules. This attractive force creates a weak bond, called a **hydrogen bond** or **H-bond,** between adjacent water molecules (fig. 1.5). These bonds are much weaker than the H—O bond within a single water molecule and are continually breaking and reforming with other water molecules. Without H-bonding between molecules, water would boil at −80° C and freeze at −100° C, making life as we know it impossible. Hydrogen bonding also accounts for many other unique properties of water. Some of these properties are summarized in table 1.2 and discussed in more detail in the following paragraphs.

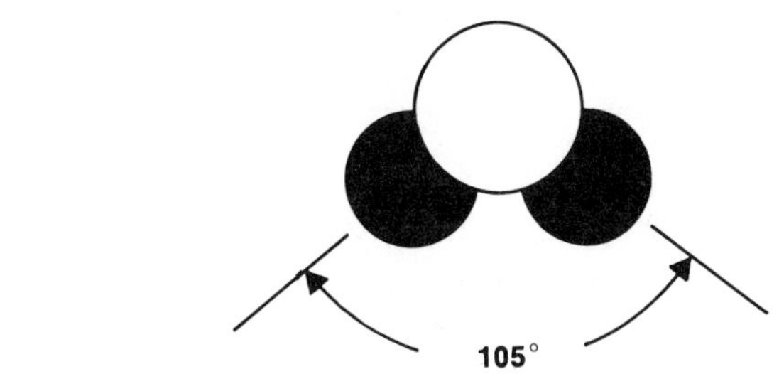

Fig. 1.4 The molecular configuration of water (H_2O). The O atom is shown in white, H in black. The oxygen end has a slight net negative charge, the other end a slight net positive charge.

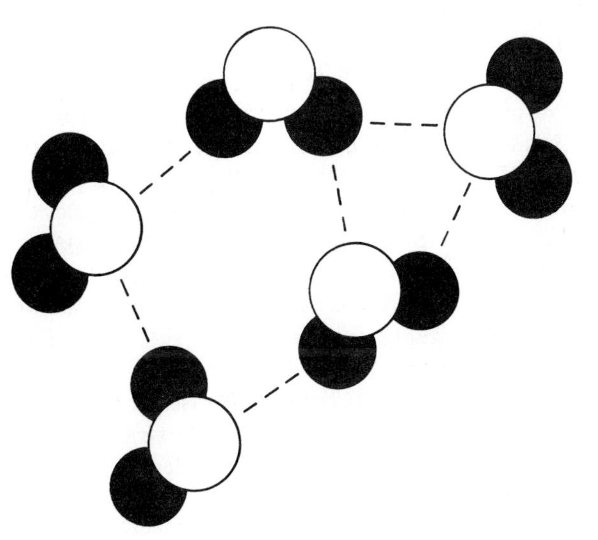

Fig. 1.5 Hydrogen bonding between adjacent water molecules. (---) represents hydrogen bonds.

Table 1.2. *Some Biologically Important Physical Properties of Water.*

Property	Comparison with Other Substances	Importance in Physical-Biological Environment
Surface tension	Highest of all liquids.	Important in physiology of the cell. Critical to position maintenance of surface organisms.
Thermal expansion	Temperature of maximum density decreases with increasing salinity. For pure water, it is at 4°C.	Fresh water and dilute seawater have their maximum density at temperatures above the freezing point. This property plays an important part in controlling temperature distribution and vertical circulation in lakes.
Heat capacity	Highest of all solids and liquids except liquid ammonia.	Prevents extreme ranges in temperature. Heat transfer by water movements is very large. Tends to maintain uniform body temperatures.
Conduction of heat	Highest of all liquids.	Although important on a small scale, as in living cells, mixing and circulation processes are far more important.
Latent heat of fusion	Highest except ammonia.	Temperature-moderating effect at freezing point owing to absorption or release of latent heat.
Latent heat of vaporization	Highest of all substances.	Large latent heat of evaporation is extremely important in heat and water transfer to atmosphere and in moderating marine temperature.
Dissolving power	In general, dissolves more substances and in greater quantities than any other liquid.	Maintains a large variety of substances together in solution.

Adapted from H. U. Sverdrup, Martin W. Johnson, and Richard H. Fleming, *The Oceans: Their Physics, Chemistry, and General Biology,* © 1942, Renewed 1970. By permission of Prentice-Hall, Inc., Englewood Cliffs, New Jersey.

Viscosity and Surface Tension

Hydrogen bonding between adjacent water molecules within the fluid mass tends to resist external forces that would separate these molecules. This property is known as **viscosity** and has a significant effect on floating and swimming marine organisms. The viscosity of water reduces the tendency of some organisms to sink by increasing the frictional resistance between themselves and nearby water molecules; but at the same time it magnifies problems of drag that must be overcome by actively swimming animals.

The mutual attraction of water molecules at the surface of a water mass (such as the air-sea boundary) creates a flexible molecular "skin" over the water surface. This is the **surface tension** of water, and is sufficiently strong to support the full weight of a water strider (fig. 1.6). Both surface tension and viscosity are temperature-dependent, increasing with decreasing temperature.

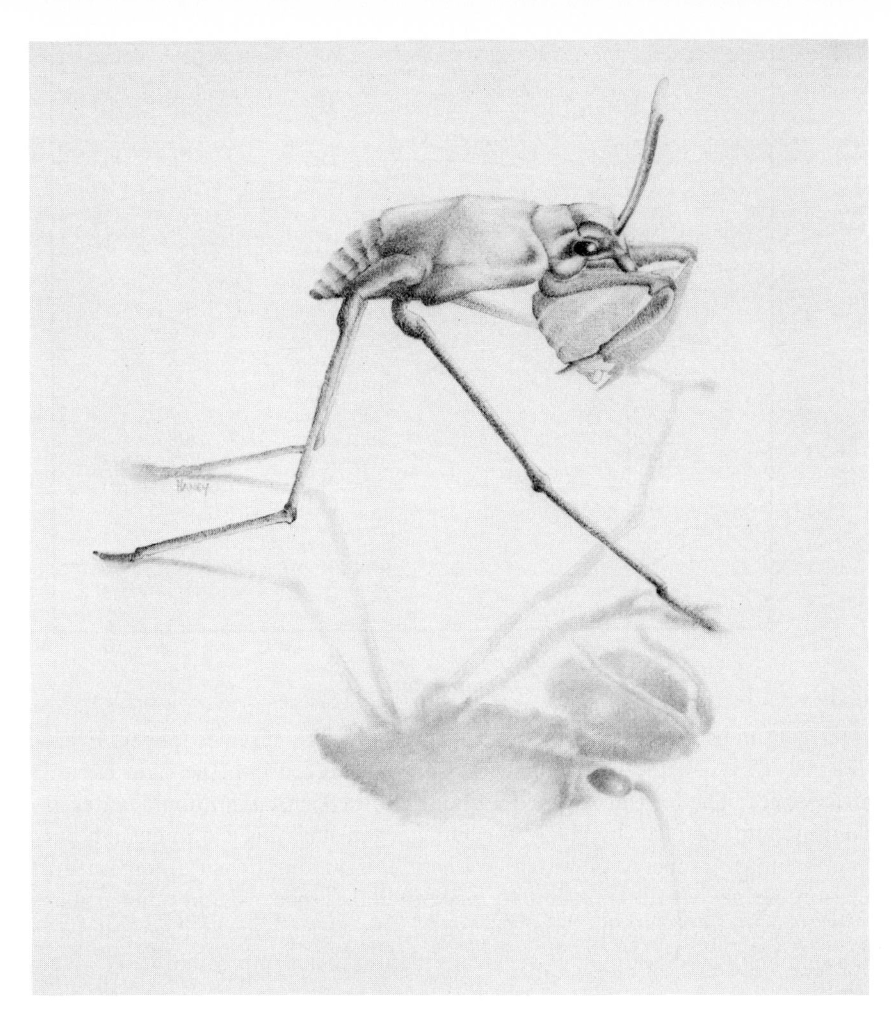

Fig. 1.6 A water strider (*Halobates*), one of the few completely marine insects, is supported by the surface tension of seawater. Redrawn from a photograph by Lana Cheng, Scripps Institution of Oceanography.

Density-Temperature Relationships

Most liquids contract and become denser as they cool. The solid form of these substances is denser than the liquid form. The structure of liquid water at low temperatures is not known, but several models have been proposed to explain its behavior. Over most of the temperature range at which water is liquid, it behaves like other liquids. The **density** increases with decreasing temperature, but only to 4° C.[1] Below 4° C, the normal density-temperature pattern reverses (fig. 1.7). One model suggests that at near-freezing temperatures, less dense icelike clusters consisting of several water molecules form and disintegrate very rapidly within the body of the liquid water. As liquid

1. The maximum density of pure water is used to define the fundamental metric measurement of mass, the gram. The gram is defined as the mass of pure water at 4° C contained in the volume of one cubic centimeter. Thus the density, the ratio of mass to volume, of pure water at 4° C is 1.000 g/cm^3.

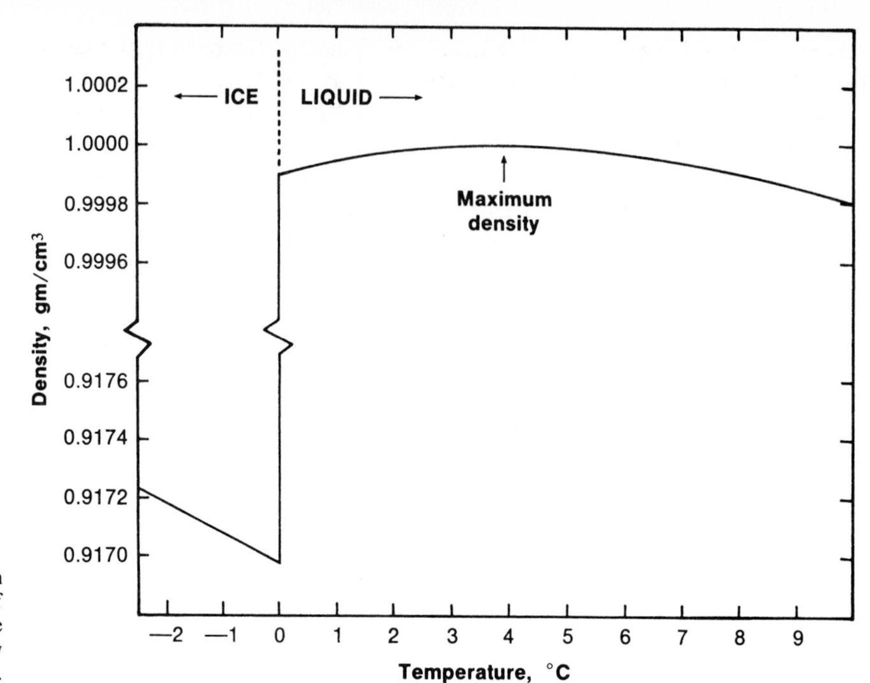

Fig. 1.7 Relationship between temperature and density of pure water. Note the large break in the vertical density scale.

water continues to cool, more clusters form and each survives longer. Eventually at 0° C, all the water molecules become locked into the rigid crystal lattice of ice. The ice thus formed is about 8% less dense than liquid water at the same temperature (fig. 1.7). For living organisms, this is an unusual, but very fortunate property of water. Without this unique density-temperature relationship, ice would sink as it formed; and lakes, oceans, and other bodies of water would freeze solid from the bottom up. Organisms living in such an environment would find winter survival difficult, if not impossible.

Heat Capacity

Heat is a form of energy, the energy of molecular motion. The source of almost all energy entering the earth's heat budget is the sun. At the surface of the sea, radiant energy is converted to heat energy. In the sea, heat is transferred from place to place primarily by **convection** (mixing) and secondarily by **conduction** (molecular exchange of heat). Heat energy is measured in **calories.**[2]

Water has the ability to absorb or give up heat without experiencing a large temperature change. To illustrate the high **heat capacity** of water, imagine a one-gram block of ice at −20° C on a heater that provides heat at a constant rate. Heating the ice from −20° C to 0° C requires 10 calories, or 0.5 calories per degree of temperature increase. However, converting one gram of ice at 0° C to liquid at 0° C requires 80 calories. Conversely, 80 calories of heat must be extracted from one gram of liquid water at 0° C to convert

2. A calorie is a unit of heat energy, defined as the quantity of heat needed to elevate the temperature of 1 g of pure water 1° C.

it completely to ice at the same temperature. This is referred to as the **latent heat of fusion.** Continued heating of the one-gram water sample from 0° C requires one calorie of heat energy for each one degree change in temperature until the boiling point (100° C) is reached. At this point, further temperature increase is halted until all the water is converted to water vapor. For this conversion, 540 calories of heat energy is necessary, and is referred to as the **latent heat of vaporization.** Figure 1.8 summarizes the energy requirements for water temperature changes. The high heat capacity and the large amount of heat required for evaporation enable large bodies of water to resist extreme temperature fluctuations. Heat is absorbed slowly by water during warm periods and gradually given up during cold periods. This process provides a temperature-moderating effect for the marine environment and adjacent land areas.

Seawater

Seawater is the accumulated product of millions of years of solvent action by water on rocks, soil, organisms, and the atmosphere. About 3.5% of seawater is composed of dissolved compounds from these sources. The other 96.5% is pure water. Traces of all naturally occurring substances probably exist in the ocean and may be separated into three general categories: (1) inorganic substances, usually referred to as salts and including nutrients necessary for plant growth; (2) dissolved gases; and (3) organic compounds usually derived from living organisms. An adequate discussion of this final category is beyond the scope of this text. Organic compounds dissolved in seawater include fats, oils, carbohydrates, vitamins, amino acids, proteins, and other substances. These compounds are thought to be an important source of nutrition for marine bacteria and several other types of organisms. Current research indicates that other organic compounds, especially synthetics such as DDT and other chlor-

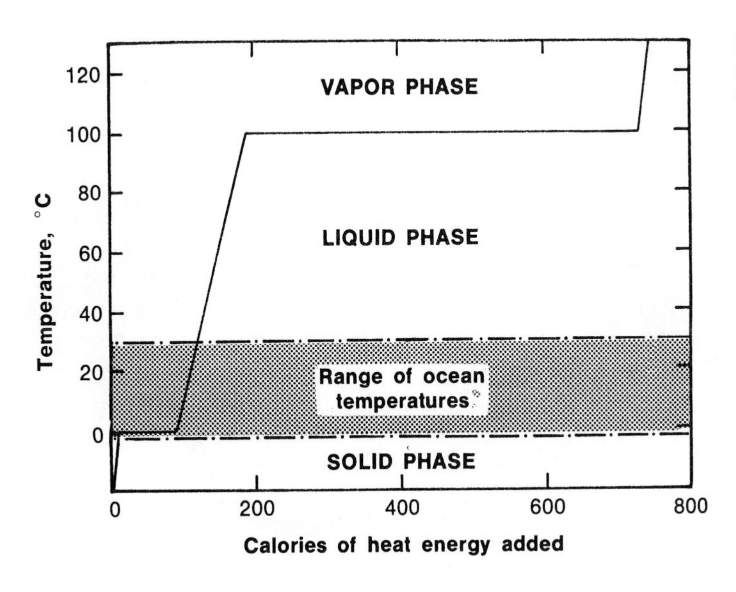

Fig. 1.8 The heat energy necessary to cause temperature and phase changes in water.

inated hydrocarbons that accumulate in seawater, have devastating effects on some forms of marine life.

Dissolved Salts

Salts account for the majority of dissolved substances in seawater. The total amount of dissolved salts in seawater is referred to as the **salinity,** which is measured in parts per thousand ($^{o}/_{oo}$). The average seawater salinity is approximately $35^{o}/_{oo}$. Salinity values range from nearly zero at river mouths to over $40^{o}/_{oo}$ in some areas of the Red Sea. Yet in open ocean areas away from coastal influences, the salinity varies only slightly over large distances (fig. 1.9). Salinity is altered by processes that add or remove salts or water from the sea. The primary mechanisms of salt and water addition or removal are evaporation and precipitation, river runoff, and freezing and thawing of sea ice. An excess of evaporation over precipitation removes water from the sea surface, thereby concentrating the remaining salts and increasing the salinity. Excess precipitation decreases salinity by diluting the sea salts. Freshwater runoff from rivers has the same effect. Figure 1.10 illustrates the average annual north-south variation of evaporation and precipitation from the sea surface. The areas with greater evaporation than precipitation (hatched portions of fig. 1.10) generally correspond to the high surface-salinity regions shown in figure 1.9. These latitudes also coincide with most of the great land deserts of the world. When seawater freezes, only the water molecules are incorporated into the developing ice crystal. The dissolved salts are excluded, thus increasing the salinity of the remaining seawater. The process is reversed when ice melts. Freezing and thawing of seawater are usually seasonal phenomena, resulting in little long-term salinity differences.

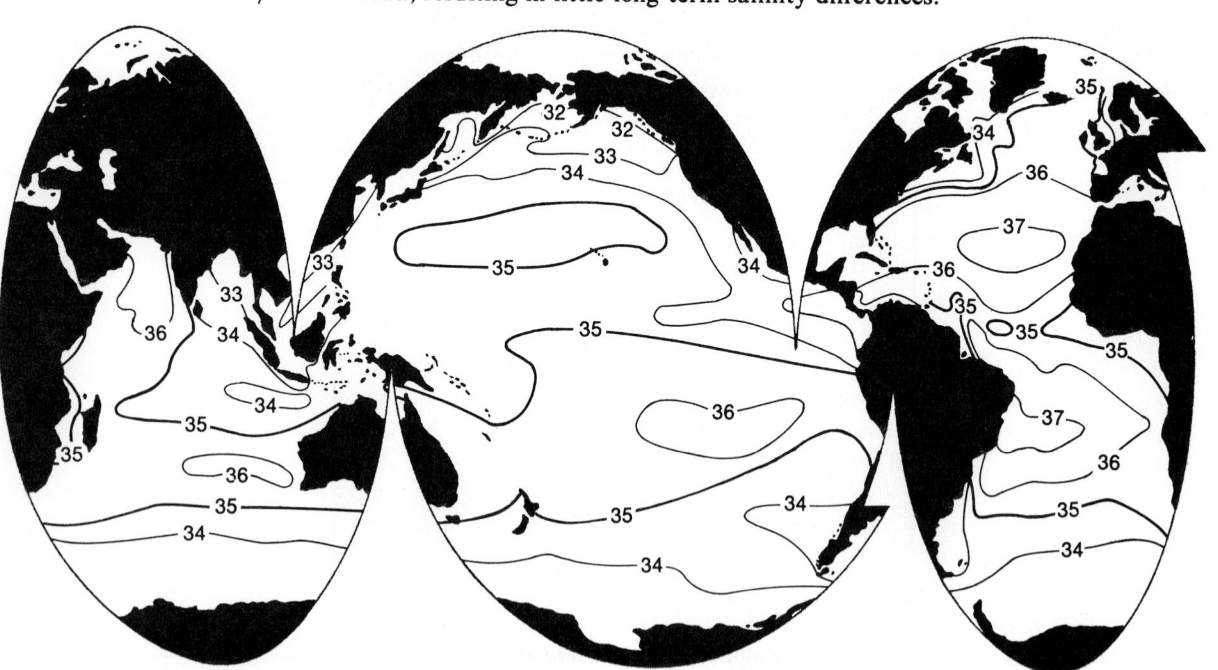

Fig. 1.9 Geographic variations of surface ocean salinities in $^{o}/_{oo}$.

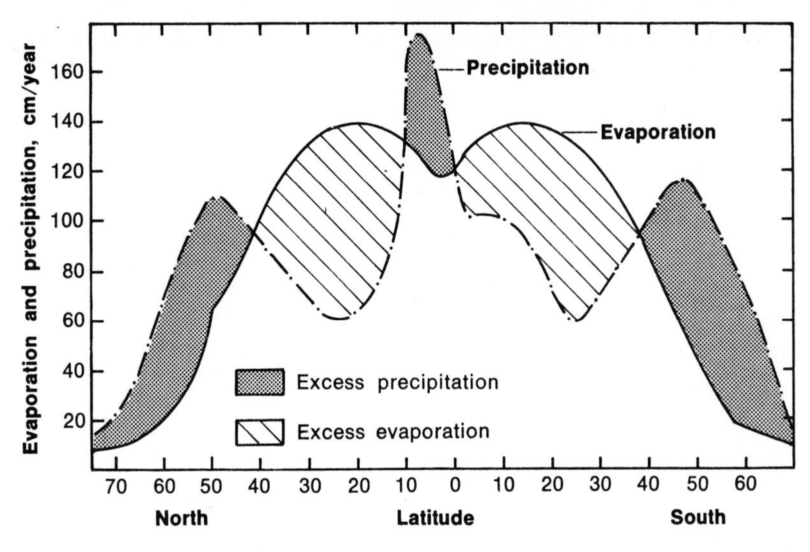

Fig. 1.10 Average north-south variation of sea surface evaporation and precipitation. Redrawn by permission of G. Dietrich, 1963, *General Oceanography*. (New York: Interscience Publishers.)

When dissolved in water, salts dissociate to produce both positively and negatively charged **ions.** For example, table salt (sodium chloride) dissociates to form positively charged sodium ions (Na^+) and negatively charged chloride ions (Cl^-). The more abundant ions found in seawater are listed in table 1.3 and are grouped as major or minor constituents according to their abundance. The major ions account for over 98% of the total salt concentration in seawater. In relation to each other, concentrations of the major ions remain remarkably constant, even though their total abundance may differ from place to place.

Seawater is a complete chemical medium for life, for it provides all the chemical substances necessary for the growth and maintenance of plant and animal tissue. Magnesium, calcium, bicarbonate, and silicate are important components of the hard skeletal parts of marine organisms. Nitrate and phosphate are required by plants for the synthesis of organic material. In addition, a vital similarity exists between the chemical composition of seawater and that of the body fluids of marine plants and animals. Most of the more abundant ions enumerated in table 1.3 are important components of the body fluids of all organisms.

It is essential to the well-being of all living things that they maintain reasonably constant internal environmental conditions. The tendency of living organisms to control or regulate fluctuations of the internal environment is known as **homeostasis.** Homeostasis is the result of the coordinated biological processes of organisms, which tend to regulate such conditions as body temperature, blood sugar level, and metabolic rate. The term homeostasis should not imply a static situation, but rather one that varies within definite and tolerable limits. Here we are particularly interested in those processes that affect the homeostasis of salt and water exchange between the body fluids of an organism and its seawater environment.

The body fluids of marine plants and animals are separated from seawater by boundary membranes that participate in many vital exchange pro-

Table 1.3. *Major and Minor Ions in Seawater of 35°/oo Salinity.*

Ion	Chemical Symbol	Concentration °/oo	
Chloride	Cl^-	19.3	Major
Sodium	Na^+	10.6	Major
Sulfate	SO_4^{-2}	2.7	Major
Magnesium	Mg^{+2}	1.3	Major
Calcium	Ca^{+2}	0.4	Major
Potassium	K^+	0.4	Major
Bicarbonate	HCO_3^-	0.1	Major
Bromide	Br^-	0.066	Minor
Borate	H_3BO_3	0.027	Minor
Strontium	Sr^{+2}	0.013	Minor
Fluoride	F^-	0.001	Minor
Silica	$Si(OH)_4$	0.001	Minor
and traces of other naturally occurring elements			

cesses, including absorption of oxygen, nutrient intake, and excretion of waste materials. Small molecules, such as water, easily pass through some of these membranes, whereas the passage of larger molecules and the abundant ions of seawater is restricted. Such membranes are said to be **selectively permeable** because they allow only small molecules and ions to pass through readily while regulating the exchange of larger molecules and ions. When substances are free to move, as they are when dissolved in seawater, the effective movement of these substances is along a gradient from regions of high concentrations to regions of lower concentrations. This type of molecular or ionic transfer is known as **diffusion.** Diffusion processes cause both water molecules and dissolved substances to move along concentration gradients within living organisms, and also across selectively permeable membranes between an organism and the surrounding seawater.

To illustrate the basic problems of salt and water balance in marine organisms, let's examine two representative animals: a sea cucumber and a salmon. Sea cucumbers avoid problems of salt and water imbalance simply by maintaining an internal fluid medium that is chemically similar to seawater (about 35°/oo dissolved salts). The sea cucumber can easily maintain this balance as long as the salt concentrations of the fluids on either side of its boundary membranes are equal and no concentration gradient exists (this is known as an **isotonic** condition). A state of equilibrium is maintained as long as water diffuses out of the sea cucumber as rapidly as it enters and the salt content of the internal fluids remains equal to that of the seawater outside.

However, consider what happens if the sea cucumber is removed from the sea and placed in a freshwater lake. The salt concentration is then greater inside the animal (still 35°/oo) than outside (the body fluids are now **hypertonic** to the lake water), and the internal water concentration (965°/oo) is correspondingly less than the concentration of the lake water (1,000°/oo). Water molecules, following the concentration gradient, diffuse across the selectively permeable boundary membranes into the sea cucumber. The movement of water across such a membrane is a special type of diffusion known as **osmosis.** The dissolved salts, now more concentrated within the animal than outside, cannot diffuse out of the sea cucumber, as this movement is blocked by the impermeability of the membranes to these salts. The net result is an increase in the amount of water inside the sea cucumber. The additional water creates an internal **osmotic pressure** that is potentially damaging, since the animal is incapable of expelling the excess water. Most other marine invertebrates and many marine plants, as well as sea cucumbers, have little or no capability for countering such osmotic stress. As a consequence, these organisms are limited to regions where salinity fluctuates little from open-ocean conditions.

In contrast to the limited control that sea cucumbers have over their osmotic situation, bony fish and some other marine animals and plants possess well-developed **osmoregulatory mechanisms.** As a result, some of these organisms are free to move between regions of varying salinities unhindered by osmotic upsets. For the present discussion, a salmon (which spends part of its life in seawater, and the remainder in fresh water) will serve as an example of how some organisms maintain a homeostatic internal fluid medium regardless of external environmental conditions (fig. 1.11).

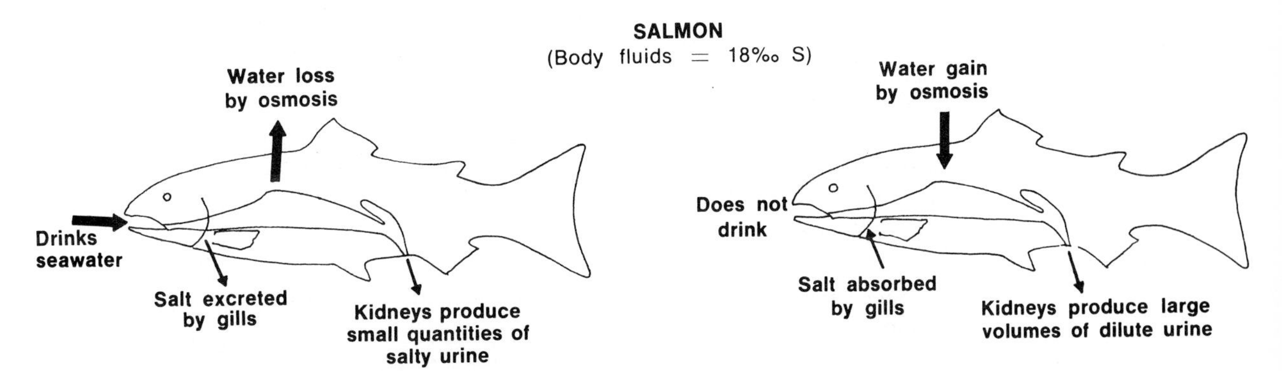

Fig. 1.11 A comparison of the osmotic conditions of a sea cucumber and a salmon in salt and fresh water.

The salt concentration of a salmon's body fluids, like those of most other bony fish, is intermediate between fresh water and seawater (about 18‰). As such, the body fluids are hypertonic to fresh water and **hypotonic** to seawater. Thus these fish never achieve an osmotic balance with their external environment. Instead, they must constantly expend energy to maintain a stable internal osmotic condition quite different from either river or ocean water. In seawater, salmon lose body water by osmosis and are constantly plagued by problems of dehydration, even though surrounded by an ocean of water. To counter this, salmon drink large amounts of seawater, which are absorbed by the digestive tract. The water is retained in the body tissues, and excess salts are actively excreted by special **chloride cells** located in the gills. Since the kidneys of salmon are unable to produce urine with a salt concentration higher than that of its body fluids, they are of no use in getting rid of excess salts.

When in freshwater rivers and lakes, the osmotic problems of salmon are completely reversed. Here the problem is largely one of osmotic water gain across the gill and digestive membranes, and a steady loss of salts to the surrounding water. Salmon drink very little fresh water, although some is inadvertently swallowed with food. To balance the inflow of water, the kidneys produce copious amounts of dilute urine after effectively recovering most of the salts from that urine. Needed salts are obtained from food and also are actively absorbed from the surrounding water through specialized cells in the gills. Thus, at a considerable expense of energy, salmon maintain a homeostatic internal fluid environment in either river or ocean water. The osmotic effects of fresh water and seawater on the salmon and sea cucumber are compared and summarized in figure 1.11.

Marine Temperatures

Temperature is a relative measure of the condition caused by heat energy and is most commonly measured in either degrees Fahrenheit (°F) or degrees Celsius (°C). Temperature is a universally important factor governing the existence and behavior of living organisms. Life processes cease to function above the boiling point of water and at subfreezing temperatures when the formation of ice crystals disrupts cellular structures. But between these absolute limits, life flourishes over a wide range of temperature regimes.

Most animals (the "cold-blooded" or **poikilothermic** forms) and virtually all plants lack mechanisms of body temperature regulation. Their body temperatures vary with, and are largely controlled by, environmental temperature conditions. Poikilotherms and plants generally have rather narrow optimum temperature ranges; bracketed on either side by wider suboptimal, but tolerable, ranges of temperatures. Relatively few animals (only birds and mammals) are **homeothermic;** that is, they maintain precisely controlled internal temperatures regardless of environmental temperatures.

Cell growth, oxygen consumption, heartbeat, and the many other physiological functions collectively termed **metabolism** proceed at temperature-regulated rates. For marine plants and poikilotherms, water temperature is the primary factor controlling their metabolic rates. Within tolerable temperature limits, the metabolic rate of many poikilotherms is roughly doubled by a 10° C temperature increase. This, however, is only a general rule of thumb; some processes may accelerate sixfold with a 10° C temperature increase, while others may not change at all. The actual effect of water temperature on the rate of development of a typical poikilothermic organism (e.g., eggs of Atlantic cod) is shown in figure 1.12. Homeotherms with reasonably constant internal temperatures are less restricted by environmental temperatures and often occur over wide temperature ranges.

The high heat capacity of water limits marine temperatures to a much narrower range than those on land (fig. 1.13). Some marine plants and animals survive in coastal tropical lagoons at temperatures as high as 40° C. A few deep-sea animals spend their lives in water perpetually less than 0° C. Penguins and a few other homeotherms well-adapted to extreme cold commonly experience air temperatures far below 0° C in polar regions. Penguins even manage to incubate and hatch eggs under these conditions. But these are unusual exceptions; most marine life thrives at water temperatures between 0° and 30° C.

The distribution of various forms of marine life is closely associated with geographical differences of seawater temperatures. Surface ocean temperatures are highest near the equator and decrease toward both poles. This temperature gradient establishes several east-west trending marine climatic zones (fig. 1.14). The approximate temperature range of each zone is included in figure 1.13.

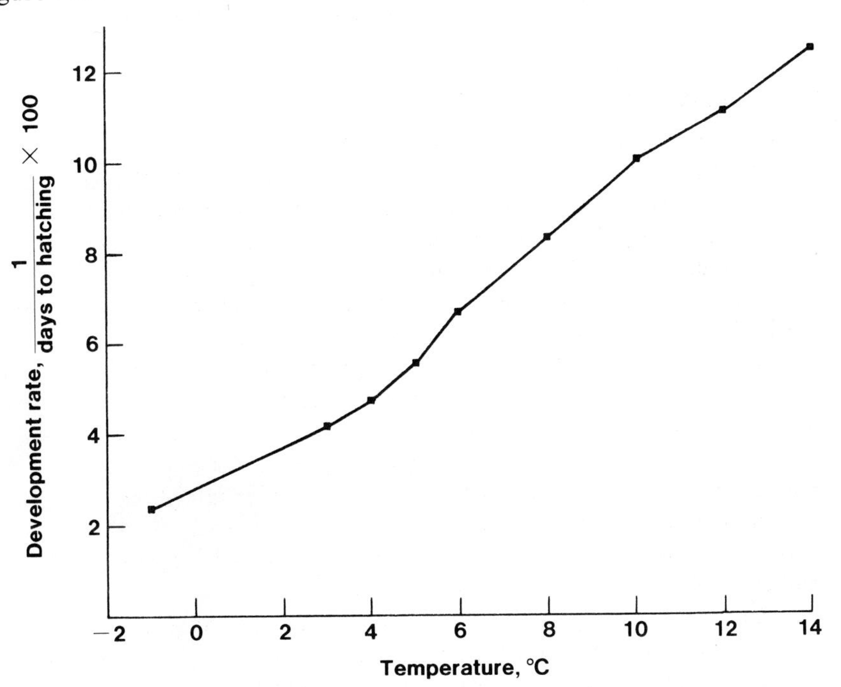

Fig. 1.12 The effect of water temperature on the rate of development of cod eggs. Data from Reibisch 1902.

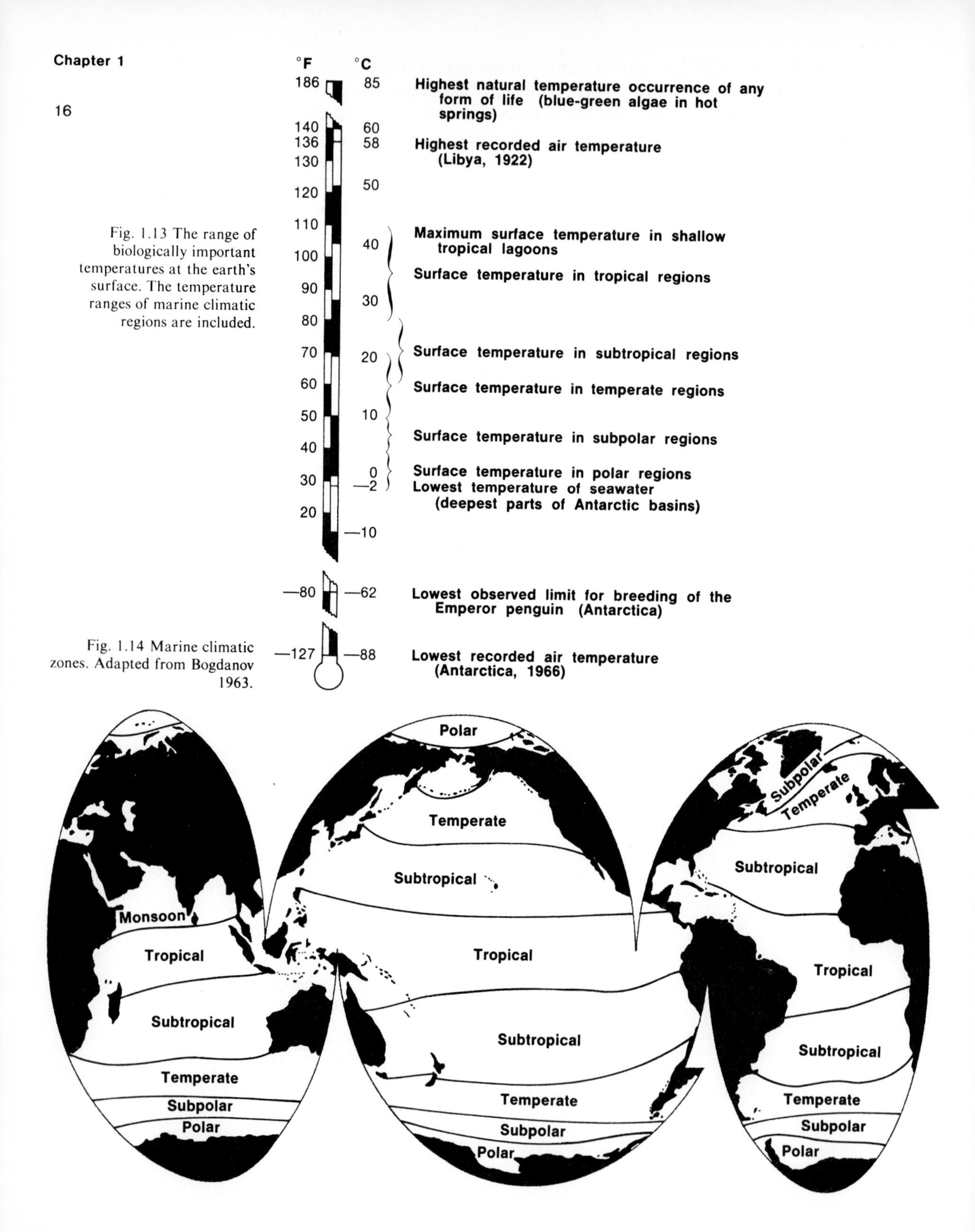

Fig. 1.13 The range of biologically important temperatures at the earth's surface. The temperature ranges of marine climatic regions are included.

Fig. 1.14 Marine climatic zones. Adapted from Bogdanov 1963.

Salinity-Temperature-Density Relationships

Seawater density is a function of both temperature and salinity. The density increases with either a temperature decrease or a salinity increase. Under normal oceanic conditions, temperature fluctuations exert a greater influence on seawater density because the range of marine temperature values is much greater (−2° C to 30° C) than the range of open-ocean salinities.

Some generalizations may also be made about the vertical distribution of ocean temperature, salinity, and density. The most dense water is found on the bottom; but the physical processes that create this dense water (evaporation, freezing, or cooling) are strictly ocean surface features. Therefore, dense bottom water must sink from the surface. These sinking processes mix deep-ocean waters and will be discussed more fully later. An obvious feature in most oceans is a **thermocline,** a subsurface zone of very rapid temperature (and density) change (fig. 1.15). The large density difference on either side of the thermocline effectively separates the oceans into a two-layered system: a thin, well-mixed surface layer above the thermocline overlying a cold, thick, stable zone. The thermocline inhibits exchange of gases, nutrients, and sometimes even organisms between the two layers. In temperate and polar regions, the thermocline is a seasonal feature. During the winter months, the surface water is cooled to the same low temperature as the deeper water. This causes the thermocline to disappear and allows seasonal mixing between the two layers.

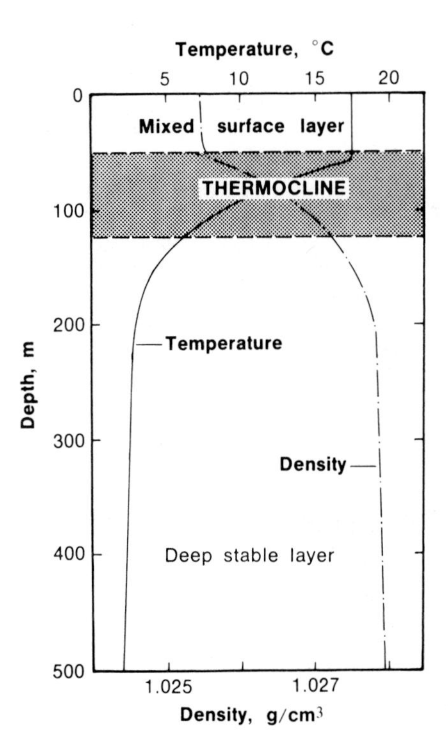

Fig. 1.15 Vertical distribution of water temperature and density in 35‰ salinity seawater.

Dissolved Gases

The solubility of gases in seawater is a function of temperature. Greater solubility occurs at lower temperatures. However, the solubility of atmospheric gases in water is limited. Nitrogen, carbon dioxide, and oxygen are the most abundant gases dissolved in seawater. Nitrogen (N_2) is comparatively inert and therefore is not involved in the basic life processes of most organisms. On the other hand, carbon dioxide and oxygen are metabolically very active. Carbon dioxide and water are utilized by green plants in photosynthesis to produce oxygen and high-energy organic compounds like sugar. Respiration by plants and animals reverses the photosynthetic process to release the usable energy incorporated in the organic components of the organism's food. Conversely, oxygen is used in respiration, and carbon dioxide is given off.

Carbon dioxide (CO_2) is abundant in most regions of the sea, and concentrations too low to support plant growth do not normally occur. Seawater has an unusually large capacity to absorb CO_2 because most dissolved CO_2 does not remain as a gas. Rather, much of the CO_2 combines with water to produce a weak acid, carbonic acid (H_2CO_3). Normally, carbonic acid dissociates to form a hydrogen ion (H^+) and a bicarbonate ion (HCO_3^-) or two H^+ ions and a carbonate ion (CO_3^{-2}). These reactions can be summarized as chemical equations:

1. $CO_2 + H_2O \rightleftharpoons H_2CO_3$
   carbon dioxide + water ⇌ carbonic acid
2. $H_2CO_3 \rightleftharpoons H^+ + HCO_3^-$
   carbonic acid ⇌ hydrogen ion + bicarbonate ion
3. $HCO_3^- \rightleftharpoons H^+ + CO_3^{-2}$
   bicarbonate ion ⇌ hydrogen ion + carbonate ion

The arrows pointing in both directions indicate each reaction is reversible, either producing or taking up H^+ ions. The abundance of H^+ ions in water solutions controls the acidity or alkalinity of that solution, and is measured on a scale of 1 to 14 pH units (fig. 1.16). The pH units are a measure of the H^+ ion concentration. One on the pH scale is very acidic and represents a high H^+ ion concentration. Fourteen is very basic (or alkaline) and denotes low H^+ ion concentrations. Neutral pH (the pH of pure water) is 7 on the scale. The carbonic acid—bicarbonate—carbonate system in seawater functions to **buffer** or to limit changes of seawater pH. If excess H^+ ions are present, the reactions above proceed to the left, removing them from solution. Otherwise the solution would become more acidic. If too few hydrogen ions are present, more are made available by the conversion of carbonic acid to bicarbonate, and bicarbonate to carbonate. In open-ocean conditions, this buffering system is very effective, limiting ocean water pH values to a range between 7.5 and 8.4.

Oxygen in the form of O_2 is necessary for the survival of most organisms (the only exceptions are some species of anaerobic microorganisms). The

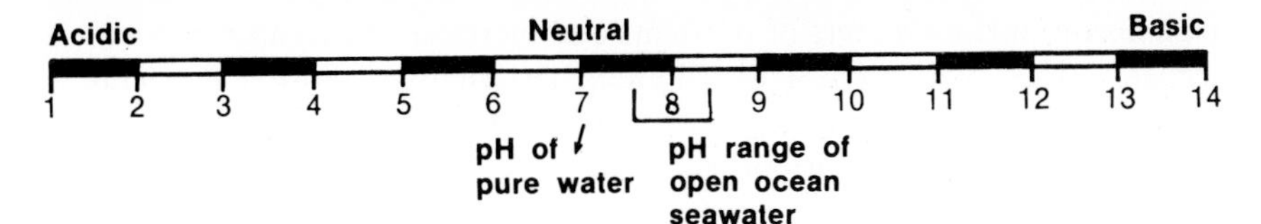

Fig. 1.16 The pH scale.

abundance or lack of O_2 in seawater strongly influences the distribution of marine life. Oxygen is utilized by organisms in all areas of the marine environment, including the deepest trenches. However, the transfer of oxygen from the atmosphere to seawater and the production of excess oxygen by marine plants are the only available methods of introducing oxygen into seawater. Both of these processes are limited to the near-surface region of the ocean. Oxygen consumed near the bottom in deep areas can be replaced only by oxygen from the surface. If replenishment is not rapid enough, available oxygen supplies may be depleted or reduced to critically low concentrations. Oxygen replenishment occurs by very slow diffusion processes from the oxygen-rich surface layers downward and also by vertical water movements that carry oxygen-enriched waters down to deep-ocean basins. At intermediate depths, animal respiration and bacterial decomposition use O_2 as fast as it is replaced, creating an O_2 **minimum zone.** Figure 1.17 illustrates a typical vertical profile of dissolved oxygen from the surface to the bottom of the sea.

Dissolved Nutrients

Nitrate (NO_3^{-2}) and phosphate (PO_4^{-3}) are the fertilizers of the sea. These and smaller amounts of other nutrients are utilized in the photosynthetic process by plants living in the near-surface waters and are excreted back into the water at all depths as animal and bacterial waste products. This process

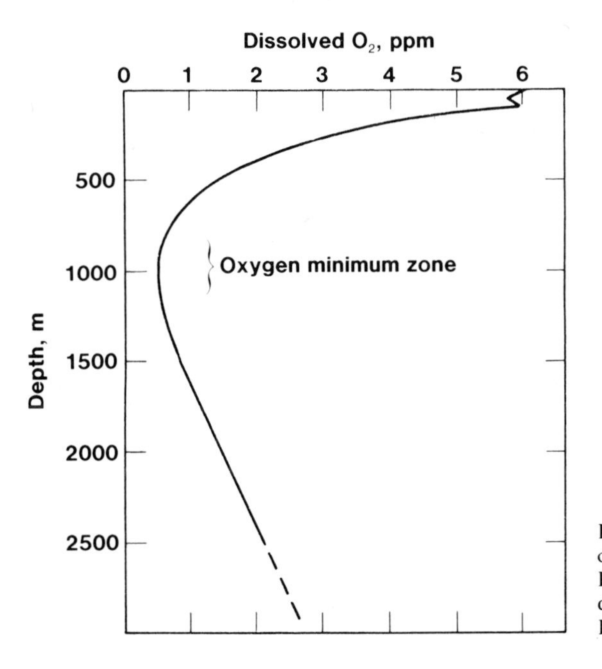

Fig. 1.17 Vertical distribution of dissolved O_2 in the North Pacific (150° W, 47° N) during winter. Data from Barkley 1968.

depletes the surface waters of nutrients and increases their concentrations in deeper waters. The vertical distribution pattern for dissolved nutrients is opposite that for dissolved oxygen, which is normally high in surface waters and low in deep waters. The opposing patterns of vertical oxygen and nutrient distribution reflect the reverse biological processes which influence their concentrations in seawater. Oxygen is normally produced by near-surface plants and consumed by animals, while nutrients are utilized near the surface by plants and excreted by animals at all depths.

The Ocean in Motion

Ocean water is constantly in motion, providing a near-uniform medium for living organisms. Such motion speeds mixing and diffusion processes to minimize variations in salinity and temperature characteristics. Oceanic circulation processes also serve to disperse swimming and floating organisms and their reproductive products. Toxic body wastes are carried away; while food, nutrients, and essential elements are replenished. The primary driving force behind oceanic circulation processes is heat from the sun, with small additional contributions from the gravitational attraction of the moon and sun. These circulation processes, so beneficial to all forms of marine life, are wave action, tides, currents, and vertical water movements.

Waves

Differential solar heating of various regions of the earth's surface and atmosphere produces winds. Winds that blow across the sea surface in turn produce **waves** and **surface currents.** The mechanism of energy transfer from the atmosphere to the ocean is poorly understood. However, it is known that the size of the waves produced is dependent on the wind's velocity, duration, and **fetch**, the extent of the area over which the wind blows. Ocean waves range in height from a few millimeters for very small capillary waves to towering storm waves over 30 m high. Waves are commonly characterized by their **period,** the time required for two successive waves to pass a reference point. Several types of ocean waves, with their periods, their causes, and their relative amounts of energy, are given in figure 1.18. Regardless of their size, period, or cause, the general features of wave motion apply equally to all ocean waves.

Once generated, waves move away from the area of formation. However, it is only the wave shape that advances, transmitting the energy forward. The water particles themselves do not advance horizontally. Instead, their paths approximate vertical circles with little or no forward motion (fig. 1.19). Waves provide a mechanism to mix thoroughly the surface layer of water. The depth to which waves produce noticeable motion is about one-half the wavelength (also fig. 1.19). As the wavelength seldom exceeds 100 m in any ocean, the depth of effective mixing by wind-driven waves is generally no greater than 50 m.

Waves entering shallow water behave differently than open-ocean waves. When the water depth is less than one-half the wavelength, bottom friction begins to slow the forward speed of the waves. This causes the waves to "bunch up," becoming higher and steeper. At some point the waves become unstable, pitch forward, and "break." Breaking waves release tremendous amounts of energy on shorelines (and on the organisms living there) and in time can alter the essential character of the shoreline.

Tides

Tides are ocean-surface phenomena familiar to anyone who has spent much time on a seashore. Actually they are very long period waves (compare these to other ocean waves in figure 1.18). But they are usually imperceptible in the open ocean and become noticeable only against coastlines where they can be observed as a periodic rise and fall of the sea surface. The maximum elevation of the tide, known as **high tide,** is followed by a fall in sea level to a minimum, the **low tide.** On most coastlines, two high and two low tides occur each day. The vertical difference between high and low tides is the **tidal range,** which varies from a few centimeters in the Mediterranean Sea to over 15 m in the long, narrow Bay of Fundy between Nova Scotia and New Brunswick. The range of tides on a coastline defines a limited but unique

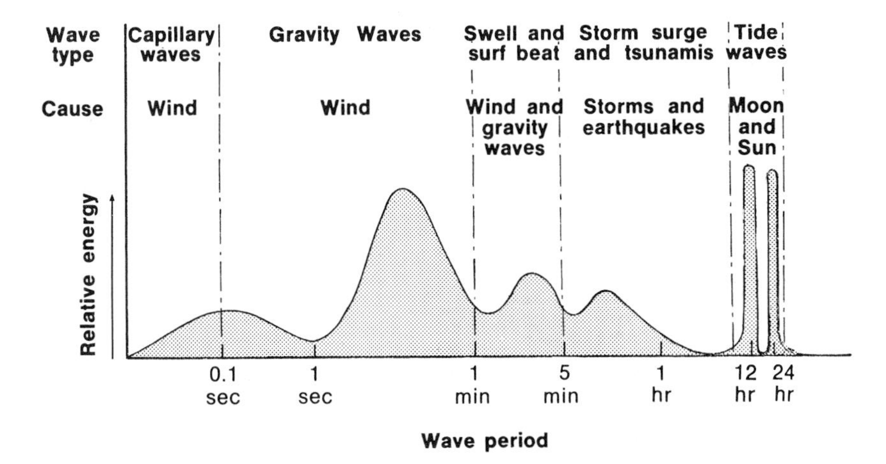

Fig. 1.18 The spectrum of ocean surface waves, based on period, cause, and the relative amount of energy available in each wave type. Adapted from Munk 1950.

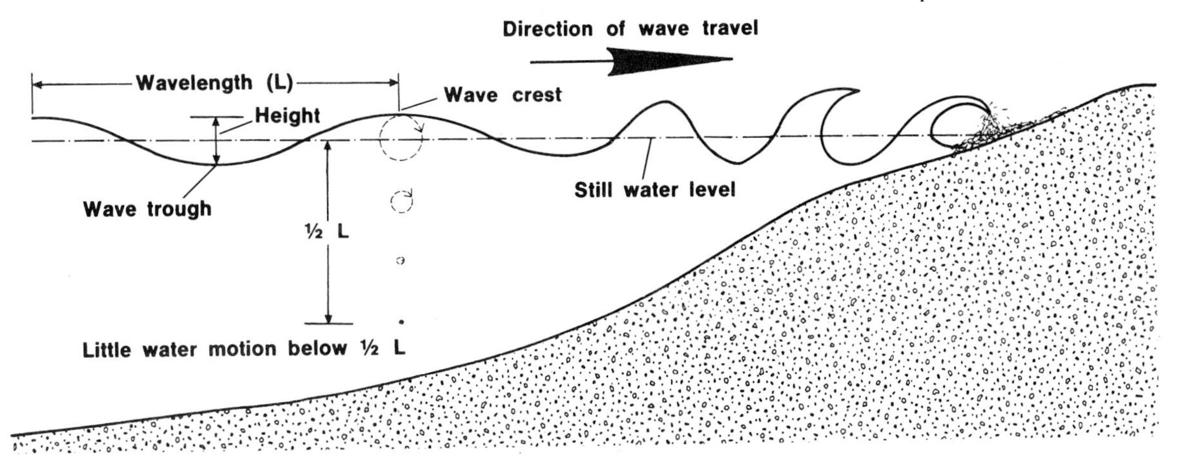

Fig. 1.19 Wave form and pattern of water motion in a deepwater wave as it moves in to shore to the right. Circles indicate orbits of water particles diminishing with depth.

marine life zone, the **intertidal.** Here, the sea, the land, and the air all play important roles in establishing the complex physical conditions to which all intertidal plants and animals must adapt.

In 1687, in his "Principia Mathematica," Sir Isaac Newton explained ocean tides as the consequence of the gravitational attraction of the moon and sun on the oceans of the earth. Newton's law of universal gravitation states that the gravitational attraction between two bodies is directly proportional to their masses, and inversely proportional to the cube of the distance between the bodies. The mass of the sun is about 27,000,000 times greater than that of the moon. Yet the moon exercises twice as much influence on the earth's tides because the earth-moon distance is only 1/400th the earth-sun distance.

The moon completes one orbit around the earth each lunar month (27.5 days). To maintain that orbit, the gravitational attraction between the earth and moon must exactly balance the centrifugal force holding these bodies apart. On earth, the centrifugal force is equal everywhere in direction and magnitude (solid arrows, fig. 1.20). Although the average gravitational attraction between the earth and moon balances the centrifugal force, the two forces are not equal at all points on the earth's surface. The moon's gravitational pull (dash-line arrows, fig. 1.20) is stronger than the centrifugal force on the side of the earth facing the moon, and weaker on the opposite side. In combination, the net effect of these two forces is a complex of tide-producing forces on the earth's surface (outline arrows, fig. 1.20).

Hypothetically, if the earth were completely covered with water, two bulges of water, or lunar tides, would pile up; one on the side of the earth facing the moon, and the other on the opposite side of the globe (fig. 1.21). As the earth makes a complete rotation every 24 hours, a point on the earth's surface (indicated by the marker, fig. 1.21) would first experience a high tide *(a)*, then a low tide *(b)*, another high tide *(c)*, another low tide *(d)*, and finally another high tide *(e)*. During that rotation, however, the moon advances in its own orbit so that an additional 50 minutes of the earth's rotation is required to bring the point directly in line with the moon again. Thus the reference point actually experiences two equal high and two equal low tides every 24 hours and 50 minutes (a lunar day).

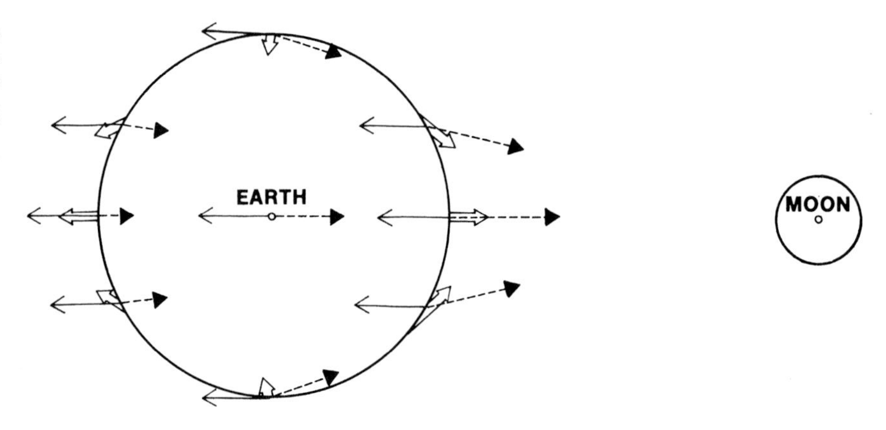

Fig. 1.20 Tide-producing forces (outline arrows) on earth are the result of centrifugal force (solid arrows) combined with the gravitational attraction of the moon (dash-line arrows).

In a similar manner, the sun-earth system also generates tide-producing forces that yield a solar tide about one-half as large as the lunar tide. The solar tide is expressed only as a variation on the basic lunar tidal pattern, rather than as an individual set of tides. When the sun, moon, and earth are in alignment (at the time of the new and full moon, fig. 1.22), the solar tide has an additive effect on the lunar tide, creating extra-high high tides and very-low low tides (**spring tides**). One week later, when the sun and moon are at right angles to each other, the solar tide partially cancels the lunar tide to produce moderate tides known as **neap tides**. During each lunar month, two sets of spring and neap tides occur.

So far, we have considered only the effects of tide-producing forces in a hypothetical ocean covering a hypothetical planet without continents. What happens when continental landmasses are taken into consideration? The continents act to block the westward passage of the tidal bulges as the earth rotates under them. Unable to move freely around the globe, these tidal impulses establish complex patterns within each ocean basin that quite often

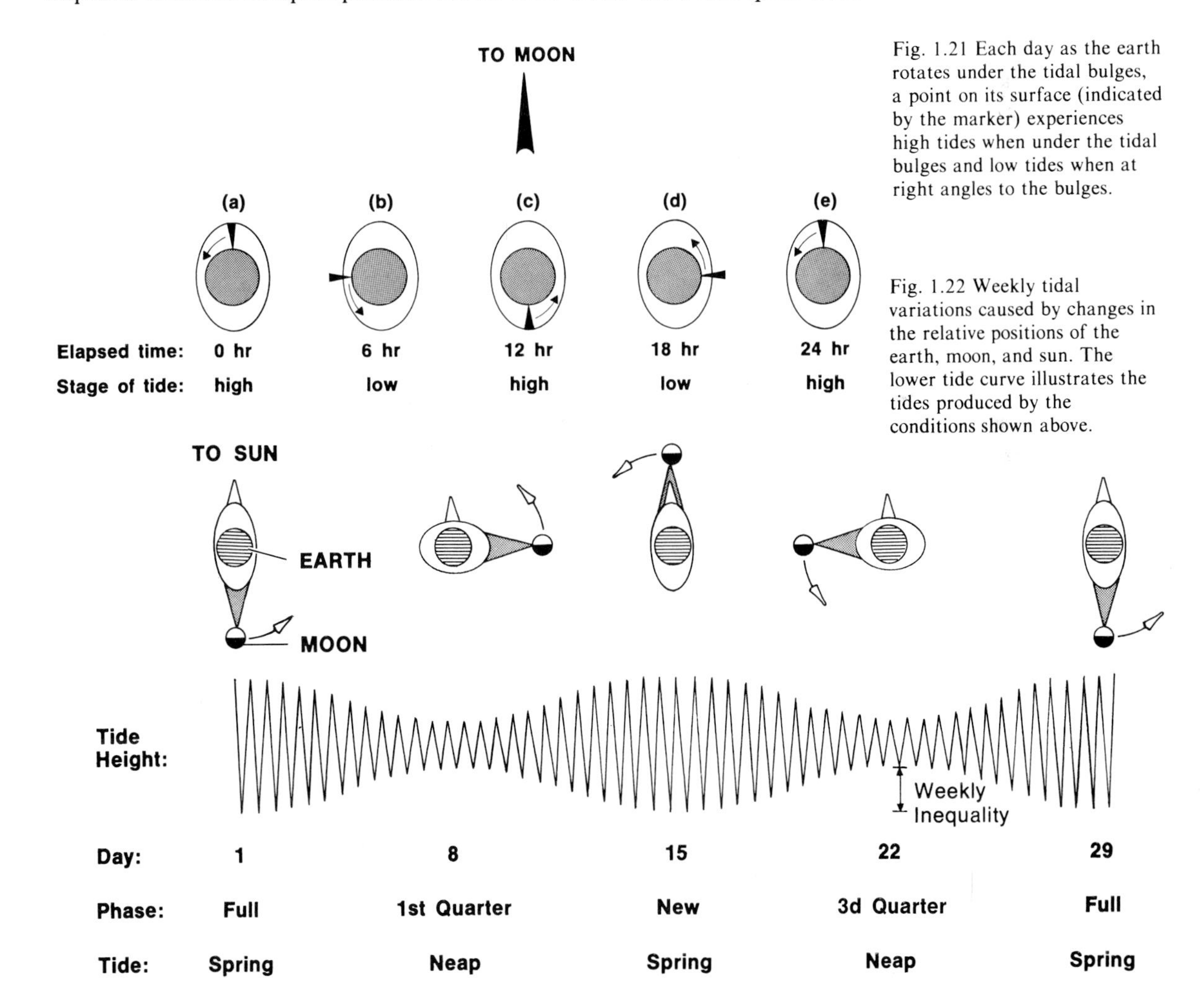

Fig. 1.21 Each day as the earth rotates under the tidal bulges, a point on its surface (indicated by the marker) experiences high tides when under the tidal bulges and low tides when at right angles to the bulges.

Fig. 1.22 Weekly tidal variations caused by changes in the relative positions of the earth, moon, and sun. The lower tide curve illustrates the tides produced by the conditions shown above.

differ markedly from the tidal patterns of adjacent ocean basins, or even other regions of the same ocean basin.

Some regional variations in the daily tidal configuration at three stations along the east and west coasts of North America are shown in figure 1.23. Portland, Maine, experiences two high and two low tides each lunar day. The two high tides are quite similar to each other, as are the two low tides. Such

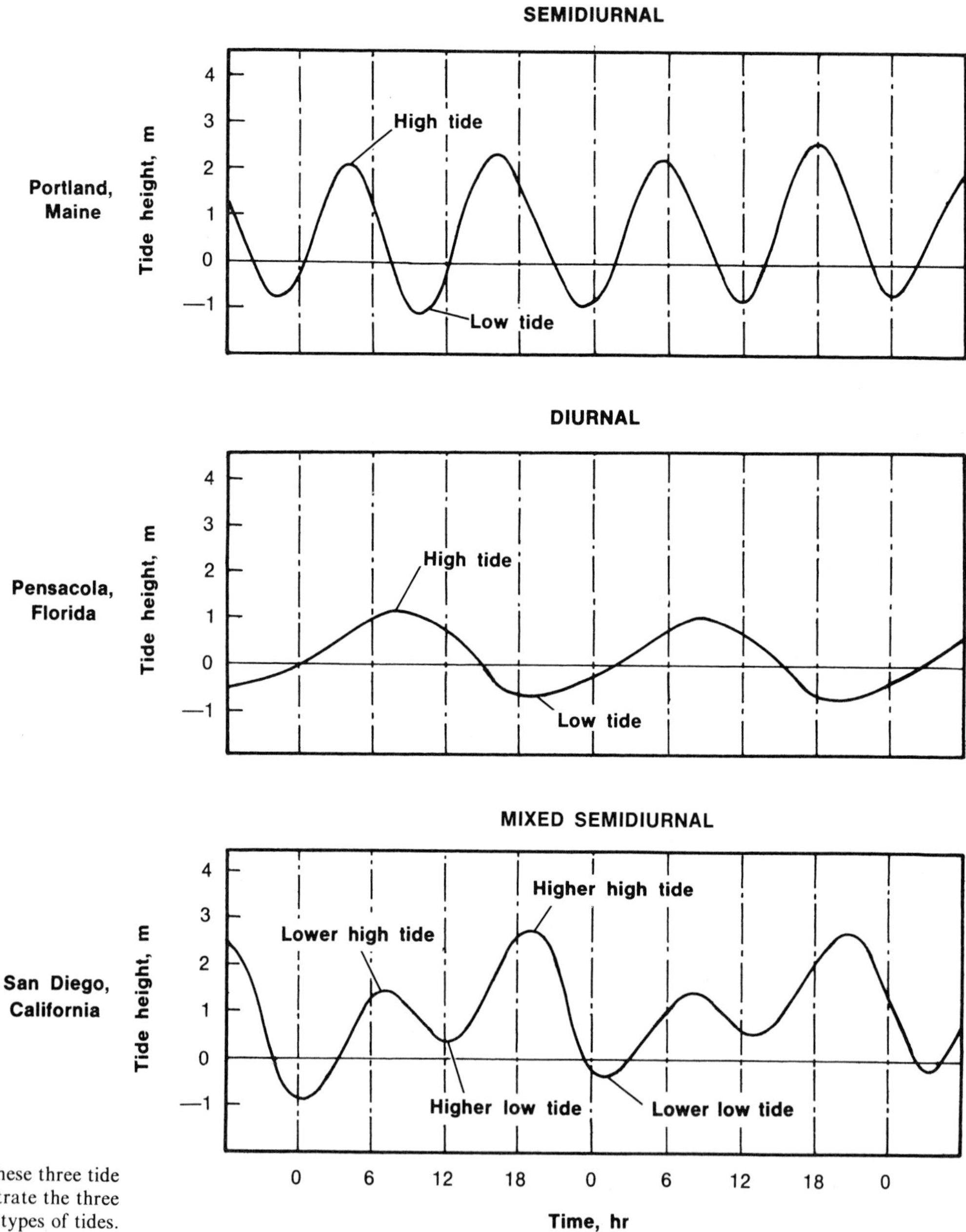

Fig. 1.23 These three tide curves illustrate the three common types of tides.

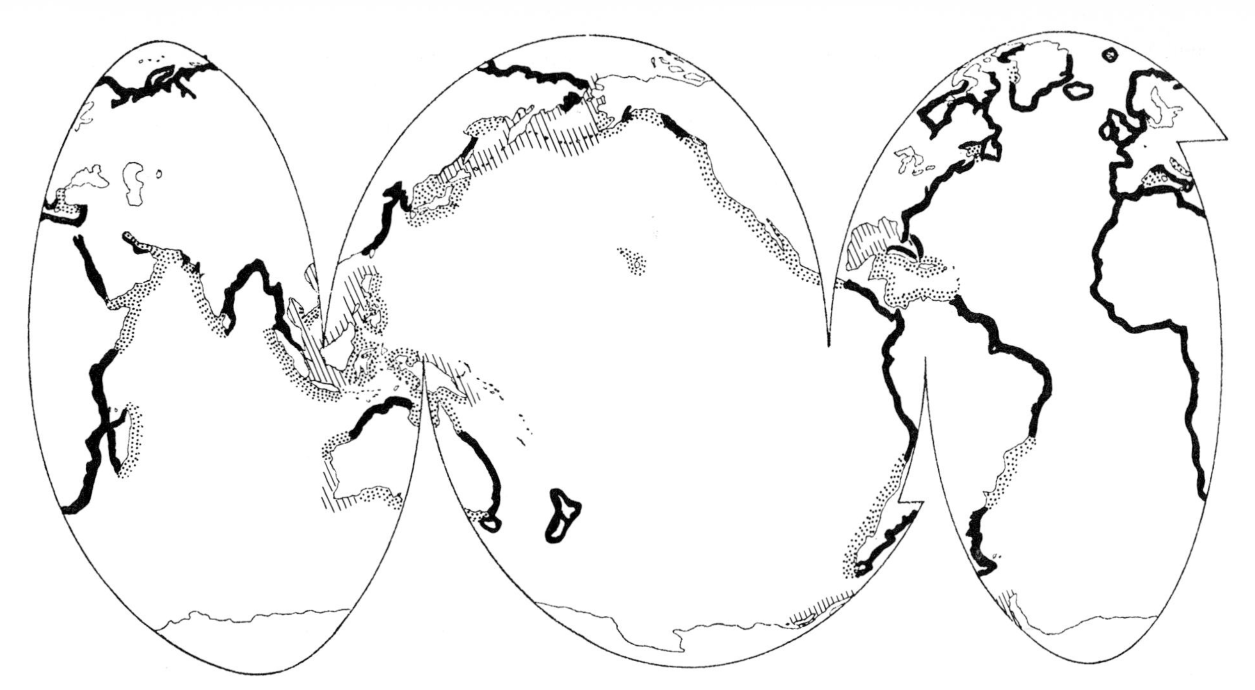

tidal patterns are referred to as **semidiurnal** (or semidaily) tides and are characteristic of much of the East Coast of the United States. The tidal pattern at Pensacola, Florida, on the Gulf Coast has only one high and one low tide each lunar day. This is a **diurnal,** or daily, tide. Different yet is the daily tidal pattern at San Diego, California. There, two high and two low tides occur each day, but successive high tides are quite different from each other. This type of tidal pattern, characteristic of the West Coast of North America, is a **mixed semidiurnal** tide. The geographical occurrence of diurnal, semidiurnal, and mixed semidiurnal tides are outlined in figure 1.24.

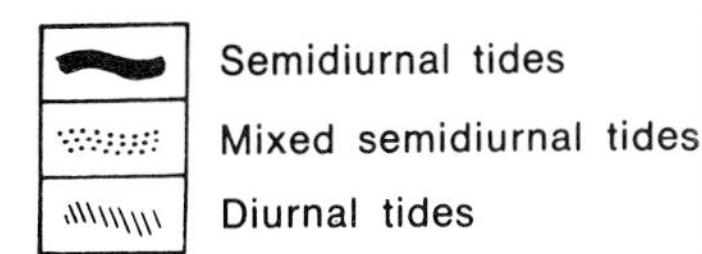

Fig. 1.24 The geographical occurrence of the three types of tides described in figure 1.23.

Tidal conditions for any day on a selected coastline can be predicted because the periodic nature of tides is easily observed and recorded. For the most part, prediction of the timing and amplitude of future tides is based on historical observations of past tidal occurrences at tide-recording stations along coastlines and in harbors around the world. The National Ocean Survey of the U.S. Department of Commerce uses information from these records to compile and publish annual "Tide Tables of High and Low Water Predictions" for principal ports and coastlines of the world.

Surface Currents

Large-scale horizontal transport of surface waters occurs in regions where winds blow over the ocean with a reasonable constancy of direction and velocity. Three major wind belts occur in the Northern Hemisphere. The **trade winds,** near 15° N latitude, blow from northeast to southwest. The **westerlies,** in the middle latitudes, blow primarily from the west-southwest. At very high latitudes, the **polar easterlies** blow from east to west. Each of these wind belts has its mirror-image counterpart in the Southern Hemisphere.

The momentum imparted to the sea by these major wind belts drives regular patterns of broad, slow, relatively shallow ocean surface currents. Some currents transport more than one hundred times the volume of water carried by all of the earth's rivers combined. Currents of such magnitude greatly affect the distribution of marine organisms and the rate of heat transport from tropical to polar regions.

As the surface layer of water is moved horizontally by the wind, momentum is transferred downward. The speed of the deeper water diminishes steadily as momentum is lost to overcome the viscosity of the water. Eventually, at depths generally less than 200 m, the speed of wind-driven currents becomes negligible.

The surface water moved by the wind does not parallel the wind direction, but experiences an appreciable deflection; to the right in the Northern Hemisphere, and to the left in the Southern Hemisphere. This deflection is known as the **Coriolis effect.** As successively deeper water layers are set into motion by the water above them, they undergo a further Coriolis deflection from the direction of the water above to produce a spiral of current directions from the surface downward (fig. 1.25). The magnitude of the Coriolis deflection of wind-driven currents varies from about 15° in shallow coastal regions to nearly 45° in the open ocean. The net Coriolis deflection from the wind headings creates a pattern of wind-driven ocean surface currents that flow primarily in an east-west direction.

Continental masses obstruct the continuous east-west flow of currents. Consequently, water transported by these currents is moved from one side of the ocean and piled up on the other. The surface of the equatorial Pacific Ocean, for example, is higher on the west side than on the east. The opposite is true in the middle latitudes of both hemispheres; the east side is higher.

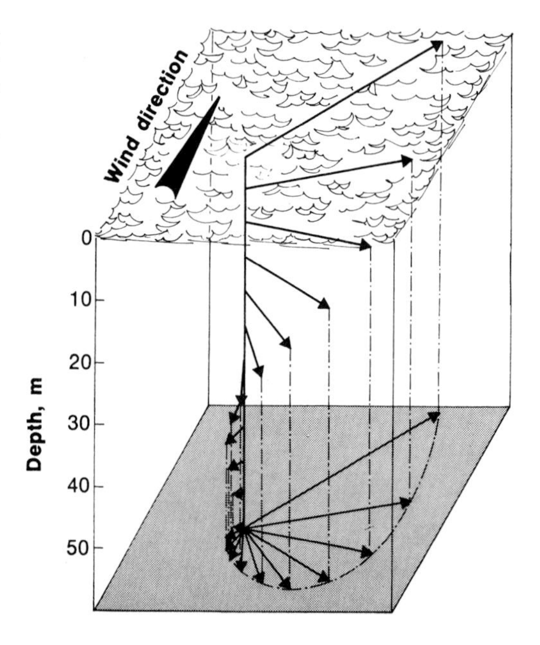

Fig. 1.25 A spiral of current directions, indicating greater deflection to the right (in the Northern Hemisphere), which increases with depth due to the Coriolis effect. Arrow length indicates relative current speed. Redrawn from H. U. Sverdrup, Martin W. Johnson, and Richard H. Fleming, *The Oceans: Their Physics, Chemistry, and General Biology*, © 1942, renewed 1970. By permission of Prentice-Hall, Inc., Englewood Cliffs, New Jersey.

Eventually, the water must flow away from areas where it has accumulated to regions where it originated. Either the water flows directly back against the established current, producing a **countercurrent;** or it flows as a **continental boundary current** in a north-south direction from areas of accumulation to areas of removal. Both these current patterns exist, but are especially obvious in the North Pacific (fig. 1.26). An east-flowing Equatorial Countercurrent divides the west-flowing North Pacific Equatorial Current. The north-south flowing continental boundary currents connect the east-west currents to produce large, circulating current **gyres**. Similar current patterns are found in the other major ocean basins (fig. 1.27).

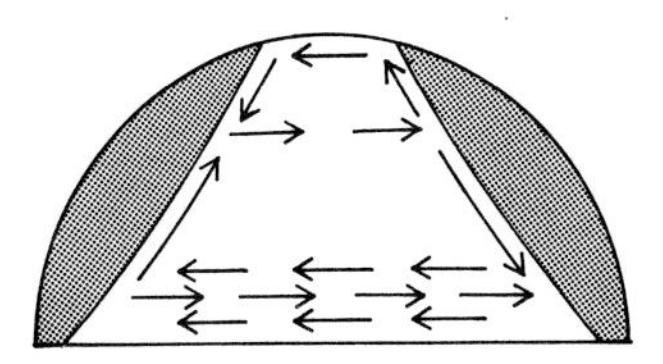

Fig. 1.26 Generalized surface-current flow in the North Pacific Ocean.

Vertical Water Movements

Vertical water movements are produced by sinking and upwelling processes. Such processes tend to break down the vertical stratification established by the thermocline. Seawater sinks when its density increases. The physical processes that increase seawater density are strictly surface features. Thus dense seawater, derived from the surface, is usually highly oxygenated. This water transports dissolved oxygen to deep areas of the ocean basins, which would otherwise be **anaerobic** (without O_2). The chief areas of sinking are located in the colder latitudes where sea surface temperatures are low. Figure 1.28 outlines the general patterns of large-scale deep-ocean circulation. These patterns of water transport are very slow and ill-defined. An estimated one thousand years are required for water that sinks in the North Atlantic to reach the surface again in the Southern Hemisphere. Similar patterns in the Pacific may require ten times as long.

Rising water masses are accounted for by different processes, usually lumped under the term "**upwelling,**" and are considered in chapter 5. Whatever the cause, all upwelling processes have the same result. They bring deeper nutrient-rich waters to the surface. The continuous availability of plant nutrients from deep water accounts for the high productivity characteristic of regions of upwelling. Many of the world's important fisheries are based in upwelling areas.

In the arid climate of the Mediterranean Sea, evaporation from the sea surface greatly exceeds precipitation and runoff. The resulting high-salinity water sinks as its density increases, and fills the deeper parts of the Mediterranean basin. The sinking of surface water provides substantial mixing and O_2 replenishment for the deep water of the Mediterranean, which is similar to the deep circulation of the open ocean. Part of this deep dense water eventually flows out of the Mediterranean over the shallow sill at Gibraltar and spreads down into the Atlantic Ocean. To compensate for the outflow and losses due to evaporation, nearly two million cubic meters of Atlantic surface water flows into the Mediterranean each second. The currents at Gibraltar can be compared to two large rivers flowing in opposite directions, one over the other (fig. 1.29).

Like the Mediterranean, the Black Sea is isolated by a shallow sill (at the Bosporus). But the Black Sea is characterized by a large excess of precipitation and river runoff. The dilute surface waters form a shallow, low

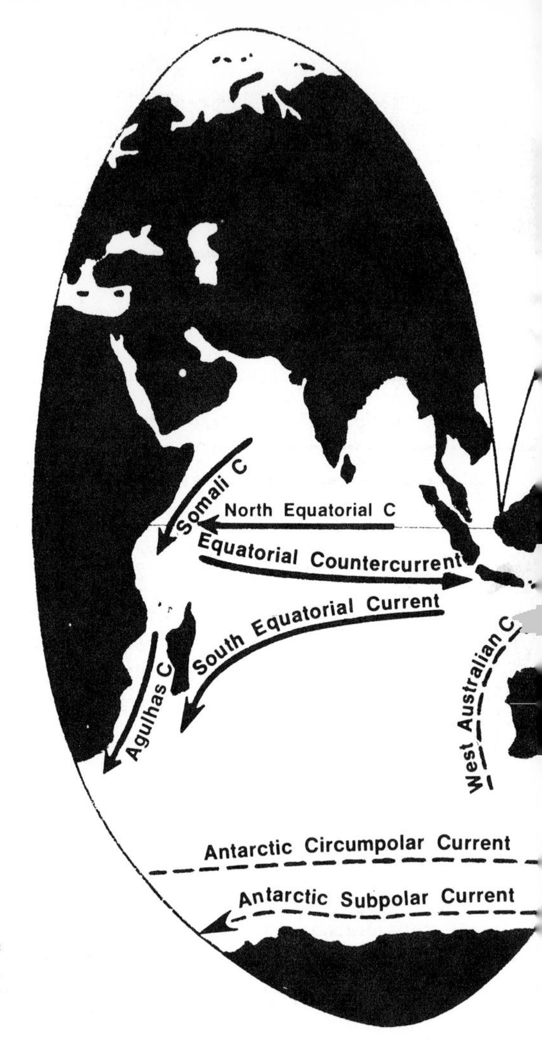

Fig. 1.27 The major surface currents of the world ocean. Cold currents are indicated by dash-line arrows.

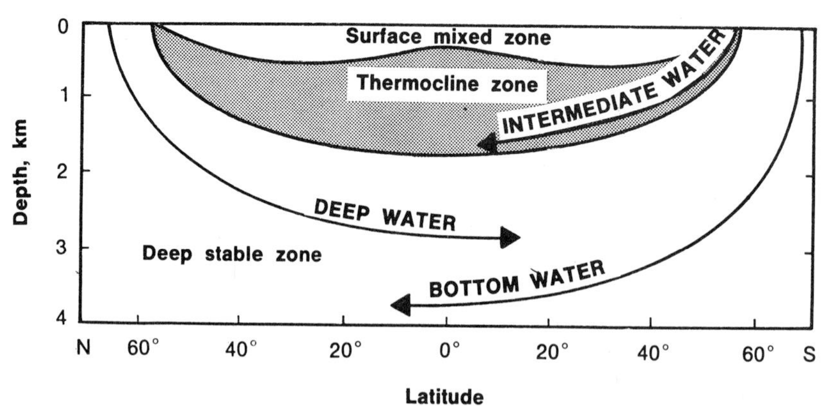

Fig. 1.28 The general pattern of deep-ocean circulation, shown in a north-south profile.

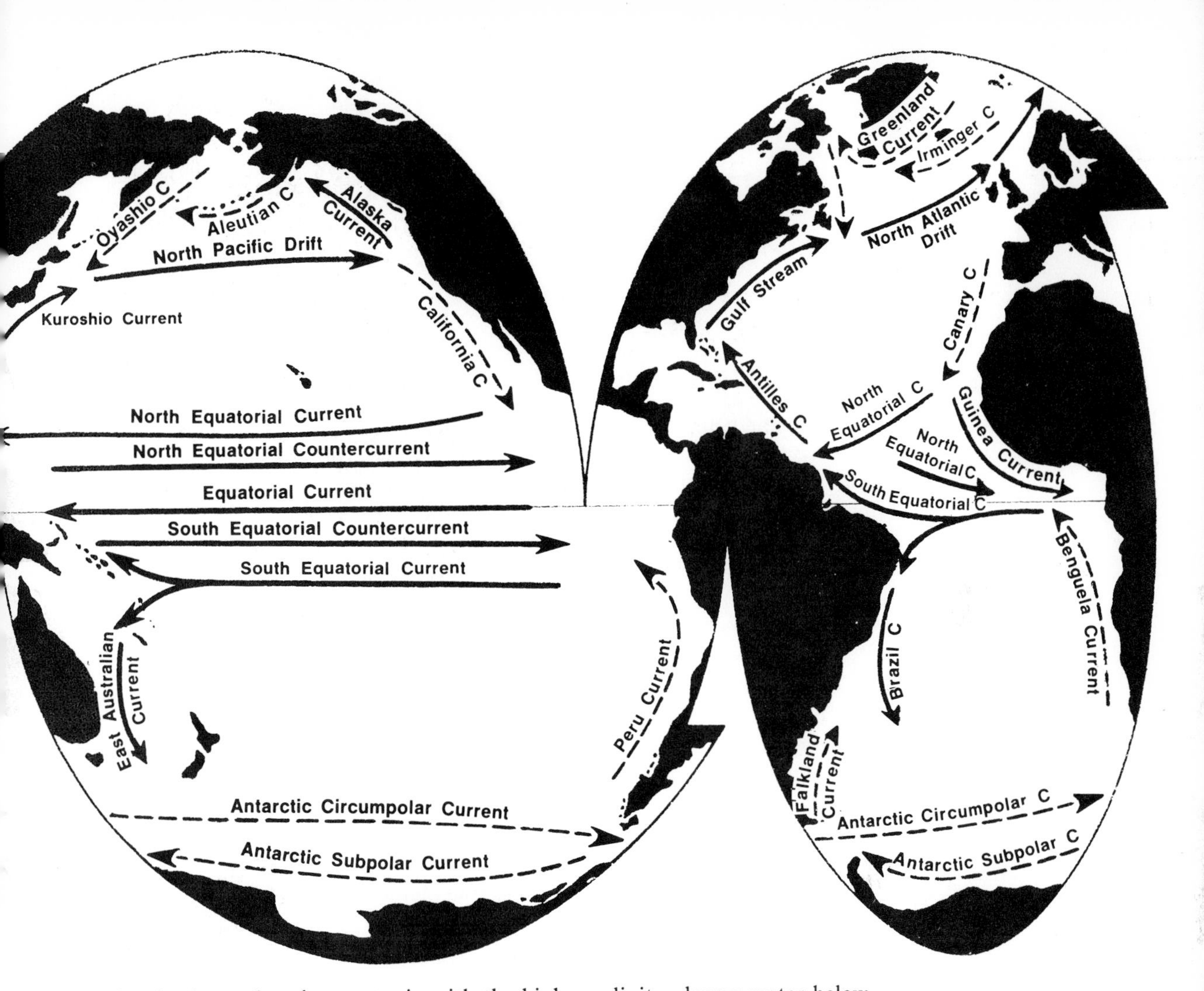

density layer that does not mix with the higher salinity, denser water below, but instead flows into the Mediterranean Sea through the Bosporus (fig. 1.29). For all practical purposes, the water below 150 m in the Black Sea is stagnant. Oxygen-rich surface water does not sink, so the more common oxygen-dependent forms of marine life are restricted to the uppermost layer. But the anaerobic deep waters of the Black Sea (over 80% of its volume) are by no means lifeless. The rain of organic remains from above has accumulated and provides abundant nourishment for numerous types of anaerobic bacteria. These bacteria exist without O_2 and in turn produce hydrogen sulfide (H_2S), which is toxic to other forms of life. Thus, the lack of deep circulation in the Black Sea limits the input of O_2, and allows the buildup of nutrients and H_2S. In this sense, the circulation of the Black Sea resembles that of some enclosed fiords of Scandinavia and the west coast of Canada.

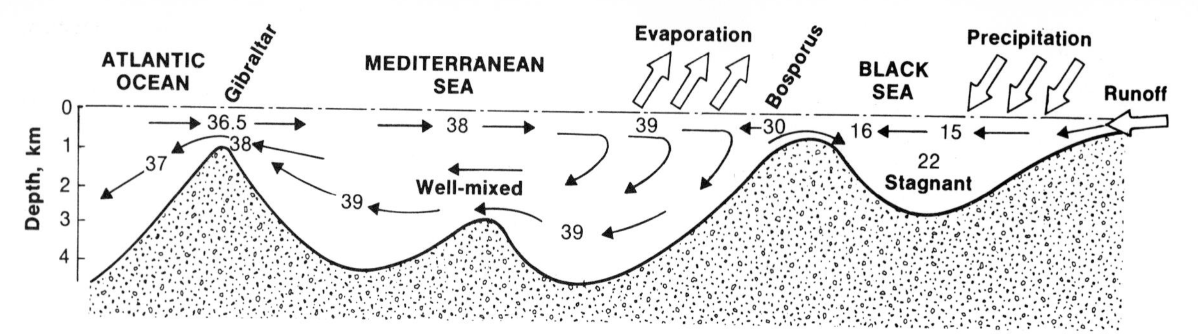

Fig. 1.29 A comparison of the deep-ocean circulation patterns of two marginal seas, the Mediterranean Sea and the Black Sea. The numbers represent salinity (‰).

Classification of the Marine Environment

The size and complexity of the marine environment make it a difficult system to classify conveniently. Thus, many various systems of classification have been proposed, each reflecting the interest and bias of the classifier. The system presented here is a slightly modified version of a widely accepted scheme proposed by Hedgpeth in 1957. The terms used in figure 1.30 designate particular zones of the marine environment, and should not be confused with the names of groups of organisms that normally inhabit these zones. The boundaries of these zones are defined on the basis of physical characteristics, such as water temperature, water depth, and available light.

The limits of the **splash** and **intertidal zones** are defined by tidal fluctuations of sea level along the shoreline. These zones and their inhabitants are examined in detail in chapters 4 and 5. The splash, intertidal, and **inner shelf** zones occur in the **photic** (lighted) **zone** where the light intensity is great enough to accommodate plant growth. The remaining zones are located in the **aphotic** (unlighted) **zone** where the absence of sunlight prohibits plant growth. The depth of the photic zone is highly variable depending on conditions that affect light penetration in water. Thus, the photic zone extends much deeper in clear, tropical waters than in murky, coastal waters of temperate areas. The average depth of the photic zone is 50-100 m.

The **benthic division** refers to the sea bottom topography. The portion of the continental shelf below the photic zone is the **outer shelf.** The **bathyal zone** is approximately equivalent to the continental slope areas. The **abyssal zone** refers to abyssal plains and other ocean bottom areas between 3,000 and 6,000 m in depth. The upper boundary of this zone is sometimes defined as the region where the water temperature never exceeds 4° C. The **hadal zone** is that part of the ocean bottom below 6,000 m, primarily the trench areas.

The **pelagic division** includes the entire water mass of the ocean. For our purposes, it will be sufficient to separate the pelagic region into two provinces: the **neritic province,** which includes the water over the continental shelves; and the **oceanic province,** the water which overlies the deep ocean basins.

Each of these subdivisions of the ocean environment is inhabited by characteristic marine plants and animals. It is these organisms, and their interaction with their immediate surroundings, that is the subject of the remainder of this book.

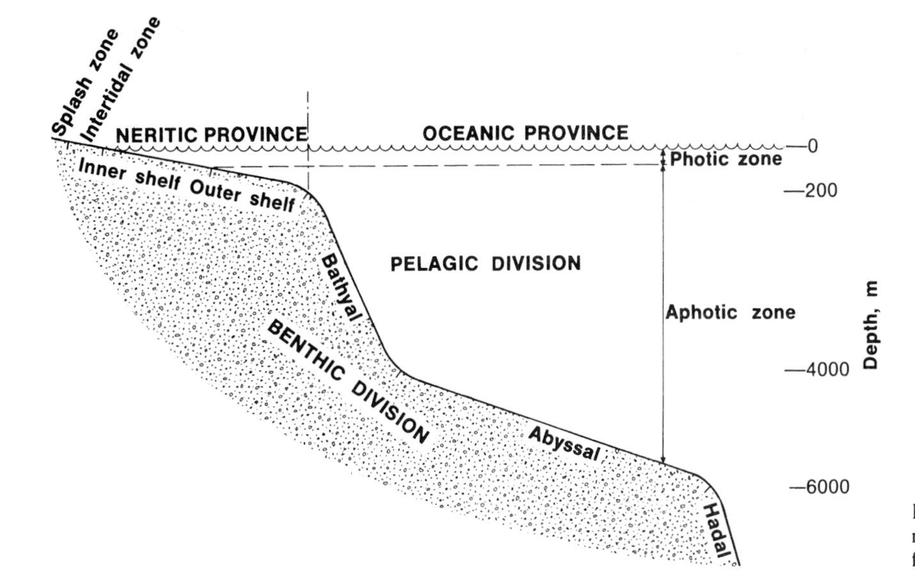

Fig. 1.30 A classification of the marine environment. Adapted from Hedgpeth 1957.

Summary

The world ocean is a large interconnected body of seawater, which covers 71% of the earth's surface. The sea bottom is smooth in some places and mountainous in others, with trenches extending beyond ten thousand m in depth.

Most of the basic properties of seawater are determined by the unusual characteristics of water itself. The asymmetrical shape of a water molecule creates an electrical charge separation that initiates hydrogen-bonding interactions with adjacent water molecules. Hydrogen bonding, in turn, affects water's basic properties, including its stability as a liquid, its viscosity, surface tension, heat capacity, solvent capability, and density-temperature relationships.

Seawater contains in solution a variety of salts, gases, and other substances that average about 3.5% of the total weight of seawater. These dissolved substances affect the density of seawater as well as its osmotic properties, buffering capacity, and other biologically significant features.

The water of the oceans is constantly in motion, mixed and moved by winds, tides, waves, currents, sinking water masses, and upwelling. The driving forces behind these mixing processes are heat from the sun and, to a much lesser extent, the gravitational pull of the moon and sun.

The marine environment is one of the most complex on earth and can be separated into two basic units, the benthic and pelagic divisions. These in turn may be subdivided into smaller, more convenient categories based on water depth, light availability, and tidal exposure.

Questions for Discussion

1. Why do surface ocean-water temperatures vary less from season to season than do air temperatures over nearby land masses?

2. List the processes which cause ice to form on seawater. Explain why these processes also establish conditions that tend to resist further freezing of the same water mass.
3. How are the surface ocean currents in the Northern Hemisphere similar to those of the Southern Hemisphere? How do they differ?
4. A drift bottle is tossed into the ocean off the north coast of Peru. Three years later the bottle is recovered on a beach in Norway. Describe the most likely path of the bottle from Peru to Norway, assuming it to have been transported solely by ocean surface currents. Do any other reasonable routes exist?
5. Describe the variation of dissolved oxygen in an oceanic water column from the surface to 2,000 m in depth. Account for the variations shown.
6. Freshwater crayfish and marine lobsters are closely related, yet each is incapable of surviving in the other's habitat. Discuss some likely reasons for this.

Suggestions for Further Reading

Books

Any recent introductory oceanography text, such as

Anikouchine, W. A., and Sternberg, R. W. 1973. *The world ocean.* Englewood Cliffs, N. J.: Prentice-Hall.

Gross, G. M. 1976. *Oceanography, a view of the earth.* Englewood Cliffs, N. J.: Prentice-Hall.

Ingmanson, D. E., and Wallace, W. J. 1973. *Oceanology: an introduction.* Belmont, Calif.: Wadsworth.

The Rand McNally atlas of the oceans. 1977. Chicago: Rand McNally.

Articles

Armi, L. 1978. Mixing in the deep ocean—the importance of boundaries. *Oceanus* 21(fall):14–19.

Bascom, W. 1960. Beaches. *Scientific American*, August: 80–91.

Byran, K. 1978. The ocean heat balance. *Oceanus* 21(fall): 18–26.

MacIntyre, F. 1970. Why the sea is salt. *Scientific American,* November: 104–15.

McDonald, J. E. 1952. The coriolis effect. *Scientific American,* May: 72–76.

Stewart, R. W. 1967. The atmosphere and the ocean. *Scientific American,* September: 27–36.

Seastar brachiolaria larva. Courtesy Carolina Biological Supply Company.

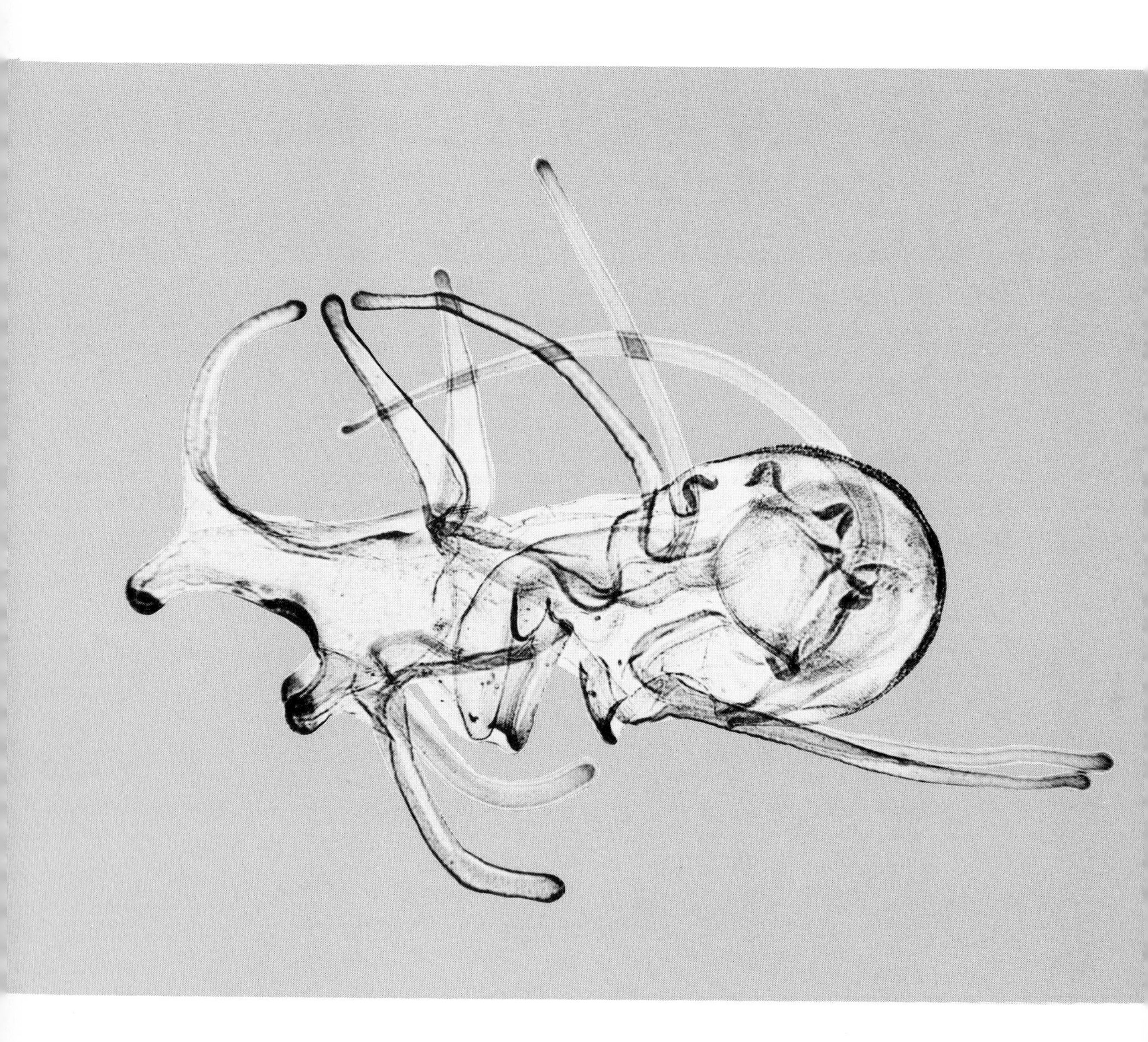

The Origin and Development of Life in the Sea

2

Life is a very special phenomenon. We can observe it, dissect it, and analyze it. We can discuss the attributes of life and can even state with a good deal of authority how living systems work. Yet our comprehension of life remains incomplete until we understand something of its origins.

Within the past two centuries, many lines of thought concerning the beginnings of life on earth have been presented and have met with varying degrees of acceptance. But in spite of several hundred years of research, the origins of living organisms still remain a matter of some speculation. The knowledge gained from these studies has, however, considerably limited the range of serious investigation and speculation accepted by biologists today. For example, the premise that life is the result of a supernatural or religious event is not considered here because it cannot be subjected to scientific examination. Such a premise must be accepted or rejected solely on the basis of faith. Equally untestable at present is the hypothesis that life forms were carried to earth from elsewhere in the universe. Until additional evidence concerning the possibility of life on other planets is available, this concept merely begs the question of life's origins by banishing the investigation to some distant and inaccessible part of the universe.

In 1924, Oparin, a Russian biochemist, and later in England, Haldane presented (independently) a very different theory of the origin of life on earth. They suggested that early life forms developed under favorable conditions from common nonliving substances that existed in the early oceans of the earth. The Oparin-Haldane hypothesis, with slight variations and some extensions, has become widely accepted by biologists and other scientists today. This hypothesis has been subjected to intense scientific scrutiny and testing; it is continually undergoing minor revision as new information becomes available.

The discussion that follows presents the central theme and general sequence of events as hypothesized by Oparin and Haldane. Several of their points, especially those requiring a detailed knowledge of biochemistry, have been intentionally omitted. The purpose here is to use the general hypothesis as a convenient framework to support some basic and unifying concepts concerning the structure and function of living organisms.

The Sea Before Life

The validity of much of the Oparin-Haldane hypothesis depends on the actual environmental conditions that existed on the earth's surface early in its history. Our solar system, including the earth, is thought to have been formed approximately 4.5 billion years ago. Modern theories on the origin of the solar system suggest that the planets aggregated from a vast cloud of cold gas and dust particles into clusters of solid matter. These clumps continued to grow as gravity attracted them together. As the earth grew in this fashion, pressure from the outer layers compressed and heated the earth's center. Aided by heat from the decay of radioactive elements, the interior of the earth melted. Iron, nickel, and other heavy metals migrated to the core, while the lighter materials floated to the surface and cooled to form a thin crust (fig. 2.1).

The vents of numerous volcanoes poked through the crust and tapped the upper mantle for the liquid material and gases that were then spewed out over the surface of the young earth. From these volcanic gases, a primitive atmosphere developed. The chemical makeup of the primitive atmosphere is a major point of controversy, but it was doubtless much different from our atmosphere today (which is composed of 78% N_2, 21% O_2, and traces of other gases). Water vapor was certainly present. As the water vapor condensed, it fell as rain and accumulated in depressions on the earth's surface to form embryonic oceans. Little or no molecular oxygen (O_2) was present, either in the atmosphere or dissolved in the seas. Carbon was probably abundant as methane (CH_4) or carbon dioxide (CO_2). Nitrogen, the most abundant gas of the atmosphere today, was probably available as ammonia (NH_3) or possibly molecular nitrogen (N_2).

Some of the gases from the early atmosphere were eventually absorbed by seawater. Ions dissolved from rocks and carried to the seas by rivers added to the mixture, creating a complex solution of H_2O, CH_4, NH_3, possibly CO_2 and N_2, plus the more abundant ions listed in table 1.3. These substances contained the basic elements that constitute the chemistry of life, but they were not in the proper chemical combination necessary for life forms to develop. All living organisms are composed of four basic types of organic compounds: **proteins, carbohydrates, DNA** and the closely related **RNA**, and

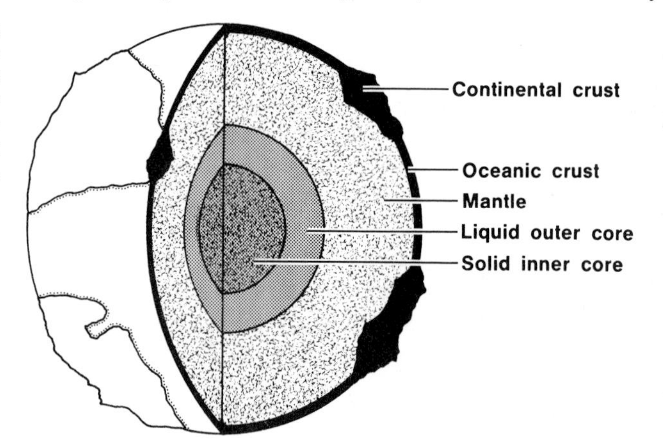

Fig. 2.1 A section through the earth, showing its density-layered interior structure. The crustal thickness is greatly exaggerated in order to show continents and ocean basins at this scale.

lipids (fatty substances). Each of these substances is structurally quite complex, yet each is composed of much simpler subunits. All proteins are derived from various combinations of some twenty **amino acids** (in much the same way that all words in the English language are developed from different combinations of the twenty-six letters of the alphabet). Carbohydrates are long, often complex chains of **sugar** molecules. In a similar fashion, **DNA** or **RNA** is constructed of various combinations of four **nucleic acids** and sugar; and **lipids** consist of **fatty acids** and **alcohol.** The point is that the complex structural components of living systems are composed of a few types of simple substances. Yet even these simple organic compounds (amino acids, sugars, nucleic acids, fatty acids, and alcohols) are much more complex than the solution of molecules found in the earth's primordial seas.

In 1953, Stanley Miller performed an instructive series of experiments that substantially narrowed the conceptual gap between a watery solution of simple molecules and the organized chemical complexity of living organisms. In a closed flask, Miller exposed a mixture of CH_4, H_2, NH_3 gases and boiling water (representing the earth's primitive atmosphere) to an electrical spark. This and other similar experiments that followed have produced, by nonbiological means, a variety of complex organic compounds normally found in living systems. Common among them were several amino acids, sugars, various organic acids, and even **ATP** (adenosine triphosphate, a source of energy in cells). Amino acids are necessary to form proteins, which in turn function as structural components (as in muscle tissue) or as **enzymes** to regulate biochemical reactions. Sugars form carbohydrates to be used as structural units or as an energy source. ATP is a high-energy compound universally used by living organisms for short-term energy storage or conversion (a single active cell often requires more than two million molecules of ATP each second to meet its energy requirements).

Several sources of energy, including lightning, ultraviolet radiation, and radioactive decay, were probably available to act on the "soup" of organic matter accumulating in the earth's early seas. These energy sources sufficed to form larger and more complex substances from the simpler ones. From amino acids, proteins capable of controlling and regulating other chemical reactions formed. Other organic compounds formed from simpler components in much the same manner.

Droplets of these compounds, in various combinations, were dispersed in seawater by waves and tides. Over immense periods of time, the less stable droplets broke up and disappeared. Only the most stable forms endured this prolonged period of chemical development. Primitive examples of growth and metabolism were exhibited by droplets that absorbed additional materials from the environment and utilized them to synthesize new substances. Certain droplets eventually achieved the proper combination of nucleic acids, which form **DNA** or **RNA**, to record critical genetic information needed to build and repair their own parts. Once capable of transferring that information to subsequent generations, they had achieved the basis of life's hereditary mechanism and the essence of true biological reproduction.

Some Characteristics of Life

But were these droplets—these "**protobionts**"—alive? Throughout this discussion, terms such as "life" and "alive" have been used with the assumption that the reader has, from past experience, developed some intuitive understanding of their meanings. Life is a difficult term to define, but it can be at least characterized. Like the chemicals from which they are made, living organisms are structurally quite complex; but their complexity is highly organized. Each level of organization within a living system is derived from several components smaller and less complex than itself. The more common levels of organization found in living systems are listed and defined in table 2.1. Life forms also use energy and break down and resynthesize complex chemical substances. The energy and materials are used by all life forms to grow and reproduce, to respond to their environment, and, in general, to maintain their organized physical and chemical state.

These are the more obvious attributes of life that are necessary for long-term survival. Except for the higher levels of organization shown in table 2.1, most of these attributes had been achieved by our "protobionts." If they can

Table 2.1. *Levels of Organization in Living Systems. Each Level Is Composed of Numerous Units From One or More Levels Below.*

Level of Organization	Definition	Examples
Ecosystem	The organisms of a particular type of area, together with the physical features of the environment in which they live	Coral reef ecosystem
Community	An ecologically integrated group, consisting of all the populations living in a given, limited area	Rocky intertidal community, beach community
Population	A group of interbreeding organisms coexisting in the same time and place	Herring school
Organism	An individual structure made up of one or more cells, that is capable of reproduction and mutation	Whale, diatom
Organ	A specific body part, consisting of several tissues associated together as an identifiable, functional unit	Heart, intestine
Tissue	An aggregation of similar cells, usually with a specific function	Muscle tissue, fatty tissue
Cell	The fundamental organizational unit of living material	Muscle cell, nerve cell, diatom
Cellular organelle	A well-defined structure within cells	Chloroplast, nucleus
Macromolecule	A very large molecule, consisting of numerous simple molecules, linked together	Proteins, carbohydrates
Simple molecule	A small chemical unit consisting of two or more atoms bonded together	Amino acids, sugars
Atom	The smallest unit of an element, indivisible by ordinary chemical procedures	C, H, O

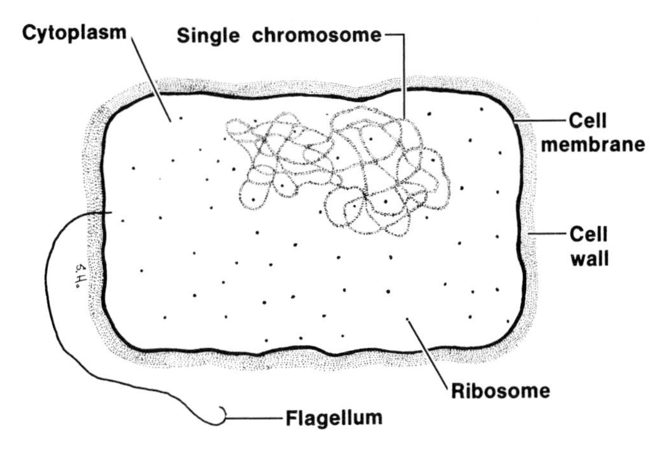

Fig. 2.2 A generalized diagram of a bacterial cell.

be considered "alive" at their primitive stage of development, what manner of life was it, and when did it exist?

Fossil evidence of complex life forms older than 600 million years is not abundant. Even so, fossil remains of simple cells over 3 billion years old have been reported from scattered sites in Africa. These microscopic organisms had achieved a level of structural organization strikingly like some modern bacteria. Like modern bacteria and blue-green algae (fig. 2.2), these early life forms lacked much of the complex subcellular structure found in other modern cells. Yet they presumably contained the necessary complement of cellular machinery needed to function as living cells. A **cell wall** provides form and mechanical support for the cell. Inside the cell wall, a selectively permeable **cell membrane** separates the internal fluid environment (the **cytoplasm**) from the exterior of the cell, and regulates exchange between the cell and its external medium. Limited movement is provided by a whiplike **flagellum.** Internally, the genetic information is coded and stored in a single, looped **chromosome.** That information is used by the small **ribosomes** to direct the synthesis of enzymes. The enzymes, in turn, control and regulate all other chemical reactions that occur in living cells.

Sources of Cellular Energy

To satisfy their energy needs, the first living organisms probably used ATP simply because it was readily available in seawater. A molecule of ATP (adenosine triphosphate) is composed, as its name implies, of an adenosine compound with three phosphate groups: [adenosine]—(P)~(P)~(P). The symbol ~ represents a high-energy chemical bond that, when broken, yields more calories of available energy than other chemical bonds. Usually, only the terminal bond is broken to release energy, a (P) unit, and [adenosine]—(P)~(P)(adenosine diphosphate or **ADP**):

$$\text{ATP} \xrightarrow{\text{enzyme}} \text{ADP} + \text{P} + \text{energy}$$

As the supply of preformed ATP was consumed and competition for it increased, biochemical systems developed to synthesize new ATP from ADP and other energy-rich compounds. In an environment with little free O_2 and abundant supplies of organic material, **anaerobic respiration** (respiration without O_2) provided a mechanism to obtain energy for use in cellular processes. Several variations of anaerobic respiration are exhibited by present-day plants and animals, yet all characteristically release energy from organic substances without using O_2. In **alcoholic fermentation,** for example, sugar is degraded, or broken down, to alcohol and CO_2. Energy is released in the form of ATP:

$$\underset{\text{sugar}}{C_6H_{12}O_6} \xrightarrow[\text{enzymes}]{\text{respiratory}} \underset{\text{alcohol}}{2C_2H_5OH} + \underset{\text{carbon dioxide}}{2CO_2} + \underset{\text{energy}}{ATP}$$

ATP is not synthesized from scratch, but is formed from lower-energy ADP and Ⓟ.

These primitive life forms, capable of renewing their store of ATP, continued to reproduce and compete for the supply of high-energy compounds available in the sea. Eventually, increased competition for dwindling food resources must have established a high survival premium on organisms that could capitalize on alternate sources of energy. Several solutions to the energy problem may have evolved; but one, **photosynthesis,** proved especially successful.

Photosynthesis is a biochemical process that uses a green pigment, **chlorophyll,** to absorb some of the abundant energy of the sun's rays. The first step in the development of photosynthesis was the direct synthesis of high-energy ATP from ADP and Ⓟ. When light energy strikes a molecule of chlorophyll, it excites an electron of the chlorophyll to a higher, unstable energy state. Another substance, which has a high affinity for electrons, leads the high-energy electron through a series of molecules collectively referred to as an **electron transport system** (ETS). The ETS eases the high-energy electron step-by-step back down to its initial energy state (fig. 2.3). Such stepwise chemical reactions are a general characteristic of biochemical systems.

Energy released by the electron as it passes through the ETS is used by enzymes to form ATP from ADP and P (fig. 2.3). The electron is eventually cycled back to the chlorophyll molecule to be used again.

Most modern photosynthetic organisms use another more complex energy-capturing process that will be described in detail in chapter 6. In this

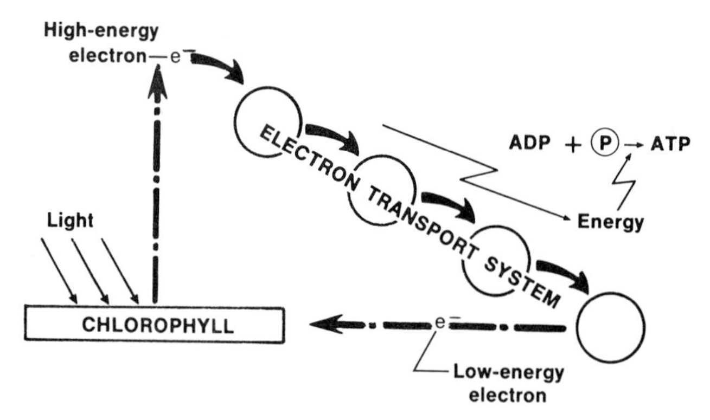

Fig. 2.3 A simple form of photosynthesis.

process, the high-energy ATP and other substances produced are immediately used to synthesize sugars, amino acids, and lipids from CO_2 and H_2O. For the present, this second type of photosynthesis can be summarized by the following general equation:

$$\underset{\text{carbon dioxide}}{6CO_2} + \underset{\text{water}}{12H_2O} \xrightarrow[\text{chlorophyll}]{\text{sunlight}} \underset{\text{sugar}}{C_6H_{12}O_6} + \underset{\text{water}}{6H_2O} + \underset{\text{oxygen}}{6O_2}$$

Fossil evidence suggests that blue-green algae or photosynthetic bacteria were the first to capitalize on photosynthesis as a solution to their energy needs. Fossil remains of blue-green algae nearly 3 billion years old indicate that photosynthesis evolved at an early stage in the development of life on earth. With a practically inexhaustible supply of energy, photosynthesizers managed to sidestep many of the energetic limitations experienced by previous forms of life. At the same time they renewed the supply of high-energy substances for other nonphotosynthetic organisms. The bodies of the photosynthesizers themselves became the primary source of high-energy organic reserves, directly or indirectly providing the nutrition for almost all other organisms.

Oxygen liberated by photosynthesizers dissolved into seawater, and significant amounts gradually found their way into the atmosphere for the first time. To some anaerobic organisms, O_2 was an intolerable metabolic poison that ultimately limited their occurrence to unoxygenated bottom muds, anoxic ocean basins, and other marginal habitats. Other nonphotosynthesizers were directly dependent on the material produced by the photosynthesizers and had to suffer the sometimes corrosive effects of increasing O_2 concentrations. Some of these organisms developed methods of using O_2 to their advantage. Respiratory processes more complex than that of anaerobic respiration evolved to completely oxidize high-energy compounds such as sugar to carbon dioxide and water, and in the process release energy:

$$\underset{\text{sugar}}{C_6H_{12}O_6} + \underset{\text{oxygen}}{6O_2} \xrightarrow[\text{enzymes}]{\text{respiratory}} \underset{\text{carbon dioxide}}{6CO_2} + \underset{\text{water}}{6H_2O} + \underset{\text{energy}}{ATP}$$

This process utilizes oxygen and is called **aerobic respiration.** In aerobic respiration, each molecule of sugar yields 19 times as much energy as it would if used in anaerobic respiration. Those organisms that metabolized food and oxygen in this manner secured a tremendous energetic edge over their anaerobic competitors.

The Cellular Structure of Life

With additional energy to expend, larger cells with increased structural complexity and greater stability developed. These are the **eucaryotic cells,**[1] char-

1. According to current scientific usage, eucaryotic is the preferred spelling. The previously used variation, eukaryotic, is also correct.

acteristic of living organisms whose cells possess a **nucleus** (bacteria and blue-green algae lack a true nucleus and are termed **procaryotic cells**). Eucaryotic cells are generally larger than procaryotes, and they house a variety of membrane-bound structures (fig. 2.4) not found in procaryotes (fig. 2.2).

The chromosomes and their surrounding **nuclear membrane** form a central structure, the **nucleus**. The enzymes involved in respiration and energy release are associated with the numerous small **mitochondria.** Many of the enzyme-synthesizing ribosomes are free in the cytoplasm, but others are organized on a membranous **endoplasmic recticulum.** Food particles are ingested through **pinocytosis channels** and stored in **vacuoles** within the cell. Other subcellular structures are involved in excretion of wastes, osmotic balance, and a number of other cellular chores. In addition, photosynthetic eucaryotes typically possess two special features: (1) **chloroplasts** serve as the sites of photosynthesis, and (2) a rigid **cell wall** provides shape and support in a manner similar to procaryotic cells.

Eucaryotic cells are the structural units of all forms of "higher" plant and animal life. It was from eucaryotic ancestors that most of our present-day plants and animals evolved.

The Changing Marine Environment

Because of their small size and relative scarcity, we have only rudimentary fossil information about life forms that existed on earth prior to 600 million years ago. Although we know little of how they lived, they apparently had a significant impact on the character of their physical environment. Oxygen was produced in increasing amounts by microscopic photosynthetic plants. The O_2 content of the atmosphere 600 million years ago was probably about 1% of its present concentration. It was not much, but it is believed to have been the turning point at which time organisms utilizing aerobic respiration became dominant, and the anaerobes declined.

Fig. 2.4 Schematic diagram of a eucaryotic cell.

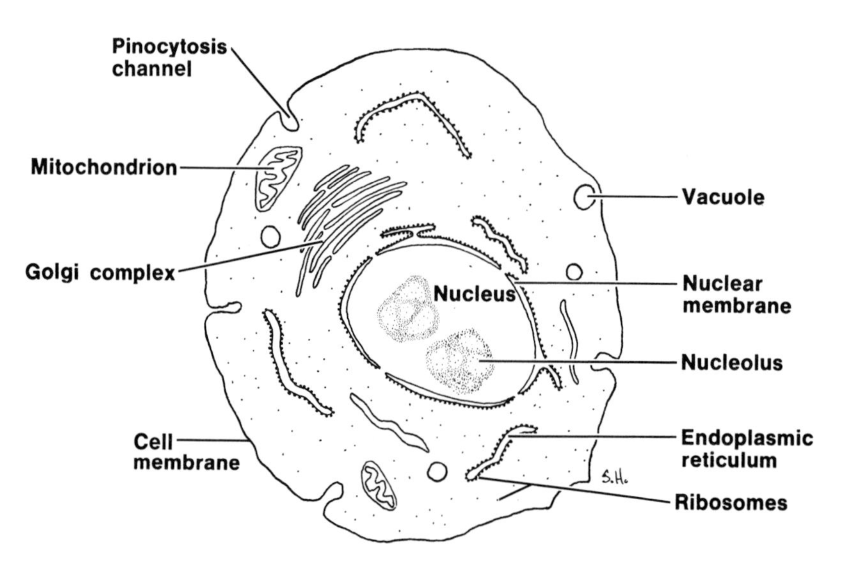

The evolution of more complex life forms using increasingly efficient methods of energy utilization set the stage for an explosion of marine life forms. By 500 million years ago, most of the major groups of marine plants and animals had made their appearance. Worms, sponges, corals, and the immediate ancestors of terrestrial animals and plants were abundant. But life could only exist in the sea at that time, where it was shielded from ultraviolet radiation by a protective blanket of seawater.

As O_2 became more abundant in the upper atmosphere, some of it was converted to **ozone** (O_3). The process of forming ozone absorbed much of the lethal ultraviolet radiation coming from the sun and prevented it from reaching the earth's surface. The O_2 concentration of the atmosphere 400 million years ago is estimated to have reached 10% of its present level. The ozone derived from the additional O_2 screened enough ultraviolet radiation to permit a few life forms to abandon their sheltered marine home and colonize the land. Figure 2.5 summarizes some of the significant events of the origin and early development of life on earth.

Since their initial formation, the ocean basins themselves have experienced considerable change. New material derived from the earth's mantle has so extended the continents that they are now larger and stand higher than at any time in the past. The oceans have kept pace, getting deeper by accumulating new water from volcanic gases and the chemical breakdown of rock.

In the early part of this century, Alfred Wegener suggested (and not too convincingly for most scientists of the time) that the oceans might be changing in other ways. Based partly on the jigsaw-puzzle fit of the continents (especially Africa and South America), Wegener proposed that our present continental masses had "drifted" apart following the breakup of a single supercontinent, **Pangaea**. It was not until the early 1960s that new and telling

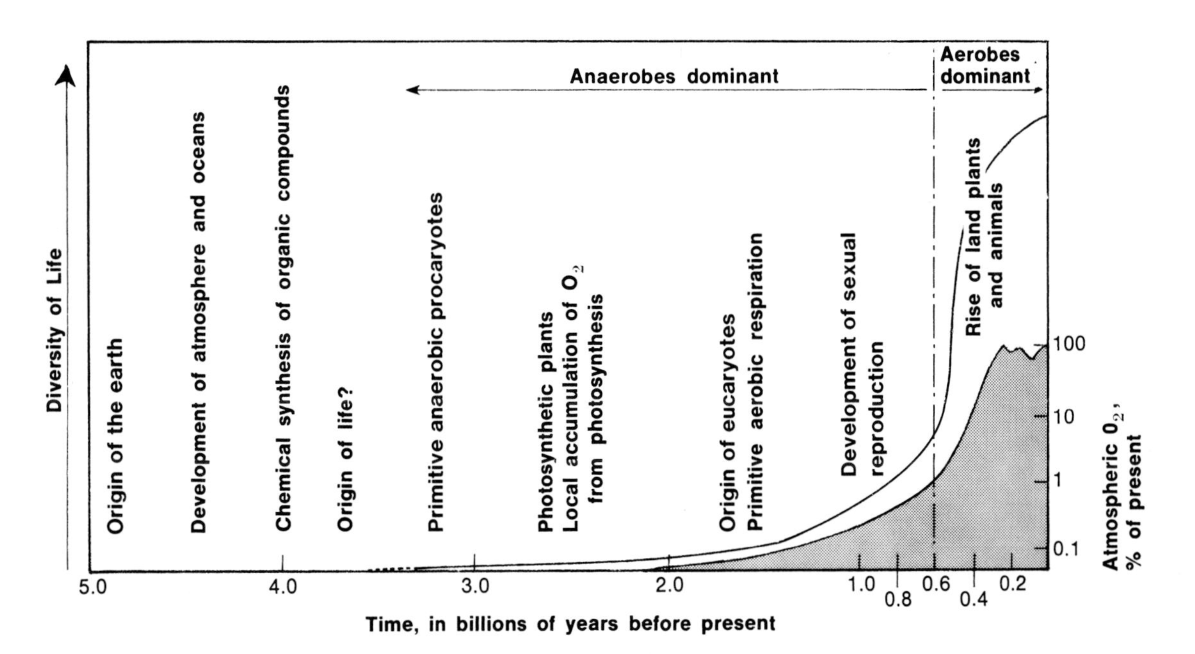

Fig. 2.5 A summary of some biological and physical milestones in the early development of life on earth. Upper curve represents the relative diversity of life; the lower curve, the O_2 concentration of the atmosphere.

evidence provided widespread endorsement for Wegener's proposal from the scientific community.

The evidence that supports the closely related concepts of **continental drift** and **seafloor spreading** indicates that the earth's crust is divided into a number of giant irregular plates. These rigid plates float on the more dense and slightly plastic mantle material beneath. Each plate includes both oceanic and continental crust and is bounded by oceanic trench and ridge systems (refer to fig. 1.3). New oceanic crustal material is thought to be formed continually along the axes of oceanic ridges and rises. As the crustal plates grow on either side of the ridge, they move laterally in opposite directions, carrying bottom sediments and attached continental masses with them (fig. 2.6).

The changes that seafloor spreading and continental drift have wrought on the shapes and sizes of the oceans have been impressive. The African continent seems to be drifting northward on a collision course with Europe, inexorably closing the Mediterranean Sea. Recent violent earthquakes in Turkey and Greece were only incidental tremors in this monumental collision of crustal plates. The rates of seafloor spreading have been determined for some oceans, and they vary widely. The South Atlantic is widening about 3 cm each year (or approximately your height in your lifetime). The Pacific Ocean is shrinking somewhat faster.

The breakup of Pangaea produced ocean basins where none existed before. The seas of 200 million years ago have changed size or even disappeared altogether. The past positions of the continents and ocean basins, based on our present understanding of the processes involved, are reconstructed in figure 2.7.

Excess crust produced by seafloor spreading is accommodated by folding into mountain ranges or by slipping down into the mantle and remelting (fig. 2.6). Unfortunately, most of the fossil deposits of early marine life forms can

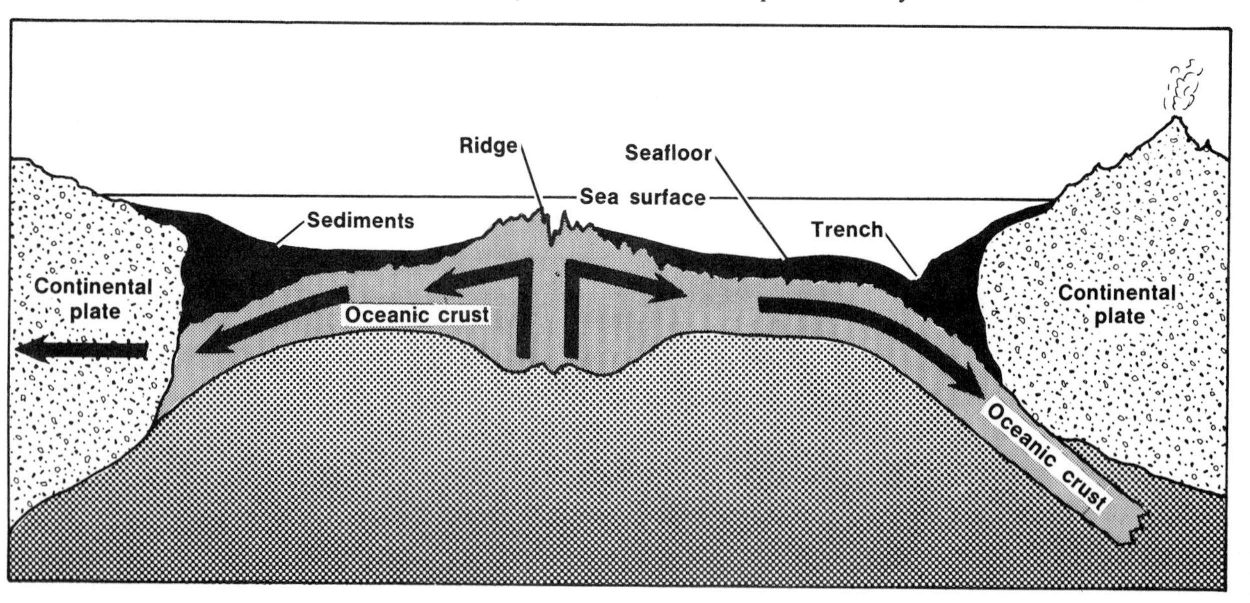

Fig. 2.6 Cross section of a spreading ocean floor, illustrating the relative motions of oceanic and continental crusts.

never be studied, for they too have been carried to destruction in the mantle by the "conveyor belt" of the seafloor crust. It is ironic indeed that the only fossil evidence we have for the first 90% of the evolutionary history of marine life is to be found on land that has been derived from ancient seabeds.

Processes of Evolution

The last half-billion years of life's history have been marked by the development and expansion of highly diverse forms of life in ever-increasing numbers.

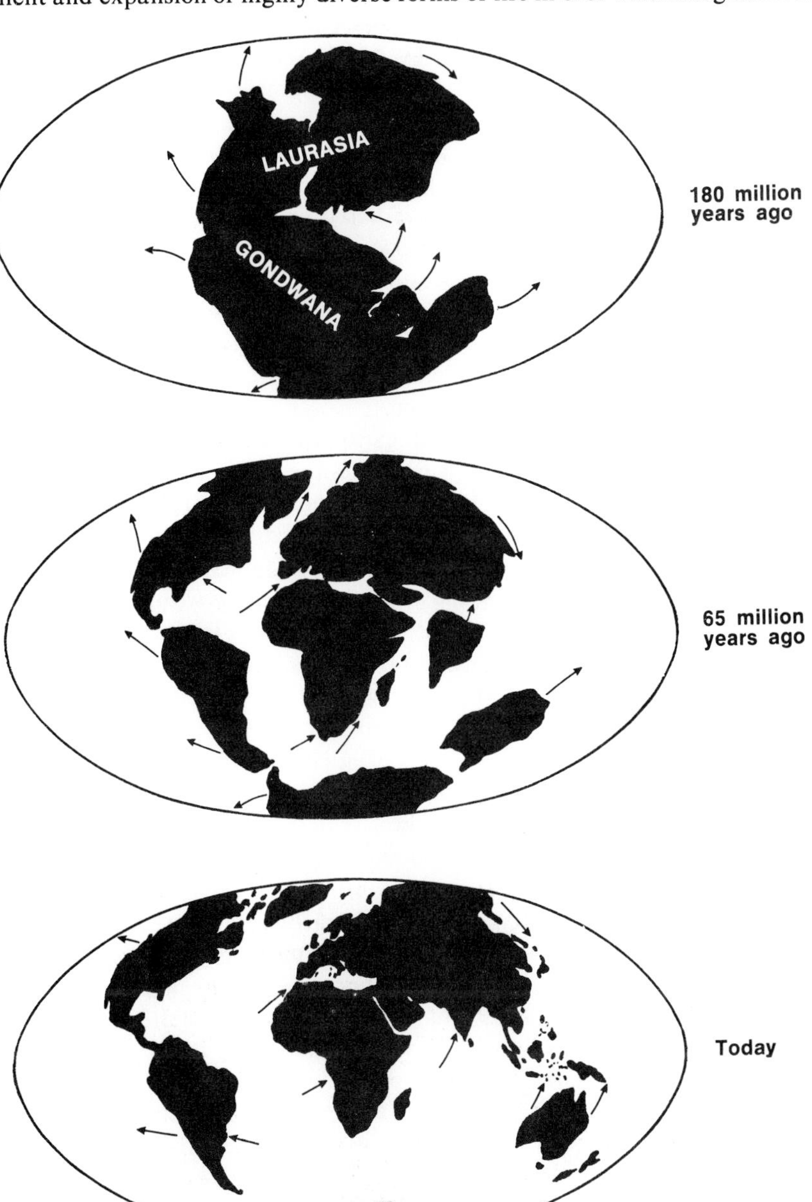

Fig. 2.7 About 200 million years ago, Pangaea separated into two large continental blocks, Laurasia and Gondwana. Since then, they have fragmented into smaller continents and drifted apart in the directions indicated by arrows. These maps outline the changing past positions of the continents and ocean basins. Adapted from Dietz and Holden 1970.

Large, multicellular plants and animals with complex structures and life processes evolved. Rigid skeletons developed to provide protection for crucial internal organs and to serve as sites for muscular attachment. Locomotion became more effective, and some animals became efficient predators—preying on their sluggish neighbors. A few types of marine plants and animals left the sea to establish their lineage on land. But most remained within the sheltered confines of the sea, to continue their evolution to the present.

Although the concept of **evolutionary change** in organisms is now strongly supported by experimental and fossil evidence, it was not always so. When the fundamental explanation of biological evolution was advanced by Charles Darwin, and independently by Alfred Wallace, in 1858, their basic assumptions were hotly contested. They were hampered by a complete lack of knowledge concerning chromosomes, genes, and the mechanism of inheritance. In spite of that, more than a century of testing and scientific scrutiny has only strengthened the basic validity of Darwin's statement.

Darwin's theory of evolution was based on two interrelated concepts. First, he rejected the idea of a sudden creation of a variety of unchanging organisms. Instead, he felt that present-day organisms had descended by gradual, but continuous, changes from ancestors different from themselves. This concept was supported by numerous bits of fossil evidence. Fossil remains of previous life forms indicated that slight changes in the structure of organisms over long periods of time were common.

The structural similarities that exist between living organisms also pointed to a common ancestry. For example, the basic skeletal pattern of a man's arm closely resembles the forelimbs of a porpoise, and even of a penguin (fig. 2.8). Granted, some of the bones are modified, but the basic similarity strongly suggests a common ancestry for all three animals.

Numerous existing plants and animals also carry within their bodies unmistakable evidence of their earlier origins. Whales, for instance, have no rear legs, and therefore have no use for a pelvis. Yet mature whales have, embedded in their body walls on either side of their genital openings, small vestigial remnants of what once was a pelvis. A more convincing confirmation of their terrestrial origins can be seen during embryonic development. Small limb buds appear where hind legs should be (fig. 2.9), then disappear again prior to birth. It seems logical to suggest that these temporary and useless structures were inherited from a four-footed terrestrial ancestor of whales.

The evidence for structural changes through time was apparent to Darwin, but the cause for the changes was not nearly so obvious. An important clue to the mechanics of evolutionary change came from breeders of domesticated plants and animals. In relatively short time spans, plant and animal breeders "developed" new strains or types of organisms quite unlike their predecessors.

In any population, be it goldfish, people, or fir trees, a certain amount of structural variation normally exists between individuals. Such variation is the physical expression of genetic differences between those individuals. **Mutations** (changes in the genetic information of an organism) establish genetic variations, and sexual reproduction rapidly multiplies and spreads the

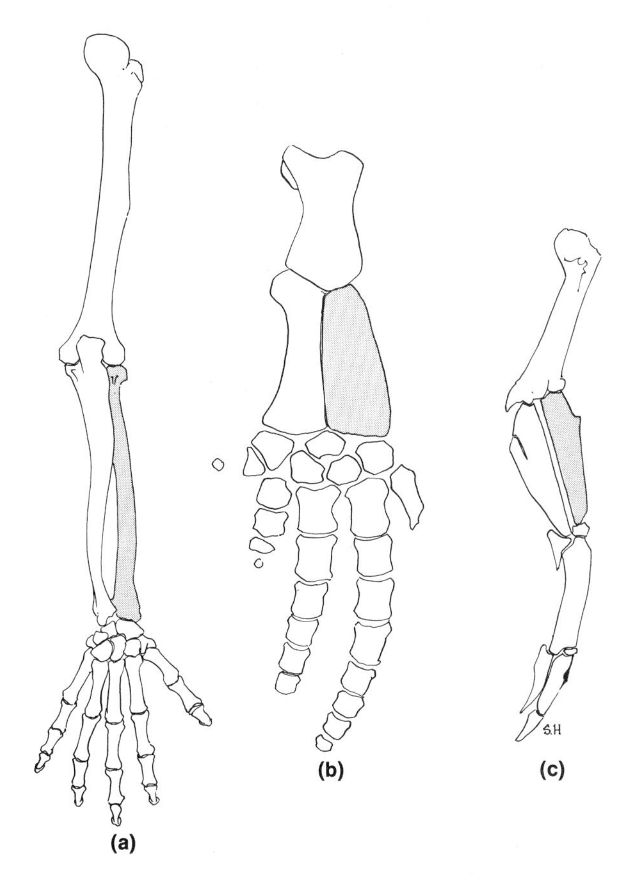

Fig. 2.8 Forelimb skeletons of (*a*) a human, (*b*) a porpoise, and (*c*) a penguin. The radius bone between the elbow and the wrist has been shaded in each.

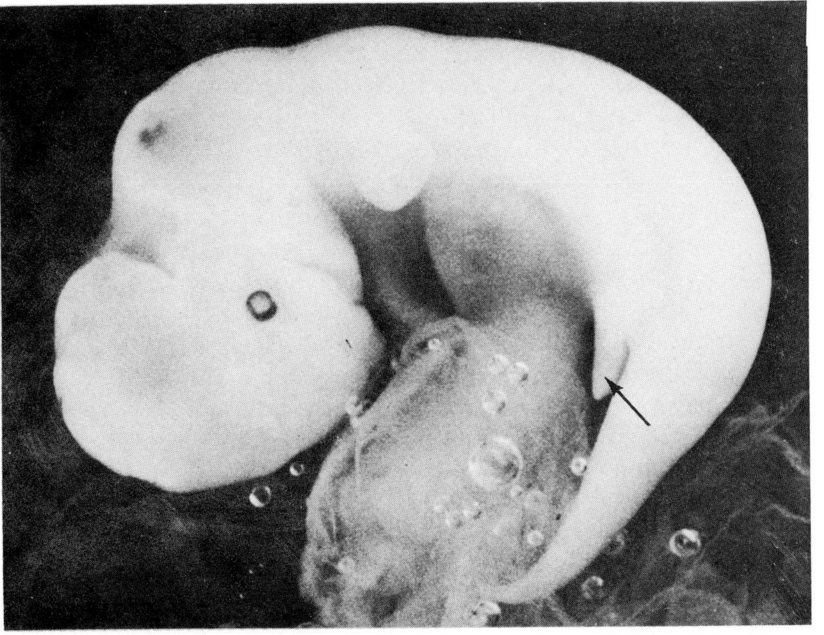

Fig. 2.9 A 70-day embryo of a gray whale. Note the definite rear limb buds (arrow). By permission from Rice and Wolman 1971. *The Life History and Ecology of the Gray Whale (Eschrichtius robustus)*. Spec. Publ. No. 3, American Society of Mammalogists.

Fig. 2.10 A variety of unusual structures (shaded parts) developed from an ancestral goldfish type (center) by intense selective breeding.

variations within a population. Oriental goldfish breeders, for example, began to capitalize on this natural variation over ten centuries ago. They started by selecting fish that best exhibited the characteristics they wanted to develop. The selected fish were allowed to reproduce, and the others were eliminated. After several generations of intensive selective breeding, characteristics that were not obvious in the first generation became quite prominent (fig. 2.10).

Since genetic variations also exist between individuals of wild populations, Darwin believed **natural selection** factors could account for evolutionary changes in nondomesticated plants and animals. More time is necessary for natural selection processes to produce significant changes in wild populations, but the time frame that supports natural evolutionary processes (often measured in millions of years) is sufficient to account for the changes produced.

Most natural populations are characterized by reproductive potentials in excess of those needed to simply maintain the population (and also in excess of the number their habitat can support). Sooner or later, expanding populations outgrow their necessary resources, and competition between individual members of the population is intensified. The individual's ability to survive and reproduce is affected by its inherent genetic and physical uniqueness. Natural conditions cause many to perish before reaching sexual maturity. Only those that are better equipped to compete and survive succeed in passing on their genetic traits to future generations of the population.

The offspring inherit characteristics that, in turn, provide an improved ability to compete and survive. This improved "fitness" may result from an increased resistance to disease, starvation, or climatic variations; or it may be simply a capacity to reproduce faster. This competition and differential survival is usually summarized in the overworked phrase "survival of the fittest." But the rules and conditions for survival change continuously and unpredictably. The selection factor for one generation might be a food shortage, but for the next generation, disease. "Survival of the fitter" might be more appropriate, as organisms seldom evolve to fit their total environment perfectly.

The basic biological units of evolutionary change, then, are populations. Evolutionary change only occurs in populations, never in individuals. Individuals perish regardless of whether or not their populations evolve. But when populations cease to adapt and change, extinction becomes inevitable. Of the untold millions of types of plants and animals that have evolved in the past 3 billion years of life's history on earth, only a tiny fraction exist at present. These are the temporary winners.

Systems of Classification

Natural systems are sometimes quite difficult to consider in their entirety. We often subdivide them into smaller, more convenient units; then categorize the units and relate them to the whole system on the basis of certain characteristics. The classification of the marine environment (fig. 1.30) is a good example. To be of value, any classification scheme must present the information in a generally accepted manner. This requires an orderly framework around which to logically classify the available information so that it becomes significantly more meaningful or useful. Whatever forms they assume, all classification schemes have one fundamental purpose: to provide a contrived, but accepted, means of treating information from complex natural systems in a useful and informative fashion.

The classification of marine plants and animals is not as simple a matter as the classification of the marine environment. Three systems of classification for marine organisms are presented here. Each system emphasizes a different aspect of the many important interrelationships that exist among living organisms, and between themselves and their environment. Very briefly, these systems are based on (1) the evolutionary relationships between organisms, (2) the spatial distribution of the organisms in the sea, and (3) the feeding or trophic relationships of marine plants and animals.

Taxonomic Classification

Nearly 1.5 million types of living organisms exist today. Due to the evolutionary processes that have operated for the past 3–4 billion years of earth history, each of these species exhibits some genetic relationship to all others. Often the relationship is obvious, as between dolphins and porpoises. However, the novice might have difficulty arriving at the correct conclusion that seals are more closely related to cats than to sea lions. The **taxonomic method** of classification deals with this vast and often confusing array of plant and animal diversity in a manner that reflects the evolutionary, or **phylogenetic,** relationships of organisms.

The purpose of taxonomic classification is to categorize organisms into natural units. One goal is to trace the lines of plant and animal evolution that have led to the diverse life forms of the present. Another is to identify and describe similarities among existing organisms. In recent years, computers have been employed to sort out the mass of information generated when large numbers of characteristics are considered. The objective classification schemes developed for computer operations form the foundation of a relatively new field known as **numerical taxonomy.**

Regardless of whether traditional or numerical methods are used, the taxonomic approach to classification consists of three basic processes. First, closely related groups of individual organisms must be recognized and described. Next, these groups, called **taxa** (singular, **taxon**), are assigned Latin names according to a rigidly prescribed procedure. Finally, the described and labeled groups are fitted into a system of larger, more inclusive classification groups.

The fundamental and smallest unit of taxonomic classification is the **species.** No precise definition of "species" is available; yet the species is a biological reality, and a working definition of a species is a practical necessity. A species can be simply defined as a group of closely related individuals that can and normally do interbreed and produce fertile offspring. The free exchange of genetic information between individuals of such groups steers them along a common evolutionary path, with the whole population adapting to environmental influences as a unit rather than as individuals. This definition of a species is widely accepted, but does pose special problems for the classification of marine organisms. Due to the environmental extremes occupied by many marine animals, they are quite often difficult, or even impossible, to study alive; and little is known of their reproductive habits. In such cases, another somewhat circuitous definition is called upon: a species is a group of closely related individuals classified as a species by a competent taxonomist on the basis of body anatomy, physiology, and other characteristics. Whatever definition is used, the species must be regarded as a functional biological unit capable of being studied and identified.

Assigning names to species or larger groups of organisms is a process more regimented than merely initially recognizing and describing the species. Common names are often effectively used in localized areas, but the lack of standardization in the use of common names detracts from their widespread usefulness and acceptance. To some people the name "dolphin" refers to an air-breathing porpoiselike marine mammal. To others, a "dolphin" is a tasty game fish. Such drawbacks of common names are eliminated when species and other taxonomic groups are assigned scientific names. These names are Latinized and are accepted by international agreement as "official" group names. Scientific names of plants and animals consist of two terms. The first is the **genus,** or generic, name followed by the species name. Conventionally, the generic name is capitalized, the species name is not. Both are either italicized or underlined. Each scientific name represents only one species of organism. Thus, there can be no confusion that *Delphinus delphis,* the common dolphin, refers only to a species of porpoiselike dolphins, and not to the dolphin fish.

The naming of a species does not complete the taxonomic classification process. The species is only part of a larger classification scheme that consists of a hierarchy of taxonomic categories:

- Kingdom
  - Phylum (Division for plants)
    - Class
      - Order
        - Family
          - Genus
            - Species

Each category is so constructed that it encompasses one or more categories from the next lower level. All of the categories above the species level are artificial, contrived for the convenient pigeonholing of similar groups of organisms. These groups are not completely arbitrary, however; but are arranged to reflect the known or assumed evolutionary relationships between organisms. It is because much of the evolutionary history of life is not known in detail that classification based on this lack of information sometimes tends to become artificial. Ideally, each genus is composed of a group of very closely related, but genetically isolated, species. **Families** include related genera that have many features in common. The cat family is a familiar example. **Orders** include related families based on generalized characteristics. **Classes, phyla** (singular, **phylum**), and **kingdoms** are even larger categories and are based on more general features. (The term **division** is used in place of *phylum* in the plant kingdom.)

Table 2.2. lists the taxonomic categories of four common marine organisms. The whale and the common dolphin, because they are members of the same class, are more closely related to each other than to either the purple sea urchin or the giant kelp. Still, the sea urchin has closer affinities to either the whale or the dolphin than to the kelp, which is in a different kingdom. In this manner, the taxonomic system of classification serves to sort out the known evolutionary information concerning plants and animals, and present it in a meaningful way.

In figure 2.11, the major phyla and divisions of marine organisms are arranged as a "phylogenetic tree" to illustrate the probable evolutionary relationships of these groups. Traditionally two kingdoms are recognized, the **Animalia** (animals) and **Plantae** (plants). The vertical dashed line separates the animal phyla on the left from the plant divisions on the right. More recent classification schemes include as many as five kingdoms to accommodate certain groups that cannot be neatly characterized as either animal or plant. The component groups of each of the five kingdoms are encircled by dashed lines in figure 2.11. In a five-kingdom system the procaryotic bacteria and blue-green algae are isolated into a third kingdom, the **Monera.** Predominantly single-celled eucaryotic organisms are grouped into the kingdom **Protista.** And the **Fungi** form the fifth kingdom. Notice that the kingdom Protista encompasses unicellular forms from both the plant and animal sides of figure 2.11.

Each scheme has its good points. The five-kingdom system better represents our present understanding of the early evolutionary relationships of living organisms. From a functional point of view, though, the two-kingdom system is simpler to employ. So for convenience, organisms that have cell walls and are photosynthetic will be rather arbitrarily referred to as plants. Organisms lacking these characteristics will be labeled animals. In the next chapter, each of the animal phyla listed in figure 2.11 is briefly discussed. Marine plants are considered in some detail in chapter 4. Only those phyla or divisions that have significant numbers of marine representatives are emphasized.

Table 2.2. *The Taxonomic Classification of Four Marine Organisms.*

Taxonomic Category	Blue Whale	Common Dolphin	Purple Sea Urchin	Giant Kelp
Kingdom	Animalia	Animalia	Animalia	Plantae
Phylum/ Division	Chordata	Chordata	Echinodermata	Phaeophyta
Class	Mammalia	Mammalia	Echinoidea	Phaeophycae
Order	Mysticeti	Odontoceti	Echinoida	Laminariales
Family	Balaenopteridae	Delphinidae	Strongylocentrotidae	Lessoniaceae
Genus	*Balaenoptera*	*Delphinus*	*Strongylocentrotus*	*Macrocystis*
Species	*musculus*	*delphis*	*purpuratus*	*pyrifera*

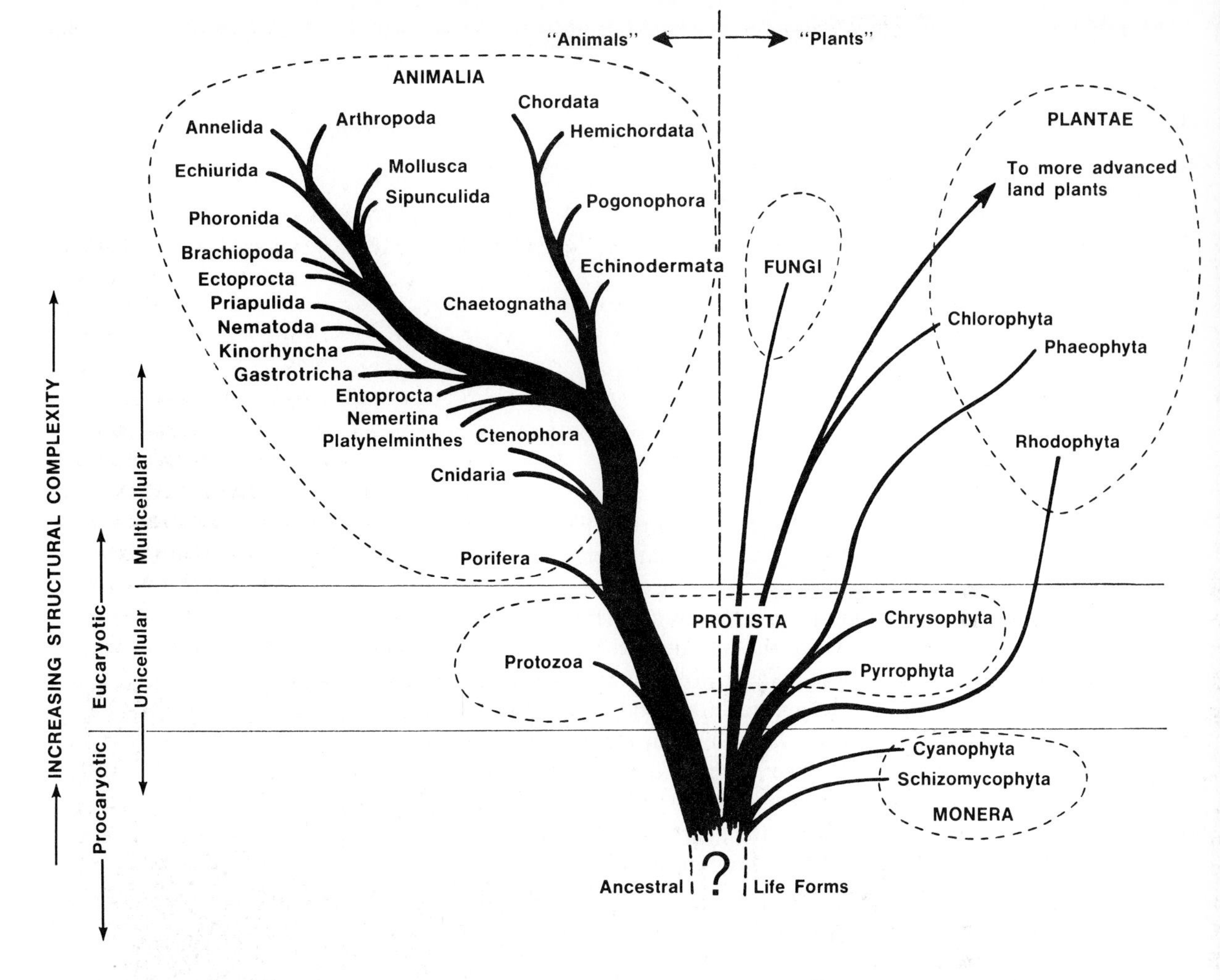

Fig. 2.11 A "phylogenetic tree," illustrating probable evolutionary relationships of the major groups of marine organisms. Each phylum and division is listed at the tips of the "branches." The five kingdoms are outlined with dashed lines.

Spatial Distribution

A much simpler way to classify marine organisms is according to where they live (fig. 2.12). The **benthos** includes the animals living on the bottom (**epifauna**) or in the sediment (**infauna**). This definition is often extended to include many types of fishes and other animals that can swim, but are generally associated closely with the ocean bottom. Benthic plants are restricted to the intertidal areas and shallow margins of the oceans. Below the photic zone, only animals exist, surviving on organic material drifting down from above.

The large, actively swimming marine animals belong to the **nekton.** This group includes marine mammals, many fish, and a few types of invertebrates such as squid and some shrimp.

Plankton (derived from the Greek term **planktos** which means 'to wander') are defined by their movements and their size. Carried about by water currents, they have little or no capability of horizontal motion, although some have remarkable vertical swimming abilities. Plankton are usually small, even

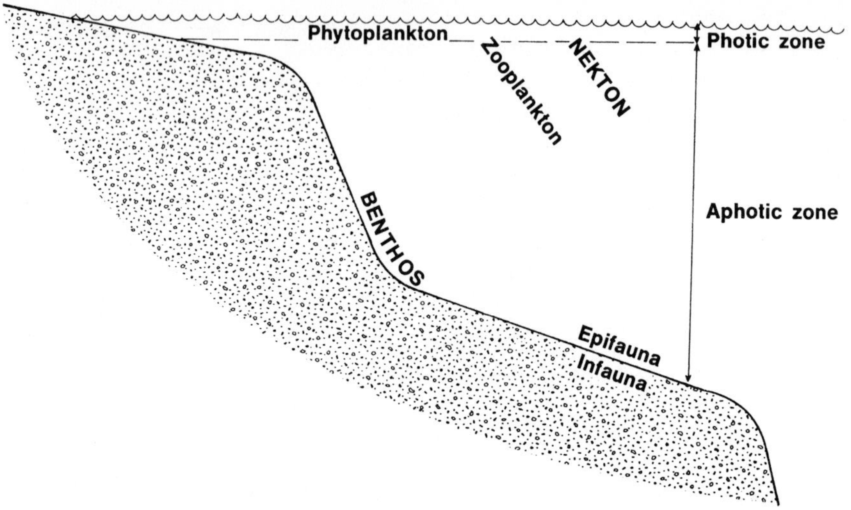

Fig. 2.12 A spatial classification of marine plants and animals. Compare this figure to the classification scheme for the marine environment, figure 1.30.

microscopic organisms, but some jellyfish may have tentacles over 15 m long and a bell 2 m in diameter. Plant members of the plankton are termed **phytoplankton.** They are nearly all microscopic, either single-celled or loose aggregates of a few cells. Phytoplankton are restricted to the sunlit, or photic, zones of the marine environment. The **zooplankton** are the animal plankton. These range in size and complexity from microscopic single-celled animals to large multicellular ones. The zooplankton are distributed throughout the pelagic division of the marine environment.

There are some situations in which these clear-cut distinctions between major groups break down. Many fish, for example, hatch from eggs as zooplankton, then gradually develop into nektonic animals as their size increases and their swimming ability improves. Even so, this system is useful for referring to major groups of marine organisms living under similar environmental conditions.

Trophic Relationships

Plants and animals can also be classified by their **trophic** associations. Basically this approach involves analysis of what an organism eats and what eats it. Living organisms require two fundamental things from their nourishment. Matter is necessary for individual growth and for reproduction. Energy is also required to perform work and to maintain the ordered chemical state that distinguishes living organisms from nonliving assemblages of similar material.

The transfer of matter and energy used for metabolic processes within the marine environment has resulted in a close interdependence of the three major kinds of marine organisms: **producers, consumers,** and **decomposers.** Plants are **autotrophic,** or self-nourishing. Plants are the producers, capable of absorbing readily available solar energy and building high-energy organic substances such as carbohydrates. In the process, they use inorganic nutrients (primarily nitrate and phosphate), water, and dissolved gases. Plants are referred to as the **primary producers** of the marine ecosystem and are placed in the first **trophic level.** The consumers and decomposers are unable to synthesize their own food from inorganic substances and ultimately must depend on plants for nourishment. These are the **heterotrophs.** Even in these groups there is some specialization in terms of nutrition. Animals adapted to feed on plants are **herbivores** and occupy the second trophic level, while those that prey on other animals are **carnivores.** The carnivores occupy the third and higher trophic levels. The decomposers, primarily bacteria and fungi, exist on **detritus,** the excrement and other waste products of all types of organisms and also the dead remains of the organisms themselves. Whatever their specialized feeding role may be, all heterotrophs metabolize the organic compounds synthesized by photosynthetic plants to gain available energy. This general process is termed **cellular respiration** and can be conducted either aerobically or anaerobically.

Organic compounds such as sugar produced by plants become the vehicle for the transport of usable energy to the other inhabitants of the ecosystem. An important distinction must be made between the flow of essential nutrients and the flow of energy in an ecosystem. The movement of nutrient compounds and dissolved gases is cyclic in nature, going from plants to animals, to decomposing bacteria, and eventually back to plants (fig. 2.13). In contrast, the energy flow in an ecosystem is unidirectional, from the sun through the plants to the consumers and decomposers. Living organisms, like most other energy-consuming systems, are not highly efficient in their use of energy. Much of the solar energy available at the sea surface is not absorbed by marine plants. Furthermore, a portion of the energy that is captured in the photosynthetic process is used by the plants for cellular maintenance, growth, and reproduction. Thus, only a fraction of the energy produced by photosynthesis is available to the herbivores. A similar decrease in available energy occurs between the herbivores and carnivores (fig. 2.14). Laboratory and field studies of marine organisms place the efficiency of energy transfer from one trophic level to the next at between 6% and 20%. In other words, only 6%–20% of the energy available to any trophic level is usually passed on to the next. A widely accepted average efficiency is 10%, although recent work on certain benthic communities and fish populations provide examples of energetic efficiencies significantly higher.

The paths of nutrient and energy flow through the living portion of the marine ecosystem are referred to as **food chains.** They may be grazing food chains, commencing with plants and leading directly through a succession of grazers and predators; or they may be parallel detritus food chains, based on the waste and death of the grazing food chains. With only a few near-shore exceptions, the first trophic level of marine food chains is occupied by widely dispersed plants of microscopic dimensions. The microscopic character of most of the marine primary producers imposes a size restriction on many of the occupants of higher marine trophic levels. Since very few animals are adapted to feed on organisms many orders of magnitude smaller than themselves, marine herbivores also are usually quite small. Invariably, large marine animals are carnivores and occupy levels far up the food chain. In contrast, the plants of the terrestrial ecosystem are generally quite large. As a result, most

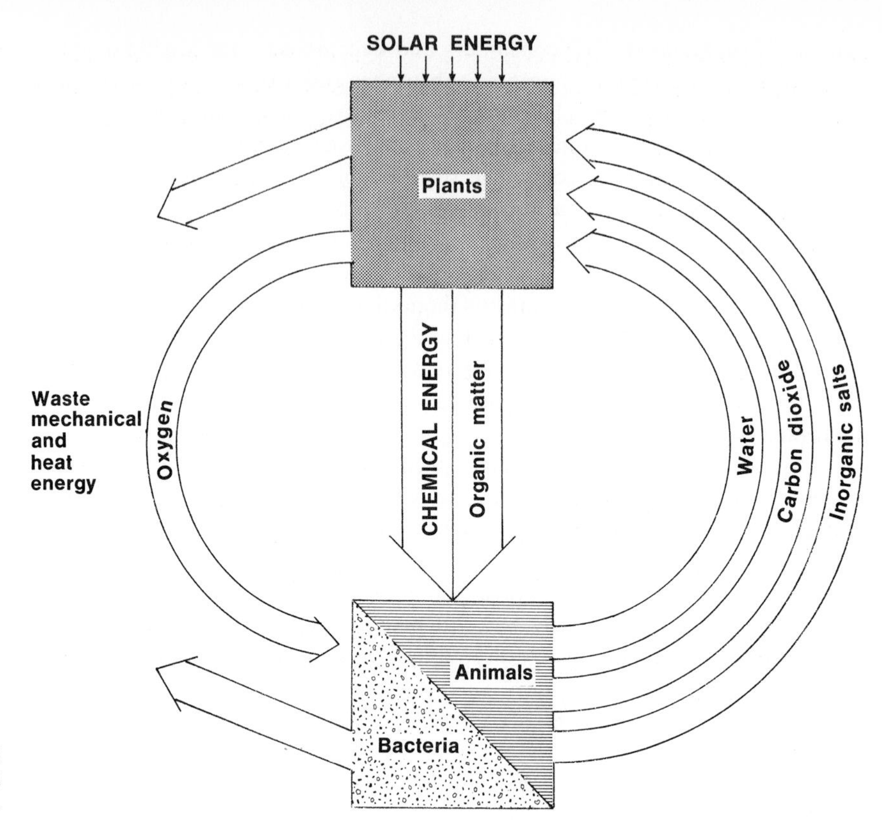

Fig. 2.13 Paths of nutrient and energy flow in an idealized marine ecosystem.

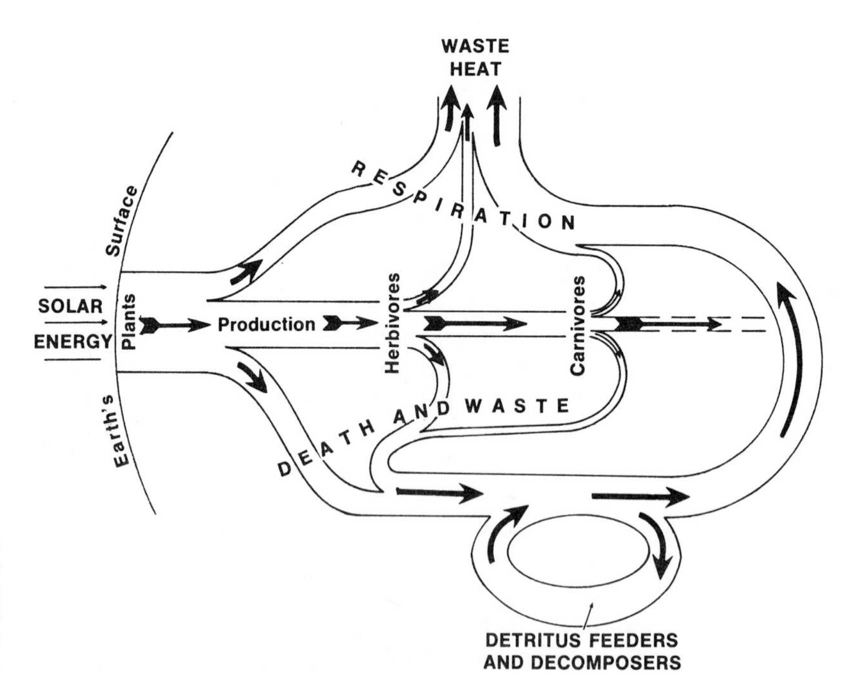

Fig. 2.14 Energy flow in an ecosystem. Solar energy utilized by photosynthetic plants is eventually degraded by cellular respiration to waste heat.

large land animals are herbivores. Food chains can be arranged in a linear fashion to illustrate the decrease in available energy and material from lower to higher trophic levels. Figure 2.15 illustrates such a food pyramid proceeding from phytoplankton to herring at the third trophic level.

Very seldom in natural systems do straight-line food chains actually occur. A more descriptive term for the complex feeding relationships of organisms is a **food web.** Figure 2.16 outlines in greater detail the major trophic relationships of the organisms leading to the herring shown in figure 2.15. The herring is a somewhat opportunistic feeder and does not specialize on only one type of food organism. The same holds true for many of the other organisms of this food web. The complex feeding relationships of the herring make it very difficult to place in a particular trophic level. When feeding on *Calanus* copepods, the adult herring occupies the third level; the fourth when feeding on sand eels; and either the fourth or fifth trophic level when feeding on the amphipod *Themisto.* Even the complex of feeding relationships outlined in figure 2.16 is an oversimplification, for it ignores other marine animals that compete with the herring for the same food sources and further confuse the total trophic picture. Such a confusion of interrelated feeding patterns often becomes quite unintelligible; we must therefore resort to the simplification of the food chain concept for a more easily understood, though admittedly incom-

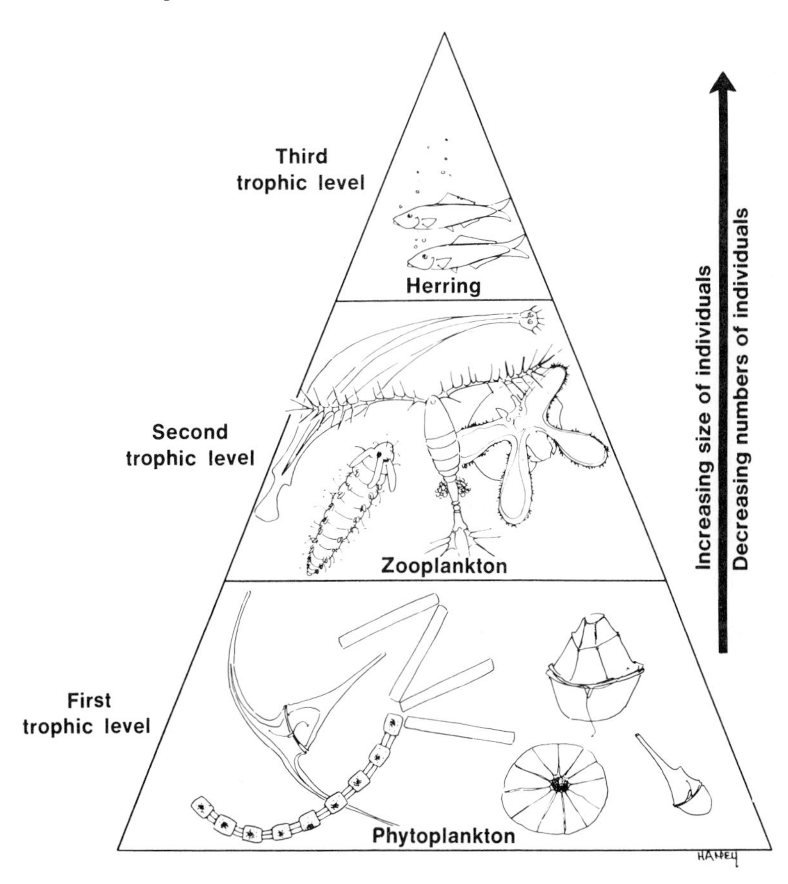

Fig. 2.15 Food pyramid leading to adult herring.

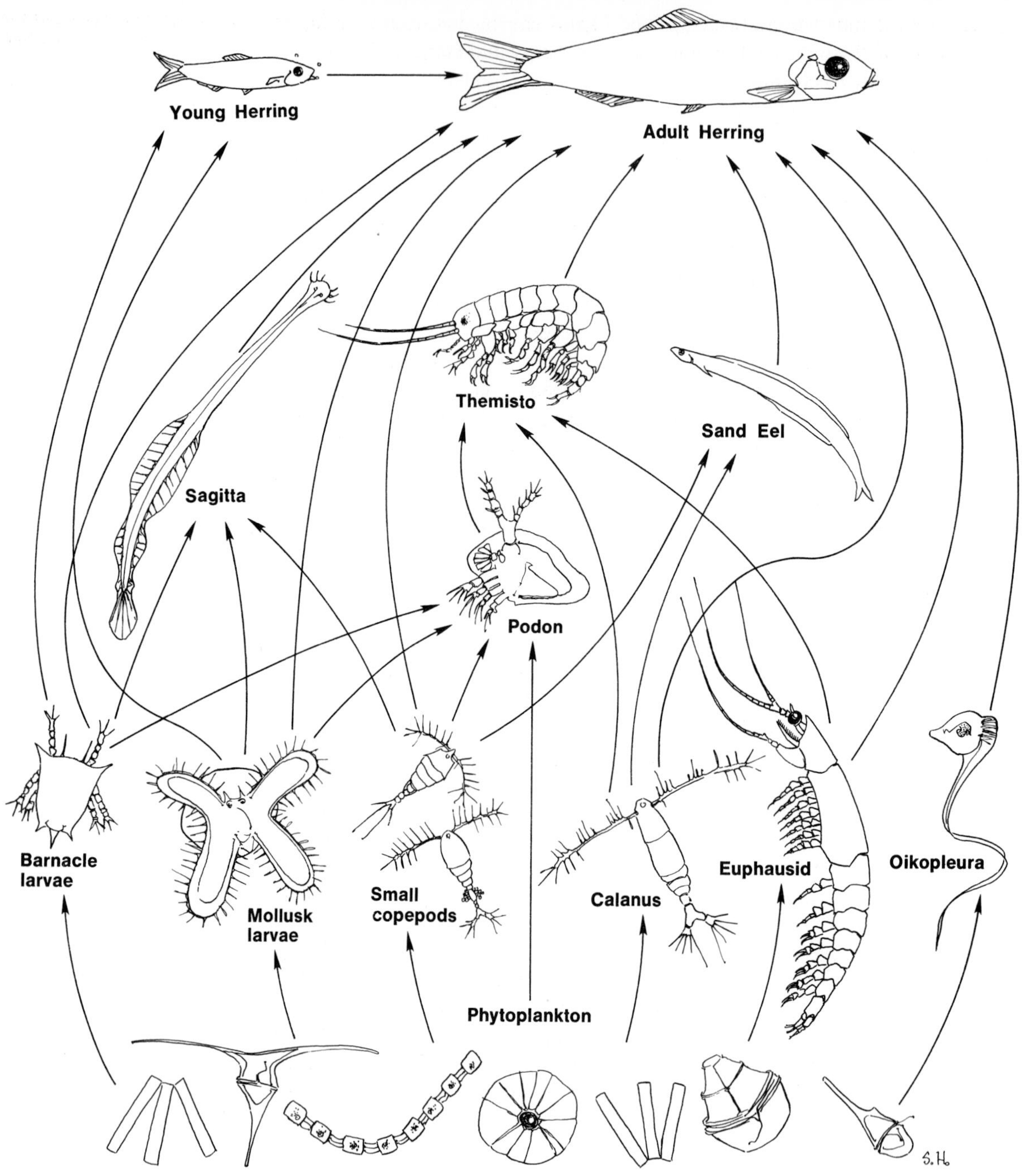

Fig. 2.16 A food web, illustrating the major trophic relationships leading to an adult herring. Adapted from Hardy 1924.

plete, explanation of the trophic relationships of marine organisms. In figure 2.17, some of the more common energy and nutrient pathways of a marine ecosystem are outlined.

The General Nature of Marine Life

Modern marine plants and animals share many basic structural and behavioral characteristics with their terrestrial relatives, but in several important ways marine life is quite unique. Marine organisms exist within a dense, circulating, interconnected medium. The movement of seawater mixes and transports organisms, their food, and their waste products so that few forms are isolated from the effects of others. Even the smallest nonswimming plants or bacteria can become widely distributed by moving currents and water masses.

It is the phytoplankton that initially establish much of the unique character of marine animals. Even in very productive areas of the open ocean, the concentration of marine plants is thousands of times more dilute than a healthy cornfield. The dispersed nature and extremely small size of the phytoplankton limit the size and abundance of animal life in the sea. Most of the animal life is congregated near the photic zone and its supply of plants. At greater depths the density of animal populations tends to decrease as the supply of food falls off. Below the photic zone, all marine life is dependent on the rain of detritus from above.

Many of the substances produced by marine plants are not consumed directly by herbivores, but are dissolved into seawater. These substances, including carbohydrates and amino acids, are eventually utilized by suspended bacteria at all depths. The bacteria, in turn, become food for animals capable of harvesting them. Thus most small marine animals and many large ones are directly dependent on microscopic phytoplankton or even smaller bacteria for their nutrition. Most marine animals, then, are **suspension feeders;** and they employ numerous techniques and devices to separate minute food particles from the sea.

The sea provides buoyancy and structural support to many strikingly beautiful plants and animals. But remove them from the water and they collapse into formless masses. It is only with the supportive aid of seawater that these organisms can continue to exist and function. Seawater also supports some impressively large animals. Deep-sea squids over 15 m long have been observed and others 20 or even 30 m in length are not improbable. Before their populations were diminished by whaling, some blue whales approached weights of 200 tons. But these animals are exceptional and stand out in sharp contrast to the general nature of life in the sea.

Summary

The past history of the world ocean is not known in great detail, yet some workable hypotheses concerning the origin and evolution of life in the sea can be formulated. These hypotheses suggest that early life forms evolved from

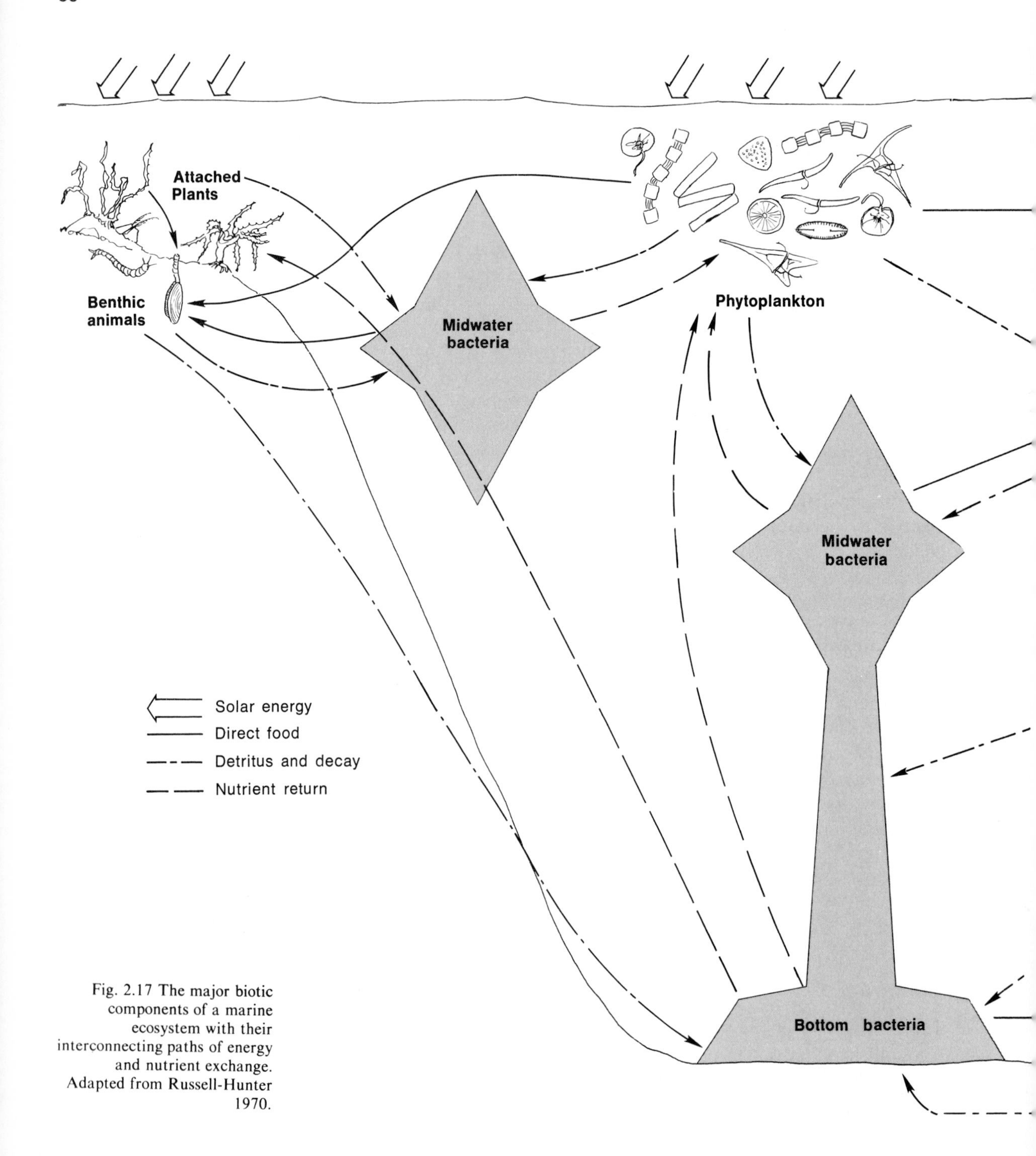

Fig. 2.17 The major biotic components of a marine ecosystem with their interconnecting paths of energy and nutrient exchange. Adapted from Russell-Hunter 1970.

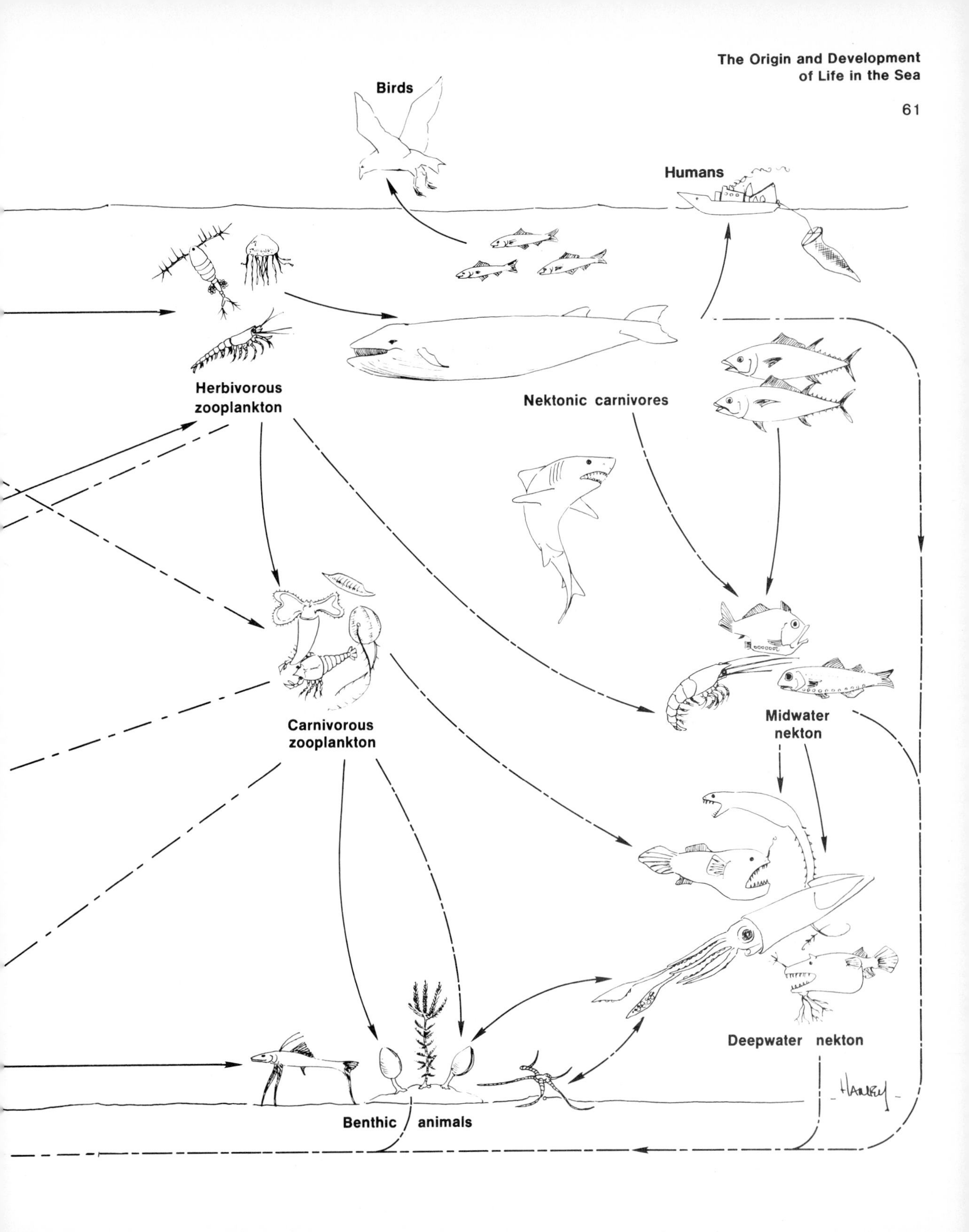
Birds
Humans
Herbivorous
zooplankton
Nektonic carnivores
Carnivorous
zooplankton
Midwater
nekton
Deepwater nekton
Benthic animals

complex organic compounds formed in the earth's early seas. These early life forms apparently possessed all the attributes of modern living organisms.

Since life originated on earth, it has been evolving, improving, and expanding in response to changes in the environment. Seafloor spreading has drastically altered the form of the ocean basins, as continents have drifted apart to form new seas and encroach on old ones. The composition of seawater and the atmosphere gradually changed, altered by the life processes of the seas' inhabitants.

Several hundred thousand kinds of living organisms inhabit the sea. They interact with each other and their nonliving environment in a multiplicity of ways. To avoid confusion, several systems are used to classify these organisms. Those stressed here are based on the evolutionary (phylogenetic) history of the organism, its spatial distribution within the sea, and its nutritional relationships with other organisms.

The relatively dense fluid environment of marine organisms promotes the existence of small and dispersed plants. They in turn influence the general nature of all other forms of marine life.

Questions for Discussion

1. List and discuss the general conditions that cause marine food chains leading to large organisms to be much longer than terrestrial food chains leading to animals of a similar size.
2. Describe the fundamental differences between procaryotic and eucaryotic cells. How do those differences affect the general functions and capabilities of the cells?
3. Describe the fundamental differences between the flow of nutrients and the flow of energy in marine ecosystems. In what form is most of the energy lost from these ecosystems?
4. Discuss some of the advantages and the drawbacks inherent in grouping living organisms into the classification schemes outlined in this chapter.

Suggestions for Further Reading

Books

Miller, S. E., and Orgel, L. E. 1974. *The origins of life on the earth.* Englewood Cliffs, N. J.: Prentice-Hall.

Russell-Hunter, W. D. 1970. *Aquatic productivity.* New York: Macmillan.

For a more complete discussion of cell structure, photosynthesis, and respiration, and evolution, consult any recent introductory biology textbook. Some recommendations are:

Curtis, H. 1975. *Biology.* New York: Worth.

Loewy, A. G., and Siekevitz, P. 1970. *Cell structure and function.* New York: Holt, Rinehart & Winston.

Wilson, E. O., et al. 1973. *Life on Earth.* Stamford, Conn.: Sinauer Associates.

Articles

Bernal, J. D., and Synge, A. 1972. The origin of life. *Oxford Biology Reader*. No. 45–9613.

McKenna, M. C. 1972. Possible biological consequences of plate tectonics. *Bioscience* 22:519–25.

Schopf, J. W. 1978. The evolution of the earliest cells. *Scientific American,* September:111–38.

Sokal, R. R. 1966. Numerical taxonomy. *Scientific American,* December: 106–16.

Vine, F. J. 1970. Sea-floor spreading and continental drift. *Journal of Geological Education* 18:87–90.

Dr. Robert D. Ballard of Woods Hole Oceanographic Institution examines a giant sea worm recovered from hot water vents in the Galapagos Rift. Photo by Jack Donnelly.

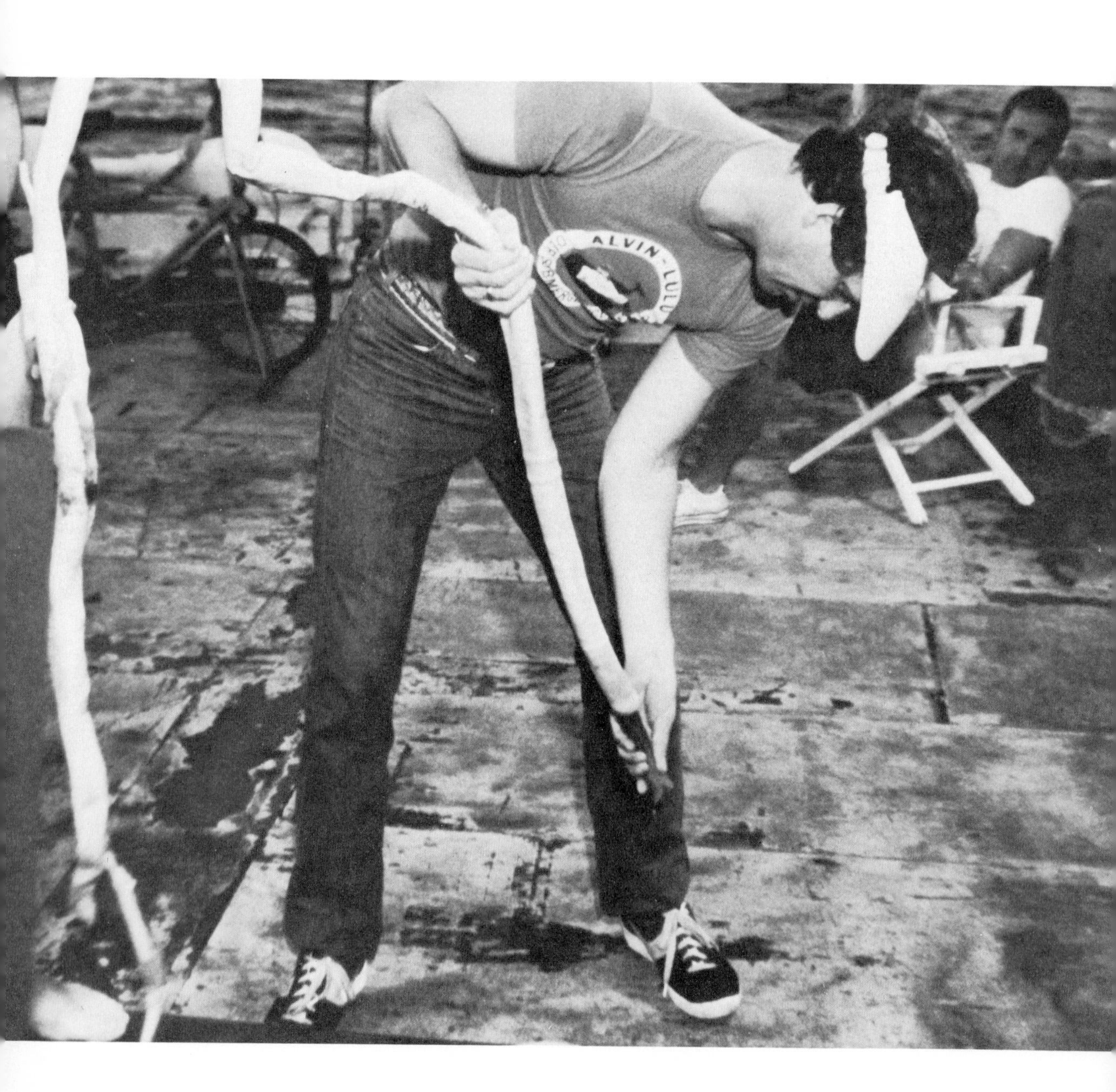

An Overview of Marine Animals

3

All of the animal phyla included in figure 2.11 have some members living in the sea. Several phyla are, and evidently always have been, restricted to the marine environment. Some are quite well known, while others are so obscure that they are unfamiliar even to many biologists.

In this chapter, the characteristics of each phylum are briefly surveyed. The purpose of their introduction here is to alleviate cumbersome descriptions as you encounter these groups in subsequent chapters. Only the more abundant and obvious phyla are emphasized. Groups that are primarily or wholly parasitic on other organisms are not included. The identifying features and habitats of the adult forms are stressed. However, many marine animals produce planktonic larval stages that appear and function quite differently than their parents. They live at different depths than the adults, feed on different foods, and generally experience quite different environmental selection pressures.

The first animals probably evolved about 700 million years ago. Since that time, numerous strategies for coping with survival in a dynamic, evolving marine environment have been tested. Of the many animal groups to make their appearance on the stage of evolution, some thirty phyla exist at present.

These phyla are presented in an order that generally corresponds to moving up the phylogenetic tree of the animal kingdom (fig. 2.11). Several significant trends in animal evolution are represented in this sequence. Increased complexity and specialization of structures are evident, especially in the systems involved in O_2 exchange, excretion, feeding and digestion, circulation, and reproduction. In the "higher" phyla, there is a greater dependence on sexual reproduction, and less on asexual budding or fragmentation. Improved sensory systems and increasingly complex brains able to integrate sensory information have led to expanding patterns of behavioral responses. Of these thirty or so phyla, only a few—in particular, the nematodes, mollusks, arthropods, and chordates—clearly dominate the animal composition of the seas and monopolize the energy flow of most marine communities.

Two main lines of animal evolution have occurred. These are represented by the main branches of figure 2.11. One branch is crowned by the arthropods, the other by the chordates. These two phyla include extremely successful representatives from both the terrestrial and marine environments. In the arthropods, insects thrive on the land as their marine counterparts, the crustaceans, do in the oceans. The chordates are represented by terrestrial mammals as well as by aquatic fishes.

Some Single-celled Forms

Protozoa

The phylum Protozoa encompasses a variety of microscopic animals. The unifying characteristic of the Protozoa is their unicellular nature. All protozoans consist of a single cell or are parts of loose aggregates of cells. Protozoans are structurally quite complex, and some biologists prefer to think of them as very small acellular animals rather than unicellular ones. This phylum includes the familiar freshwater *Amoeba* and *Paramecium,* some parasites, and many marine forms.

Marine protozoans are abundant in the plankton and also on the bottom. Asexual reproduction by cell division is common. Sexual reproduction, when it occurs, is often quite complex.

The order Foraminiferida is mostly marine. Its members are common in the plankton, but most are benthic or live attached to plants and other animals. Most "forams" are microscopic, although individuals of a few species are several mm in size. They have internal chambered shells which usually are composed of calcite ($CaCO_3$) or cemented sand grains. Penetrating this shell, or **test,** are numerous strands of cytoplasm called **pseudopodia** (fig. 3.1). The pseudopodia are used for locomotion and for collecting food.

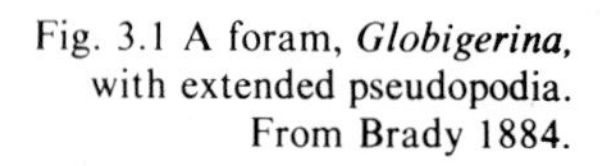

Fig. 3.1 A foram, *Globigerina,* with extended pseudopodia. From Brady 1884.

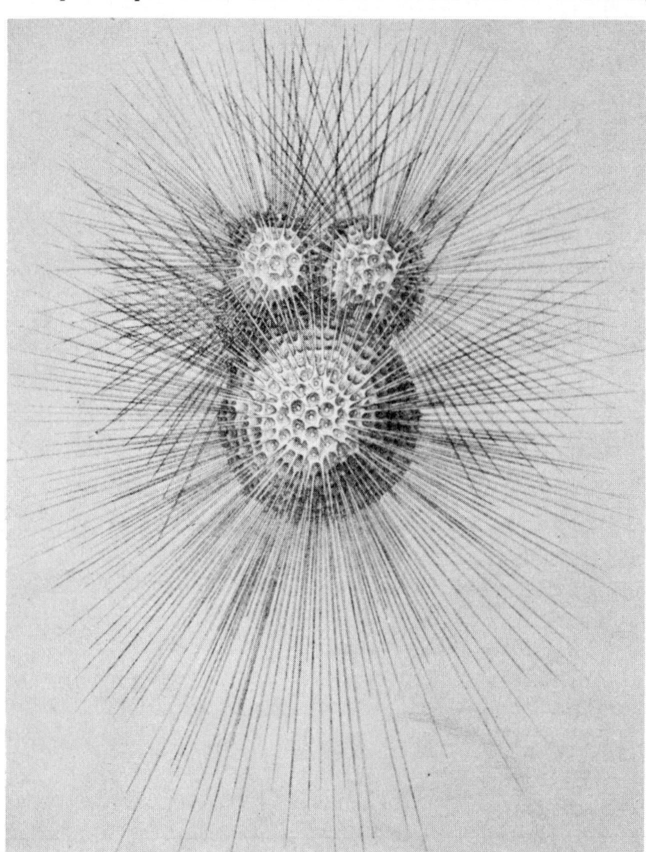

Some planktonic forams, such as *Globigerina* (fig. 3.1), are so widespread and abundant that their tests blanket large portions of the seafloor. After thousands of years of accumulation, this **globigerina ooze** may form deposits tens of meters thick. The famous chalky cliffs of Dover, England, are composed mainly of foram tests that accumulated on the seafloor and were subsequently uplifted above sea level.

The order Radiolaria is entirely marine and most members are planktonic. They are similar in size to planktonic forams. The beautiful symmetry often associated with radiolarians (fig. 3.2) is formed by an internal skeleton of silica (SiO_2).

Members of the order Tintinnida are the most abundant free-living group of marine ciliates (organisms that possess tiny hairlike projections, or cilia). The tintinnid cell is partially enclosed in a vase-shaped **lorica** made of cemented particles or of a material secreted by the cell. Ciliated tentacles at one end of the cell are used for feeding. A large variety of other ciliates exist

Fig. 3.2 A highly magnified scanning electron micrograph of a variety of radiolarian skeletons. Courtesy of Scripps Institution of Oceanography.

in the sea. Some are free-living, but most are parasitic on or in other marine animals.

An Evolutionary Sideline

Porifera

The Porifera is one of the few animal phyla with a widely accepted common name—the sponges. The sponges are among the simplest multicellular animals. Each sponge consists of several types of loosely aggregated cells but lacks the cellular specialization and organization characteristic of other multicellular animals. They thus represent an evolutionary sideline not followed by any other group of living animals. In spite of their simplicity, they share several advantages with other multicellular animals. Unlike the single-celled Protista, cells within each individual can be replaced to permit larger size and longer lifespan. In addition, sponges can be specialized to more efficiently handle food collection, protection, and other diverse chores of survival.

The name Porifera stems from the numerous pores, holes, and channels that perforate the bodies of sponges. Water is circulated through these openings into an internal cavity, the **spongocoel,** where food and O_2 are extracted. The water then exits through a large excurrent pore, the **osculum** (fig. 3.3).

Fig. 3.3 An encrusting sponge with prominent excurrent water openings, or oscula.

Fig. 3.4 Silicate skeletons of two glass sponges, *Euplectella.* Courtesy of American Museum of Natural History.

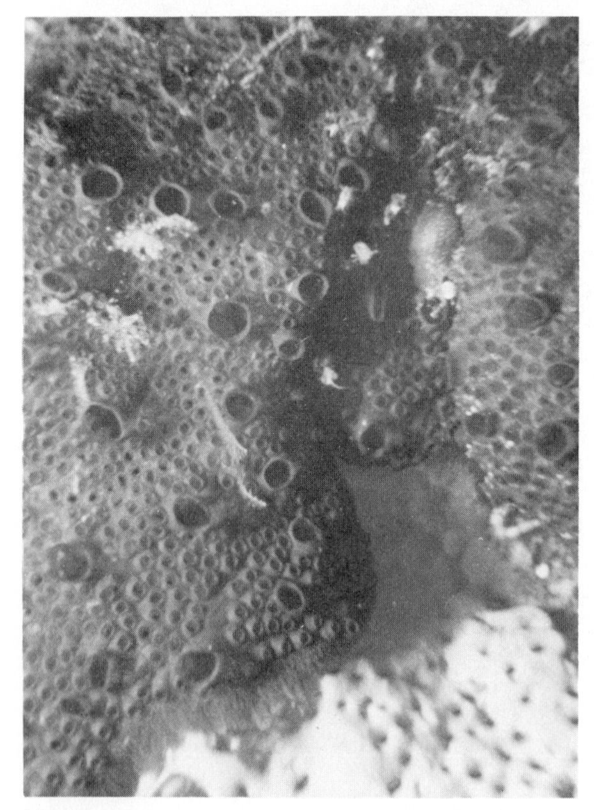

Fig. 3.3

Fig. 3.4

Sponges are mostly marine and are usually found attached to hard substrates such as rocks, pilings, or animal shells. Sometimes they are radially symmetrical, but more commonly they conform to the shape of the substrate. Some sponges are supported internally by a network of flexible **spongin** fibers. The commercial bath "sponge" is actually the spongin skeleton with all of the living material removed. Other sponges have skeletons composed of spongin and hard mineralized **spicules.** The spicules are either calcareous ($CaCO_3$) or siliceous (SiO_2) in chemical composition. The spicule skeleton of the deep-water glass sponge, *Euplectella,* is one of the most complex and beautiful of all sponges (fig. 3.4).

Radial Symmetry

Members of the phyla Cnidaria and Ctenophora exhibit radially symmetrical body plans. The circular shape of radially symmetrical animals provides several different planes of symmetry to divide the animal into mirror-image halves (fig. 3.5). The mouth is located at the center of the body on the **oral** side; the opposite side is the **aboral** side. Without a head or tail, there is neither a right nor left side. Radially symmetrical animals possess a relatively simple diffuse nerve net without a central brain to process sensory information and organize appropriate responses.

Cnidaria

The phylum Cnidaria (sometimes referred to as Coelenterata) includes a large, diverse group of relatively simple, yet versatile, marine animals, such as jellyfish, sea anemones, corals, and hydroids. In all cnidarians, the inner and outer body walls are separated by a gelatinous layer called the **mesoglea.** A centrally located mouth leads to a blind digestive tract, the **gastrovascular cavity.** The mouth is surrounded with tentacles capable of capturing and ingesting a wide variety of marine animals. The tentacles and, to a lesser extent, other parts of the body, are armed with batteries of microscopic structures, the **nematocysts.** Nematocysts are produced in special cells, the **cnidoblasts**, and are unique to this phylum. They are discharged when stimulated

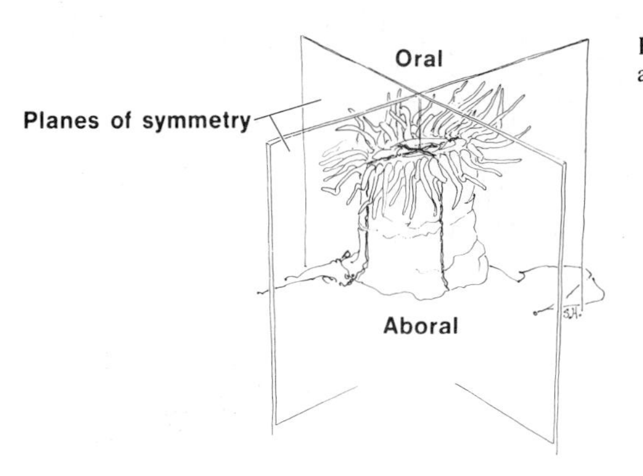

Fig. 3.5 Planes of symmetry in a radially symmetrical animal.

by other organisms. Some nematocysts are adhesive and stick to the prey, others become entangled in the prey's bristles or spines, and another type (fig. 3.6) pierces the prey and injects a paralyzing toxin.

Cnidarians exist as free-swimming **medusae** or sessile benthic **polyps.** Both forms have essentially the same body organization. The oral end of the medusa, bearing the mouth and tentacles, is oriented downward. The mesoglea of most medusae is well developed and jellylike in consistency. This feature has earned them the descriptive, if inappropriate, name of jellyfish. In the polyp, the mouth and tentacles are directed upwards. Many species of cnidarians alternate between a swimming medusoid generation and an attached benthic polypoid generation. In a generalized cnidarian life cycle (fig. 3.7), polyps can produce medusae or additional polyps by budding. The medusae in turn produce eggs and sperm that, after fertilization, develop into the polyps of the subsequent generation.

The phylum Cnidaria consists of three classes, each characterized by its own variation of the basic cnidarian life cycle shown in figure 3.7. The Hydrozoa includes colonial hydroids and siphonophores, such as the Portuguese man-of-war, *Physalia*. Hydrozoans usually have well-developed medusoid and polypoid generations. Various individuals of the polypoid colony are specialized for particular functions, such as feeding, reproduction, and defense.

In the class Scyphozoa, the polyp stage is reduced or completely absent. This class includes most of the larger and better-known medusoid jellyfish (fig. 3.8). In the third class, the Anthozoa, it is the polyp form that dominates and the medusoid generation is absent. Many anthozoans, such as corals and sea fans, are colonial, but some anemones exist as large solitary individuals (fig. 3.9). Unlike most cnidarians, the corals and some other anthozoans produce external, often massive, deposits of $CaCO_3$.

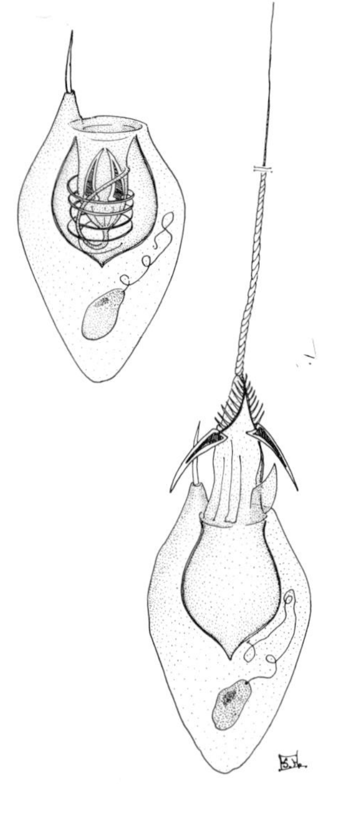

Fig. 3.6 Undischarged (left) and discharged (right) penetrant nematocysts.

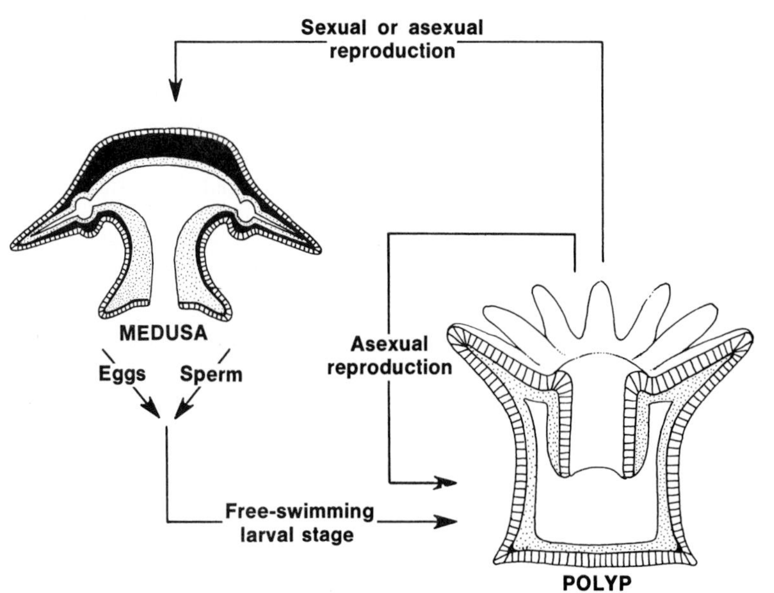

Fig. 3.7 Generalized cnidarian life cycle.

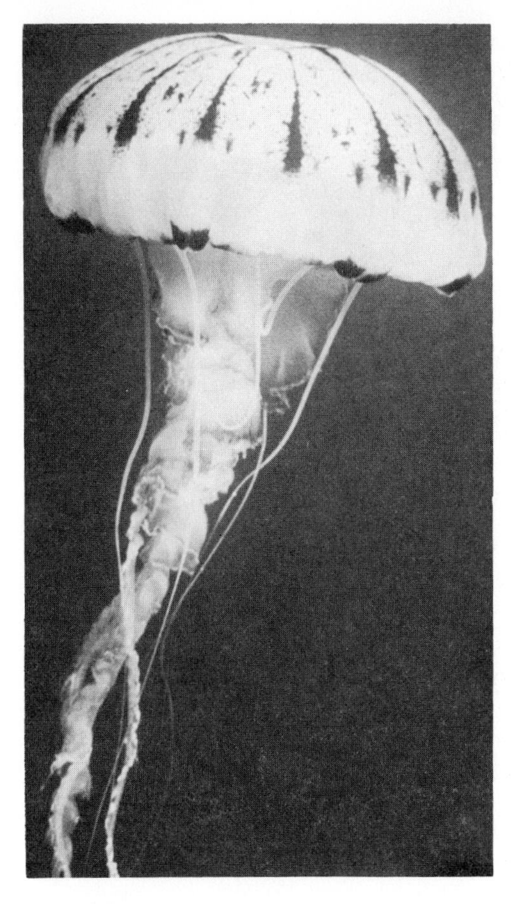

Fig. 3.8 A large jellyfish, *Pelagia.* Official photograph U.S. Navy.

Fig. 3.9 A large, solitary sea anemone with its mouth at the center. Courtesy Carolina Biological Supply Company.

Ctenophora

The phylum Ctenophora consists of about eighty species. All are marine and most are planktonic, usually preying on small zooplankton. Most individuals are smaller than a few cm in size, but one tropical genus *(Beröe)* may be found up to 20 cm in length.

The ctenophores are closely allied to cnidarians. They have radial body symmetry, a gelatinous medusalike body, and, in some, **colloblast cells** that resemble cnidarian nematocysts. One species of ctenophore, *Euchlora rubra,* has been found to possess true nematocysts.

Members of this phylum are characterized by external longitudinal bands of cilia, called **ctenes** (fig. 3.10). Locomotion is provided by the wavelike movements of the ctenes. Tentacles armed with colloblasts are used to capture food.

Evolutionary Advances

With one exception (the echinoderms), the remainder of the animal phyla exhibit **bilateral body symmetry.** Bilateral symmetry refers to a basic animal

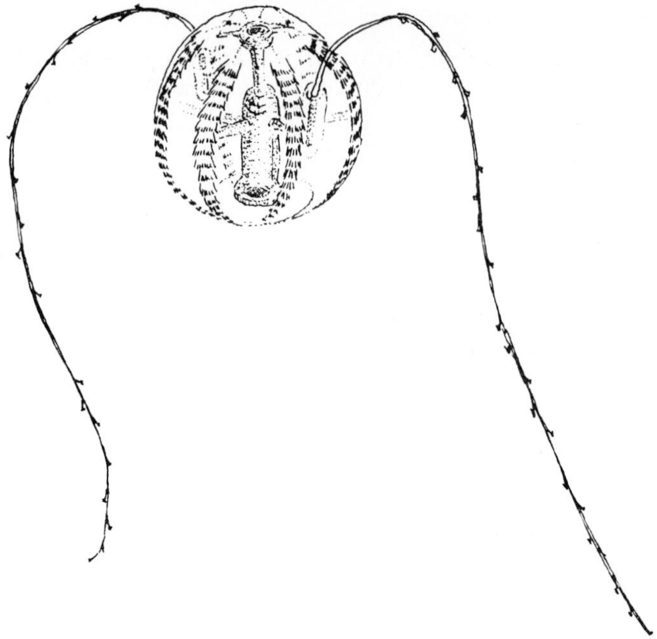

Fig. 3.10 A ctenophore, *Pleurobranchia,* with tentacles and four radial rows of ctenes visible.

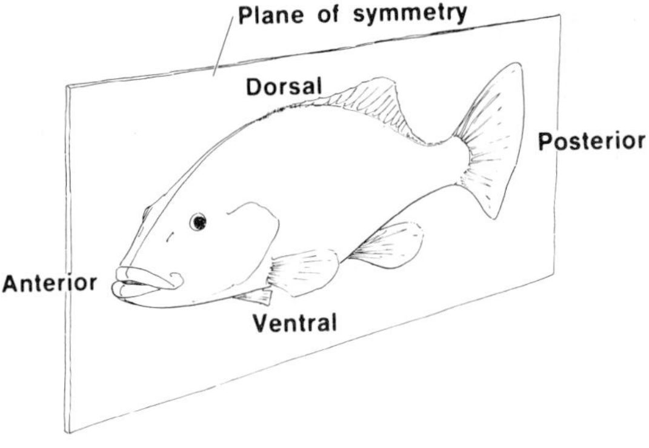

Fig. 3.11 Plane of symmetry in a bilaterally symmetrical animal.

body plan through which only one plane of symmetry can pass to create two mirror-image halves (fig. 3.11). Such animals exhibit definite head (anterior) and rear (posterior) ends, as well as right and left sides, and a top (dorsal) and bottom (ventral). These animals possess sophisticated sensory systems capable of one-way conduction of nerve impulses, and an increasingly complex mass of nerve cells necessary to process the widening scope of sensory information. Accompanying this evolutionary trend toward an anterior brain has been the development in the head region of specialized sensory receptors (organs) for vision, smell or taste, and hearing.

The simplest groups of bilaterally symmetrical animals are composed of small, elongate, mostly wormlike creatures. These animals fall into seven phyla: the Platyhelminthes (flatworms), Nemertina, Gastrotricha, Kinorhyncha, Nematoda, Priapulida, and Entoprocta. Most members of these phyla are benthic, living in soft bottom deposits, except for the entoprocts, which attach to hard substrates.

Platyhelminthes

Most Platyhelminthes, or flatworms, are parasitic (this group includes flukes and tapeworms). Only in the class Turbellaria are free-living flatworms found. They are primarily aquatic, and the great majority of turbellarians are marine. There are a few planktonic species of flatworms, but most are bottom dwellers in sand or mud, or on hard substrates (fig. 3.12*a*).

Marine flatworms are usually less than 10 cm long, thin, and leaf shaped. The outer surface of flatworms is generally covered with cilia, which are best developed on the underside. These cilia provide a gliding type of locomotion for moving over the bottom. The mouth is usually centrally located on the underside and leads to a blind digestive tract. Turbellarians are carnivorous, preying on other small invertebrates.

Nemertina

The nemertines are wormlike benthic animals. They are closely related to the flatworms, but are somewhat more organized in body structure (fig. 3.12*b*). They have a simple circulatory system, a complex nervous system, and a complete digestive tract ending in an anus. Individuals of one species are over 2 m long, but most are much smaller. These shallow-water animals are equipped with a remarkable **proboscis** for defense and food gathering. The proboscis is everted rapidly from the anterior part of the body to ensnare prey. The proboscis of some nemertine worms is fixed with a piercing stylet to stab the prey and inject a toxin.

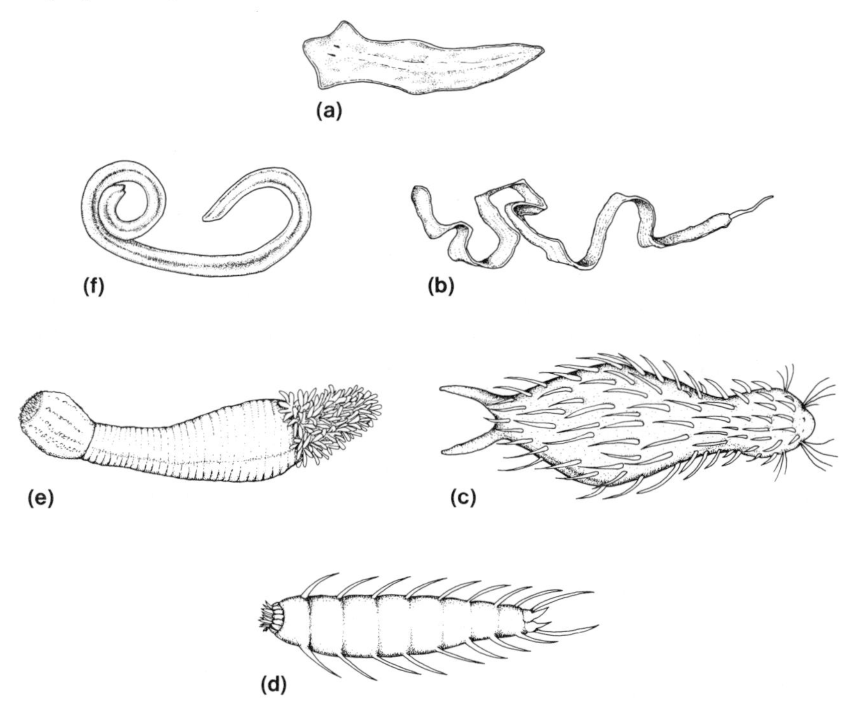

Fig. 3.12 Some simple wormlike animal phyla: (*a*) flatworm, (*b*) nemertine, (*c*) gastrotrich, (*d*) kinorhynch, (*e*) priapulid, and (*f*) nematode.

Gastrotricha and Kinorhyncha

Gastrotrichs and kinorhynchs contain a large variety of marine species, but most are so small (usually less than one mm) that they go virtually unnoticed by most observers. They are cylindrical and elongated with a mouth, feeding structures, and sensory organs at the anterior end (fig. 3.12*c* and *d*). Marine gastrotrichs and kinorhynchs inhabit sand and mud deposits in shallow water, where they feed on detritus, diatom films, or other small animals.

Priapulida and Nematoda

More wormlike in appearance are the priapulid worms and nematode worms (fig. 3.12*e* and *f*). Only three species occur in the phylum Priapulida. They live buried in intertidal sediments of polar and subpolar waters. Individuals seldom exceed 10 cm in size. Priapulid worms are carnivorous, feeding on soft-bodied invertebrates, which are captured with an eversible proboscis.

The nematode worms are among the most common and widespread multicellular animals. Some are parasitic, but many are free-living. Most marine nematodes live in the bottom sediments and are found at virtually all water depths. In fact, nematodes are probably the most abundant multicellular animals in the marine benthic environment. Locomotion is not well developed. Crawling and bending motions are common. Nematodes are cylindrical in cross section and greatly elongated. They seldom exceed a few cm in length.

Entoprocta

Entoprocts are benthic, living on rocks, shells, sponges, and seaweeds. Most are colonial. Superficially, they resemble small colonial hydroids. Their external appearance is also quite similar to that of members of another phylum, the Ectoprocta.

At one time, entoprocts and ectoprocts were combined in a single phylum, the Bryozoa (moss animals). But studies of internal structures have shown that these two groups are only distantly related, and two separate phyla are warranted. Individuals of both groups have U-shaped digestive tracts. Projecting from the upper surface is a crown of tentacles. The mouth and anus of entoprocts open within the ring of tentacles (hence the name Entoprocta—inner anus). The ectoproct mouth is located within the tentacles, but the anus is not. The crown of ciliated feeding tentacles of ectoprocts is known as a **lophophore** and is also characteristic of two other marine phyla.

The Lophophore Bearers

The lophophore is the feeding organ of three structurally dissimilar phyla of marine animals: the Ectoprocta, Phoronida, and Brachiopoda.

Ectoprocta

The ectoprocts are a major animal phylum, with 4,000 freshwater and marine species. They are primarily members of shallow-water benthic communities,

Fig. 3.13 A branched colony of ectoprocts with feathery lophophores extended.

occupying the same general habitats as entoprocts. All ectoprocts are colonial and form encrusting or branching masses of small individuals (fig. 3.13).

Phoronida

The phylum Phoronida consists of about 15 species of elongate, burrowing animals. All are marine and live in tubes in shallow water. During feeding, the lophophore projects out of the tube, but it can be retracted rapidly for protection. The phoronids seldom exceed 20 cm in length and have no appendages except for the lophophore.

Brachiopoda

The brachiopods, or lamp shells, have been exceedingly abundant animals for much of the past half-billion years. Over 30,000 extinct species have been described, but fewer than 300 presently exist. All brachiopods are benthic and live cemented to the bottom or attached by a stalk (fig. 3.14). The outer calcareous shell superficially resembles that of a bivalve mollusk. However, the symmetry of the shells is quite different. Bivalve shells are positioned to the sides of the soft internal organs. In contrast, brachiopod shells are located above and below the soft parts.

Most living brachiopods inhabit waters less than 200 m deep. As in the phoronids and ectoprocts, the ciliated lophophore is used to gather minute suspended material from seawater for nutrition.

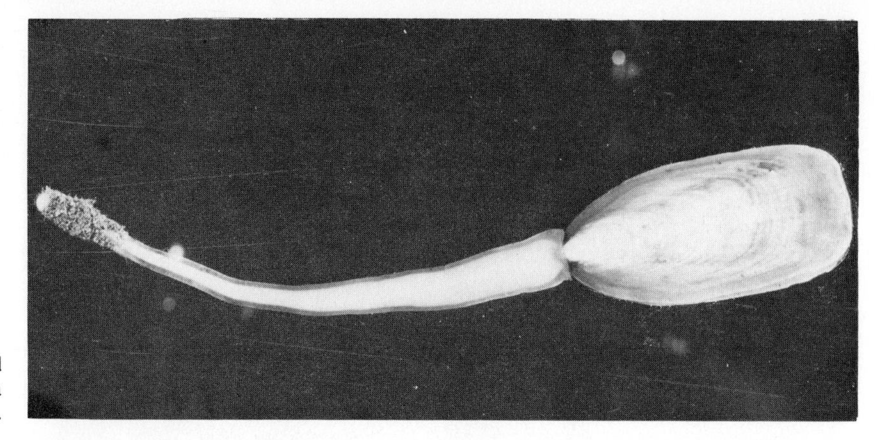

Fig. 3.14 The brachiopod *Lingula*. Courtesy Carolina Biological Supply Company.

The Mollusks

Mollusca

The mollusks are among the most abundant and easily observable groups of marine animals. They have adapted to all the major marine habitats. It is difficult to characterize such a large and diverse group as the phylum Mollusca. In general, mollusks are unsegmented animals with well-developed sensory organs, often concentrated in the head region. Most mollusks have a hard external shell surrounding the soft body. A large muscular foot is used for locomotion, anchorage, and securing food.

This phylum is composed of six classes. Representatives of five of the six classes are quite common and are shown in figure 3.15. The sixth class, the Monoplacophora, is a rare group that was thought to have been extinct for 400 million years. In 1952, a few living specimens were collected from deep water off the coast of Costa Rica. Since then, additional specimens have been collected and carefully studied. Alone among the mollusks, the monoplacophorans exhibit some body segmentation and are thought possibly to represent an ancestral relationship between mollusks and the segmented annelid worms.

Chitons belong to the class Amphineura. They are characterized by eight calcareous plates embedded in their dorsal surfaces. These animals are found in rocky intertidal areas, using their large foot to cling to protected depressions in rocks. Chitons feed by grazing algae from rocks with a rasping tonguelike organ, the **radula.**

The class Gastropoda includes snails and slugs (marine, freshwater, and terrestrial), limpets, abalones, and nudibranchs. Although one-piece shells are characteristic of this class, several types of gastropods completely lack shells. Most gastropods are benthic; only a few without shells, or with very light ones, have successfully assumed a pelagic life-style. Many gastropods graze on algae much as chitons do. Others feed on detritus and organic-rich sediments. Several are even successful carnivores.

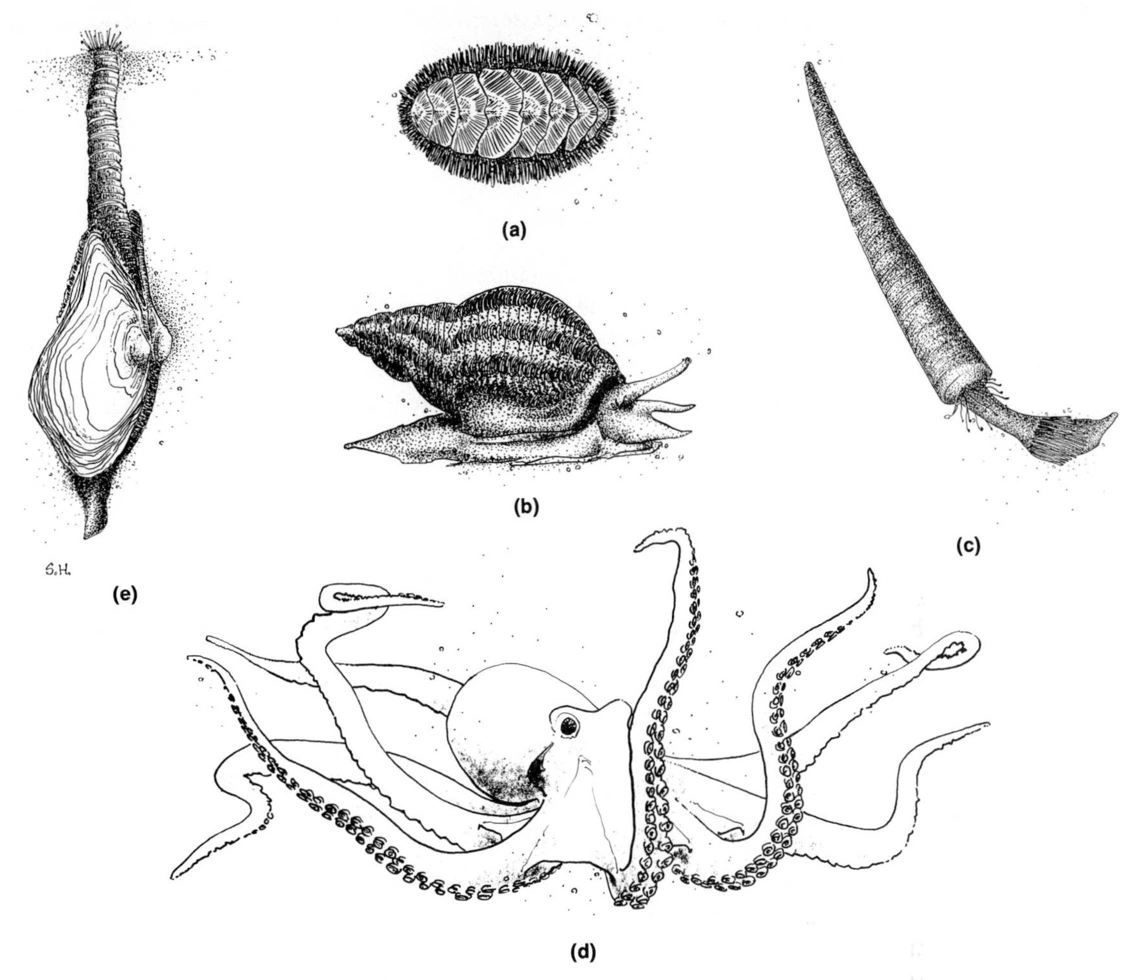

Fig. 3.15 Representatives of the common classes of mollusks: (*a*) Amphineura, (*b*) Gastropoda, (*c*) Scaphopoda, (*d*) Cephalopoda, and (*e*) Pelecypoda.

The 200 species of tusk shells, class Scaphopoda, are found buried in sediments in a wide range of water depths. As the common name implies, the shells of these animals are elongated and tapered, somewhat like an elephant's tusk. The head and foot project from the opening at the larger end of the shell. Microscopic organisms from the sediment and water are captured by adhesive tentaclelike structures.

The Pelecypoda, which include mussels, clams, oysters, and scallops, have hinged two-piece, or bivalve, shells. As adults, most are rather slow-moving benthic animals. But some, such as mussels and oysters, live cemented to hard substrates. This class has an extensive depth range, from intertidal areas to below 5,000 m. Most feed on sediment deposits or on suspended plankton and detritus from the water.

Molluscan evolution has reached its zenith in the class Cephalopoda, the squids and octopuses. Members of this class are highly organized, carnivorous predators with sucker-lined tentacles, well-developed sense organs, and reduction or loss of the external shell. A unique propulsion system, using high-speed jets of water, provides speeds greater than those of other marine invertebrates. Cephalopods are also larger than most other invertebrates. The giant squid, *Architeuthis,* may reach 20 m in length, by far the largest living invertebrate species.

More Wormlike Phyla

The wormlike body structure of the phyla discussed previously has been an extremely successful evolutionary adaptation. Before introducing the remaining phyla of marine "worms," we should examine the reasons of this success. Most of the members of the wormlike phyla dwell in soft mud or sand deposits. Their elongate body forms permit effective burrowing movements in spite of a lack of rigid internal skeletons to support the muscles of locomotion. Burrowing actions and other body movements are accomplished by muscles in the body wall working against the enclosed fluid contents of the body. These fluids cannot escape and are essentially incompressible. As such they provide a **hydrostatic skeleton** for the muscles of the body wall. In the more effective burrowing worms, these muscles are arranged in two sets; circular muscle bands around the body and longitudinal muscles extending the length of the body. Like all other muscles, these can exert force only by contraction. Thus when the circular muscles of a worm's body contract, its diameter decreases. But, as its fluid volume remains the same, its hydrostatic skeleton experiences a slight pressure, forcing the body to elongate. If the rear of the body is anchored, contracting the circular muscles results in a forward movement. The circular muscles resume their precontraction state by relaxing and allowing the longitudinal muscles to shorten the body and make it fatter. These two types of muscles continue to work in opposition to each other to provide an effective sediment burrowing motion for a large variety of marine worms.

Sipunculida

Another major phylum of wormlike creatures, Sipunculida, can be found throughout the world ocean. The 250 species of sipunculids, or peanut worms, are entirely marine. Most are found in the intertidal zone, but their distribution extends to abyssal depths. Peanut worms are benthic. They live in burrows, crevices, or other protected niches, often in competition with other wormlike animals. They range from 2 mm to over 50 cm in size. The body is usually cylindrical and is capped by a ring of ciliated tentacles surrounding the anterior mouth (fig. 3.16).

Echiuroidea

This is a small phylum of benthic marine worms, which resemble peanut worms in size and general shape. Echiuroids are common intertidally, but occasionally are found to depths exceeding 6,000 m. Most echiuroids live in burrows in the mud. One remarkable feature of this group is an extendible

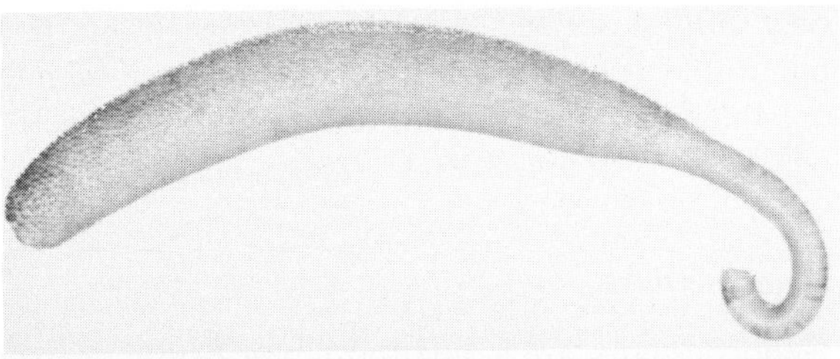

Fig. 3.16 A sipunculid worm, *Sipunculus*. Courtesy Carolina Biological Supply Company.

Fig. 3.17 The fat innkeeper, *Urechis*, shown within a glass-walled burrow.

proboscis, a feeding and sensory organ that projects from the anterior end of the worm. In some species the proboscis is longer than the remainder of the body and is quite effective for gathering food while the worm remains in the protected confines of its burrow.

Urechis, an echiuroid of the California coast, has a very short proboscis. The proboscis is used to secrete a mucus net from the animal to the wall of its U-shaped burrow (fig. 3.17). Water is pumped through the burrow by repeated waves of contractions along the worm's body wall. As water passes through the mucus net, extremely fine particles are trapped. When the net is clogged with food, the worm consumes it and constructs another.

Pogonophora

Pogonophorans are almost exclusively deep-water, tube-dwelling marine worms (80% of the known species live between 200 and 4,000 m). This obscure phylum was not even discovered until 1900. Since then about 70 species have been fully described. Adult sizes range from 10–35 cm in length. Pogonophorans are noted for their complete lack of an internal digestive tract. They are thought to use their anterior ciliated tentacles to collect food particles, which are then digested externally and absorbed directly by the tentacles.

Hemichordata

Hemichordates are a small group of benthic marine worms that seem to be closely related to the pogonophorans. They have an anterior proboscis and a soft, flaccid body up to 50 cm long. These worms live in protected areas under rocks or in tubes or burrows. Most are found in shallow water.

Fig. 3.18 A chaetognath, *Sagitta.*

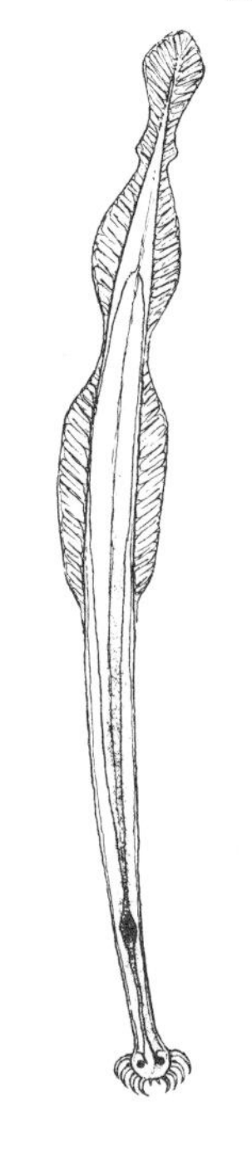

Chaetognatha

In contrast to the general benthic habitat of most marine worms, chaetognaths, or arrowworms, are torpedo-shaped planktonic carnivores (fig. 3.18). Although they seldom exceed 3 cm in length, they very effectively prey on other zooplankton. Arrowworms swim with rapid darting motions and capture prey with the bristles that surround the mouth. Only about 60 species of arrowworms exist, but they are frequently very abundant in the zooplankton. Certain species of arrowworms apparently respond to, and associate with, subtle chemical or physical characteristics of seawater. As such they serve as useful biological indicators of particular oceanic water types.

Segmentation

Annelida

The annelids are usually represented by the familiar terrestrial earthworm. However, this phylum also contains a diverse and successful group of marine forms, the class Polychaeta, with over 5,000 species. Polychaete worms, like other annelids, are segmented. The body cavity and internal organs contained in it are subdivided into a linear series of structural units called **metameres.** The result of segmentation in polychaete worms is a sequential compartmentalization of the worm's hydrostatic skeleton and surrounding muscles. This permits a greater degree of localized changes in body shape and ultimately a more controlled and efficient form of locomotion.

Fig. 3.19 The filtering structures of a tube-dwelling polychaete worm. Courtesy C. Farwell, Scripps Institution of Oceanography.

Some polychaetes ingest sediment to obtain nourishment, others are carnivorous, and many use a complex tentacle system (fig. 3.19) to filter microscopic bits of food from the water. Suspension-feeding polychaetes often occupy partially buried tubes. They are common in intertidal areas but are also found in deeper water. One polychaete, *Tomopteris,* is planktonic throughout its life cycle.

Arthropoda

Like annelids, arthropods are linearly segmented. In addition to the advantages of segmentation, arthropods possess a distinctive hard **exoskeleton.** The exoskeleton is largely composed of a complex organic substance, **chitin.** This rigid outer skeleton serves not only as an impermeable barrier against fluid loss and bacterial diseases, but also as a multiple lever system for muscle attachment. Its structure resists deformations induced by contracting muscles, allowing faster responses and greater control of movements. Flexing of the body and appendages is limited to thin membranous joints located between the rigid exoskeletal plates. The exoskeleton also restricts continuous growth. Periodically the old exoskeleton is shed and is replaced by a new larger one as the animal quickly expands to fill it (fig. 3.20).

Members of the phylum Arthropoda account for over 75% of all existing animal species identified. Most belong to the class Insecta, which is almost exclusively nonmarine. However, three classes of this phylum, the Crustacea, Merostomata, and Pycnogonida, are primarily or completely marine in distribution.

Two of these classes of arthropods are completely marine, but their diversity is very restricted. The first class, Merostomata, has an extensive fossil history that includes extinct water scorpions 3 m long. Modern representatives include the horseshoe crab, *Xiphosura,* an inhabitant of the Atlantic and Gulf coasts of North America (fig. 3.21). The sea spiders of the class Pycnogonida are long-legged bottom dwellers with very reduced bodies (fig. 3.22). Small pycnogonids only a few mm in size are quite common intertidally. They can be collected from hydroid or bryozoan colonies, or the blades of intertidal algae. Deep-sea pycnogonids are often much larger than their intertidal relatives. Some have leg spans of 60 cm.

The third class, the Crustacea, is an extremely abundant and successful group of marine invertebrates. Obvious and well-known crustaceans include shrimps, crabs, and lobsters. These large, mostly benthic, crustaceans are not representative of the entire class, however. Most marine crustaceans are very small and are a major component of the zooplankton.

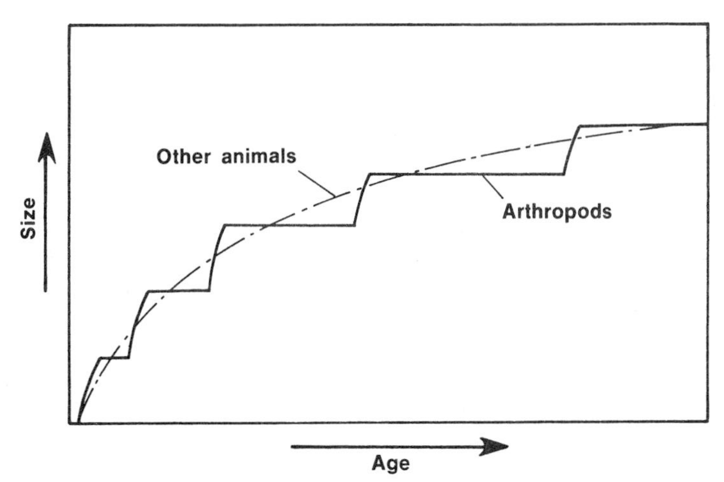

Fig. 3.20 Patterns of arthropod and nonarthropod growth. In contrast to the smooth curve of other animals, arthropods rapidly increase their body size in steps following each molt of the exoskeleton.

Fig. 3.21 Two horseshoe crabs, *Xiphosura*. Official photograph U.S. Navy.

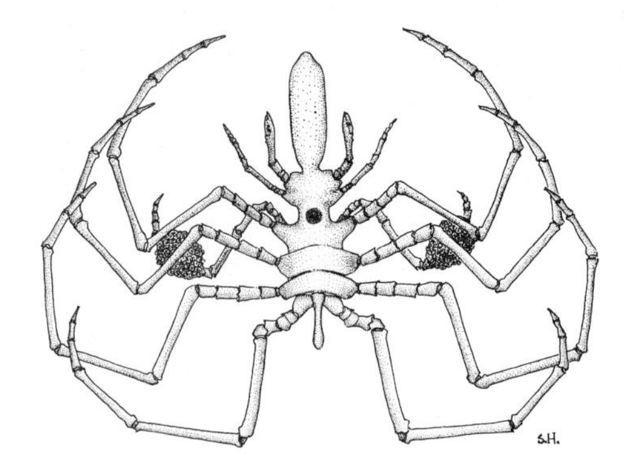

Fig. 3.22 A deep-sea pycnogonid.

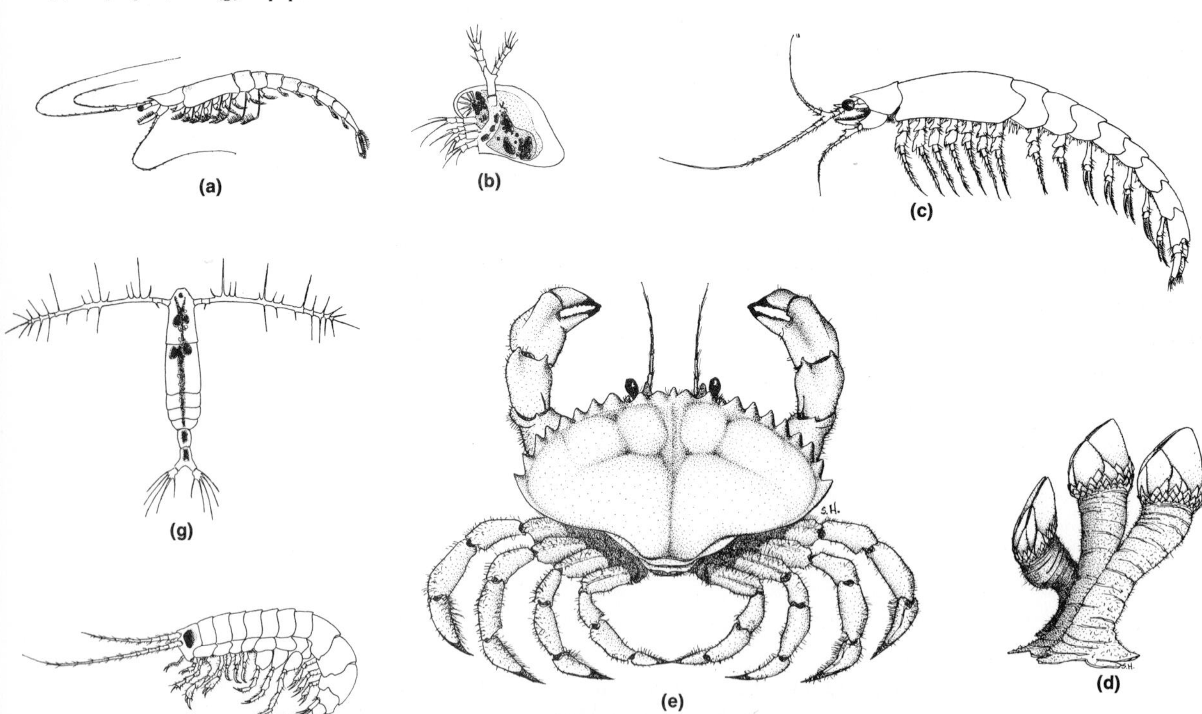

Fig. 3.23 A variety of marine crustaceans: (*a*) mysid, (*b*) cladoceran, (*c*) euphausiid, (*d*) barnacle, (*e*) crab, (*f*) amphipod, and (*g*) copepod.

Crustaceans are arthropods with two pairs of **antennae.** Few other useful generalizations can be made concerning this class. Its members exhibit a tremendous diversity in body structure and mode of feeding (fig. 3.23). The range of habitats also vary greatly, from burrowing ghost shrimp to planktonic copepods and parasitic barnacles.

Radial Symmetry Revisited

Echinodermata

The echinoderms, an exclusively marine group of animals, are widely distributed throughout the sea. They are common intertidally and are also abundant at great depths. Almost all forms are benthic as adults. Most are characterized by a calcareous skeleton, external spines or knobs, and a five-sided, or **pentamerous,** body symmetry (fig. 3.24). In this phylum, radial body symmetry is a secondary condition, as echinoderms characteristically develop from bilaterally symmetrical planktonic larval stages. Other aspects of their evolutionary history place them higher on the phylogenetic tree of animal groups (fig. 2.11) than those phyla characterized by primary radial body symmetry. A unique internal **water-vascular system** hydraulically operates the numerous tube feet. The tube feet extend through the skeleton to the outside and serve multiple functions as respiratory, excretory, sensory, and locomotor organs.

Five classes of echinoderms currently exist. Representatives of each are shown in figure 3.25. The Echinoidea are spiny, inflated herbivores or sediment ingesters variously known as sea urchins, heart urchins, and sand dollars. The Asteroidea, or sea stars, are usually five-armed, but the number may vary. Six-, ten-, and twenty-one-armed sea stars are known. Most sea stars are carnivorous, but a few are known to use cilia and mucus to collect fine food particles. Feather stars and sea lilies (class Crinoidea) are usually attached with the mouth oriented upward. Plankton and detritus are trapped by the arms and mucus secretions. Sea cucumbers of the class Holothuroidea are sausage-shaped echinoderms with the mouth located at one end. The body wall is muscular, with reduced skeletal units and spines. A few sea cucumbers feed on plankton, but most ingest sediment. The brittle stars (class Ophiuroidea) are surprisingly common animals in soft muds, through which they sort and selectively ingest particles of organic material.

The Chordates

Chordata

The phylum Chordata exhibits a remarkable variety of body forms and habitats. Yet at some stage in their development, all members of this phylum possess a supportive **notochord** made of cartilage, a **hollow dorsal nerve cord,** and **pharyngeal slits,** or **arches.**

The subphylum Urochordata includes animals such as benthic filter-feeding sea squirts (fig. 3.26) and the planktonic gelatinous salps. Another

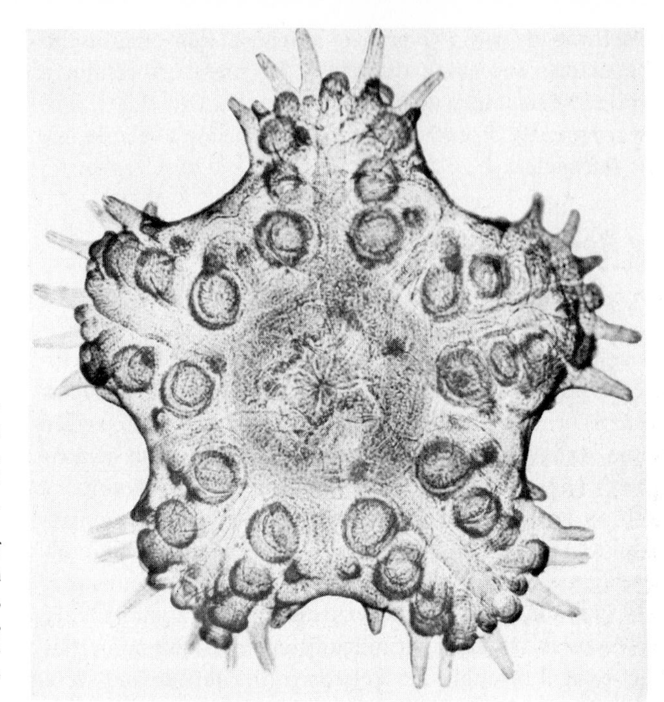

Fig. 3.24 A very young sea star with numerous tube feet projecting from its body. Courtesy Carolina Biological Supply Company.

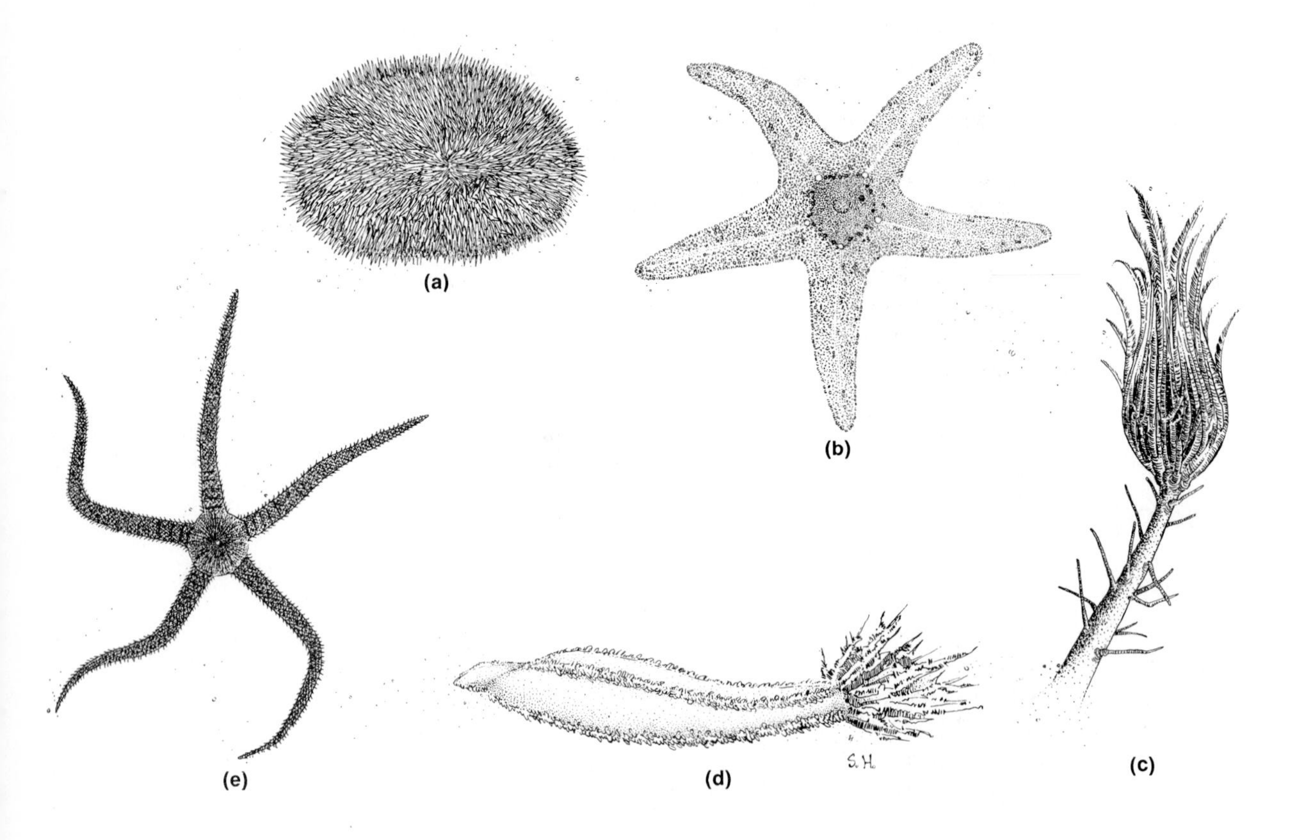

Fig. 3.25 Representatives of the five living echinoderm classes: (*a*) Echinoidea, (*b*) Asteroidea, (*c*) Crinoidea, (*d*) Holothuroidea, and (*e*) Ophiuroidea.

subphylum of the chordates is the Cephalochordata, which includes the lancelet *Amphioxus*. These animals are small and tadpole-shaped. They live partially buried tailfirst in near-shore sediments.

The unique feature of the third subphylum, the Vertebrata, is the **vertebral column** that extends through the main axis of the body for support. This single feature is used arbitrarily (and unfortunately) to divide the animal kingdom into two disparate portions, the invertebrates and the vertebrates. The vertebrates (fig. 3.27) include three classes of "fish" as well as four classes of "tetrapods." Fish are difficult to precisely characterize; but generally they are aquatic, streamlined in form, swim with fins, and utilize gills for oxygen and CO_2 exchange.

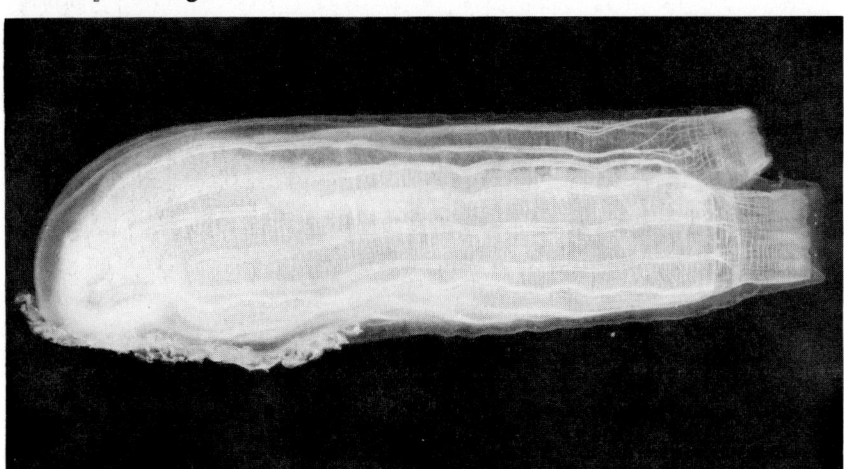

Fig. 3.26 The sea squirt *Ciona*. Courtesy Carolina Biological Supply Company.

Fig. 3.27 Marine vertebrate classes: (*a*) Agnatha (hagfish); (*b*) Chondrichthyes (shark); (*c*) Osteichthyes (bass); (*d*) Reptilia (turtle); (*e*) Aves (pelican); and (*f*) Mammalia (porpoise).

More species of fish exist than in all other vertebrate groups combined, and a large portion of these are marine. Existing fish are usually separated into three classes. The class Agnatha exhibits a mixture of primitive and specialized characteristics. They lack paired fins and biting jaws. As adults both types of living agnathans, the lampreys and hagfish, are parasitic or scavengers on other fish. The class Chondrichthyes (cartilaginous fish) includes sharks, skates, and rays. Bony fish (class Osteichthyes) account for essentially all other living fish.

Tetrapods are essentially four-limbed, air-breathing vertebrate animals with a terrestrial evolutionary history. Yet a few types of reptiles, birds, and mammals have left their land habitats and returned to the sea. A few species of marine turtles and snakes are quite successful. The same is true for birds. Penguins, for instance, spend most of their lives in the ocean, leaving only to rear their young. Many other birds are semimarine and utilize the sea as a source of food. Mammals exhibit varying degrees of adaptations to the marine environment. Polar bears differ little from their terrestrial relatives. Others, such as seals and sea lions, show affinities for both the land and the sea. At the apex of marine mammal evolution are the very successful whales, dolphins, and porpoises.

Summary

The animal kingdom is well represented in the marine environment. All major and most minor phyla have at least some marine representatives. Several phyla are found only in the sea. Each phylum is briefly described to provide the means for acquiring a working familiarity with marine animal groups as quickly as possible. The phyla are introduced in an order generally corresponding to an ascent of the phylogenetic tree shown in figure 2.11. Increasingly complex and specialized structures for feeding, reproduction, locomotion, circulation, excretion, and sensory perception are apparent in this sequence.

Questions for Discussion

1. What survival advantages might an animal such as a sea anemone with radial body symmetry have over one with bilateral symmetry? What might be some disadvantages?
2. Why do you think many critical sense organs are concentrated in the head region of "higher" animals rather than in other parts of their bodies?
3. Many common marine animals have wormlike body forms. What survival advantages does this body shape create for mud or sand dwellers?
4. Compare the rigid arthropod exoskeleton with the fluid hydrostatic skeleton of annelid worms. List and discuss the advantages and disadvantages of each.

Suggestions for Further Reading

Books

Fingerman, M. 1976. *Animal diversity.* New York: Holt, Rinehart & Winston.

Russell-Hunter, W. D. 1968. *A biology of lower invertebrates.* New York: Macmillan.

———1969. *A biology of higher invertebrates.* New York: Macmillan.

Warner, G. F. 1977. *The biology of crabs.* New York: Van Nostrand Reinhold.

Wells, M. J. 1978. *Octopus: physiology and behavior of an advanced invertebrate.* New York: John Wiley.

Yonge, C. M., and Thompson, T. E. 1976. *Living marine molluscs.* London: William Collins Sons.

Articles

Murphy, R. C. 1962. The oceanic life of the Antarctic. *Scientific American,* September: 186–99.

Valentine, W. 1978. The evolution of multicellular plants and animals. *Scientific American,* September: 140–58.

Pacific starfish. Photo by Visual Research/Roger Klocek.

Life on the Bottom—The Benthos

4

Over 90% of the animal species found in the ocean, and nearly all of the larger marine plants, live in close association with the sea bottom. These organisms are the benthos. Benthic marine plants are restricted to the shallow, near-shore fringe where the bottom coincides with the photic zone. Without the plant's need for sunlight, benthic animals range from high intertidal zones to cold, perpetually dark trenches more than 10,000 m deep. The variety of benthic animal species reflects the extreme diversity of environmental conditions that they experience living on the sea bottom.

Benthic organisms exist at or very near the thin interface between the sea bottom and the overlying water. The environmental demands they must meet for survival are defined by the characteristics of the bottom and the water above them, the exchange of substances between the sediments and the overlying water, and conditions established by the other living members of their community.

Living Conditions on the Bottom

Benthic animals that crawl about on the surface of the sea bottom, or sit firmly attached to it are referred to as the epifauna (fig. 4.1). Epifauna are associated with rocky outcrops or the surface of firm sediment deposits. Other benthic animals, the infauna, find food or protection within the bottom rather than on it. Infaunal clams, worms, and crabs are macroscopic and are familiar to anyone who has spent a few moments digging in a sandy beach or mudflat. These **macrofauna** either swallow or displace the sediment particles around themselves as they move. Less obvious, but no less important, are numerous microscopic infauna. Those less than 50 μm in size are considered **microfauna**. Intermediate in size between the macrofauna and microfauna is a very interesting and abundant group of animals, the **meiofauna**. The meiofauna are also referred to as **interstitial animals**, as they occupy the spaces (the interstices) between sediment particles.

Seafloor Characteristics

The sea bottom is a crucial part of the habitat of benthic organisms. It supports the weight of many organisms that are considerably denser than

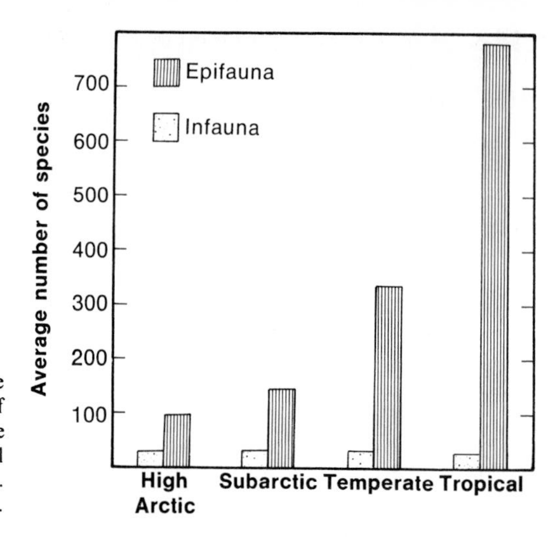

Fig. 4.1 Variations in the average number of species of several bottom invertebrate groups from equal-sized coastal areas in different latitudes. Adapted from Thorson 1957.

seawater. Some animals excavate burrows in the bottom material, or construct tubes of it. On hard bottoms, animals and plants secure a firm attachment to resist the tug of waves and currents.

The bottom also functions as a mechanical barrier to collect and accumulate plankton, waste material, and other plant and animal debris sinking from the productive, sunlit waters above. Fallout of organic detritus from the photic zone is, in some regions, the only source of food for the bottom inhabitants. A variety of worms, mollusks, echinoderms, and crustaceans obtain their nourishment by ingesting the accumulated detritus and digesting its organic material. Benthic organisms are adapted for life on or in particular bottom types; and the character of life there, to a large extent, is dependent on the properties of the bottom material. This material varies from solid rock surfaces to very soft, loose deposits. Rocky bottoms are most commonly found around the edges of the ocean basins where waves erode and remove finer sediment particles. Rocky outcrops also occur in deep ocean basins, but they are comparatively small and geographically isolated.

Most of the sea bottom is covered with small sediment particles, along with other debris, that have settled from the surface. Marine sediments are derived from three principle sources. A few minerals precipitate from their dissolved state in seawater to produce irregular deposits on the seafloor. Manganese nodules are well-known examples of this type of deposit. Such deposits may have some economic importance as a source of minerals useful to man, but they are not widespread on the seafloor and probably have little effect on the life-styles of benthic organisms.

Marine sediments nearshore and on the continental shelves are largely the products of erosion on land and subsequent transport by rivers (and, to a lesser extent, winds) to the sea. Once in the ocean, suspended sediment particles are carried and sorted by current and wave action according to their size and density. Larger, dense sand grains quickly settle to the bottom near shore. Very fine clay particles are often carried several hundred km out to sea before settling.

Much of the sedimentary material found in the deep ocean basins away from continental margins is composed of mineralized skeletal remains of single-celled plant and animal plankton. These deposits are known as oozes and are characterized by their chemical composition. Siliceous oozes contain cell walls of diatoms and the internal silicate skeletons of planktonic radiolarians (see figure 3.2). The skeletons of other planktonic protozoans, the foraminifers, constitute most of the extensive calcareous oozes found on the ocean floor. These oceanic oozes accumulate very slowly, approximately 1 cm of new sediment every 1,000 years. In the deep sea, oceanic oozes exhibit distributional patterns that reflect the surface abundance of their plant and animal sources. These patterns are shown in figure 4.2.

Animal-Sediment Relationships

Benthic animals play an important role in mixing and sorting the sediments by their burrowing and feeding activities. Oxygen and water from the sediment surface are circulated down into the sediment through these tubes and burrows. Further modification of sedimentary characteristics is accomplished by cementing particles together to form tubes and by compacting sediments together as fecal pellets and castings. On rocky bottoms, the grazing activities

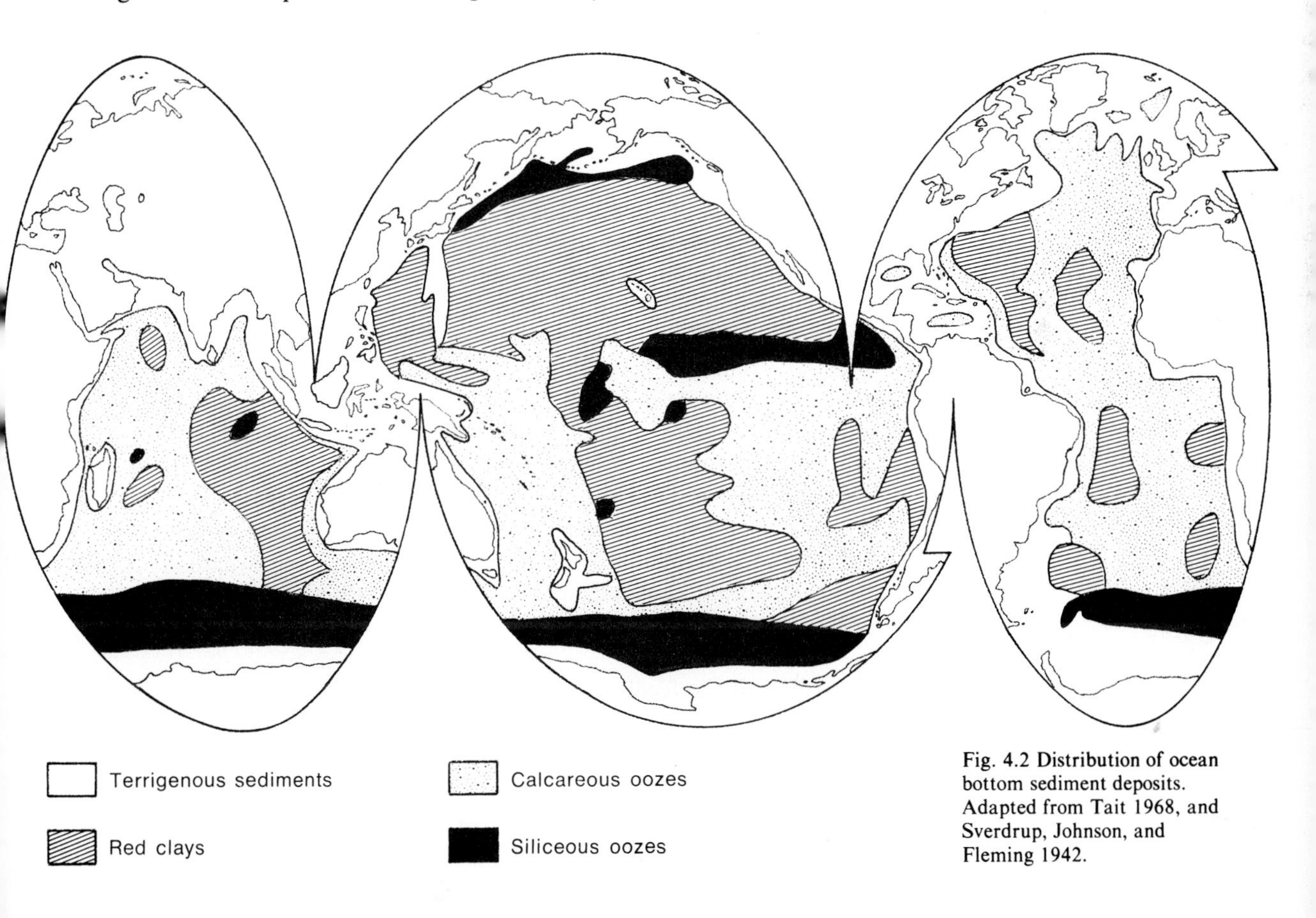

Fig. 4.2 Distribution of ocean bottom sediment deposits. Adapted from Tait 1968, and Sverdrup, Johnson, and Fleming 1942.

of chitons and sea urchins aid the erosive processes of waves by scraping away rock particles as well as food (fig. 4.3). There are even a few benthic animals, such as pholad clams, that are especially adapted for boring into solid rock.

The distributional patterns of benthic plants and animals are strongly influenced by the firmness, texture, and stability of their substrate. These features govern the effectiveness of locomotion or, for nonmotile species, the persistence of their attachment to the bottom. Epifauna are most frequently associated with firm or solid bottom material. When found on softer muds, they often display elongated, stiltlike legs that extend into or along the sediment for better support and traction.

The particle size and organic content of the bottom material limit the versatility, and thus the distribution of specialized feeding habits. **Suspension feeders** depend on small plankton or detritus for nutrition. A filtering device is employed (fig. 4.4) to separate minute suspended food particles from the water. These animals generally require clean water to avoid clogging their filters with indigestible particles. Therefore they are usually found on rocks or associated with coarse sediments.

In deep-ocean basins, mudflats, and other soft-bottom areas, **deposit feeding** is common. Deposit feeders engulf masses of sediments and process them through their digestive tracts. They extract nourishment from the included organic material in much the same manner as earthworms do. Some deposit feeders indiscriminately ingest any available sediments. Others select organically rich areas for consumption to increase the nutritive value of what they eat.

A few remarkable animals are even capable of extracting sufficient nourishment from sediments by conducting digestive processes outside their bodies. The products of digestion are absorbed either through specialized organs or across the general body wall. Pogonophorans are believed to depend on this type of **absorptive feeding**, as are numerous echinoderms. Most sea stars are carnivorous, but a few species are quite opportunistic. *Patiria miniata*, the Pacific Coast bat star, eats almost anything. When feeding on bottom sediments, it extrudes its stomach outside its body, then digests and absorbs the organic matter from the sediments. The omnipresent bacteria also depend on extracellular digestion. As they absorb nutrients and grow, they in turn become a significant source of particulate food for deposit feeders.

The benthic environment abounds with **predators** and **scavengers**, feeding on the residents of the bottom, or on their remains. Most bottom predators and scavengers are permanent members of the benthos, and eventually are eaten by other benthic consumers. However, fish and birds often make temporary but serious inroads into accessible benthic animal populations (fig. 4.5).

Regardless of the feeding habit employed by benthic animals, the ultimate source of food is the primary producers of the photic zone. Intertidal and shallow-water benthic plants provide direct sources of nutrition for the abundant herbivorous **algal grazers**. Some grazers nibble away bits of the larger seaweeds (fig. 4.6). Most, however, rasp filmy growths of diatoms, blue-green algae, and other small encrusting plants from rocky substrates. Sea

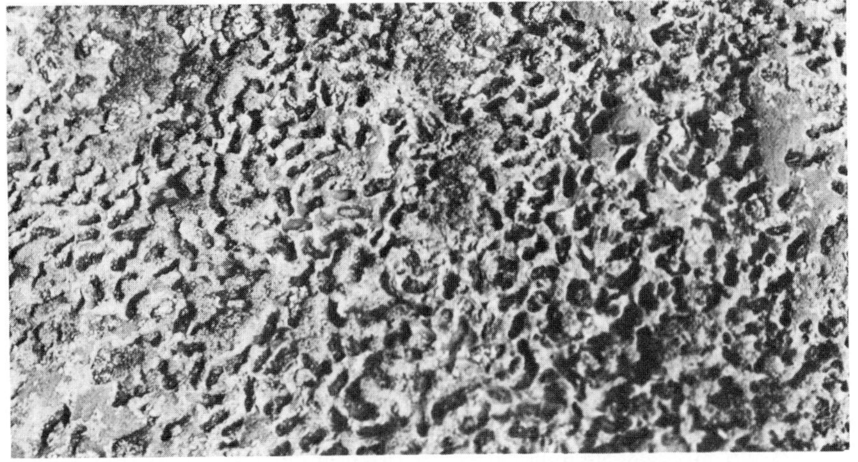
Fig. 4.3

Fig. 4.4

Fig. 4.5

Fig. 4.6

Fig. 4.3 Erosion pits in sandstone created by the rasping actions of small chitons.

Fig. 4.4 Stalked barnacles with their feathery filtering appendages extended. Courtesy Carolina Biological Supply Company.

Fig. 4.5 A godwit feeding in the intertidal.

Fig. 4.6 A small limpet, *Acmaea*, grazing on stipes of *Egregia*. Previous grazing scars are visible.

urchins use their five-toothed Aristotle's lantern to remove algal growths. Similar results are accomplished with the filelike radula of herbivorous gastropods and chitons.

Larval Dispersal

A benthic life-style need not preclude extensive geographic ranges for sedentary bottom creatures. One-fifth of the common rocky intertidal animal species occurring at San Diego, California, can also be found along the entire west coast of the United States and into British Columbia. Several other benthic species are even more widely dispersed, often in similar ecological conditions on opposite sides of the same ocean basin. *Mytilus edulis*, variously known as the bay mussel, blue mussel, or edible mussel, is common to temperate coasts of both sides of the Pacific and Atlantic oceans.

A few animals, such as barnacles, often hitch rides on floating debris, the hulls of ships, or even an occasional passing whale to cross an otherwise impassable ocean. An Australian barnacle, *Elminius modestus*, was apparently introduced to England on the hulls of supply ships during World War II. It has since colonized the coasts of Ireland, France, Belgium, the Netherlands, Germany, and Denmark. In many sheltered reaches of these coastlines, *E. modestus* is competing with and replacing native barnacle populations.

A far more popular method of extending the geographical limits of temperate- and warm-water benthic species relies on the production of temporary planktonic larval stages (also known as **meroplankton**). These small, feeble swimmers, bearing little resemblance to their parents (fig. 4.7), drift with the ocean's surface currents for some time before they metamorphose and assume their benthic life-styles. Thorson estimated that about 75% of shallow-water benthic invertebrate species produce larvae that remain planktonic for two to four weeks. Over 5% of the species Thorson examined had planktonic larval stages exceeding three months, and a few were as long as six months in duration (fig. 4.8). Our understanding of ocean currents suggests that none but the most prolonged larval stages can make direct transoceanic trips before settling to the bottom. For each extra day the larvae remain in the plankton, they are exposed to additional threats of predation, increased pressures of finding food, and greater possibilities of being carried by the currents to areas where survival is unlikely. Yet the perils of planktonic pursuits are apparently profitable, for the parents of so many very successful species produce planktonic prototypes of themselves.

Even in very slow ocean currents, drifting planktonic forms may spread far beyond the geographical limits of the adult population. Many are swept into unfavorable areas and perish. But the survivors may expand their parents' original range, or settle into and mix with other populations and reduce their genetic isolation.

During their planktonic existence, many types of larvae react positively to sunlight and remain near the sea surface and their basic food supply, the phytoplankton. As their pelagic life draws to a close and they seek their

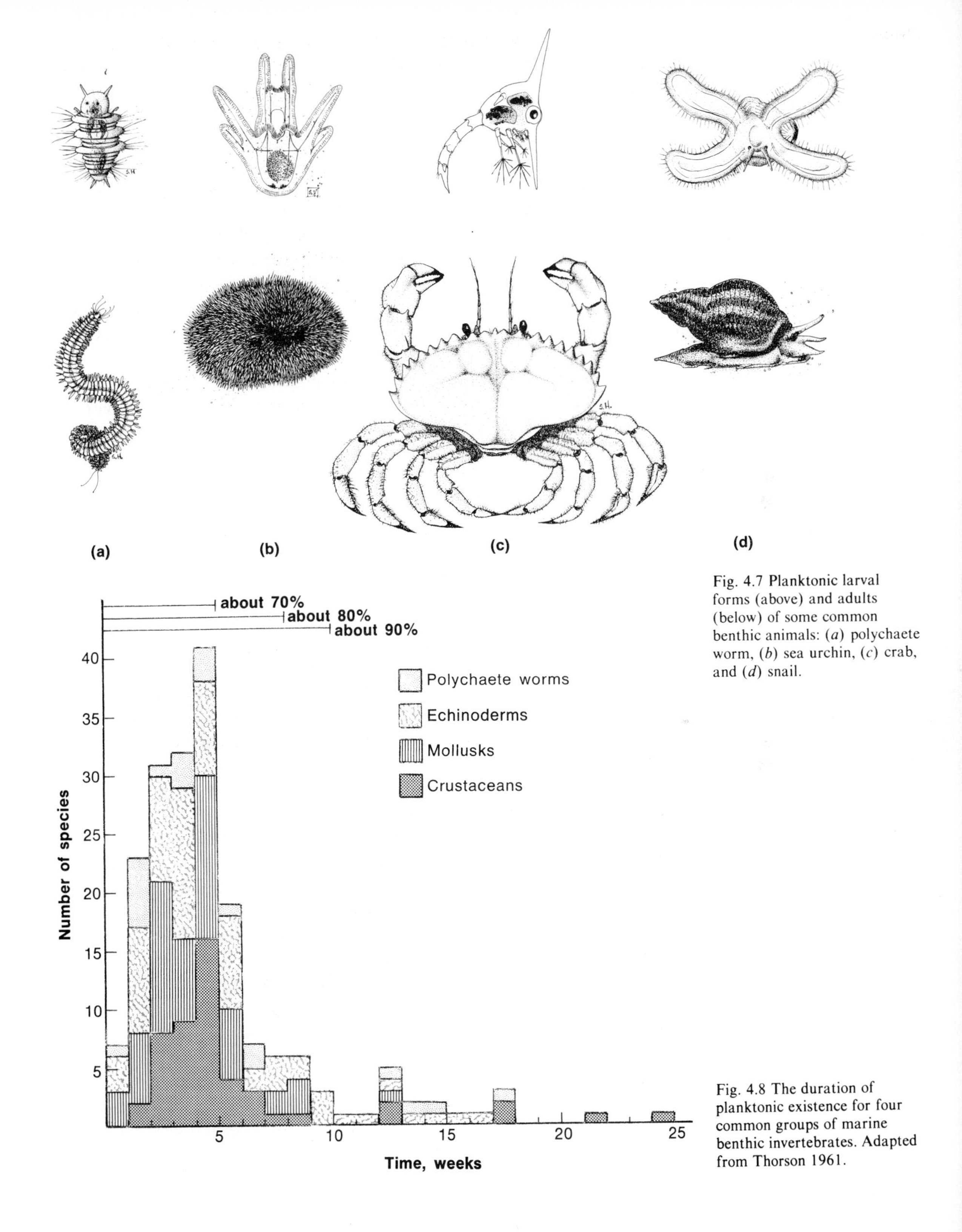

Fig. 4.7 Planktonic larval forms (above) and adults (below) of some common benthic animals: (*a*) polychaete worm, (*b*) sea urchin, (*c*) crab, and (*d*) snail.

Fig. 4.8 The duration of planktonic existence for four common groups of marine benthic invertebrates. Adapted from Thorson 1961.

permanent homes on the bottom, some remain near the sea surface and ride into the intertidal on waves and tides. Others shun the light and swim near the bottom. Most enter a swimming-crawling phase, during which a larva settles to the bottom, investigates it, and if it is not suitable, swims up again to be carried elsewhere.

Just how a larva knows when a suitable substrate is encountered is an important, but as yet unanswered, question. Texture of the bottom, chemical attractants, types of bottom material, and effects of light are at best only partial answers to the question. Specific bottom types, such as sand or hard rock, do not attract larvae from a distance to settle there. Bottom types are found by chance, but once the appropriate bottom type is encountered, the larva may be induced to remain and quickly metamorphose into a young bottom stage. In contrast, chemical substances diffusing from established populations of some attached animals, including oysters and barnacles, seem to attract larvae of their own species. This may be beneficial for oyster and barnacle larvae, for the presence of adults in the settling site insures that the physical conditions there are appropriate for survival. However, for many other larvae, settling among their adults is certain to be catastrophic. Older, established individuals generally have relatively lower demands for food and oxygen, have more stored energy, and in general, can effectively compete for resources with the newly settled young. In times of shortages, the younger individuals are the first to suffer.

Until they settle to the bottom, planktonic larvae are not in competition for food or space with the adults of their species. Even so, competition for food among the plankton is often rigorous. About 10% of the species with long larval phases produce large yolky eggs that provide the larvae with most or all of their nutritional supply. However, most species hatch from very small eggs and must begin feeding and competing with each other almost immediately.

Some benthic species spawn all year long; others have short and well-defined spawning seasons. In the latter group, the timing of reproduction or spawning is geared to produce young at times most advantageous to their survival. For many species of benthic animals, the spawning periods are timed to place their larvae in the plankton community when phytoplankton is abundant and readily accessible. In shallow waters, temperature and day-length provide two of the more obvious cues for timing reproduction. The gonads of spring and summer spawners develop in response to rising water temperatures or lengthening days. Oysters, for instance, refrain from spawning until a particular water temperature is reached.

Regardless of how many eggs are produced, the reproductive success of a population requires that the **fecundity** (the production of eggs or offspring) of a population must exceed its **mortality** (the rate at which individuals are lost). Any population, the mortality of which consistently exceeds its fecundity, will shrink and eventually disappear for want of new recruits. Adaptations that increase fecundity and/or reduce mortality improve the chances for successful reproduction.

The fecundity of some shallow-water benthic animals is truly awesome. The females of many of these species each produce over ten million eggs annually. A moderate-size sea slug *(Aplysia)* produced an estimated 478 million eggs during five months of laboratory observations. Such excessive reproductive enthusiasm would quickly place any shoreline knee-deep in sea slugs if the spawning efforts of only a few adults were all to survive.

Obviously, egg and larval mortality in these species are extremely high. Of the millions of potential offspring produced, very few attain sexual maturity. In some benthic animals, internal fertilization is accomplished before the eggs are released into the water. Some species of snails, crabs, sea stars, and other invertebrates retain their larvae internally or in special brood pouches, then release them at reasonably advanced stages of development. For some of these invertebrates, brooding may be an adaptive consequence of small adult size. Smaller species of benthic invertebrates, with correspondingly smaller gonads, are less likely to produce sufficient planktonic larvae to equal their larger competitors. So internal fertilization and larval incubation are employed to reduce offspring mortality to some extent. Even so, many of the abundant and familiar seashore animals simply spew great quantities of eggs and sperm into the surrounding water where fertilization occurs.

Fertilization in these mass spawners is not as haphazard as it may seem. Unidentified chemical substances (sometimes referred to as **pheromones**) are present in the egg or sperm secretions of sea urchins, oysters, and presumably many other marine invertebrates. When shed into seawater, these pheromones induce other nearby members of the population to spawn, and they in turn stimulate still others until much of the population is spawning simultaneously. As you might guess, spawning pheromones are quite specific. For instance, the sperm secretions of a species of sea urchins induce females of the same species to spawn, but have no effect on female oysters. Another chemical substance is contained in the heads of sea urchin sperm cells and unites only with the surface coat of sea urchin eggs (fig. 4.9). Together with pheromones, these substances regulate the timing of spawning, the specificity of sperm for eggs of the same species, and ultimately the overall prospects for successful fertilization by mass spawners.

It is distressing to note that, for many years, smashing sea urchins has been a popular and sporting method of removing these so-called "pests" from the kelp beds on which they feed. Diving clubs frequently organized competitions, with prizes going to the club killing the most urchins in a specific time. The impact of these eradication programs on sea urchin populations is questionable, for a smashed sea urchin (if it was ready to spawn) releases not only its own eggs or sperm, but also pheromones that cause its neighbors to do likewise. Thus a Sunday afternoon's efforts to elimate a few thousand urchins may, in fact, trigger a mass-spawning of billions of sea urchin eggs (enough to replace the animals destroyed with more than a few left over). Worse yet, such activities tend to promote the myth that man is capable of interfering with and correctly altering the character of natural systems to fit his own needs without first understanding the basic functions of those systems.

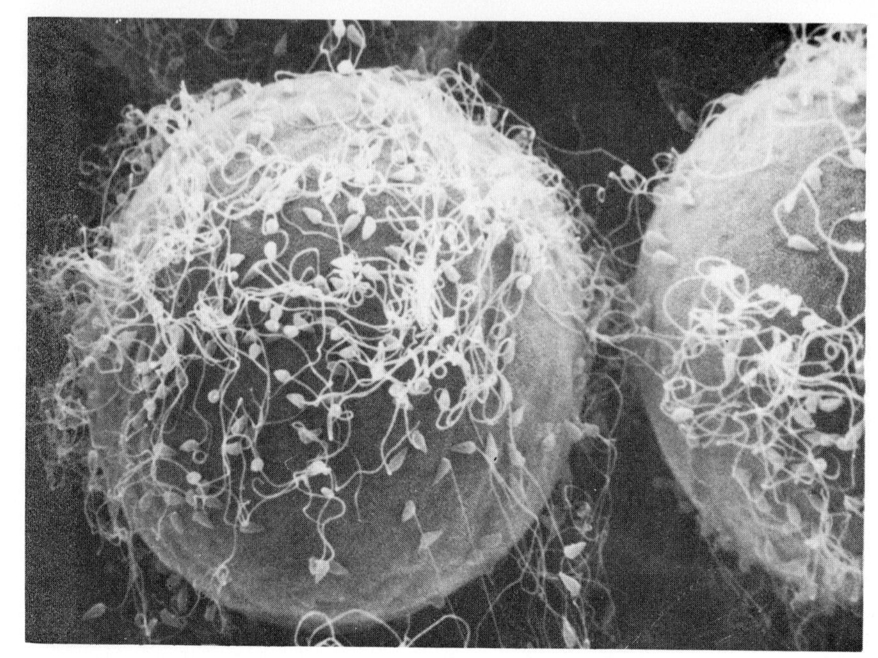

Fig. 4.9 A scanning electron micrograph of a sea urchin egg covered with sperm cells. Courtesy M. Tegner, Scripps Institution of Oceanography.

The Intertidal Zone

The coastal strip where land meets the sea is home for some of the richest and most complex marine communities to be found anywhere. The organisms here are easily observed and sampled, yet their biology is complicated by several overlapping and interrelated physical factors. Only in the coastal zone does sunlight penetrate with sufficient intensity to support plant growth on the bottom. Seaweeds as well as phytoplankton thrive and provide a rich food supply for abundant animal populations. A few of these plants will be referred to in the discussions to follow, but a more detailed examination of benthic plants occurs in chapter 5.

The periodic rise and fall of the tides imposes some dramatic effects on a portion of the coastal zone known as the intertidal, or **littoral**, zone. Tidal fluctuations of sea level often expose intertidal plants and animals to severe environmental extremes, alternating between complete submergence in sea-water and nearly dry terrestrial conditions. Local characteristics of the tides, including their vertical range and their frequencies, determine the amount of time intertidal plants and animals are out of water. Still, most intertidal regions have exposure curves which resemble figure 4.10 regardless of their locations.

For most intertidal plants and animals, low tide is a time of physiological stress. When the tide is out, exposed organisms are subjected to wide variations of atmospheric conditions. The air may dry and overheat their tissues in hot weather or freeze them during winter months. Rainfall and freshwater runoff create severe osmotic problems as well. Predation by land animals, such as birds, rats, and raccoons, make their presence felt even in the intertidal zone

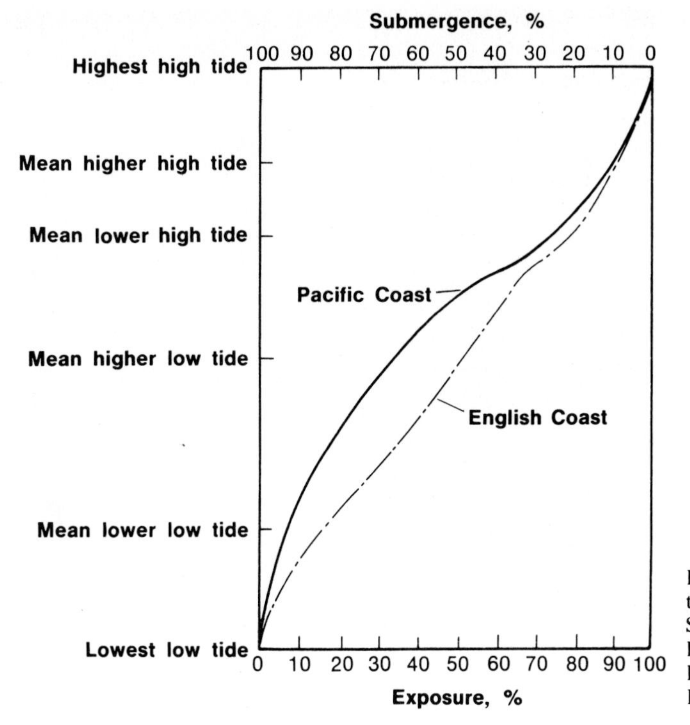

Fig. 4.10 Exposure curves for the Pacific coast of the United States and the Atlantic coast of England. Adapted from Ricketts and Calvin 1968, and Lewis 1964.

at low tide. Only at high tide are truly marine conditions restored to the intertidal zone. The returning waters moderate the temperature and salinity fluctuations brought on by the previous low tide. Needed food, nutrients, and dissolved oxygen are replenished, and accumulated wastes are washed away.

Accompanying the beneficial effects of seawater is the physical assault of waves and surf. The influence of wave shock on the distribution of intertidal plants and animals is apparent on all exposed coastlines of the world. Surf, storm waves, and surface ocean currents shift and sort sediments, transport suspended food, and disperse reproductive products. Much of the wave energy expended on the shore (and the organisms living there) eventually serves to shape and alter the essential character of the shoreline itself. Continually modified by the power of ocean waves, shorelines have assumed a variety of forms (fig. 4.11). Rocky shorelines are constantly swept clean of finer sediments by heavy surf or strong currents. Beaches are characterized by waves that remove fine silt and clay particles but leave the sand grains behind. These finer materials are washed out to sea or are deposited in the quiet, protected waters of bays and lagoons.

The variety of tidal conditions, bottom types, and wave intensities along the shore combine to create a boundless assortment of living conditions for coastal plants and animals. It is difficult to characterize the prevailing conditions on long stretches of shoreline without risking overgeneralization. The west coast of North America, for instance, has many rugged rocky cliffs exposed to the full force of wave action. Yet interspersed between these cliffs and headlands are numerous sandy beaches and quiet mud-bottom bays and

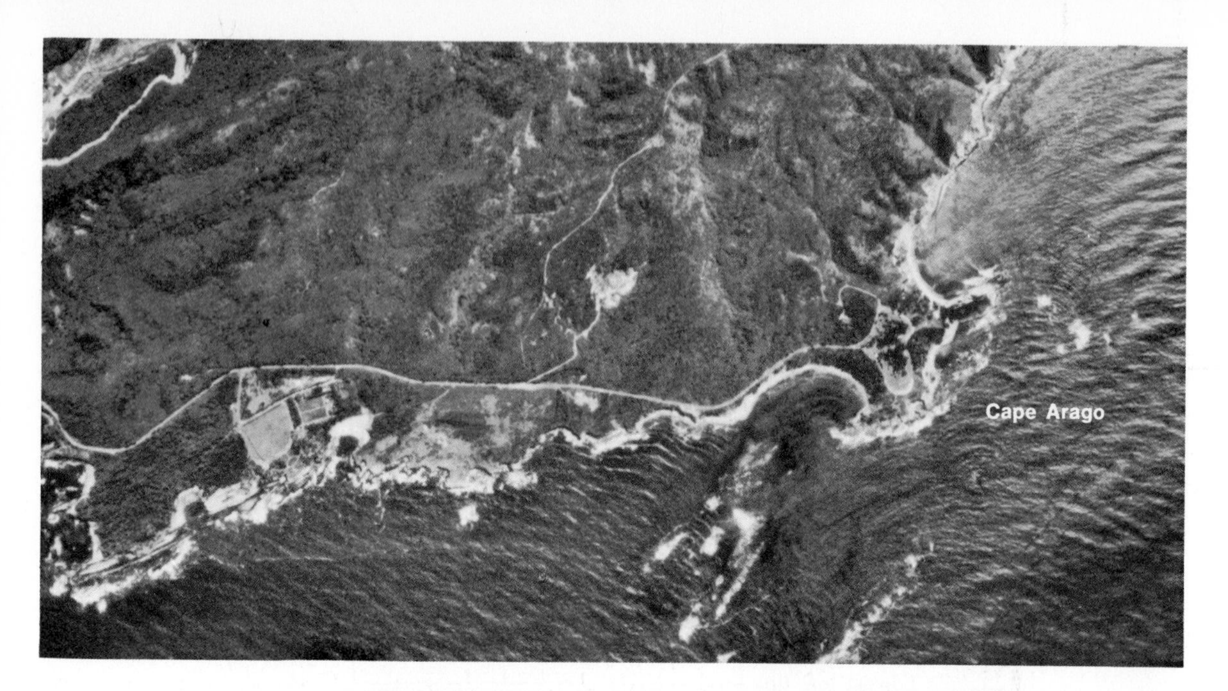

Fig. 4.11 An aerial photograph of a portion of the Oregon coast with protected coves, exposed headlands (Cape Arago), and offshore rocky reefs. Courtesy U.S. Geological Survey.

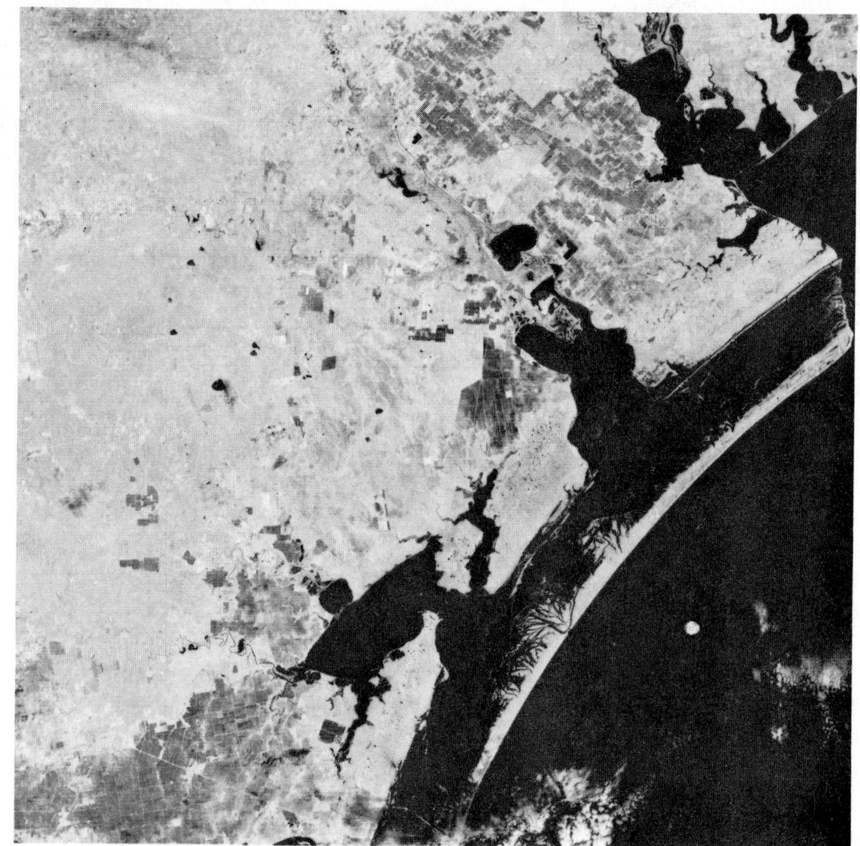

Fig. 4.12 A portion of the Texas Gulf coast showing a large barrier island (Matagorda Island). Photographed by the Earth Resources Technology Satellite.

estuaries. On the East Coast, conditions vary from the spectacular rugged coastline of northern New England and the Canadian Maritime Provinces to extensive sandy beaches in the mid-Atlantic states. From Chesapeake Bay south to Florida, numerous coastal marshes are protected from extensive wave action by long, low barrier islands that parallel the mainland. Similar conditions, but with smaller tidal ranges, exist along much of the Gulf Coast (fig. 4.12).

The southern tip of Florida is the only shoreline on the continental United States to experience tropical conditions. Tropical shorelines are typically marked by large coral reefs or by extensive swampy woodlands of mangroves. Florida lacks well-developed living coral reefs; however, mangroves occur in abundant profusion along the state's southern coast. Mangroves actually include several types of shrubby and treelike plants that often grow together to form impenetrable thickets. Their branching prop roots trap sediments and detritus to extend existing shorelines or even form new low-lying islands.

Within a particular type of coastal environment, the interrelated influences of tidal exposure, bottom type, and intensity of wave shock produce an infinitely varied set of vertically arranged habitats. The vertical distribution of coastal plants and animals reflect the vertical changes in environmental conditions of the shoreline. Different species tend to occupy different levels or zones within the intertidal. Quite often, each zone is sharply demarcated from adjacent zones by the color, texture, and general appearance of the species living there. The result is a well-defined vertical series of horizontal life zones, sometimes extending for lengthy distances along a coastline.

The vertical distribution of intertidal plants and animals is governed by a complex set of environmental conditions that vary along gradients above and below the sea surface. Temperature, wave shock, light intensity, and "wetness" are some of the more important physical factors that vary along such gradients. Additionally, several biological factors, including predation and competition for food and space, are superimposed on these physical gradients to further delineate the life zones of the shoreline. This combination of physical and biological factors frames and limits the range of existence of an organism. It, as well as the biological role the organism plays in its habitat, defines the organism's **niche**. The complex interplay of physical and biological conditions and the variety of shore life itself create a nearly unlimited selection of niches for intertidal plants and animals.

As the tides advance and recede over the intertidal portion of the shoreline, so do the vertically graded changes in temperature, light intensity, degree of predation, and other environmental factors. Vertically arranged series of plant and animal populations are not unique to intertidal regions. They can be found elsewhere: on mountainsides, in the sea beneath low tide, and in tideless lakes and ponds. Ocean tides, then, do not cause **vertical zonation** within the intertidal, but simply modify and spread out the pattern of zonation to make it more pronounced.

For years marine biologists have wrestled with the intricate problems of defining and identifying specific subzones within the intertidal. However, the multiplicity of factors influencing intertidal zonation have seriously compounded the task. As a result, each of the major subzones are frequently further subdivided on the basis of locally abundant plant or animal populations. The makeup of intertidal populations may vary from place to place, causing the patterns of zonation to change; yet vertical zonation remains a visible unifying feature on all shorelines. It therefore seems to be a logical and appropriate basis on which to compare and describe the marine life of a few selected shores.

Rocky Shores

It was emphasized in chapter 2 that ecosystems have two complementary pathways for energy transfer, a grazing food chain and a detritus food chain (refer to fig. 2.14). The grazing food chain routes energy and nutrient material from the primary producers through the grazers and predators. Detritus eaters utilize the bits and pieces of dead and decaying matter available within the ecosystem. Within the coastal zone, neither rocky shores nor sandy beaches appear to be complete ecosystems by themselves. The trophic relations within rocky shore communities exhibit well-developed and complicated grazing food chains, but very little in the way of detritus food chains. The erosional nature of rocky shores simply prohibits the accumulation of detritus and, of course, the existence of those animals dependent on it for food.

Patterns of distribution and abundance, as well as trophic relationships, in rocky intertidal communities are complex and sometimes change dramatically over short distances and from season to season. A shaded northern exposure, for example, usually harbors several species absent from nearby sunny slopes. Tide pools contain an assemblage of plants and animals quite different from that of surrounding well-drained platforms. The variety of life on one side of a boulder may differ markedly from that on the other side. And if you look under the boulder, still other species are to be found.

With such a bewildering array of niches available on even a small stretch of shoreline, it might seem improbable to find recurring themes of vertical zonation on widely separated shorelines. Yet similar patterns of zonation do exist on rocky shores, whether it is New England, Australia, British Columbia, or South Africa. Vertical zonation is such a compelling feature of life on rocky shores that considerable effort has been expended devising schemes to identify and describe distinct intertidal subzones and their inhabitants. Most of these descriptions are useful on a regional basis only, and no real purpose would be served by reviewing them here. If you desire a detailed account of life on intertidal rocky shores, several works with regional emphasis are listed at the end of this chapter.

The following general discussion is not inteneded as a rock-by-rock, barnacle-by-barnacle examination of the marine life of rocky shores. Rather, some of the more conspicuous plants and animals, and the adaptations that permit them to remain conspicuous, are examined. Only three rather ill-defined zones, the upper, middle, and lower intertidal zones, are employed for reference. As the boundaries separating these zones are artificial, they are frequently and consistently violated by their residents. You are likely to see species that dominate one zone scattered through other zones as well.

The Upper Intertidal

In the upper intertidal, living conditions are sometimes nearly as terrestrial as they are marine. Often only a vague demarcation separates land and marine vegetation. This area is wetted only infrequently by high spring tides and splash from breaking waves. The upper intertidal is only sparsely inhabited by marine plants and animals. Dark mats of blue-green algae *Calothrix* or the lichen *Verrucaria* frequently form a noticeable band or series of tarlike patches to mark the uppermost part of the rocky intertidal. Small tufts of a filamentous green algae, *Ulothrix*, may also extend into the highest parts of the intertidal. These plants are tolerant to large temperature changes and are unusually adept at resisting desiccation. The small, tangled filaments of *Calothrix* are embedded in a gelatinous mass to maintain their store of water and to reduce evaporation. Lichens, such as *Verrucaria*, are symbiotic associations of a fungus and a unicellular alga (fig. 4.13). In the case of *Verrucaria*, the fungal part absorbs and holds several times its weight of water. The water is used by the fungus as well as the photosynthetic algal cells that produce food for the entire lichen complex.

Grazing on the sparse and scattered vegetation of the upper intertidal are only a few species of snails, limpets, and occasional crustaceans (fig. 4.14). Unlike its other close marine relatives, the small littorine snail, *Littorina*, is an air-breather. In place of gills, a highly vascularized mantle cavity is used in much the same manner as land snails for O_2 and CO_2 exchange. Some species of *Littorina* are so well-adapted to an air-breathing existence that they drown if forced to remain underwater. Like the littorines, limpets of the upper intertidal (especially *Acmaea*) are amazingly tolerant to temperature changes. Both can seal the edges of their shell openings against rock surfaces to anchor themselves and to retain moisture. Littorines and limpets are algal grazers

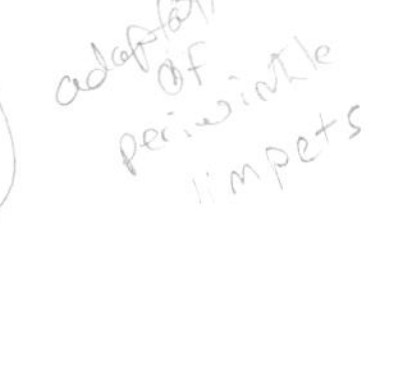

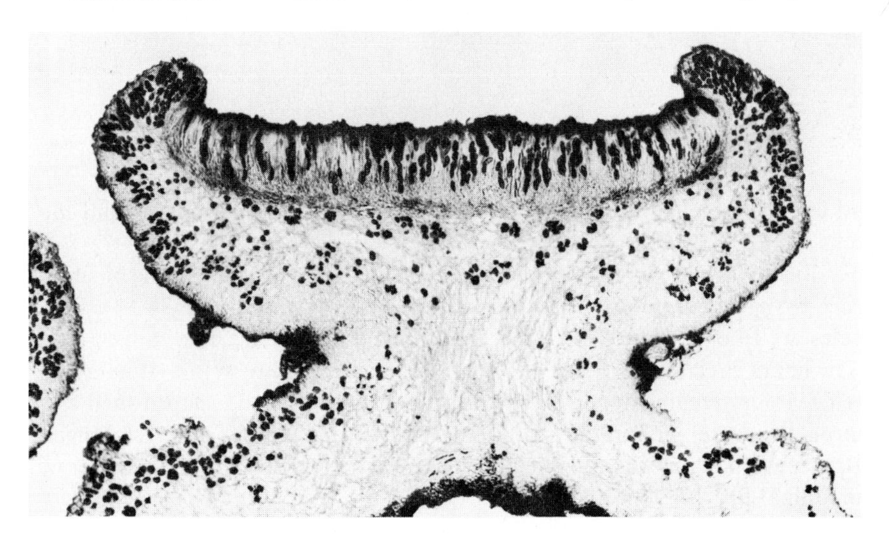

Fig. 4.13 Magnified cross section of a lichen with algae cells (dark spots) embedded in fungal filaments (light stands). The cup-shaped feature is an ascocarp, a reproductive structure. Courtesy Carolina Biological Supply Company.

Fig. 4.14 Two members of the sparsely populated rocky upper intertidal: the shore crab, *Pachygrapsis,* and the littorine snail, *Littorina.* Official photograph U.S. Navy.

Fig. 4.15 Stunted acorn barnacles, *Chthamalus,* survive in the shallow depressions of Mike's name.

and use their filelike radulae to scrape the small algae and lichens from the rocks.

Just below the lichens and blue-green algae, a conspicuous zone of small acorn barnacles, *Balanus* or *Chthamalus*, frequently appears (fig. 4.15). Barnacles are filter-feeders, but in the high intertidal, they are able to feed only a few hours each month when wetted by high spring tides. While submerged, their feathery feeding appendages extend from their volcano-shaped shell and search the water or minute plankton. Between high tides, a set of hinged calcareous plates blocks the entrance to the shell and seals the remainder of the animal in.

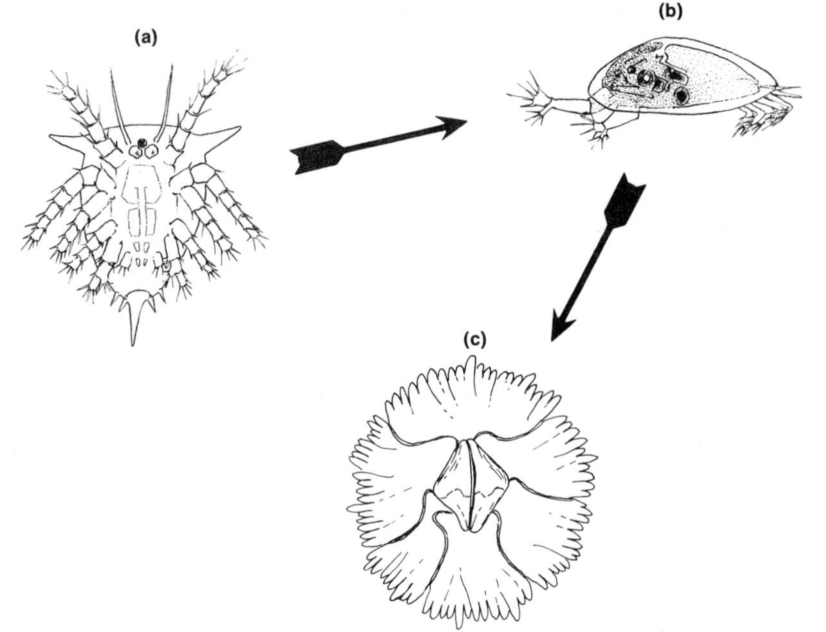

Fig. 4.16 Planktonic and early benthic stages of the barnacle *Balanus:* (*a*) nauplius stage, (*b*) cypris stage, and (*c*) early benthic stage.

Most barnacles are **hermaphroditic;** that is, individuals contain gonads of both sexes. Yet each generally refrains from fertilizing its own eggs. During mating, a long tubular penis is extended into a neighboring barnacle, and the sperm are transferred to fertilize the neighbor's eggs. The eggs develop and hatch within the barnacle's shell and are released as microscropic free-swimming planktonic stages known as **nauplii,** shown in figure 4.16*a*. After several molts of its exoskeleton, the nauplius develops into a **cypris larva** (fig. 4.16*b*). The cypris eventually settles on the bottom, selects a permanent homesite, then cements itself to the bottom with a secretion from its antennae. Cypris larvae are attracted by the presence of other barnacles, thus insuring settlement in areas suitable for barnacle survival. Soon after settling, the cypris turns over, loses its planktonic appearance, and begins to surround itself with a wall of calcareous plates (fig. 4.16*c*).

The Middle Intertidal

The middle intertidal is occupied by greater numbers of individuals and species than the upper intertidal zone. This zone is sufficiently inundated by tides and waves to provide an abundance of plant nutrients as well as 0_2 and plankton food for filter-feeding animals. The lush growths of green, red, and especially brown algae furnish a bountiful supply of locally produced food for grazers too.

Occasional small, but permanent, tide pools protect hermit crabs, snails, and the more fragile nudibranchs and anemones from exposure and the physical assault of the surf. The upper range of anemones is usually determined by their tolerance to desiccation. Aggregate anemones of the Pacific Coast *(Anthopleura elegantissima)* are known to withstand internal temperatures as great as 13°C above the surrounding air temperature. Yet serious water loss will destroy them. These anemones combat extreme desiccation and temperature fluctuations by retracting their tentacles and attaching bits of light-colored stone and shell to themselves, presumably to reflect light and heat. The clumped mats, so characteristic of the aggregate anemone (fig. 4.17) are the result of a peculiar mode of asexual reproduction. To divide, these anemones literally pull themselves apart by simultaneously creeping in opposite directions. Each half quickly regenerates its missing portion, producing two new individuals to replace the original. These anemones also reproduce sexually by releasing eggs and sperm into the water.

The dominant and conspicuous members of the middle intertidal (fig. 4.18) are mussels *(Mytilus)*, barnacles (usually *Balanus*), some chitons and limpets, and several species of brown algae (especially *Fucus* and *Pelvetia)*.

Fig. 4.17 The aggregate sea anemone, *Anthopleura elegantissima.* Individuals above the waterline have retracted their tentacles.

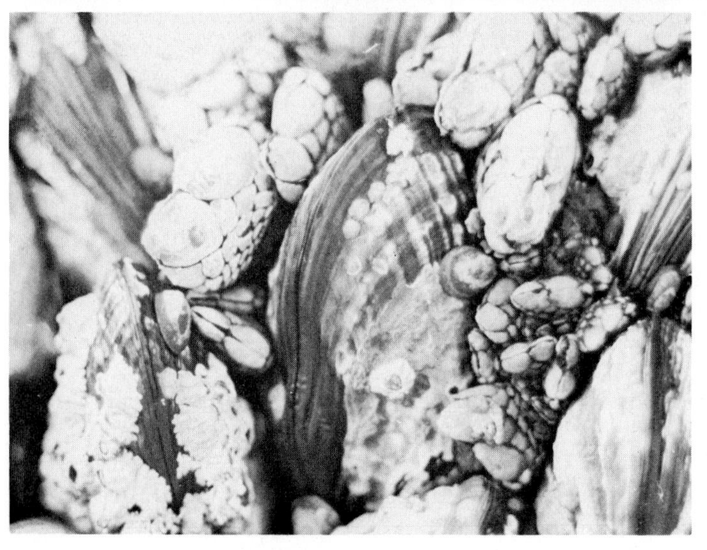

Fig. 4.18 Close-up view of mussels, acorn barnacles, and gooseneck barnacles of the middle intertidal.

The animals are securely anchored to the substrate, and present low, rounded profiles to minimize resistance to breaking waves. The plants are secured by strong holdfasts and usually have sturdy but flexible stipes to absorb much of the wave shock. Both *Fucus* and *Pelvetia* have thickened cell walls to resist water loss during low tide (fig. 4.19).

In the densely populated middle intertidal, mussels, barnacles, brown algae, and other sessile creatures are limited by two commonly shared resources: the solid substrate on which they live and the water above which provides their dissolved nutrients and suspended food. Mussels, barnacles, and algae compete for these critical resources in different ways. In regions where physical factors permit each to survive, these three competing groups interact by dominating the available attachment space, or by overgrowing their competitors and monopolizing the resources available from the water (fig. 4.20).

Available space on the rock surfaces of the middle intertidal is crucial for survival, yet seldom is it fully utilized. Patches of open space are periodically provided by a number of interacting biological and physical processes. Small areas of barnacles and mussels are continually removed by their chief predators—sea stars and predatory snails. Seasonal die-offs of algae, and even battering by heavy surf and drifting logs, also create cleared patches for future settlement and competition.

Most of the middle intertidal inhabitants have free-swimming larval stages, capable of settling almost anywhere within the intertidal zone. Algal spores and barnacle larvae simultaneously settling on bare rock eventually grow and compete for the space available. Because of the space limitations that may exist on exposed coasts, the algae are usually squeezed out as the barnacles increase in diameter and dislodge or overgrow them. On some sheltered rocky coasts, though, recruitment of barnacle larvae is prevented by the sweeping action of wave-tossed algal blades. Only in this manner can *Fucus* achieve and maintain spatial dominance over barnacles. If the barnacles are not removed before they are securely cemented into place, they quickly escape

Fig. 4.19

Fig. 4.20

Fig. 4.19 *Fucus*, a brown alga, thrives next to small, black mussels (*Mytilus*) on a Maine intertidal rock.

Fig. 4.20 A bed of acorn barnacles (*Balanus*) severely deformed because of crowding. Inhibited by their neighbors from expanding laterally, they grew upward instead.

the adverse effects of algal blades through growth, and eventually force *Fucus* off the rocks.

Barnacles are not necessarily safe once they have outgrown or overgrown their algal competitor. They are consumed in prodigous numbers by sea stars and carnivorous snails. Even herbivorous limpets have a detrimental, and sometimes severe, impact on barnacle populations. Young barnacles are eaten or dislodged by limpets as they bulldoze their way through their grazing activities. Limpets seem to have less effect on the small crack-inhabiting *Chthamalus* than on the larger more exposed *Balanus* individuals. Thus in the presence of limpet disturbance, *Chthamalus* gains a slight competitive advantage over the otherwise dominant *Balanus*.

The larval stages of mussels do not require bare rock exposures and will settle on algae, barnacles, and among aggregations of adult mussels. After settling, the young mussels crawl over the bottom, seeking improved conditions before they attach themselves with several strong elastic **byssal threads**. Byssal threads are formed from a fluid secreted by an internal byssal gland. The fluid flows down a groove in the small tongue-shaped foot, and onto the substrate. On contact with seawater, the fluid quickly toughens to form a thread. Then the foot is moved slightly and additional threads are formed.

If left undisturbed, mussels eventually overgrow barnacles and algae. Seldom, however, do rocky intertidal conditions remain undisturbed for long. Mussels are extensively preyed on by sea stars (such as *Pisaster* on the Pacific Coast and *Asterias* on the Atlantic). These sea stars are quite sensitive to desiccation, and their impact on mussel populations is much more severe in the lower portions of the mussels' intertidal range. Young mussels are also devoured by *Thais* and other predatory snails. They survive these predatory onslaughts by numerically swamping an area with more individuals than the local predators can consume. In time, the mussels, too, escape through growth, becoming so large that the snails are incapable of drilling through their shells to consume the soft flesh within.

As patches of mussels are cleaned out by predators or broken off by waves, they are temporarily replaced by algae or barnacles, then gradually the mussels regain their ascendancy. It is ultimately the dynamic balance resulting from competition between these dominant organisms, and the patterns of disturbance that affect their survival, that shape the biological character of the middle intertidal. These organisms, in turn, influence the distribution and abundance of numerous other plant and animal species. A cursory examination of mussel beds reveals two other conspicuous animal species, filter-feeding gooseneck barnacles and predatory sea stars. But living on the mussel shells or among the thick masses of byssal threads beneath is an extremely complex community of more fragile and often unseen animals. This submussel habitat protects several common species of clams, worms, shrimps and other crustaceans, crabs, hydroids, and many types of algae. Many of these species utilize mussel shells as available substrate for attachment. Others exist because they are unable to survive in the same area without the protection afforded by the canopy of mussels overhead.

This complex association of plants and animals is wholly dependent on the existence of thick masses of well-anchored mussels. This is the culmination, the **climax** stage, of a long succession of plant and animal populations that begins on bare rock and progresses through a sequence of population changes (fig. 4.21). Eventually this process of **biological succession** reaches the stable climax stage; in this case, the mussel bed-gooseneck barnacle-sea star community. When natural disturbances remove the mussels and disrupt the stability of the community, they are quickly replaced by a predictable succession of nonmussel populations (outlined in fig. 4.21). Thus the structure of communities such as those dominated by mussels are seldom stable for long, but rather achieve a state of dynamic equilibrium between the stabilizing effect of succession and the many disruptive factors which reduce that stability.

The Lower Intertidal

The biological character of lower intertidal rocky coasts differs markedly from the zones above. It is difficult for some species and impossible for others to succeed in the upper and middle intertidal zones. Those few that do are often present in vast numbers. In the lower intertidal, the emphasis changes to a community with an unbridled diversity of species, but without the conspicuous dominant types so characteristic of the middle and upper intertidal.

The lower intertidal usually abounds with seaweeds. Brown, red, and even a few species of green algae of moderate size spread a protective canopy of wet blades over much of this zone, as shown in figure 4.22*a*. In other places extensive beds of surf grass or eelgrass achieve a similar effect (fig. 4.22*b*). Carpeting many of the rocks are tufts of small filamentous brown and red algae. Calcareous red algae become especially prolific at these levels. The pinkish hue of *Lithothamnion* encrusting rocks and lining the sides of tide pools is a common sight.

The animals of the lower intertidal include at least a few species from all the major and several minor phyla. It is here that one can truly appreciate the diversity, complexity, and sheer beauty of intertidal marine life. On the

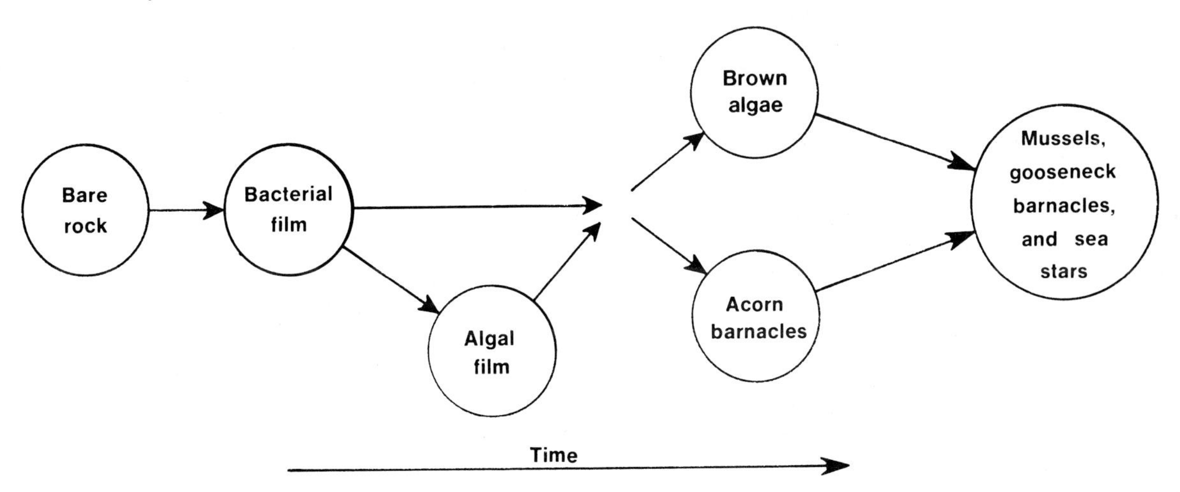

Fig. 4.21 Succession on temperate rocky shores, leading to the mussel-barnacle-sea star climax community at right.

(a)

(b)

Fig. 4.22 (*a*) A brown algal canopy in the lower intertidal. (*b*) Sea grasses in the same lower intertidal.

east coast of North America, a large white anemone, *Metridium,* occurs in tide pools and on exposed portions of the lower intertidal. *Anthopleura xanthogrammica,* a beautiful green anemone (fig. 4.23) occupies a similar niche on the West Coast. Although securely anchored by discs at their bases, they are active predators of planktonic animals and small fish. Prey is captured by discharging many microscopic nematocysts from special cells in the anemone's tentacles. The nematocysts of *Metridium* and *Anthopleura* are small. When touched with a finger they produce a slight tingling, sticky sensation. Other anemones are not so gentle, and several of the larger tropical species can inflict serious, painful injuries to humans.

Fig. 4.23 The green anemone *Anthopleura xanthogrammica.*

Fig. 4.24 A ventral view of the nudibranch *Hermissenda.* Long fingerlike cerata project from its upper surface.

The batteries of nematocysts found on anemone tentacles effectively discourage hostile intentions of most predators, but still do not guarantee complete immunity against predation. A few snails and sea spiders penetrate the sides of anemones and feed on the unprotected tissues there. Eolid nudibranchs also commonly graze on anemones and the closely related hydroids. These nudibranchs possess mechanisms, not yet completely understood, which block the discharge of the toxic nematocysts. During digestion the undischarged nematocysts are preserved and passed to special storage sacs in the rows of fingerlike **cerata** along the back (fig. 4.24). There they probably serve as independent defensive mechanisms against nudibranch predators. Some of these nudibranchs are extremely selective, preserving only the most effective nematocysts and somehow digesting the others.

The echinoderms are another familiar group of animals in the lower intertidal. Sea stars, sea urchins, brittle stars, and sea cucumbers are all generally quite sensitive to desiccation and salinity changes, and are seldom seen in abundance above the lower intertidal zone. Although slow-moving, sea stars are nevertheless voracious predators of mussels, barnacles, snails, an occasional anemone, and even other echinoderms.

When approached by some species of sea stars, many of these normally sessile species execute some remarkable escape responses. Pectens swim jerkily away, clams and cockles leap clear of the sea star, and sea urchins and limpets crawl rapidly away. Sea anemones, like *Stomphia* and *Actinostola* from Puget Sound, detach themselves and somersault or roll aside when touched by certain sea stars (fig.4.25). These sea stars continously liberate substances that initiate alarm reactions in their prey; actual contact usually leads to even more vigorous escape movements. Prey species apparently recognize and identify their sea star predators by the substances they exude. They react violently to the touch or presence of sea stars that usually prey on them, but seldom respond to those not encountered in their normal habitat.

At the low tide line, the lower intertidal merges with the uppermost part of the inner shelf zone. Where rocky bottoms extend below the low tide line and are not covered by sediments, the transition from intertidal to subtidal is often gradual. Many of the plant and animal species common to the lower intertidal are also abundant in neighboring shallow subtidal regions. But rocky substrates eventually give way to soft sediments. In protected stretches of coastlines or below the sea surface, wave action is diminished and loose sediments and detritus begin to accumulate. Plants and animals of the rocky shore disappear and are replaced by those typical of sand or mud bottoms.

Sandy Beaches and Muddy Shores

Beaches and mudflats are the depositional features of the coastal zone. They are unstable and tend to shift and conform to conditions imposed by changing forces of waves and currents. These coastal features provide the ecological complement to rocky shores. Large plants find the shifting nature of soft sediments difficult to cope with, and few exist here. The few plants that have managed to adapt support even fewer grazers. It is on these depositional shores

Fig. 4.25 A "swimming" anemone, *Actinostola*, evading a predatory sea star. The anemone has detached itself from the bottom and is somersaulting away. Photo by C. Birkland, courtesy P. Dayton, Scripps Institution of Oceanography.

that the other half of the marine coastal ecosystem, the detritus food chains, dominate. Bits of organic material washed off adjacent rocky shores and the surrounding land, or drifted in from kelp beds further offshore, sustain the detritus eaters of sandy and muddy shores.

Beaches are made of whatever loose material is locally available. Quartz grains, black volcanic sand, or pulverized carbonate plant and animal skeletons are most common. Beaches occur where waves are sufficiently gentle to allow sand to accumulate, but still strong enough to wash the finer silts and clays away. A good portion of the sand on many beaches is temporarily eroded away by large winter waves and deposited as underwater sandbars offshore. Smaller waves the following summer move the sand back on shore. Beach sands are also slowly moved parallel to the shore by longshore currents. In response, populations of beach inhabitants may fluctuate widely from season to season and from one year to the next.

Mudflats are somewhat more stable than beach sands, but they too may also be altered by seasonal variations in current patterns and wave activity. Intertidal mudflats are typically confined to estuaries or quiet reaches of bays and lagoons. Only in these protected coastal environments can significant amounts of finer silt and clay particles settle out. Mudflats contain some sand, but it is mixed with varying amounts of finer silt and clay particles to produce mud. The terms sand, silt, and clay have widely accepted general meanings, but each also refers to a specific range of sediment particle sizes (fig. 4.26).

Several properties of marine sediments are critical to organisms living in close association with them. In general, these properties are established by the size and shape of sediment particles. The size of spaces between sediment particles (the interstitial spaces) decreases with finer sediments. Interstitial space size, in turn, regulates the porosity and permeability of sediments to water. In coarse sands, water flows freely between sand grains, recharging the

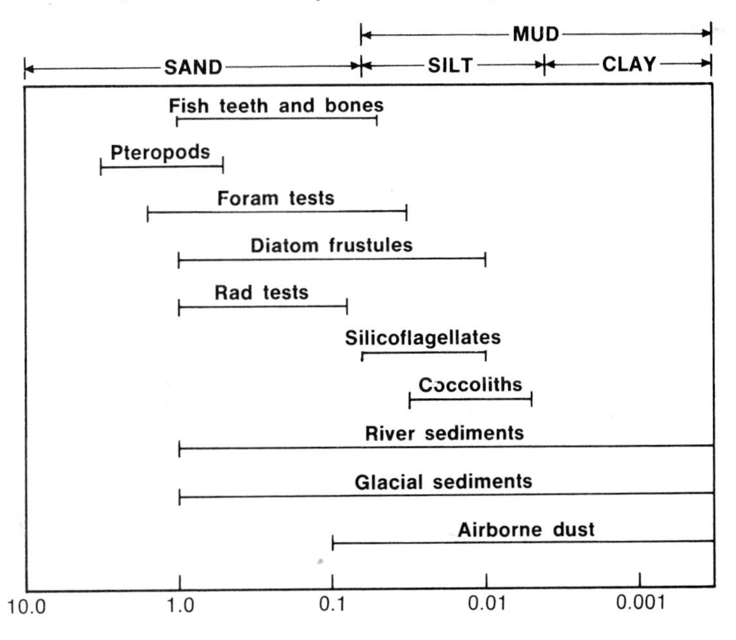

Fig. 4.26 Particle size ranges for some common sources of marine sediments. Most contribute to all three categories, sand, silt, and clay. Adapted from Gross 1972.

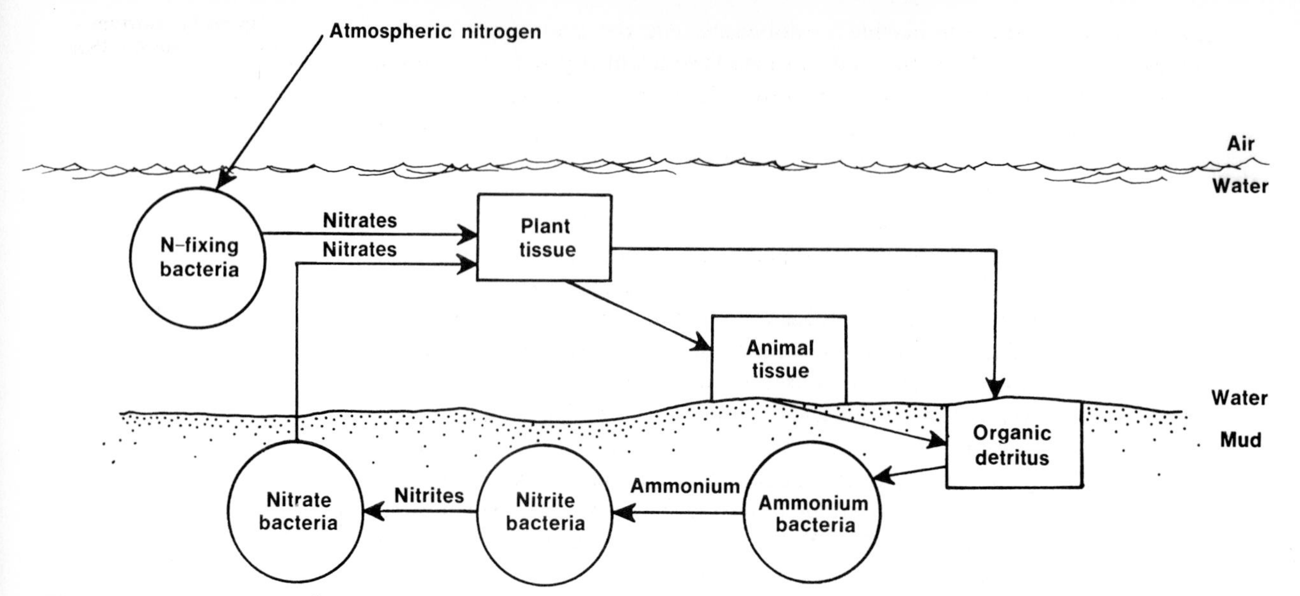

Fig. 4.27

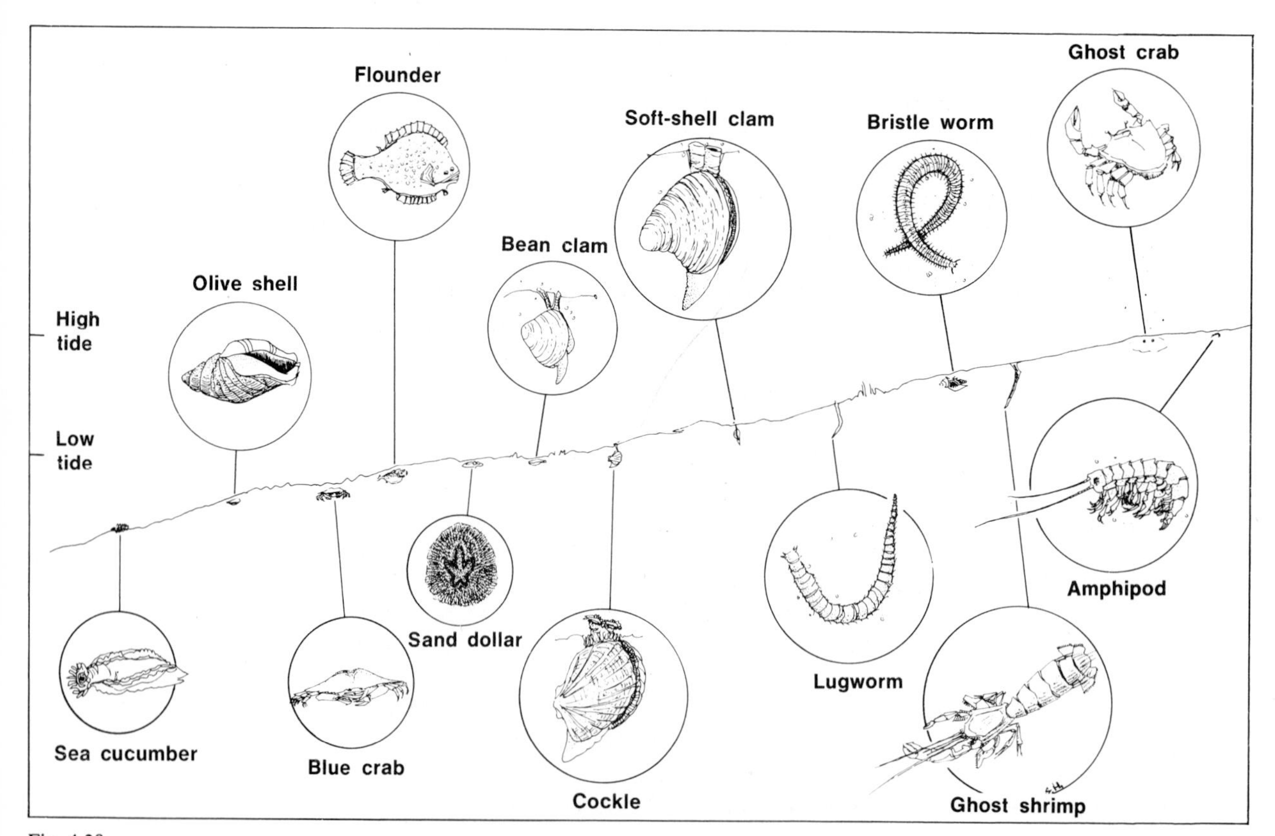

Fig. 4.28

supply of dissolved 0_2 and flushing away wastes. On the other hand, beaches are usually steeper than mudflats, so they drain and dry out much more quickly. In fine-grained muds, sediment particles are packed so tightly that little water can percolate through. With the exchange of interstitial water restricted, 0_2 used by mud dwellers is not rapidly replenished, nor are their wastes quickly removed.

In contrast to porous sands that accumulate little organic material, fine-grained muds with small interstitial spaces are effective traps for particles of organic debris. Much of the accumulated bottom organic material is found in a thin, brownish surface layer about 1 cm thick. Below this layer, the organic content of the muds usually decreases as animals and decomposing bacteria and fungi consume it. Respiration by the inhabitants of the muds also diminishes the available dissolved 0_2 supply of the interstitial waters. Seldom does dissolved 0_2 from the water above penetrate more than one or two cm into any but the coarsest sandy sediments. The lower limit of 0_2 penetration in organic-rich sediments is usually apparent as a color change. The sediments are light colored in the oxygenated surface layer, and change to a dark or even black color in the anaerobic zone below. The anaerobic conditions of deeper muds inhibit, but do not halt, decomposition of the organic material.

Bacteria and fungi are the major groups of marine organisms capable of utilizing the rich organic accumulations in the anaerobic portion of muddy sediments. Without 0_2, these anaerobic decomposers are obliged to use other available elements for their respiratory processes. Sulphate is an abundant ion in seawater, and is commonly reduced to hydrogen sulphide (H_2S) by these anaerobes. The H_2S is responsible for the "rotten-egg" smell and black color so characteristic of anaerobic marine muds.

Not all benthic bacteria and fungi are anaerobic, however. Aerobic decomposers dominate the surface oxygenated layer of mud, but their numbers decline rapidly with depth. Beneath the oxygenated layer, the anaerobes are active down to 40-60 cm, then their numbers also dwindle rapidly. The overwhelming abundance of aerobic and anaerobic decomposers are responsible for the preponderance of chemical changes that occur in marine sediments. The results of these chemical reactions include the decomposition of organic material, consumption of dissolved 0_2 near the bottom, and the ultimate return of critical plant nutrients to the water (fig. 4.27).

When compared to the teeming populations of the rocky intertidal, beaches appear to be quite desolate. Macroscopic algae are rare, as are large and obvious epifauna. Shifting, unstable sands are unsuitable platforms for surface anchorage, and nearly all the permanent residents of the beach dwell underground. Patterns of zonation are more difficult to demonstrate, yet under the sand, life zones comparable to those on rocky shores are distinguishable (fig. 4.28).

The upper portions of sandy beaches along temperate coasts are occupied by a few species of talitrid amphipods, particularly *Talitrus* or *Orchestoidea*. The common name of "beach hopper" reflects the unusual bounding mode of locomotion of these small crustaceans. Beach hoppers are most active at night,

Fig. 4.27 The nitrogen cycle of a soft bottom marine community. Several types of bacteria sequentially reduce and excrete nitrogen compounds for reuse by marine plants. Similar cycles for carbon, phosphorus, and other nutrient elements also exist.

Fig. 4.28 Under-sand zonation along the East Coast of the United States. The species change rapidly from the portion permanently under water at left to the dry part of the beach above high tide at right.

and prefer to burrow a few cm into the sand during the day. Occasionally, they make excursions down the beach face as the tide recedes.

In the upper parts of tropical beaches, talitrids are replaced by ghost crabs (*Ocypode*). Like the talitrids, they are nocturnal scavengers. Ghost crabs live in burrows and only infrequently return to water to dampen their gills. Like the nearly terrestrial littorine snails of the upper rocky intertidal zone, ghost crabs are well adapted for long stays on the upper beach without contact with water.

The middle beach is frequently populated by a variety of other amphipods, lugworms (*Arenicola*), dense concentrations of isopod crustaceans (*Eurydice*), and the mole crab, *Emerita*. The latter three demonstrate the fundamental feeding methods employed by the larger members of the beach community. *Arenicola* occupies a U-shaped burrow with its head usually buried just below a sand-filled surface depression. The burrows are more or less permanent, for waves stir up and move sediment and detritus to the head region where they are consumed. Mounds of coiled castings indicate the location of the other end of this sediment ingester.

The small isopods are usually less than 1 cm long. They actively prey on even smaller interstitial animals that inhabit the pore spaces between sand grains. Nearly every animal phylum is represented in the interstitial fauna of beaches; and a few groups such as harpacticoid copepods and gastrotrichs are practically confined to the interstices of beach sands. In spite of their divergent backgrounds, most interstitial animals show the basic adaptations needed for life between sand grains. They are elongated, small (no more than a few mm) and move with a sliding motion between sand grains without displacing them. Some examples of interstitial animals from different phyla are shown in figure 4.29. Some interstitial animals are carnivorous, others feed on detritus deposits and material in suspension. Another specialized feeding habit, unique to interstitial animals, is sand-licking. Individual sand grains are manipulated by the animals' mouth parts to remove minute bacterial growths and thin films of diatoms.

The mole crab, *Emerita*, represents a third mode of feeding common to many beach macrofauna. When feeding, *Emerita* burrows tail first in the sand and faces down the beach. Only its eyes and a pair of large feathery antennae protrude above the sand. When a wave breaks over the crab and begins to recede, the antennae are extended against the rush of water (fig. 4.30). Entrapped phytoplankton (and possibly even large bacteria) are swept from the filtering antennae and moved to the mouth by other feeding appendages.

In the lower portion of intertidal beaches, the variety of life increases. Polychaete worms, still other amphipods (such as *Haustorius*), and an assortment of clams and cockles occur. Many of these lower beach inhabitants, such as soft-shelled clams (*Mya*) and cockles (*Cardium*) of the Atlantic coast, represent the upper fringes of much larger subtidal populations. The small wedge-shaped bean clam, *Donax*, of the Atlantic and Gulf coasts (but not the Pacific coast species) migrates up and down the beach with the tides; yet it is usually considered an inhabitant of the lower beach. *Donax* responds to the

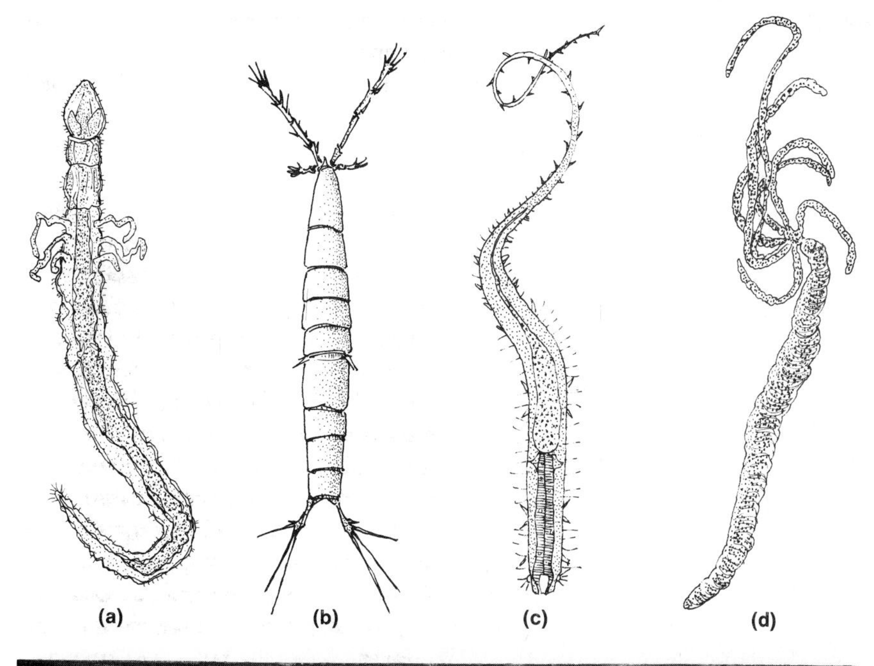

Fig. 4.29 A few examples of the interstitial fauna of sandy beaches. Each is of a different phylum, yet all exhibit the small size and worm-shaped body characteristic of interstitial fauna: (*a*) a polychaete, *Pasmmodrilus,* (*b*) a copepod, *Cylindropsyllis,* (*c*) a gastrotrich, *Urodasys,* and (*d*) a hydra, *Halammohydra.* Redrawn in part from Eltringham 1972.

Fig. 4.30 The sand crab *Emerita* with feeding antennae extended. Photograph by D. Garcia.

agitation of incoming waves of rising tides by emerging from the sand. After the wave carries the clam up the beach, it digs in to await the next wave and another ride. During ebb tides, the behavior is reversed. *Donax* emerges only after a wave breaks and begins to wash back down the beach. So, with little energy expenditure of its own, this small clam capitalizes on the abundance of available wave energy to carry it up and down the beach face.

Donax is one of many sandy beach inhabitants to exhibit a rhythmicity of behavior that is in phase with the tidal cycle. Fiddler crabs (*Uca*) quietly sit out submergence by high tides, then emerge from their burrows at low tide to feed or engage in social activities. When fiddler crabs are removed to the laboratory, their activity rhythms persist for some time in concert with the changing tidal cycle in spite of the absence of tidal cues.

Most organisms, and possibly all of them, have an innate time sense, usually referred to as a "**biological clock.**" Rhythmic cycles of body temperatures, activity levels, 0_2 consumption, and a host of other physiological variations occur independently of changes in the external environment. These are outward manifestations of internal biological clocks. The internal "mechanism" of the clock is not known, but its existence has been demonstrated in a wide variety of organisms ranging from single-celled diatoms to humans.

The tide-related cycle of activity exhibited by the fiddler crab is known as a **circalunadian rhythm**; tidal cycles repeat every lunar day (24.8 hours). The coloration of fiddler crabs also depends on **circadian rhythms** (based on a solar day of 24 hours). They are light-colored at night, but darken during the day.

Clean sandy beaches quite commonly grade into intermediate muddy sand, or sandy mud deposits, and eventually to the muddy shores of bays, estuaries, and other sheltered coastal environments. Here a complication arises, for concepts of vertical zonation, in the sense that they were applied to the sloping faces of beaches and rocky shores, become inappropriate on the nearly level expanses of mudflats. The epifuana of mudflats are dominated by mobile species of gastropod mollusks, crustaceans, and polychaete worms. They sometimes range over wide areas of the mudflat and demonstrate only blurred, weakly established patterns of lateral zonation.

However, mud-dwelling organisms do occupy zones arranged vertically in the sediment. A few cm below the mud surface, the interstitial water is generally devoid of available 0_2, and the infauna are obliged to obtain their 0_2 from the water just above the mud or do without. The numerous openings of tubes and burrows on the surfaces of estuarine mudflats (fig. 4.31) attest to an unseen wealth of animal life beneath. Bivalve mollusks extend tubular siphons through the anaerobic mud to the oxygenated water above. The depths to which these animals can seek protection in the mud are limited largely by the lengths of their siphons, and indirectly, by their ages. Other infauna utilize the sticky consistency of fine-grained organically rich muds to construct permanent burrows with connections to the surface (figs. 4.28 and 4.38).

During high tides, the submerged portions of intertidal beaches and mudflats are visited by shore crabs, shrimps, fish, and other transients from deeper water. Some come to forage for food; others find the protected waters ideal for spawning. Their forays are only temporary, however, for they leave with the ebbing tide and surrender the intertidal to the shorebirds. During low water, the long-billed curlews and avocets probe for the deeper infauna, while sandpipers and other short-billed shorebirds concentrate on the shallow infauna and small epifauna. In this way, the birds effectively partition their available food resources and reduce competition among themselves. The

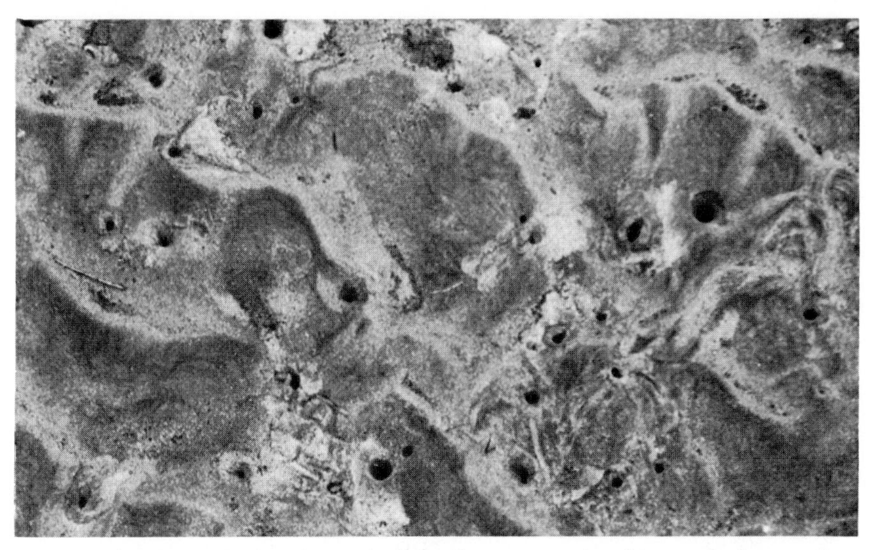

Fig. 4.31 The barren surface of a mud flat, with tubes, openings, burrows, and other evidence of an abundance of animal life beneath.

impact of these aerial predators is difficult to assess, but it must be impressive, for a single oyster-catcher may eat as many as 300 cockles each day.

When the tide is out, the infauna of muddy shores also must cope with an absence of available 0_2. Some switch from aerobic to anaerobic respiration. In so doing they must reduce their metabolic activities to compensate for the relative inefficiency of anaerobic respiration as an energy-yielding process. Larger infauna exist anaerobically only temporarily, and revert to aerobic respiration as soon as they are again covered by the tides. But for many of their smaller burrowing neighbors with no direct access to the oxygen-laden waters above, anaerobic respiration is a permanent feature of their infaunal existence in intertidal muds.

Estuaries

The problems of zonation are further complicated by estuarine conditions that overlie so many of the muddy shore environments in temperate regions. Estuaries, like lagoons and bays, are partially enclosed bodies of water that maintain free connections to the open sea (fig. 4.32). Estuarine waters are the special result of fresh water from land drainage discharging into and mixing with tidal influxes of seawater. Within an estuary, complex gradients of salinity, water temperature, turbidity, and current action occur. Salinity values normally decrease inland from the mouth of an estuary, as seawater experiences increasing dilution by the river from the upstream end. Vertical salinity gradients are also established, for the less dense fresh water usually flows out along the surface and only partially mixes with the more saline wedge of seawater beneath. Rotation due to the Coriolis effect also confuses the picture by forcing seawater further upstream on the left sides (when looking out to sea) of northern hemisphere estuaries and on the right sides of estuaries in the southern hemisphere. The salinity gradients of a hypothetical estuary are shown in figure 4.33. If you can now visualize the general pattern

Fig. 4.32 Estuary of the Columbia River between Oregon and Washington. Photographed by the Earth Resources Technology Satellite.

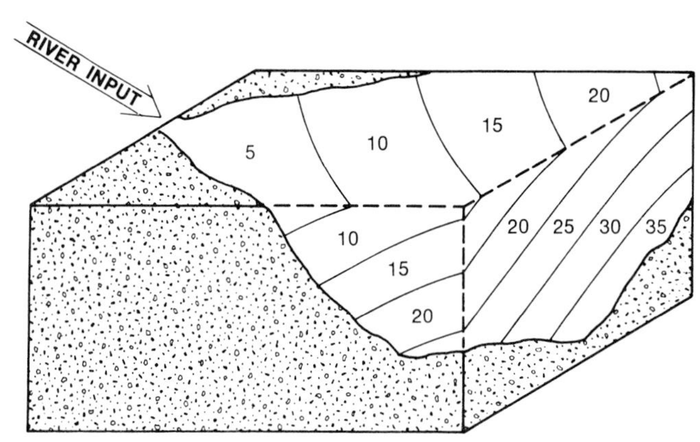

Fig. 4.33 Diagram of horizontal and vertical salinity gradients in a hypothetical estuary of the Northern Hemisphere. Numbers refer to salinity in ‰.

of estuarine salinity gradients shown in figure 4.33 as a dynamic system, changing with the tides as the bottom wedge of seawater moves in and out of the estuary, you can appreciate the complexity of salinity gradients the less mobile forms of estuarine life must contend with to survive.

As a general rule, marine animals and plants penetrate estuaries to their limits of tolerance to low and rapidly changing salinity conditions. Some have poorly developed osmoregulatory capabilities and avoid osmotic problems by not venturing too far into estuaries. These include many of the same species found on nearby sandy beaches and nonestuarine mudflats.

In the brackish water portions of estuaries where salinities dip to very low values, fewer species survive, although they may be individually quite abundant. A small fraction of brackish water species (insect larvae and a few snails and polychaete worms) originated in fresh water; the remainder have evolved from marine forms (fig. 4.34). These animals employ a number of adaptive strategies to overcome the osmotic problems of recurring exposure to low and variable salinities of estuarine waters. Some of these adaptations are merely modifications of structural or physical systems already imperative for survival on exposed intertidal shorelines. Many bivalve mollusks, for instance, simply stop feeding and close their shells when subjected to osmotic stresses of low salinity water. Isolated within their shells, they maintain the integrity of their body fluids and await the return of more saline water at high tide.

Tunicates, anemones, and several other soft-bodied estuarine epifauna are **osmotic conformers**. That is, they tolerate large variations of internal ionic concentrations without serious damage. Osmotic conformers are unable to control the osmotic flooding of their tissues when subjected to low salinities, so their body fluids fluctuate and remain isotonic with the water around them.

The most successful and abundant groups of estuarine animals have evolved mechanisms to regulate and stabilize the water and ion concentrations of their body fluids independently of external variations. These mechanisms are as varied as the organisms themselves; yet all involve systems to acquire essential ions from their external medium and to excrete excess water as it diffuses into the body.

The osmoregulatory devices used by bony fish have already been described in chapter 1. The body fluids of estuarine crabs remain nearly isotonic with their external medium in normal seawater, but become progressively hypertonic as the seawater becomes more dilute. When in dilute seawater, additional ions are actively absorbed by the gills of these animals to compensate for those lost in their urine (fig. 4.35). These and most other estuarine crustaceans are osmotic conformers at higher salinities and osmoregulators in dilute seawater.

Only a few of the more hardy species of estuarine organisms are **euryhaline**, capable of withstanding excessively high as well as low salinities. Limited numbers of these species are found in hypersaline lagoons and aberrant estuaries that fringe some of the world's arid coastlines. Lagoons such

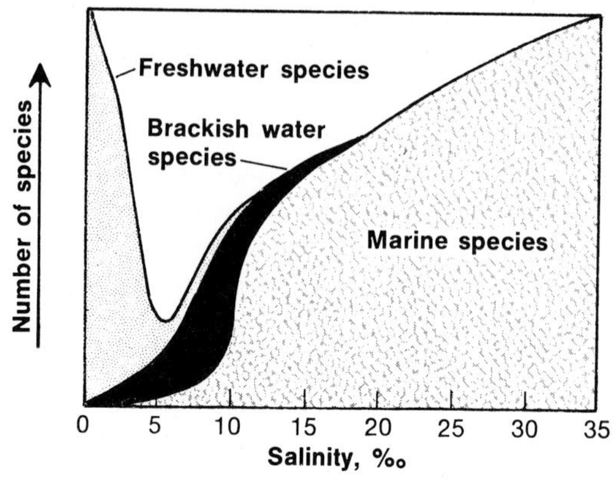

Fig. 4.34

Fig. 4.34 Relative contributions of marine, freshwater, and brackish water species to estuarine fauna. Redrawn from Remane 1934.

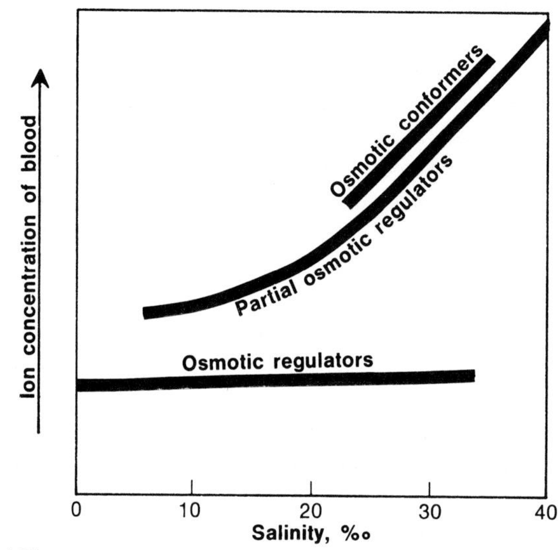

Fig. 4.35

Fig. 4.35 Variations in ion concentrations of body fluids or blood with changing external water salinities for osmotic conformers, osmotic regulators, and partial regulators.

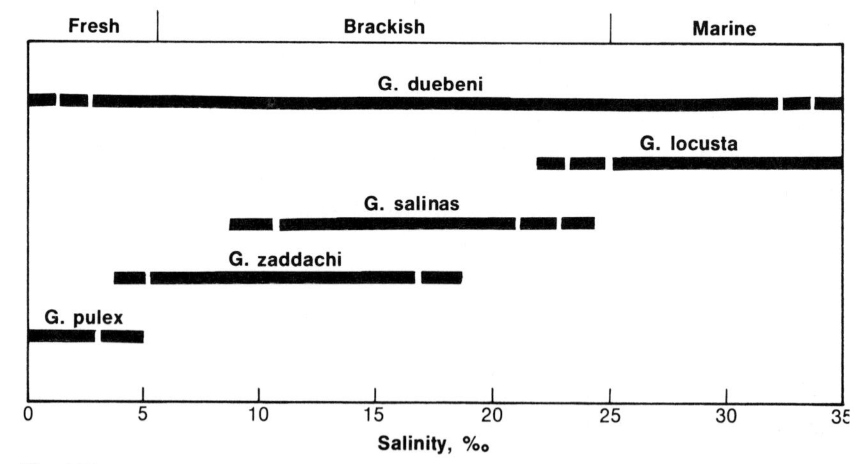

Fig. 4.36

Fig. 4.36 Salinity tolerances of five species of amphipods (*Gammarus*). Four of the five have limited and exclusive salinity tolerances. Only *G. duebeni* is euryhaline, capable of living in fresh water or seawater. Adapted from Nicol 1967.

as those along the coasts of Texas and northeast Mexico, and the Sivash (locally known as the Putrid Sea) on the western side of the Sea of Azov have shallow bottoms, high summer temperatures, excessive evaporation, and, naturally, high salinities. Here, the osmotic problems are similar to those encountered by bony fish in seawater and are so severe that successful reproduction seldom occurs. The lagoon populations are sustained by continued immigration of euryhaline species from estuaries.

Most other estuarine animals are **stenohaline;** they tolerate exposure only to restricted salinity ranges. For instance, gammarid amphipods are common inhabitants of estuaries, yet each species occupies only a selected portion of the entire range of salinity regimes available (fig. 4.36). The distributional patterns of amphipods and other estuarine animals are not governed solely by salinity considerations. Food and sediment preferences, current action, and interspecific competition are also factors in establishing and maintaining patterns of horizontal zonation in estuarine mudflats.

The inflow of rivers into estuaries contributes more than just low salinity water. Suspensions of sand and mud, plus appreciable quantities of particulate and dissolved organic material, are delivered from the river's watershed and deposited in extensive mudflats along the sides of the estuary.

These mudflats support extensive beds of submerged sea grasses as well as a variety of emergent salt-marsh plants. Yet these abundant primary producers are seldom grazed directly by herbivores. Rather, they are targets of the microbial activity of profuse decomposing bacteria. Ultimately the bacteria break down the plant matter to particulate detritus, convert some of it to form more bacterial cells, and release dissolved organic material to the waters of the estuary. Other bacteria scavenge this dissolved organic material and incorporate it into still more bacterial cells.

Thus, decomposing bacteria, as well as the phytoplankton of the overlying waters, contribute heavily to the production of small energy-rich detrital food particles. These then become the major source of food for large populations of particle consumers living on and in the bottom of an estuary (fig. 4.37). The particle consumers, in turn, produce still more particles in the form of feces and rejected food items, eventually to be recolonized by bacteria and cycled back into the particle pool of the estuary.

With estuarine bacteria playing a central role in the production of small food particles, numerous species of nonestuarine animals also exploit these food resources to further complicate the trophic relationships within estuaries. Several types of shrimps, crabs, fish, and other coastal species make spawning migrations to exploit estuaries as nurseries for their young. Although such reproductive behavior benefits from the abundant estuarine food supply, little is known about the physiological costs of living in the stressful environment of an estuary.

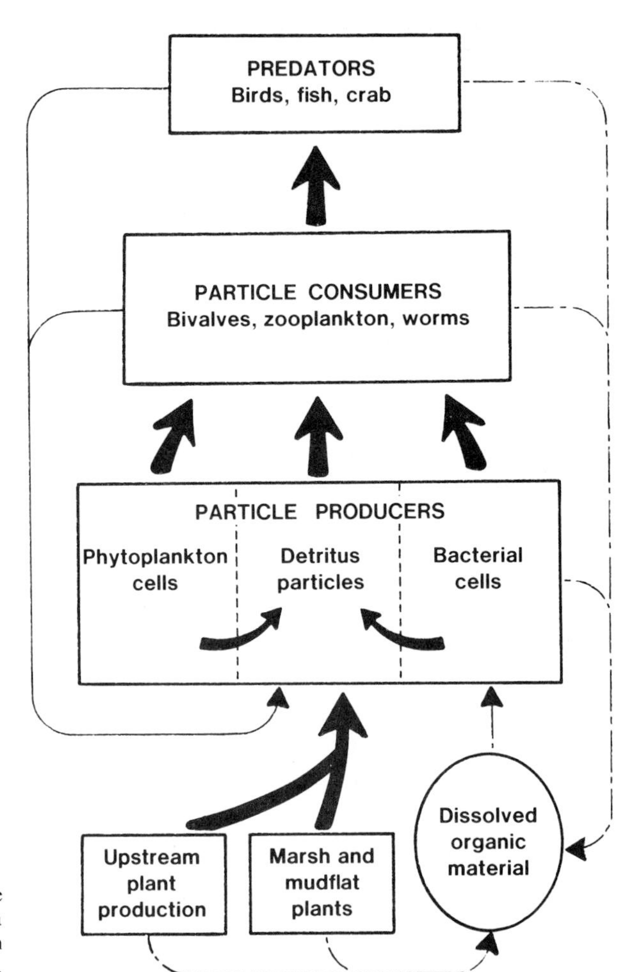

Fig. 4.37 Food particle production and utilization in a typical estuary. Adapted from Correll 1978.

Below the Tides

Below the intertidal zone, living conditions on the sea bottom change gradually as wave action, light intensity, and water temperature diminish with increasing depth. Sand and mud deposits become quite extensive and, in fact, dominate the seafloor below the low tide line. The soft bottoms of the continental shelves are comparatively level and are characterized by a uniformity and simplicity of environmental conditions not found along the intertidal shoreline. Benthic plants are largely restricted to occasional small reefs, rocky outcrops, and kelp forests on the inner shelf. Nearly all the bottom fauna are dependent on the slow rain of plankton and detritus from the sunlit photic zone above. Here, filter-feeders and deposit-feeders are well established, as are their predators.

Extensive studies of the life in shallow water soft bottoms were initiated by the Danish biologist, C. G. J. Petersen, in the early part of the twentieth century. His intent was to evaluate the quantity of food available for flounders and other commercially useful bottom fish. After sorting and analyzing thou-

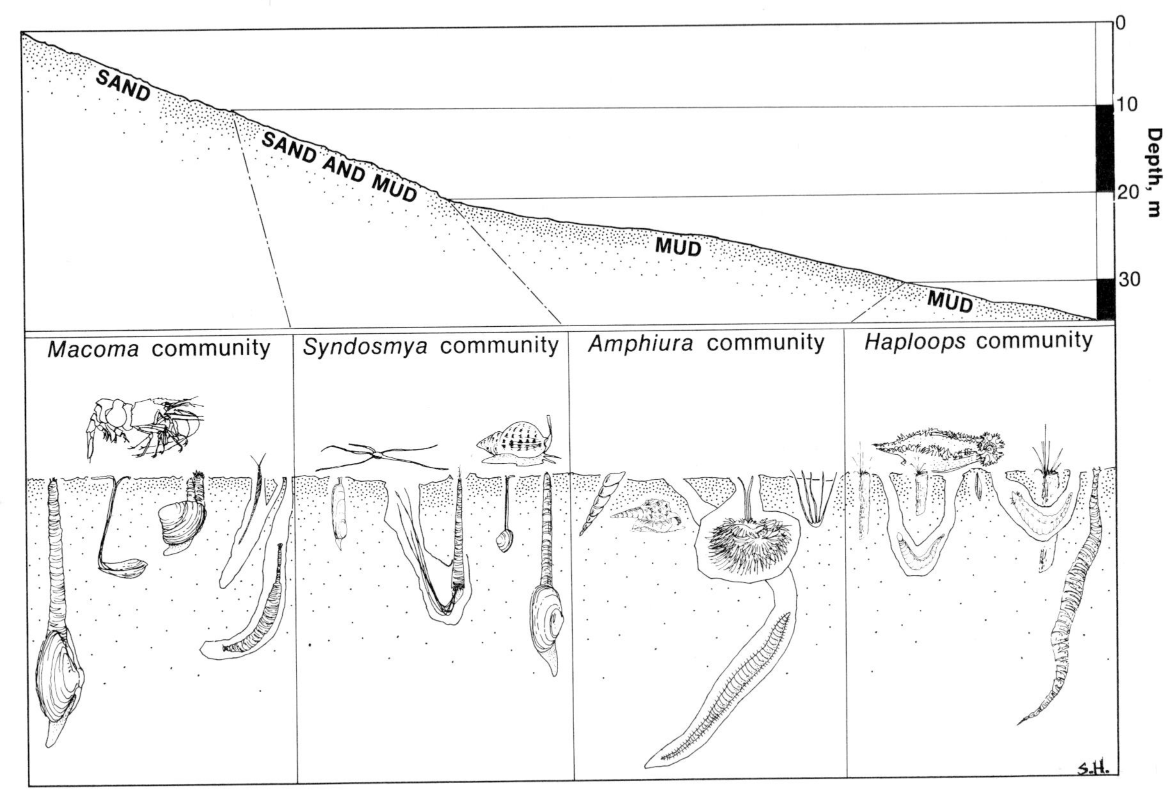

Fig. 4.38 A series of soft-bottom benthic communities in Danish seas. Adapted from Thorson 1968.

sands of bottom samples from Danish seas, Petersen concluded that large areas of the level sea bottom are inhabited by recurring associations, or communities, of infaunal species (fig. 4.38). Each community has a few very conspicuous or abundant macrofauna as well as several less obvious forms. On other bottom types, distinct communities of other species can be found. When exposed to similar combinations of environmental conditions, even widely separated shallow bottom communities in temperate waters closely resemble each other in structure and species composition (fig. 4.39). Although Petersen considered his communities statistical units only, these recurring and predictable links between certain animal species and particular environmental features led G. Thorson to invoke sound arguments for the recognition of Petersen's communities as biological realities.

Since Petersen's time, a prime objective of many benthic ecologists has been to describe the manner in which the benthos is distributed on the seafloor, and how this distribution is related to the sediments, the overlying water, and the influence of community members on each other. Using diving gear for direct observations in shallow water, and an assortment of dredges, trawls, and grabs to obtain bottom samples in deeper water, they have found parallel shallow water communities in much of the cold and temperate regions of the world ocean. However, Petersen's concept of parallel communities breaks down in tropical and subtropical waters. Here, large numbers of species exist, but seldom does a single species dominate a community as it might in colder waters.

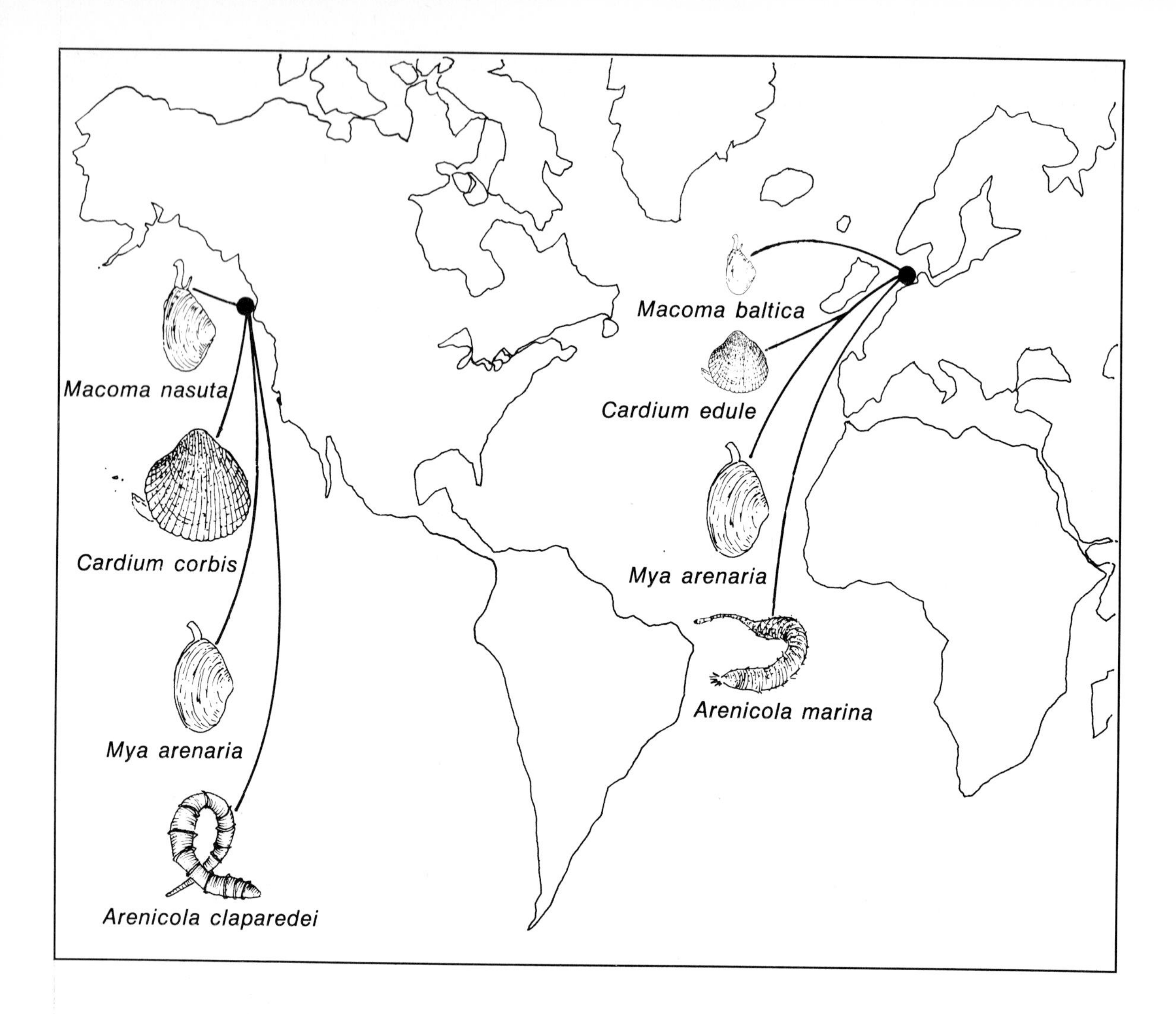

Fig. 4.39 Diagram showing the close similarity of soft-bottom communities in the northeast Pacific and the northeast Atlantic. Adapted from Thorson 1957.

Coral Reefs

Synonymous with the tropics in the minds of many is a unique type of shallow water marine ecosystem—the coral reef. Corals are cnidarians, closely related to sea anemones. They too are radially symmetrical, capture prey with nematocyst-armed tentacles, and are permanently attached to a solid substrate. A major difference between corals and anemones is the nature of their substrates. Coral polyps sit in calcareous skeletal cups, or **corallites,** of their own making (fig. 4.40). Radiating from the center of each corallite are several bladelike **septa.** Periodically, the coral polyp withdraws its soft parts from the bottom portion of the corallite and secretes a partition. The partition provides a new elevated bottom in the corallite. As the coral polyp grows, it may bud off new polyps asexually or produce planktonic larvae by sexual reproduction.

Like anemones, corals are ubiquitous. They can be found in the deep sea as well as on temperate and tropical shores. However, **hermatypic,** or reef-

Fig. 4.40 The skeletal bases, or corallites, of a coral. Official photograph U.S. Navy.

forming corals, are restricted to tropical and a very few subtropical regions where the water temperature never dips below 18°C. Hermatypic corals are much more abundant and diverse in the Indian and Pacific oceans (about 700 species) than in the Atlantic (about 35 species).

Vigorously growing reef corals also require clean water, a firm bottom, moderately high salinities, and plenty of sunlight. Consequently, corals do not thrive near river mouths with their discharges of fresh water and suspended sediments. Many corals are quite adept at cleaning their surfaces of suspended sediments, but may be growth-limited in turbid waters because they cannot find a suitable foundation on the muddy seafloor. Corals require clear water for still another reason. Living in the surface tissues of all hermatypic corals are masses of symbiotic **zooxanthellae**. Zooxanthellae are unicellular plants (actually modified dinoflagellates) that, like all other photosynthetic organisms, require light. They occur in such concentrations that they often provide most of the color seen in corals.

Each participant of the zooxanthellae-coral association derives several benefits from the other. Corals provide the plant cells with a constant, protected environment and an abundance of nutrients ($C0_2$ and nitrogenous and phosphate wastes from cellular respiration of the coral). In return the corals gain 0_2 and avoid the necessity of excreting many of their cellular wastes. Some controversy exists concerning the role zooxanthellae play in the nutrition of their hosts. Corals are apparently unable to consume zooxanthellae directly, for they lack the enzymes needed to digest the plants' cellulose cell walls. Even so, recent experiments using radioactive C^{14} indicate that labeled CO_2 is taken from seawater by the photosynthetic zooxanthellae and eventually is transferred as carbohydrates to the coral tissue. Corals possess an unidentified substance that stimulates zooxanthellae to secrete products of their photosynthetic activity. In living corals, then, the plant cells themselves are not digested, but sometimes as much as 40% of the organic material they manufacture photosynthetically is translocated to the host coral tissue. This has been shown to be sufficient to satisfy the daily energy needs of several species of corals. On some reefs, the total contribution of symbiotic zooxanthellae to the energy budget of the reef is several times higher than phytoplankton production occurring in the waters above the reef.

In spite of the nutritional contribution of zooxanthellae, coral polyps remain superbly equipped to utilize external sources of food. Corals with large polyps and tentacles, such as *Favia* or *Mussa,* feed exclusively on small fish and larger zooplankton. Species with smaller polyps use ciliary currents to collect small plankton and detritus particles. Most coral polyps, large or small, may be capable of harvesting organic particles as small as suspended bacteria, bits of drifting fish slime, and even organic substances dissolved in seawater.

The two principal limitations of hermatypic corals, sunlight and water temperature, restrict the development of coral reefs to shallow tropical waters. New corals develop from swimming, drifting, planktonic larvae. Each larva contains a supply of zooxanthellae. The larvae settle and thrive only if they encounter the preferred bottom conditions. When they do, the reef form they eventually create depends on existing environmental conditions as well as the developmental history of the reef.

Coral reefs occur as three general types; **fringing reefs, barrier reefs,** and **atolls.** As the name implies, fringing reefs form borders just along the shore-

Fig. 4.41 Palao Atoll, capped with four small low-lying islands, in the Caroline Islands, tropical Pacific. Courtesy U.S. Geological Survey.

line. Some of the Hawaiian reefs are of this type. Barrier reefs are further offshore and separated from the shore by a lagoon. The Great Barrier Reef of Australia is by far the largest single biological feature on earth. It borders some 2,000 km of Australia's northeast coast. Less impressive barrier reefs are common in the Caribbean Sea. Atolls are generally ring-shaped reefs from which a few low islands project above the sea surface (fig. 4.41)

While serving as a naturalist aboard the H.M.S. *Beagle* in the 1830s, Charles Darwin had an opportunity to study the reef forms of several oceanic islands. From his observations, he proposed that essentially all oceanic coral reefs were supported by volcanic mountains beneath. Fringing reefs, barrier reefs, and atolls, he suggested, are related but separate stages in the sequence of island reef development. Darwin's argument went like this. Within the tropics, newly formed volcanic islands (and submerged volcanoes that almost reach the sea surface) are eventually populated by coral larvae from other near-by coral islands. The larvae settle and grow near the surface and close to shore, forming a fringing reef, as in figure 4.42*a*. The most rapid growth occurs on the outer sides of the reef where food and oxygen-rich waters are more abundant. Waves break loose pieces of the reef and move them down the slopes of the volcano. On this debris, more corals establish themselves and grow toward the surface.

The weight of the expanding reef, as well as the immense burden of the volcano itself, actually depresses the ocean floor and the island slowly sinks. If the upward growth of the reef keeps pace with the sinking island, the coral maintains its position in the sunlit surface waters. Otherwise, the reef sinks into the cold darkness of the depths and expires. As the island sinks away from the growing reef, many of the massive corals left in the quiet waters behind the reef die. They are soon covered with reef debris to form a shallow lagoon. Delicate coral forms survive in the lagoon, protected from the waves by what is now a barrier reef, as in figure 4.42*b*. With further sinking, the volcanic core of the island may disappear completely beneath the reef cap and leave behind a chain of low-lying atoll islands encircling a shallow lagoon.

Darwin's concept of coral reef formation is, with a few modifications, widely accepted today. Test drilling on several atolls have revealed, as Darwin predicted, thick caps of carbonate reef material overlying submerged volcanos. Two test holes drilled on Eniwetok Atoll (the site of United States H-bomb tests in the 1950s) penetrated over 1,000 m of shallow-water reef deposits before reaching the basalt rock of the volcano. For the past 30 million years, Eniwetok apparently has been slowly subsiding as the reef grew up around it.

For the past several hundred thousand years, the formation and melting of mammoth continental glaciers have produced extensive world-wide fluctuations in sea level. Darwin was unaware of these fluctuations, and had no means of predicting their effects on coral reef development. Seventeen thousand years ago, when the glaciers of the last ice advance were at their greatest, average sea level was about 100 m below its present stand. As the ice melted, sea level gradually rose (about 1 cm each year) until it reached its present level about 6,000 years ago. Many coral reefs did not grow upward quickly enough and perished. Those that did keep up with the rising sea are the living reefs we see today.

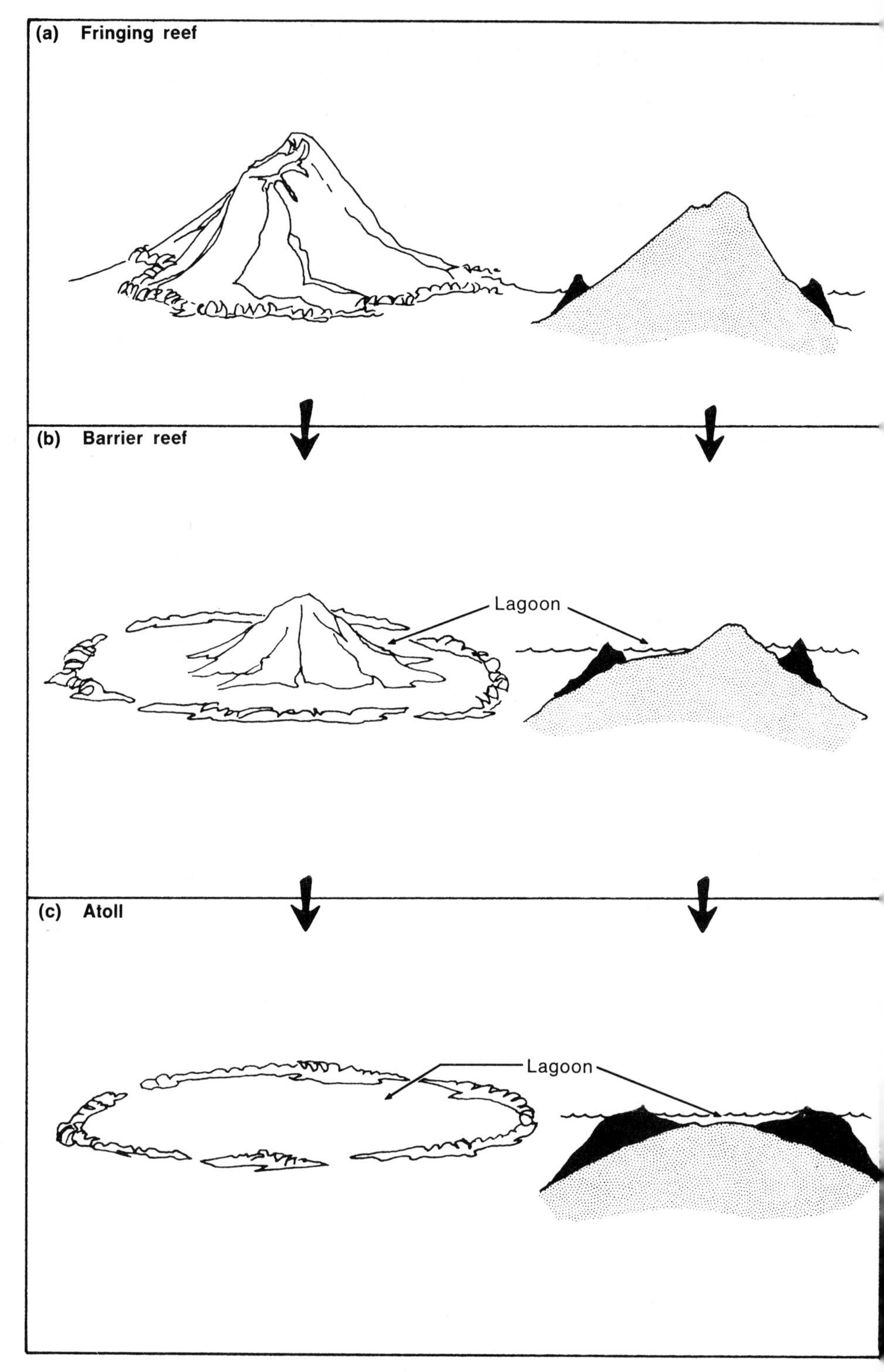

Fig. 4.42 The developmental sequence of fringing (*a*) barrier, (*b*) atoll, and (*c*) reefs. Reef forms are shown at left. In the cross sections at right, volcanic island material is stippled, reef formations are black.

Coral reefs are not constructed exclusively of the skeletons of hermatypic coral. These corals play a major, but not exclusive, role in the formation of most "coral" reefs. A large contribution of calcium carbonate also comes from several types of encrusting and segmented calcareous red (and a few species of green) algae, skeletons of single-celled foraminifers, mollusk shells, sea urchin tests and spines, and the calcareous remains of other reef inhabitants. From this encrusted, integrated base of skeletal remains, coral reef ecosystems have evolved as the most complex of all benthic associations.

The living richness of coral reefs stands in obvious contrast to the generally unproductive nature of surrounding tropical oceans. The precise trophic relationships between producers and consumers on the reef are largely unknown, but oceanic reefs appear to function as highly efficient autotrophic systems. They produce more organic material than they consume. Odum and Odum, working on Eniwetok Atoll, found that the average coral colony contained three times as much plant as animal material. Zooxanthellae constituted only 4% of the total. The remainder was filamentous green algae living within the coral skeleton.

Coral colonies function as a complete and highly efficient trophic system, each with its own photosynthetic, herbivorous, and carnivorous aspects. Critical nutrients are rapidly recycled between the producer and consumer components of the coral colony. As much of the nutrient cycling is accomplished within the coral tissues, little opportunity exists for the nutrients to escape from the coral production system. Internal nutrient losses are reduced and localized productivity on the reef remains high.

Zonation on Coral Reefs

Environmental conditions that favor some coral reef inhabitants over others in a particular habitat depend a great deal on wave force, water depth and temperature, salinity, and a host of other biological factors. These conditions vary greatly across a reef and provide for both horizontal and vertical zonation of the coral and algal species that form the reef. Parallel, but less well-defined zonation of associated plants and animals also occurs. Figure 4.43 is a cross-

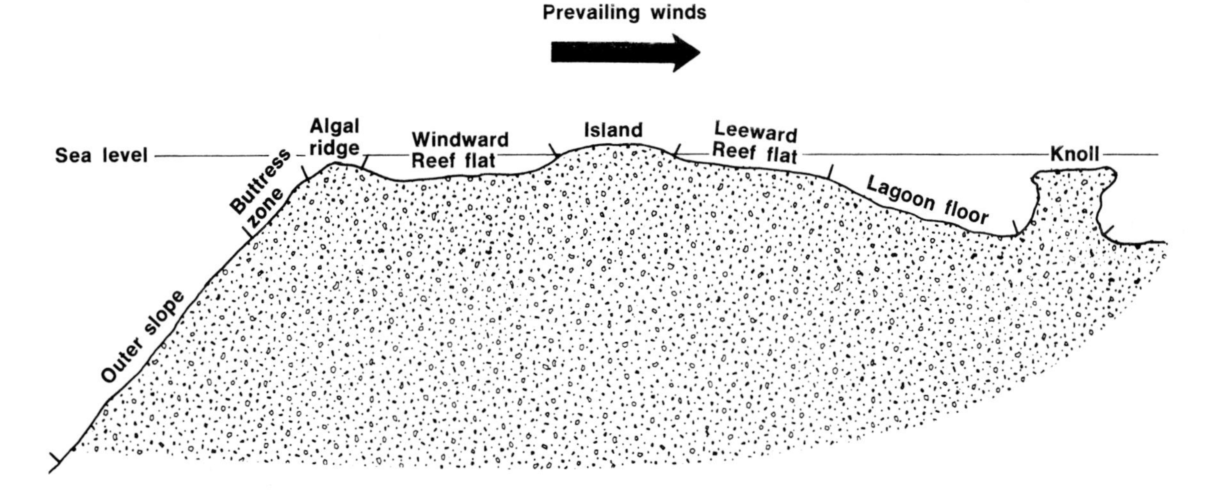

Fig. 4.43 Major life zones across a typical Indo-Pacific coral reef.

section of an idealized Indo-Pacific coral reef, including the major features and zones of the reef.

The living base of a coral reef begins as deeply as 150 m below sea level. Between 150 and 50 m on the outer reef slopes, a few small, fragile species, such as *Leptoseris,* exist. Fewer still thrive because little sunlight penetrates at these depths. Above 50 m, and extending up to the base of vigorous wave action (approximately 20 m), is a zone of transition between deep and shallow water associations. Here, the corals and algae receive adequate sunlight, yet are sufficiently deep to avoid the adverse effects of surface waves. Several of the delicately-branched species commonly found in the protected lagoon waters, including *Acropora*, also occur here (see plates 1 and 2).

From a depth of about 20 m to just below the low tide line is a rugged zone of spurs, or **buttresses,** radiating out from the reef. Interspersed between the buttresses are grooves that slope down the reef face. These grooves drair debris and sediment off the reef and into deeper water. Continual heavy surf has limited detailed studies of the buttress zone, but it is known to be dominated by massive coral growths (such as *Acropora*) and by several species of encrusting coralline algae. The massive corals thrive in this zone of breaking waves, intense sunlight, and abundant oxygen. Many of the larger fish of the reef—sharks, jacks, barracudas, and tunas—patrol the buttresses and grooves in search of food. Smaller fish seem to be in every hole and crevice on the reef.

A large portion of the geographical range of coral reefs is swept by the broad reaches of the trade winds. The waves generated by these winds crash as thundering breakers on windward sides of reefs. On the opposite, or leeward sides, the reefs experience the surge of ocean swell, but not the severe pounding so typical of windward reefs. Windward reefs are usually characterized by a low, jagged **algal ridge**. The algal ridge suffers the full fury of the incoming waves. In this severe habitat a few species of calcareous red algae, especially *Porolithon* and *Lithothamnion,* flourish and produce the ridge. These encrusting algae produce new reef material as rapidly as the waves erode it away. A few snails, limpets, and the slate-pencil urchin, *Heterocentrotus* (plate 7), can also be found here. Slicing across the algal ridge are surge channels that flush bits and fragments of reef material off the reef and down the seaward slope.

Extending behind the algal ridge to the island (or, if it is not developed, to the lagoon) is a **reef flat**, a nearly level surface barely covered by water at low tide. The reef flat may be narrow or very wide and consist of several subzones. The variety of coral species and growth forms found here is immense. In places where the water deepens to a meter or so, small raised **microatolls** occur. Microatolls are produced by a half-dozen different genera of corals and, with other coral growth forms, provide the framework for possibly the richest and most varied habitat on the reef. Burrowing sea urchins (*Echinometra*) are common. The calcareous green alga, *Halimeda*, and several species of large foraminifers thrive and add their skeletons to the sand-sized deposits on the reef flat. The sand, in turn, provides shelter for other urchins, sea cucumbers, and burrowing worms and mollusks.

Plate 1a. Bush coral, *Acropora* (Guam Island). Photo by M. Weeks.

Plate 1b. Plate coral, *Acropora* (Palau Island). Photo by M. Weeks.

Plate 1c. Leaf coral, *Montipora*, surrounded by various growth forms of *Acropora* (Palau Island). Photo by M. Weeks.

1a.

1b.

1c.

Plate 2a. Staghorn coral, *Acropora* (Palau Island). Photo by M. Weeks.

Plate 2b. *Porites* (Oahu Island). Photo by H. Bertsch.

Plate 2c. Organ-pipe coral, *Tubipora* (Guam Island). Photo by M. Weeks.

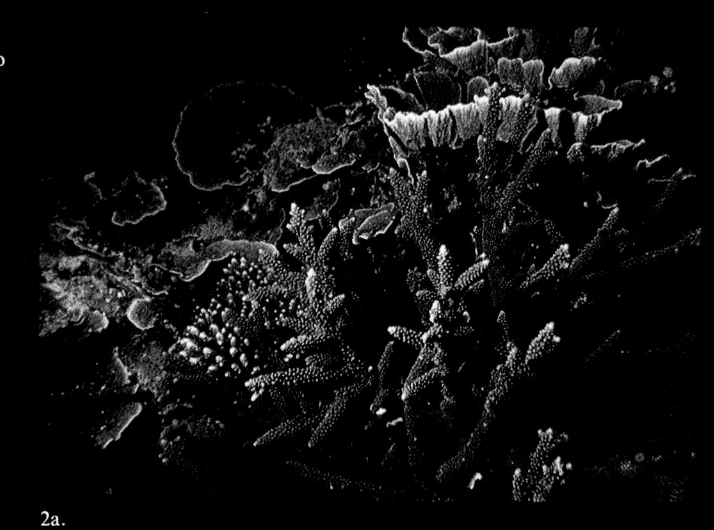

2a.

2b.

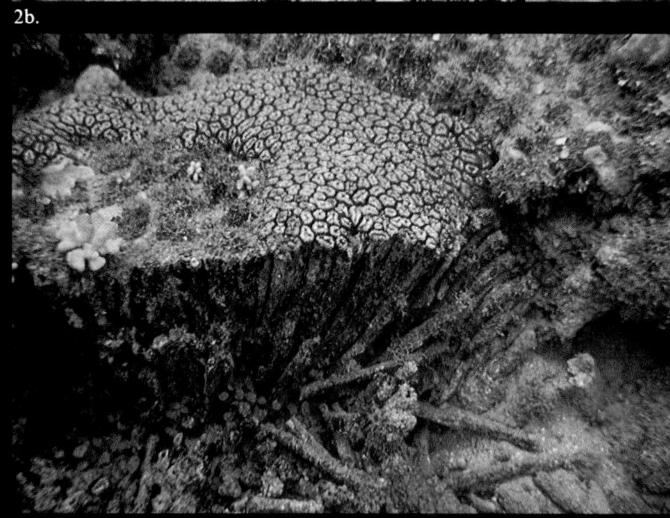

2c.

3a.

3b.

Plate 3a. Mixed corals and sponges (Oahu Island). Photo by H. Bertsch.

Plate 3b. *Zoanthus* with polyps fully extended (Oahu Island). Photo by H. Bertsch.

Plate 3c. *Tubastrea* with some polyps extended (Oahu Island). Photo by H. Bertsch.

Plate 4a. Extended polyps of the soft coral *Telesto* (Oahu Island). Photo by H. Bertsch.

Plate 4b. Red branching gorgonian *Melithaea* with a giant clam *Tridacna* below (Palau Island). Photo by M. Weeks.

4a.

Plate 5a. Sponge overgrowin
coral (Oahu Island). Photo by
H. Bertsch.

Plate 5b. Black-hole sponge
and encrusting red algae (Oah
Island). Photo by H. Bertsch.

Plate 5c. Sponge (Oahu
Island). Photo by H. Bertsch.

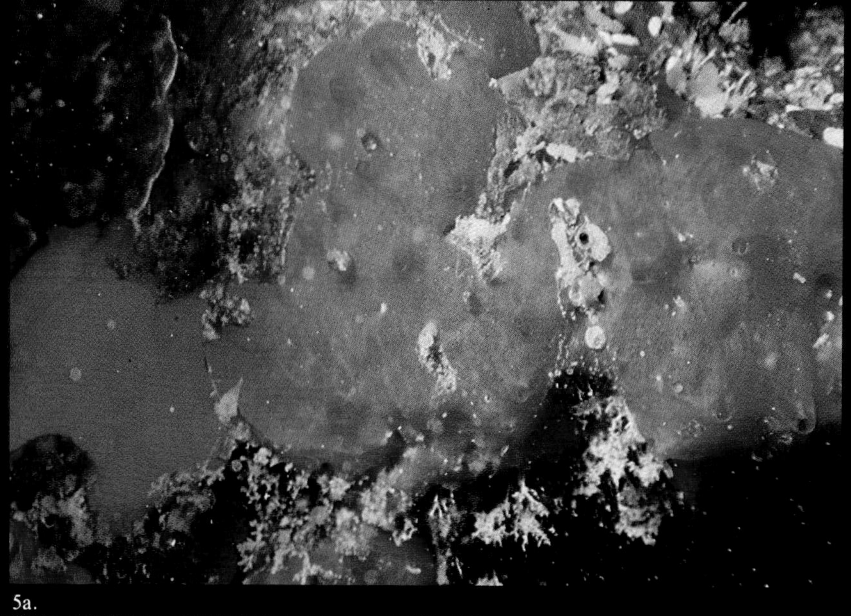

5a.

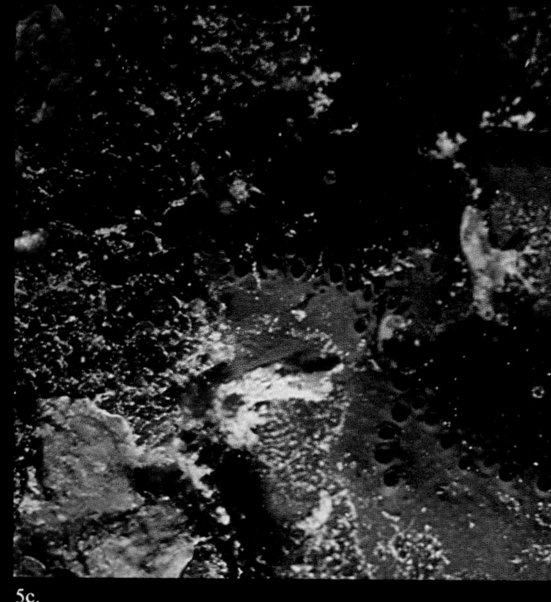

5c.

Plate 6a. Three species of *Chromodoris* nudibranchs (Oahu Island). Photo by H. Bertsch.

Plate 6b. Nudibranch *Chromodoris imperialis* (Oahu Island). Photo by H. Bertsch.

Plate 6c. Nudibranch *Chromodoris godeffroyana* (Oahu Island). Photo by H. Bertsch.

Plate 6d. Nudibranch *Halgerda graphica* (Oahu Island). Photo by H. Bertsch.

6a.

6b.

Plate 7a. Crown-of-thorns sea star, *Acanthaster* (Oahu Island). Photo by H. Bertsch.

Plate 7b. *Acanthaster* tube feet (Oahu Island). Photo by H. Bertsch.

Plate 7c. Pencil urchin, *Heterocentrotus*, on *Porites* coral (Oahu Island). Photo by H. Bertsch.

Plate 7d. *Heterocentrotus* (Oahu Island). Photo by H. Bertsch.

7a.

7b.

Plate 8a. Mixed reef fishes (Guam Island). Photo by M. Weeks.

Plate 8b. Nearly transparent leaf fish, *Taenianotus* (Oahu Island). Photo by H. Bertsch.

Plate 8c. Moorish idol, *Zanclus cornutus* (Guam Island). Photo by M. Weeks.

Plate 8d. Yellow butterfly fish, *Chaetodon auriga* (Palau Island). Photo by M. Weeks.

8a.

8b.

8c.

Possibly the most spectacular animal of the reef flat is the giant clam *Tridacna*. The largest species of this genus occasionally exceeds a meter in length and weighs over 100 kg. Some tridacnids sit exposed atop the reef platform. Others slowly rock and work themselves partially into the growing coral structure beneath (plate 4). Like corals, and many other invertebrates, tridacnids house zooxanthellae in specialized tissues, particularly the enlarged siphons that line the edges of the shell. When the shell is open, the pigmented siphonal tissues, with their zooxanthellae, are exposed to the full impact of the tropical sun. Tridacnid clams were long thought to "farm" their zooxanthellae in blood sinuses within the siphons, then transport them to the digestive glands where they were digested by single-celled **amebocytes**. Using elaborate staining and electron microscope techniques, P.V. Fankboner has recently demonstrated that the digestive amebocytes of *Tridacna* selectively cull and destroy old or degenerate zooxanthellae of questionable nutritive value. Presumably, healthy zooxanthellae are maintained to provide products of their photosynthetic efforts in solution to their hosts.

The tranquil waters of the lagoon protect two general life zones: the lagoon reef and the lagoon floor. The lagoon reef forms the shallow margin of the lagoon proper. It is a leeward reef, free of severe wave action. It lacks the algal ridge characteristic of the windward reef and, in its place, has a more luxuriant stand of corals. Other algae, some specialized to burrow into coral, flourish here. So do uncountable species of crustaceans, echinoderms, mollusks, anemones, gorgonians, and some representatives of nearly every other animal phylum (plates 4, 5, 6, and 7). In this gentle, protected environment, single coral colonies of *Porites* and *Acropora* achieve gigantic proportions, as in plates 1 and 2. Branching bush and treelike forms extend several meters from their bases. The plating, branching, and overtopping structures common in the protected lagoon are most likely structural adaptations evolved in response to competition for particulate food and sunlight, two resources vital to the survival of reef-forming corals.

Associated with the reef and lagoon, but with the mobility to escape the limitations of a benthic existence, are literally thousands of species of reef fishes (a few are shown in plate 8). They find protection on the reef, prey on the plants and animals living there, and sometimes nibble at the reef itself. Several genera are common to all the major regions characterized by coral reefs. These include moray eels (*Gymnothorax*), porcupine fish (*Diodon*), butterfly fish (*Chaetodon*), squirrel fish (*Holocentrus*), groupers (*Epinephelus*), trigger fish (*Xanthichthys*), gobies, wrasses, surgeonfish, sea horses, and an abundant supply of sharks, skates, and rays.

Symbiotic Relationships in Coral Reef Fish

Countless marine organisms exist together in symbiotic relationships that provide protection, or food, or both, to at least one of the participants. The term **symbiosis** is presently used to denote an intimate and prolonged contact between two (or more) organisms in which at least one partner obtains some benefit from the relationship. Zooxanthellae in corals and tridacnid clams have already been discussed as examples of symbiosis.

Symbiotic relationships can, for simplicity, be reduced to three broadly overlapping categories (fig. 4.44). **Commensalism** provides an obvious benefit to one partner (the **symbiont**) without seriously affecting the **host** one way or another. In **mutualism,** both the symbiont and the host benefit from the association. **Parasitism** is a third, highly evolved symbiotic relationship in which the parasite lives on or in the host and obtains food benefits at the expense of the host. Parasites do not usually kill their hosts (those that do might be considered "imperfect" parasites), but they can make their presence felt by reducing the host's food reserves, resistance to disease, and general vigor. The infected host then is more likely to become a casualty to infection, starvation, or predation, but not to the parasite directly.

Excellent examples of all three types of symbiosis can be found in many of the abundant animal groups of the coral reef environment. But rather than bog down in a futile attempt to describe them all, this discussion is limited to some of the better-known symbiotic relationships involving coral reef fish. They span the entire range, from very casual commensal associations to highly evolved parasitic relationships.

Small schools of the pilot fish (*Naucrates*) form loose commensal associations with large predatory sharks. They swim below and in front of their hosts and scavenge bits of food from the shark's meal. Neither the pilot fish nor the shark show any structural specialization for this relationship. The remoras (*Remora* and *Echeneis*, fig. 4.45) also associate with large sharks and occasionally even whales and turtles. The remora's first dorsal fin is actually a sucking disc and is used to attach itself to its host. From its attached position it feeds on leavings of the host.

The small shrimpfish (*Aeloiscus*) are often observed swimming head down among the long sharp spines of the sea urchin, *Centrechinus* (fig. 4.46). From the urchin they acquire protection without altering the urchin's behavior. A similar association exists between small man-of-war fish (*Nomeus*) and the Portuguese man-of-war (*Physalia,* fig. 7.8). In this case, *Physalia's* long venomous tentacles provide a protected retreat for the small fish.

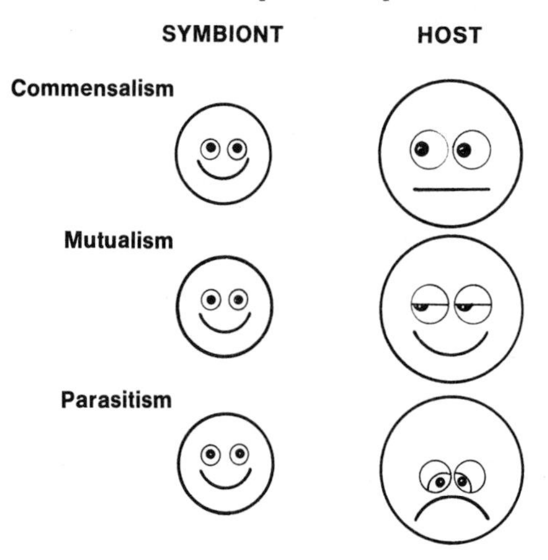

Fig. 4.44 Three aspects of symbiotic associations: commensalism, mutualism, and parasitism.

Fig. 4.45 Two remoras, with their modified dorsal fins visible. Courtesy M. Weeks.

Fig. 4.46 Shrimpfish seeking shelter amid the spines of a sea urchin.

The brightly colored clown fish, *Amphiprion,* finds equally effective shelter by nestling among the stinging tentacles of the sea anemones *Stoichactis* and *Actinia* (fig. 4.47). This relationship is somewhat more complex than those just described, and is probably a mutualistic one. Clown fish, in return for the protection they obtain, assume the role of "bait" to lure other fishes within reach of the anemone. They have been observed to collect morsels of food and in at least one instance, catch another fish and feed it to the host anemone. In this very close partnership, the anemones may be nutritionally dependent on the clown fish, for they do not thrive without their guests. Clown fish apparently are not immune to the venemous nematocysts of the host. Yet they display a peculiar habit of mouthing and nibbling the anemone's tenta-

Fig. 4.47 A clownfish, *Amphiprion*, nestled in the tentacles of its host anemone. Courtesy L. Ford, Scripps Institution of Oceanography.

Fig. 4.48 The small wrasse *Labroides* cleaning external parasites from a turkey fish. Courtesy C. Farwell, Scripps Institution of Oceanography.

cles. Nibbling seems to accustom the anemone to the presence of the fish against its tentacles. Substances contained in the mucus of the fish's skin may provide the mechanism to inhibit nematocyst discharge.

The increased popularity of skin and scuba diving in the past two decades has revealed some remarkable cleaning associations involving a surprising number of animals. **Cleaning symbiosis** is generally considered a form of mutualism; with one partner picking external parasites and damaged tissue from the other. The first gets the parasites to eat, the other has an irritation removed.

The behavioral and structural adaptations of cleaners are well developed in a half dozen species of shrimps and a few groups of small fishes. Tropical cleaning fishes include the butterfly fish (*Chaetodon*), the young stages of the gray angelfish (*Pomacanthus*), gobies (*Elecatinus*), and several wrasses (*Bodianus* and all four species of *Labroides*, fig. 4.48). All are brightly marked and are equipped with pointed pincerlike snouts and beaks. Generally they are solitary (a few live in pairs) and occupy a cleaning station around an obvious rock outcrop or coral head.

Host fish approach these cleaning stations, frequently queuing up and jockeying for position near the cleaner. They often assume unnatural and awkward poses somewhat reminiscent of some courtship displays. As the cleaner fish moves toward the host, it inspects the host's fins, skin, mouth, and gill chambers. It then picks away parasites, slime, and infected tissue around wounds.

In the Bahamas, C. Limbaugh tested the cleaner's role in subduing parasites and infections of other reef fishes. Two weeks after removing all known cleaners from two small reefs, the areas were vacated by nearly all but the territorial fish species. Those that remained showed signs of increased parasitism, frayed fins, ulcerated skin, and an overall ratty appearance. Limbaugh concluded that symbiotic cleaners are essential in maintaining healthy fish populations in his study area.

Similar studies by G. Losey were conducted on a Hawaiian reef. In this case the small cleaning wrasse, *Labroides phthirophagus* (the major cleaner on the reef) was excluded from the study site for more than six months. During that time, no increase in the level of parasite infestation was observed. This experiment suggests that, for some cleaner-host associations, the role of the cleaner is not a crucial one. The cleaner may be dependent on the host for food, but the host's need for the cleaner seems to be quite variable.

The fine line separating mutualistic cleaning of external parasites and actual parasitism of the host fish is crossed occasionally by cleaning fish such as *Labroides*. In addition to unwanted parasites and diseased tissue, they are not above taking a little extra healthy tissue or scales or grazing on the skin mucus secreted by the host. Thus the total range of associations displayed by cleaning fishes encompasses mutualism, commensalism, and infrequently, parasitism.

Parasitism is such a widespread way of life in the sea that few fish avoid contact with parasites at some time in their lives. The groups notorious for creating parasitic problems in humans—viruses, bacteria, flatworms, roundworms, and leeches—also plague marine fish.

In spite of the bewildering array of parasites that infest fish, very few fish have become full-time parasites themselves. One remarkable exception is the small needle fish (*Carapus*). It finds refuge in the intestinal tracts of sea cucumbers and sometimes the stomachs of certain sea stars. When seeking a host, needle fish apparently detect a chemical substance from the cucumber, then orient toward the respiratory current coming from the cucumber's anus. (Sea cucumbers draw in and expel water through their anus for gas exchange.) The fish enters the digestive tract tail-first via the anus. The hosts are not altogether willing participants in this relationship. They are sometimes seen ejecting their digestive and respiratory organs in an attempt to rid themselves of the symbiont. Once this association is established, the fish assume a parasitic existence, feeding on and seriously damaging the host's respiratory structures and gonads.

Color

Against the colorful background of their coral environment, reef fish have evolved equally brilliant hues and striking color patterns. The colors are derived from skin or internal pigments and from iridescent structural features (like those of a bird's feathers) with optical properties that produce color effects. Most fish apparently form accurate visual images of what they see, and many see those images in color. Like humans, fish probably are susceptible to misleading visual images and camouflage.

Our interpretation of the adaptive significance of color in fish falls into three general categories: concealment, disguise, and advertisement. Some seemingly conspicuous fish resemble their coral environment so well that they are nearly invisible when in their natural setting (fig. 4.49). Extensive color changes often supplement their basic camouflage when moving to different surroundings. Rapid color changes are accomplished by expanding and contracting pigmented cells (**chromatophores**) in the skin. These changes are governed by the direct action of light on the skin, by hormones, and by nerves to each chromatophore. As the chromatophore expands, its pigment granules become more obvious as they spread through the branching processes of the cell (fig. 4.50). When contracted, the pigment retreats to the center of the cell and little of it is visible. Other cells, called **iridocytes**, contain reflecting crystals of guanine. Iridocytes can, within a few seconds, produce an entire spectrum of colors.

Several distinctive fish conceal themselves with color displays reminiscent of disruptive coloration, or dazzle camouflage, used to disguise military hardware. Bold, contrasting lines, blotches, and bands tend to disrupt the fish's image and draw the observer's attention away from recognizable features, such as eyes. One common strategy masks the eye with a dark band across the black staring pupil so it appears continuous with some other part of the body (fig. 4.51). To carry the deception even further, masks around the real eyes are sometimes accompanied by fake eye-spots on other parts of the body or fins. Eye-spots are obviously intended as visual attention getters. They are usually set off by concentric rings to form a bull's-eye. Presumably, predators are drawn away from the eyes and head and toward less vital parts of the body.

The flashy color patterns of cleaning fish serve a very different function. If they are to attract any business, they must be conspicuous. So they advertise themselves and their location with bright startling color combinations. Similar reasoning applies to the clown fish, which acts as a flashy lure to attract other fish within reach of the host anemone's tentacles.

Bold advertisement displays are also useful for sexual recognition. In certain species, one or both sexes assume bright color patterns during the breeding season. The colors play a prominent role in the courtship displays, which lead to spawning. During this period, the positive value gained from sexual displays must at least offset the adverse impact of attracting hungry predators. Between breeding seasons, these fish usually assume a drab, less conspicuous appearance.

Fig. 4.49

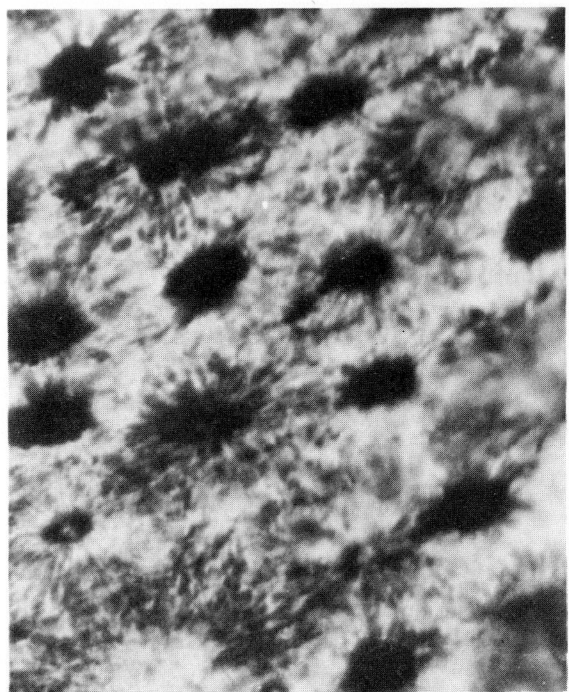

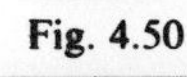

Fig. 4.50

Fig. 4.51

Fig. 4.49 The stonefish *Synanceja horrida* is almost impossible to see when it rests on the bottom. Courtesy C. Farwell, Scripps Institution of Oceanography.

Fig. 4.50 Magnified chromatophores from a section of fish skin. The pigments of some are expanded and diffuse; others are densely concentrated in small spots.

Fig. 4.51 A butterfly fish, *Chaetodon,* with well-developed disruptive counter-shading. Courtesy C. Farwell, Scripps Institution of Oceanography.

Advertisement displays are also employed to warn would-be predators of fish carrying sharp or venomous spines (see fig. 4.48), poisonous flesh, or other features that would be painful or dangerous if eaten. Predatory fish recognize the color patterns of unpalatable fish and soon learn to avoid them.

Occasionally, a species capitalizes on the advertisement displays of another fish by closely mimicking its appearance. The cleaner wrasse, *Labroides*, for example, is nearly immune to predation because of the useful function it performs for its potential predators. Over much of its range, *Labroides* lives in close proximity to a small blenny (*Aspidenotus*). The blenny so closely resembles *Labroides* in size, shape, and coloration (fig. 4.52), that it fools many of the predatory fish that approach the wrasse's cleaning station. Not content to share *Labroides* immunity to predation, the blenny uses its disguise to prey on fish that mistakenly approach it for cleaning.

Only in the clear waters of the tropics and subtropics does color play such a significant role in the lives of shallow water animals. In the productive and turbid waters of temperate and colder latitudes, light does not penetrate as deeply, nor is the range of colors available. In coastal waters and kelp beds, monotony and drabness of appearance rather than brilliance is the key to camouflage (fig. 4.53). In the deep ocean, color is even less important. Without light to illuminate their pigments, it matters little whether deep-water organisms appear red, blue, black, or chartreuse when viewed at the surface. In the abyss, they all assume the uniform blackness of their surroundings.

The Abyss

Beyond the continental shelves, the sea bottom descends sharply to the stygian depths of the deep-sea floor. Three-quarters of the ocean bottom (the abyssal and hadal zones of fig. 1.30) lie at depths below 3,000 m, yet this immense area is home for less than 1% of the life in the sea. Studies of deep-sea life have been fragmentary, retarded by the great expense of sampling the ocean's deeps and by the difficulties of bringing healthy deep-sea animals to the surface for direct observations. Captured animals encounter extreme temperature and pressure changes when hauled from the bottom. By the time they reach the surface, they are usually dead or seriously injured.

The deep sea is one of the most rigorous and constant environments on earth. There is no sunlight, and therefore no living plants. The bottom, with very few exceptions, is composed of fine-grained clays and accumulated skeletal remains of near-surface plankton. The water is cold, averaging 2°C and dipping slightly below 0°C in polar regions. Pressures created by the burden of overlying water are tremendous; they vary between 300 and 600 atmospheres on the abyssal seafloor and exceed 1,000 atm in the deepest trenches (each 10 m of water depth adds another **atmosphere** of pressure; 1 atm is approximately equal to 1 kg/cm^2 or 15 lb/in^2). These pressures may be sufficient to alter some enzymatic reactions. Laboratory studies have confirmed that metabolic rates of deep-sea bacteria are much lower at pressures normally experienced on the seafloor than at sea surface pressures. Less is known about the response of multicellular organisms to high pressures, but the results of

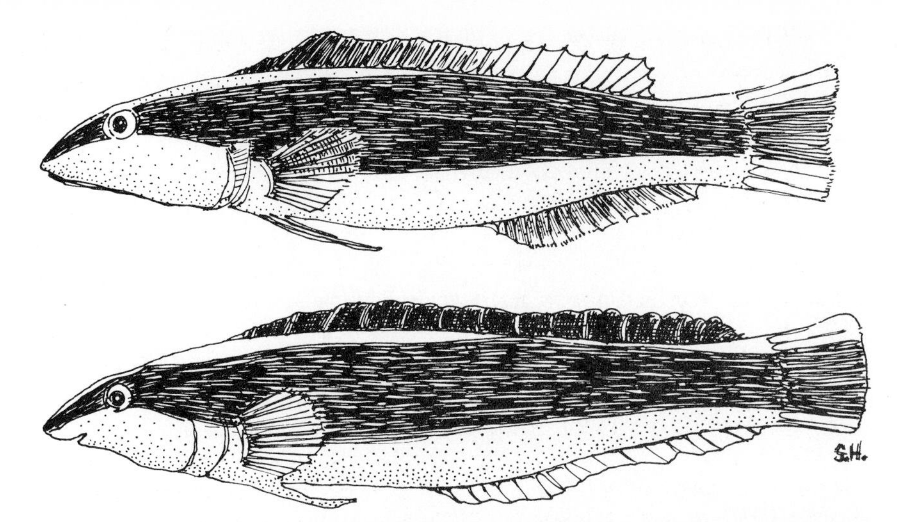

Fig. 4.52 The small cleaner *Labroides* (above) and its mimic, *Aspidenotus* (below).

Fig. 4.53 A round stingray, *Urolophus,* camouflaged on the bottom. Official photograph U.S. Navy.

a few studies suggest pressure induced reductions in metabolic rates lead to lowered reproductive capacities and increased life spans in the deep sea. It has been suggested that the gigantism found in some deep-sea species is due to metabolic adjustments to the extreme pressures. Such speculation may be premature, for the effects of extreme pressures on growth rates and maximum sizes of deep-sea animals are not yet known (fig. 4.54).

The inhabitants of the deep-sea floor are a distinctive group, even though few exhibit structural adaptations that make them appear notably different from their shallow-water relatives. Instead, a shift in dominant taxonomic groups occurs in deeper water. Echinoderms (especially sea cucumbers), polychaete worms, pycnogonids, and isopod and amphipod crustaceans

Fig. 4.54 A group of very large crustacean amphipods feeding on bait in the Peru-Chile Trench at a depth of 7,000 m. For scale, the cable at right is just over 6 cm in diameter. Courtesy Scripps Institution of Oceanography, Marine Life Research Group.

become abundant whereas sea stars, bivalves, and other mollusks decline in numbers. Some groups are virtually absent until relatively great depths are reached. Most species of pogonophorans, for instance, are found below 3,000 m, and 30% of them are restricted to trenches.

It is not possible to establish a precise global depth boundary between the animals of the deep sea and the shallow-water fauna of the continental shelves. Generally, the boundary exists as a vague region of transition on the continental slopes bordering the deep-sea basin. However, animals of the "deep sea" commonly extend into shallower water in polar seas; on occasion even to the inner portions of continental shelves.

Here, in the physically stable environment of the deep sea, patterns of reproduction are thought to differ strongly from those of shallow-water benthic animals. Very few deep-water benthic species produce planktonic larvae, for their chances of reaching the food-rich photic zone several km above, then successfully returning to the ocean floor for permanent settlement, are extremely remote. To compensate for the absence of a dependable external food supply, fewer but larger eggs are produced. The larvae are supplied with adequate yolks to develop directly to fairly advanced stages prior to hatching. Brood pouches, incubating chambers, and other similar adaptations further enhance the chances of survival by protecting the eggs until they hatch. Consequently, the larvae have a reasonable chance of making it on their own in one of the most severe environments on earth.

Low temperatures and high pressures, combined with a limited food supply, led to an early and widespread belief that the rigorous and specialized climate of the deep sea would not support a highly diversified assemblage of animals. Instead it was assumed that only a few highly adapted animals could succeed in the abyss. But because of recent improvements in sampling devices, deep-sea communities have been found to contain a wide diversity of species equivalent to soft-bottom communities in shallow inshore waters. To explain the unexpected diversity of deep-sea life, researchers have hypothesized that the number of deep-sea species has gradually increased as the species adjusted to each other and assumed narrower, more specialized niches within their stable environment.

A most critical and variable resource in the deep sea is food. In the open ocean, food for deep-sea benthic communities, by necessity, comes from above; but little is known of its condition when it arrives at the bottom. After being repeatedly consumed by pelagic scavengers and bacteria, small plankton particles may be of little nutritive value by the time they settle to the bottom. However, before leaving the photic zone, much of the near-surface plankton production is apparently aggregated into larger compact fecal pellets of zooplankton, which settle more rapidly to the bottom. This fecal fallout serves to accelerate the transport of organic material to the abyss, falling from the surface waters in a few days rather than the weeks or months of settling time necessary for the smaller plankton particles.

Large, rapidly sinking particles, including squids, fish, and even an occasional whale, may provide a significant, although unpredictable supply of food to the inhabitants of the deep-sea floor. If large food parcels do contribute significantly to the energy budget of the deep sea, they are probably rapidly consumed by various wide-ranging scavenger-predators (fig. 4.55). Most seem to be swift enough to evade bottom trawls and are best known from photographs taken by underwater cameras baited with food. They seem to be food generalists, capable of rapidly locating and dispatching large food items as they arrive on the bottom. Some of the food is eventually dispersed as detritus and fecal wastes to the remainder of the bottom community.

A portion of the smaller edible material settling to the bottom is immediately claimed by suspension feeders. However, the majority of benthic animals in the deep sea are infaunal deposit feeders. Analyses of their stomach contents indicate that they indiscriminately engulf sediments containing smaller infauna and bacteria as well as some dead organic material. Claude Zobell estimated that 30–40% of the organic material available at the bottom is first absorbed by benthic bacteria, which are in turn consumed by larger animals.

Dayton and Hessler have proposed the general term **"cropper"** for deep-**sea animals that have merged the roles of predator and deposit feeder** (fig.

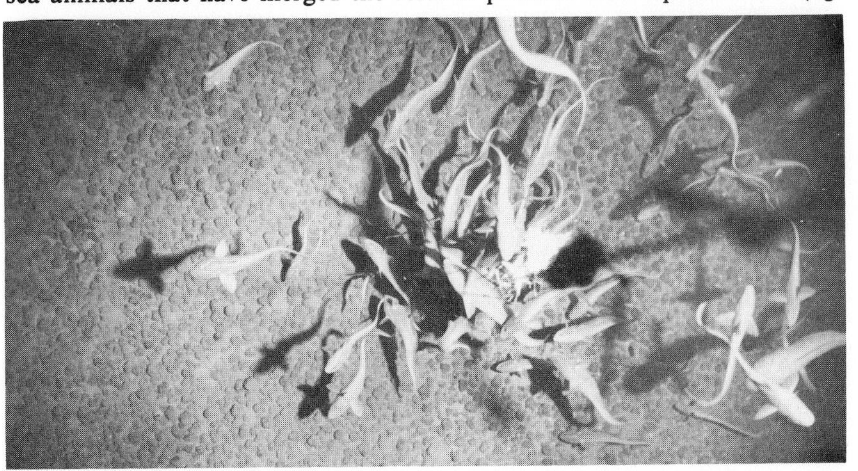

Fig. 4.55 Macurid fish scavenging around a bait can (center) lowered 5,850 m to the sea bottom north of Hawaii. Courtesy Scripps Institution of Oceanography, Marine Life Research Group.

4.56). They suggest that these croppers, by heavily preying on populations of smaller deposit feeders, are responsible for reducing competition for food and for permitting coexistence between species sharing the same food resource. Thus, even though a deep-sea community as a whole is food-limited, populations within the community need not be so long as they are heavily preyed upon. With competition for food reduced by cropping, fewer species are pushed to extinction and the diversity of the community remains high. The disruptive effects of large croppers on smaller ones can be compared to predators, or ice, or logs, as disturbance mechanisms in rocky intertidal communities. By nonselectively reducing competition, they lessen the possibility of a species being excluded from a community, or from existence, by resource competition.

Early in 1977, a team of researchers studying the Galapagos Rift Zone west of Equador discovered several small but remarkable assemblages of benthic animals nearly 3 km deep. Dense aggregations of mussels, crabs, pogonophorans, and giant clams were found clustered around hot water vents emanating from the sea floor. The Galapagos Rift is a site of active seafloor spreading, with extensive lava flows so young that very little sediment has had a chance to accumulate. The hot vents are the product of seawater circulating through the many cracks and fissures in the newly formed hot lava crust.

Close observations of these vents made from the deep-diving submersible, *Alvin*, established an intriguing link between the plumes of warm water and the presence of numerous animals on an otherwise barren seafloor. The water coming from the vents is warm, turbid, and rich in hydrogen sulfide. Apparently much of the normal load of sulfate ions in seawater is converted to hydrogen sulfide as it percolates through hot crustal rocks, ultimately to be discharged through the vents at the crust surface.

As it leaves the vents, the hydrogen sulfide in these warm plumes is absorbed quickly by bacteria and oxidized to sulfur. The energy released in this cellular reaction is then used to synthesize the complex organic compounds necessary for bacterial growth and reproduction. These bacterial cells then form the base of simple food chains leading to the large clams, mussels, and other obvious vent animals. In this manner, these few limited populations of benthic animals have tapped into an unusual energy source—the chemicals

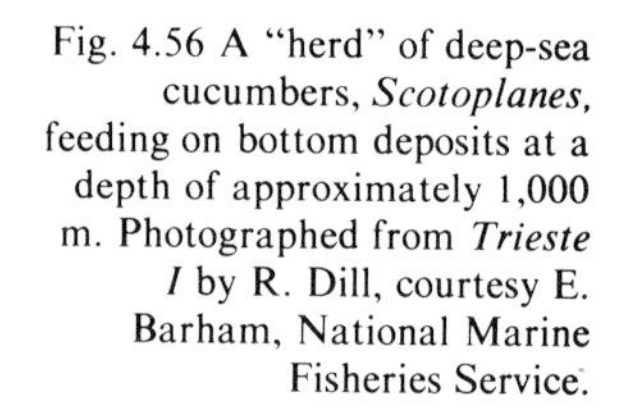

Fig. 4.56 A "herd" of deep-sea cucumbers, *Scotoplanes*, feeding on bottom deposits at a depth of approximately 1,000 m. Photographed from *Trieste I* by R. Dill, courtesy E. Barham, National Marine Fisheries Service.

of the earth's crust—and achieved a nutritional emancipation from the fallout products of the photic zone above.

Summary

The sea bottom is one of the most varied and, in places, rigorous habitats on earth. The variety of benthic life forms attest to the diverse range of niches available on the bottom. The seafloor, the water just above the bottom, and other living plants and animals all help to shape the environmental conditions faced by the benthos. Feeding, locomotion, and reproduction are all strongly influenced by characteristics of the sea bottom.

Dispersal of many shallow-water benthic species is accomplished with planktonic larval forms that are usually quite different in appearance from their parents. During their planktonic existence, these larvae experience environmental pressures often unknown to their bottom-dwelling adults.

Plants and animals of the intertidal zone experience the added complication of periodic exposure to the atmosphere. In the upper intertidal, desiccation and an intermittent food supply are major problems. The organisms of the more densely populated middle intertidal experience a much less restrictive physical environment, but encounter increased interspecific competition. In the lower intertidal, the emphasis on a few well-adapted and dominant species is replaced by a much more diversified assemblage of plants and animals.

Sandy beaches and muddy shores are depositional environments, characterized by deposits of loose sediments and organic detritus. Patterns of vertical zonation do occur, but they are as apparent within the sediment as along its surface. In estuaries, these distributional patterns are complicated by the discharge of fresh water from coastal streams and rivers into the sea.

Coral reefs form the framework for exceedingly complex communities of tropical marine plants and animals. Symbiotic associations are common, and numerous examples of commensalism, mutualism, and parasitism are apparent. The brightly colored patterns of coral reef fish illustrate the advertisement, disguise, and concealment roles of brilliant coloration in a coral reef environment.

The benthic animals of the abyss are not well known. They experience little in the way of fluctuations in their physical environment and are limited primarily by the absence of a constant and abundant food supply. Most are thought to have very generalized feeding habits, and function either as wide-ranging predator-scavengers or as sedentary croppers.

Questions for Discussion

1. The existing tidal cycle and pattern directly influence many physical factors that in turn affect an intertidal animal's ability to successfully adapt and survive. Discuss as many of these physical factors as you can in relation to their influence or effect upon the animal.
2. Why is it crucial to local marine life that at least a few coastal wetlands, estuaries, and sloughs be maintained in natural conditions?

3. Discuss the ecological and survival advantages of planktonic larval stages for benthic animals living in shallow water. Why are planktonic larval forms not equally advantageous for benthic animals of the abyss?
4. Coral reefs give the appearance of highly productive ecosystems, yet they exist in oceanic regions with very low production rates and standing crops. Why are coral reefs so productive?

Suggestions for Further Readings

Books

Darwin, C. 1962 (orig. publ. 1842). *The structure and distribution of coral reefs.* Berkeley, Calif.: Univ. of California Press.

Eltringham, S. K. 1972. *Life in mud and sand.* New York: Crane, Russak & Co.

Lewis, J. H. 1964. *The ecology of rocky shores.* London: English Universities Press.

McLusky, D. S. 1971. *Ecology of estuaries.* London: Heinemann Educational Books.

Newell, R. C. 1970. *Biology of intertidal animals.* New York: American Elsevier.

Ricketts, E. F., and Calvin, J. 1968. *Between Pacific tides.* 4th ed. Edited by J. W. Hedgpeth. Stanford, Calif.: Stanford Univ. Press.

Stephenson, T. A., and Stephenson, A. 1972. *Life between tidemarks on rocky shores.* San Francisco: W. H. Freeman.

Teal, J., and Teal, M. 1974. *Life and death of the salt marsh.* Boston: Little, Brown.

Weins, H. J. 1962. *Atoll environment and ecology.* New Haven, Conn.: Yale Univ. Press.

Articles

Corliss, J. B., and Ballard, R. D. 1977. Oases of life in the cold abyss. *National Geographic* 152:441-53.

Epel, D. 1977. The program of fertilization. *Scientific American,* November: 129-38.

Feder, H. M. 1972. Escape responses in marine invertebrates. *Scientific American,* July: 92-100.

Harger, J. R. E. 1972. Competitive coexistence among intertidal invertebrates. *American Scientist* 60:600-607.

Goreau, T. F., Goreau, N. L., and Yonge, C. M. 1971. Reef corals: autotrophs or heterotrophs? *Biological Bulletin* 141:247-60.

Grassle, J. F. 1978. Diversity and population dynamics of benthic organisms. *Oceanus* 21 (winter): 42-49.

Jannasch, H. W., and Wirsen, C. O., 1977. Microbial life in the deep sea. *Scientific American,* June: 42-52.

Limbaugh, C. 1961. Cleaning symbiosis. *Scientific American.* August:42-49.

Menge, B. A. 1975. Brood or broadcast? The adaptive significance of different reproductive strategies in the two intertidal sea stars *Leptasterias hexactis* and *Pisaster ochraceus. Marine Biology* 31:87-100.

Muscatine, L., and Porter, J. W. 1977. Reef corals: mutualistic symbiosis adapted to nutrient-poor environments. *Bioscience* 27:454-60.

Palmer, J. D. 1975. Biological clocks of the tidal zone. *Scientific American,* February: 70-79.

Schener, P. J. 1977. Chemical communication of marine invertebrates. *Bioscience* 27:644-68.

Scott, R. D., and Jitts, H. R. 1977. Photosynthesis of phytoplankton and zooxanthellae on a coral reef. *Marine Biology* 41:307-15.

Fronds of the giant kelp, *Macrocystis*.
Official photograph of U.S. Navy.

Marine Plants

5

Members of the abundant plant groups so familiar on land—the ferns, mosses, and seed plants—are poorly represented or totally absent from the marine environment. Yet the sea does not lack for its primary producers. The majority of marine plants are quite different in structure and in many functions from their terrestrial counterparts. At the beginning of this century most marine plants were referred to collectively as *algae* and were lumped together in a single division, the Thallophyta. By the 1920s it was recognized that the algae were comprised of several related, yet distinct, groups of marine plants.

At the present time, marine species from eleven plant divisions have been recognized and described. These divisions are characterized by their own unique combinations of photosynthetic pigments, cell wall structures, storage products, and growth forms (table 5.1). Of these, only five: the Chrysophyta, Pyrrophyta, Phaeophyta, Rhodophyta, and Cyanophyta, are predominantly marine. The Chlorophyta, Anthophyta, and Schizomycophyta also contribute to the total marine flora. Members of these seven plant divisions are grouped according to whether they are planktonic or benthic (the Schizomycophyta and Mycophyta have not been included because they are generally nonphotosynthetic), and will be the subject of this and the following chapters.

Benthic Plants

Some forms of benthic marine plants are quite familiar to even the casual observer of seashore life. Most are conspicuous because they are commonly found in intertidal or shallow subtidal zones near shore. These plants, like the phytoplankton, are confined to the photic zone by their need for sunlight. But their additional requirement of a solid bottom for anchorage restricts their distribution to a very narrow fringe around the periphery of the marine environment. Some attached algae are even more conspicuous because of their large size, while others are small, sometimes even microscopic. Whatever their size, their role as producers of plant material to sustain other forms of near-shore marine life is a critical one and should not be overlooked.

Table 5.1. *Marine Plant Divisions and Their General Characteristics.*

Division (common name)	Approx. No. of Living Species	Proportion of Species Marine (%)	General Size and Structure	Photosynthetic Pigments	Storage Products	Habit
Chrysophyta (golden-brown algae) (coccolithophores) (silicoflagellates) (diatoms)	 650 200 ? 6,000–10,000	 ±20 96 most 30–50	Unicellular, often flagellated, microscopic	Chlorophyll *a, c* Xanthophylls Carotenes	Chrysolaminarin Oils	Planktonic and benthic
Xanthophyta	60	15	Filamentous, microscopic	Chlorophyll *a* Xanthophylls Carotenes	Chrysolaminarin Fats	Benthic
Pyrrophyta (dinoflagellates)	1,100+	93	Unicellular or colonial, flagellated, microscopic	Chlorophyll *a, c* Xanthophylls Carotenes	Starch Fats Oils	Planktonic
Euglenophyta (euglenoids)	400	3	Unicellular, flagellated, microscopic	Chlorophyll *a, b* Xanthophylls Carotenes	Starch Fats	Benthic
Chlorophyta (green algae)	7,000	13	Unicellular and multicellular, microscopic to macroscopic	Chlorophyll *a, b* Carotenes	Starch	Mostly benthic
Cyanophyta (blue-green algae)	200	±75	Unicellular, prokaryotic, nonflagellated, microscopic	Chlorophyll *a* Carotenes Phycobilins	Starch	Mostly benthic
Phaeophyta (brown algae)	1,500	99.7	Multicellular, macroscopic	Chlorophyll *a, c* Xanthophylls Carotenes	Laminarin and others	Mostly benthic
Rhodophyta (red algae)	4,000	98	Unicellular and multicellular, mostly macroscopic	Chlorophyll *a* Carotenes Phycobilins	Starch and others	Benthic
Anthophyta (flowering plants)	250,000	0.018	Multicellular, macroscopic	Chlorophyll *a* Carotenes	Starch	Benthic
Schizomycophyta (bacteria)	1,500	12	Unicellular, prokaryotic, nonflagellated, microscopic	Nonphotosynthetic	------	Planktonic and benthic
Mycophyta (fungi) (lichens)	 75,000 16,000	 0.4 0.1	Microscopic	Nonphotosynthetic Variable	------	Intertidal benthic

Adapted from Dawson 1966, and Scagel *et al.* 1965

Cyanophyta

Blue-green algae (division Cyanophyta) are found almost everywhere light and water are available. But marine forms are usually inconspicuous in comparison to other marine plants. Little diversity of form is apparent in blue-green algae. These plants are individually microscopic, but they may aggregate to produce macroscopic colonies. One abundant coral reef form, *Lyngbya,* develops long strands or hollow tubes of cells nearly a meter in length. Reproduction of blue-green algae is usually accomplished by cell division. Occasionally the growing colony will fragment to disperse the cells. More complex modes of reproduction, involving motile or resistant stages, are also known.

On temperate seashores, a few species of blue-green algae (fig. 5.1) are sometimes noticeable as tarlike patches encrusting rocks in the intertidal or splash zones. Others can be found in abundance on mudflats of coastal marshes and estuaries. Blue-green algae are also commonly associated with tropical coral reefs. Several types of abundant reef-dwelling blue-green algae, including *Lyngbya,* have been implicated in **ciguatera** poisoning of fish and humans on some tropical Pacific islands.

A few species of blue-green algae, including *Calothrix,* are capable of utilizing atmospheric nitrogen (N_2) to satisfy their metabolic nitrogen needs. The process of **nitrogen fixation** in marine plants is poorly understood, but it is known to be limited to blue-green algae and several types of bacteria. Field studies have shown that nitrogen-fixing blue-green algae, either alone or in association with other plants, contribute significantly to the nitrogen economy of their communities.

Blue-green algae demonstrate a strong tendency to form intimate associations with other organisms. Various examples of symbiosis with animals are common. Two genera can even be found inhabiting marine planktonic diatoms, such as *Rhizosolenia.* Many blue-greens live as **epiphytes,** attached to other larger plants. Some blue-green epiphytes, for example those inhabiting turtle grass beds along the Gulf Coast of the United States, are also nitrogen-fixers. As such, they play an important role in the fertility and productivity of these sea-grass beds.

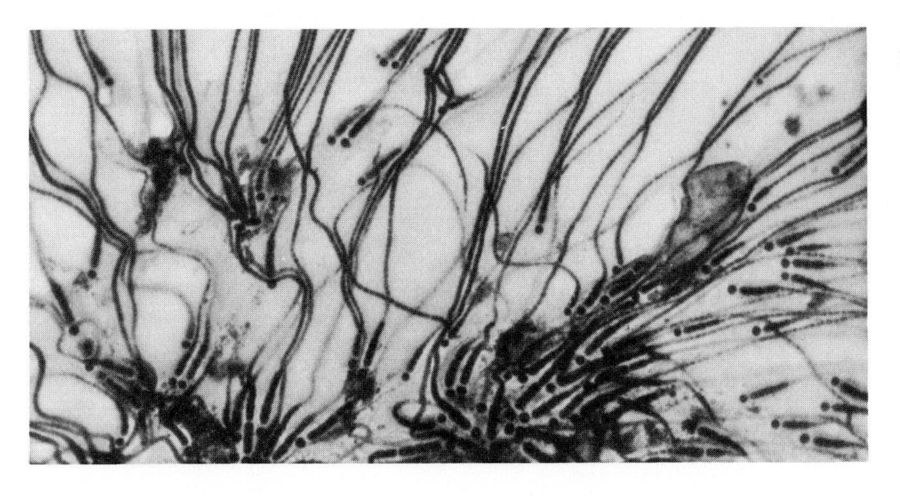

Fig. 5.1 Micrograph of the blue-green alga *Rivularia.*

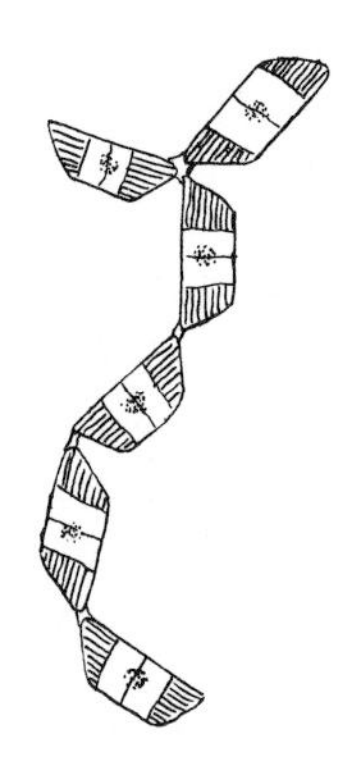

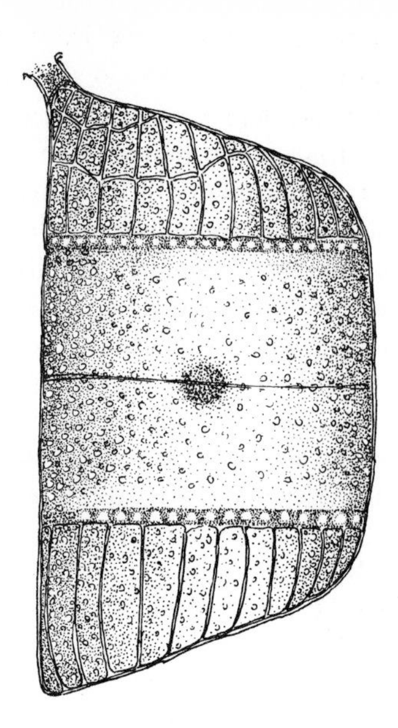

Fig. 5.2 A benthic diatom, *Isthmia,* forming long, complex chains of cells. A close-up of a single cell is shown at right.

Benthic Diatoms

Bottom-living diatoms closely resemble their planktonic counterparts (to be discussed later in this chapter) in cell structure, modes of reproduction, and other general characteristics. These plants can be found on almost any solid substrate in shallow seawater: on mud surfaces, rocks, larger marine plants, man-made structures, and the hard shells of marine animals. One type, *Cocconeis,* even makes a home on the undersides of blue whales. Many of the benthic diatoms secrete a mucilage pad that connects adjacent cells into complex chains and branching forms (fig. 5.2). In this manner, macroscopic diatom colonies a few cm long are formed.

When compared to planktonic diatoms, the geographical distribution of benthic diatoms is severely restricted because of their need for solid substrates. Still, they make a significant contribution to the total amount of plant production in estuaries, bays, and other localized shallow-water areas. Some species of these diatoms are also a key factor in the succession of plants and animals that culminates in a rich growth of fouling organisms on docks, boats, and other man-made structures. A number of studies have indicated that marine bacteria are usually the first life forms to settle and grow on new or freshly denuded underwater structures. Development of a diatom film quickly follows, and is in turn succeeded by more complex populations of larger plants and animals.

Anthophyta

Marine flowering plants are abundant in localized areas along some seashores and in backwater bays and sloughs. The sea grasses often live entirely submerged, whereas salt marsh plants and mangroves are seldom completely inundated by seawater. These plants represent a minor reinvasion of the marine environment by a few species of a predominantly terrestrial plant group—the flowering plants (division: Anthophyta).

Fourteen common genera, including about 45 species, of sea grasses are dispersed around coastal waters of the world. Many of these species also inhabit freshwater lakes and streams. Most are restricted to the tropics and subtropics. Three common genera in the United States are *Thalassia, Zostera,* and *Phyllospadix. Thalassia* (fig. 5.3*a*), or turtle grass, is common in quiet waters along most of the Gulf Coast from Florida to Texas. Eelgrass, *Zostera marina* (fig. 5.3*b*), is widely distributed along both the Atlantic and Pacific Coasts of North America. *Zostera* normally inhabits quiet shallow waters but is occasionally found as deep as 50 m. Less widespread in distribution is the surf grass, *Phyllospadix* (fig. 5.3*c*), which is found on either side of the North Pacific. Surf grass inhabits the lower intertidal and shallow subtidal rocks subjected to considerable wave and surge action.

Most sea grasses produce horizontal **rhizomes** that attach the plants in soft sediments or to rocks (fig. 5.3). From the buried rhizomes, many erect grasslike shoots develop to form thick green masses of vegetation. These plants are a staple food for many near-shore marine animals and migratory birds. Densely matted rhizomes and leaves also effectively trap and accumulate nutrients and organic debris to further enhance the living conditions of the area.

Many sea grasses reproduce vegetatively by sprouting additional vertical leaves from the lengthening horizontal rhizome. In addition, seeds are produced in incomplete flowers. The seeds of each type of sea grass are well suited to their environment. Eelgrass seeds simply drop into the mud and take root

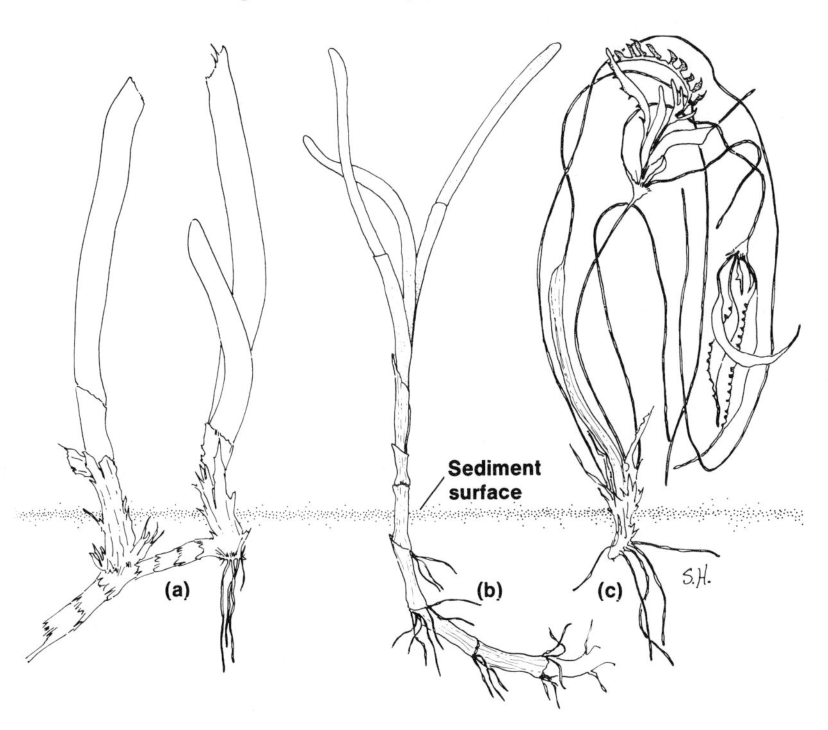

Fig. 5.3 Three common sea grasses: (*a*) turtle grass, *Thalassia;* (*b*) eelgrass, *Zostera;* and (*c*) surf grass, *Phyllospadix.* Adapted from Dawson 1966.

near the parent plant. In contrast, the fruits of *Thalassia* may float for long distances before releasing their seeds in the surf. The fruits surrounding individual seeds of *Phyllospadix* are equipped with projections lined with bristles. When shed into the surf, these bristles snag small branches of algae and the seeds germinate in place.

Several other species of flowering plants commonly exist partially submerged on bottom muds of quiet coastal salt marshes. These plants are usually situated so that their roots are periodically, but not constantly, exposed to tidal flooding. In essence, they are terrestrial plants that have evolved various degrees of tolerance to excess salts from sea spray and water. Some even have special structural adaptations for their semimarine existence. The cord grass, *Spartina,* for example, actively excretes excess salt through special two-celled salt glands on the leaves. Even so, several species of *Spartina* have higher experimental growth and survival rates in fresh water than in seawater. This strongly suggests that the salt marsh does not provide optimum growth conditions for *Spartina,* even though the salt marsh is its natural habitat. Competition with other land and freshwater plants may have forced *Spartina* and other salt-tolerant species into the restricted areas of the salt marshes.

The Seaweeds

By far the majority of the large, conspicuous forms of attached marine plants are the seaweeds. The term *seaweed* has sometimes been used in confusing ways to indicate a group of larger marine plants normally attached to the bottom in relatively shallow coastal waters. The term is used here in a more restrictive sense, referring only to macroscopic members of the plant divisions Chlorophyta (green algae), Phaeophyta (brown algae), and Rhodophyta (red algae). Table 5.1 includes a summary of some major characteristics of each division.

Seaweeds are extremely abundant in intertidal zones and commonly extend to depths of 30–40 m. In clear tropical seas, some forms of red algae thrive at depths as great as 200 m. Many seaweeds tolerate extreme surf action on exposed rocky intertidal outcrops as long as they are securely fixed to the solid substrate. Where they are abundant, the seaweeds greatly influence and modify existing environmental conditions for other types of shallow-water marine life by providing food, protection from waves, shade, and sometimes a substrate on which to attach.

Each group is characterized by specific combinations of photosynthetic pigments that are reflected in the common name of each division. The adaptive significance of these pigment variations is discussed in the following chapter. The bright, grass-green color characteristic of green algae is due to the predominance of chlorophyll over other accessory pigments. Green algae vary in structure from simple filaments (*Chaetomorpha,* fig. 5.4*a*) to flat sheets and diverse complex branching forms (*Codium,* fig. 5.4*b*). They are usually less than .5 m long, but one species of *Codium* from the Gulf of California occasionally grows to 8 m in length. When compared to brown and red algae, the Chlorophyta have fewer marine species. But their sheer numbers often compensate for their limited diversity.

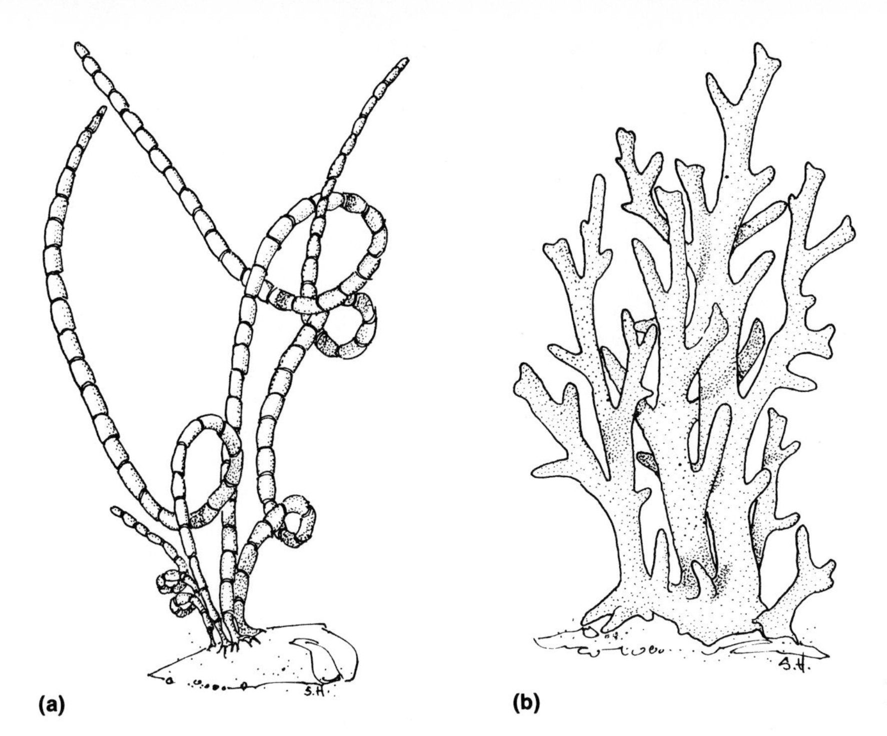

Fig. 5.4 Two marine forms of green algae: (*a*) *Chaetomorpha* and (*b*) *Codium.*

The chlorophyll pigments of the Phaeophyta sometimes can be seen as a greenish hue. But more often the green is partially masked by the golden xanthophyll pigments, especially **fucoxanthin,** which is characteristic of this division. This blend of green and brown pigments usually results in a drab, olive-green color. Many of the larger and more familiar algae of temperate seas belong to this division (fig. 5.5). A number of species are quite large, and are sometimes collectively referred to as **kelp.** In temperate and high latitudes, they usually dominate the marine benthic vegetation. Numerous smaller, less obvious brown algae also are common in temperate and cold waters, as well as in tropical areas.

Red algae, with red **phycoerythrin** and blue **phycocyanin** pigments as well as chlorophyll, exhibit a wide range of colors. Some are bright green and others are sometimes confused with brown algae. However, most red algae living below low tide vary from soft pinks to various shades of red. Red algae are as diverse in structure and habitat as they are in coloration. Seldom, though, do red algae exceed a meter in length, and none compare in size to the larger brown kelps.

Structural Features of Seaweeds

Seaweeds are not as complex as the flowering plants. They lack roots, flowers, seeds, and true leaves. Yet within these structural limitations seaweeds exhibit an unbridled diversity of shapes, sizes, and structural complexity. Nearly microscopic filaments of green and brown algae can be found growing side by side with encrusting forms of red algae and flat sheetlike members of all three divisions. Many of the larger members of all three seaweed divisions develop

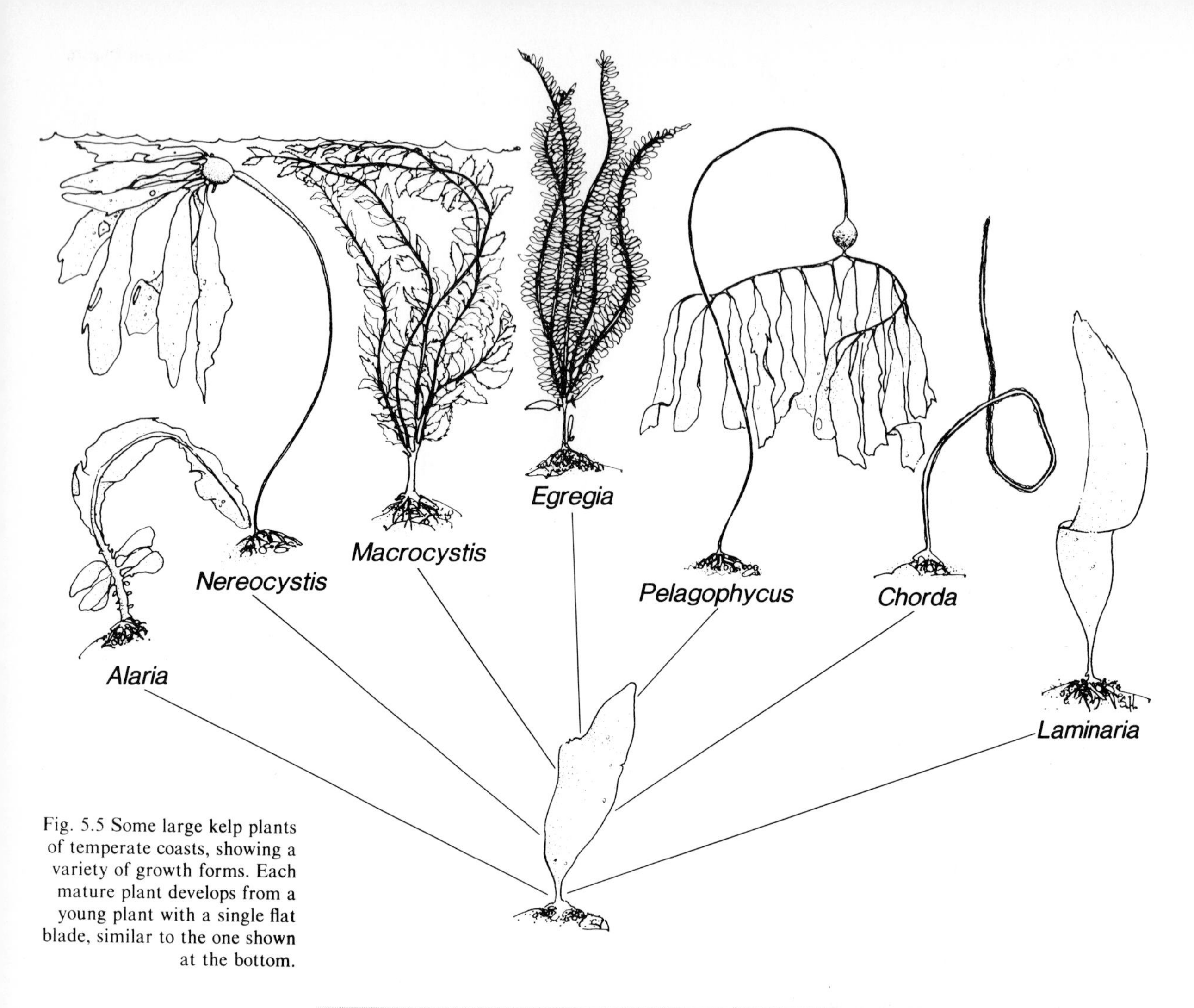

Fig. 5.5 Some large kelp plants of temperate coasts, showing a variety of growth forms. Each mature plant develops from a young plant with a single flat blade, similar to the one shown at the bottom.

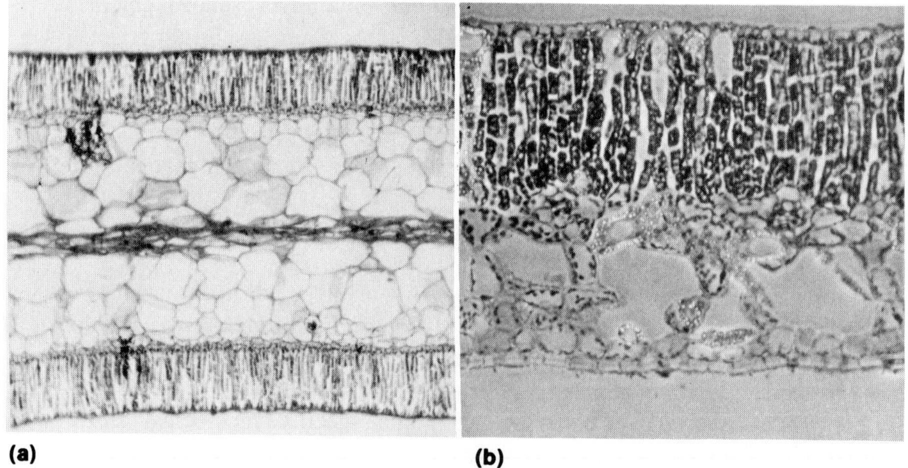

Fig. 5.6 Cross sections of (*a*) a blade of a typical marine alga, *Nereocystis,* and (*b*) a flowering plant leaf. Note the contrasting symmetry patterns of the two cross sections.

into mature plants with similar general forms, each consisting of a blade, stipe, and holdfast.

The Blade The flattened, usually broad, leafy structures of seaweeds are known as **blades.** Seaweed blades frequently achieve a complex level of branching and cellular arrangement. Large forms of brown algae produce distinctive blade shapes and patterns of blade arrangement (fig. 5.5); yet each begins as a young plant with a single, unbranched, flat blade nearly identical to other young kelp plants.

The blades house photosynthetically active cells, but photosynthesis commonly occurs in the stipes and holdfasts as well. In cross section (fig. 5.6) seaweed blades (*b*) are structurally quite unlike the leaves of terrestrial plants (*a*). The cells nearer the surface of the blade are capable of absorbing more light, and so are photosynthetically more active than those cells near the center of the blade. "Veins" of conductive tissue usually are lacking in the blades of seaweeds, as are distinctions between the upper and lower surfaces of the blade. The flexible blades usually droop in the water or float erect, so there is no permanent upper or lower surface. Each side of the seaweed blade is generally equally exposed to sunlight, nutrients, and water; and is therefore equally capable of conducting photosynthesis. Unlike seaweeds, the flowering plants (including sea grasses) exhibit an obvious asymmetry of leaf structure, with a dense concentration of photosynthetically active cells crowded near the upper surface (fig. 5.6*b*). Below the upper surface is a spongy layer of cells separated by large spaces to enhance the exchange of CO_2, which is often 100 times *less* concentrated in air than in seawater.

Pneumatocysts Several of the large kelp plants have gas-filled floats, or **pneumatocysts,** to buoy up the blades near the more abundant sunlight of the surface. Again, a large diversity in size and structure is noted. The largest pneumatocysts belong to *Pelagophycus,* the elkhorn kelp (fig. 5.5). Each elkhorn kelp plant is equipped with a single pneumatocyst, sometimes as large as a basketball, to support six–eight immense drooping blades, each of which may be 1–2 m wide and 7–10 m long.

Sargassum produces numerous small pneumatocysts (fig. 5.7). A few species of *Sargassum* lead a pelagic life afloat in the middle of the North

Fig. 5.7 A portion of *Sargassum,* with numerous small pneumatocysts.

Atlantic Ocean (the "Sargasso Sea"). In the Sargasso Sea, *Sargassum* seasonally produces large patches of floating plants that are the basis of a complex *Sargassum* community of crabs, fish, shrimp, and other animals uniquely adapted to living among the *Sargassum*. In the Sea of Japan, other species of attached intertidal *Sargassum* break off and also become free-floating for extended periods of time.

Pneumatocysts are filled with the gases most abundant in air: N_2, O_2, and CO_2. Surprisingly though, the pneumatocysts of some kelp plants also contain relatively large concentrations (over 2%) of carbon monoxide, CO. The source of the CO is not known, but is believed to be a by-product of metabolism.

The Stipe A flexible, stemlike **stipe** serves as a shock absorber between the wave-tossed upper parts of seaweeds and the securely anchored holdfast at the bottom. An excellent example is *Postelsia*, the sea palm (fig. 5.8) that grows attached to rocks only in the most exposed, surf-swept portions of the intertidal zone. Its hollow, resilient stipe is remarkably well suited for yielding to the waves without breaking.

The blades of some seaweeds grade into the holdfast without forming a distinct stipe. In others, the stipe is very conspicuous, and occasionally

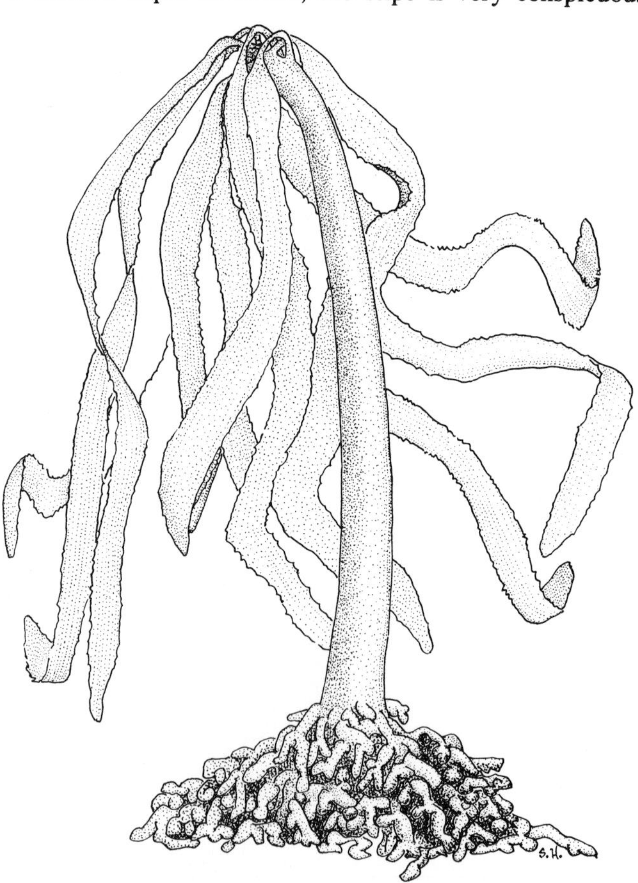

Fig. 5.8 The northern sea palm *Postelsia* (Phaeophyta) is equipped with a relatively large stipe and a massive holdfast.

extremely long. The single long stipes of *Nereocystis* and *Pelagophycus* (fig. 5.5) provide a kind of slack-line anchoring system, and commonly exceed 30 m in length. The complex multiple stipes of *Macrocystis* (also fig. 5.5) are often even longer.

Special cells within the stipes of *Macrocystis* and a limited number of other brown and red algal species form conductive elements that are strikingly similar in form to those present in stems of terrestrial plants. Radioactive tracer studies have shown that these cells definitely transport the products of photosynthesis from the blades to other parts of the plant. In smaller seaweeds with photosynthetic stipes and holdfasts, the necessity for rapid, efficient transport through the stipe is minimal.

The Holdfast **Holdfasts** of the larger marine algae often superficially resemble root systems of terrestrial plants. However, the basic function of the holdfast is to attach the plant to the bottom. Seldom does the holdfast absorb nutrients for the plant as true roots do. Holdfasts are well adapted for getting a grip on the substrate and resisting violent wave shock and the steady tug of tidal currents and wave surges. The holdfast of *Eisenia* (fig. 5.9), composed of many short, sturdy, rootlike **haptera,** illustrates one of several types found on solid rock.

Other holdfasts are better suited for loose substrates. The holdfast of *Macrocystis* has a large, diffuse mass of haptera to penetrate sandy bottoms and stabilize a mass of sediment for anchorage. *Penicillus* does the same thing on a much smaller scale, with many fine filaments embedded in sand or mud bottoms (fig. 5.10).

A variety of small red algae demonstrate special adaptations for attaching themselves to other marine plants. Figure 5.11 illustrates two common red algal epiphytes attached to strands of the surf grass, *Phyllospadix.* Using other marine plants as substrates for attachment is a common habit of many smaller forms of red algae.

Reproduction and Growth

Reproduction in seaweeds as well as in most other plants can be either sexual, involving the fusion of **gametes** (sperm and eggs), or simply a vegetative regrowth of new individuals (asexual reproduction). Some seaweeds reproduce either way, but a few are limited to vegetative reproduction only. The pelagic species of *Sargassum,* for instance, maintain their populations by an irregular vegetative growth followed by fragmentation. The dispersed fragments of *Sargassum* are capable of continued growth and regeneration. Sexual reproduction is lacking in the pelagic species of *Sargassum,* but not in the attached benthic forms.

Much of the structural variety observed in seaweeds is derived from complex patterns of sexual reproduction, which define the life cycles of seaweeds. For our purposes, these complex life cycles can be simplified to three fundamental patterns. The sexual reproduction examples of the first two types described here are not meant to cover the entire spectrum of seaweed life cycles, but to develop a basic pattern that underlies the complexity and variation involved in sexual reproduction of seaweeds.

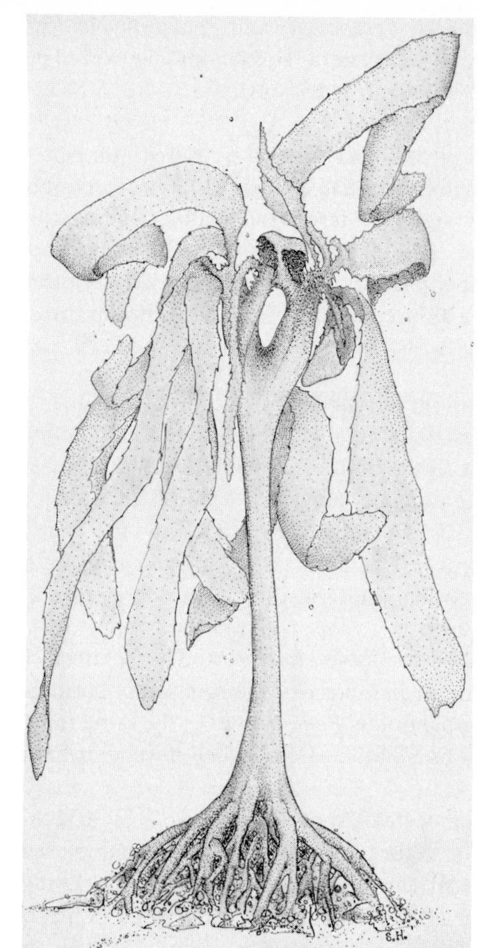

Fig. 5.9

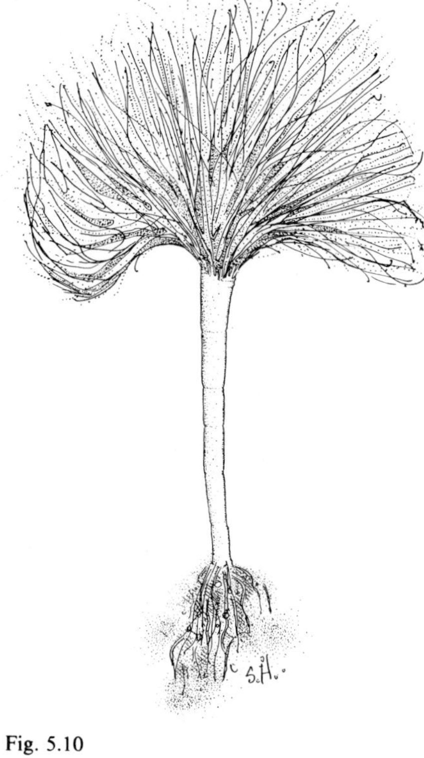

Fig. 5.10

Fig. 5.9 The southern sea palm *Eisenia*. (Phacophyta).

Fig. 5.10 *Penicillus* (Phaeophyta) with fine hairlike haptera for anchoring in loose sediments.

Fig. 5.11 Two red algal epiphytes: (*a*) *Smithora* and (*b*) *Chondria* attached to a strand of *Phyllospadix*.

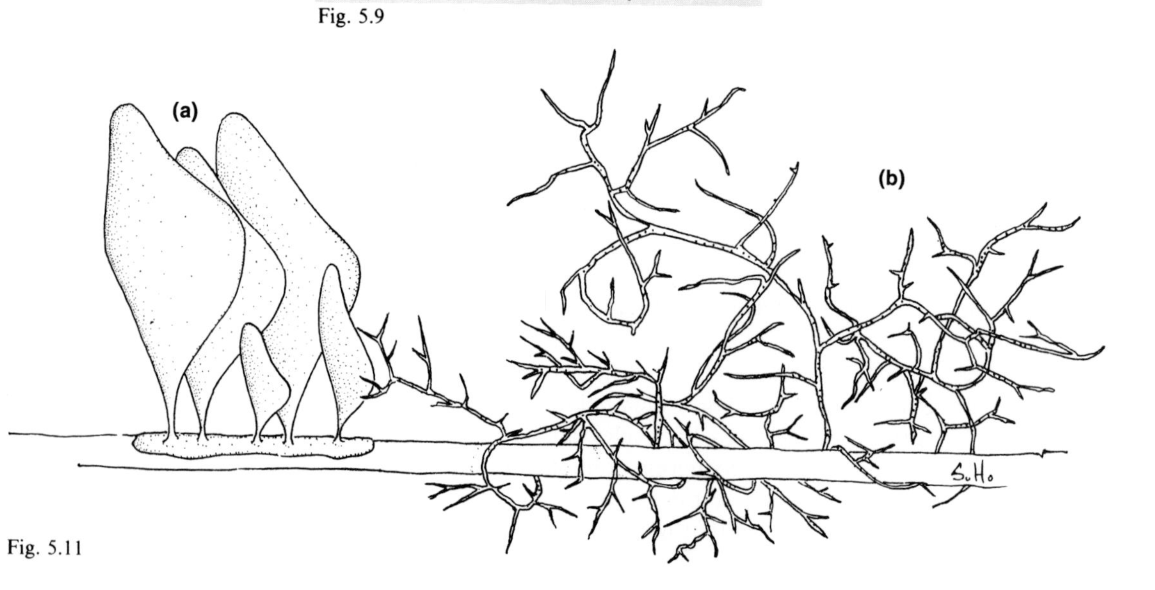

Fig. 5.11

In the life cycle of most of the larger seaweeds, an alternation of **sporophyte** and **gametophyte** generations occur. The green alga, *Ulva,* represents one of the simplest patterns of alternating generations (fig. 5.12). This basic life cycle, with minor modifications, is common to many brown and green algae. The cells of the macroscopic sporophyte are **diploid;** that is, each cell contains two of each type of chromosome characteristic of that species. Certain cells of the *Ulva* sporophyte undergo a special type of cellular division known as **meiosis** (or **reduction division**) to produce single-celled, flagellated **zoospores.** As a result of meiosis, these zoospores contain only one chromosome of each pair that was present in the diploid sporophyte, and are said to be **haploid.**

The zoospores are capable of limited swimming, then settle to the bottom. There they immediately germinate by a series of simple, or **mitotic,** cell divisions to produce a large multicellular, haploid gametophyte. Special cells of the gametophyte in turn produce flagellated, haploid gametes that are released into the water. When two gametes from different gametophytes meet, they fuse to produce a diploid, single-celled **zygote.** By repeated mitotic divisions, the zygote germinates and completes the cycle by producing a large sporophyte once again. The sporophyte and gametophyte generations are identical in appearance. The only difference between the two forms is the number of chromosomes in each cell; the diploid sporophyte has double the chromosomal complement of the haploid gametophyte cells.

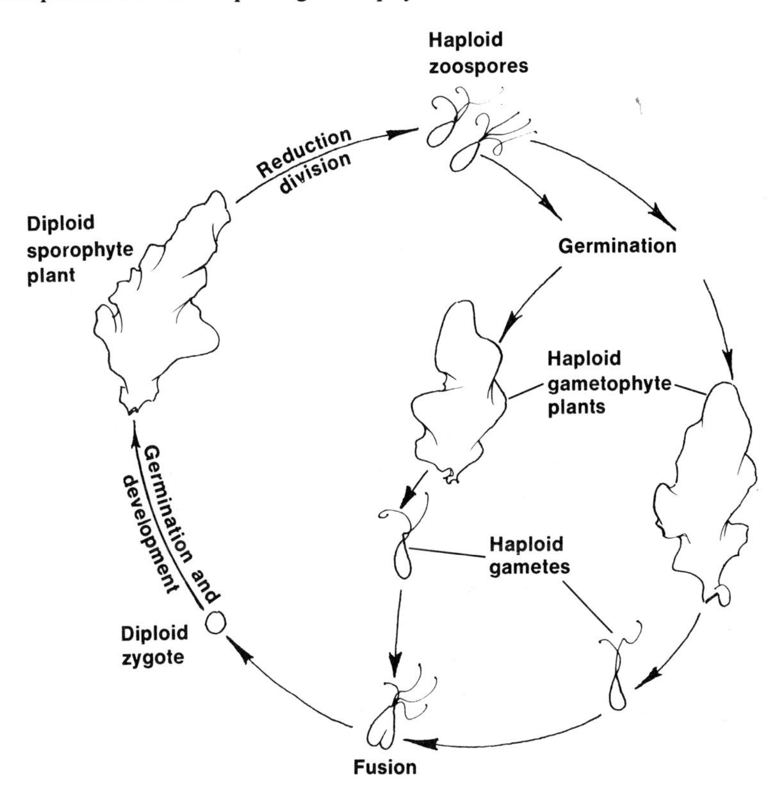

Fig. 5.12 The life cycle of the green alga *Ulva,* alternating between diploid sporophyte and haploid gametophyte generations. Adapted from Dawson 1966.

The life cycles of numerous other seaweeds are characterized by a suppression of either the gametophyte or the sporophyte stages. In the green alga *Codium* and the brown alga *Fucus* the multicellular haploid generation is completely absent. The only haploid stages are the gametes. In other large brown algae, the gametophyte stage is reduced. The life cycle of *Laminaria* is similar to most other large kelp plants and serves as an excellent generalized example of seaweeds with a massive sporophyte that alternates with a diminutive, often unnoticed, gametophyte (fig. 5.13). Specialized cells (called **sporangia**) on the blades of the diploid sporophyte undergo meiosis to produce several flagellated, microscopic zoospores. These haploid zoospores swim to the bottom and quickly attach themselves. They soon germinate into very small gametophytes composed of several cells. The gametophytes are of two types. The female gametophyte produces large, nonflagellated gametes, or eggs. The egg cells are fertilized in place on the female gametophyte by flagellated male gametes, the **antherozoids** (or sperm cells), produced by the male gametophyte. After fusion of the gametes, the resulting zygote germinates to form another large sporophyte.

The zoospores of green algae are characterized by four flagella; each gamete has two flagella. Either way, the flagella are equal in length and project from one end of the cell. The flagellated reproductive cells of brown algae always have two flagella of unequal lengths, and they insert on the sides of the cells rather than at the ends.

Red algae completely lack flagellated reproductive cells. This group is dependent on water currents to transport the male gametes to the female

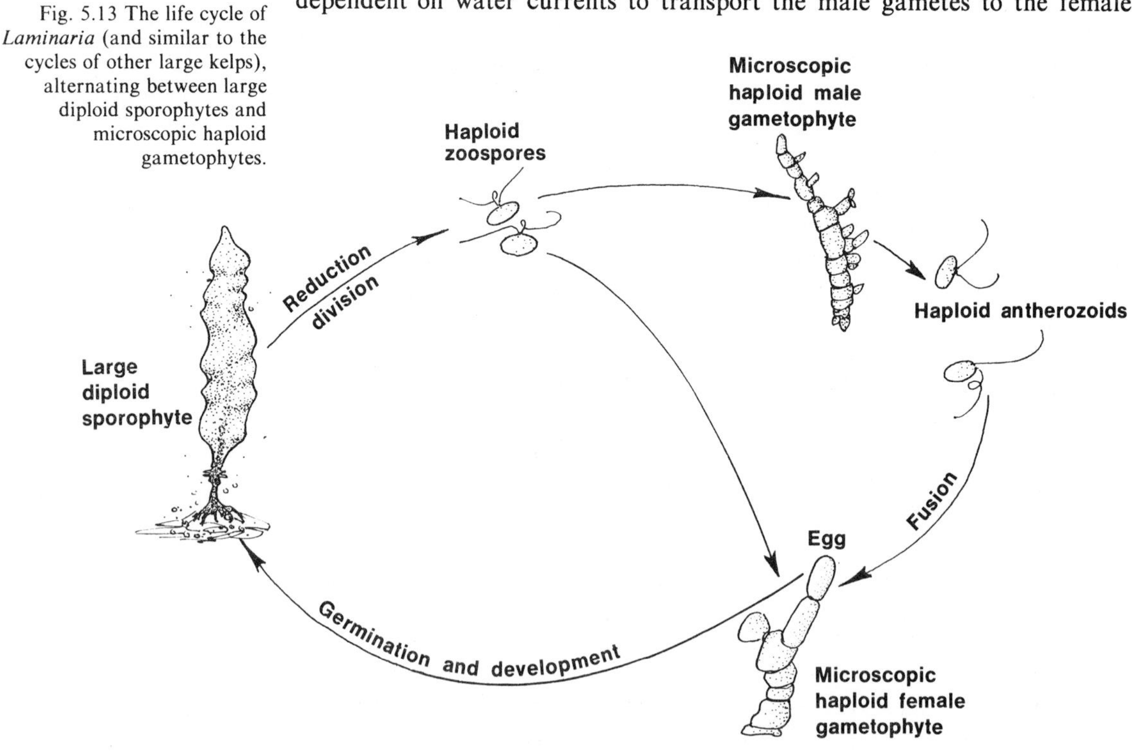

Fig. 5.13 The life cycle of *Laminaria* (and similar to the cycles of other large kelps), alternating between large diploid sporophytes and microscopic haploid gametophytes.

reproductive cells. The most common life cycle of red algae is the triphasic type, with three distinct generations. It is somewhat reminiscent of the reproductive cycle outlined for *Ulva* (fig. 5.12). A diploid sporophyte produces haploid spores that germinate into haploid gametophytes. Instead of producing a new sporophyte, however, the gametes from the gametophytes fuse and develop into a third phase unique to the red algae, the **carposporophyte.** The carposporophyte then produces **carpospores** that develop into sporophytes, and the cycle is completed.

The development of a large multicellular seaweed from a single microscopic cell is essentially a process of repeated mitotic cell divisions. Subsequent growth and differentiation of these cells produces a complex plant with many types of cells, each specialized for particular functions. Once the plant is developed, additional cell division and growth does occur; for instance, to replace tissue lost to animal grazing or wave erosion. However, such cell division is commonly restricted to a few specific sites within the plant that contain **meristematic** tissue with a capacity for further cell division. These meristems frequently occur at the upper growing tip of the plant. In kelp plants and some other seaweeds, additional meristems situated in the upper and lower portions of the stipe provide for elongation of the stipe and blades (fig. 5.14). During periods of rapid growth in the spring months, the rate of stipe elongation in *Nereocystis, Pelagophycus,* and *Macrocystis* often exceeds 30 cm per day.

Fig. 5.14 An idealized large brown alga illustrating the meristematic regions (indicated by arrows) of rapid cell division and growth.

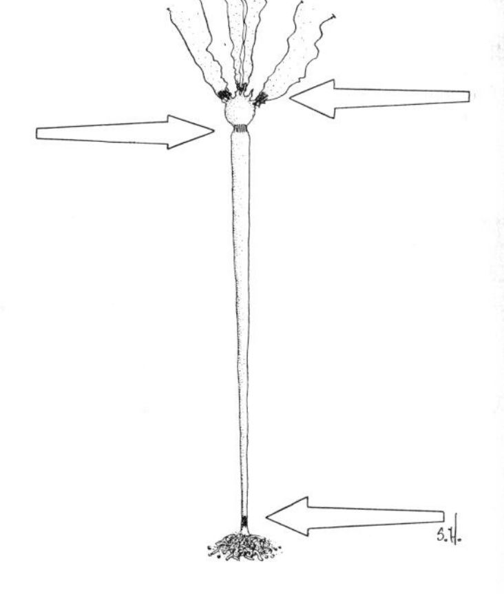

The meristematic activity of a cell layer at or near the surface of some kelp stipes provides lateral growth to increase the thickness of the stipe. The stipes of a few perennial species of kelp, including *Pterygophora* and *Laminaria,* retain evidence of this secondary lateral growth as concentric rings that superficially resemble the annual growth rings of trees.

Geographical Distribution

An interplay of a multitude of physical, chemical, and biological variables influences and controls the distribution of marine plants on a local scale. For instance, on an exposed rock in the lower intertidal zone on the Oregon coast, *Postelsia* may thrive; but 10 m away the conditions of light, temperature, nutrients, tides, surf action, and substrate may be such that *Postelsia* cannot survive. Yet on an ocean-wide scale, relatively few factors seem to control the presence or absence of major groups of seaweeds. Significant among these are water and air temperature, tidal amplitude, and the quality and quantity of light.

With these factors in mind, a few generalizations can be made concerning the geographical distribution of benthic plants. In marked contrast to the impoverished seaweed flora of the Red Sea, the tropical western coast of Africa, and the western side of Central America, seaweeds thrive in abundant profusion along the coasts of southern Australia and South Africa, on both sides of the North Pacific, and in the Mediterranean Sea. The West Coast of the United States is somewhat richer in seaweed diversity than the East Coast. From Cape Code northward, the East Coast is populated with typically subarctic seaweeds. South of Cape Cod, the effects of the warm Gulf Stream become more and more evident, until a completely tropical flora is encountered in southern Florida.

The red algae are not rare in cold water regions, but are more plentiful in the tropics and subtropics. **Coralline** or calcareous forms of red algae, characterized by extensive deposits of $CaCO_3$ within their cell walls, (fig. 5.15*a*) are even more abundant and conspicuous in the tropics. The use of calcium carbonate as a skeletal component by warm water marine algae is apparently related to the decreased solubility of $CaCO_3$ in water at higher temperatures. In the tropics plants expend less energy to extract $CaCO_3$ from the water. Here the coralline algae are extremely important in the formation and maintenance of coral reefs. Encrusting coralline algae grow over coral rubble, cementing and binding it into a mass that can resist the pounding of heavy surf. Coralline algae also contribute substantial amounts of $CaCO_3$ to coral reefs. In fact, some Indian Ocean "coral" reefs completely lack coral animals and are entirely constructed and maintained by coralline algae. The few calcareous forms of green algae that exist (fig. 5.15*b*) are also limited to warm water and play a large role in the production of $CaCO_3$ on some coral reefs.

Fig. 5.15 Two types of calcareous algae: (*a*) *Bossiella* (Rhodophyta) and (*b*) *Halimeda* (Chlorophyta).

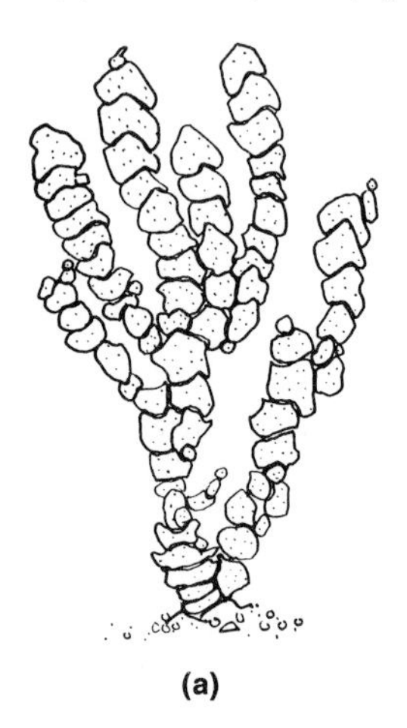

(a)

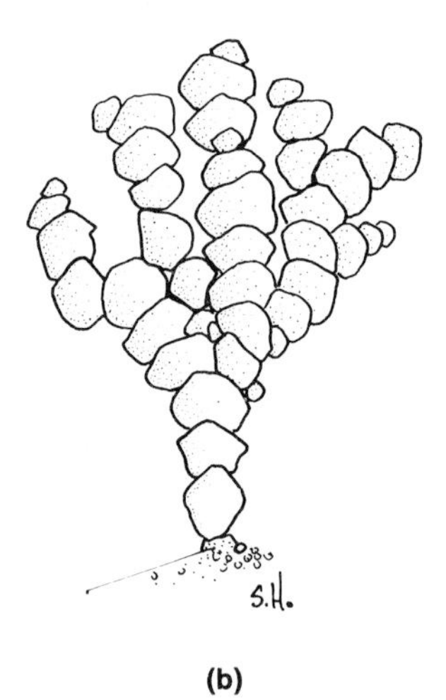

(b)

The brown algae are a temperate-to-cold-water group, with few tropical representatives. Seldom are extensive kelp beds found nearer to the equator than 30° N or 30° S latitude. The large kelps are especially abundant in the North Pacific. Cord grass and other grassy salt marsh plants are also generally found outside warm tropical or subtropical regions. In similar protected mud-bottom habitats between 30° N and 30° S latitudes, salt marshes give way to extensive and impenetrable thickets of shrubby mangroves (fig. 5.16).

Fig. 5.16 The dense thickets of mangrove trees are confined to shallow, protected tropical coastlines.

Phytoplankton

The most obvious plant members of the plankton community are the Pyrrophyta and the golden-brown Chrysophyta, with minor contributions from the green and blue-green algae (Chlorophyta and Cyanophyta). The planktonic members of these groups are microscopic and live suspended in the water. Although they are small, these plants account for most of the primary production in the marine environment.

Chrysophyta

The marine members of this division are single-celled plants. Like all other eukaryotic plants, their primary photosynthetic pigment is chlorophyll *a*. In addition, members of this division have accessory chlorophyll *c* and golden or yellow-brown **xanthophyll** pigments. Most have mineralized cell walls or internal skeletons of silica or calcium carbonate. Some species possess flagella for motility, but like other planktonic organisms, can do very little to counter horizontal transport by water currents. This division consists of two classes: the Chrysophyseae and the Bacillariophyseae.

The Chrysophyseae are found predominantly in fresh water. However, two groups, the **coccolithophores** and **silicoflagellates**, are relatively abundant in some marine areas. They are not well known because of their very small size. Most marine coccolithophores and silicoflagellates are classed as **nannoplankton,** with cell sizes smaller than the 60 μm mesh opening of a fine-mesh silk plankton net. As a result, **net plankton** collections do not contain representative members of these smaller forms.

Coccolithophores are single-celled plants with numerous small calcareous plates, or **coccoliths,** imbedded in their cell walls (fig. 5.17). Coccoliths

Fig. 5.17 Scanning electron micrograph of a coccolithophore, *Coccolithus huxleyi,* with a dense covering of coccoliths (× 4,500). Note the isolated coccoliths at lower left. Courtesy Elizabeth Venrick, Scripps Institution of Oceanography.

have been studied and described from seafloor sediments, but it was not until 1898 that the algal cells producing them were discovered. It has been suggested that coccoliths may function to reflect much of the ambient light in clear tropical waters, permitting these organisms to thrive in areas of very high light intensity. Coccolithophores are found in all warm and temperate seas. In these regions, they may account for a substantial portion of the total primary productivity. In the Sargasso Sea, for instance, a single species, *Coccolithus huxleyi* seems to be responsible for most of the photosynthesis there. However, their photosynthetic role in the total marine ecosystem is not yet well defined.

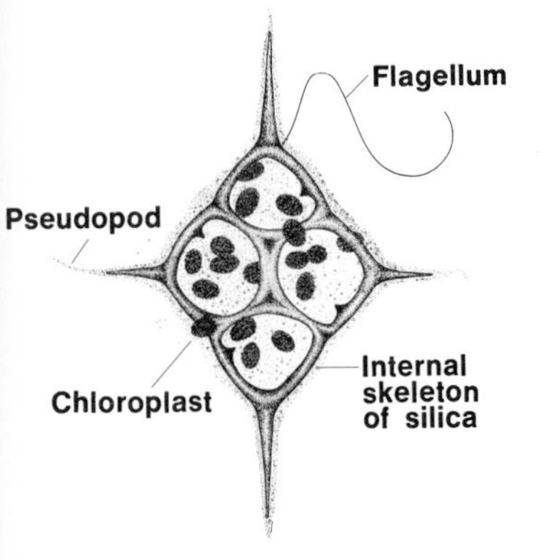

Fig. 5.18 A silicoflagellate, *Dictyocha.*

The silicoflagellates, like the coccolithophores, were first recognized and identified from their fossil skeletons in marine sediments. Silicoflagellates have internal, and often ornate, skeletons composed of silica. They have one or two flagella and many small chloroplasts (fig. 5.18). The significance of silicoflagellates as marine primary producers has not been evaluated, but their contribution is thought to be small.

The most obvious and often the most abundant members of the phytoplankton are the **diatoms** (class: Bacillariophyseae). These plants are unicellular, but may occur in chains or other loose aggregates of cells. Cell sizes range from less than 15 μm in length to the giants of the diatom world, which approach 1 mm. Most diatoms are between 50 and 500 μm in size. Diatoms have a cell wall, or **frustule,** composed of pectin with large amounts (up to 95%) of silica. The frustule actually consists of two closely fitting halves, the **epitheca** and a slightly smaller **hypotheca** (fig. 5.19). The cytoplasm of the cell is located just inside the frustule and surrounds one or more vacuoles. Planktonic diatoms usually have many small chloroplasts scattered throughout the cytoplasm, but in low light intensities the chloroplasts may become aggregated near the exposed cell ends.

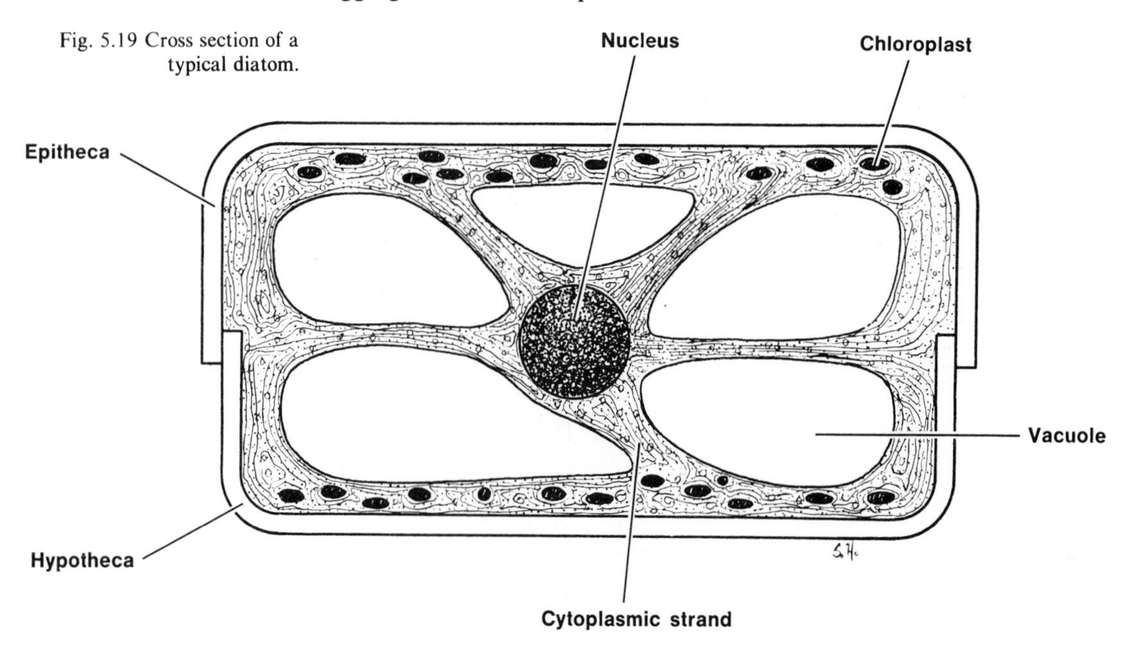

Fig. 5.19 Cross section of a typical diatom.

Diatoms exist in an immense variety of shapes (fig. 5.20) derived from two basic patterns of cell shape. The frustules of most planktonic species appear radially symmetrical from an end view. Circular, triangular, and modified square shapes are common. These are known as **centric** diatoms. Other diatoms, especially benthic forms, display varying types of bilateral symmetry and are termed **pennate** diatoms. Only the pennates are capable of locomotion. The mechanism for locomotion is not fully understood, but is believed to involve a wavelike motion on the cytoplasmic surface that extends through a groove (the **raphe**) in the frustule. This flowing motion is accomplished only when the diatom is in contact with another surface. As one might anticipate, diatoms capable of locomotion are generally restricted to shallow water sediments or to the surfaces of larger plants and animals.

Fig. 5.20 A variety of centric and pennate diatoms arranged in a striking geometric pattern.

The silicate frustules of diatoms are partially perforated by large pores arranged irregularly or in striking geometric patterns (fig. 5.21*a*). Each large pore penetrates a structural unit of the cell wall, usually hexagonal in shape, called the **areolus** (fig. 5.21*b*). The large outer pore connects with fine inner pores to facilitate water, nutrient, and waste exchange between the diatom's cytoplasm and the external environment.

Diatoms and most other unicellular plants and animals reproduce by simple cell division. An individual parent cell divides in half to produce two daughter cells (fig. 5.22), and each of these grows to repeat the process. Generally, no exchange of genetic material with other cells is involved. This method of reproduction can yield a remarkably large number of diatoms in a very short period of time. When conditions for growth are favorable, rates of cell division greater than once each day are not uncommon. By dividing every day, a single diatom requires less than three weeks to produce one million daughter cells. Populations of diatoms and other rapidly dividing unicellular plants thus have a special capacity to respond rapidly to improved growth conditions.

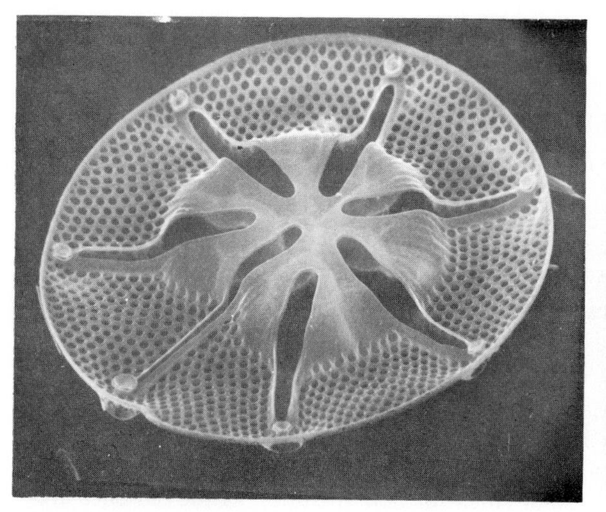

(a)

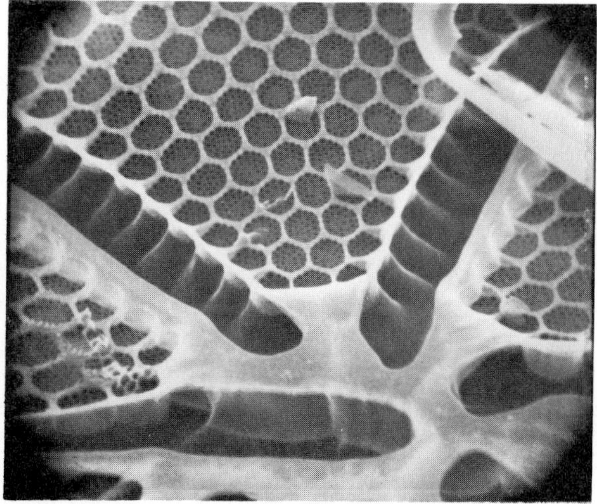

(b)

Fig. 5.21 Scanning electron micrographs of a centric diatom, *Asteromphalus heptacles*. (*a*) The entire cell (× 4,700); (*b*) a highly magnified portion of a similar cell, showing the character of perforations through the frustule. Courtesy Elizabeth Venrick, Scripps Institution of Oceanography.

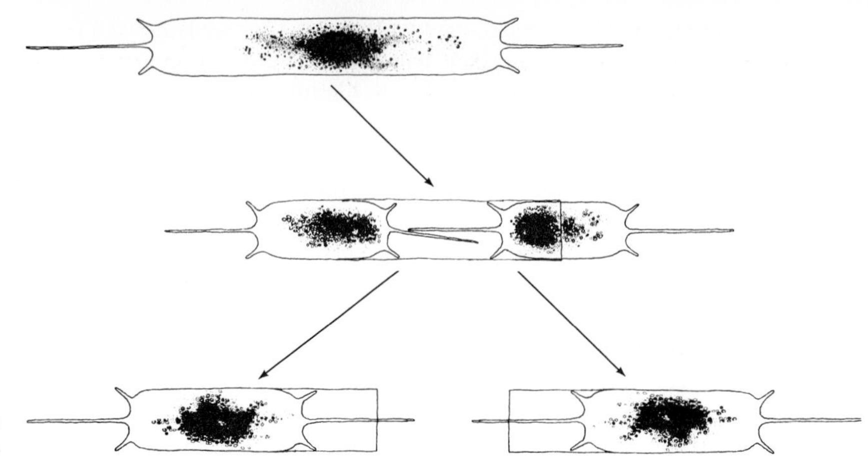

Fig. 5.22 Cell division in *Ditylum*, a centric diatom.

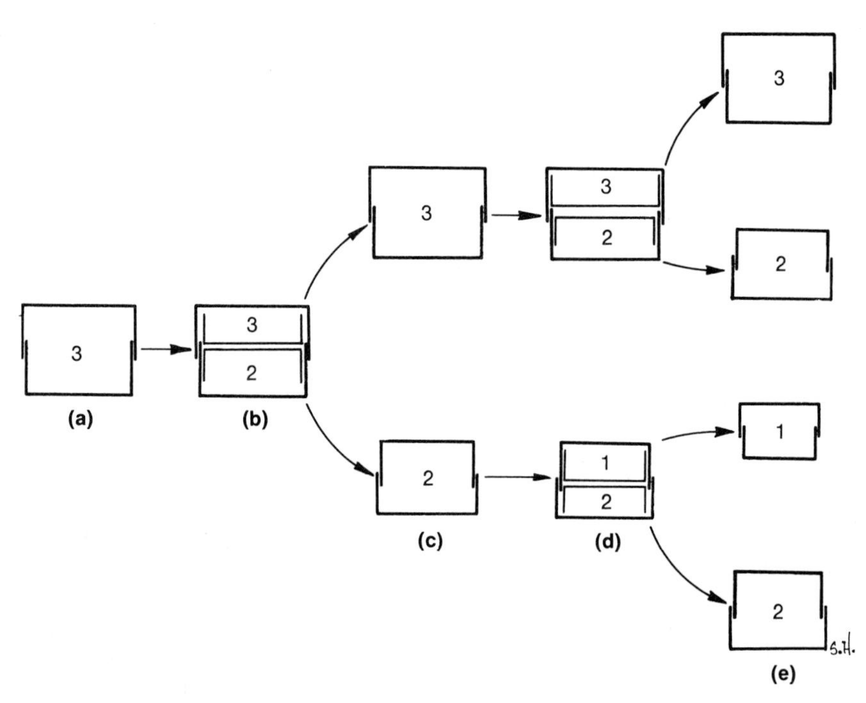

Fig. 5.23 Cell division and subsequent size reduction in diatoms. Numerals represent distinct cell sizes.

Restrictions of size and shape imposed upon diatoms by the rigid frustule create a peculiar problem of cellular reproduction (fig. 5.23). During diatom cell division, two new frustule halves are formed inside the original frustule (*b*). One is the same size as the hypotheca of the parent cell (*a*) and is destined to become the hypotheca of the larger daughter cell (*c*). The other frustule half becomes the new hypotheca for the other daughter cell. Each daughter cell receives its epitheca from the original frustule of the parent cell. The daughter cells grow (*c*) and repeat the process (*d, e*). This method of cell division is efficient in the use of silica for new frustules, as the old ones are not discarded. However, a definite decrease in the average cell size results

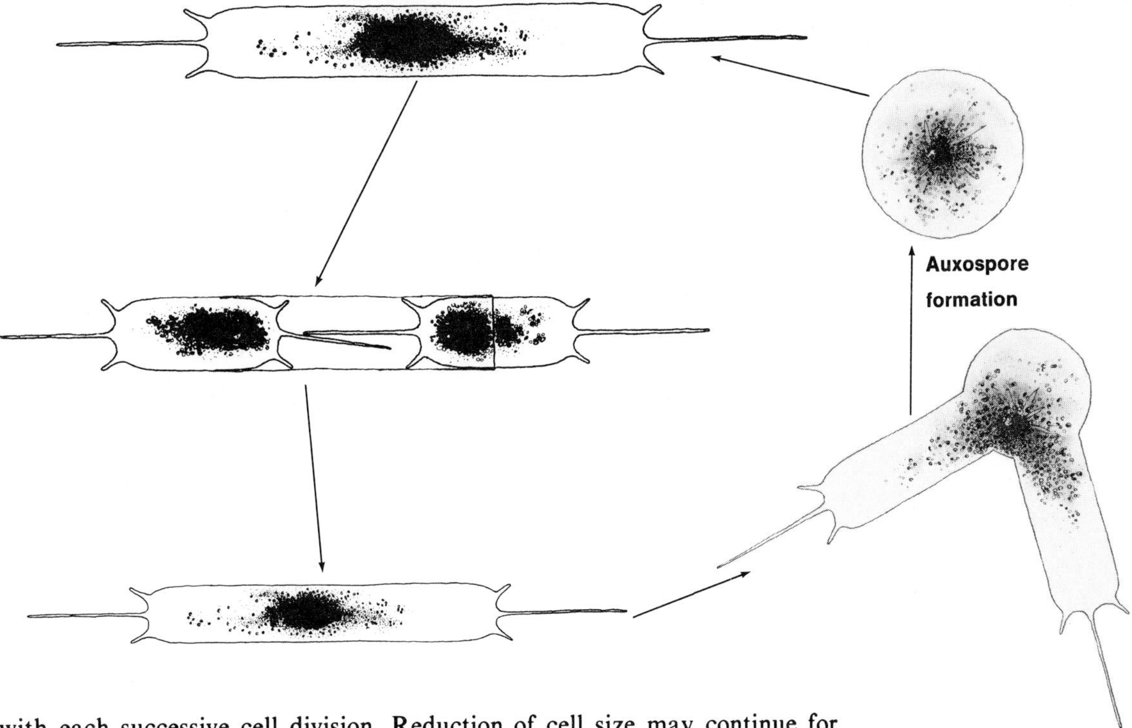

Fig. 5.24 Cell division of *Ditylum* showing reduction in cell size, auxospore formation, and eventual enlargement to its original size.

with each successive cell division. Reduction of cell size may continue for many months, eventually reaching a minimum of about 25% of the original cell size.

This size reduction is not observed in all natural diatom populations, indicating that continual readjustment of cell diameter occurs in some species. When the minimum cell size is reached, the small diatom then sheds its enclosing frustule (fig. 5.24), and the naked cell, known as an **auxospore,** flows out. The auxospore enlarges to the original cell size, forms a new frustule, and begins dividing again to repeat the entire sequence. Auxospores are also formed by the fusion of gametes in sexual reproduction.

The variety of planktonic diatom species that exist in temperate waters is impressive. Figures 5.25 and 5.28 illustrate a few of the more common diatoms of temperate waters.

Pyrrophyta

Certain characteristics of the division Pyrrophyta have convinced many taxonomists to include these organisms as part of the animal kingdom. Some species are not photosynthetic, but obtain energy from organic compounds dissolved in seawater or even by ingesting particulate bits of food. Most are motile, using a pair of flagella. Finally, some species (the unarmored forms) even lack cell walls. Despite these nonplant features, most marine Pyrrophyta (or **dinoflagellates**) are photosynthetic and must be functionally characterized as plants. Their share of the total marine plant production is significant; in warmer seas, it often surpasses that of diatoms.

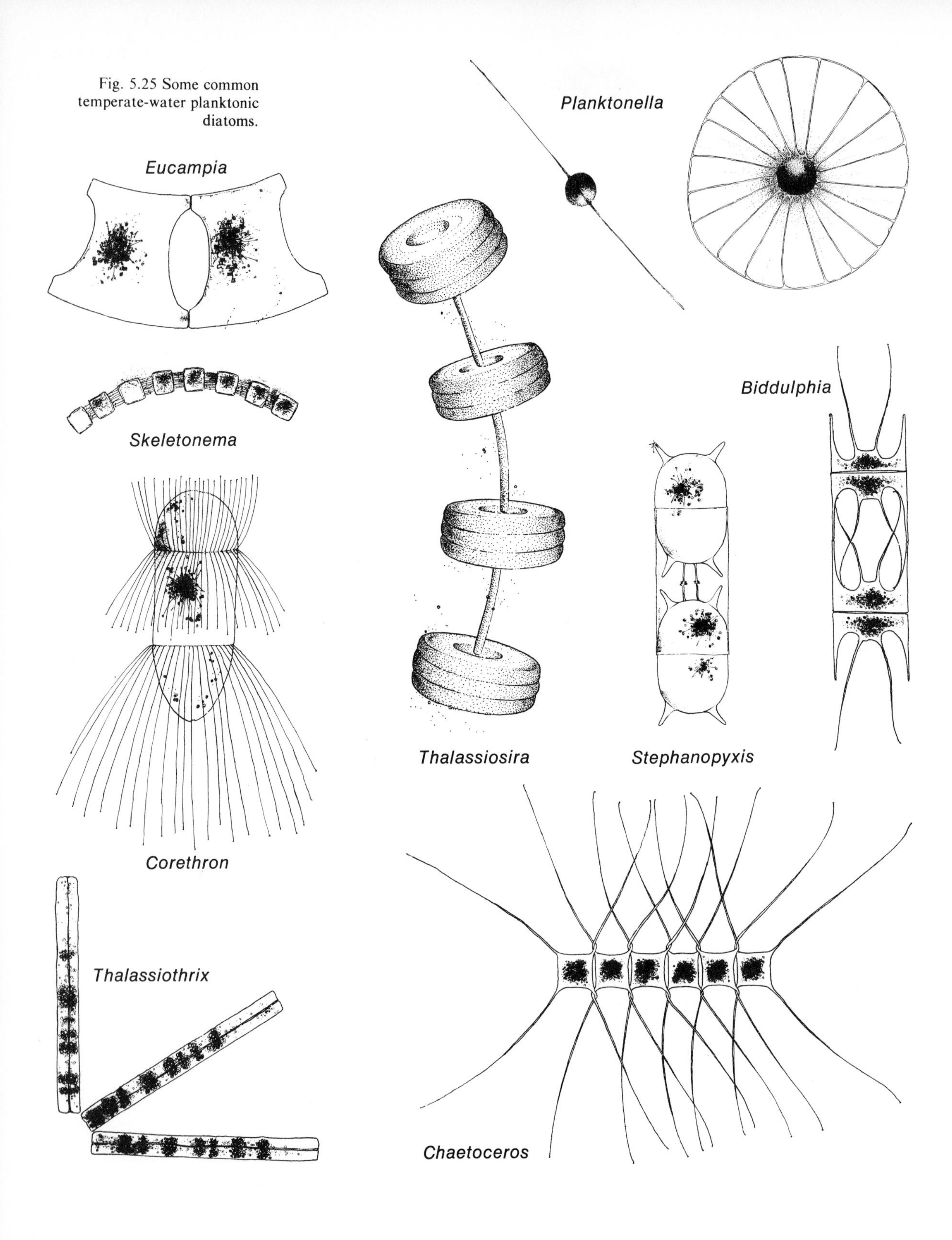

Fig. 5.25 Some common temperate-water planktonic diatoms.

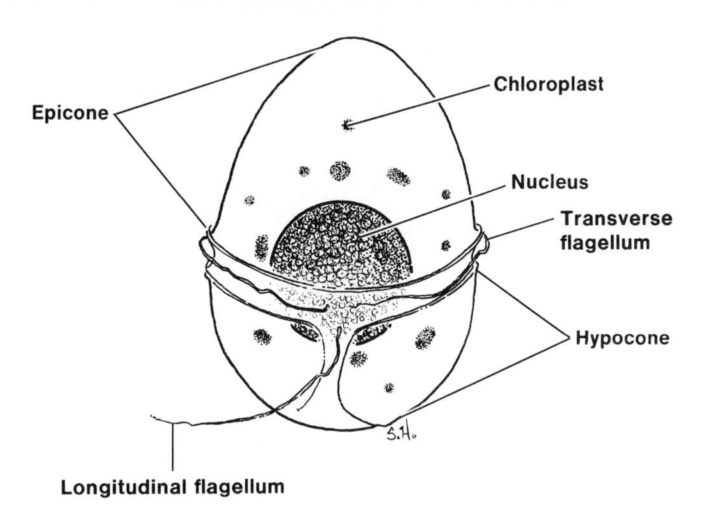

Fig. 5.26 Structural features in an idealized dinoflagellate.

Dinoflagellates are typically unicellular, with a large nucleus, two flagella (fig. 5.26), and several small chloroplasts containing photosynthetic pigments similar to those of diatoms. One broad, ribbonlike flagellum encircles the cell in a transverse groove that divides the cell into an anterior **epicone** and a posterior **hypocone.** The other, a longitudinal flagellum, projects forward and pulls the cell to provide forward motion. Cell sizes range from 25–500 μm. In armored forms, the cell wall consists of articulating cellulose plates arranged irregularly over the cell surface. The plates may be perforated by many pores. Spines, wings, horns, or other ornamentations may also decorate the cell wall. Figure 5.27 illustrates a few common marine dinoflagellates.

Dinoflagellates reproduce by longitudinal cell division. Each new daughter cell retains part of the old cell wall and quickly rebuilds the missing part after cell division. Consequently, a reduction in size does not occur. Sexual reproduction has been reported in a few species, but confirmation is needed. The rate of reproduction may approach that of diatoms. Dense concentrations of dinoflagellates are quickly produced under optimal growth conditions. Cell concentrations in these **blooms** are often so dense that they color the water red, brown, or green.

At night dense blooms of luminescent species (such as *Noctiluca* or *Ceratium*) become visible as a faint glow when disturbed by a ship's bow, a swimmer, or a wave breaking onshore. This luminescent glow is often highlighted by pinpoint flashes of larger crustaceans or ctenophores. This biological production of light, or **bioluminescence**, occurs in all major groups of marine animals, in some marine bacteria, and in several species of dinoflagellates. Light is produced when luciferin, a relatively simple organic compound, is oxidized in the presence of the enzyme luciferase. This reaction is a very efficient process, creating light entirely within the visible spectrum while producing almost no heat. In some species of *Gonyaulax,* light production follows a circadian rhythm, with maximum light output occurring just after midnight.

A dozen species of dinoflagellates are known to produce toxins that, in bloom condition known as **red tides,** cause serious mortality in other forms of marine life. Most dinoflagellate toxins interfere with nerve functions and result

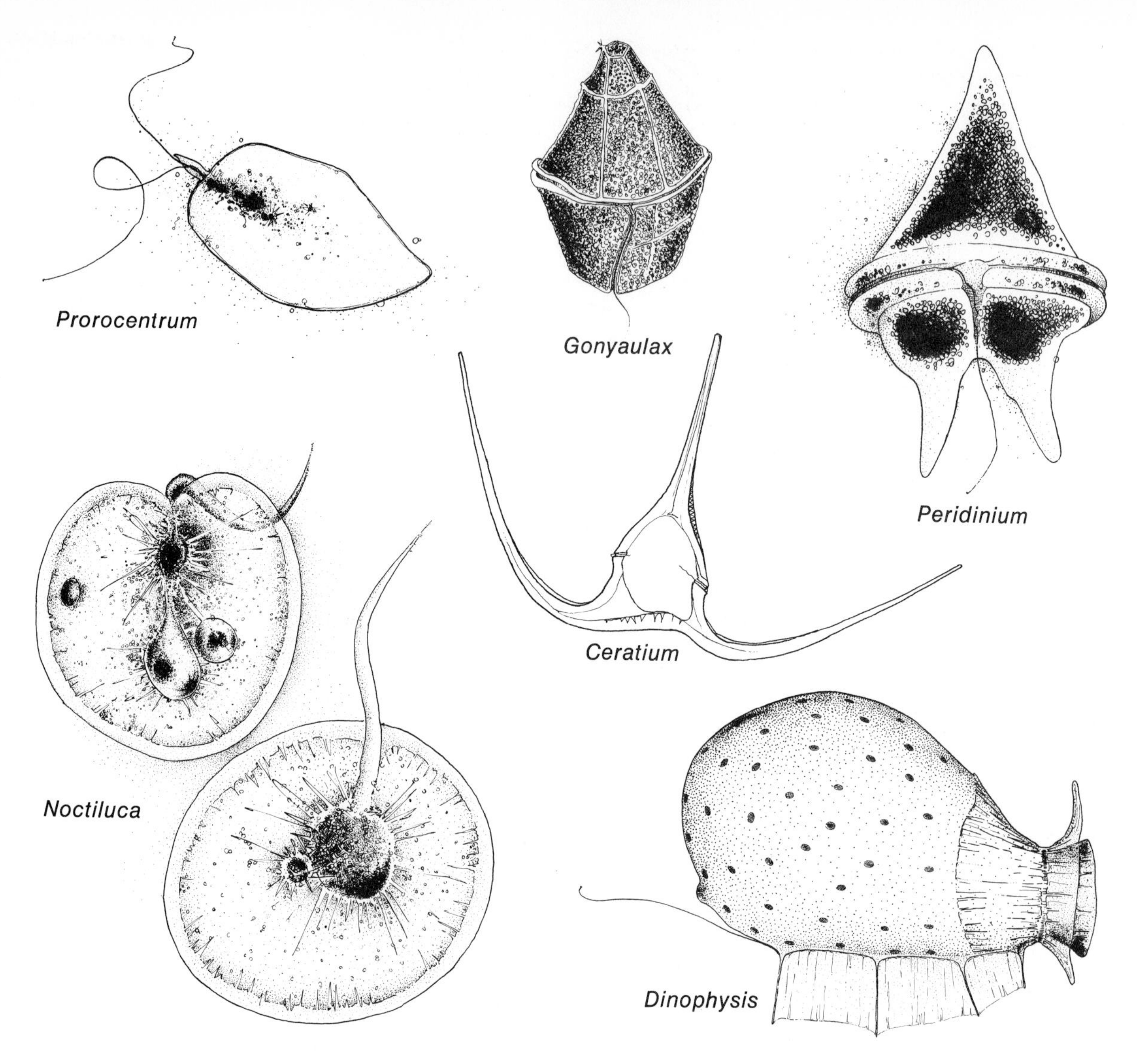

Fig. 5.27 Some common marine dinoflagellates.

in paralysis. Fish and other vertebrates seem especially susceptible to these toxins. At low dinoflagellate cell densities, the toxins may accumulate in animals (particularly shellfish) and render the flesh toxic. For instance, people who eat butter clams (*Saxadoma*) during the summer months occasionally experience paralytic shellfish poisoning from **saxitoxin.** However, this toxin is actually produced by the dinoflagellate *Gonyaulax* when it has been ingested and concentrated by *Saxadoma*. Saxitoxin is fifty times more lethal than two better-known plant toxins, curare and strychnine (table 5.2).

Recent studies have cast doubt on the long-held assumption that the blue-green alga *Lyngbya* is the source of the ciguatera toxin in tropical red snappers. *Lyngbya* does cause an occasional contact dermatitis known as "swimmer's itch" in Hawaii during summer months, but its involvement in

Table 5.2. *A Comparison of Lethal Dosages (for Mammals) of Some Marine Organisms. A Few Familiar Nonmarine Toxic Organisms (*) Are Included to Provide a More Complete Comparison.*

Source	Toxin	Minimum Lethal Dose (μg toxin/kg body wt)
*Bacteria *(Clostridium tetani)*	tetanus toxin	.0001
*Rattlesnake (*Crotalus* sp.)	(from bite)	.2
Butterclam *(Saxidoma giganteus)* and other shellfish; initially produced by dinoflagellates (*Gonyaulax* sp.)	saxitoxin	9
Stonefish *(Synanceja horrida)*	(from spines)	15
Yellow-bellied sea snake *(Pelamis platurus)*	(from bite)	40
Red snapper *(Lutjanus bohar)*	ciguatera	80
Eels (*Anguilla, Conger,* and *Muraena* sp.)	(from bite)	150
*Flowering plant	strychnine	500
California stingray *(Urolophus halleri)*	(from sting)	1,000

the production of ciguatera toxin has been seriously questioned. An as yet unidentified species of dinoflagellate seems a more likely candidate.

Other Phytoplankton

The occurrence of other plant divisions in the plankton is usually limited, but is certainly not uncommon. Some types of blue-green algae produce dense blooms in warm-water regions. The red phycobilin pigment in dense blooms of *Trichodesmium* is responsible for the color and the name of the Red Sea. *Trichodesmium* blooms are not toxic and should not be equated with the poisonous red tides caused by dinoflagellates.

Small unicellular planktonic forms of green algae apparently exist in some abundance because chlorophyll *b* (found only in green algae) is commonly found in filtered seawater samples. Yet few cells are found in the open sea, so their importance as primary producers is not known. Dense concentrations are common, however, in near-shore, high nutrient conditions, especially near areas contaminated with sea lion or bird excrement.

Special Adaptations for a Planktonic Existence

The evolutionary success of all phytoplankton hinges on their ability to obtain sufficient nutrients and light energy from the marine environment. Phytoplankton cells must be widely dispersed in their seawater medium to increase their utilization of dissolved nutrients. Yet they must congregate and remain in the relatively restricted photic zone to absorb sufficient sunlight. These opposing conditions for a successful planktonic existence have established some fundamental characteristics to which all phytoplankton, and indirectly, all other marine life have become adapted.

Size

One of the most characteristic features of all phytoplankton is their size. Almost without exception they are microscopic, which suggests that a strong selective advantage accompanies smallness in marine plants. Why? In contrast to land plants, phytoplankton are constantly bathed in a medium that not only provides nutrients and water, but also carries away waste products. Exchange of these materials in a fluid medium is accomplished by diffusion in either direction across the cell membrane of the plant.

The quantity of materials required from the external environment by the cell is dependent on a number of factors such as the rate of photosynthesis and growth. But if these and other variables are held constant, the basic material requirements of the cell are nearly proportional to the size, or more accurately, to the volume of the cell. However, the ability of the cell to satisfy its material requirements is a function, not of the volume, but of the extent of cell surface through which the materials can diffuse.

Let us examine a hypothetical phytoplankton cell to understand how a change in the size influences both its nutrient requirements and its capacity to satisfy those requirements. To simplify computations, we will begin with a cell shaped like a cube and measuring 1 mm on each side. This cell must absorb nutrients to sustain a volume of cell material equal to 1 mm^3. Our hypothetical cell has 6 mm^2 of surface area through which nutrient absorption can take place.

If the cell size is doubled to 2 mm, the surface area increases to 24 mm^2. However, the volume, which is a function of the size, has increased eightfold to 8 mm^3. This larger cell has an average of only 3 mm^2 of cell surface for each mm^3 of cell volume. By doubling the size of the cell, the surface area:volume ratio is reduced by half. Ultimately, a maximum size limit exists for all single-celled organisms. If that size is exceeded, the surface area of the cell will not be sufficient to sustain the enclosed volume of protoplasm.

Now, reverse the example and imagine a cell with sides of 0.5 mm. It has a surface area of 1.5 mm^2 and a volume of only 0.125 mm^3. Each mm^3 of protoplasm is supplied by 12 mm^2 of cell surface. Thus, as far as diffusive exchange across the cell membrane is concerned, a tremendous advantage belongs to those organisms that achieve high surface area:volume ratios. The results of these computations are summarized in table 5.3.

Reduction of phytoplankton cell size is a very effective and widespread means of achieving high surface area:volume ratios, but there are many others. Many cells assume more complex shapes that increase the surface area while

Table 5.3. *The Relationship Between Surface Area: Volume Ratios and Changing Size of a Cube-shaped Cell.*

Cell Size	Volume	Surface Area	Surface Area / Volume
1 unit	1 $unit^3$	6 $units^2$	6:1
2 units	8 $units^3$	24 $units^2$	3:1
0.5 units	.125 $units^3$	1.5 $units^2$	12:1

adding little or nothing to the volume. Cell shapes resembling ribbons, leaves, or long bars, and cells with bristles or spines are all common mechanisms to increase the amount of surface area relative to the volume. Cell vacuoles filled with seawater are common in diatoms (refer to fig. 5.19). These cells are large, but the actual volume of protoplasm requiring sustenance is only a fraction of the total volume of the cell.

Flotation

Phytoplankton, with their protoplasm and varying amounts of cell wall material, have an average density somewhat greater than that of seawater. Some of these cells eventually tend to sink out of the optimum light conditions of the photic zone. Lacking the means to actively swim upward to counter their general sinking tendency, some fraction of diatom populations sink slowly while cell numbers sufficient to continue reproducing the population are carried upward by vertical mixing of surface water.

Phytoplankton exhibit many adaptations to slow the sinking rate and prolong their trip through the photic zone. One of the most effective adaptations is simply to increase the frictional resistance to their passage through water by increasing the surface area:volume ratio. Reduced cell sizes accomplish this as do the production of horns, wings, or other cellular projections.

Other cells reduce their sinking rates by tracing zigzag or long spiral paths down through the water column. *Asterionella* and *Rhizosolenia*, shown in figure 5.28, demonstrate these adaptations. *Asterionella* forms long curved chains of cells that spiral slowly through the water as it sinks. *Eucampia, Chaetoceros* (fig. 5.25), and many other diatoms form similar twisted chains of cells. The asymmetrically pointed ends of *Rhizosolenia* create a "falling-leaf" pattern as it sinks; again to prolong its stay in the photic zone.

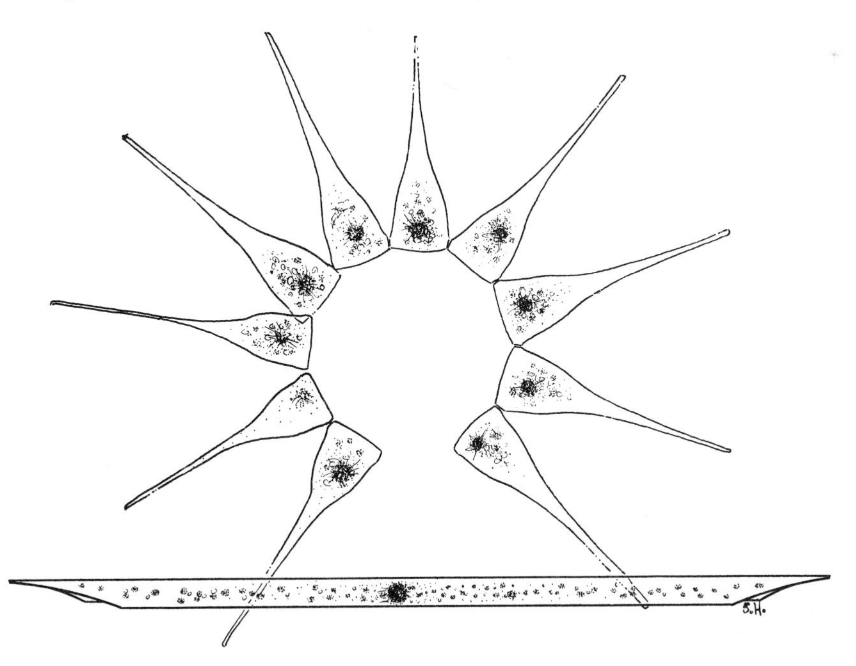

Fig. 5.28 A spiral chain of *Asterionella* (above) and a single elongate *Rhizosolenia* cell (below).

Adaptations for reducing the sinking rate are not limited to structural variations. Mechanisms that reduce the average cell density by "lightening the load" are also evident in some phytoplankton. Planktonic diatoms generally produce thinner and lighter frustules than do benthic diatoms. *Ditylum* is capable of excluding higher density ions (calcium, magnesium, and sulphate) in its cell fluid and replacing them with less dense ions. Other species may also do this, but *Ditylum* has been more thoroughly studied in this respect because of its larger size. Finally, the production and storage of low-density fats and oils may also be helpful to slow the rate of sinking.

Trichodesmium and some other planktonic blue-green algae have evolved sophisticated (for prokaryotic cells) internal gas-filled vesicles to provide flotation. The walls of these vesicles are constructed of small protein units, which can withstand outside water pressures experienced anywhere within the photic zone.

Adjustments to Unfavorable Environmental Conditions

The effects of locally worsening environmental conditions are minimal for species with an extensive geographical range. Plankton with little or no capability of large-scale horizontal propulsion must depend on the ocean's surface currents for dispersal. All of the adaptive features discussed above that extend the residence time of plankton in the horizontally moving surface currents also serve to increase their geographical distribution.

For protection, long spines and horns render phytoplankton less palatable to herbivorous grazers. There is some evidence to suggest that copepods, for instance, prefer nonspiny diatoms to spiny ones. Slimy gelatinous masses that sometimes surround large colonies of *Chaetoceros* and other diatoms also discourage herbivores.

The optimum growth period for phytoplankton in nonupwelling temperate and polar seas is seasonally restricted because of reduced sunlight in winter and limited nutrient supplies in summer. Faced with the prospect of weeks or even months with reduced photosynthesis, phytoplankton in these regions have a few alternatives. They can move, switch to other energy sources, or simply hang on until conditions improve. The first choice does not generally apply to diatoms; but motility, limited as it is, is extremely important to flagellated plant cells. A swim of merely one or two cell lengths is often sufficient to place the cell away from its excreted wastes and into an improved nutrient supply. Toxic dinoflagellates occasionally improve their own nutrient supply by poisoning their neighbors and thus accelerating the renewal of needed nutrients. These toxins may also serve to discourage predation by herbivores.

Species with alternate sources of energy have a crucial survival advantage. During poor growing conditions some dinoflagellates, and possibly even a few species of diatoms, can survive by absorbing dissolved organic compounds from seawater. Strictly photosynthetic plants rely on stored food reserves (fats, oils, and starch) for a temporary energy supply. When these give out some species still have other alternatives. Phytoplankton populations can enhance their survival in unfavorable light conditions by producing more

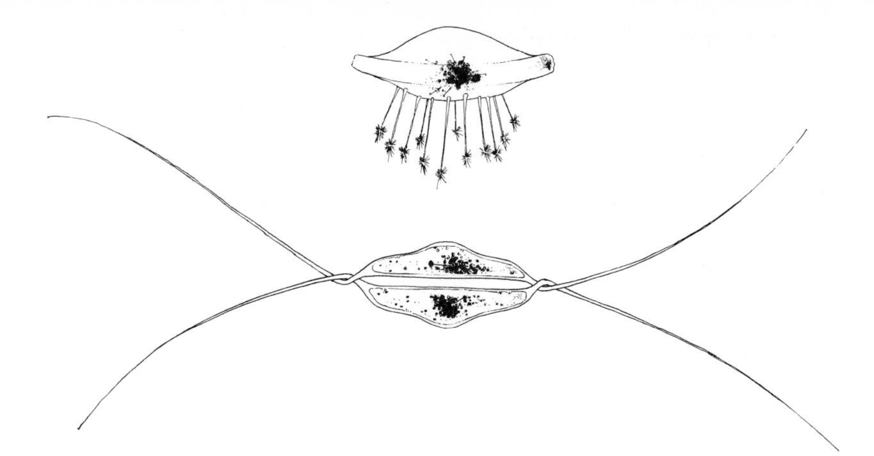

Fig. 5.29 Inactive resistant stages of two species of *Chaetoceros* (see fig. 5.25 for the active growth form).

chlorophyll and more photosynthetic enzymes in each cell. Finally, a variety of diatoms produce special stages with reduced metabolic activity and increased resistance to environmental extremes (fig. 5.29). A few species of dinoflagellates are also known to secrete gelatinous coats around themselves to form a resistant cell. With the return of improved growing conditions, these resistant stages germinate and commence photosynthesis and growth. At this point, the growing plant populations come under the regulatory influence of complex physical and biological factors to be considered in the next chapter.

Summary

Representatives of eleven plant divisions live in seawater. Of these, only five divisions are predominantly marine. Each group has a unique complement of photosynthetic pigments, storage products, cell wall characteristics, and habitats.

Benthic marine plants are subject to quite different environmental limitations than are phytoplankton. Most are attached to the sea bottom or to other organisms, and several achieve quite large sizes. Plants from nearly every division are included in this group, but the dominant groups are green algae (Chlorophyta), brown algae (Phaeophyta), red algae (Rhodophyta), and flowering plants (Anthophyta). Benthic plants are limited to the very narrow fringe around the periphery of the sea, and therefore produce less plant material than do phytoplankton.

The Chrysophyta (diatoms, coccolithophores, and silicoflagellates) and Pyrrophyta (dinoflagellates) comprise the major share of the phytoplankton. They are microscopic, usually unicellular, and generally exist dispersed throughout much of the photic zone. Members of both groups can reproduce extremely rapidly by asexual cell division. Their small size and complex cell shapes promote high surface area:volume ratios that accelerate exchange of nutrients and waste materials as well as increase the cells' frictional resistance to sinking.

Questions for Discussion

1. How can you account for the relatively small contribution that seaweeds are thought to make to the total marine plant production system?
2. Diatoms exhibit many adaptations that function to slow their sinking rate through the water. Why is it critical to diatoms to decrease their sinking rates?
3. What adaptations permit dinoflagellates to succeed in warm waters where diatoms do not thrive?
4. Why do thriving populations of phytoplankton tend to be dispersed throughout the photic zone rather than crowded together at the sea surface?
5. What adaptations to decrease sinking rates are found in marine phytoplankton?

Suggestions for Further Reading

Books

Dawson, E. Y. 1966. *Marine botany, an introduction.* New York: Holt, Rinehart & Winston.

Odum, E. P. 1971. *Ecology.* New York: Holt, Rinehart & Winston. Chapters 5 and 6.

Raymont, J. E. 1963. *Plankton and productivity in the oceans.* New York: Pergamon Press. Chapter 5.

Round, F. E. 1973. *The biology of algae.* New York: St. Martins Press.

Teal, J., and Teal, M. 1975. *The Sargasso Sea.* Boston: Little, Brown.

Articles

Dale, B., and Yentsch, C. M. 1978. Red tide and paralytic shellfish poisoning. *Oceanus* 21(summer): 41–49.

Echlin, P. 1966. The blue-green algae. *Scientific American,* June:74–81.

Foster, M. S. 1975. Algal succession in a *Macrocystis pyrifera* forest. *Marine Biology* 32:313–29.

Lipps, J. H. 1970. Plankton evolution. *Evolution* 24:1–22.

Mann, K. H., and Breen, P. A. 1972. The relation between lobster abundance, sea urchins, and kelp beds. *Journal of the Fisheries Research Board of Canada* 29:603–9.

Phillips, R. C. 1978. Sea grasses and the coastal environment. *Oceanus* 21(summer):30–40.

Pickett-Heaps, J. 1976. Cell division in eukaryotic algae. *Bioscience* 26:445–50.

Pomeroy, L. R. 1974. The ocean's food web, a changing paradigm. *Bioscience* 24:499–504.

Sorokin, Yu. I. 1971. Bacterial populations as components of oceanic ecosystems. *Marine Biology* 11:101–5.

Walsby, A. E. 1977. The gas vacuoles of blue-green algae. *Scientific American,* August:90–97.

Dinoflagellate, *Dinophysis,* completing cell division.

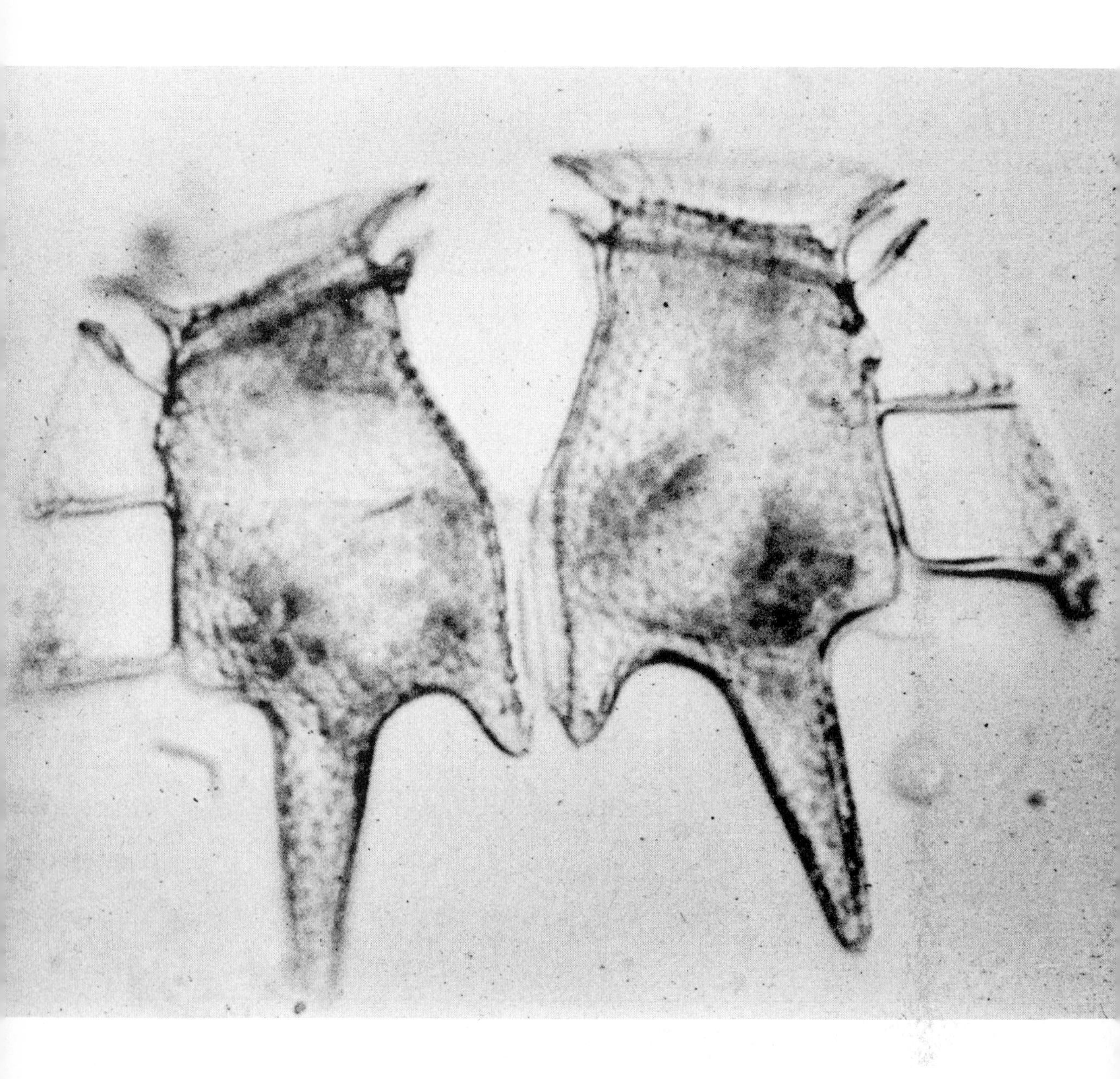

Primary Production in the Sea

6

Primary production is the biological process of creating high-energy organic material from CO_2, H_2O, and other nutrients, at the expense of solar energy. Primary production is a term often used interchangeably with plant production or photosynthesis. The organic material synthesized by the primary producers ultimately becomes transformed and transferred to other trophic levels of the ecosystem. The total amount of organic material produced in the sea by photosynthesis represents the **gross primary production** of the marine ecosystem. In nature, gross primary production is sometimes difficult to measure; yet it is nonetheless useful as a base of reference for understanding the production potential of the marine ecosystem.

A portion of the organic material produced by photosynthesis is utilized directly by the plants themselves for respiration. Any excess production is applied to growth, reproduction, and losses due to death, and is referred to as the **net primary production.** Net marine primary production represents the amount of organic material that is available to support the animals and decomposers of the sea. Rates of gross and net primary production are usually reported in units of grams of carbon fixed by photosynthesis under a square meter of sea surface per day or year ($gC/m^2/day$ or $gC/m^2/year$).

Attached benthic algae are restricted to a shallow, narrow zone around the continental fringes, but the phytoplankton are dispersed throughout the entire expanse of the ocean's photic zone. Thus, most of the primary production in the sea is accomplished by phytoplankton. The actual portion, though, is a current topic of debate. Although phytoplankton have been credited with as much as 98% of the total marine plant production, recent studies indicate that the photosynthetic contribution of benthic algae may have been seriously underestimated.

The following discussion of some global aspects of marine plant production focuses on production by phytoplankton, with less reference to the larger forms of attached algae.

Measurements of Primary Production

Theoretically, the net photosynthetic rate of a phytoplankton population can be estimated by measuring the rate of change of some chemical component of the photosynthetic reaction, such as the rate of O_2 production or CO_2 consumption by the phytoplankton.

For many years, the **light and dark bottle technique** has been used to study primary production in marine phytoplankton. With this method, measured changes in O_2 consumption and production are used to compute phytoplankton respiration and photosynthetic rates. In its simplest form, this is how it works. Seawater samples (including their natural phytoplankton populations) are collected from several depths within the photic zone of the study area. The samples from each depth are divided and placed into three bottles: a **light bottle (LB)** that is transparent to light, an opaque **dark bottle (DB)** covered with foil or black tape to exclude light, and an **initial bottle (IB).**

The O_2 concentrations of the water in the initial bottles are determined immediately to establish the initial conditions of dissolved oxygen in the light and dark bottles at each depth. Each pair of light and dark bottles are then lowered back to the depth at which they were collected. There, the phytoplankton cells within the bottles are allowed to incubate at normal conditions of temperature and (for the light bottle) light intensity (fig. 6.1). After a period of time (usually a few hours), the light and dark bottles are hauled to the surface and the O_2 concentration of the water in each bottle is quickly measured.

Deprived of light in the dark bottle, the phytoplankton are unable to photosynthesize, but still use O_2 in cellular respiration. The decrease of dissolved O_2 in the dark bottle (IB–DB) is a measure of that respiration. The O_2 produced by photosynthetically active cells in the light bottle (LB–IB) is an indicator of net primary production only; as some of the photosynthetic prod-

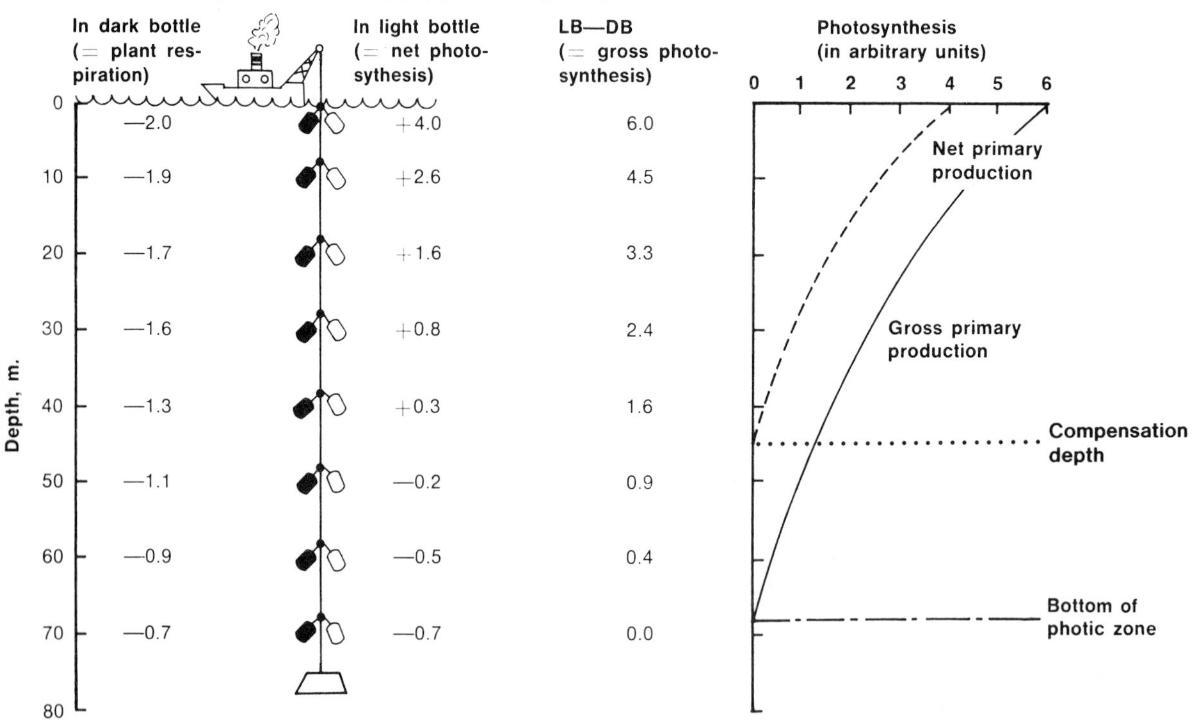

Fig. 6.1 The results of a hypothetical light and dark bottle experiment. Water samples from 10m depth increments are replaced at original depths in paired light and dark bottles. After a period of time, the bottles are retrieved and changes in O_2 are determined. DB values indicate O_2 decrease at each depth due to plant respiration without photosynthesis. LB values represent O_2 changes from photosynthesis and respiration (net primary production) in the light. The difference between the two values (LB-DB) is the gross primary production. With these values, net and gross primary production curves (at right) can be drawn to represent the variation in photosynthesis with depth.

ucts, including O_2, are quickly reused by the plants themselves. The gross primary production at any depth can be estimated by combining the net primary production (LB–IB) and plant respiration (IB–DB). Figure 6.1 illustrates some hypothetical results of a light and dark bottle productivity experiment.

The precision of the light bottle, dark bottle technique hinges on the validity of a few critical assumptions. First, it is assumed that respiratory O_2 consumption in the dark bottle is the same as that in the light bottle. This may be true at optimum or below optimum light conditions, but is usually not a correct assumption for phytoplankton in high light intensities. Changes in their general activity and physiological condition, as well as differential changes of phytoplankton population sizes in the light and dark bottles due to unequal rates of cell reproduction or death, might lead to further sources of error. Significant amounts of O_2 may also be consumed by zooplankton or bacteria included in the light or dark bottles.

Some of the problems inherent in productivity estimates based on O_2 changes in light and dark bottles are avoided by determining rates of CO_2 uptake instead. In the early 1950s, Steemann Nielsen first used a procedure that employed radioactive carbon (C^{14}) as a carbon tracer in photosynthesis. In the following decades, improved C^{14} measurements have become the preferred method for marine primary production studies.

In practice, the C^{14} procedure is similar to the O_2 evolution technique, but it is more sensitive when productivity is very low. Paired light and dark bottles are used. Each bottle is injected with a known quantity of bicarbonate containing the labeled C^{14}. After a period of incubation at the proper depth, the samples are recovered. The phytoplankton of each sample are collected on membrane filters and dried. The amount of radioactive carbon assimilated by the phytoplankton in the bottles is measured with a radioactivity counting device. By convention, dark bottle radioactivity is subtracted from light bottle radioactivity to correct for all nonphotosynthetic effects. Net primary production is then computed using an appropriate conversion factor.

In all photosynthetic plants, except photosynthetic bacteria, chlorophyll *a* is necessary to catalyze photosynthetic reactions. One might assume, then, that the gross primary production in a volume of seawater is proportional to the amount of chlorophyll *a* contained in the living phytoplankton of the water sample. Such a relationship between gross primary production and chlorophyll *a* concentrations has been established, but only in an approximate fashion.

Chlorophyll *a* concentration is a good indicator of the amount of plant material in a volume of seawater at any one time. This total amount of plant material is termed the **standing crop.** Standing crop sizes at any given moment are governed by a balance between crop increases (cell growth and division) and crop decreases (sinking and grazing). Most of the gross primary production of a healthy, actively growing phytoplankton population is not used in respiration, but instead contributes to the existing standing crop. In contrast, old populations, or healthy cells in poor growing conditions, use a large portion of their gross production in respiration; and net production declines. If a net loss occurs, the population will eventually disappear.

The standing crop of a healthy phytoplankton population measured on successive days may demonstrate little or no increase, suggesting that no net production occurred from one day to the next. A more likely explanation is that significant net production did occur, but it only replaced the portion of the crop lost to grazers and to sinking. Thus, the relationship between standing crop and productivity depends to a large degree on the **turnover rate** of newly created plant material.

The turnover rate of phytoplankton populations is extremely rapid. Many species of phytoplankton are capable of dividing once each day, and several of the smaller species divide even faster. The coccolithophore shown in figure 5.17, for instance, can undergo almost two divisions per day. Their populations are completely replaced, or turned over, twice each day, so comparatively little plant material exists in the water at any one time. High turnover rates also occur in benthic algae. Growth rate estimates of some kelp plants on the east coast of Canada indicate that the kelp blades resemble moving belts of plant tissue, growing at the base and eroding back at the tips. At any one time, the plant itself (the standing crop) represents as little as 10% of the total plant material produced during a year.

Short-term estimates of either primary production rates or standing crop sizes alone provide only a limited picture of the intensity and dynamics of phytoplankton production. However, if both plant productivity and standing crop size are measured simultaneously, a **productivity index** can be calculated:

$$\text{Productivity Index (P. I.)} = \frac{\text{primary production rate}}{\text{standing crop}}$$

Such an index, adjusted to a given light intensity, is more useful than either of its components as it provides a distinction between the production potentials of large, long established phytoplankton populations, and small, actively growing ones with high productivity characteristics. Unfortunately, the few P.I. values that have been reported are insufficient to formulate a global picture of the dynamics of phytoplankton production based on productivity indexes.

A more static, but still very useful summary of the annual rate of net phytoplankton production, based primarily on C^{14} productivity estimates, is presented in the final section of this chapter.

Some Factors That Affect Primary Production

The continued synthesis of organic material by marine phytoplankton depends on a set of interacting physical, chemical, and biological conditions. If nutrients, sunlight, space, and other parameters necessary for growth are unlimited, phytoplankton population sizes increase in an exponential fashion (fig. 6.2).

In nature, phytoplankton populations do not continue to grow unchecked as figure 6.2 suggests. Rather, their sizes are controlled either by their limits of tolerance to certain environmental factors, or by the availability of substances for which there is a minimum need. Any condition that exceeds the limits of tolerance, or does not satisfy the basic material needs of an organism,

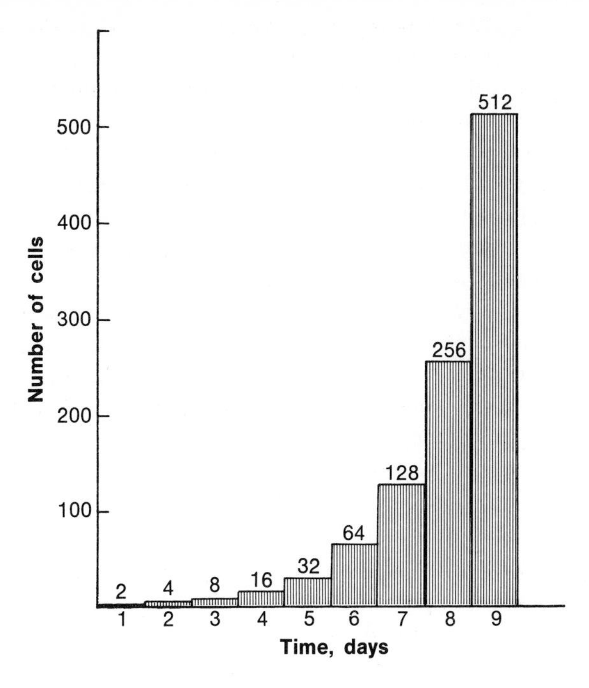

Fig. 6.2 Unlimited growth of a phytoplankton population, beginning with a single cell and dividing once a day.

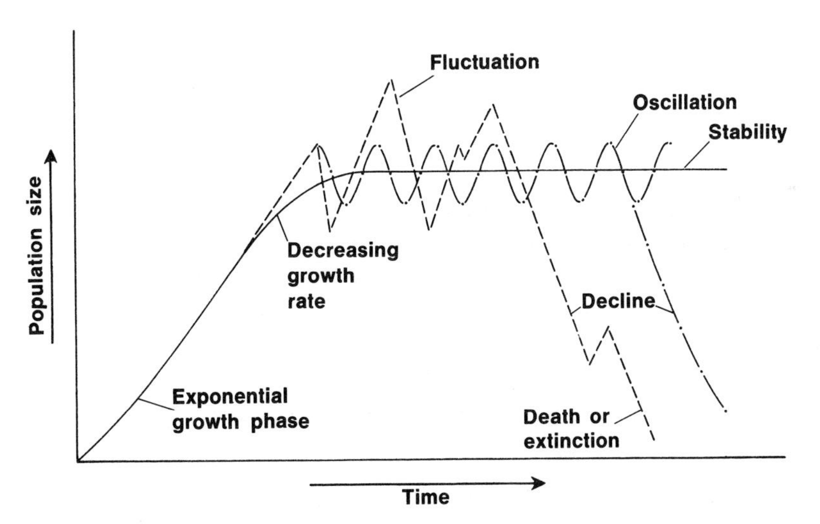

Fig. 6.3 Some common growth patterns exhibited by phytoplankton populations when subjected to one or more growth-limiting factors. The population may level off and stabilize, fluctuate wildly, or undergo periodic oscillations.

establishes a check on further population growth, and is said to be a **limiting factor.** Important limiting factors for phytoplankton are light, nutrient availability, and grazing by herbivores. Phytoplankton populations limited by one or a combination of these factors are forced to deviate from the exponential growth curve shown in figure 6.2. Some of the possible termination fates of a growth-limited population are portrayed in figure 6.3.

Light

The requirement for light imposes a fundamental limit on the distribution of all marine plants. To live, they must remain in the upper region of the ocean (the photic zone), where solar energy sufficient for photosynthesis will reach them. The depth of the photic zone is determined by the capacity of sunlight to penetrate seawater. This in turn is influenced by a variety of conditions: the atmospheric absorption of light, the angle between the sun and the sea surface, and water transparency.

The amount of energy reaching the sea surface depends on varying atmospheric conditions, such as dust, clouds, and gases that absorb, reflect, and scatter a portion of the incoming solar radiation. On an average day, about 65% of the incident radiation arriving at the outer edge of our atmosphere reaches the earth's surface. The magnitude of incoming solar radiation is reduced when the angle of the sun is low, as in winter, or at high latitudes.

A portion of the light that makes it through the atmosphere is reflected back out into space by the sea surface itself. Below the sea surface, still more light energy is lost. Dissolved substances, suspended sediments, and even plankton populations diminish the amount of light available for photosynthetic activity (fig. 6.4).

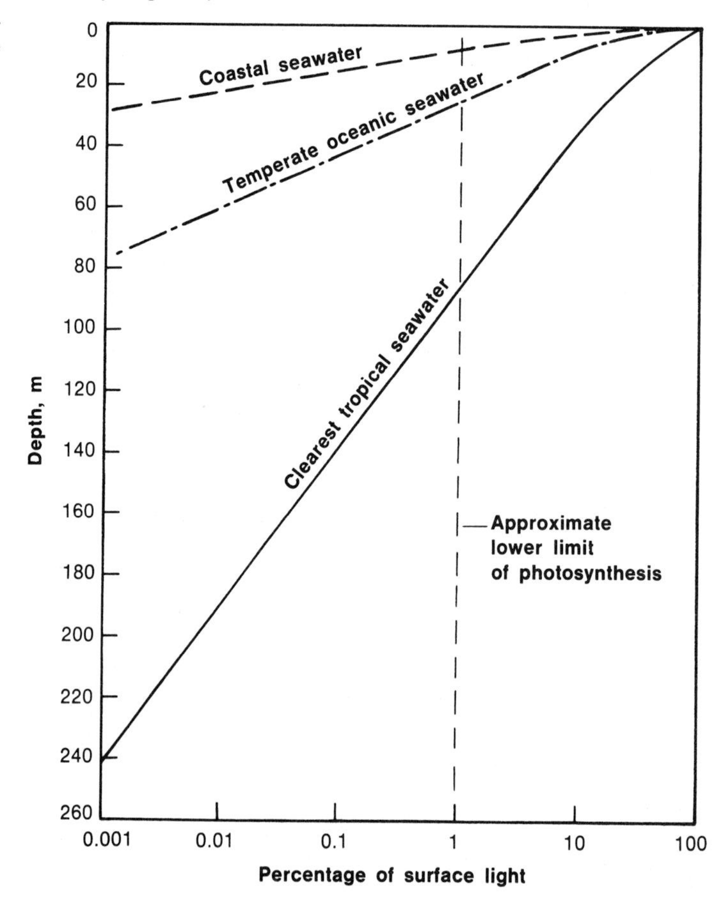

Fig. 6.4 Relative penetration of sunlight in varying types of seawater. Note the logarithmic scale for percentage of surface light. Adapted from Jerlov 1951.

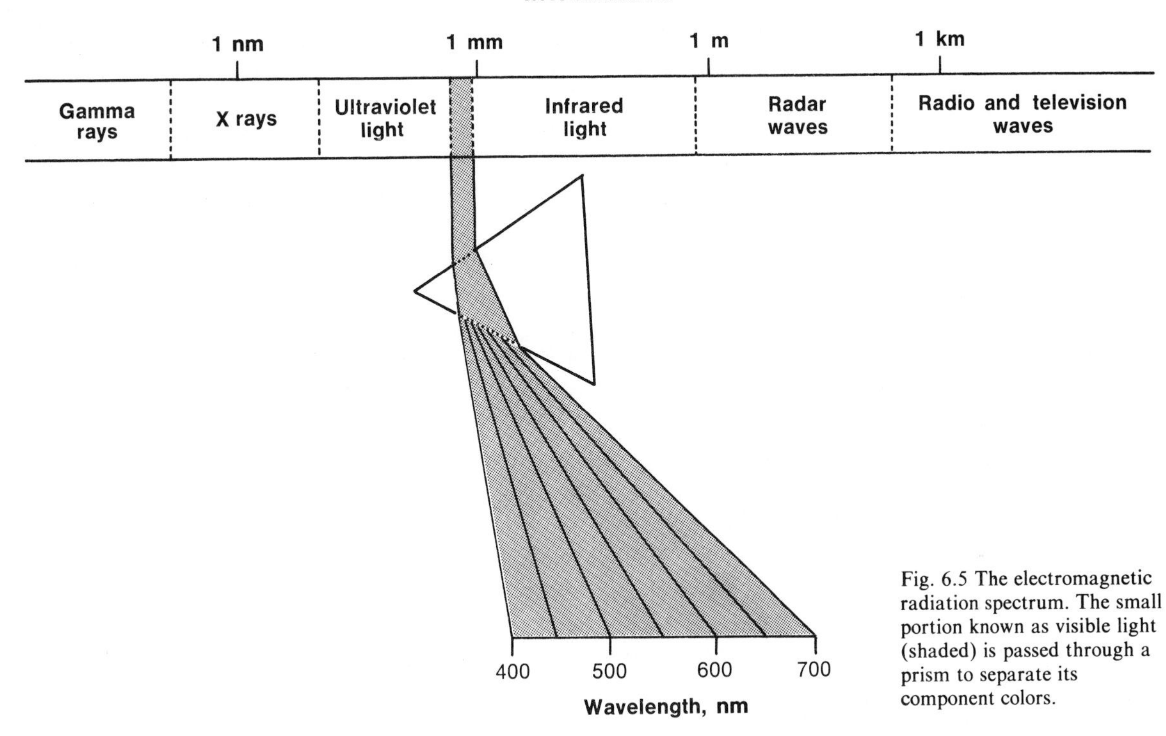

Fig. 6.5 The electromagnetic radiation spectrum. The small portion known as visible light (shaded) is passed through a prism to separate its component colors.

Sunlight, in its travel from outer space into the sea, is significantly altered qualitatively in addition to being reduced quantitatively. Visible light, as we perceive it, comprises only a very small segment of the much more extensive **electromagnetic radiation spectrum** (fig. 6.5). The range of electromagnetic radiation extends from very short wavelength, high-energy rays to radio waves that have wavelengths greater than one km.

Sunlight, or "white light," arriving at the sea surface, includes all colors of the visible spectrum from violet to red (fig. 6.5, bottom). Each color is characterized by a range of wavelengths measured in nanometers (nm).

Seawater quickly alters the color characteristics of light by differentially absorbing portions of the visible spectrum. In general, the violet and the orange-red ends of the spectrum are the first to be absorbed. Clear seawater is most transparent to the blue and green portions of the spectrum (450–550 nm), but this light too is eventually absorbed or scattered (fig. 6.6). In even the clearest tropical waters, almost all of the red light is absorbed in the upper 10 m; whereas 10% of the blue light penetrates to 100 m.

The greater penetration and eventual back-scattering of blue light account for the characteristic blue color of clear, tropical seawater. Coastal waters are commonly more turbid, with a greater load of suspended sediments and dissolved pigmented substances derived from land runoff. Here, there is a shift in the relative penetration of light energy, with green light penetrating deepest. In many coastal regions green light is reduced to 1% of its surface intensity in less than 30 m. Thus, the cumulative effects of differential absorp-

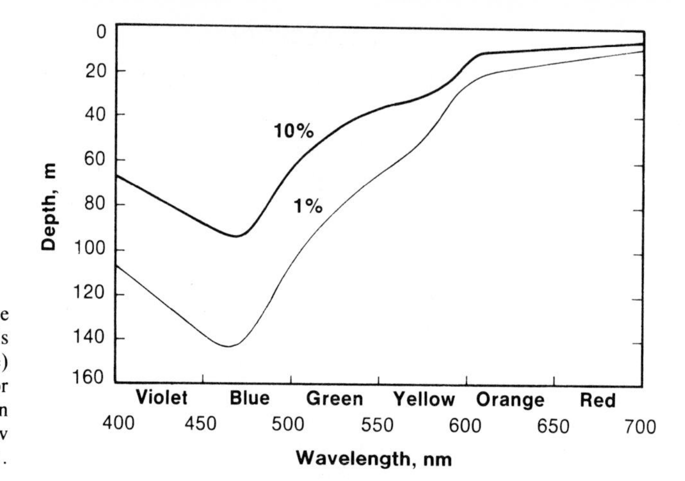

Fig. 6.6 Depths at which the surface radiation of light is reduced to 10% (upper curve) and 1% (lower curve) for various colors in clear ocean water. Adapted from Jerlov 1951.

tion and scattering of sunlight by seawater reduce the intensity and spectral width of the light available below the sea surface.

At some depth the light intensity is so faint that no photosynthesis will occur. This depth defines the bottom of the photic zone and varies from a few meters deep in coastal waters to over 200 m in clear tropical seas. At a depth somewhat above the bottom of the photic zone, the rate of photosynthesis is just balanced by plant respiration. This depth of no net primary production is the **compensation depth** (see fig. 6.1). The compensation depth is approximately equivalent to the depth at which the available light is reduced to 1% of its surface intensity (fig. 6.4). In clear tropical waters the compensation depth often extends below 100 m throughout the year. In higher latitudes, it may reach 50–60 m in midsummer, but nearly disappears during the winter months. However, these are average compensation depths for mixed phytoplankton assemblages composed of many different species, each with its own peculiar compensation depth.

In moderate and low light intensities photosynthesis by phytoplankton is largely light limited and exhibits a direct relationship to light intensity (fig. 6.7, curve a). At higher light intensities, photosynthesis ceases to follow the light intensity curve; it may stabilize or even decrease nearer the sea surface because of **photoinhibition** by strong light (fig. 6.7, curve b). Between the light-limited and light-inhibited portions of the photosynthetic curve b shown in figure 6.7 is a zone of optimum, or **saturation light intensity.** At this point, photosynthesis no longer increases in proportion to increasing light intensities. The photosynthetic machinery of phytoplankton cells is saturated with light, and higher light intensities nearer the sea surface fail to elicit proportionate increases in photosynthesis.

Phytoplankton from different environments exhibit some degree of photosynthetic adjustment to varying light intensities. Therefore the saturation light intensity for any phytoplankton population is not constant, but changes with changing sets of environmental conditions. Variations in saturation light intensities are also found among major phytoplankton groups. Dinoflagellates, in general, seem to be better adapted than diatoms to intense light (fig. 6.8). As a result their relative contribution to the total marine primary production is much greater in tropical and subtropical regions.

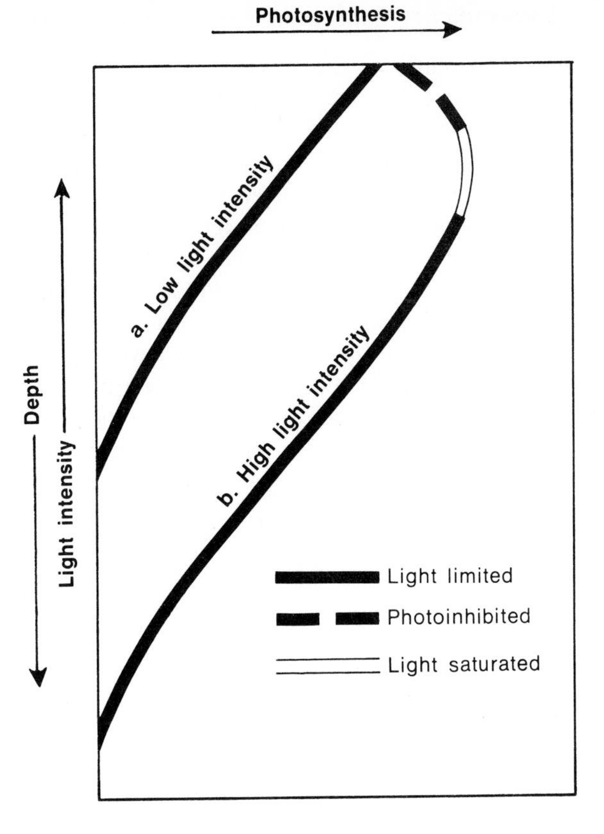

Fig. 6.7 Relationship between photosynthesis and depth at low and high light intensities.

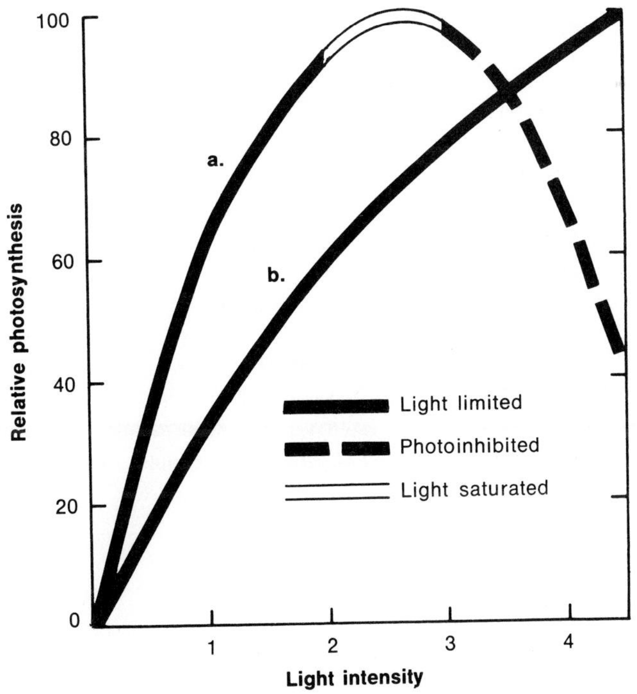

Fig. 6.8 A comparison of photosynthetic responses of two phytoplankton species to varying light intensities. The diatom *Planktonella* (curve *a*) shows marked photoinhibition at high light intensities; whereas the photosynthetic rate of *Dinophysis*, a dinoflagellate (curve *b*), continues to increase even at high light intensities. Adapted from Qasim *et al.* 1972.

Photosynthetic Pigments

The photosynthetic apparatus of all marine plants except blue-green algae and bacteria is located in the chloroplasts of actively photosynthesizing cells. It is in the chloroplasts (or the whole cells of bacteria and blue-green algae) that the pigment systems containing chlorophyll and varying amounts of other photosynthetic pigments listed in table 5.1 are located. There they absorb light energy and initiate its conversion to forms of chemical energy usable by the plant and eventually by other organisms.

Primitive photosynthetic plants, such as bacteria, rely on the simple photosynthetic system shown in figure 2.3 to produce ATP and completely satisfy their limited energy needs. Eucaryotic plants, however, employ a more elaborate photosynthetic process involving more complex pigment systems and two distinct sets of chemical reactions. In the first set, the **light reaction,** light energy is absorbed and two high-energy substances, ATP and $NADPH_2$, are produced (fig. 6.9). In addition, a molecule of water is split, releasing oxygen and two H ions, while freeing two electrons to replace those leaving pigment system II. As the term implies, light is needed to drive the light reaction; without light, it ceases.

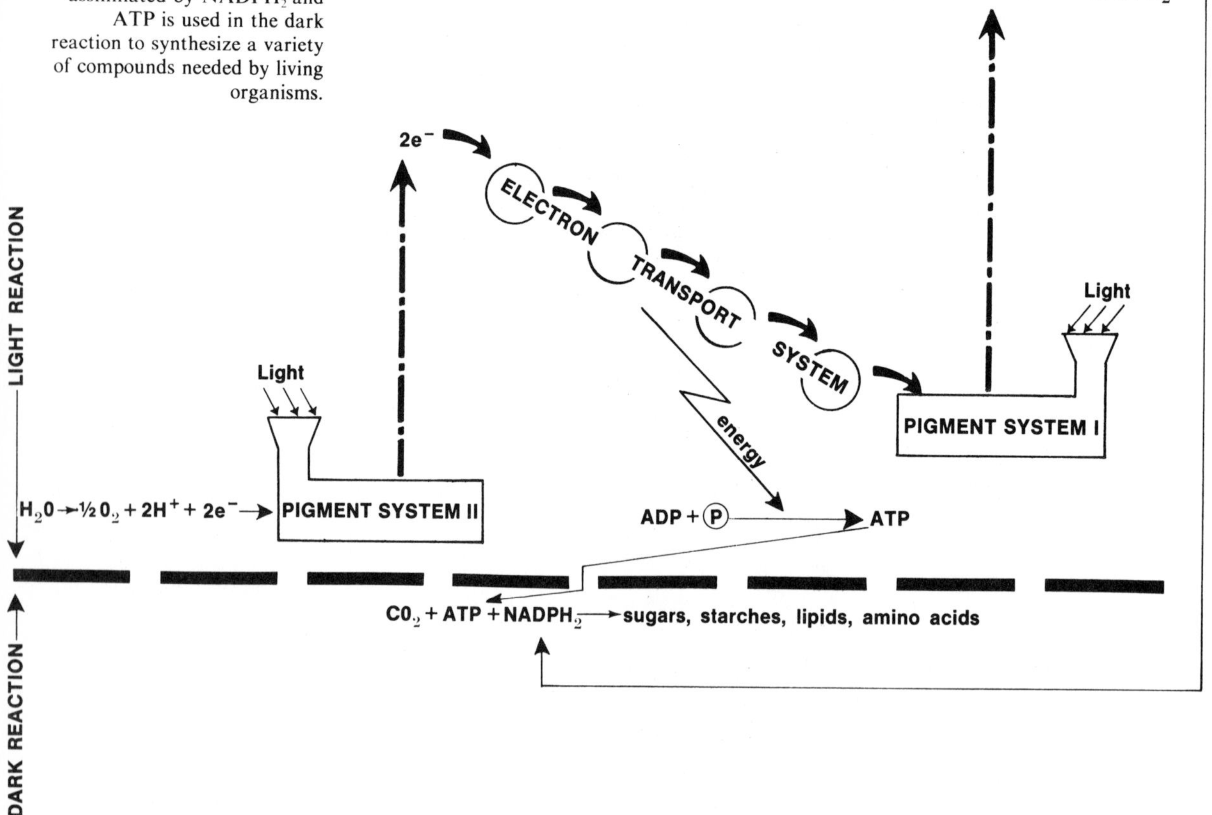

Fig. 6.9 The photosynthetic mechanism of eucaryotic plants. The heavy horizontal line separates the light reaction (above) from the dark reaction (below). Electrons activated by light are not returned to their sources, but instead combine to form a high energy substance $NADPH_2$. The chlorophyll electrons are replaced by electrons gained from splitting H_2O molecules. The energy assimilated by $NADPH_2$ and ATP is used in the dark reaction to synthesize a variety of compounds needed by living organisms.

The pigment systems and enzymes involved in the light reaction are situated on membranes within the chloroplast. Between these membranes is the biochemical apparatus for the **dark reaction** part of photosynthesis. Light energy is not necessary to maintain the dark reaction, but the high-energy ATP and $NADPH_2$ produced by the light reaction are. Energy from these substances is used in the dark reaction to synthesize sugars and a variety of other organic compounds needed by the cell.

Chlorophyll *a*, the one photosynthetic pigment common to all eucaryotic plants, appears green for the same reason coastal seawater appears green. Both absorb more of the available light energy from the violet and red ends of the spectrum, leaving the green light nearly unaffected (fig. 6.10). Chlorophyll serves efficiently as the basic energy-absorbing pigment for land plants. However, a few meters of seawater absorbs much of the red and violet portions of the visible spectrum before it reaches the chloroplasts of most marine plants. Since chlorophyll best absorbs energy from red and violet light, its effectiveness is greatly reduced in seawater.

The evolutionary response of most marine plant groups has been to supplement the light-absorption potential of chlorophyll with a variety of **accessory pigments**. These pigments function as light-gathering antennae to absorb light energy over a wide range of wavelengths, then transfer the energy to chlorophyll for introduction into the light reaction. Accessory pigments absorb light from spectral regions where chlorophyll cannot. Figure 6.10 also illustrates the complementary effect of the accessory pigment, **fucoxanthin,** which is found in brown algae and diatoms. Fucoxanthin absorbs light primarily from the blue-green region of the spectrum, the region where chlorophyll absorbs least effectively. In combination, chlorophyll and fucoxanthin are capable of absorbing energy from most of the visible light spectrum. Other common accessory pigments found in red algae are **phycocyanin,** which absorbs orange and red light; and **phycoerythrin,** which absorbs blue and green light. These and other accessory pigments listed in table 5.1 have enabled various groups of marine plants to adapt to the limited conditions of light availability in seawater.

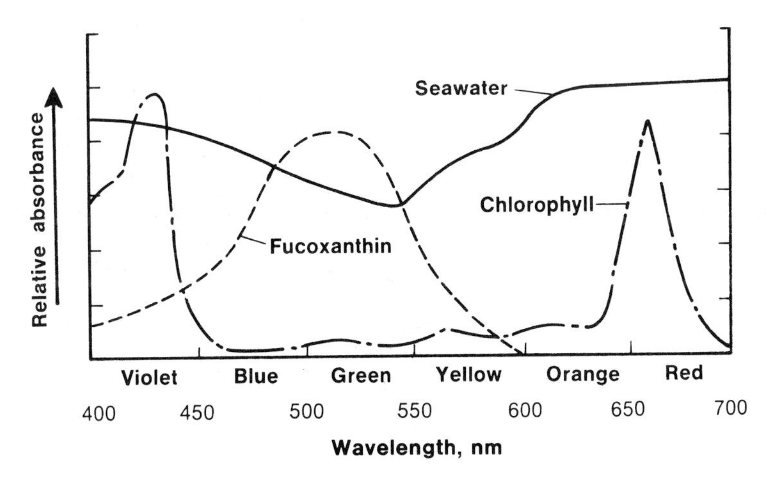

Fig. 6.10 Light absorption by seawater (———) reduces the energy available to chlorophyll (——— - ———). Accessory pigments such as flucoxanthin (----) greatly enhance a plant's light-absorbing capabilities in spectral regions where chlorophyll is inefficient.

The depth changes normally experienced by marine phytoplankton expose them to a wide variety of submarine light conditions. Their arrays of pigments are capable of absorbing light energy at almost any depth within the photic zone. The attached benthic algae commonly exhibit well-defined patterns of vertical distribution. The green algae, with a predominance of chlorophyll pigments, are restricted to relatively shallow waters by their inability to absorb much of the deeper penetrating green and blue wavelengths. The brown algae, characterized by an abundance of xanthophyll pigments (including fucoxanthin, fig. 6.10) as well as chlorophyll, survive well in intertidal regions, but are also common to depths of 50 m. The phycoerythrin and phycocyanin accessory pigments of red algae account for the greatest depth range of any algal group, from high intertidal rocks to depths as great as 200 m in clear tropical waters.

Nutrient Requirements

The nutrients required by all plants are a bit more complex than the general photosynthetic equation (p. 41) might indicate. Proper growth and maintenance of plant cells depend on the availability of more than just water and carbon dioxide, because plants are composed of a myriad of compounds that cannot be assembled from C, H, and O alone.

The nutrient requirements of plants can be understood best by determining the basic composition of the plant itself. Chemical analysis of a hypothetical "average" marine plant might yield the results shown in figure 6.11.

Generally, marine plants experience no difficulty in securing an adequate supply of water. Most are continuously and completely bathed by seawater, and few cells of any marine plant are seriously isolated from the external

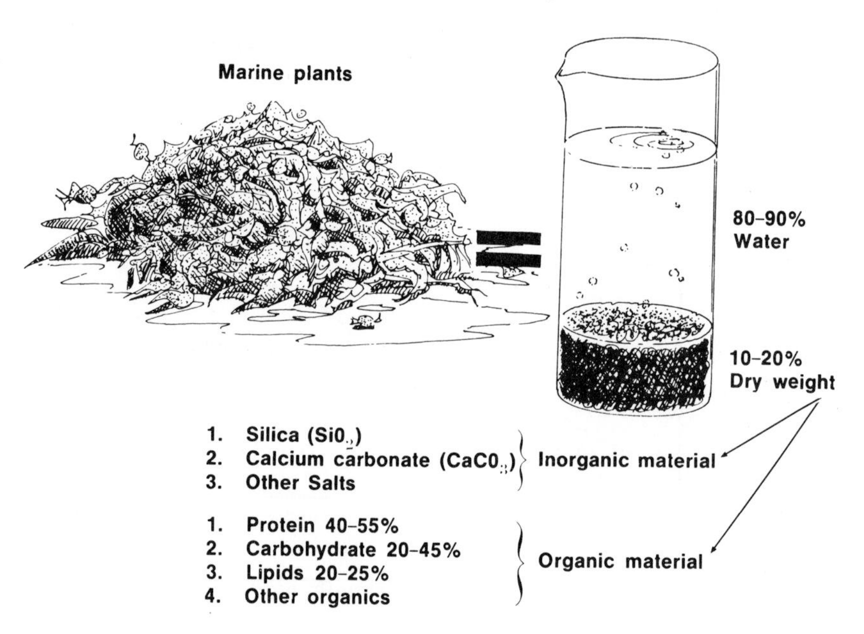

Fig. 6.11 Chemical composition of a hypothetical "average" marine plant.

water environment. Some species living in the intertidal zone are subject to a degree of desiccation at low tide. These plants exhibit both resistance to and tolerance of water loss. Infrequently, though, combinations of low tides and dry winds from the land do occur to seriously damage intertidal plants. In southern California, extreme low tides on autumn afternoons occasionally combine with hot, dry desert winds (known locally as Santa Ana winds) to dry out and eventually denude portions of the higher rocky intertidal regions.

Many types of marine plants are equipped with mineralized cell walls or internal skeletons of either calcium carbonate ($CaCO_3$) or silica (SiO_2). Carbon dioxide for carbonate formation and for photosynthesis exists in seawater primarily as carbonic acid (H_2CO_3, actually a combination of one H_2O and one CO_2 molecule), bicarbonate (HCO_3^-), and carbonate (CO_3^{--}). The abundance of these ions is influenced by photosynthesis, respiration, water depth, and pH. However, the concentration of total CO_2 present in seawater is not low enough to inhibit photosynthesis or the formation of $CaCO_3$. Calcium ions (Ca^{++}) necessary for calcium carbonate formation are also very abundant in seawater at all depths.

Silica occurs in skeletal and cell wall components of silicoflagellates and diatoms. Concentrations of dissolved silica are generally low in surface waters (fig. 6.12) and occasionally become so depleted that the growth and reproduction of these plant groups are inhibited.

Fig. 6.12 Concentrations of dissolved silica at various depths in the three major ocean basins. From H. U. Sverdrup, Martin W. Johnson, and Richard H. Fleming, *The Oceans: Their Physics, Chemistry, and General Biology*, © 1942, renewed 1970. By permission of Prentice-Hall, Inc., Englewood Cliffs, New Jersey.

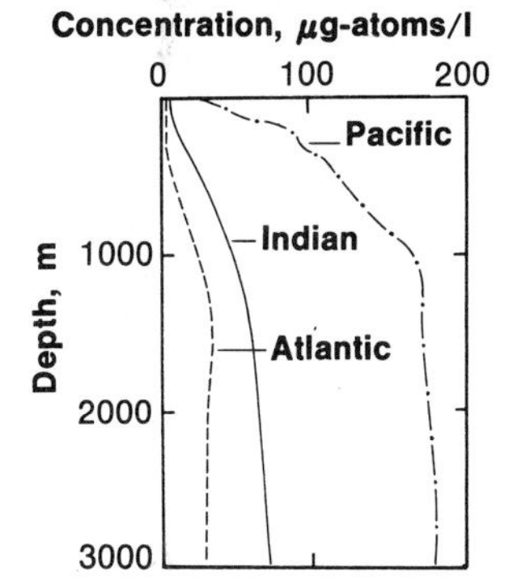

Organic matter is a widely used term applied collectively to those biologically synthesized compounds that contain C, H, usually O, lesser amounts of N (nitrogen) and P (phosphorus), and traces of many other elements necessary for the maintenance of life. Proteins, carbohydrates, and lipids are the most abundant types of organic compounds in living systems. Each contains carbon, hydrogen, and oxygen in varying ratios. In addition, lipids often include P, whereas proteins contain both N and P.

How much of each of these elements is required by plants? Elemental analyses of phytoplankton whole-cell cultures grown under various light conditions provide an average atomic ratio of approximately 110C:230H:75O:16N:1P. The sources of these elements for marine plants are various. Carbon, hydrogen, and oxygen are abundantly available from carbonate (CO_3^{--}) or bicarbonate ions (HCO_3^-) and water (H_2O). Nitrogen is much less plentiful but is present in seawater principally as nitrate (NO_3^{--}), with lesser amounts of nitrite (NO_2^-), and ammonium (NH_4^+). High concentrations of molecular nitrogen (N_2), which constitute 78% of the earth's atmosphere, are also dissolved in seawater. However, most marine organisms are not metabolically equipped to utilize this source of N. The exceptions are a few species of marine nitrogen-fixing blue-green algae. They may, however, contribute a substantial portion of the total N used by the phytoplankton in nutrient-depleted seas.

Phosphorus, present principally as phosphate (PO_4^{---}), is even less abundant in seawater than is nitrate. However, the biological demands on phosphate are less. The ratio of usable N and P in seawater is similar to the ratio of 16N:1P of living plant material.

The distribution of nitrate and phosphate in seawater (fig. 6.13) is similar to that of silicate (fig. 6.12). These nutrients are usually in short supply in the photic zone because of continual plant utilization. In periods of rapid phytoplankton growth, needed quantities of one or more of these nutrients may not be available. In such circumstances, continued plant growth is limited by the rate of nutrient regeneration.

In addition to the nutrient elements just mentioned, growing marine plants require several other elements in minute amounts. These **trace elements** include iron, manganese, cobalt, zinc, copper, and others. Depletion of iron in English Channel waters has been observed during spring diatom blooms, suggesting that iron availability may limit the size or composition of phytoplankton populations. But in most cases, it is not known whether natural concentrations of other trace elements commonly dip to values sufficiently low to inhibit marine plant growth.

Vitamins too are crucial for proper plant growth and reproduction. Some species of diatoms, for example, apparently require more vitamin B_{12} during auxospore formation than at other times. Some species of diatoms can synthesize their own vitamin B_{12}, while others are dependent on bacteria to provide the needed amount.

Nutrient Regeneration

Some plant material consumed by herbivores is used for growth or converted to fecal wastes. Most of it eventually sinks below the photic zone and accumulate at greater depths. Other nutrients are excreted as N-containing urea and ammonia wastes and are recycled back to the phytoplankton as quickly as they are excreted. Regeneration of the nutrients initially used to produce plant material is dependent on respiration by consumers, but more importantly on decomposition of organic material by bacteria and some fungi living in the water column and on the bottom. Bacterial action decomposes organic material and returns phosphates and nitrates, as well as other limiting nutrients, to seawater in inorganic form for reuse by the primary producers (refer to fig. 2.13). Bacteria and fungi also absorb dissolved organic compounds from sea-

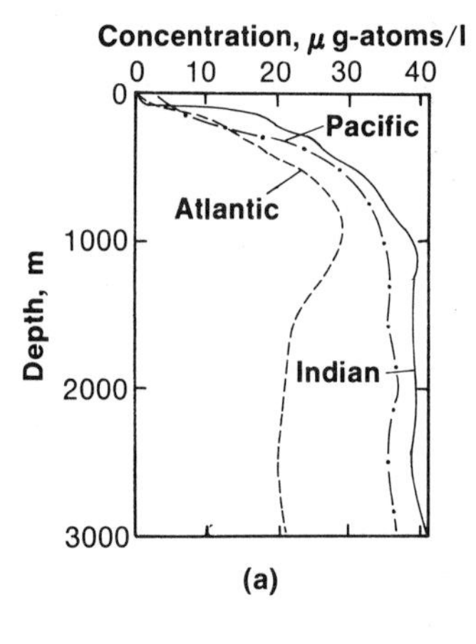

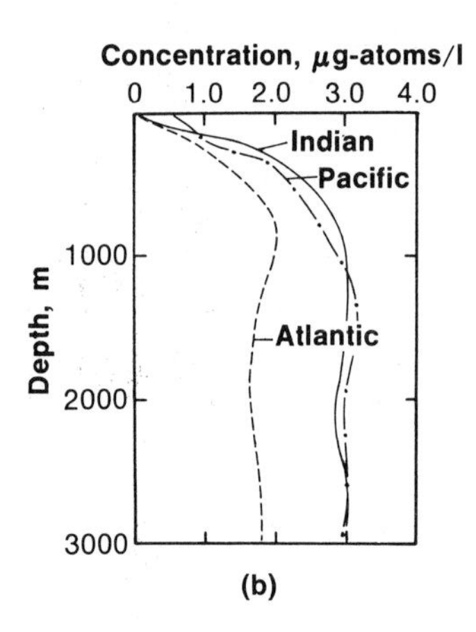

Fig. 6.13 Distribution of (*a*) nitrate and (*b*) phosphate with depth in the three major ocean basins. From H. U. Sverdrup, Martin W. Johnson, and Richard H. Fleming, *The Oceans: Their Physics, Chemistry, and General Biology*, © 1942, renewed 1970. By permission of Prentice-Hall, Inc., Englewood Cliffs, New Jersey.

water and convert them to living cells that become an additional food source for many benthic and small planktonic animals.

Figures 6.12 and 6.13 indicate that major concentrations of limiting nutrients reside below the photic zone where they cannot be utilized by photosynthetic plants. Upward molecular diffusion only accounts for a slow and not very substantial return of nutrients to the photic zone. Much more significant to the rapid and continued growth of marine plants are large-scale mixing processes, including turbulence and vertical water movements, which rapidly transport nutrient-rich deep water upward.

Wind and tide waves create turbulence in near-surface waters (see fig. 1.19) and mix deeper nutrients upward. Turbulent mixing is most effective over continental shelves where the shallow bottom prevents the escape of nutrients into deeper water. Tidal currents in the southern end of the North Sea and the eastern side of the English Channel are sufficient to mix the water almost completely from top to bottom. As a result, summer phytoplankton productivity there remains high as long as sunlight is sufficient to maintain photosynthesis.

In subtropical latitudes of most oceans, the strong permanent thermocline near the base of the photic zone imparts a high degree of vertical stability to the water column and inhibits upward mixing of nutrient-rich waters. These regions generally have very low rates of primary production, comparable to deserts on land.

Thermoclines also develop in temperate waters to restrict the return of deep-water nutrients, but only on a seasonal basis (fig. 6.14). During winter months, the surface water cools and sinks. The thermocline disappears (*a*) and deeper nutrient-rich water is mixed to the surface. As solar insolation increases in the spring, the surface water warms and the thermocline is reestablished (*b*). A well-developed summer thermocline (*c*) resembles the permanent thermocline of subtropical waters, and creates an effective barrier blocking nutrient return to the photic zone. With decreased daylength and cooler weather in autumn (*d*), the thermocline weakens and disappears into winter. This process of **convective mixing** is a seasonal phenomenon in temperate regions, continuing from late fall to early spring. But in high latitudes, continuous heat loss from the sea to the atmosphere produces year-round convective mixing. Low light conditions rather than scarce nutrients usually limit plant growth in these polar regions.

Subsurface water is carried to the photic zone by several processes collectively termed **upwelling.** One type, known as coastal upwelling, is produced by winds blowing surface waters away from a coastline. The surface waters are replaced by deeper waters rising to the surface (fig. 6.15). Nearshore currents, which veer away from the shoreline, produce the same result. Four major coastal upwelling areas occur in the California, Peru, Canary, and Benguela Currents. Minor upwelling areas are scattered along many other coastlines.

Another type of upwelling is more limited in extent, and normally exists only in the central Pacific Ocean. The Pacific Equatorial Current flows westward, straddling the equator. The Coriolis effect causes a slight displacement

Fig. 6.14

(a) Winter

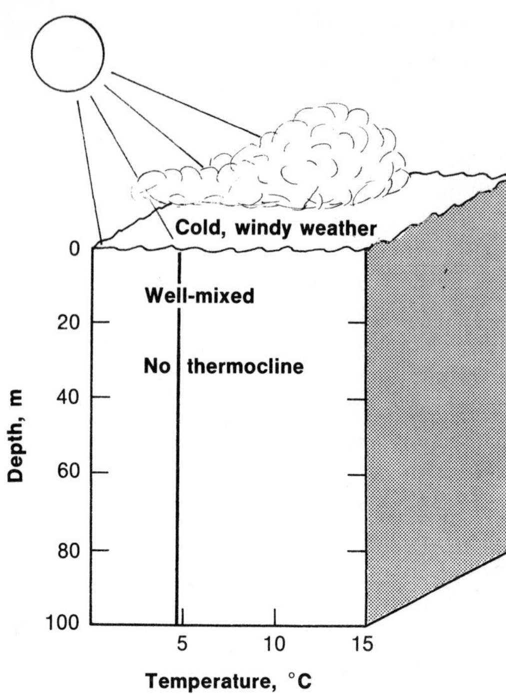

(b) Spring

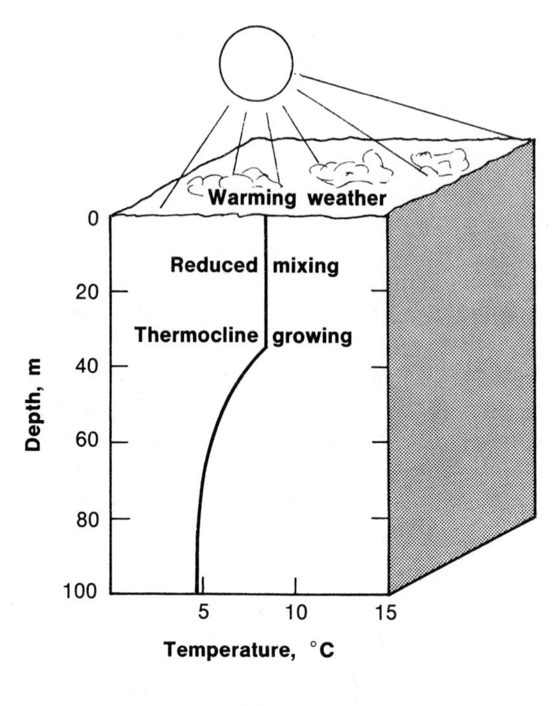

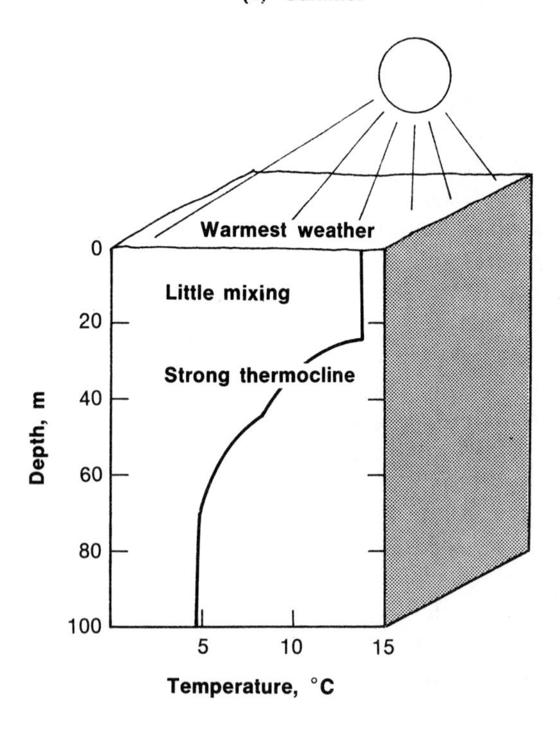

(d) Autumn

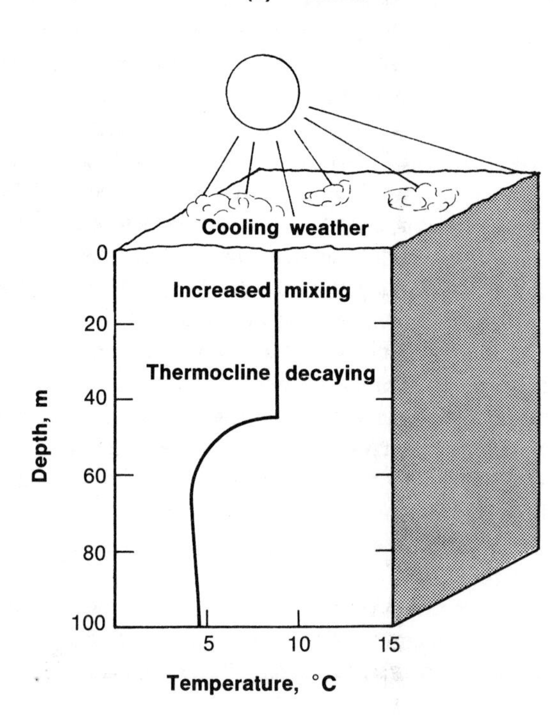

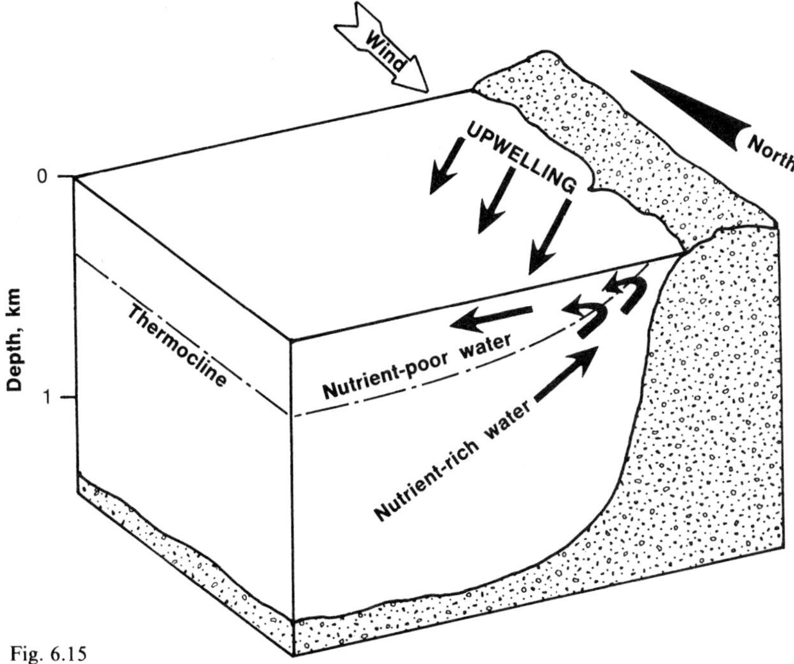

Fig. 6.15

Fig. 6.14 Growth and decline of the thermocline in temperate ocean waters. Adapted from Dodimead *et al.* 1963, for ocean station "P" off the west coast of North America at latitude 50°N, longitude 145°W.

Fig. 6.15 Coastal upwelling in the Northern Hemisphere.

to the right of the portion of the current in the Northern Hemisphere (refer to fig. 1.25). The portion of the current in the Southern Hemisphere is displaced to the left. The resultant divergence of water away from the equator creates an upwelling of deeper water to replace that which has moved away. This area of upwelling is the basis for an important Japanese long-line tuna fishery.

Major upwelling areas also occur around the Antarctic continent. In these regions, water that sinks in the Northern Hemisphere and flows south at mid-depth again surfaces, bringing with it a thousand-year accumulation of nutrients (fig. 6.16 and refer also to fig. 1.28). The extraordinary fertility of the Antarctic seas stands in sharp contrast to the barrenness of the adjacent continent. Consequently, almost all Antarctic life, whether terrestrial or marine, is dependent upon the marine food chain supported by this massive upwelling.

On a reduced scale, a pattern of upwelling also occurs in estuaries. A portion of the nutrient-laden seawater flowing into the bottom of an estuary is mixed upward into the less dense outflow of surface freshwater. This upwelling serves to continually replenish the plant nutrients utilized by growing populations of estuarine primary producers.

Langmuir cells (named after Irving Langmuir who first clarified their structure after he observed *Sargassum* in the North Atlantic floating in long rows parallel to the wind direction) are parallel pairs of counter-rotating convection cells driven by surface winds (fig. 6.17). Langmuir convection cells set up alternating zones of divergence and convergence, and sometimes sweep organic detritus and plankton to the lines of convergence between adjacent

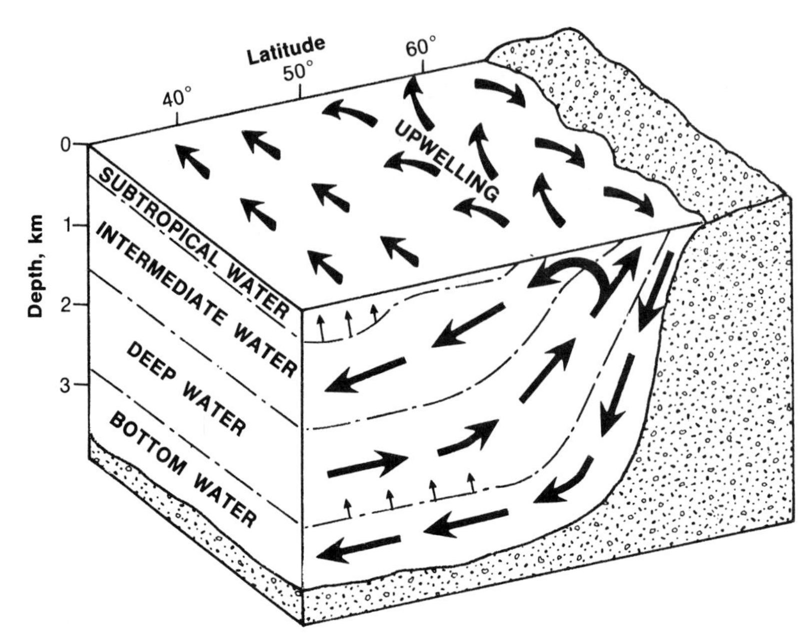

Fig. 6.16 Upwelling and deep-ocean circulation in the Antarctic.

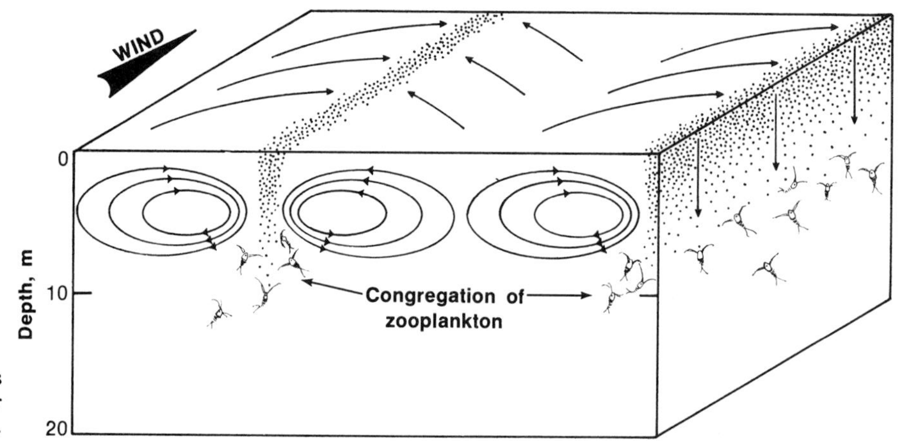

Fig. 6.17 Circulation patterns of wind-driven Langmuir convection cells.

cells. This material is often evident at the surface as long parallel "slicks," foam lines, or rows of floating debris. Similar accumulations may be created by internal waves and other factors. Langmuir cells extend only a few meters deep and are not important for nutrient upwelling from deep water. However, these convection cells may create nutrient traps under the convergences. Phytoplankton and particulate debris that accumulate there attract grazing zooplankton in concentrations often 100 times more dense than those in adjacent areas.

Grazing

The trophic interrelationships of marine phytoplankton and small herbivores (mostly zooplankton and small fish) can be quite complex. Grazing may decrease the standing crop and thus the productivity of a phytoplankton population. On the other hand, such grazing might also improve the overall survival conditions for phytoplankton by reducing competition for resources and accelerating nutrient regeneration.

The capacity of herbivorous zooplankton to quickly decimate a phytoplankton population is shown in table 6.1. With initial conditions of a phytoplankton population having a density of one million cells/liter and reproducing once each day, the herbivore population density was adjusted to achieve a grazing rate that just held the phytoplankton population constant. When the zooplankton population density was doubled, the phytoplankton population was reduced to slightly over 100,000 cells/liter in three days and to 27,000 cells in five days. At a density five times that necessary to hold the phytoplankton population constant, the zooplankton reduced the phytoplankton cell density to 24 cells/liter in three days, and the culture was essentially eliminated in five days.

Ideally, grazing rates should adjust to the magnitude of primary productivity to insure a balance between plant and animal populations. Rates of photosynthesis do limit the average size of the animal populations they support, yet short-term fluctuations of both plant and animal populations often occur. The magnitude of these fluctuations tends to be moderated somewhat by stabilizing **feedback mechanisms** between plant and grazer populations. An abundant food supply permits the grazers to reproduce and grow rapidly. Eventually, however, they consume the plants more quickly than the plants can reproduce themselves. Overgrazing reduces the phytoplankton population and its photosynthetic capacity, causing food shortages and reductions of the enlarged herbivore populations. When grazing intensity is reduced because of food shortages, the phytoplankton population may recover, increase in size, and again set the stage with an abundant food source to cause a repeat of the entire cycle. Such oscillations of population size may extend through many trophic levels of the food web.

Table 6.1. *Changes in a Phytoplankton Population With a Constant Rate of Cell Division at Varying Grazing Intensities.*

	Phytoplankton Population Density (cells/liter)		
Time in Days	*Initial Grazing Intensity*	*Grazing Intensity Doubled*	*Grazing Intensity Increased Five-fold*
0	1,000,000	1,000,000	1,000,000
1	1,000,000	487,000	62,000
2	1,000,000	237,000	3,900
3	1,000,000	106,000	240
4	1,000,000	56,000	15
5	1,000,000	27,000	1

Adapted from Fleming 1939

In most cases, a time delay exists between population peaks of the consumed and the consumer. The extent of the time lag depends largely on the consumer's reproductive response to an increasing food supply. In favorable conditions, asexually reproducing phytoplankton can divide rapidly and can increase their population size more quickly than larger, sexually reproducing zooplankton. Phytoplankton can therefore achieve a greater population size before the zooplankton catch up, and may experience larger population fluctuations than the more slowly breeding herbivores.

In addition to the temporal patchiness suggested above, marine phytoplankton commonly display a large measure of localized spatial, or geographical, patchiness. Dense patches of phytoplankton often tend to alternate with concentrated patches of zooplankton. The inverse concentrations of phytoplankton and zooplankton densities stem in part from the effects of grazing and of differences in their reproductive rates. A dynamic model of phytoplankton growth, grazing, and subsequent zooplankton migration that establishes and effectively maintains the alternating patchy distribution of marine phytoplankton and zooplankton, is presented in figure 6.18. This is but one of many models used to explain phytoplankton patchiness. Initially, a dense patch of phytoplankton provides favorable growth conditions for herbivores that are attracted from adjacent water into the phytoplankton patch (*a*). The grazing rate increases in the area of the patch, but declines elsewhere. Production in the original patch soon decreases because of overgrazing and increases in adjacent areas. Eventually, the original phytoplankton patch is eliminated by the dense concentration of grazers. The adjacent areas become the new phytoplankton patches (*b*) attracting herbivores from the recently overgrazed region, and repeating the entire sequence. In addition to grazers, phytoplankton patches may also succumb to nutrient depletion or be dispersed by water turbulence.

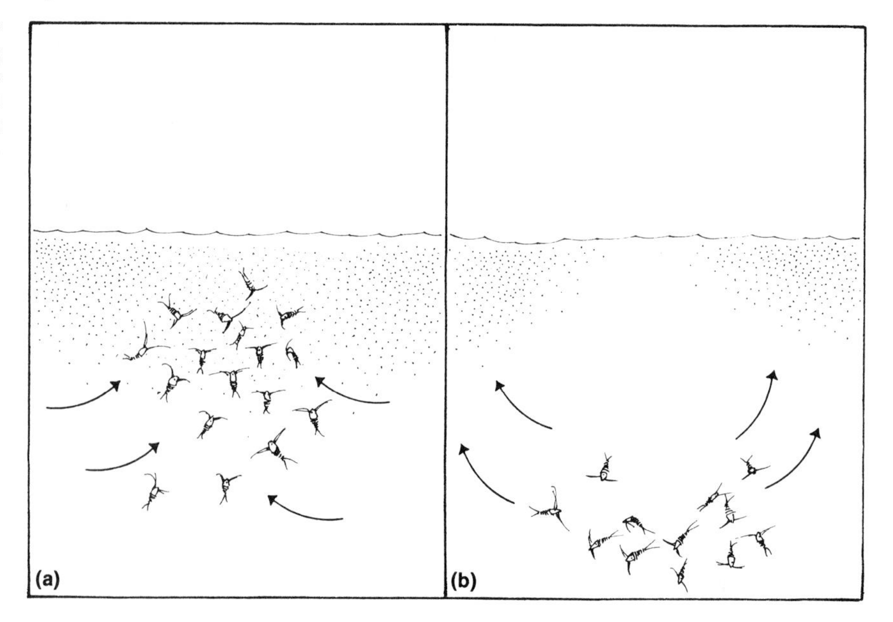

Fig. 6.18 A dynamic model for establishing and maintaining patches of marine phytoplankton and zooplankton. Adapted from Bainbridge 1953.

Some species of zooplankton are attracted by particular phytoplankton species and repelled by others. External metabolites secreted by the plants have been suggested as one cause for selective grazing. Detection of phytoplankton patches by the quality of light passing through them is another possibility. Some copepods, when exposed to light that is predominantly red, display a "red dance," with most of their movements oriented vertically. But in light with a strong proportion of blue, the same copepods exhibit a "blue dance," moving horizontally. The horizontal movements have been interpreted as hunting or searching. Horizontal motions eventually bring the copepods into or under a phytoplankton patch, where increased chlorophyll concentrations decrease the relative proportion of blue light. The copepods then shift to the vertical "red dance" that maintains their position with the phytoplankton patch.

Seasonal Aspects of Marine Primary Production

A prominent feature in the production cycle of temperate and cold seas is the spring diatom increase (often referred to as a **bloom**). Diatom blooms are the result of combined seasonal variations of water temperature, light and nutrient availability, and grazing intensity. In early spring, water temperature and available light increase, nutrients are abundant in near-surface waters, and grazing pressure is diminished. In a word, conditions are ideal for rapid and abundant plant growth. But if the bottom of the mixed layer extends below some critical depth (determined by light penetration), near-surface turbulence will distribute the phytoplankton cells randomly through this mixed layer.

Cells in the deeper portions of the mixed layer receive insufficient light, and no net production occurs. The spring bloom commences only after the growing thermocline thins the mixed layer to a level above the critical depth. In general, bloom conditions in the open ocean occur as a broad band of plant production sweeping poleward with the onset of spring. The standing crop of diatoms increases quickly to the largest of the year and begins to deplete nutrient concentrations. The grazers respond to the additional pasturage, although more gradually, by increasing their numbers.

As spring warms into summer, sunlight becomes more plentiful, but the developing seasonal thermocline effectively reduces nutrient return from deeper water. Coupled with increased grazing, the diatom population declines and remains restricted throughout the summer. With food more scarce, the summer zooplankton population also drops off. Unlike diatoms, the dinoflagellate population increases slowly during the spring, remains healthy throughout the summer, and decreases in autumn with diminished light intensity.

Cooler autumn air temperatures begin to break down the summer thermocline and allow convection to renew nutrients to the photic zone. The phytoplankton respond with another bloom, which, although not as remarkable as the spring bloom, is sufficient to initiate another upswing of the zooplankton population. The autumn bloom is cut short by decreasing light and reduced temperatures as winter approaches. As production goes down, resistant over-wintering stages of both phytoplankton and zooplankton become

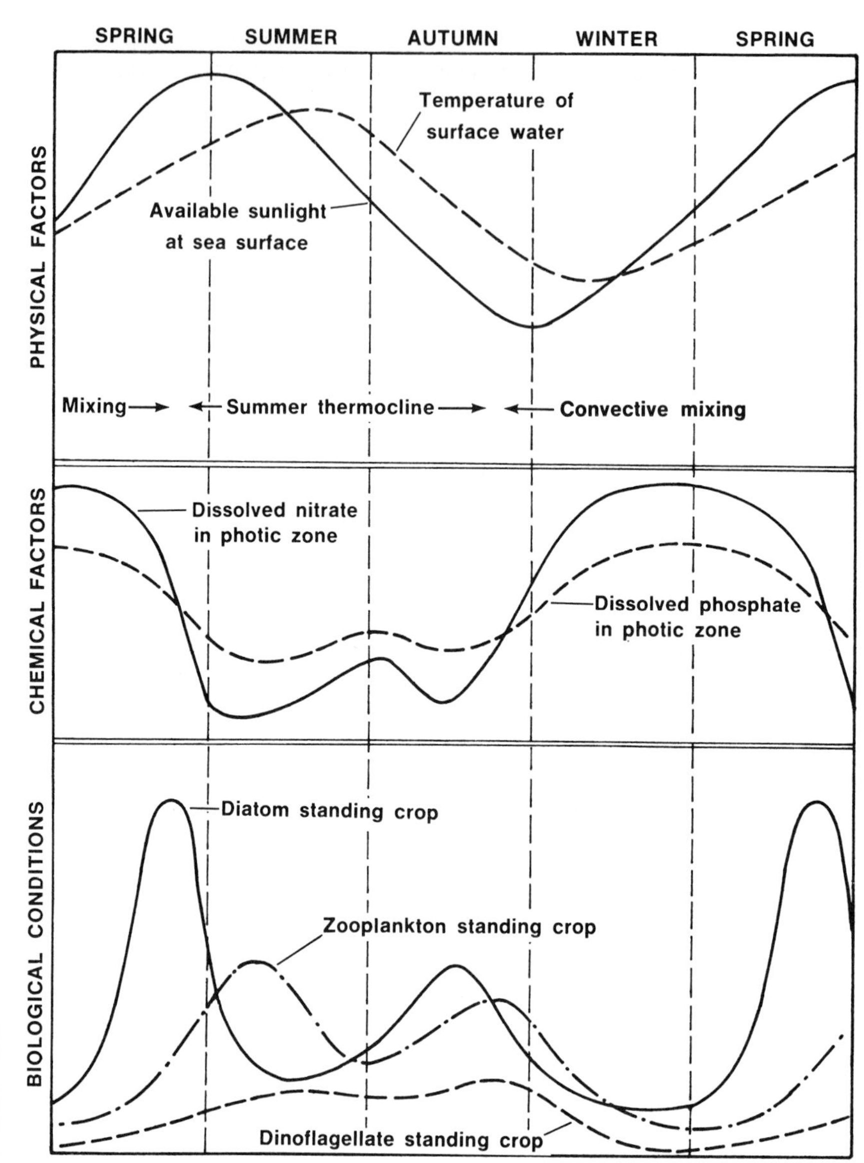

Fig. 6.19 Seasonal fluctuations of some physical and chemical factors of temperate seas, which in turn influence phytoplankton and zooplankton population sizes.

more abundant. Convective mixing continues to recharge the nutrient load of the surface waters in readiness for a repeat of the entire performance the following spring. The cyclic fluctuations of physical, chemical, and biological features of a temperate sea are graphically summarized in figure 6.19.

The production characteristics of tropical and subtropical waters closely resemble those of continuous summer in temperate regions. Sunlight is available in abundance, yet production is low due to a strong permanent thermocline that resists vertical mixing of nutrients. The low rate of nutrient return is partially compensated by a year-round growing season and a deep photic zone. Regions of tropical upwelling, especially in the Equatorial Pacific, that are provided with a continuous supply of nutrients as well as plentiful sunlight, differ from most tropical and subtropical regions by being reasonably rich in marine life.

Coastal upwelling in temperate seas alters the generalized picture presented in figure 6.19 by replenishing nutrients during the summer when they would otherwise be depleted. As long as light is sufficient and upwelling continues, high phytoplankton production occurs and is reflected in abundant local animal populations. In some areas, the duration and intensity of coastal upwelling fluctuate with variations in atmospheric circulation. Along the Washington and Oregon coasts, the instability of spring and summer wind patterns produces sporadic upwelling interspersed with short periods of no upwelling and low primary productivity. Off the coast of Ecuador, a relaxation of upwelling every six or seven years produces a disastrous change in local current patterns. Warm nutrient-poor water of the Equatorial Countercurrent extends farther south than usual and mixes with the normally cold and very productive Peru Current flowing north. Nutrient-rich water is excluded from the surface, and the plant and animal populations are destroyed. The decomposing organic matter sinks, depleting the available dissolved oxygen and producing hydrogen sulphide (H_2S), which poisons much of the remaining marine life. The effects of this situation (known locally as "El Niño" or "The Child" because it usually occurs around Christmas time) extend throughout the food web, killing large numbers of carnivores and greatly reducing fishery yields.

Sea surface temperatures in polar regions are always low. The thermocline, if one exists at all, is only poorly established, and is not an effective barrier to nutrient return from deeper waters. Light, or more correctly the lack of it, thus becomes the major limiting factor for plant growth in polar seas. Ample light to sustain high phytoplankton growth rates lasts only for a few months during the summer. Even so, photosynthesis can continue around the clock during those few months to quickly produce huge phytoplankton populations. As the light intensity and day-length decline, the short summer diatom bloom declines rapidly. Winter conditions closely resemble those of temperate regions, except that in polar seas they endure much longer. There the complete cycle of production consists of a single short period of plant growth, equivalent to a typical spring bloom immediately followed by an autumn bloom and decline alternating with an extended winter of reduced net production.

Predictive Modeling

The cause-and-effect interactions between organisms and their environment suggest that a **predictive model** of primary production in the marine ecosystem can be devised if those interactions can be measured and studied. In itself, the ability to make accurate predictions is a useful tool for analyzing and wisely using natural resources. Moreover, the ability to design a qualitatively and quantitatively accurate predictive model indicates that we understand something of how the system works. These models are not meant to be exact duplicates of nature. Instead they remain as crude simplifications of the real world, but, which in their simplicity reveal some fundamental processes of the system. Information regarding only a relatively small number of variables is often a sufficient basis for a workable model because only a few key factors often control or dominate a significant part of the action.

Several attempts have been made to reduce to relatively simple mathematical expressions the multiplicity of environmental factors that affect the rate of primary production in the sea. The work of G. A. Riley serves as a useful example of the general applicability of predictive models for marine production systems. Over three decades ago, Riley presented a rather rigorous mathematical equation for computing a theoretical seasonal growth curve for phytoplankton. His equation included expressions for phytoplankton population size, average surface light intensity, extinction coefficient of light in seawater, depth of the photic zone, rate of nutrient depletion, phytoplankton respiration rate, water temperature, and grazing rate by herbivores.

Riley's equation can be reduced to the following much simpler expression by combining many functions into single constants, using average values for these constants, and making other simplifying assumptions:

$$\frac{dP}{dt} = P(a\text{-}r\text{-}g\text{-}m)$$

where, $\frac{dP}{dt}$ = rate of change of the phytoplankton population with time

P = phytoplankton population
a = gross primary productivity
r = plant respiration rate
g = rate of grazing loss
m = rate of cell mortality from other causes (mostly sinking)

In effect, this equation states that the rate of change in the size of the phytoplankton population is dependent on the rate of gross primary productivity minus plant respiration and cell losses to grazing and sinking. Using this model, Riley calculated the expected changes in the phytoplankton population of Georges Bank for a full year. Figure 6.20*a* demonstrates a substantial agreement between Riley's predicted values and the actual observed values of the phytoplankton crop.

These predictive techniques were not limited in application to plants alone. Riley also devised a similar equation for changes in the standing crop of zooplankton on Georges Bank. Again, the predicted and observed values of the herbivore population size were in close agreement (fig. 6.20*b*).

In the past few years, Riley's simplistic models have been superceded by massive computerized attempts to model larger segments of pelagic ecosystems (for example, Steele's recent attempt to model the time course of the dynamic interactions between phytoplankton and their herbivorous grazers in the North Sea). But rather than attempt to evaluate them here, the interested reader is directed to references at the end of this chapter. The point to be made here is that, in spite of the problems inherent in evaluating equations

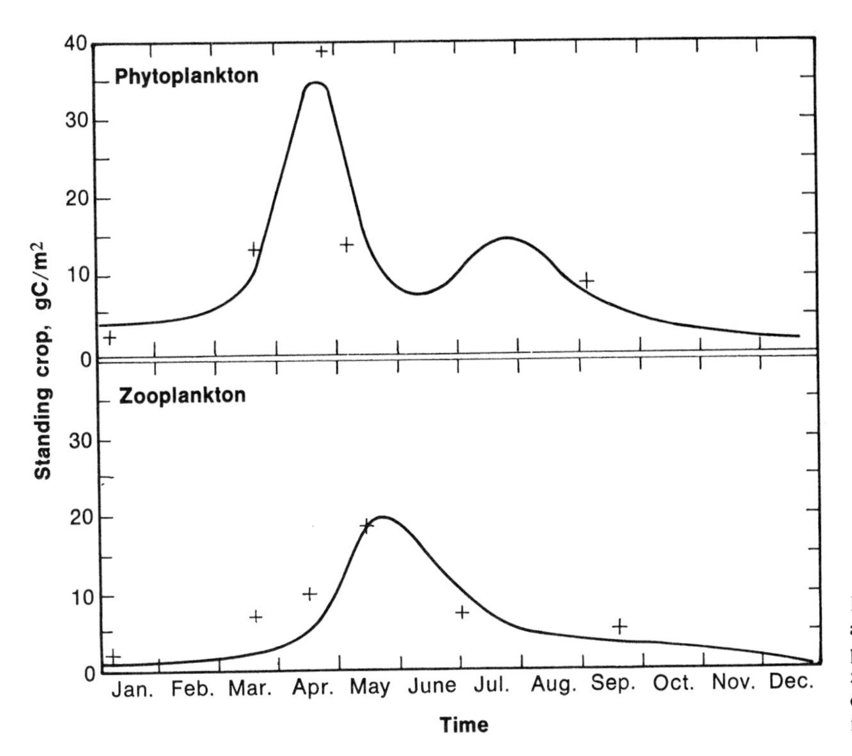

Fig. 6.20 Predicted (———) and observed (+) values of phytoplankton (*a*) and zooplankton (*b*) standing crops on Georges Bank. Redrawn from Riley 1946 and 1947.

that are in part based on unsubstantiated assumptions and sparse data, the predicted productivity values are generally within ±25% of the actual measured values. And they are improving all the time, as our understanding of the processes that govern the dynamics of marine populations continues to expand.

Global Marine Plant Production

High latitudes, shallow regions, and zones of upwelling generally support large marine plant populations, but most of this production is accomplished during the warm summer months when light is not a growth-limiting factor. Open ocean regions, especially in the tropics and subtropics where a strong thermocline is a permanent feature, tend to have low annual rates of plant production. Figure 6.21 illustrates the general geographical distribution of marine plant production on a global scale.

John H. Ryther recently defined three general primary production provinces for the marine environment: open ocean, coastal zone, and upwelling areas. For each of these production provinces, he provided estimates of phytoplankton production rates based primarily on accumulated C^{14} productivity determinations. The contribution to the total primary production by benthic algae is assumed to be small, but as mentioned earlier, that assumption is presently a subject for reevaluation.

Open ocean regions, which encompass about 90% of the ocean's area, support rates of net primary production that range from 25 to 75 $gC/m^2/year$

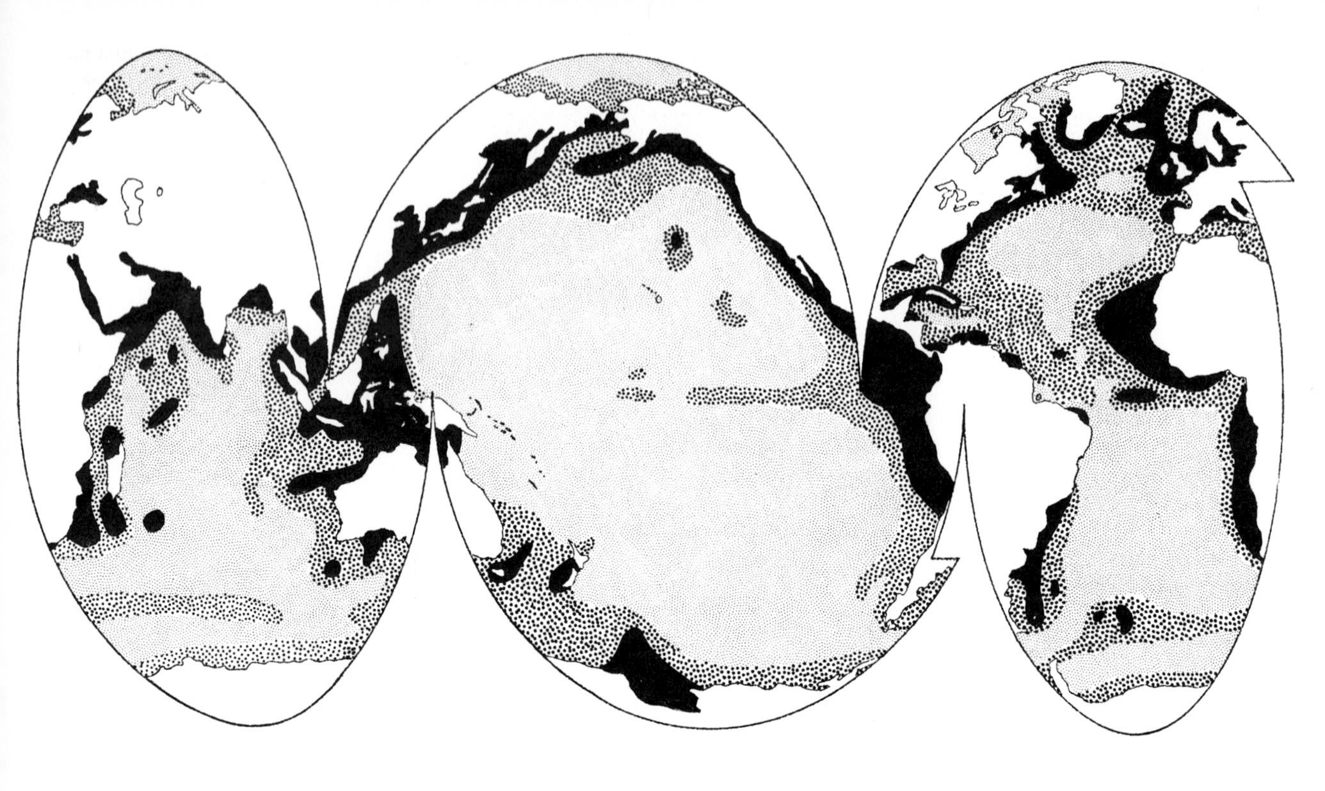

Fig. 6.21 The geographic distribution of marine plant production. Adapted from FAO 1972.

and average roughly 50 $gC/m^2/year$, according to Ryther. Although productivity is low, this province accounts for over 80% of the total plant production in the sea because of its vastness. Coastal zones, including some offshore areas of high productivity, are less extensive in area but more productive than the open sea. Nearly 10% of the marine environment is included in this province. Net productivity of 100 $gC/m^2/year$ is about average for the coastal province, but extremely productive reefs and estuaries are known to yield new plant material at rates exceeding 1000 $gC/m^2/year$. A few isolated areas of the very restricted upwelling province occasionally achieve production rates of 10 $gC/m^2/day$. However, much of this production is seasonal, and a reasonable annual average rate for upwelling areas is approximately 300 $gC/m^2/year$ (or somewhat less than 1 $gC/m^2/day$). Table 6.2 summarizes Ryther's productivity values for the various marine production provinces mentioned above, as well as more recent ones by Whittaker and Likens.

A significant point of disagreement between the two productivity estimates listed in table 6.2 is the reported production figures for the coastal zone. The data of Whittaker and Likens are likely to be more accurate as they take into account the results of several recent studies on the productivity of kelp beds and estuaries.

Table 6.2. *Rates of Net Phytoplankton Production For Each Marine Primary Production Province.*

Province	% of Ocean	Average Productivity (g of carbon/m^2/year)	Total Net Productivity (10^9 tons of carbon/year)		
Open Ocean	90	50	16.3	18.7	cont. shelf = 4.3
Coastal Zone	9.9	100	3.6	6.0	estuaries = 1.0
Upwelling Areas	0.1	300	0.1	0.1	algal beds = 0.7
		Total =	20.0*	24.8*	

Compiled from Ryther 1969 (Columns 1, 2, and 3), and Whittaker and Likens 1973 (Column 4)
*Total plant production assumed to be 10 × carbon production.

The general agreement between the two sets of productivity estimates presented in table 6.2 suggests that they represent a reasonably accurate estimate of the annual net plant production of the sea: 20–25 billion tons of carbon, or 200–250 billion tons of total plant material. For comparison, the entire human population of the earth requires something on the order of 3 billion tons of food annually to sustain itself. And many members of that population are hungrily eying the bounty of the sea. But for several reasons (discussed in chapter 9), this abundant profusion of plant material will probably never be utilized on a scale sufficient to alleviate the serious nutritional problems already rampant in much of our population. Instead, this vast amount of organic material will continue to fuel the metabolic machinery of the animal members of the marine trophic organization.

Summary

Rates of photosynthesis by marine plants (gross primary production) and rates of net primary production are measured with light and dark bottle O_2 evolution techniques or radioactive C^{14} techniques. These techniques analyze the effect of several environmental factors on the rates of primary production in the sea. Significant among these factors are light intensity and quality, nutrient availability, and grazing pressure.

Several marine plant groups complement the light-absorbing capabilities of chlorophyll with various accessory pigments that give them their characteristic coloration. The light and nutrient requirements of marine plants are usually spatially separated in the sea; light is available at the sea surface, yet great stores of dissolved nutrients are concentrated in waters below the photic zone. Only in areas where upwelling and mixing occur to return the deep-water nutrients to the photic zone do marine plants thrive.

The cumulative effects of cyclic grazing pressures and varying light intensity and nutrient availability create a pattern of seasonal and geographical plant production. But, taken as a single production system, the marine environment produces approximately 200–250 billion tons of plant material each year.

Questions for Discussion

1. Describe the important processes that influence nutrient return to the photic zone of the ocean. Relate these processes to the geographical distribution of plant production in the sea.
2. Discuss in detail why large attached marine plants have a variety of photosynthetic pigments. Relate this to their general depth distribution.
3. In areas of upwelling, the rate of marine plant productivity may often be comparable to good farmland, although the amount of plant material present may be very low. Explain why, in terms of general characteristics of marine phytoplankton.
4. What advantages does the C^{14} method for measuring primary productivity have over the O_2 evolution method used earlier?

Suggestions for Further Reading

Books

Raymont, J. E. 1963. *Plankton and productivity in the oceans*. New York: Pergamon Press. Chapters 6–11.

Russell-Hunter, W. D. 1970. *Aquatic productivity*. New York: Macmillan.

Steele, J. H. 1974. *The structure of marine ecosystems*. Cambridge: Harvard Univ. Press.

Steemann Nielsen, E. 1975. *Marine photosynthesis*. New York: Elsevier.

Articles

Correll, D. L. 1978. Estuarine productivity. *Bioscience* 28:646–50.

Landry, M. R. 1976. The structure of marine ecosystems: an alternative. *Marine Biology* 35:1–7.

Levine, R. P. 1969. The mechanism of photosynthesis. *Scientific American*, December: 58–70.

Malone, T. C. 1971. The relative importance of nannoplankton and netplankton as primary producers in tropical oceanic and neritic phytoplankton communities. *Limnology and Oceanography* 16:633–39.

Mann, K. H. 1973. Seaweeds: their productivity and strategy for growth. *Science* 182:975–81.

Moorish idol. Photo by Doug Wallin/
Taurus Photos.

7 Life at Large—The Pelagic Animals

Life in the pelagic division of the marine environment exists in a three-dimensional, nutritionally dilute medium. Both microscopic plants and the major groups of small herbivores and many of their larger predators live in near-surface waters. The general distribution of pelagic animals reflects their nutritional dependency on the primary producers of the sea. Like marine plants, they are concentrated in regions of upwelling, over continental shelves and other shallows, and elsewhere in or near the photic zone. The upper few hundred meters of the sea teem with animal life. At greater depths, population densities diminish rapidly but never completely disappear.

The animals of the pelagic division include the zooplankton and nekton. Most nektonic animals begin life as members of the zooplankton community. As they grow and improve their swimming capabilities, they eventually graduate to the status of "nekton." As no practical basis exists for precisely separating pelagic animals into functional plankton and nekton groups (see p. 55, chap. 2), they will be discussed together in this chapter.

Zooplankton Feeding and Distribution

Although a few larger invertebrates, such as shrimp and squid, are nektonic as adults, the nekton is dominated by vertebrates. Fish are the most common members of the nekton, along with several species of mammals and a few regionally abundant species of birds and reptiles. Zooplankton are represented by a variety of permanent planktonic forms (the **holoplankton**) and by temporarily planktonic larval stages (the **meroplankton**) of shallow-water invertebrates, which are discussed in chapter 4.

The great variety of meroplankton reflects the diversity of their sedentary adult stages. The meroplankton, like their parents, are concentrated in the nearshore neritic province. Their abundance is related to the seasonal productivity cycles of local phytoplankton communities. Meroplankton seldom occur in significant numbers in oceanic waters.

The holoplankton are recruited from several animal phyla. Prominent among these are the protozoans, cnidarians, ctenophores, some mollusks, chaetognaths, abundant crustacean arthropods, and invertebrate chordates. Yet fewer than five thousand species of holoplankton, and a similar number of nektonic species, exist in the world ocean. This restricted diversity of pelagic animal life is partially an evolutionary response to living in a near uniform, constantly moving fluid environment. Small scale variations in temperature or chemical features are minimized by local mixing and diffusive processes. Additionally, the pelagic pool of nonliving organic material is mostly in dissolved form, with less available as particulate debris. There are no pelagic equivalents of mud flats or rocky reefs to interrupt the monotonous uniformity of the water medium and increase the variety of discrete microhabitats available to pelagic animals.

The most numerous and widespread species of holoplankton are the crustaceans. Copepods, euphausiids, amphipods, decapods, and ostracods (figs. 3.23 and 7.5) all contribute greatly to near-surface plankton communities. Calanoid copepods, such as *Calanus* and *Acartia*, account for the bulk of herbivorous zooplankton in the 1–5 mm size range. Copepods, like all other arthropods, are equipped with an exoskeleton and numerous jointed appendages. All adult calanoid copepod species are similar in body form and general feeding behavior, suggesting a very successful, functional form.

Although copepods prey on large phytoplankton cells when they are available, calanoid species typically capture smaller, more abundant phytoplankton by means of a basketlike filtering mechanism derived from the complex feathery head appendages (fig. 7.1). The hairlike setae on the appendages of *Calanus* are fine enough to retain food particles larger than about 10 μm. Laboratory observations have revealed that food particles are carried into the filter basket by a series of water vortices (defined by arrows in fig. 7.1), which are generated by the feeding appendages and the five pairs of thoracic swimming legs. Special long setae on the feeding appendages remove the trapped particles and direct them to the mouth. With this filtering mechanism, *Calanus* is capable of exploiting quite a size range of food particles.

Calanus and other small pelagic particle grazers are normally exposed to a wide spectrum of food particle sizes, between 1 and 100 μm. These particles range from abundant minute bacteria through the common types of phytoplankton to rare, large particles. This size spectrum of food particles presents an opportunity for small versatile particle grazers to specialize by adopting a feeding strategy that involves selectivity of optimum-sized food items. Presently there is little detailed information about lower trophic level linkages in even the simplest of pelagic food webs. It can only be suggested that *Calanus* employs efficient selective feeding strategies and does not simply blunder through the ocean indiscriminantly consuming all particle sizes.

Many noncrustacean holoplankton are translucent or even transparent. Whatever ambient light exists in their immediate environment simply passes through them without forming a silhouette to alert potential predators. These species lack large muscle masses and skeletal tissue, giving their bodies a watery or gelatinous consistency. Some are extremely fragile and are nearly impossible to collect intact. These gelatinous forms include single-celled protozoans, cnidarian medusae ("jellyfish"), ctenophores, planktonic mollusks, and salps and appendicularians. The larger jellyfish and ctenophores prey on zooplankton and small fish, whereas many of the smaller forms exhibit sophisticated filter-feeding adaptations which rival those of copepods in their efficiency and complexity.

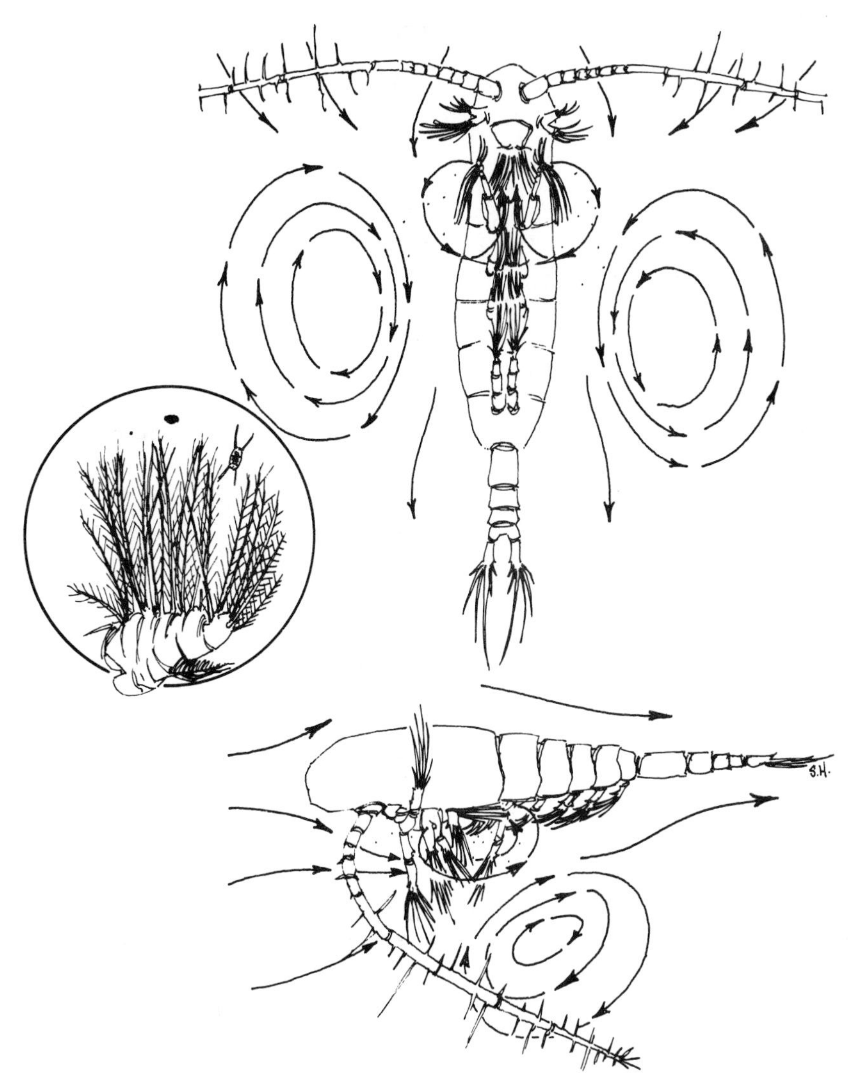

Fig. 7.1 The filter-feeding mechanism of *Calanus,* shown from a ventral (above) and a side view (below). The fine setae of the feeding appendages are compared to a 50 μm diatom (inset). Adapted from Russell-Hunter 1969.

Numerous gelatinous herbivores rely on nets or webs of mucus to ensnare food particles. One highly evolved example is *Gleba*, a planktonic pteropod mollusk. When feeding, *Gleba* secretes a mucous web, often exceeding 2 m in diameter. The free-floating web spreads horizontally as it is produced, maintaining a single point of attachment at the mouth of the snail. As the animal and web slowly sink, small plankton and other particles are trapped in the mucus. The web with its load of food is then formed into a mucous string, directed to the mouth, and ingested.

Another elaborate mucous feeding system is found in appendicularians, small, tadpole-shaped invertebrate chordates. Most appendicularians live totally enclosed within delicate, transparent mucous bubbles (fig. 7.2). At one end of the bubble are openings through which food-laden water enters, pumped by the tail beat of the occupant. The incurrent openings are screened with fine-meshed grills to exclude large phytoplankton cells. Smaller cells enter the

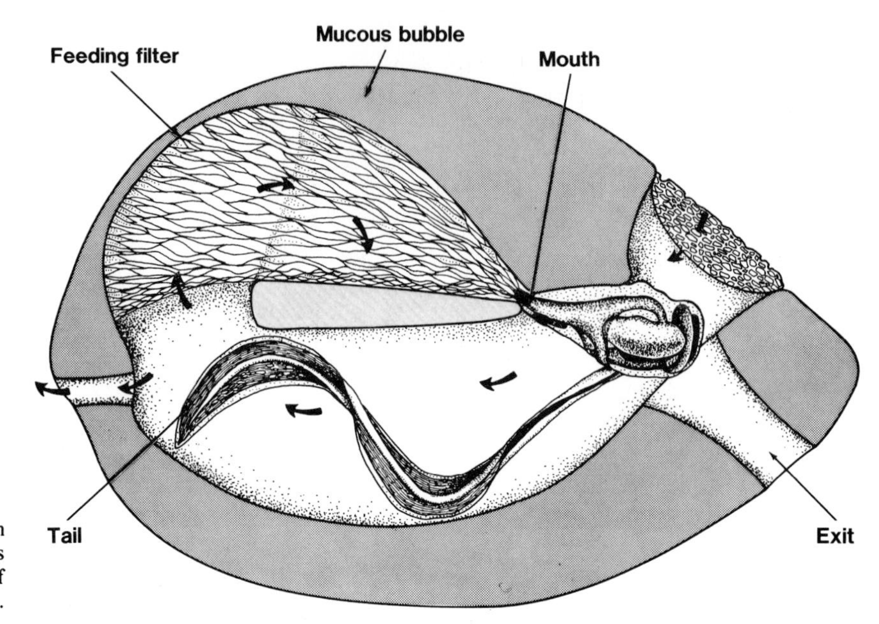

Fig. 7.2 The appendicularian *Oikopleura* within its mucous bubble. Arrows indicate path of water flow.

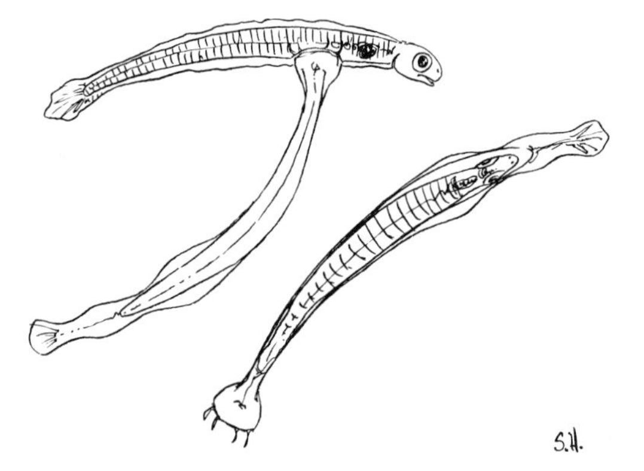

Fig. 7.3 A small chaetognath, *Sagitta*, capturing and consuming a fish larva its own size.

bubble and are trapped on a complex internal mucous feeding filter. Every few seconds the animal sucks the particles off the filter and into its mouth. When the incurrent filter becomes clogged or the interior is fouled with feces, the entire bubble is abandoned, and a new one constructed, sometimes in as little as ten minutes.

The small, soft-bodied chaetognaths are voracious predators of other zooplankton. This group of planktonic animals is frequently referred to as a minor phylum, for only about sixty species exist. Yet they are found throughout the world ocean, often in numbers sufficient to decimate whole broods of young fish (fig. 7.3). In addition to their significant role in pelagic food chains, some species of chaetognaths are well-known biological indicators of distinctive types of surface ocean water. So too are many species of crustaceans, pteropods, and other pelagic animals.

Away from the influences of continental borders, zooplankton in the upper 200 m of the world ocean drift along slowly in large, semienclosed current gyres. This upper layer of the oceanic province is the **epipelagic zone.** In marked contrast to the myriad of life zones available to animals on the sea bottom, the epipelagic zone can be partitioned into only a few major habitats. Each is broadly defined by its own unique combination of temperature and salinity characteristics. These major epipelagic habitats are reflective of the major marine climatic zones shown in figure 1.14. Each is inhabited by a suite of zooplankton species that, over a long period of time, have adapted to the special set of environmental conditions which exist there.

The distribution patterns of six species of planktonic euphausiids are mapped in figure 7.4. These patterns closely resemble the general large-scale distribution of many other epipelagic animal species as well. As noted in figure 7.4, there is the tendency for each species to be distributed in broad latitudinal bands across one or more oceans. Well-defined patterns of tropical (*E. diomediae*), subtropical (*E. brevis*), and south polar (*E. superba*) distribution are evident. Some species, such as *E. diomediae* and *E. brevis*, are broadly tolerant to their environmental regimes and occupy wide latitudinal bands. Others (*E. longirostris, T. gregaria,* and *E. superba*) occupy narrower latitudinal ranges. Similar regimes in both the Northern and Southern Hemispheres are frequently inhabited by the same species. This **biantitropical distribution** is exhibited by the subtropical *E. brevis* and the temperate water *T. gregaria.* Often these lower latitude species extend into all three major ocean basins (*E. brevis* and *T. gregaria* do), but occasionally they do not (*E. diomediae*

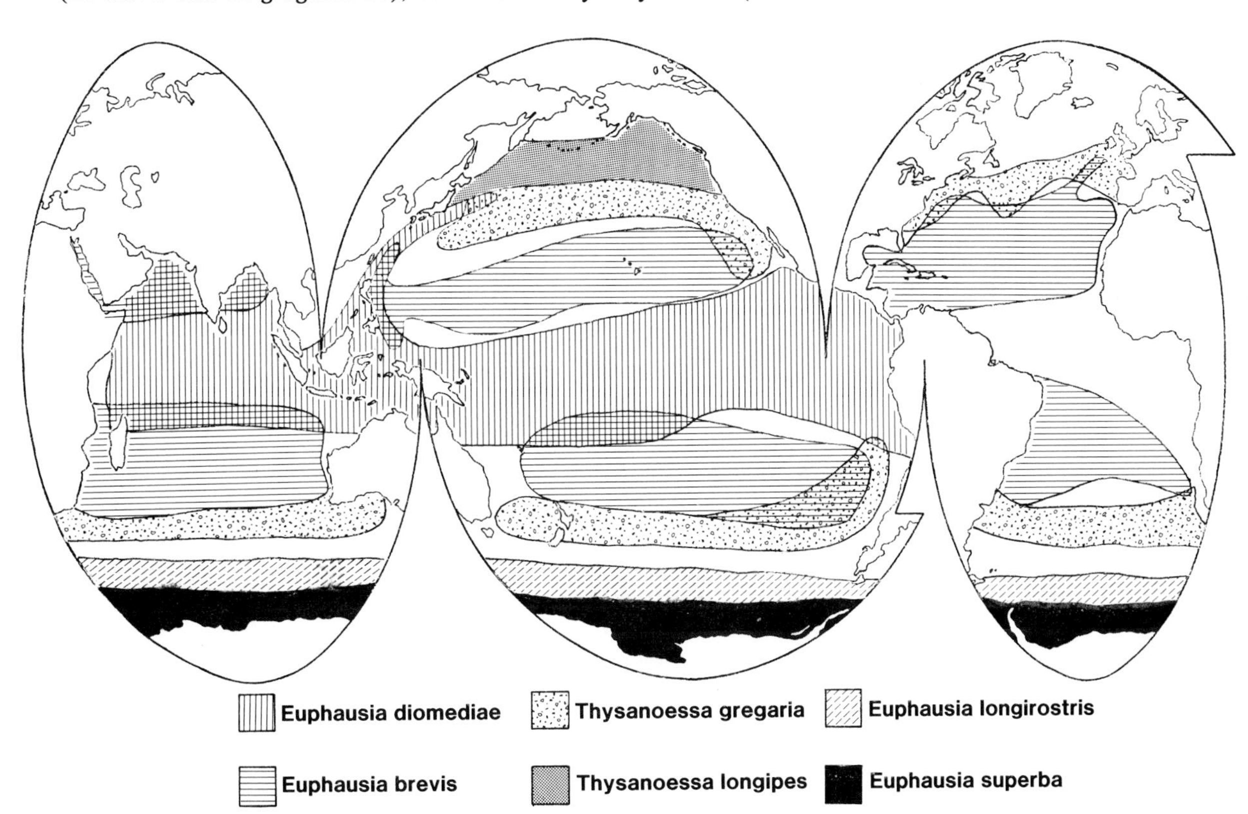

Fig. 7.4 The global distribution of six species of epipelagic euphausiids.

is conspicuously absent from the tropical Atlantic). The distribution of *E. diomediae* suggests that although comparable latitudes in the Atlantic, Pacific, and Indian Oceans provide similar environmental conditions, each ocean still retains significant individual differences.

High latitude species in the Southern Hemisphere (*E. longirostris* and *E. superba*) also commonly extend around the globe, aided by extensive oceanic connections between Antarctica and the other southern continents. Similar circumglobal distributions are less common in higher latitudes of the Northern Hemisphere (*T. longipes* is restricted to the North Pacific).

There exists some slight overlap of the boundaries of these zones; but analyses of the distribution patterns of numerous other species of zooplankton and nekton have confirmed that these boundaries define in a very real way the major epipelagic habitats of the oceanic province.

Below the epipelagic zone we know considerably less about the distribution of pelagic animals. But regardless of where they live, these creatures experience environmental conditions and problems of survival that are different than those of bottom dwellers. They have solved, with varying degrees of success, the fundamental problem of staying off the bottom. Consequently, many have become divorced from the sluggish life-style of the benthos. For some nekton, high-speed locomotion has become a critical aspect of existence. Efficient locomotion and highly developed senses for orientation and navigation have made possible effective small- and large-scale migrations to seek food and otherwise improve conditions for survival.

Buoyancy

Living in the water free from the solid bottom presents some buoyancy problems for pelagic marine animals, since most of the tissues of these animals are somewhat more dense than seawater (which has a specific gravity of 1.02–1.03). The specific gravity of muscle is near 1.05; of bone, scale, and shell, 2.0; of cartilage, 1.1; and of fat, wax, and oil, 0.8–0.9. The solutions to this problem are even more varied and complex than those exhibited by phytoplankton.

Increased Frictional Resistance

Our previous definition of zooplankton was based largely on their weak swimming ability. The smaller zooplanktonic forms especially do not move around much under their own power. In this respect they are much like phytoplankton. As you might expect, many of the flotation and buoyancy devices employed by zooplankton are similar to those found in phytoplankton. Most zooplankton are characteristically small, but are able to increase the frictional resistance to the water by increasing the surface area of the animal relative to its minute volume. Increased frictional resistance to sinking is also derived from a profusion of spines, hairs, "wings," and other surface extensions (fig. 7.5).

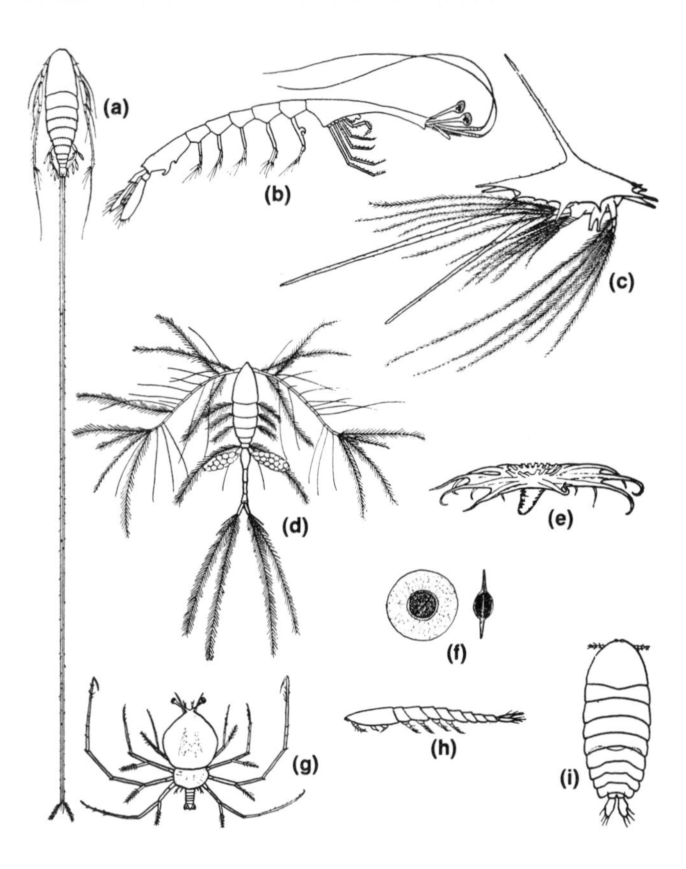

Fig. 7.5 Some structural adaptations for flotation in planktonic animals: (*a*) copepod *(Aegisthus)*; (*b*) decapod *(Lucifer)*; (*c*) barnacle nauplius; (*d*) copepod *(Oithona)*; (e) holothurian *(Pelagiothuria)*; (*f*) pelagic egg of copepod *(Tortanus)*; (*g*) phyllosoma larva of lobster; (*h*) copepod *(Sapphirina)* side view and (*i*) top view. From H. U. Sverdrup, Martin W. Johnson, and Richard H. Fleming, *The Oceans: Their Physics, Chemistry, and Biology*, © 1942, renewed 1970. By permission of Prentice-Hall, Inc., Englewood Cliffs, New Jersey.

For larger, faster-moving animals, however, increased frictional resistance is counterproductive to high speeds in water. As a result, the evolutionary trends in fish and other nekton have been toward a variety of other buoyancy mechanisms, but these mechanisms are found in many zooplankton as well.

Reduction of Heavy Body Tissues

Reduced bone and muscle tissue is especially common in deep-ocean fish. Many species of deep-living fishes have flabby, soft, nearly transparent flesh supported by very weak bones (fig. 7.6). The bodies of these fishes serve as little more than appendages to move their over-sized mouths feebly from one victim to the next.

Salps, ctenophores, jellyfish, arrowworms, and many other zooplankton with gelatinous, watery body consistencies produce lift by actively eliminating heavier sulphate ions from their body fluids and replacing them with chloride ions to maintain osmotic equilibrium. *Cranchia scabra,* a squid, excludes divalent ions from its body fluids and replaces them with less dense ammonium ions derived from metabolic wastes. Another squid, *Chiroteuthis,* has one of its four pairs of arms filled with low density body fluids. These arms, which have less muscle than the other arms and appear swollen, are located on the

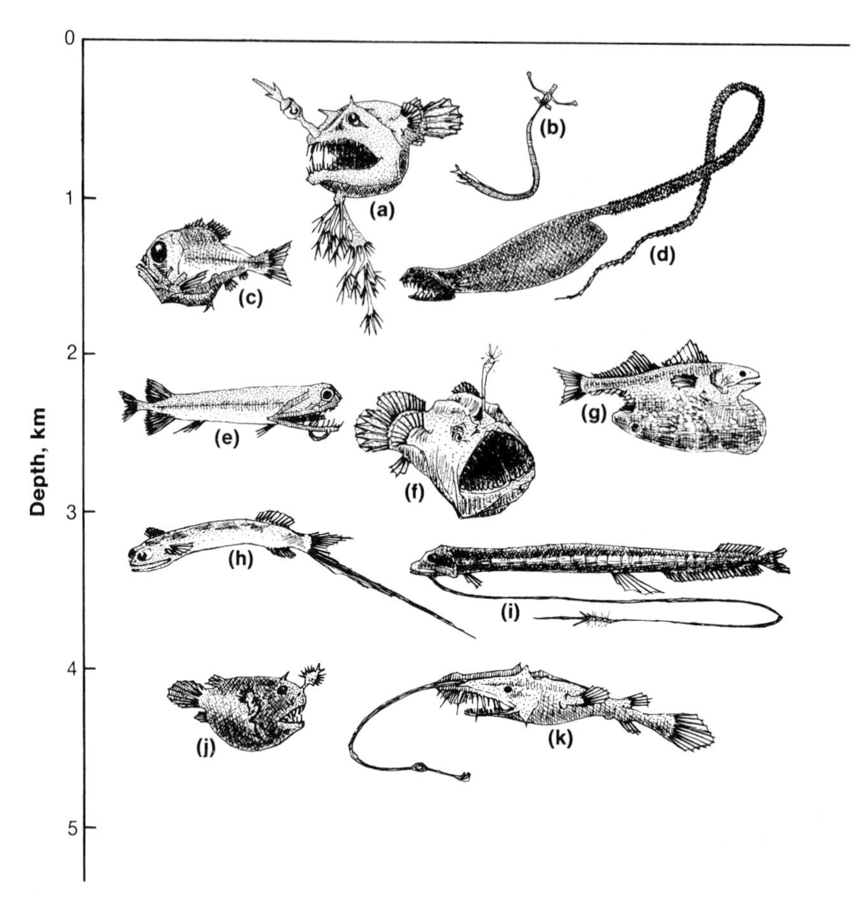

Fig. 7.6 A few fish of the deep sea, shown at their usual depths. Most have reduced bodies, large mouths, and lures to attract prey. (*a*) An angler, *Linophyrne*, (*b*) young *Idiacanthus* with eyes on stalks, (*c*) a hatchetfish *Argyropelecus*, (*d*) a gulper, *Saccopharynx*, (*e*) a widemouth, *Malocosteus*, (*f*) another angler, *Melanocetus*, (*g*) the "great swallower," *Chiasmodus*, with a larger fish in its stomach, (*h*) a giant tail *Gigantura*, (*i*) *Eustomias*, (*j*) *Borophyrne*, an angler, and (*k*) another angler, *Lasiognathus*.

ventral side of the animal. As they are lighter than seawater, they may cause *Chiroteuthis* to swim and float upside down.

Stored fats and oils, with specific gravity values ranging from 0.8–0.9, are also quite common buoyancy devices in large as well as small pelagic marine animals. Whales, elephant seals, and other large marine animals maintain thick blubber layers just under the skin. The average blue whale is about 18% blubber, and approximately 80% of the blubber is fat (the remainder is connective tissue and blood vessels). Blubber also functions to streamline these animals and insulate them against heat loss. Many sharks and a variety of bony fishes store great quantities of oils, primarily in the liver and muscle tissue. In some species of sharks, the liver accounts for more than one-quarter of the body weight.

Gas Inclusions

Fats, oils, and body fluids of reduced densities, although widely employed for buoyancy, are still only slightly less dense than seawater. This poses a serious problem for many small but active nektonic species. They cannot energetically afford to pack around a huge oily liver or a thick blubber layer; nor can they sacrifice muscle and bone to lighten the load. This problem is neatly solved for many marine animals with an internal gas-filled flotation organ. The chief advantage of a gas inclusion for buoyancy is its density. At sea level, air is only about 0.1% as dense as seawater. Thus, a small gas volume provides a relatively large amount of lift.

The amount of lift that can be derived from a volume of gas depends on the volume of seawater the gas displaces. Unlike water, gases are very compressible, and so occupy different volumes at varying pressures (and depths). At sea level, the pressure created by the earth's envelope of air is about 1 kg/cm^2 or 15 lb./in.^{2} or 1 atmosphere (atm) of pressure. Below the sea surface, the water pressure increases about one atm for each 10 m depth increase. Thus the total pressure experienced by a fish at 5,000 m is 501 atm (more than 3.5 tons/in.^{2}).

The gas-filled buoyancy organs of some marine animals are rigid and strong and can structurally resist increased water pressures found at great depths. Others maintain their buoyancy in flexible, compressible containers.

Rigid Gas Containers

Rigid-walled gas containers are found only in a few types of cephalopods. All cephalopods are believed to have evolved from an ancestral stock that had an external shell (fig. 7.7). *Nautilus* is the only living cephalopod that has retained its external shell. The shells of other living cephalopods are either reduced to an internal chambered structure, as in the cuttlefish (*Sepia*) and

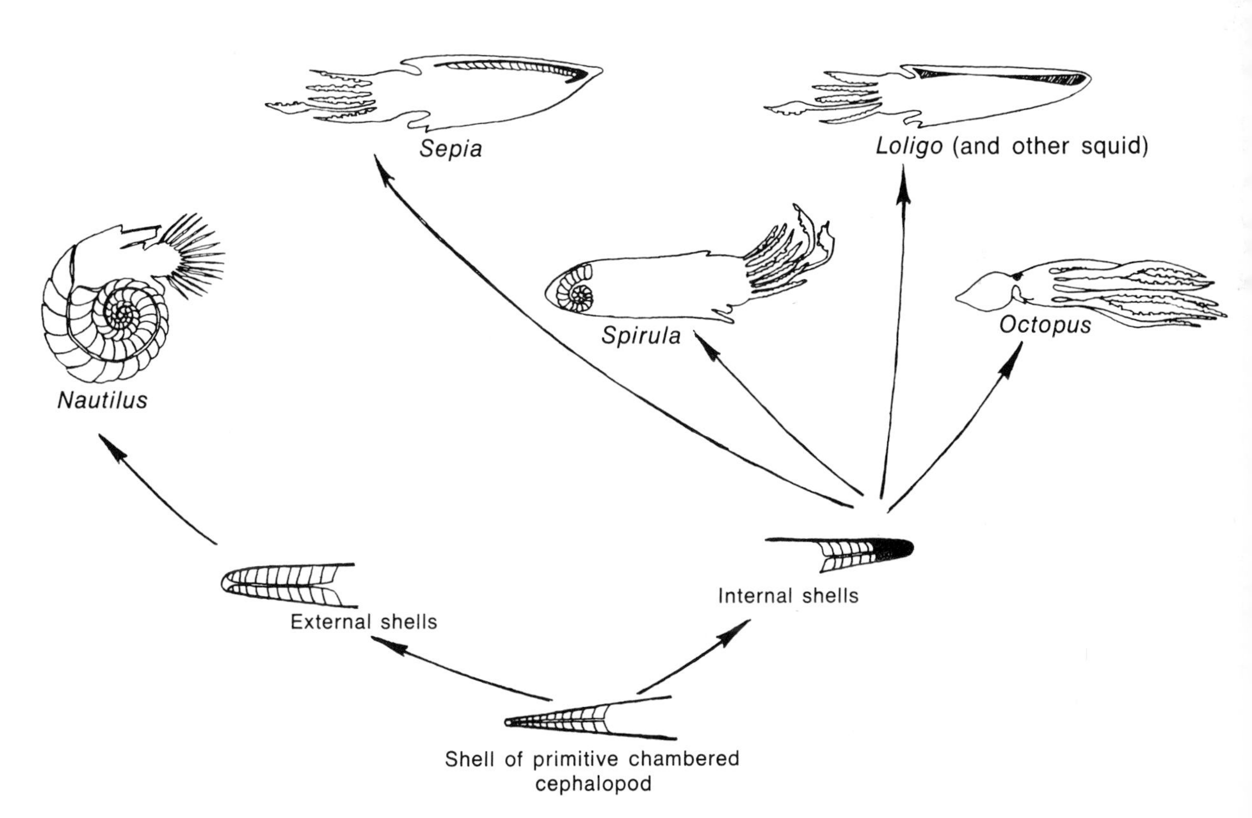

Fig. 7.7 The probable evolutionary relationships of living and extinct cephalopods. The shape and structure of the chambered shells is emphasized. Darkened areas represent structural support.

Spirula (a deep-water squid); or are absent entirely, as in *Octopus*. In squids other than *Spirula*, a thin chitinous structure (the **pen**) extends the length of the mantle tissue, and represents the last vestige of what was once an internal shell.

Nautilus, *Sepia*, and *Spirula* all have hard transverse **septa** that separate adjacent chambers of the shell. In *Nautilus*, only the last and largest chamber is occupied by the animal. As *Nautilus* grows, it moves forward in its shell and adds a new chamber by secreting another transverse septum across the area it just vacated. The chambers are connected by a central tubelike tissue, the **siphuncle.** The siphuncle of *Nautilus* removes salts from the fluids left behind when a new chamber is formed. Water within the chamber then diffuses into the siphuncle because of the osmotic gradient maintained by the siphuncle. As water leaves, it is replaced by gases (mostly N_2) from tissue fluids. Gases are not "pumped" into the chambers, but are simply allowed to diffuse in. As the total pressure of the gases dissolved in seawater never exceeds 1 atm, neither does the gas pressure within the chambers. The lift obtained from the gas inclusion very effectively offsets the weight of the shell in water, and *Nautilus* becomes neutrally buoyant. *Sepia* and presumably *Spirula* evacuate fluids from their chambered shells in a similar manner.

These chambered cephalopods are confronted with the same depth-limiting factor that plagues submarines. Their depth range is seriously limited by the resistance of their shells to increased water pressure. Each species has a critical implosion depth where the external water pressure becomes too great for the design and strength of its shell, and it collapses. The implosion depth of *Nautilus* shells is somewhat below 500 m, yet this animal does not normally live below 240 m.

Nonrigid Gas Inclusions

A few genera of siphonophores (a type of colonial cnidarian), as in figure 7.8, maintain neutral or even positive buoyancy by secreting gases into a float, or **pneumatophore.** *Velella* (sometimes called by-the-wind sailor, Jack-by-the-wind, or simply purple sail), and the larger Portuguese man-of-war, *Physalia* (7.8*a*), have large pneumatophores and float at the sea surface. The pneumatophore also acts as a simple sail to catch surface breezes that transport the colony long distances. Both *Velella* and *Physalia* have a worldwide distribution, with only one species in each genus.

Other siphonophores with gas floats are neutrally buoyant and can easily change their vertical position in the water column by swimming (7.8*b*). A gas gland within the pneumatophore secretes gas into the float. Excess gases are vented through a small pore that is opened and closed by a sphincter muscle.

A little planktonic snail, *Glaucus*, has a different solution to its buoyancy problems. It simply produces and stores large amounts of intestinal gases to offset the weight of its shell. *Ianthina*, another planktonic snail, forms a cluster of bubbles to which it clings at the surface. This adaptation is apparently related to its preference for feeding on the soft parts of *Velella* (which also floats at the surface).

(a)

(b)

Fig. 7.8 Two siphonophores with gas-filled air floats for buoyancy: (*a*) *Physalia*, the Portuguese man-of-war with the commensal fish *Nomeus*; (*b*) a midwater physonect siphonophore. (*a*) Courtesy of the American Museum of Natural History; (*b*) Courtesy of E. Barham, National Marine Fisheries Service.

Many bony fish, especially active species with extensive muscle and skeletal tissue, have body densities about 5% greater than that of seawater. To achieve neutral buoyancy, many of these fishes have an internal swim bladder filled with gases (mostly N_2 and O_2). The swim bladders of modern bony fish develop embryonically from an out-pouching of the esophagus (fig. 7.9).

The connection between the esophagus and swim bladder, called the **pneumatic duct,** is present during the larval or juvenile stages of most bony fish. In some species, the pneumatic duct remains unchanged in the adult (**physostomous** condition). In other primarily marine species, the duct disappears as the fish matures (**physoclist** condition, fig. 7.10). However, nearly half of the more than 20,000 species of bony fishes, when mature, lose not only the pneumatic duct, but the swim bladder as well. Swim bladders are notably lacking in bottom fish and very active, continuously swimming fish like some tuna.

Swim bladders are not rigid structures. As such, the volume of water they displace is subject to changing water pressures at different depths. A fish

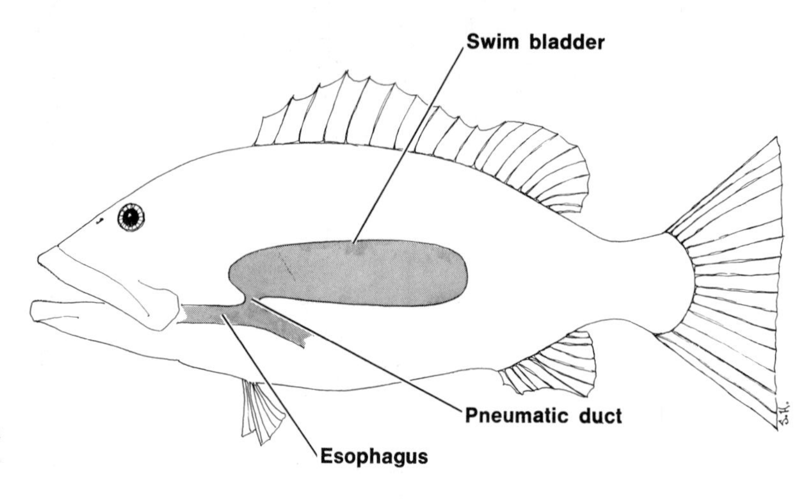

Fig. 7.9 Position of the swim bladder in bony fish.

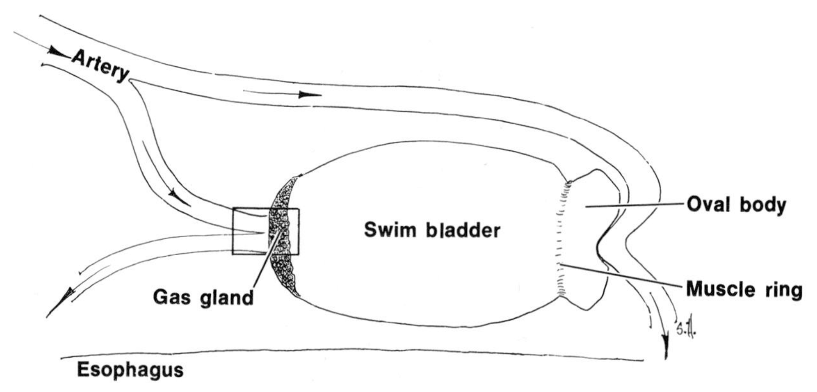

Fig. 7.10 A physoclist swim bladder. Arrows indicate the direction of blood flow. Note the lack of any connection between the bladder and the esophagus. The area within the rectangle is diagrammed in greater detail in figure 7.15.

that swims downward experiences greater external water pressures, which compress the swim bladder and reduce its volume. The quantity of gas in the bladder must then be increased to compensate for the pressure change. Conversely, an ascending fish must get rid of swim bladder gases as rapidly as they expand. Some physostomous fish fill their swim bladders simply by gulping air at the sea surface. Excess gases from physostomous swim bladders are also expelled through the pneumatic duct and eventually out the mouth or anus. Lacking a pneumatic duct, a fish with a physoclist swim bladder reabsorbs excess gases into the bloodstream. These bladders have a specialized region, the oval body (refer again to fig. 7.10), which is richly supplied with blood vessels for resorption of gases. The oval body is isolated from the remainder of the swim bladder by a muscle ring that regulates access of the bladder gases to the oval body.

In most cases, both types of swim bladders have a gas gland that secretes gas from the blood into the bladder when these fish have no access to air. But again there are occasional exceptions. Herring, for example, lack gas glands, and are restricted to reasonably shallow waters. The capacity of fish with physoclist swim bladders to quickly add or remove bladder gases to compensate for a rapid depth change is limited. If a deep-water fish rapidly ascends, the decreased water pressure allows the gases within the somewhat elastic swim bladder to expand and reduce the overall density of the fish. The density decrease may be so great that the fish is unable to descend for some time. This fact is well illustrated by the appearance of many deep-water fish brought to the surface (unwillingly, of course) in trawls. It is not unusual for the swim bladders of such fish to expand and force their stomachs into their mouths (fig. 7.11), causing severe internal organ damage.

In shallow water, the gas composition of swim bladders resembles that of air, about 20% O_2 and 80% N_2. At greater depths, the concentration of both gases increases to match the increasing water pressure. Fish with gas-filled swim bladders have been taken from depths as great as 7,000 m. The gas pressure needed within the swim bladder to balance the water pressure at that depth (5 tons/in.^{2}) is about 700 atm. Such extreme gas pressures are achieved primarily by a dramatic increase in the O_2 concentration of the bladder gases. Oxygen commonly accounts for more than 50%, and occasionally exceeds 90%, of the gas mixture of swim bladders of deep-ocean fish (fig. 7.12).

The general picture of swim bladder gas composition presented in figure 7.12 poses two intriguing questions concerning the mechanism for filling the

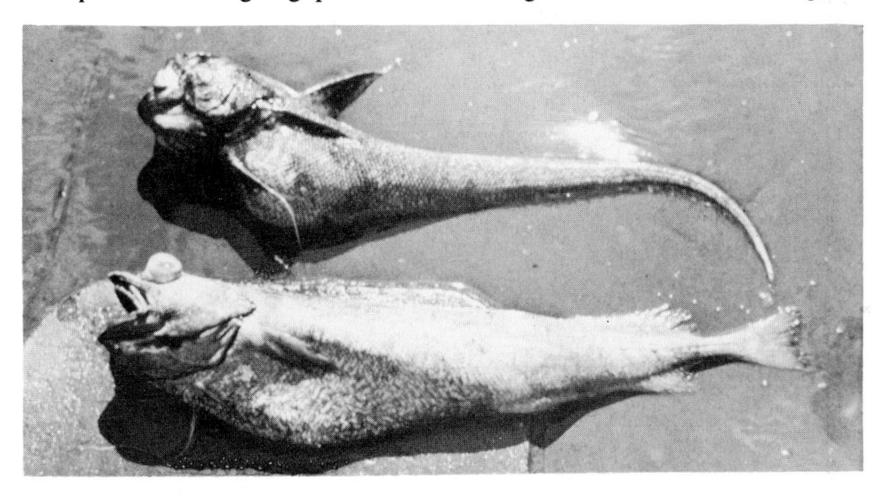

Fig. 7.11 Two deep-sea fish on the deck of a ship after being hauled up from a depth of 800 m. Both were seriously damaged and distorted by the rapid expansion of gases in their swim bladders on the way up.

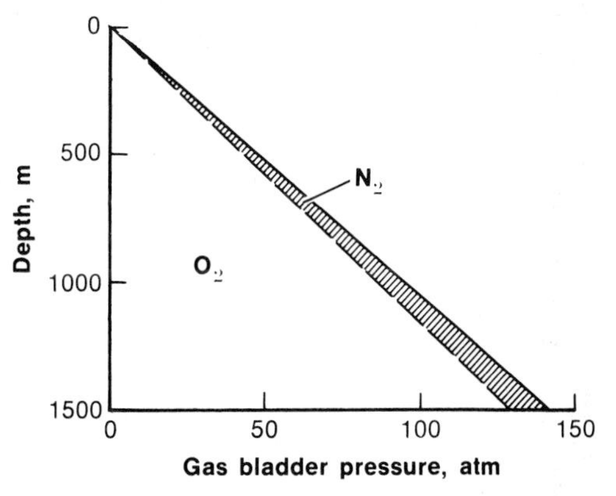

Fig. 7.12 Variation of O_2 and N_2 (shaded) pressures in swim bladders with increased depth. Below a few hundred meters, O_2 dominates. Adapted from Kanwisher and Ebeling 1957.

swim bladder in deep water. First, how are O_2 and N_2, which are dissolved in seawater at pressures no greater than 1 atm, concentrated in swim bladders at pressures as great as 700 atm? Secondly, why is O_2 so much more abundant than N_2 within swim bladders at great depths, when N_2 is more common than O_2 in seawater (often 10 times more abundant)? In some instances, O_2 is at least 1,000 times as concentrated within the swim bladders of deep fish as in the water just outside the fish. Nitrogen is generally concentrated by a factor of 10–20 times.

Deep-water fish fill their swim bladders by absorbing N_2, O_2, and traces of other gases from seawater at the gills. These gases are transported in the blood to the gas gland of the swim bladder, then secreted into the bladder at pressures equal to external water pressures. A full explanation of this process requires a brief digression from swim bladders to some aspects of gas exchange in fish.

Fish take water and dissolved gases into the mouth and pump it back over the gills. Each **gill arch** supports a double row of bladelike **gill filaments** (fig. 7.13). Each flat filament bears numerous even smaller **secondary lamellae** to further increase the area available for gas exchange. Active fishes, like mackerel, may have up to 10 cm^2 of gill surface area for each gram of body weight, which approaches 10 times the entire surface area of the body. Relative gill surface areas are notably less in sedentary bottom fish.

Minute capillaries circulate blood very near the inner surface of the secondary lamellae. As long as the O_2 concentration of the blood is less than that of the water passing over the gills, O_2 continues to diffuse across the very thin walls of the lamellae and into the bloodstream. In fish gills, the efficiency of O_2 absorption into the blood is enhanced by the direction of water flow over the gill lamellae (arrows, fig. 7.13), which is the reverse of the blood flow within the lamellae. Oxygen-rich water moving opposite to the flow of O_2-depleted blood establishes a very effective **countercurrent system** for O_2 exchange (fig. 7.14). Oxygen-deficient blood returning from the body enters the lamellae adjacent to water that has already given up much of its O_2 to blood in other parts of the lamellae. As the blood moves across the lamellae, it continually encounters water with greater O_2 concentrations, and picks up more O_2 as it goes. In this manner, the blood, as it flows through the lamellae, is always adjacent to water with a slightly greater O_2 content. Thus, O_2 continually diffuses from the water into the blood along the entire length of the capillary bed within the lamellae. With such a countercurrent O_2 exchanger, some fish are capable of extracting up to 85% of the dissolved O_2 present in the water passing over the gills. In contrast, air-breathing vertebrates like humans use less than 25% of the O_2 that enters their lungs.

Oxygen is transported in vertebrate blood, not as dissolved O_2, but rather in chemical combination with the red pigment **hemoglobin** contained within red blood cells. Nitrogen is also absorbed by the gills, but remains dissolved in the fluids of the blood. Antarctic ice fish and a few types of eel larvae are among the very few fish that lack hemoglobin for O_2 transport. Hemoglobin functions by combining with O_2 at high O_2 levels found at the gills (or lungs in other vertebrates), and releasing O_2 to the body tissues at low O_2 concen-

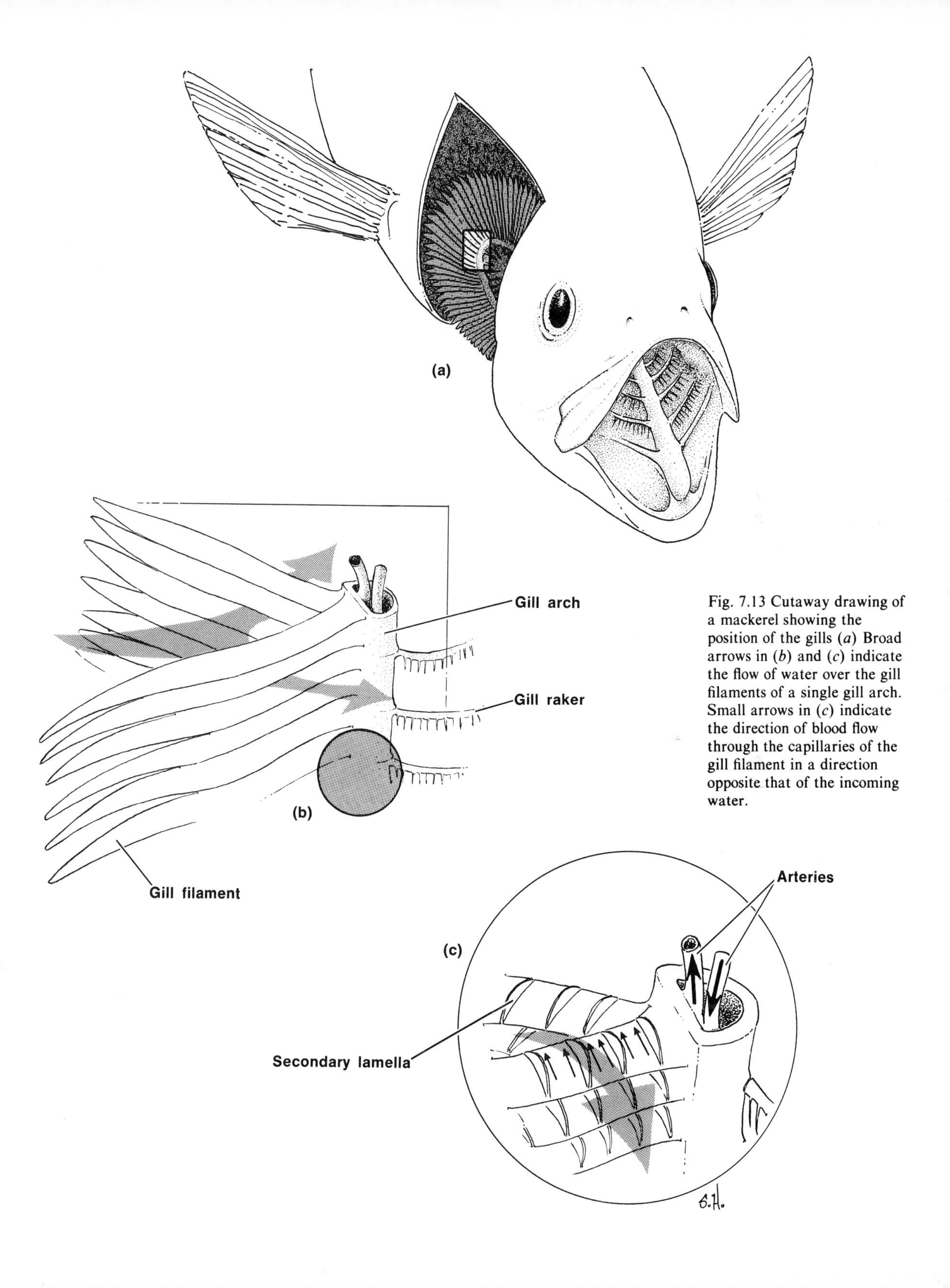

Fig. 7.13 Cutaway drawing of a mackerel showing the position of the gills (*a*) Broad arrows in (*b*) and (*c*) indicate the flow of water over the gill filaments of a single gill arch. Small arrows in (*c*) indicate the direction of blood flow through the capillaries of the gill filament in a direction opposite that of the incoming water.

trations. The quantity of O_2 carried by hemoglobin depends on the O_2 concentration of the water flowing over the gills, and of the O_2 demand by the tissues where it is used.

When hemoglobin loaded with O_2 reaches the gas gland of the swim bladder (refer to fig. 7.10), it must be induced to leave the hemoglobin and diffuse into the swim bladder, even in the face of high O_2 pressures within the bladder. The role of the gas gland in this process is simple, but critical. As oxygenated blood enters the gas gland, lactic acid is produced to lower the pH of the blood. Lower pH conditions reduce the O_2-carrying capacity of hemoglobin and induce it to dump part of its O_2 load. The unloaded O_2 has not yet left the blood; it is simply no longer associated with the hemoglobin. Additional lactic acid production creates lower blood pH conditions and encourages hemoglobin to release a substantial portion (up to 50%) of its O_2 load, even against a large pressure gradient. It is estimated that the total effects of lactic acid on hemoglobin are sufficient to produce about two atm of O_2 pressure at the gas gland.

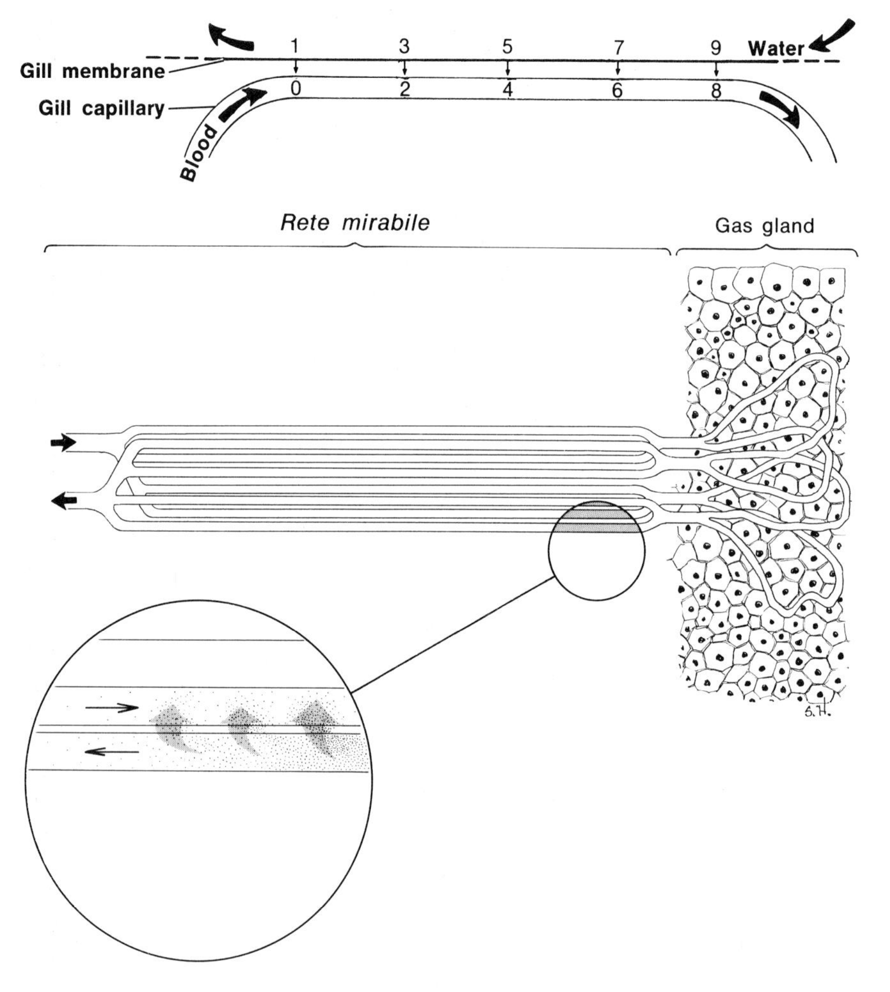

Fig. 7.14 A counter-current gas exchange system of fish gills. Nearly all the O_2 from water flowing right to left diffuses across the gill membrane into the blood flowing in the opposite direction. Numbers represent arbitrary O_2 units.

Fig. 7.15 A simplified diagram of the *rete mirabile* and gas gland associated with the swim bladders of bony fish. Inset illustrates the counter-current arrangement of blood flow (small arrows) and the diffusion of O_2 from outgoing to incoming blood vessels (broad arrows). Adapted from Hoar 1966.

Eventually the O_2 will diffuse into the swim bladder if the O_2 pressure there is not greater than 2 atm. However, this mechanism alone is not capable of producing the very high gas pressures found in the swim bladders of deep-water fish. All deep-water fish with gas-filled swim bladders have an extensive network of capillaries, called the **rete mirabile** (wonderful net), leading to and away from the gas gland (fig. 7.15, and refer to fig. 7.10). The capillaries that approach the gas gland carrying O_2-rich hemoglobin are situated adjacent to and parallel with other capillaries leaving the gas gland. Often a rete system contains as many as 200,000 such capillary channels. These complex rete systems form another countercurrent exchange system that operates on the same principle as that described for the gills.

Large amounts of O_2 forced to dissociate from hemoglobin by lactic acid at the gas gland may be blocked from diffusing into the swim bladder because of the high gas pressures there. If the O_2 leaves the region of the gas gland via a capillary of the rete system, it is not lost. Rather, it diffuses across the capillary walls to the incoming blood of adjacent capillaries. The O_2 forced off the hemoglobin is thus trapped in this recycling system as it leaves the gas gland, but before it escapes the rete system. Eventually, the pressure of O_2 in the capillaries is mechanically concentrated until it surpasses even the very high pressures of the swim bladder, and O_2 diffuses from the gas gland into the bladder.

As one might expect, a longer rete is capable of concentrating more O_2 at the gas gland. Still the rete need not be unmanageably long. It has been estimated that a rete only 1 cm long could secrete O_2 at pressures up to 2,000 atm, well in excess of the swim bladder pressures needed even in the deepest parts of the sea.

The rete mirabile concentrates N_2 as well as O_2. However, the lack of a specialized transport system for N_2 (as hemoglobin is for O_2) relegates N_2 to the role of a minor gas in swim bladders at great depths. One notable exception worth mentioning is the deep-living freshwater whitefish that has been collected with N_2 as high as 99% of the swim bladder gas mixture. The mechanism used to accomplish this feat simply is not known.

As the pressure of gases inside swim bladders increases, so do their densities. At 7,000 m, the gas within a swim bladder is so compressed that its specific gravity is about 0.7, or similar to that of fat. For some fish at great depths, the constant energy expenditure necessary to maintain a full swim bladder becomes unrealistic. So rather than battle the problems of maintaining a gas-filled swim bladder at great depths, some fish have evolved fat-filled swim bladders. They provide almost as much buoyancy as gases do at 7,000 m, but have few of the attendant maintenance problems. Fat-filled swim bladders are also found in mesopelagic fishes that live at intermediate depths (to 1,000 m) and may migrate vertically several hundred meters each day.

Locomotion

It is impossible in a chapter such as this to examine representative modes of locomotion in even the major groups of pelagic marine animals. Instead, locomotion of larger marine animals whose continued existence depends upon speed and agility in the water will be stressed. This is the group of pelagic animals that, primarily because of their ability to move, make up the nekton. For the most part, this section will be concerned with locomotion in fish, but will also include references to a few nektonic invertebrates and to other marine vertebrates.

Animals move to improve or optimize their conditions for survival. Specifically, such movements are made to find food, avoid predators, reproduce, migrate, obtain lift, aerate the gills, and for a host of other reasons. Structural or behavioral adaptations that permit animals to swim with reduced energy expenditures mean that more energy can be diverted to increased growth and reproduction, thus improving the reproductive potential of the species.

Swimming is accomplished in many ways by different marine organisms. But all efficient, high-speed, swimming nekton have two characteristics in common: a streamlined body profile and an effective organ of propulsion.

Body Form

The streamlined shape of most fish and other fast nektonic species is actually a compromise between various possible body forms that allows the animal to slip through the water with as little resistance, or drag, as possible. Three separate components of drag must be considered, first individually, then collectively. **Frictional drag** results from the interaction of the animals's surface with the water surrounding its body. If frictional drag alone is to be reduced, the ideal shape would be a sphere, which has a minimum surface area for the animal's volume, shown in figure 7.16*a*. However, an animal swimming through water must overcome more than just frictional resistance. As it swims forward, an amount of water equal to the size of the animal's cross-sectional area (from a head-on view) must be displaced to permit the animal to progress. Considered by itself, this **form drag** is minimized with a shape that has a small cross-sectional area; that is, a body shaped like a long, thin cylinder (fig. 7.16*b*). The actual shape of a fast swimmer like a tuna or porpoise is neither spherical nor does it resemble a wire, but is a compromise form between the two (fig. 7.16*c*). One additional drag factor, that of **turbulence,** must also be considered. Wind tunnel tests have demonstrated that the ideal shape of a high-speed body in a fluid medium, be it fish, missile, or torpedo, is one that has a length about 4.5 times its greatest diameter. Additionally, it should be roundly blunt at the front end, tapered to a point in the rear, and round in cross-section (fig. 7.16*d*). The form shown in figure 7.16*d* is the best overall shape to minimize the total drag resulting from friction (a function of surface area), form (a function of cross-sectional area), and turbulence (a function of streamlining). Most fast marine animals, excluding their fins, very closely approximate this ideal shape (fig. 7.17).

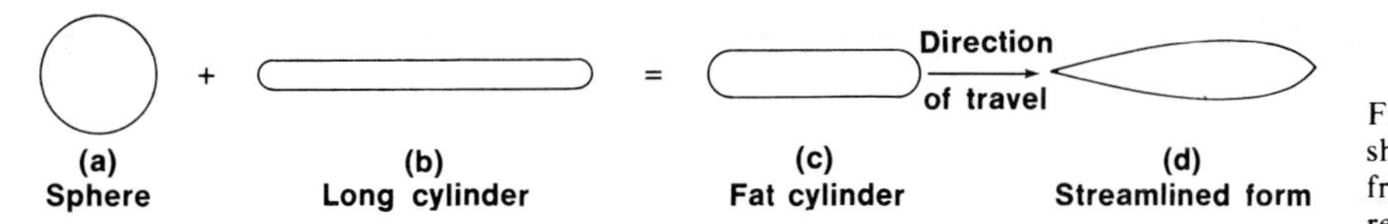

Fig. 7.16 The combination of shapes needed to minimize frictional, form, and turbulent resistance to a body moving through a fluid results in the streamlined shape (*d*).

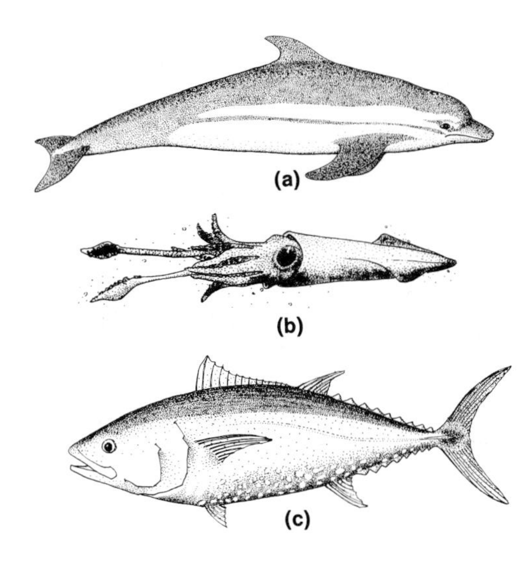

Fig. 7.17 Swift pelagic animals with streamlined body forms: (*a*) bottlenosed porpoise, *Tursiops;* (*b*) squid *Loligo;* and (*c*) tuna *Thunnus.*

Many other fish live in situations, especially near the bottom, on coral reefs, or in kelp beds, where speed is not critical for survival, but maneuverability and camouflage are. They often exhibit a wide variety of adaptive body forms (fig. 7.18) quite unlike those shown in figure 7.17.

Propulsion

The push, or thrust, needed for swimming generally comes from the sides and fins of the animal's body, especially the enlarged **caudal fin** at the posterior end of the body (fig. 7.19). The bending motion of the anterior part of the body is initiated by contraction of a few muscle segments (**myomeres**) on one side to throw the body into a curve. This curve, or wave, passes backward over the body by sequential contraction and relaxation of the myomeres. The contraction of each myomere in succession reinforces the wave form as it passes toward the tail. Immediately after one wave has passed, another starts near the head on the opposite side of the body, and the entire sequence is repeated in rapid succession. Forward thrust is developed almost entirely by the backward component of the pressure of the animal's body and fins against the water.

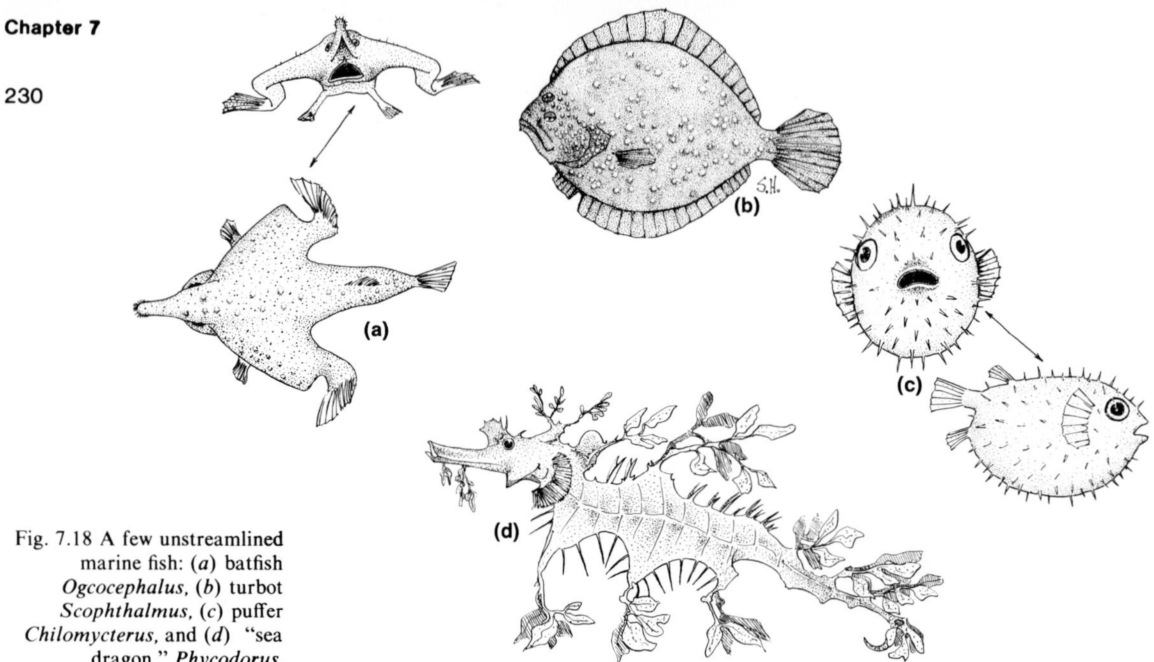

Fig. 7.18 A few unstreamlined marine fish: (*a*) batfish *Ogcocephalus,* (*b*) turbot *Scophthalmus,* (*c*) puffer *Chilomycterus,* and (*d*) "sea dragon," *Phycodorus.*

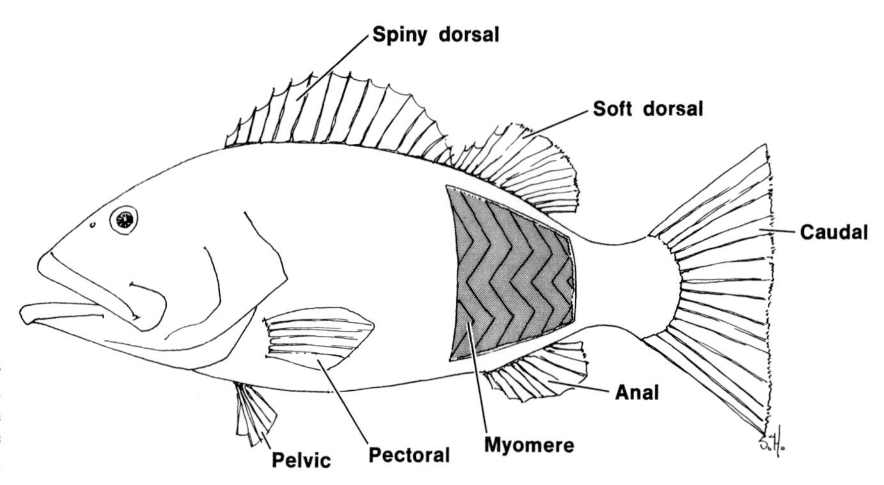

Fig. 7.19 Positions and names of principal fish fins. A portion of the musculature has been exposed to show the arrangement of myomeres.

Caudal Fins

Caudal fins typically flare dorsally and ventrally to provide additional surface area to develop thrust. However, increased fin size also increases the total frictional drag of the fish. The ratio of thrust to drag changes with the shape of the caudal fin. One index of the propulsive efficiency of the fin, based on its shape, is the **aspect ratio:**

$$\text{Aspect ratio} = \frac{(\text{fin height})^2}{\text{fin area}}$$

The caudal fins of most pelagic fish fit into five general profile categories: **rounded, truncate, forked, lunate,** and **heterocercal** (fig. 7.20); each with a different aspect ratio.

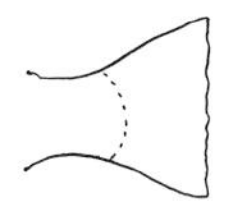
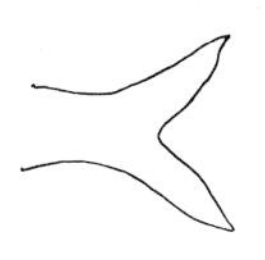
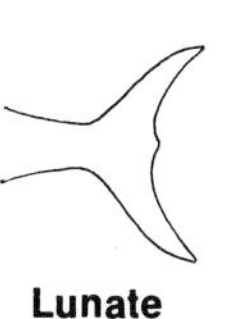
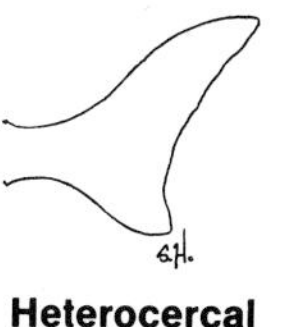

Fig. 7.20 Some examples of caudal fin shapes and their aspect ratios.

The sculpin has a rounded caudal fin that is soft and flexible and has a very low aspect ratio (approximately 1). When the fin moves laterally, it bends and allows water to "slosh" past it. This flexibility permits the caudal fin to be used effectively for accelerating and for other maneuvers. Truncate and forked fins have intermediate aspect ratios, produce less drag, and are generally found on faster fishes. But these fins are also flexible for maneuverability.

The lunate caudal fin characteristic of tuna, sailfish, marlin, and swordfish has a high aspect ratio (up to 10 in swordfish) for reduced drag at high speeds. The shape closely resembles the swept-wing design of high-speed aircraft. These fishes are among the fastest marine animals. The caudal fin is quite rigid for high propulsive efficiency, but is poorly adapted for slow speeds and maneuvering. Fish with high aspect ratio caudal fins (especially forked and lunate types) are capable of continuous swimming.

The heterocercal tail (fig. 7.20) characteristic of sharks has a shape very different from that of most bony fish (which are **homocercal,** or symmetrical about the long axis of the body). The heterocercal tail is quite asymmetrical. When the caudal fin is moved from side to side, a forward thrust develops. But, because of the asymmetry of the tail, it produces some lift as well (fig. 7.21*a*). The paired pectoral fins of sharks are flat and large, and extend horizontally from the body like wings of an aircraft (fig. 7.21*b*). The ventral side is nearly flat in front and combines with the flat extended pectoral fins to produce a large hydrofoil surface. This hydrofoil meets the water at an angle, and lift for the front part of the body develops to balance the lift produced by the tail. Pelagic sharks and other cartilaginous fishes lack swim bladders and need this lift to maintain their position in the water column. But

(a)

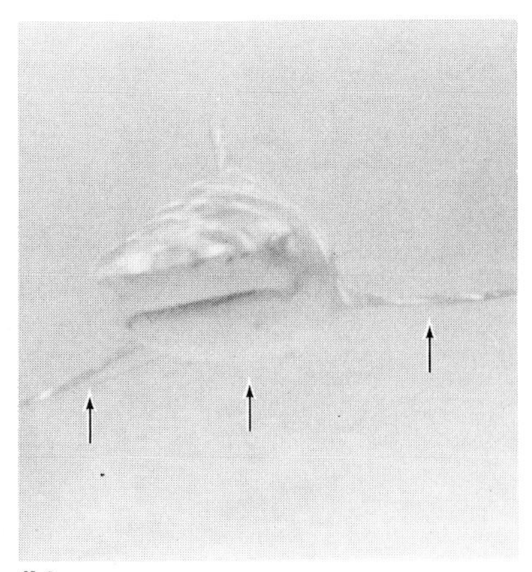
(b)

Fig. 7.21 Side (*a*) and front (*b*) views of a typical shark. Arrows indicate lift derived from the herterocercal tail and the large pectorals extending from the flat underside. Official photographs U.S. Navy.

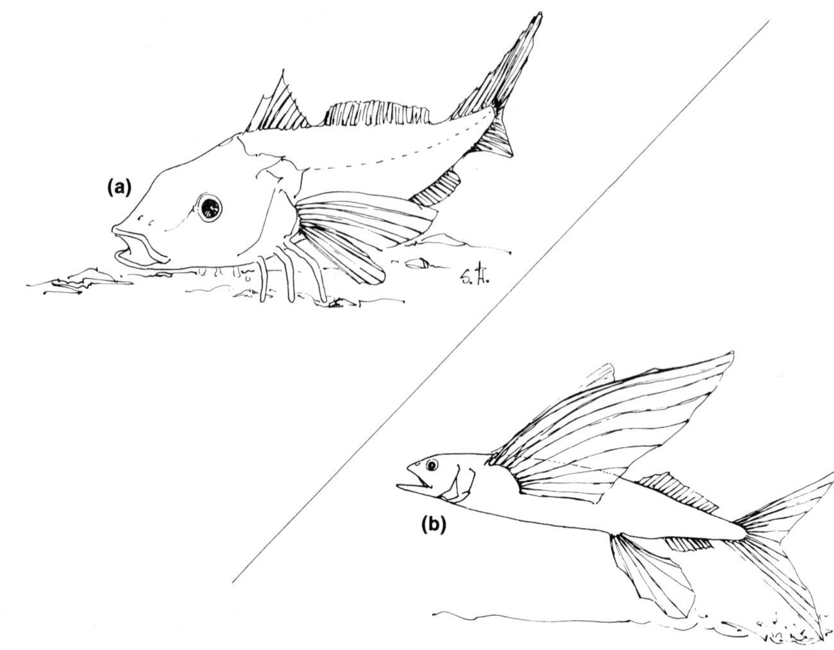

Fig. 7.22 (*a*) A gurnard *(Trigla)* that walks on the bottom using its fingerlike pectoral spines. (*b*) A flying fish (*Exocoetus*) with enlarged pectoral fins for gliding.

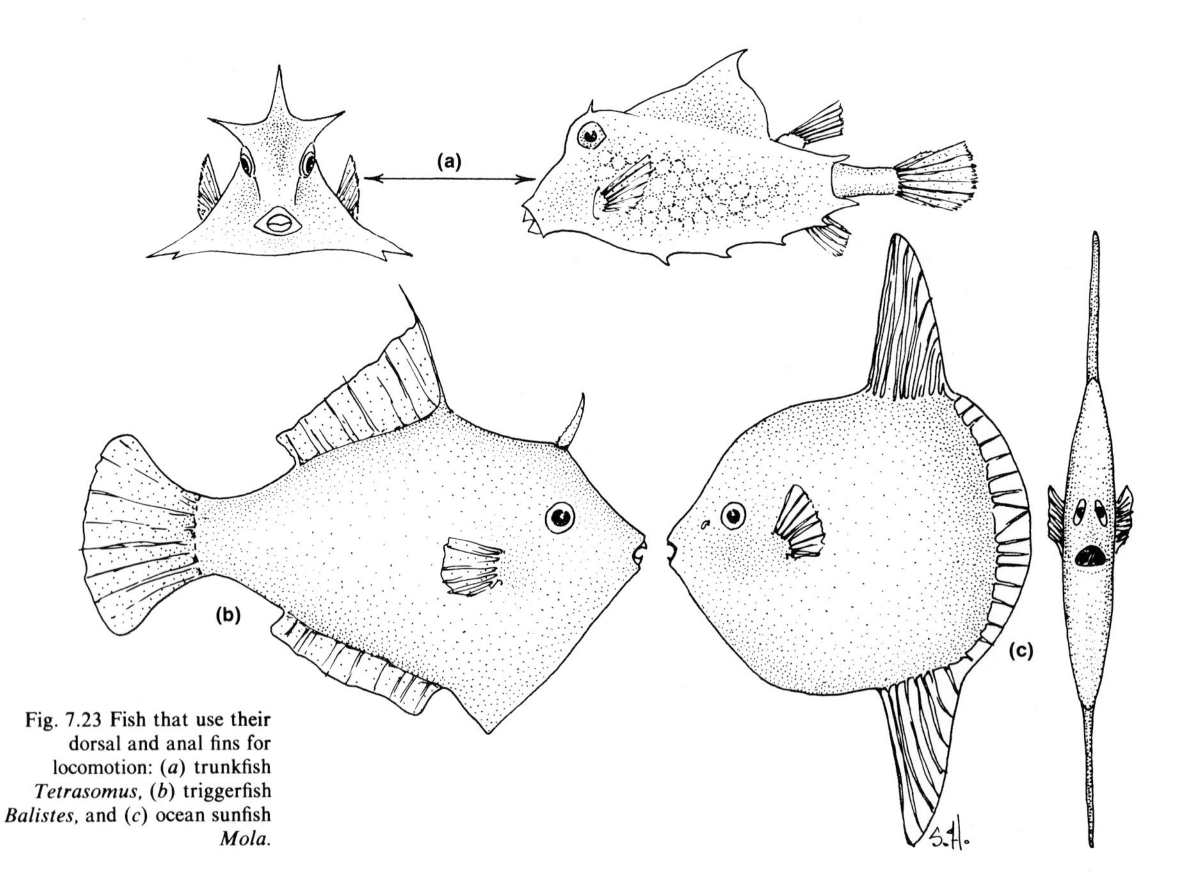

Fig. 7.23 Fish that use their dorsal and anal fins for locomotion: (*a*) trunkfish *Tetrasomus*, (*b*) triggerfish *Balistes*, and (*c*) ocean sunfish *Mola*.

this mechanism for achieving lift does have its disadvantages. These fish cannot stop or hover in midwater. To do so would cause them to settle to the bottom, a bottom that may be some distance away in open ocean areas. Maneuverability is also reduced because the paired fins must be large and rigid to function as hydrofoils, and are not well suited for making fine position adjustments.

Paired Fins

Unlike sharks, bony fish equipped with swim bladders or other buoyancy devices have their pectoral and pelvic fins free for other uses. In most, the paired fins are used solely for turning, braking, balancing, or other fine maneuvers. When swimming rapidly, these fins are folded back against the body. Wrasses and sculpins, however, swim with a jerky, fanning motion of their pectorals while the remainder of the body is held straight. Some skates and rays swim by gracefully undulating the edges of their flattened pectoral fins, or in the cases of manta and eagle rays, by flapping the pectorals like large wings.

Many fish associated with the bottom, including scülpins, use their pectorals to clumsily walk about. Gurnards and sea robins (fig. 7.22*a*) go them one better and move over the bottom using fingerlike pectoral fin rays. These rays can move independently of each other and can even bend and flex. The pectoral and pelvic fins of the little batfish take the form of muscular "legs" (fig. 7.18) for crawling about the bottom.

The greatly enlarged pectoral fins of the flying fish in figure 7.22*b* do not allow this animal to actually "fly," but merely to glide for long distances. Flying fish build up considerable speed while just under the sea surface, then leap upward with the pectorals extended. The pectorals do not flap during flight, so the length of the glide is dependent on wind conditions and the initial speed when the fish leaves the water. These "flights" are apparently a means of escaping predators, and glides up to 400 m have been reported.

Anal and Dorsal Fins

Triggerfish *(Balistes)*, ocean sunfish *(Mola)*, and trunkfish *(Tetrosomus)* all swim by undulating their anal and dorsal fins (fig. 7.23). These fins extend along much of the triggerfish's body *(b)*, but are quite restricted in the rigid-bodied trunkfish *(a)*. The large sunfish *(c)*, which reaches lengths of nearly 3 m and weighs up to a ton, is a sluggish fish that is often seen "sunning" at the surface. The little swimming that it does is accomplished by the long dorsal and anal fins with a little help from the foreshortened caudal fin.

The sea horse *(Hippocampus)* usually swims vertically with its head at right angles to the rest of its body. The prehensile tail tapers to a point and is used to cling to coral branches and similar objects. Sea horses and the closely related pipefish are propelled by rapid vibrations of the dorsal fin on the back (fig. 7.24).

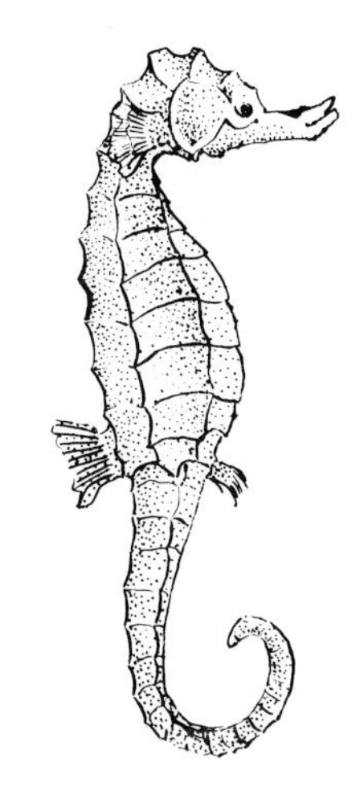

Fig. 7.24 The sea horse *Hippocampus* swims vertically using its dorsal fins for propulsion.

Other Means of Propulsion

Numerous marine animals lacking "fins" for propulsion are nonetheless effective swimmers. Marine invertebrates are not generally well known for their

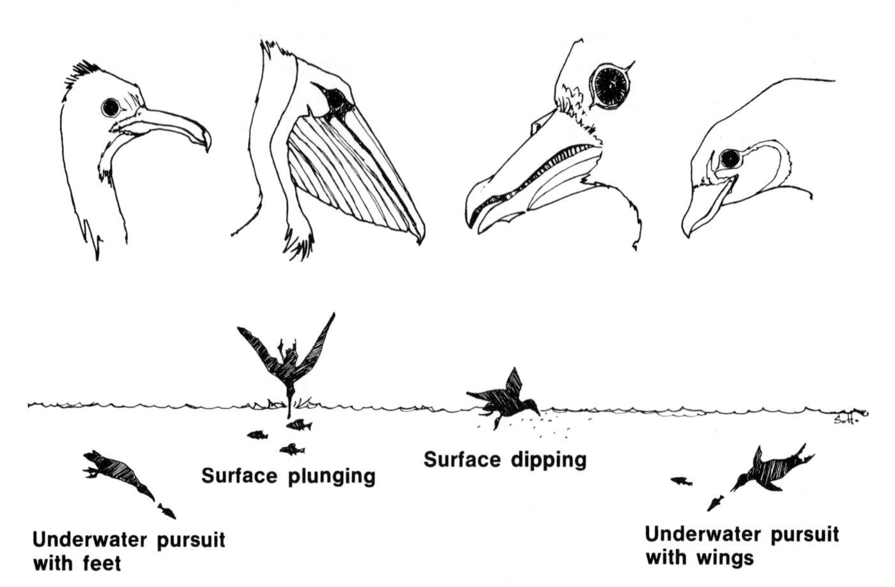

Fig. 7.25 Pursuit patterns (below) and bill shapes (above) of some marine birds. From left to right: cormorant *(Phalocrocorax);* pelican *(Pelecanus);* whale bird *(Pachyptila);* and penguin *(Pygoscelis).*

speed, but a few are fast and maneuverable enough to be successful nektonic animals. Shrimps and prawns use their abdominal paired appendages (**pleopods**) and their tail fan for swimming. Perhaps the most unusual propulsion system belongs to squids and other cephalopods. These animals take water into their mantle cavities, then expel it at high speeds through the nozzlelike **siphon.** The siphon can be aimed in any direction for rapid course corrections and a high degree of maneuverability.

Some birds also feed extensively in neritic waters. Their patterns of pursuit as well as their bill shapes differ greatly (fig. 7.25). Some, like cormorants and penguins, pursue their prey underwater using either feet or wings for propulsion. Pelicans, on the other hand, plunge from several meters above the surface to snare their food. The filter-feeding whale bird paddles at the surface, and need only dip its head to scoop up crustaceans with its unusual bill.

Speed

Several species of nektonic animals have recently become subjects of much research related to their almost unbelievable swimming speeds. *Stenella,* an oceanic porpoise, has been clocked in controlled tank situations at better than 40 km/hr (approximately 22 mi/hr) for a few seconds. Top speeds of killer whales are estimated to be 40–55 km/hr. A barracuda only 1 m long has been clocked at 40 km/hr. As a comparison, consider that human Olympic-class swimmers achieve sprint speeds of only 6–7 km/hr. To clock fish that can easily outdistance a speeding ship, specially designed fishing poles have been developed to measure the speed at which the fishing line is stripped from the reel. When a fish takes the bait and flees, its speed is measured and recorded. In this manner, investigators clocked a yellowfin tuna *(Thunnus albacares)* less than 1 m long at a maximum speed of 74.6 km/hr (45 mi/hr) for 0.19

second. A tunalike wahoo *(Acanthocybium)*, slightly more than 1 m in length was clocked at 77 km/hr for about 0.1 second. Russian fishery workers have suggested that large tuna are capable of speeds in excess of 110 km/hr (70 mi/hr). This may not be as farfetched as it seems, since some species of tuna achieve lengths of 4 m and presumably would be much faster than a fish only 1 m long. This 110 km/hr speed estimate has yet to be confirmed, however.

What enables tuna to swim so fast? The exceptional swimming abilities of tuna and tunalike fishes go beyond simply having a streamlined body form and an efficient caudal fin. The streamlined body form is complemented by other friction-reducing features. The first dorsal fin can be retracted into a slot and out of the path of water flow when not needed for maneuvering. Skin scales of tuna are reduced to minimize friction with the water. The eyes do not bulge beyond the profile of the head and are covered with an adipose eyelid to further reduce turbulence. Numerous small median **finlets** on the dorsal and ventral sides of the rear part of the body probably function to reduce turbulence in that region. The body itself is quite rigid and provides little of the forward thrust.

Most of the caudal flexing is localized in the region of the **caudal peduncle,** where the caudal fin joins the rest of the body. The caudal peduncle is flattened in cross section, and produces little resistance to lateral movements. Lateral keels on the peduncle guide the water posteriorly toward the caudal fin, rather than allowing it to slosh over the peduncle. The rigid caudal fin is lunate in shape, with a high aspect ratio (usually greater than 7). The tail beats rapidly with relatively short strokes. This type of caudal fin creates little drag, but also provides very little maneuverability.

Nearly 75% of the total body weight of a tuna is devoted to muscles for swimming. In tuna, each myomere overlaps several body segments and is anchored securely to the vertebral column. Tendons extend from the myomeres across the caudal peduncle and attach directly to the caudal fin.

Fish muscle is composed of red and white muscle fibers. Structurally, red muscle fibers are much smaller in diameter (25–45 μm) than white muscle fibers (135 μm), and are rich in **myoglobin** (a red pigment with a strong chemical affinity for O_2 similar to that of hemoglobin). The small size of the red muscle cells provides additional surface area that, in conjunction with myoglobin, greatly facilitates O_2 transfer to the red muscle cells. Physiologically, red muscle cells respire aerobically; whereas white muscle usually operates anaerobically, converting glycogen to lactic acid.

The metabolic rate (and power output) of tuna red muscle, and probably of red muscle in other fishes, is about six times as great as that of white muscle. The relative amount of red and white muscle a fish has depends on the general level of activity the fish experiences. A slow-moving grouper has almost no red muscle. At the other extreme are tuna, with over 50% of their swimming muscles composed of red muscle fibers. It is worth noting that the red muscles of sculpins, which fan their pectorals, and puffers, which swim by fanning their anal and dorsal fins, are concentrated at the bases of their respective swimming fins.

Electrodes can be inserted into red and white muscle tissue of small sharks and some tuna to measure muscle activity. At slow normal cruising speeds, only red muscles contract. Only at above normal speeds do white muscles come into play. Top speeds of about ten body lengths/second can be maintained only for about one second, but cruising speeds of 2–4 body lengths/second can be continued almost indefinitely (fig. 7.26). Apparently, the power for continuous swimming comes from the red muscle, with white muscle being held in reserve for peak power demands. White muscle does not require an immediate O_2 supply, but can operate anaerobically and accumulate lactic acid during stress situations. The lactic acid later can be converted back into glycogen or some other substance when the demand for O_2 has diminished. Tuna, with greater proportions of red muscle, are able to maintain indefinitely a cruising speed faster than most other fish.

Fish are generally thought to be poikilothermic ("cold-blooded") animals. The heat generated by metabolic processes within the body may elevate the body temperature slightly above the ambient water temperature, but is quickly lost to the surrounding seawater (table 7.1, left col.). However, a few exceptionally fast fish have body temperatures that are much warmer than the surrounding water (table 7.1, right col.). The magnitude of body temperature elevation above the water temperature is usually consistent for each

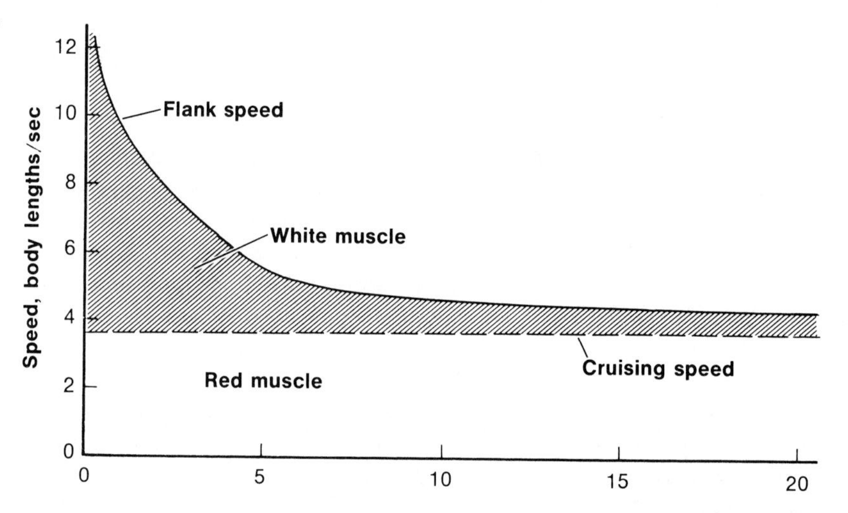

Fig. 7.26 Duration of swimming speeds for white and red muscles. White muscle is used for short bursts at flank speed and tires rapidly; red muscle maintains continuous cruising speeds. From Bainbridge 1960.

Table 7.1. *Elevation of Body Temperatures Above Seawater Temperatures for Some Marine Fish.*

Fish With Slightly Elevated Body Temperatures		Fish with Dramatically Elevated Body Temperatures	
Yellowtail *(Seriola)*	+1.4°C	Mackerel shark *(Lamna)*	+7.8°C
Mackerel *(Scomber)*	+1.3°C	Mackerel shark *(Isurus)*	+4.5°C
Bonito *(Sarda)*	+1.8°C	Tuna *(Thunnus)*	+ 5 to +13°C, occasionally to + 23°C

species. The one well-studied exception is the bluefin tuna *(Thunnus thynnus)*, which has a consistently high body temperature, regardless of the water temperature. In water of 25°C, for example, the internal body temperature was near 32°C and declined only slightly to 30°C when the animal was moved to seawater at 7°C.

Within certain limits, metabolic processes including muscle contractions occur more rapidly at higher temperatures. So the power output of a warm muscle can be greater than that of a cold muscle. Tuna and mackerel sharks exhibit some behavioral characteristics that elevate and control their internal temperatures to some extent. The distribution of these fishes is limited primarily to tropical and subtropical regions where differences between body and water temperatures are not great. More important though, are the heat-conserving anatomical features evident in tuna and mackerel sharks. In most bony fish, the swimming muscles receive blood from the dorsal aorta just under the vertebral column. The major blood source for the red muscle masses of mackerel sharks and most tuna is not the dorsal aorta, but rather a **cutaneous artery** just under the skin on either side of the body (fig. 7.27). The blood flows from the cutaneous artery to the red muscle then returns to the **cutaneous vein.** Between the cutaneous vessels and the red muscles are exten-

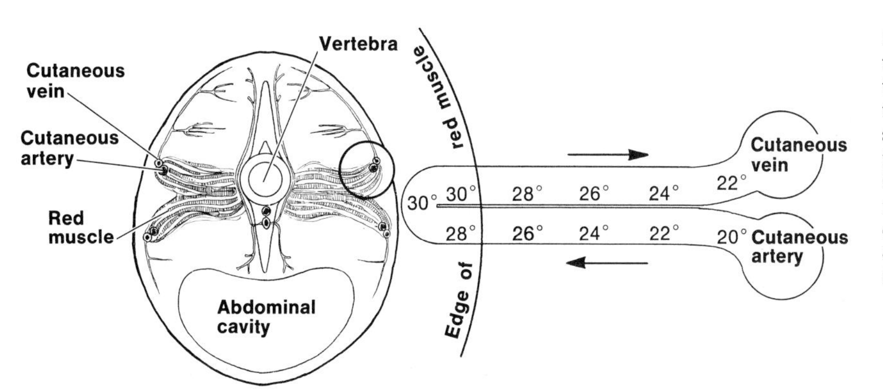

Fig. 7.27 Cross section of a tuna, showing the position of the red muscles (shaded) and the countercurrent system of small arteries and veins serving the red muscles. The numbers in the blood vessels represent temperatures within an enlarged portion of the countercurrent system. From Carey 1973.

Fig. 7.28 A skipjack *(Katsuwonus)* in a school of baitfish. Courtesy Honolulu Laboratory, National Marine Fisheries Service, NOAA, Department of Commerce.

Table 7.2. *Functional Comparison of Some Features That Influence Swimming Speeds of a "Lunger" (Rockfish) and a "Cruiser" (Tuna).*

Characteristic	Lunger	Cruiser
Body Features		
Shape		
Front view		
Rigidity	Flexible body	Rigid body
Scales	Abundant large scales	Reduced scales
Eyes	Bulging eyes	Covered with adipose lid
% of thrust by body	50%	Almost none
Dorsal fin	Broad-based and high	Generally smaller, fits into slot
Caudal Peduncle		
Form	Broad	Restricted
Cross-sectional shape		
Keels	Absent	Present
Finlets	Absent	Present
Caudal Fin		
Aspect ratio	Low, 3	High, 7–10
Rigidity	Flexible	Rigid
Maneuverability	Good	Poor
Tail beat frequency	Low	High
Tail beat amplitude	Large	Small
Swimming Muscles		
% of body wt	50–65%	75%
% red muscle	20%	50% or more
Body temperature	Ambient	Elevated

Modified from Fierstine and Walters 1968

sive countercurrent heat exchangers to facilitate heat retention within the red muscle. Cold blood enters the countercurrent system and is warmed by the blood leaving the warm red muscle. In this way, very little of the heat generated in the red muscles is lost.

All the features described above collectively function to provide tuna and other similar fish with the capability of cruising continually at moderate speeds and to be the efficient pelagic predators they are (fig. 7.28). Table 7.2 summarizes these features and provides a general comparison with a normally noncruising fish (a "lunger") that typically lies in wait for its prey.

Schooling

For most pelagic animals, the diffuse three-dimensional distribution of food items in the water makes active predation and filter-feeding popular means of securing food. The fast and maneuverable animals are, for the most part, active predators. They may be larger than a tuna or smaller than a chaetognath. Filter feeders too come in all sizes, from minute zooplankton to the largest of the whales.

The successful use of filter-feeding techniques by large whales, numerous fish, and even a few birds and seals, is dependent on the presence of abundant and dense aggregations of smaller animals. Patches of zooplankton occur partly in response to the patchy spatial distribution of their food source, the phytoplankton. However, hundreds of species of smaller fish, plus a few types of squid and larger crustaceans form well-defined social organizations called **schools.**

Schools occur in sizes varying from a few fish (fig. 7.29) to enormous, yet continuous, populations of herring occasionally extending over several km^2. Schools usually consist of a single species with all members of a similar size. Larger fish swim faster than smaller ones, and mixed populations quickly sort themselves out according to their size. The spatial organization of individuals within a school remains remarkably constant as the school moves or changes direction. They line up parallel to each other, swim in the same direction, and maintain fixed spacings between individuals. When the school turns, it turns abruptly, with the animals on the flank assuming the lead. The spatial arrangement within schools seems to be maintained by visual contact with adjacent fish within the school. Individual visibility may be enhanced by a pattern of coloration known as **countershading**. The upper surfaces of these animals are darkly pigmented while the sides and ventral surfaces are silvery or only lightly pigmented. When viewed from above, the pigmented upper surfaces of counter-shaded fish blend in with the darker background below. From beneath, the silvery undersides are difficult to distinguish from the ambient light coming from the sea surface. Thus, from either view, these fish tend to visually blend into rather than stand out against their watery background. Not only does countershading protect the school against predators, but the flashing of silvery bellies or dark backs during abrupt turns may serve to alert individuals in the school to the larger maneuvers of the whole school.

Why band together to be so conveniently eaten by larger predators (as shown in fig. 7.28)? Ironically, part of the answer seems to be simply that for small animals with no other means of individual defense, schooling behavior actually provides a degree of protection from predators.

Fig. 7.29 A small school of barracuda *(Sphyraena)*. Note the regular spacing and consistent body alignment. Courtesy M. Weeks.

Much of the present thinking concerning the survival value of schooling behavior is based on conjecture, because experiments with natural populations are exceedingly difficult to conduct and evaluate. Even so, a few points can be made. Predatory fish have less chance of encountering a prey if it is a member of a school because the individuals of the prey species are concentrated in compact units rather than dispersed over a much larger area. When a predator does occasionally encounter a school, it can only eat to its feeding capacity; then it must stop, even if more prey are available. Thus, large schools have less chance of being completely decimated by predators than do smaller schools or dispersed individuals. Large numbers of fish in a school may achieve additional survival advantages by confusing predators with continually shifting and changing positions; they might even discourage hungry predators with the illusion of an impressively large and formidable opponent.

Laboratory studies with fish that school instinctively also indicate that, when isolated at an early age and prevented from schooling, these fish are not as quick to learn, begin feeding later, grow more slowly, and of course are more prone to predation than are their siblings who are allowed to school. Schooling is also thought to serve as a mechanism to keep reproductively active members of a population together. Schooling species typically reproduce by shedding large numbers of eggs, which are fertilized in the water and left with no parental care or attention. Dense concentrations of mature individuals spawning simultaneously insure a high proportion of egg fertilization, and probably greater larval survival (for the same reasons that large numbers of their parents survived to produce them).

Migration

Numerous species of larger marine animals exhibit well-defined migratory movements. For some, the distances involved are truly oceanic in scale. Some California gray whales, for instance, accomplish an impressive 18,000 km (11,000 mi.) roundtrip journey each year.

The migratory patterns of marine animals are quite variable, yet a few generalizations can be made. These migrations seem to be an adaptation for increased population size. The available food in spawning areas may be appropriate for larval stages, but might not support the mature members of the population also. So the adults congregate in rich feeding areas that may be unsuitable for the survival of the younger stages. The actual migratory routes link the feeding areas with regions used for reproduction.

The migratory patterns of marine animals also exhibit a strong similarity to surface ocean currents. Some of the migration routes are in the same direction as the currents, others oppose the current direction. It is not uncommon for the larval stages of some species to be passively carried long distances by ocean currents. Adults may also utilize currents for a free ride, but many types of larvae are absolutely dependent on current drift for their migratory movements. The downstream drift of young stages may, by necessity, require the adults to make an active, compensatory return migration upstream against the current flow to return to the spawning grounds.

Seldom can migrations of oceanic animals be observed directly. They often move below the sea surface and well away from the coast. Most of our understanding of oceanic migrations has been inferred from tagging studies and distributional patterns of eggs and subsequent developmental stages. Tagged animals yield valuable information concerning their migratory routes and speeds, but only if the tags are recovered. The application of tagging programs is thus limited to animals that can be recaptured in large numbers. These are generally commercially important species for which a powerful economic incentive for their capture exists.

Migratory patterns may also be determined by analyzing the distribution of eggs, larvae, young individuals, and adults of a species. When a general progression of developmental stages from egg to adult can be found extending from one oceanic area to another, a migratory route between those areas may be inferred. Recently, new techniques, such as radio-tracking of individual animals, have added to our present store of knowledge concerning oceanic migrations.

Some Examples of Extensive Oceanic Migrations

The skipjack tuna, *Katsuwonus pelamis,* is widely distributed in the warm waters of the world ocean. Several genetically distinct populations probably exist, but only the east Pacific population will be considered here. The migratory pattern of the east Pacific skipjack is not as well known as the patterns of many other fish, yet the general outline of its migrations can be described.

These skipjack spawn in surface equatorial waters west of 130° longitude (fig. 7.30) during the summer. For several months, the young fish remain in the central Pacific spawning grounds. After reaching lengths of approximately 30 cm, they either actively migrate or are passively carried to the east in the North and South Equatorial Countercurrents. These adolescent fish remain in the eastern Pacific for about one year as they mature. Two feeding grounds, one off Baja California and another off Central America and Ecuador, are the major centers of skipjack concentrations in the eastern Pacific.

As the skipjack approach sexual maturity, they leave the Mexican and Central-South American feeding grounds and follow the west-flowing Equatorial Currents back to the spawning area. After spawning, the adults move from the central Pacific to forage, following the Equatorial Countercurrents as they did when adolescent. However, the feeding adults are seldom found as far to the east. Subsequent returns to the spawning area follow the general pattern established by the first spawning migration.

Six species of salmon *(Oncorhynchus)* occur in the North Pacific. They are the sockeye, pink, chum, masu, coho (or silver), and chinook (also known as the king, tyee, spring, or quinnat salmon). All are **anadromous;** that is, they spend much of their lives at sea, then return to freshwater streams and lakes to spawn. The eggs are deposited in beds of gravel where they remain through the winter. Soon after spawning the adult salmon die.

The migratory patterns of the various types of salmon are similar, so only that of the sockeye salmon will be described. After hatching in the spring,

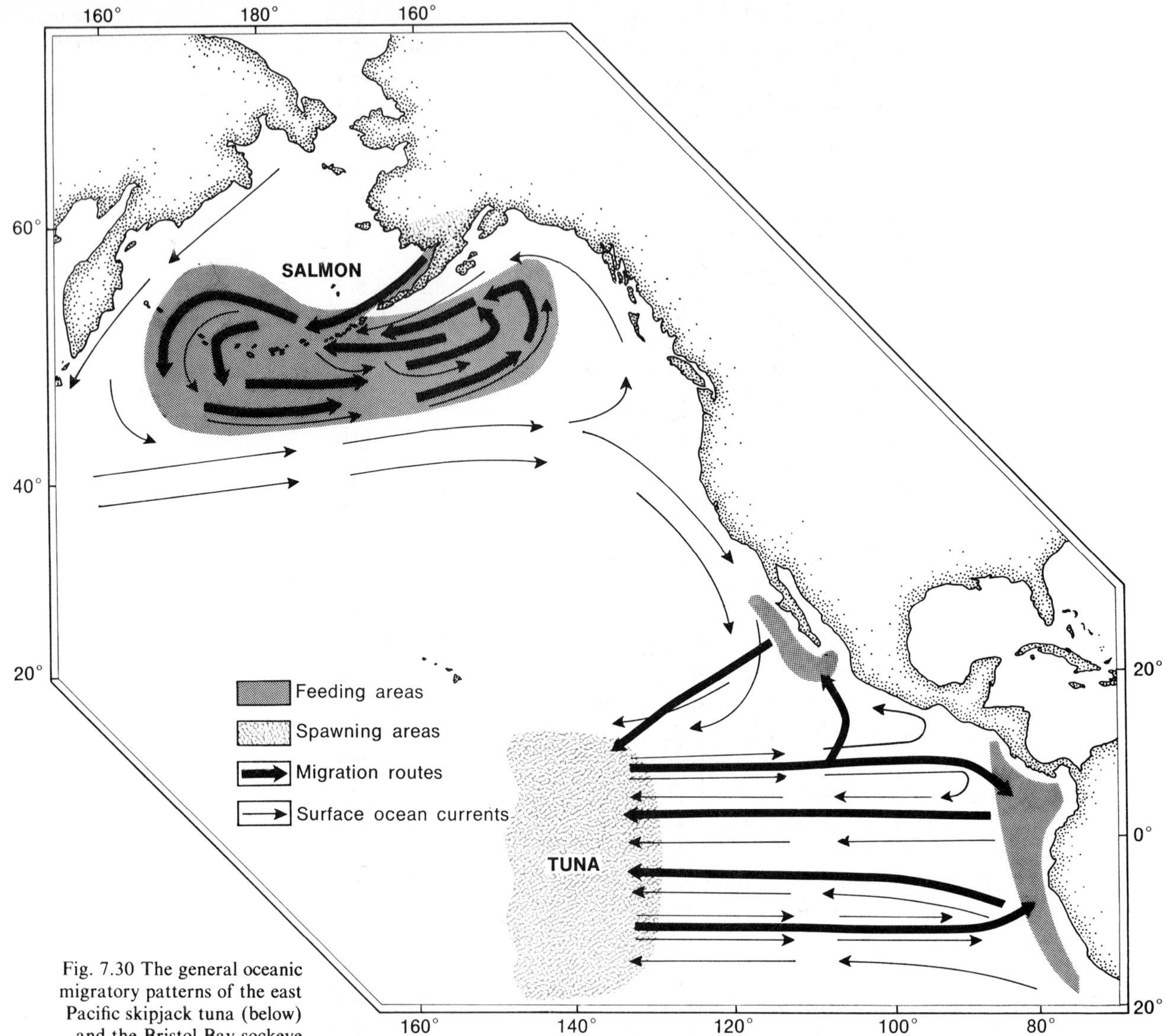

Fig. 7.30 The general oceanic migratory patterns of the east Pacific skipjack tuna (below) and the Bristol Bay sockeye salmon (above). Note the strong relationship between these migratory patterns and the surface ocean currents. These currents are identified in figure 1.27. Adapted from Royce, Smith, and Hartt 1968, and Williams 1972.

the young sockeye remain in freshwater streams and lakes for about two years as they develop to a stage known as a **smolt.** The smolts then migrate downstream and into the sea, and enter a period of heavy feeding and rapid growth.

Accumulating evidence indicates that the sockeye, as well as other salmon, follow well-defined migratory routes, usually 10–20 m deep, during the oceanic phase of their migrations. These migrations closely follow the surface current pattern in the North Pacific (fig. 7.30), but are faster than the currents. After several years at sea, the sockeye approach sexual maturity, move toward the coast, and seek out freshwater streams. Strong evidence supports the **"home stream theory"** that each salmon returns to precisely the same stream and tributary in which it was spawned. There it spawns for the first and only time, and then dies.

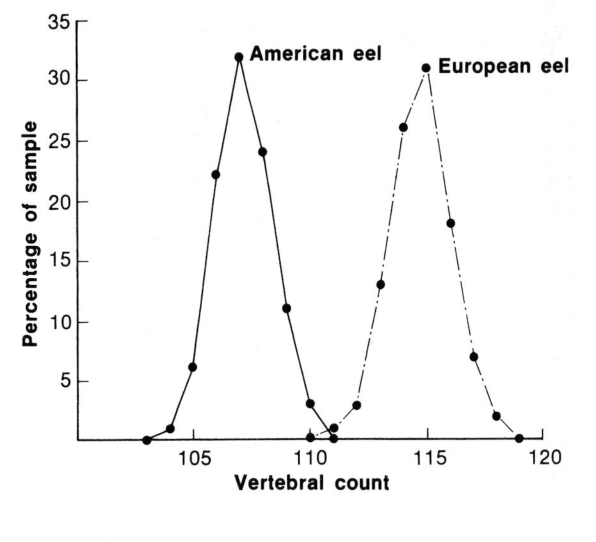

Fig. 7.31 Variation in vertebral counts of anguillid eels collected in America and Europe. Redrawn from Cushing 1968.

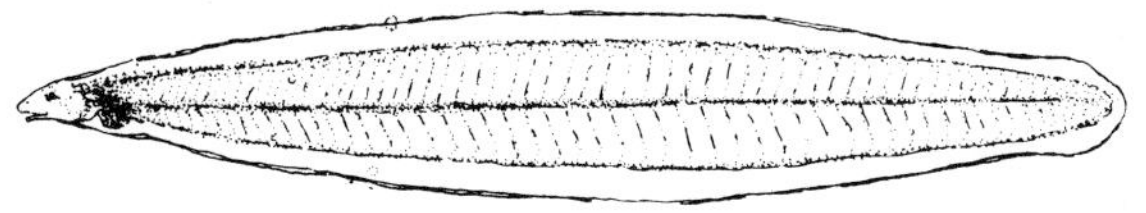

Fig. 7.32 An early leptocephalus larva of the eel *Anguilla*.

The Atlantic eel *(Anguilla)* exhibits a migratory pattern just the reverse of the Pacific salmon migration. This eel also migrates between fresh and salt water. But, in complete contrast to salmon, Atlantic eels are **catadromous.** They spawn at sea, then migrate into lakes and streams where they grow to maturity. Two species of the Atlantic eel are thought to exist, the European eel *(A. anguilla)* and the American eel *(A. rostrata)*. The distinction is based on the geographical distribution and anatomical differences of the adults (fig. 7.31).

Both species spawn in the Sargasso Sea region of the North Atlantic. The eggs hatch in the spring to produce a leaf-shaped, transparent **leptocephalus larva** about 5 mm long (fig. 7.32). The leptocephalus larvae drift out of the Sargasso Sea and to the north and east in the Gulf Stream. After one year of drifting, the American eels metamorphose and the young elvers move into rivers along the east coast of North America. The European eel larvae continue to drift for another year across the North Atlantic to the European coast (fig. 7.33). There, most enter rivers and move upstream. The remainder of the European population requires still another year to cross the Mediterranean Sea before entering fresh water.

After several years (sometimes as many as ten) in fresh water, the mature eels (now called "yellow eels") undergo physical and physiological changes in preparation for their return to the sea as "silver eels." Their eyes enlarge and they assume a silvery and dark color pattern characteristic of midwater marine fish. Then they migrate downstream and presumably return to the Sargasso Sea where they spawn and die.

Very few adult silver eels have been captured in the open sea, and none have been taken from the spawning area itself. Thus, the spawning migration

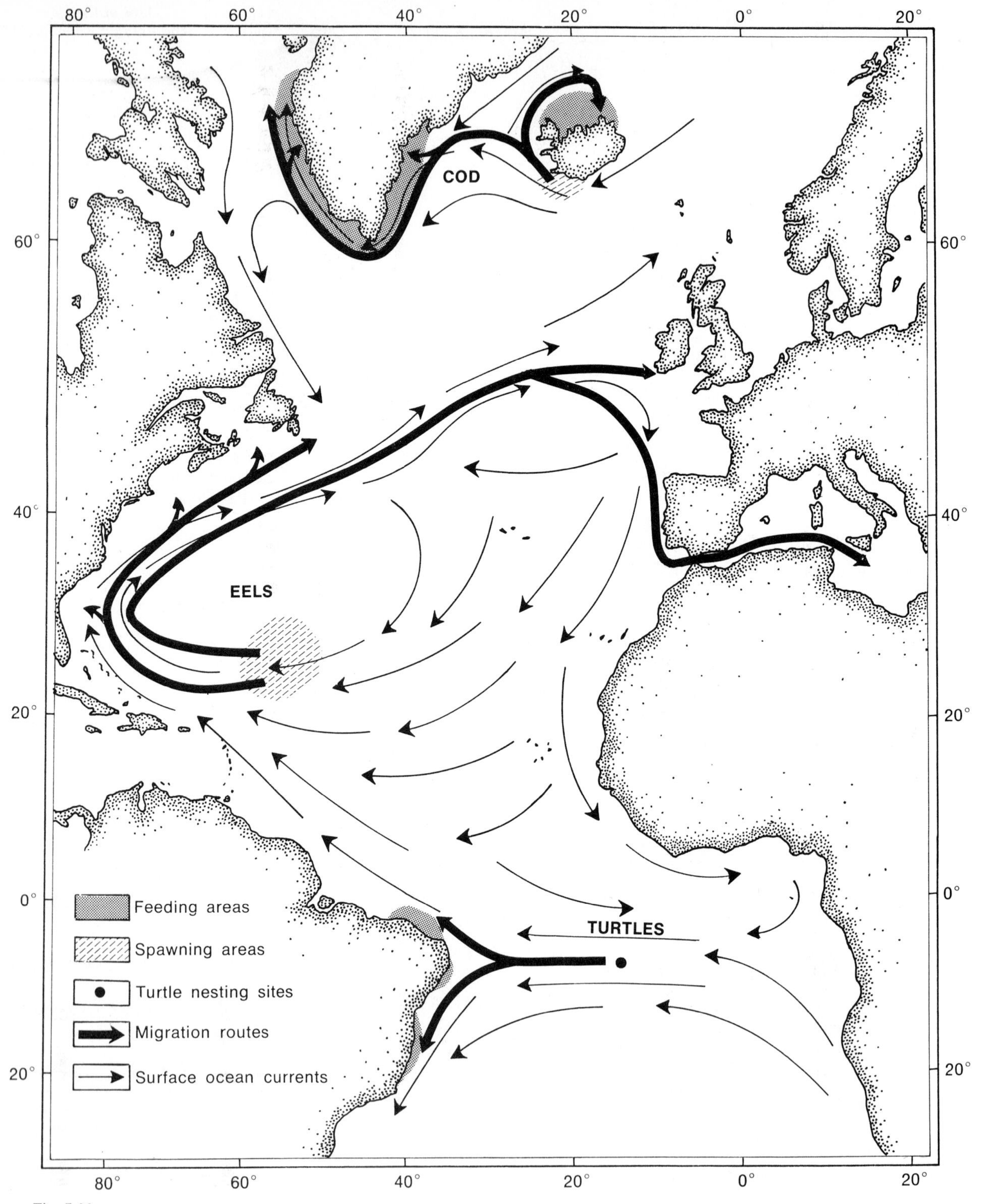
80°
60°
40°
20°
0°
20°
COD
EELS
TURTLES
Feeding areas
Spawning areas
Turtle nesting sites
Migration routes
Surface ocean currents

Fig. 7.33

back to the Sargasso Sea is still a matter for supposition. The European eels might backtrack the path they followed as leptocephalus larvae. However, doing so would require increased energy expenditures to swim against the substantial current of the Gulf Stream. A more likely route would take them into the south-flowing Canary Current after leaving European rivers, then west in the North Atlantic Equatorial Current and eventually to the region of the Sargasso Sea (fig. 7.33). The spawning migration of adult American eels is apparently accomplished by swimming across the Gulf Stream to their spawning area.

An alternative, and quite novel, hypothesis has been presented by D. W. Tucker. He suggests that European eels never return to the Sargasso Sea spawning grounds, but instead perish in the coastal waters off Europe. Tucker maintains that both the European and American *Anguilla* stocks are recruited from leptocephalus larvae produced only by spawning American eels. If Tucker's ideas prove to be correct, then the anatomical differences between the American and European eels, as suggested by figure 7.31, must be caused by the different environmental regimes encountered by the eggs and larvae as they drift across the North Atlantic. Water temperature differences, in particular, are known to cause differences in such anatomical features as the numbers of fin rays and vertebrae.

Several attempts have been made to analyze genetic variations by comparing blood proteins between European and American eels. So far, no reliable evidence to support or refute Tucker's hypothesis has been found. Until such evidence is available, several questions concerning the migration of *Anguilla* remain open.

The Atlantic cod *(Gadus morhua)*, shown in figure 7.34, is common in much of the North Atlantic ocean. It is a cold-water fish, preferring water temperatures between 1° and 5°C. Several distinct cod populations occur in the North Atlantic, and each has its own range and migratory route. In this discussion, only the Icelandic cod population will be considered.

The Icelandic cod spawning grounds are located in the warm Irminger Current to the south and west of Iceland (fig. 7.33). The cod spawn there during the late winter and spring months, and sometimes again later in the year. Each female produces from 1 to 15 million eggs over a period of a few days. Just before release, the eggs absorb fluids to increase their volume and reduce their density. The total volume of eggs produced is often as large as

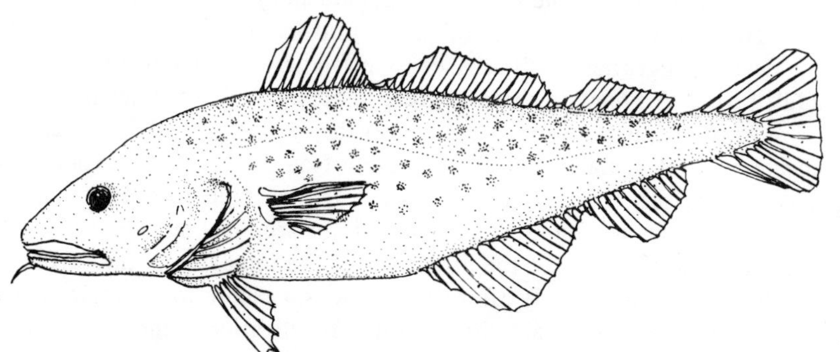

Fig. 7.33 Migratory routes of the larvae and young of anguillid eels (center), Icelandic cod (top), and green turtles (bottom). The return migrations of their respective adults have been omitted for clarity. Adapted from Carr 1965, Cushing 1968, and FAO 1972.

Fig. 7.34 The Atlantic cod *Gadus morhua*.

the female producing them! The eggs float and drift about in the water, and hatch in about two weeks, depending on the water temperature (see fig. 1.12).

The cod larvae remain in midwater for several months as they drift out of the spawning area. Some are carried to the north and east coasts of Iceland. Others enter the East Greenland Current and are transported to the southeast and southwest coasts of Greenland, a distance of over 1,600 km (fig. 7.33). Drift-bottle experiments indicate that three to four months are sufficient to make the trip solely by drift.

The movements of sexually immature cod are not well known. They may undertake local onshore-offshore movements on a seasonal basis, but are thought to remain more or less in one place. They reach sexual maturity at eight or nine years of age, then join the mature cod for their initial spawning migration.

The spawning migration of the Icelandic cod is not completely known, but is thought to be essentially the reverse of the larval drift pattern (fig. 7.33). The adults generally move along the bottom (but occasionally in midwater or even near the surface) back to the spawning area. They spawn, then return to the north Iceland and south Greenland feeding grounds. Thereafter, the cod migrate and spawn during each of the remaining ten years of their lives.

Sea turtles are common members of tropical and subtropical marine communities. In the green sea turtle, *Chelonia,* a strong tendency exists to migrate from coastal feeding grounds to remote, isolated islands for nesting. These islands apparently lack many of the predators that would harass the turtles and raid their nests on mainland beaches. The best documented feats of island-finding by green turtles are migrations between the east coast of Brazil and Ascension Island. Ascension Island is a mere dot of land, only 8 km wide, in the Atlantic Ocean midway between Brazil and Africa (fig. 7.33).

These turtles lay their eggs in warm, sandy beaches along the north and west coasts of Ascension Island. Immediately after hatching, the young turtles instinctively dig themselves out of the sand, scurry into the water, and head directly out to sea. Once they are beyond the hazards of surf and shoreline, they presumably are picked up by the South Atlantic Equatorial Current and are carried toward Brazil at speeds of 1–2 km/hr. Less than two months are needed to passively drift to Brazil, yet nothing is known af the young turtles' whereabouts or activities for their first year.

As they mature, the turtles congregate along the mainland coast where they graze on turtle grass and other sea grasses in shallow flats. Features of the nesting migration back to Ascension Island are not well known, but the adult turtles do show up there in great numbers during the nesting season.

Mating apparently occurs only near the nesting ground. Either the males accompany the females on their migration from Brazil to Ascension, or they make a precisely timed, but independent, trip on their own. Either way, the males get to the nesting area; and they can be seen just outside the surf zone, splashing and fighting for the attentions of the females. As the turtles mate just before or immediately after the females go ashore to lay their eggs, it is unlikely that the mating activities result in fertilization of the current season's eggs. Instead, the female probably stores the sperm to fertilize the eggs of the following nesting season.

The females go ashore several times during the nesting season and deposit about 100 eggs each time. This provides the only opportunity researchers have to capture and tag large numbers of turtles at their nesting sites. As the males do not leave the water, only females are tagged. Thus, almost nothing is known about the migratory behavior of the male turtles. The tagging results indicate that the females leave Ascension Island after laying, and return to the Brazilian coast. Two or three years later, they return to the tiny island of Ascension to again mate and lay their eggs.

Several of the larger marine mammals undertake impressive seasonal migrations. The large whales alternate between cold-water summer feeding grounds and warmer breeding and calving grounds in the winter. The annual migration of the California gray whale has been extensively studied and is the best known of the large whale migrations. These whales spend the summer months in the Bering Sea and adjacent areas of the Arctic Ocean as far north as the edge of the pack ice. Their habit of feeding on bottom invertebrates limits them to the shallow portions of these seas.

The southward migration is initiated as pack ice begins to form over the feeding grounds in September. The migration is in fact a procession of gray whales segregated according to age and sex. The first to leave are the pregnant females. These are followed by nonpregnant females, the immature females, adult males, and finally immature males. After they pass through the Aleutian Islands, their precise route is in doubt. They may follow the longer, curving shoreline of Alaska, or they may strike out diagonally across the Gulf of Alaska (fig. 7.35). The observations necessary for the clarification of this point simply have not been made.

South of British Columbia, the whales can be observed traveling reasonably close to the shoreline (in water usually less than 200 m deep). However, a few travel well offshore in water over 1,000 m deep. The average speed of southbound gray whales is 8 km/hr, or 200 km/day. At that speed most of the whales reach the warm protected coastal lagoons of Baja California by late January.

It is in these lagoons that the pregnant females give birth. Here also the males and nonpregnant females mate. The new mothers remain with their calves in the lagoons for about two months. During that time the nursing calves rapidly put on weight to face the rigors of a long migration back to the chilly waters of the Bering Sea.

In early spring, the northward migration begins, and is much the reverse of the previous southbound trip. Females with calves may travel farther offshore than the rest of the herd, as they are seldom observed. Traveling at a more leisurely pace than when going south, the whales reach their Arctic feeding grounds in the late spring. There they spend the summer rapidly restoring their depleted fat and blubber reserves in preparation for their next migratory performance a few months later.

From these examples of long-distance migrations of marine animals (and there are many more that could have been included), a few generaliza-

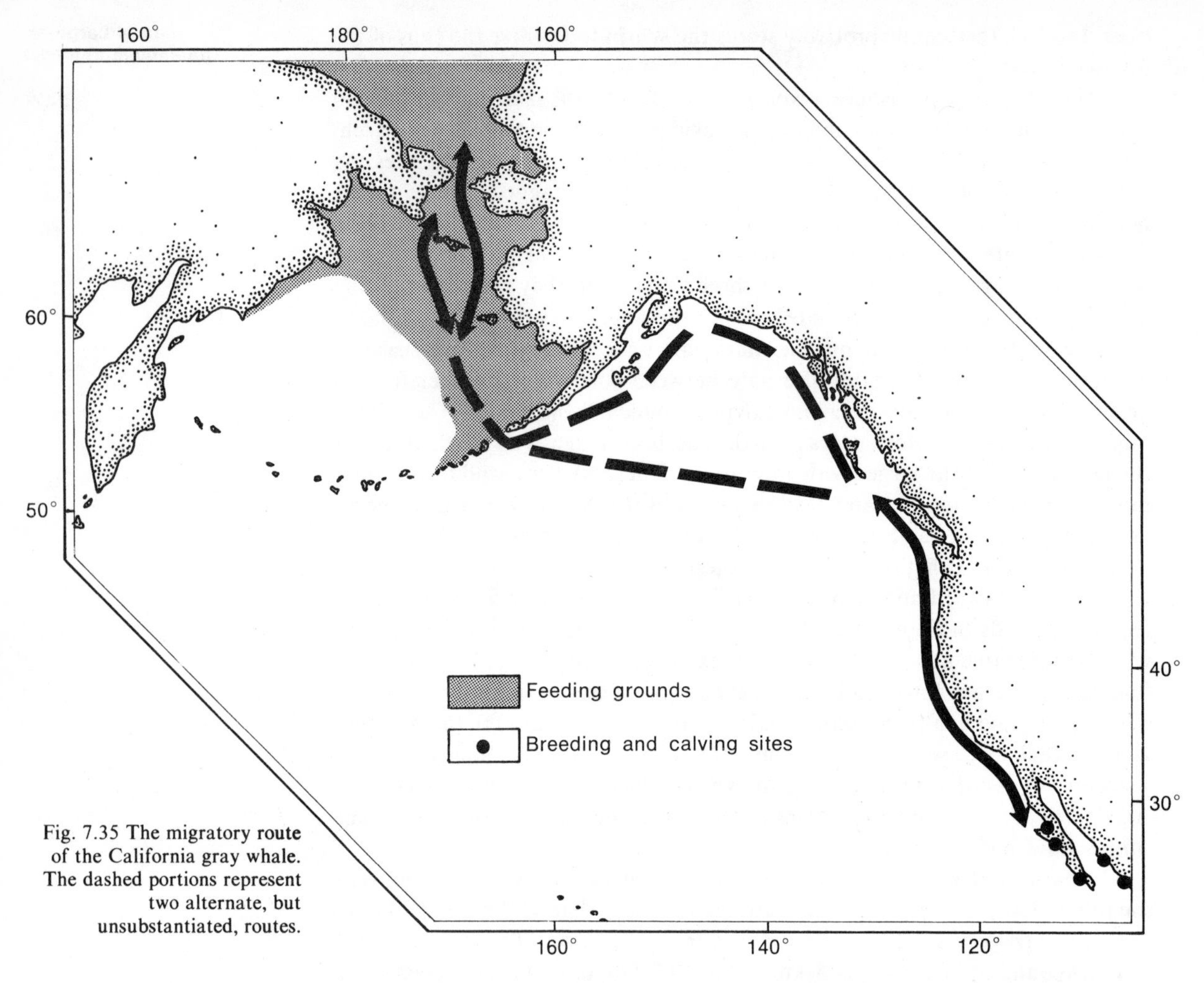

Fig. 7.35 The migratory route of the California gray whale. The dashed portions represent two alternate, but unsubstantiated, routes.

tions can be made. For many migrating species, timing or precise routes followed are simply not known. In some cases (for example, the eel *Anguilla*), it has not even been established beyond doubt that the adult European eels make a spawning migration to the Sargasso Sea. In spite of these sometimes glaring gaps in our information, we do know that numerous species of marine animals do undertake and successfully accomplish long and sometimes complex migrations. Generally the migrations link areas that insure reproductive success with other areas that provide an abundance of food.

Vertical Migration

Just below the sunlit surface waters of most oceanic areas is a twilight world inhabited by a unique assemblage of pelagic animals. This is the **mesopelagic zone,** extending from the bottom of the epipelagic zone to about 1,000 m.

The mesopelagic zone offers some distinct advantages over life nearer the sea surface. Predators may find it more difficult to see their prey in the dim light. Decreased water temperatures at mid-depths lower the metabolic rates, and thus the food and O_2 requirements of the mesopelagic animals. The cold water, with its increased density and viscosity, also slows the sinking rates of food material from above.

Large numbers of mesopelagic animals periodically migrate a few tens or hundreds of meters to feed in the near-surface waters, rather than waiting passively for food to sink. The most common pattern of vertical migration occurs on a daily cycle. At dusk, these midwater animals ascend to the photic zone and feed throughout the night. Prior to daybreak, they begin migrating back down to deeper, darker waters to spend the day. The following evening, the pattern is usually repeated. In the productive Antarctic, the daily pattern of vertical migration often breaks down, and the animals generally remain in the photic zone during the summer, and spend the winter in deeper waters.

The general pattern of daily, or **diurnal, vertical migration** has been deduced from numerous sources of information. Net collections of animals from several depths at different times throughout the day have shown that more animals are near the surface at night while fewer are at greater depths (fig. 7.36). Opposite distributions are sometimes found during the day. Direct observations from submersible vehicles support the conclusions drawn from net sampling.

Another tool has been used extensively to study the behavior of vertically migrating animals. Underwater sound pulses from ship-mounted echosounders are partially reflected by concentrations or layers of midwater animals. These sound-reflecting **deep scattering layers** can be observed to ascend nearly to the surface at dusk and break up (fig. 7.37). At daybreak, the layers reform and descend to their usual daytime depths (200–600 m). Often three or more distinct layers are discernible over broad oceanic areas.

The composition of the deep scattering layer has been and still is an unsettled question. Most inhabitants of the mesopelagic zone are simply too small or too sparsely distributed to strongly reflect sound signals. Net tows and observations from manned submersibles suggest three groups of animals as likely candidates for causing the deep scattering layers: euphausiid crus-

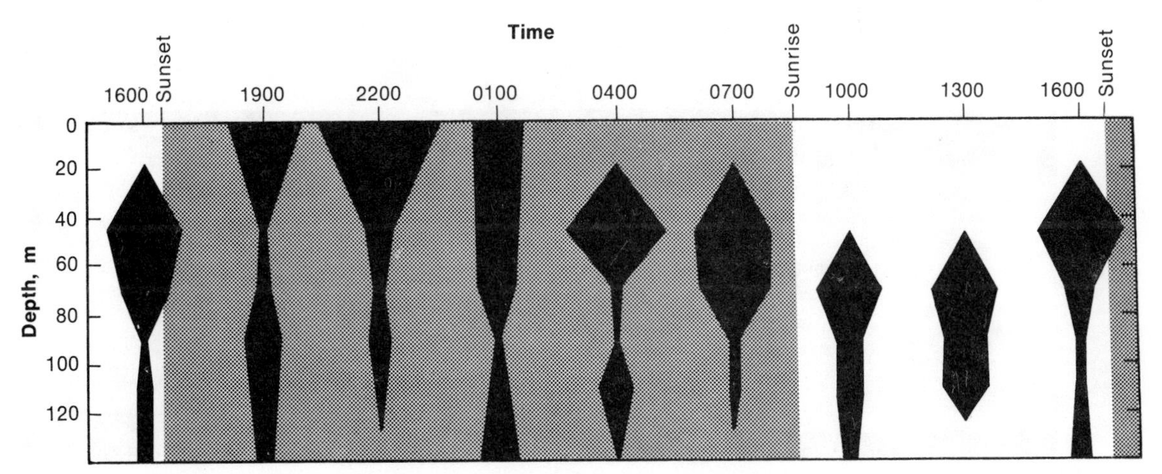

Fig. 7.36 A kite diagram of net collections of adult female copepods, *Calanus finmarchicus*, during a complete diurnal vertical migration cycle. Hours of darkness have been shaded. Adapted from H. U. Sverdrup, Martin W. Johnson, and Richard H. Fleming, *The Oceans: Their Physics, Chemistry, and General Biology*, © 1942, renewed 1970. By permission of Prentice-Hall, Inc., Englewood Cliffs, New Jersey.

taceans (fig. 3.23), fishes (primarily myctophids), and siphonophores (fig. 7.8*b*). The first two are often abundant members at depths where the deep scattering layers occur. Euphausiids may number over 100 animals in a m^3 of seawater. They also have very wide geographical distributions. The strong echoes of sound pulses may, in part, be due to the resonating qualities of the gas-filled myctophid swim bladders and siphonophore air floats. Relatively few are necessary to produce strong echoes at certain sound frequencies.

Whatever the composition of the deep scattering layers may be, they are merely sound-reflecting indicators of a much more extensive vertically migrating assemblage of animals that is not detected by echolocation. Members of the deep-scattering layer doubtless graze on smaller vertical migrators, and are, in turn, preyed upon by larger fish and squid.

These migrations, although only a few hundred meters in extent, are accomplished in a short period of time and at an appreciable expenditure of energy. The copepod *Calanus,* for example, is only a few mm long, yet it swims upward at 15 m/hr and descends at 50 m/hr. Larger euphausiids (2 cm long) move in excess of 100 m/hr. If diurnal vertical migrations are foraging trips from below into the productive photic zone, why do these ani-

Time, hrs

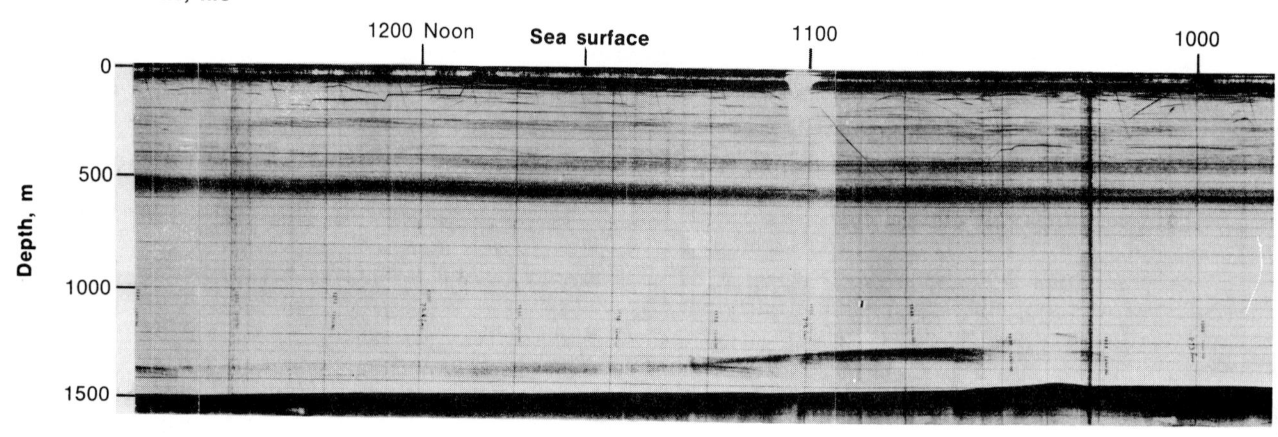

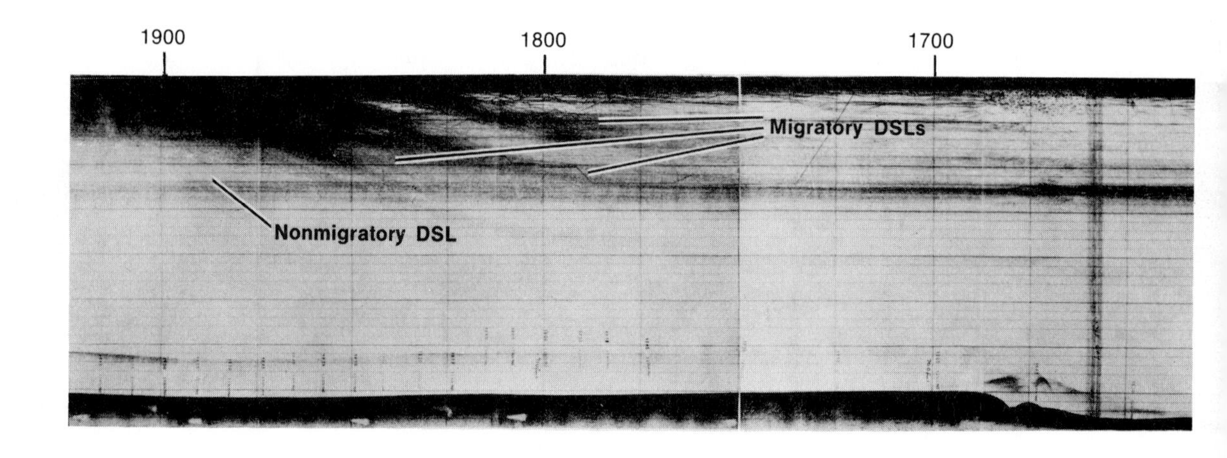

Fig. 7.37 A 13-hour record of several distinct sound scattering layers at a station near the Canary Islands on 11 November 1965. Except for slight drift corrections, the recording ship remained stationary. The time scale reads from right to left. Multiple layers begin migrating downward at daylight (0700 hrs), remain near 500 m throughout the day, then migrate upward in the evening (1800–1900 hrs.). Courtesy E. Kampa, Scripps Institution of Oceanography and the National Institute of Oceanography.

mals descend after feeding, rather than remain in the photic zone? Many explanations for vertical migration have been offered, and all probably provide a portion of the complete picture.

One plausible explanation is that diurnal vertical migration provides a means for animals to capitalize on the more abundant food resources of the photic zone in the dark of the night, then escape visual detection by predators in the refuge of the dimly-lit mesopelagic zone during the day. But vertical migration can be useful in other ways. It was mentioned earlier that lower water temperatures at depth reduce an animal's metabolic rate and its energy requirements. The energy thus conserved may be sufficient to offset the lack of food during the day and the energy expenditures incurred during the actual migration.

Vertical migration also plays an important role in the horizontal distribution of zooplankton and smaller nekton. Most of these animals are incapable of swimming long distances under their own power; they are simply too small and too slow. By swimming toward the surface at night, however, they can take advantage of surface ocean currents and get a free ride to a new habitat some distance away by morning.

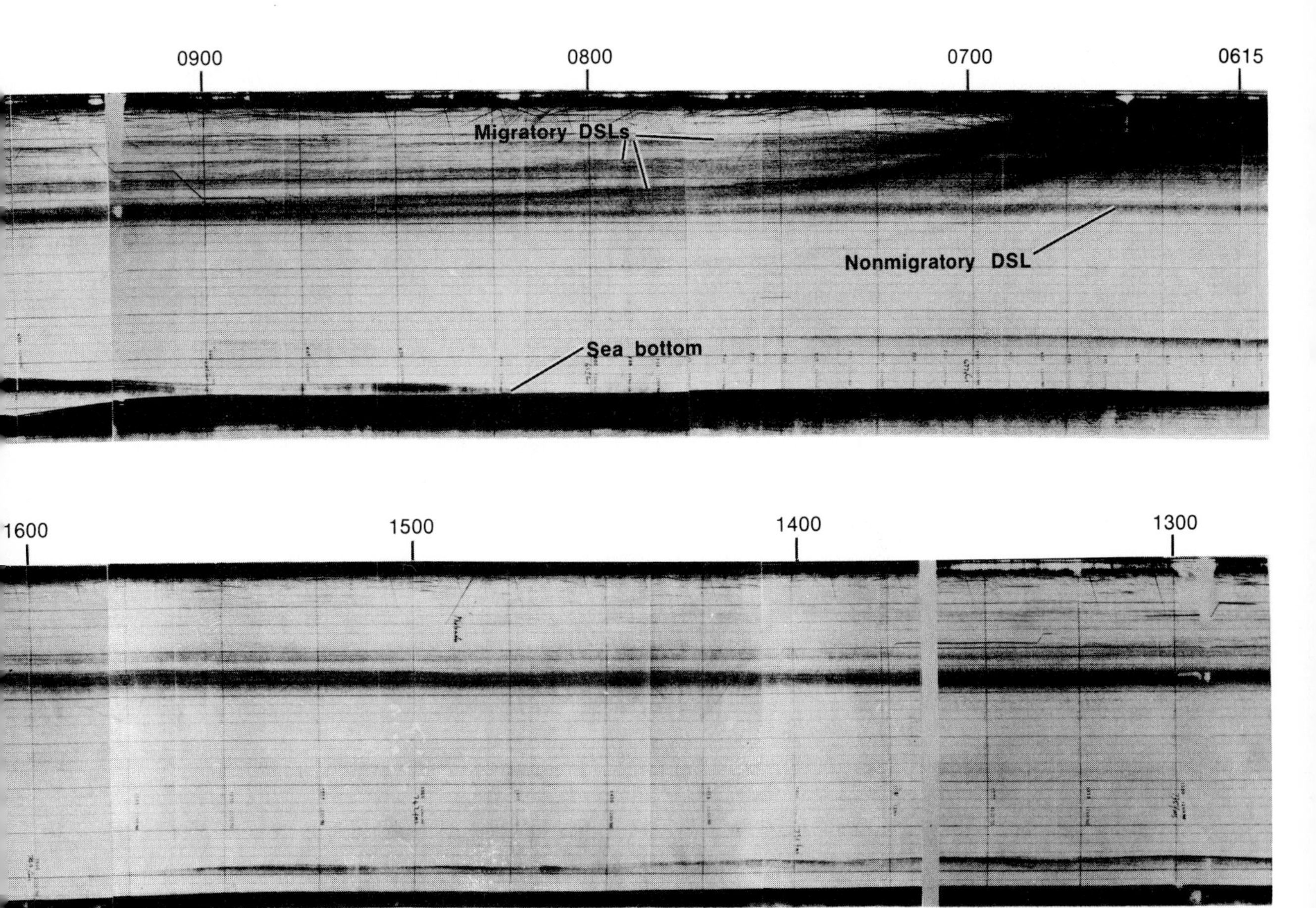

The animals are largely below the surface currents during the day and do not drift much, but the phytoplankton nearer the surface continue to drift with the currents. The daytime drift of phytoplankton patches in the photic zone is usually faster and in a different direction (refer to fig. 1.25) than the deeper animal groups. Animals that miss a phytoplankton patch one night are likely to encounter one the next evening. Conversely, a heavily-grazed phytoplankton patch may find respite from overgrazing by drifting away from the deeper grazers during the day.

Orientation

One aspect of migration that has not yet been considered is the "how" of it. How do migratory species orient themselves to determine where they are and where they are going? Before an animal can successfully accomplish a directed movement from one place to another, it must orient itself, both in time and in space.

Biological clocks operating on circadian and longer period rhythms (discussed in chapter 4) are important factors in the orientation process. A variety of environmental factors seem to be necessary as cues to adjust or "reset" the timing of these rhythms. Well known among these timing factors is the day length that changes with monotonous and predictable regularity on seasonal cycles. Day length, as well as water temperature and food availability, might serve as useful cues for following the passage of the seasons. These and other factors have been suggested as cues to trigger the seasonal migrations of marine animals.

Daily changes in light intensity seem to be the most likely cues for vertical migration. A certain low light intensity may trigger an upward swimming reaction and a higher light intensity may induce a downward swimming reaction. At dusk, sunlight does not penetrate the water as well, and the animals react by swimming upward, then disperse near the surface at night. As the light intensity increases in the morning, the migrators respond by swimming downward. Electric lights lowered into the water at night have actually driven the deep scattering layers downward from 60 m to 300 m. Bright moonlight has the same effect. Solar eclipses cause the opposite to occur; vertical migrators move toward the surface during an eclipse, even at midday.

Large-scale experiments with mixed coastal zooplankton populations have demonstrated that, under constant light and temperature conditions, some species of copepods maintained their diurnal migratory behavior as a circadian rhythm without relying on external cues such as light intensity. Other species did not migrate, and apparently required light or another external stimulus to induce vertical migration.

Orientation in space can be somewhat more complex than time orientation. Terrestrial animals and birds are known to use recognizable landmarks to orient themselves. Much of the gray whale migration occurs within sight of land, and these whales frequently exhibit a "spying" behavior by thrusting their heads vertically out of the water (fig. 7.38). It has been suggested that

Fig. 7.38 A California gray whale executing a spy hop. Photo by W. Burns, courtesy of R. Gilmore.

this behavior is a means of getting visual bearings on coastal headlands and other recognizable landmarks. Gray whales might also follow ocean bottom contours of the continental shelf, as they usually stay inside the 200 m depth contour. However, an additional and much more complex system for open ocean orientation is necessary if the gray whales cross the Gulf of Alaska rather than following the shore.

Several species of birds are capable of accurately navigating over completely unfamiliar terrain. Some recent studies by W. T. Keeton found evidence that homing pigeons somehow sense the direction of the earth's magnetic field. When he attached small magnets to the birds' necks, to disrupt the earth's magnetic field, they lost their homing ability. Control birds with nonmagnetic bars on their necks homed correctly under the same conditions. Comparable experiments to determine if marine animals have a magnetic compass sense have not been performed.

Some species of birds are also known to navigate at night using only a few stars for guidance. Directional information derived from the apparent position of the sun, moon, and stars might also be useful to migrating marine animals, but only if they can see the sky. Air-breathing whales and turtles are frequently at the surface and could then get their bearings and make course corrections using celestial cues.

A straightforward navigation system using the sun has been hypothesized for adult green turtles on their spawning migration back to their Ascension Island nesting sites. Ascension Island lies due east of the bulge of Brazil at 8°S latitude. The adult turtles could conceivably utilize the height of the noonday sun to judge latitude, swim to the east at 8°S latitude, and eventually make landfall on Ascension Island. Though still hypothetical, this system allows the turtles to make course corrections if they wander or drift to the north or south of the 8°S latitude line. Island-finding by the turtles might be improved if, once they were within about 50 km of Ascension Island on the downstream side, they detected a characteristic chemical given off by the island. No one is sure how well green turtles can use celestial cues (if at all), or how well they can smell and taste. Until these questions are answered, the guidance system of green turtles must remain hypothetical.

It is known that eels, salmon, sharks, and many other fish have extremely keen senses of smell, or **olfaction.** In the past twenty years, an impressive body of evidence has been gathered to support the idea that salmon use olfactory cues to guide them to their home stream. Rather than assuming that each stream and tributary has its own characteristic odor that is detectable some distance out to sea, F. R. Hardin-Jones has postulated a slightly different **sequential odor hypothesis** for migrating salmon. He suggests that young salmon smolt are imprinted with a sequence of stream odors during their downstream trip to the ocean. When returning as adults, the remembered cues are played back in reverse. Hardin-Jones also suggests that the odors in the river are not "homed" on as they are encountered, but rather they act as a sequence of **sign stimuli** that releases a positive response to swim upstream.

The chemical nature of the characteristic odors in stream water are still unidentified. However, these or similar odors are not likely to be concentrated sufficiently in the open ocean to guide the oceanic phase of the salmon's migration. What then are the "guideposts" available to marine fish migrating well below the sea surface across huge expanses of open ocean?

Currents are among the most stable regional features of the oceans. And the migratory patterns of many fish and other marine animals seem closely related to surface current patterns. But how can a fish detect the direction or speed of an ocean current if it can see neither the surface nor the bottom? The sharp temperature and salinity gradients often found at the edges of ocean currents might be detected by some fish, but only if the fish leaves the current. Most of the available evidence suggests that salmon, tuna, and possibly adult eels migrate within currents and not along their edges.

Fish may be able to detect ocean surface currents by visually observing the speeds and direction of horizontally moving debris and plankton (fig. 7.39). In the ocean, the water velocity generally decreases with depth. Fish near the bottom of the current should see particles above them moving in the direction of the current. Slower-moving particles below the fish would appear to move backward as the fish was carried forward by the current. In this manner, the fish could judge the current direction and orient its swimming motions either in the same direction or directly against it.

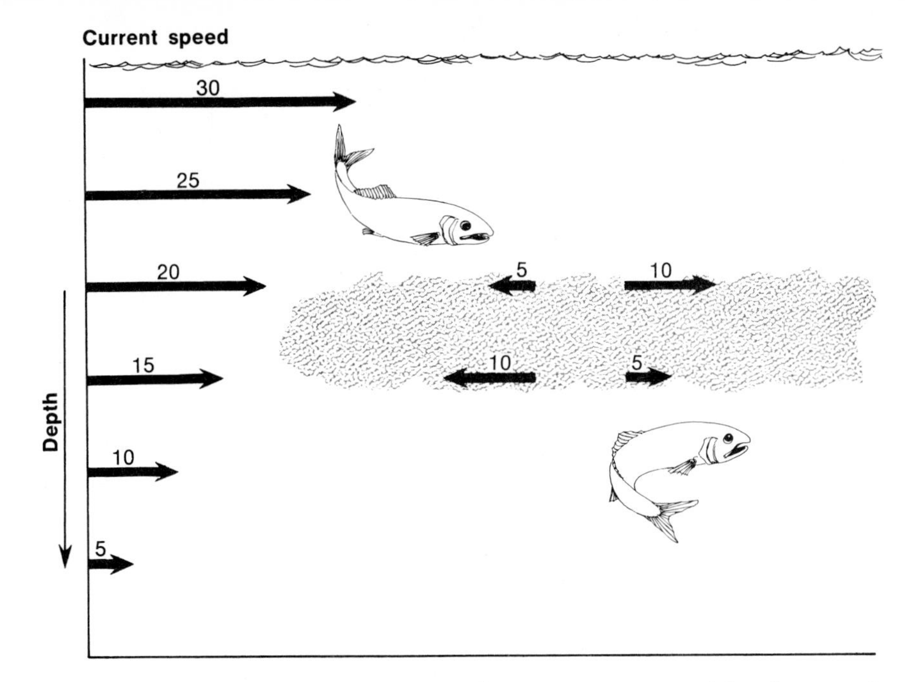

Fig. 7.39 Possible speed and direction cues for fish in an ocean current. To a nonswimming fish above an accumulation of debris and plankton (shaded region), the debris appears to move backward. From below, the debris appears to be carried forward in the direction of the current.

When electrically-charged ions of seawater are moved by the ocean's currents through the magnetic field of the earth, a weak electric potential is generated (the process is similar to the operation of an electrical generator). These ocean current potentials have been measured with ship-towed electrodes, and are used to compute current speeds. Some preliminary laboratory evidence suggests that both the Atlantic eels *(Anguilla)* and Atlantic salmon *(Salmo)* are sensitive to electrical potentials of the same magnitude as those generated by ocean currents. In addition, they are most sensitive to the electrical potential when the long axes of their bodies are aligned with the direction of the current. If fish can also detect these potentials in the ocean, some, at least, have an extremely accurate system for locating and following ocean currents.

Some sharks, skates, and rays are also known to have the requisite sensitivity to detect low-intensity electrical fields. Most studies to date have been directed toward elucidating the capability of sharks to sense and respond to weak bioelectric fields emanating from the body surfaces of their prey. These electroreceptors could also be used to detect electrical fields generated by the flow of ocean currents. Even the movement of a shark swimming through the earth's magnetic field is thought to be sufficient to induce an electrical field that is well within the sensory capabilities of the animal. It is conceivable that at least some sharks, skates, and rays utilize a magnetic compass sense as well as an ocean current detector.

Reproduction

Reproduction in pelagic animals usually proceeds as in most other animal groups. The eggs of the female are fertilized by the male either in the water or within the female's reproduction tract, and embryonic development leads to a new generation. Breeding, spawning, and other reproductive activities are generally periodic and most often associated with higher water temperatures and greater primary production of spring and summer months.

Nonseasonal Reproduction

Those species that deviate from annual cycles do so for a couple of general reasons. Deep-water species experience little in the way of seasonal changes in their environment and may breed or spawn irregularly. Yet we know so little about the reproductive features of deep-ocean pelagic animals that we can do little more than guess.

Other species vary from seasonal reproductive patterns either because small size permits them to reproduce more frequently, or because their very large size prohibits them from meeting an annual reproductive schedule. Smaller zooplankton with life spans of a few months ordinarily reproduce several times during the summer months (fig. 7.40). At the other extreme are the large whales that, after reaching maturity, breed only every second or even every third year. Their **gestation period** (the time between fertilization and birth) is slightly over one year, and the energetic demands that a year of pregnancy followed by six months of nursing make on the mother are enormous. So most of the larger species of whales include a year of rest and recovery between pregnancies.

The grunion *(Leuresthes tenuis),* a small fish common to coastal waters of southern California, exhibits a curious and unusual spawning behavior (fig. 7.41). On the second, third, and fourth nights after each full or new moon of

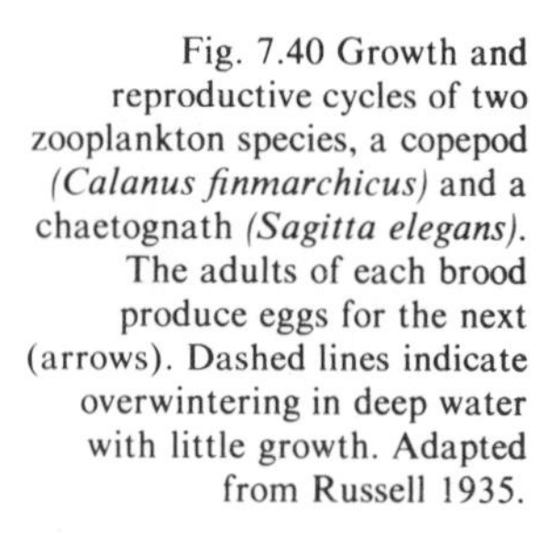

Fig. 7.40 Growth and reproductive cycles of two zooplankton species, a copepod *(Calanus finmarchicus)* and a chaetognath *(Sagitta elegans)*. The adults of each brood produce eggs for the next (arrows). Dashed lines indicate overwintering in deep water with little growth. Adapted from Russell 1935.

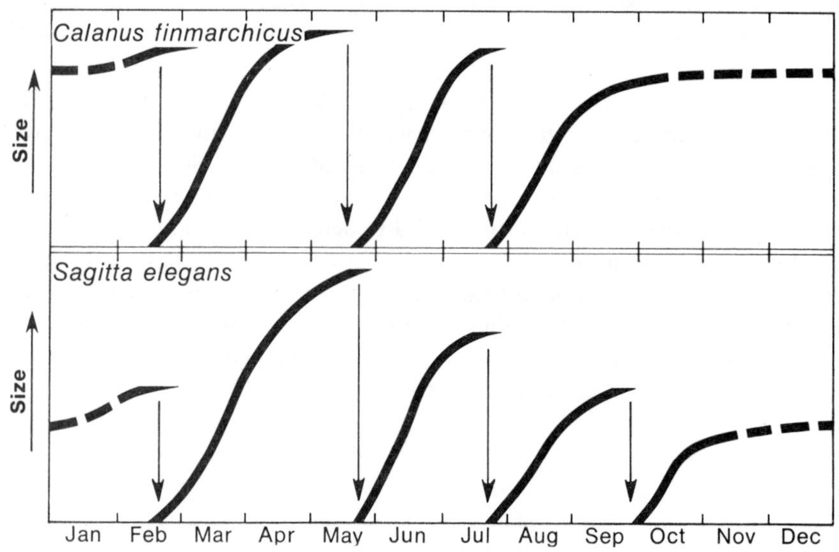

Fig. 7.41 Grunion *(Leuresthes)* spawning in the sands of a California beach. The male is curled around the female who is depositing eggs beneath the sand. Courtesy Dan Garcia.

the spring and summer spawning season, the grunion come up on the beach by the thousands to deposit their eggs in the sand, completely out of water. Even more remarkable is their precise timing, for they spawn only one to three hours immediately following the highest part of the high tide. During the spring and summer months these tides occur only at night.

As the highest spring tides occur at the time of full and new moons, the grunion spawn immediately after high tides, but on successively lower tides each night (fig. 7.42). Thus, the eggs are buried by sand tossed up on the beach by the succeeding lower tides, and are not washed out of the sand until the next series of spring tides. Nine or ten days after the last night of the run, tides of increasing height reach the area where the lowest eggs were buried (fig. 7.42). Wave action erodes the sand away and bathes the eggs with seawater. Almost immediately after being agitated and wetted by the waves, they hatch and the young grunion swim out to deeper water. There they feed and grow, reaching sexual maturity about one year later.

From Yolk Sac to Placenta

The act of giving birth to live young (a process labeled **viviparity**) is a trait often considered characteristic of mammals. Fish, on the other hand, are generally thought to be egg layers (**oviparity**). Many fish are, and some are quite prolific at it. A mature female cod may lay as many as 15 million eggs in a single season. These eggs are small, hatching into planktonic larval stages. As you might expect, the mortality rate of these eggs and larvae is extremely high. In contrast, skates, rays, and benthic sharks usually produce only a few very large eggs (fig. 7.43). A single egg of a whale shark often measures 30 cm in length. The developing embryos are protected by a durable outer case and are well nourished by the abundant yolk inside. When they hatch (sometimes requiring several months after laying), the young fish are well developed and quite capable of surviving on their own.

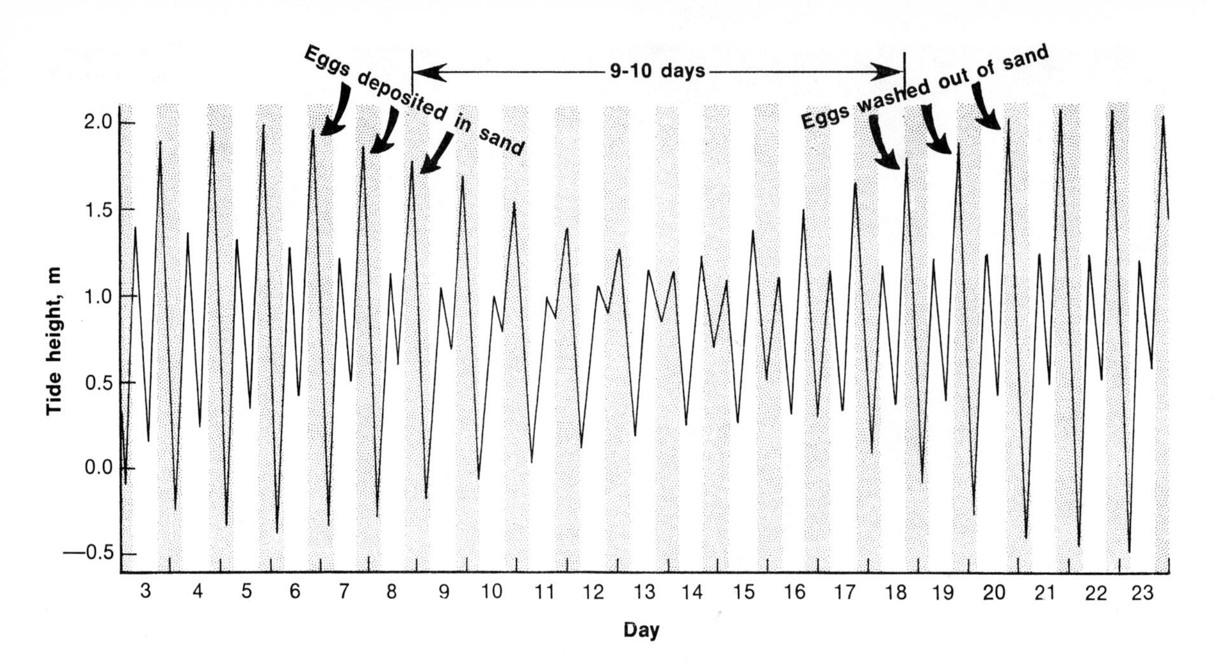

Fig. 7.42 Predicted tide heights for May 3–23, 1974, at San Diego, California. Spring tides appropriate for grunion spawning occurred on May 6, 7, and 8 (arrows at left). Nine to ten days later, the next set of spring tides (arrows at right) washed the eggs from the sand and caused them to hatch. Shaded portions indicate night hours.

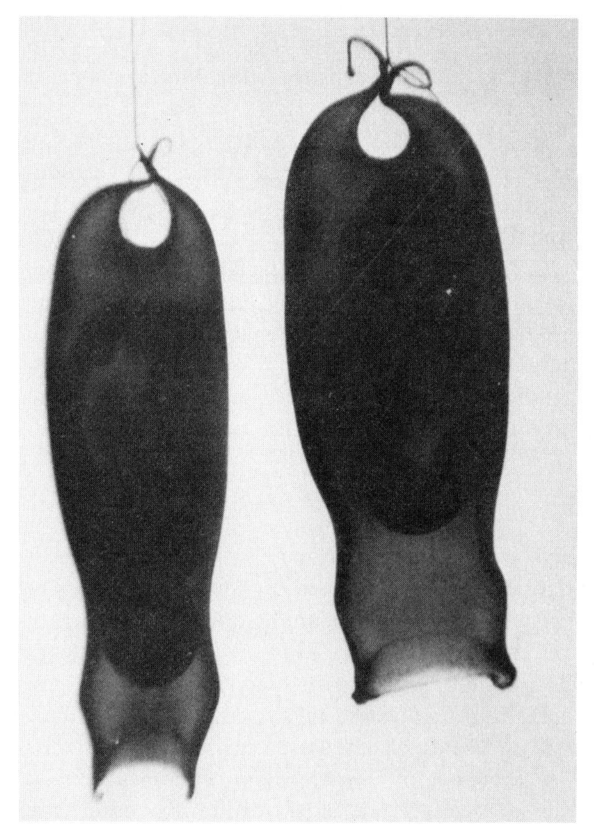

Fig. 7.43 Developing horn shark embryos *(Herterodontus)* enclosed in tough, protective egg cases. Courtesy Sea World, San Diego.

Other sharks and a few bony fish produce eggs that are maintained within the reproductive tract of the female until they hatch. They are thus delivered alive into the world, but the developing embryos obtain all of their nourishment from the yolk of their own eggs (fig. 7.44). None comes directly from their mothers. This intermediate condition between viviparity (live birth) and oviparity (egg-laying) is known as **ovoviviparity.** Ovoviviparity is essentially a method for incubating the eggs internally, and functionally differs little from the pouch-brooding habit of sea horses and pipefishes. Only it is the male sea horse and pipefish that are equipped with abdominal brood pouches. The eggs are deposited in these pouches by the females to remain for the eight to ten day incubation period.

Extending the practice of internal security for developing embryos are several species of ovoviviparous fish that provide embryonic nutrition in addition to that contained in the yolk. The oviducts and uterus of pelagic sharks and rays are usually lined with numerous small projections called **villi.** The villi secrete a highly nutritive **uterine milk** for the embryos. In the stingray *(Pteroplatea),* the secreting villi of the uterus extend down into the esophagus of the embryo. Thus nourished, the young of *Pteroplatea* at birth are fifty times larger than the initial size of their yolk sacs. Other fish, such as the white-tip shark *(Carcharhinus)* absorb nutrients through a placentalike connection between the yolk sac and the uterine wall. The embryos of surfperches are equipped with large, vascularized fins for the same purpose, to absorb additional nutrients from the mothers' ovaries.

Between the ovoviviparous fish (such as *Squalus*) and those that are obviously viviparous exists a continuum of reproductive conditions, some of which are rather exotic and do not fit neatly into either category. The embryos of the mackerel shark, *Lamna,* for instance, have no structures to absorb nutrients from the reproductive tract of the female. When the oldest embryo within a female *Lamna* has used its own yolk, it simply turns on the other eggs within the oviduct and consumes them. With the nutrition gained from its potential siblings, the single embryo is developmentally much better prepared for a pelagic existence before leaving the protective confines of its mother.

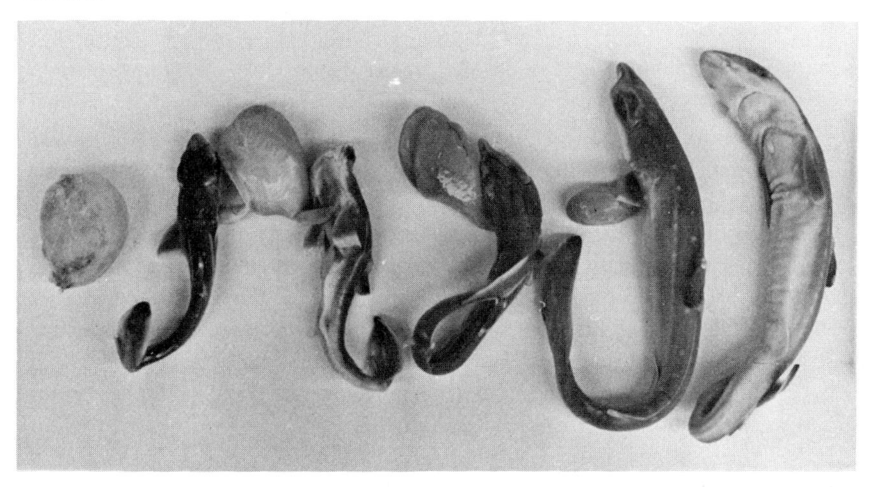

Fig. 7.44 A developmental series of the dogfish shark, *Squalus,* from an egg (left) to a completely formed embryo ready for birth (right). Note the twins (second from left) joined to a common yolk.

Some Alternatives to Conventional Sex Ratios

Most species of sexually-reproducing animals include approximately equal numbers of females and males. The "maleness" or "femaleness" of many animals is determined by the individual's complement of **sex chromosomes.** In humans, the nucleus of each cell houses 23 pairs of chromosomes; one pair is the sex chromosomes, the other 22 pairs are **autosomes** unrelated to sex determination. A human female has two large, similar sex chromosomes (an XX condition), males have one large X and one small Y chromosome. The same is true for all other mammals. Sex in birds is also established by a pair of sex chromosomes; but the pattern is opposite that of mammals. Male birds have two similar sex chromosomes; those of female birds differ in size and shape.

The influence of sex chromosomes on the sexuality of fish is less straightforward and, in fact, is quite variable. Guppies, for instance, generally reflect the mammalian pattern of sex chromosomes; XX is female and XY is male. Infrequently, though, an XX guppy occurs as a sexually functional male, and an XY individual occasionally ends up as a female. The sex chromosomes of fish lack the absolute control over sex determination found in birds and mammals. The genes involved in sex determination of fishes are, unlike mammals and birds, also carried on the autosomes. In some fishes, these autosomal sex genes apparently influence and even regulate the production of sex hormones, especially **androgen,** a male hormone, and **estrogen,** a female hormone. These hormones, in turn, influence the expression of several sexual characteristics and even the determination of sex. Fisheries' scientists have found that a high percentage of salmon eggs treated with estrogen will hatch as females. Treated with androgen, most hatch as males.

The fluid and unfixed nature of sex determination in fishes has been effectively exploited through the evolution of a broad range of sex ratios and reproductive habits not apparent in other vetebrate groups. Part of this sexual diversity is due to the separation of sexes. Separate sexes housed in different individuals eliminate any possibility of self-fertilization and its accompanying reduction in genetic variation. Even in hermaphroditic fishes such as the sea basses, *Serranus* and *Serranelus* (which do fertilize their own eggs when alone), behavioral interactions with others of the same species insure that cross-fertilization will occur much of the time. Some deep-sea fish also function simultaneously as both males and females. As the paths of these fish cross infrequently in the deep sea, encounters between two hermaphrodites will be eminently more successful than similar meetings between individuals belonging to the same sex.

Other variations have evolved as improvements on the 1 male:1 female sex ratio so characteristic of sexually reproducing animals. Males are often quite capable of fertilizing the eggs of several females. This is especially true of species that exercise little parental care after the eggs are fertilized. Thus, in a reproductive sense, some of the males of some fish populations are sexual excesses, and the reproductive potential of the population would be better served were they females instead.

A few fish species are exceptions to the 1:1 sex ratio. These species produce offspring that are all of one sex. They mature; then, at some point in their lives, some or all of them undergo a complete and functional reversal to the opposite sex. These fish are also hermaphroditic, but unlike *Serranus,* they are **sequential hermaphrodites.** The entire gonad functions first for one sex, then changes to the opposite sex. In the California sheephead, *Pimelometopon,* the fish (all females) become sexually mature at four years of age. Those that survive to seven or eight years undergo sex reversal, become functional males, and mate with the younger females. The actual ratio of females to males depends on the survival curve of the population (fig. 7.45) and the age at which sex reversal occurs. For the sheephead it is approximately five females to one male. In *Labrus* (belonging to the same family, Labridae, as the sheephead) sex reversal is size dependent. They are all born female and remain so until they reach a length of 27 cm. Beyond that size half change to males, the other half continue as females. A few species of sea basses do this in reverse, beginning life as males, then changing to females.

The ultimate example of matching the sex ratio to the reproductive needs of the population is found in *Labroides* (also in the family Labridae). This inhabitant of the Great Barrier Reef of Australia occurs in small social groups of about ten individuals. Each group consists of one dominant male; the remainder are females. The single male accommodates the reproductive needs of all the females. This type of social and breeding organization is termed **polygyny** (the counterpart of polygamy in humans). In polygynous

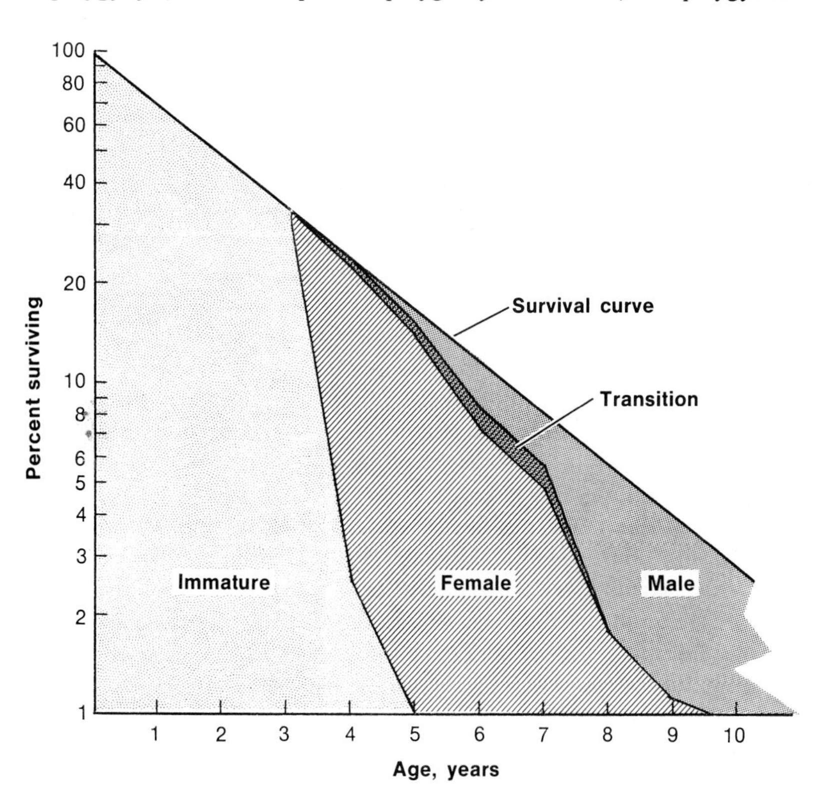

Fig. 7.45 Distribution of sexes according to age of the Catalina Island sheephead population. The survival curve is based on an assumed 30% annual mortality rate. The ages of sexual maturity and sex reversal determine the relative numbers of females and males in the population at any one time. Adapted from Warner 1973.

populations, only the dominant, most aggressive individual functions as the male, and by himself contributes half the genetic information to be passed on to the next generation.

In the event the dominant male of a *Labroides* population dies or is removed, the most dominant of the remaining females immediately assumes the behavioral role of the male. Within two weeks, her (his?) color patterns change, the ovarian tissue is replaced with testicular tissue, and the population has a new male. In this manner, males are produced only "on demand" as they are needed, and then only from the most dominant of the remaining members of the population.

These sex changes seem to be controlled by the relative amounts of androgen and estrogen produced by the gonads as the fish grows and matures. Young female sheepheads, when artificially injected with the male sex hormone androgen change to males at a younger age than normal. Injections of estrogen delay sex reversal and maintain the individual in a prolonged state of femaleness. Conditions of social stress imposed by the dominant male *Labroides* may induce estrogen production in the females to inhibit sex reversal.

These examples are but a few of the vast array of reproductive habits available to pelagic animals. In the course of evolution, the selective advantage of each has been tested and retested innumerable times. Whether the reproductive strategy of a particular species relies on millions of small eggs or a few large ones, oviparity or viviparity, separate sexes or hermaphroditism, each in its own way has contributed to the biological success of that species.

Summary

The animals of the pelagic division, the zooplankton and nekton, are drawn from many animal phyla. The temporary meroplankton represent the reproductive efforts of a large variety of shallow water benthic invertebrates, whereas the holoplankton consist of a relatively few major animal groups. Especially dominant holoplankton forms are the filter-feeding crustaceans and several soft-bodied, or gelatinous, animal groups. The limited diversity of holoplankton is restricted by the number of major habitats available in the epipelagic zone.

Pelagic animals have solved the fundamental problem of buoyancy in seawater. Some of the strategies employed by zooplankton are reminiscent of those used by phytoplankton, but they are useless for the well-muscled and streamlined nekton.

For these animals, gas-filled flotation devices provide buoyancy with very little additional volume. Air-filled floats are reasonably simple devices for animals that do not change depths or have rigid gas containers, such as siphonophores and cephalopods. However, air and other gas mixtures are compressible, and if the container is also (as are swim bladders in bony fish), some pressure-compensating mechanism is needed. The gas gland and associated countercurrent *retia mirabile* of some bony fish are capable of concentrating gases from the blood into their swim bladders at tremendous pressures.

With their buoyancy problems solved, many nektonic animals have assumed a mode of existence dependent upon speed and agility in the water. Streamlined body form and an effective organ of propulsion are basic to high speeds underwater. These are best demonstrated by tunas and tunalike fishes.

Migrations are commonly employed by motile animals to optimize conditions for survival. Long-distance migrations generally link areas that are appropriate for reproduction with the feeding areas of the adults. These are often thousands of km apart. Some zooplankton and smaller nekton undertake daily or diurnal vertical migrations to and from the food-rich photic zone to feed and to escape predators. Several factors, from coastal landmarks and ocean currents to stars and the sun, may be employed as navigational cues by the animals that undertake these migrations.

Reproductive patterns vary immensely in pelagic animals. Some spawn frequently and produce large numbers of eggs. Others reproduce infrequently and conservatively. Some are oviparous, some ovoviviparous, others viviparous. A few even undergo sex reversal. Regardless of the differences in reproductive strategies, the goal is the same: to produce offspring that will achieve maturity and eventually reproduce themselves.

Questions for Discussion

1. How do fish achieve extremely high concentrations of gases in their swim bladders? Why is N_2, the most abundant gas in air, of relatively minor importance in swim bladders of fish at great depths?
2. Explain the structural and physiological adaptations that account for the high swimming speeds achieved by tuna and similar "cruising" fish. It might be helpful to compare the "cruiser" to a typical "lunger" such as a bass or grouper.
3. Describe the structural and physiological differences that allow a greater work output from red fish muscle than from a similar amount of white muscle.
4. Discuss and compare the life cycles and migratory patterns of the European eels and the sockeye salmon. What are the probable orientation cues used by these fish during the oceanic phase of their migration?
5. Describe the role of the deep scattering layer in the exchange of nutrients and energy between the epipelagic zone and deeper water masses.
6. Why are the large-scale oceanic habitats of many epipelagic animals arranged in similar latitudinal bands in all oceans?
7. Do you think that similar patterns of distribution occur in the mesopelagic zone? Why?

Suggestions for Further Reading

Books

Alexander, R. McN. 1970. *Functional design in fishes.* London: Hutchinson.

Briggs, J. C. 1974. *Marine zoogeography.* New York: McGraw-Hill.

Greenwood, P. H., and Norman, J. R. 1976. *A history of fishes.* New York: Halsted Press.

Hardy, A. 1971. *The open sea: Its natural history. Part I: The world of plankton. Part II: Fish and fisheries.* Boston: Houghton Mifflin.

Idyll, C. P. 1976. *The abyss: The deep sea and the creatures that live in it.* London: Thomas Nelson Ltd.

Marshall, N. E. 1966. *The life of fishes.* New York: Universe Books.

Marshall, S. M., and Orr, A. P. 1972. *The biology of a marine copepod.* New York: Springer-Verlag.

Articles

Alldredge, A. 1976. Appendicularians. *Scientific American,* July:94–102.

Benson, A. A., and Lee, R. F. 1975. The role of wax in oceanic food chains. *Scientific American,* March:76–86.

Carey, F. G. *et al.* 1971. Warm-bodied fish. *American Zoologist* 11:137–45.

Denton, E. 1960. The buoyancy of marine animals. *Scientific American,* July:118–28.

Dietz, R. S. 1962. The sea's deep scattering layers. *Scientific American,* August:44–50.

Gray, J. 1957. How fishes swim. *Scientific American,* August:48–54.

Kalmijn, A. J. 1977. The electric and magnetic sense of sharks, skates, and rays. *Oceanus* 20:45–52.

Perutz, M. F. 1978. Hemoglobin structure and respiratory transport. *Scientific American,* December:92–125.

Rommel, S. A., Jr., and Stasko, A. B. 1973. Electronavigation by eels. *Sea Frontiers* 19:219–23.

Rosen, M. W., and Cornford, N. E. 1971. Fluid friction of fish slimes. *Nature* 234:49–51.

Scholander, P. F. 1957. "The wonderful net." *Scientific American,* April:96–107.

Shaw, E. 1962. The schooling of fishes. *Scientific American,* June:128–36.

Pacific white-sided dolphin, *Lagenorhynchus obliquidens*. Courtesy K. Balcomb.

Marine Mammals

8

Marine mammals are a diverse lot, ranging from the abundant and widespread cetaceans (whales, dolphins, and porpoises) and pinnipeds (seals, sea lions, and walruses) to the much less common sea otters, manatees, and dugongs. Each of these groups depends on the sea for food and spends most or all of its time in the water. They have evolved independently of each other, yet each group has some four-footed terrestrial predecessor lurking in its dim evolutionary past.

The modern whales are of two distinct types. The filter-feeding baleen whales (order: Mysticeti) lack teeth and, in their place, rows of comblike **baleen** project from the outer edges of their upper jaws (fig. 8.1). All except the gray whale feed on planktonic crustaceans or small shoaling fish. The character of the baleen, as well as the size and shape of the head, mouth, and body, differ markedly between species of baleen whales (fig. 8.2). Right and bowhead whales (*Balaena* spp.) have very fine, long baleen well adapted to collect *Calanus* and other small copepods less than 1 cm in size. Most of the rorquals (*Balaenoptera* spp.) and the humpback whale (*Megaptera novaen-*

Fig. 8.1 A right whale *(Balaena)* hauled up at a Canadian whaling station. Photo by G. Pike, courtesy S. Leatherwood, Naval Undersea Center, San Diego.

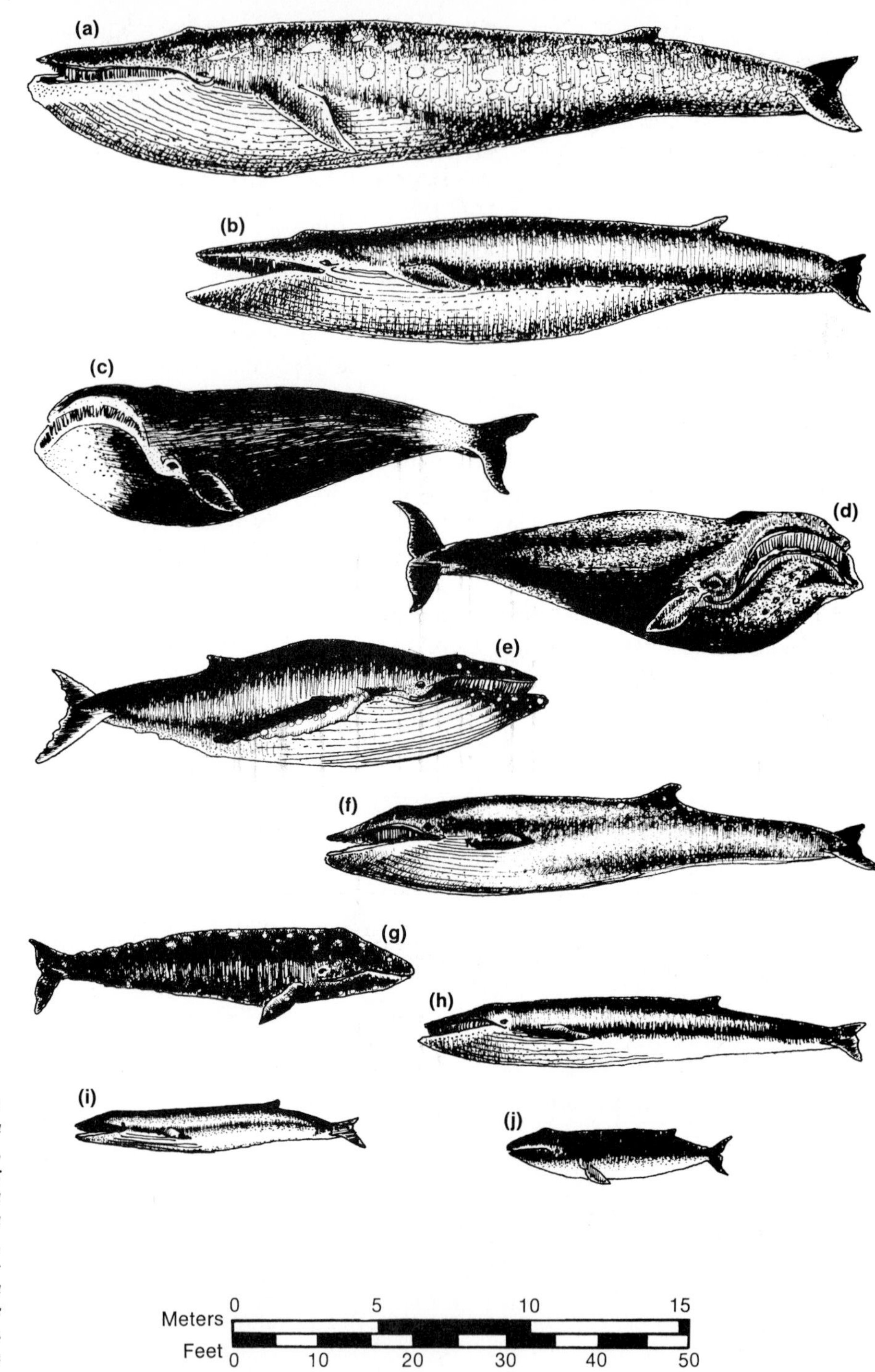

Fig. 8.2 Baleen whales: (*a*) blue, *Balaenoptera musculus;* (*b*) fin, *Balaenoptera physalus;* (*c*) bowhead, *Balaena mysticetus;* (*d*) right, *Balaena glacialis;* (*e*) humpback, *Megaptera novaeangliae;* (*f*) sei, *Balaenoptera borealis;* (*g*) gray, *Eschrichtius robustus;* (*h*) Bryde's *Balaenoptera edeni;* (*i*) little piked, *Balaenoptera acutorostrata;* and (*j*) pygmy right, *Caperea marginata.*

gliae) have generally coarser baleen fibers and feed on larger crustaceans, especially *Euphausia superba,* and other euphausiids. The California gray whale (*Eschrichtius robustus*) has the coarsest baleen of all mysticetes.

In his extensive studies of feeding behavior in baleen whales, T. Nemoto observed three generalized feeding patterns. The right, humpback, and larger rorquals (blue and fin whales) open their mouths as they swim into a shoal of crustaceans. The ventral grooves of the throat expand, increasing the capacity of the mouth. Several tons of water (and plankton) are quickly engulfed by the mouth. The gigantic muscular tongue acts as a piston to force the water out through the baleen. Numerous small animals are trapped inside the baleen, and are quickly swallowed. Sei whales swim rapidly below the surface for some distance with their jaws partially open. Small fish and large plankton become trapped in the exposed baleen and are wiped off with the tongue and swallowed.

Gray whales exhibit the most unusual feeding behavior of all mysticetes. In their shallow summer feeding grounds of the Bering and Arctic seas, these medium-sized whales feed on bottom invertebrates, especially amphipod crustaceans. It was thought that gray whales feed by dredging up mouthfuls of soft sediment and the resident invertebrates, then flushing the mud out through the coarse baleen. But observations on the feeding behavior of "Gigi," a young gray whale held in captivity in San Diego in 1971, suggest that these animals may instead sweep their heads over the surface of the mud to disturb the amphipods. As the amphipods leap off the bottom to escape, they are sucked into the side of the whale's mouth and swallowed.

All other living whales (including porpoises and dolphins) are toothed whales (order: Odonticeti), as in figure 8.3*a* and *b*. They lack baleen, are generally smaller than mysticetes, and are well equipped to catch fish, squid, and other slippery morsels of food. The stomach contents of one 15 m sperm whale yielded an intact giant squid (*Architeuthis*) 10.5 m in length. However, a study of sperm whale stomach contents by R. Clarke indicated that squid ingested by sperm whales averaged about 1 m in length. The slightly smaller killer whales have gained a reputation as voracious predators, particularly on other marine mammals. In a recent study by D. Rice, stomachs of 10 killer whales taken off the West Coast of the United States were examined. They contained the remains of 1 minke whale, 7 sea lions, 7 elephant seals, 4 porpoises, 2 sharks, a squid, and assorted large fish. The larger seals and sea lions had been dismembered, but smaller ones were swallowed whole.

The smaller odontocetes, especially, are very social and are thought by many to be highly intelligent animals. Their actions often seem purposeful and intelligent, as the following description of care-giving behavior directed to a captive Pacific common dolphin during birth demonstrates.

On December 13, 1963, a female Pacific common dolphin, *Delphinus bairdi* Dall, arrived in Marineland. . . .The common dolphin is difficult to maintain in a captive environment. This species appears to be peculiarly emotional and particularly sensitive to the competitive feeding behavior normally demonstrated by larger, more aggressive forms. This specimen, however, appeared to adapt rapidly to an enclosure shared with delphinids of four other genera. Dolphins in the latter stages of pregnancy normally display a pronounced distention of the inguino-abdominal region. The small common dolphin failed to show these signs. It was, therefore, a surprise when, at approximately 11:50 A.M. on February 15, observers saw a small tail protruding from her birth canal. The birth progressed very rapidly and by 12:05 P.M. the entire posterior portion of the fetus had been expelled. The umbilical cord, which seemed stretched and taut, was clearly visible.

The striped dolphins and false killer whale followed the laboring female. The dolphins showed particular interest and nosed the female's abdominal region on several occasions.

The dorsal fin of the calf appeared to obstruct its further passage. In normal births the dorsal fin folds at its base either to the right or left, but in this case it remained erect and caught internally at the apex of the vaginal introitus.

At 12:15 P.M. one of the striped dolphins grasped the fetal tail flukes in its mouth and withdrew the infant from the parental birth canal. A discharge of amniotic fluid and a little blood followed the delivery.

The infant was stillborn, and delayed expulsion at a critical phase of parturition was no doubt incriminated in this fetal death. . . .

Our common dolphin, attended by the striped dolphins, carried her dead infant's body to the surface. These efforts were, however, terminated by the male pilot whale, who seized the body by its head. The pilot whale devoured the small cadaver, entire, after carrying it to and from the surface for 38 minutes.

The common dolphin at first seemed little affected by the intervention of the pilot whale, but appeared greatly distressed by its ingestion of the cadaver. Whistling constantly, she moved rapidly around the tank, swimming in an erratic manner, apparently searching for her calf.

The animal quickly resumed a more normal swimming pattern, in the company of the striped dolphins, but she continued to vocalize intermittently for several hours.

Since 1:00 P.M., continuous uterine contractions had caused a three-inch length of the umbilical cord to move in and out of the female's urogenital opening. At 4:06 P.M., the common dolphin sought the company of the female false killer whale. She was observed at this time to deliberately avoid the company of the striped dolphins and begin to swim on the west side of the tank quite close to the surface. The false killer whale swam to the little dolphin and, after an apparent deliberate examination of her genital area gently grasped the umbilical remnant in her mouth, and with a lateral movement of her head withdrew this tissue some six inches from the common dolphin's body. The dolphin rolled on her back and broke away from the larger animal, but then returned and again waited for the false killer whale. Once more, the whale seized the placenta and repeated the behavior previously described and withdrew the membrane another three inches. The common dolphin during these periods was observed to actively flex her body and appeared to try to assist the false killer whale in its attempts to remove the afterbirth. At the third attempt, the female false killer whale was successful and withdrew the entire placental membrane from the smaller animal. This was released and immediately both animals resumed normal activity in the tank.[1]

The interpretation of such behavior as "intentional" or "intelligent" acts to provide assistance to another animal in distress, appealing though the concept is, is not strongly supported by behavioral evidence. These and other apparent

1. D.H. Brown, D.K. Caldwell, and M.C. Caldwell, 1966. By permission of Los Angeles County Museum of Natural History, *Contributions in Science*, pp.7–12.

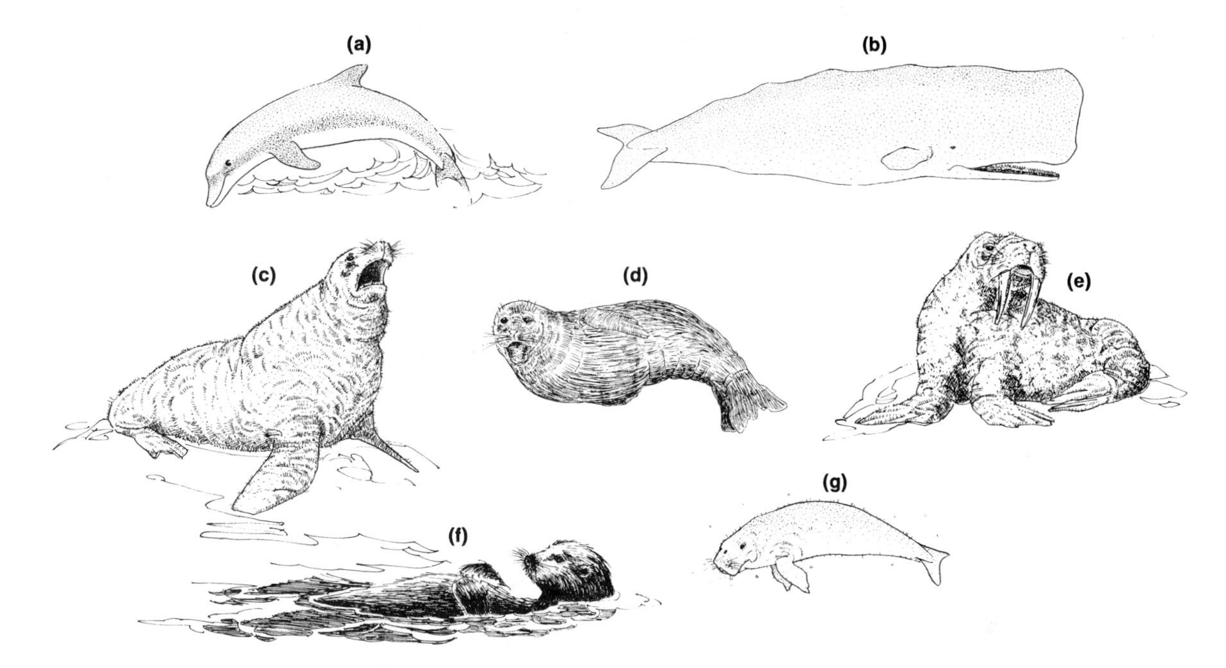

Fig. 8.3 Other marine mammal groups (not drawn to scale): (*a*) porpoise, (*b*) sperm whale, (*c*) sea lion, (*d*) seal, (*e*) walrus, (*f*) sea otter, and (*g*) dugong.

"intelligent" acts may have an adaptive purpose for the survival of the population. But to attribute these acts to an intentional purpose, with the animals "knowing what they were doing," requires evidence which is presently just not available.

Pinnipeds, also in figure 8.3*c, d,* and *e* evolved from terrestrial carnivores and, in the sea, have maintained their predacious habits. Only one species of walrus (*Odobenus rosmarus*) survives today. Walruses are found in shallow Arctic waters of the Pacific and Atlantic oceans where they feed on benthic mollusks. Seals and sea lions are not as easily distinguished from each other as they are from the walrus. Like walruses, sea lions and eared seals have large front flippers and can rotate their rear flippers beneath their bodies to provide a clumsy walking gait when on land. In the water, sea lions swim using a slow, underwater "flying" motion of their front flippers. The earless seals, as their name implies, lack external ears. They have smaller front flippers, and when out of water, their rear flippers trail uselessly behind. Seals propel themselves when swimming with side-to-side movements of their rear flippers.

Sea otters (*Enhydra lutris*), figure 8.3 *f*, have retained a strong resemblance to their fish-eating relatives of freshwater lakes and streams. Sea otters prefer to eat sluggish benthic invertebrates found along the shallow edges of the North Pacific. At some point in their evolutionary past, sea otters entered a tool-using stone age of their own. Using rocks carried to the surface with their food, they float on their backs and crack open the hard shells of sea urchins, crabs, and mussels to get at the soft insides.

Manatees, dugongs, and sea cows (order: Sirenia), figure 8.3 *g*, are large, ungainly creatures with paddlelike tails and no rear flippers. They are docile, herbivorous animals, completely restricted to shallow coastal waters where they can secure an abundance of large marine vegetation. They inhabit coastal regions along both sides of Africa, across southern Asia and the Indo-Pacific, and the western Atlantic from South America to Florida. Formerly, the Steller's sea cow occupied parts of the Bering Sea and the Aleutian Islands. It took hunters and whalers less than thirty years from the time the explorer Bering discovered these slow, quiet animals in 1741 to completely exterminate the species.

These mammalian groups have experienced varying degrees of adaptation and modification in their evolutionary transition from land to life in the sea. Sea otters differ little from their nonmarine relatives. At the other extreme are the cetaceans. Their evolution from terrestrial ancestors has culminated in a remarkable assemblage of structural, physiological, and behavioral changes to meet the challenges of a totally marine existence. In contrast to typical mammals, cetaceans lack hair and rear legs (or flippers), breathe through a dorsal blowhole, are streamlined, and propel themselves with broad horizontal tail flukes.

Yet in spite of these obvious specializations, cetaceans are still mammals and they (and other marine mammals) exhibit several less apparent but no less important adaptations to satisfy their basic mammalian requirements. Like other mammals, they are homeotherms, but they exist for the most part in cold seawater. They are air breathers in an environment where air is only intermittently available at the sea surface. Many successfully prey on other active animals even though they have no sense of smell and only limited vision. Mammals, marine or terrestrial, have body fluids that are hypotonic to seawater, and marine mammals tend to lose water to the environment by osmosis. As fresh water is seldom readily available to marine mammals, their food must satisfy their entire water needs. It seems a paradox that, with these limitations imposed by their mammalian condition, several groups of mammals have invaded the sea and have done it very successfully.

Solutions to particular problems stemming from a marine existence are often remarkably integrated with solutions to other problems. Streamlined bodies, for instance, obviously improve swimming efficiencies, but they also reduce body surface areas and rates of heat loss, thus easing the problems of maintaining high body temperatures in cold seawater. Large size, streamlined bodies, blubber layers, and systems of echolocation (a kind of biological sonar) to "see" in dark or murky waters, have evolved independently in several marine mammal groups.

Echolocation

Vision is a well-developed and useful sense for most mammals. Yet several mammalian groups function well in conditions where the lack of light renders vision nearly useless. A surprisingly large number (about 20% of all mammal species) have overcome the problems of orienting themselves and locating objects in the dark by producing sharp sounds and listening for reflected echoes as they bounce off objects. Bats are well-known echolocators, but so too are some shrews, golden hamsters, flying lemurs, and of course many marine mammals.

Soon after the first microphone was lowered into the sea, it became apparent that whales and pinnipeds are capable of generating a tremendous repertoire of underwater vocalizations. Many of the moans, squeals, and wails are evidently for purposes of communication. Some have a fascinating musical quality, such as the "songs" of the humpback whale (*Megaptera*).

The sounds most useful for echolocation are neither squeals nor songs, but rather trains or pulses of clicks of very short duration. Much more is known about the echolocating capabilities of the smaller whales, such as *Tursiops truncatus,* the bottle-nosed porpoise, for they are easily and frequently maintained in captivity. The bottle-nosed porpoise uses clicks consisting of sound frequencies audible to man as well as higher frequency clicks well beyond the upper range of human hearing. Each click lasts only a fraction of a millisecond and is repeated as often as 800 times each second. Click repetition rates are adjusted to allow the click echo to return to the animal during the very short lull between outgoing clicks. As each click strikes a target, a portion of it is reflected back to the source (fig. 8.4). The time required for a click to travel from an animal to the reflecting target and back again is a measure of the distance to the target. As that distance varies, so will the time necessary for the echo to return. Continued evaluation of returning echoes from a moving target can indicate its speed and direction of travel.

Low-frequency clicks seem to serve as orientation or "scanning" clicks for surveying an animal's general surroundings. Higher-frequency clicks always occur in situations where fine discriminations must be made. Relying solely on their echolocating abilities, blindfolded bottle-nosed porpoises have repeatedly demonstrated an aptitude for discriminating between objects of a similar nature: two fish of the same general size and shape, plates of different metals, and even between pieces of metal differing only slightly in thickness. In the wild, these animals must, while accoustically surveying their surroundings, simultaneously distinguish their own echolocation clicks from the cacophony of other sounds so frequently present in large herds of wild porpoises (fig. 8.5).

The echolocation clicks of the much larger sperm whales are lower in frequency and generally have a slower repetition rate. They can be quite powerful and may carry for several kilometers in the sea. Each "click" lasts

Fig. 8.4 Pattern of click production for echolocation. Outgoing clicks (black) are spaced to allow echoes (stippled) returning from the target to be received with little interference.

Fig. 8.5.

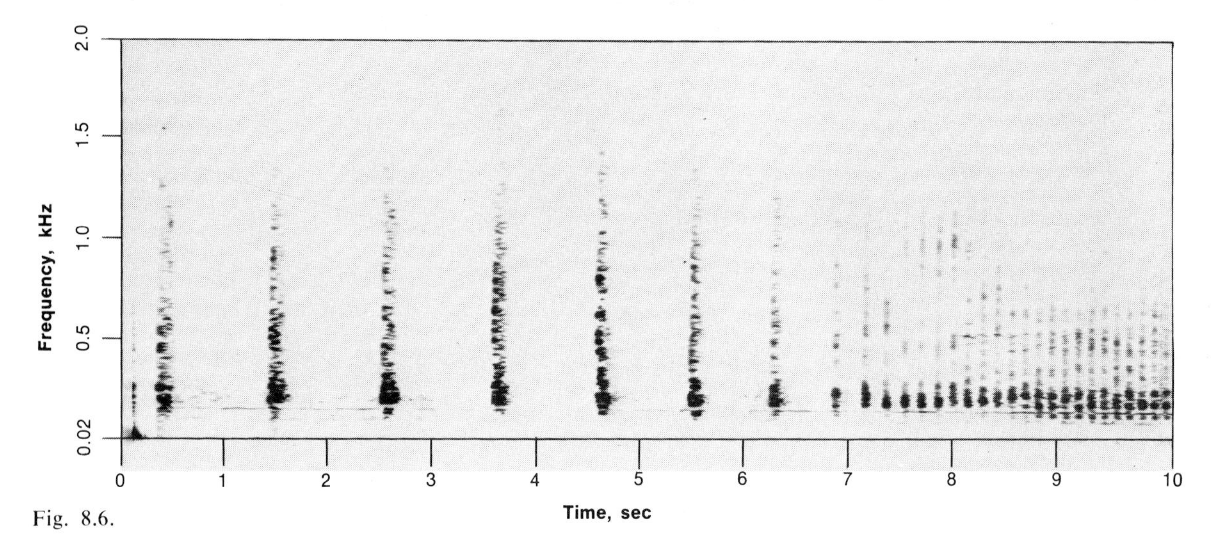

Fig. 8.6.

Fig. 8.5 A herd of porpoises at sea. Official photograph U.S. Navy.

Fig. 8.6 A sonogram of the echolocation click pulses of a sperm whale approaching a recording hydrophone. Note the accelerating pulse repetition rate. Courtesy J. Fish, Naval Undersea Center, San Diego.

about 24 milliseconds and is actually composed of a pulse or burst of up to nine separate clicks. Figure 8.6 is a sonogram of a portion of a train or sequence of click pulses emitted by a sperm whale at sea. The boat from which the recording hydrophone was suspended was apparently the target of the whale's echolocation efforts. As the whale swam toward the boat to investigate, the time required for successive pulses to travel from the whale to the boat and return decreased. The whale compensated by increasing the repetition rate of click pulses (middle of fig. 8.6) to keep the echoes returning between the outgoing sound pulses. Near the boat the click pulses were being emitted very rapidly, then abruptly ceased as the whale passed beneath the boat and presumably came within visual range.

The powerful, long-range echolocation systems of sperm whales may partially explain their success as efficient predators of the larger squid of mid-water depths. One can visualize these whales cruising along at the sea surface with all the air they need, periodically "scanning" the unseen depths below with a short burst of echolocation click pulses. Only when a target worthy of pursuit is detected and its location pinpointed does the whale depart from its air supply and go after its meal. In addition to their likely function in echolocation, there is some evidence to suggest that the click trains of sperm whales may also serve as a means of communication between individual whales during dives.

Despite our reasonably detailed understanding of the character of echolocation sounds made by cetaceans, we still don't have the answers to two very fundamental questions: How do whales produce the sounds involved in echolocation, and how do they receive and process the echoes? The larynx of toothed whales is well muscled and complicated in structure, yet it lacks vocal cords. The elongated tip of the larynx extends across the esophagus into a common tube leading to the blowhole at the top of the head. This arrangement completely separates the pathways for food and air; consequently, underwater feeding and sound production can occur simultaneously.

At the blowhole are a pair of heavily-muscled valves, the **nasal plugs**. These plugs, with an associated complex of air sacs branching from the nasal passage, are thought by some investigators to be the site of click production in the smaller toothed whales. Intensities of emitted clicks measured over the surface of the head tend to be centered above the margins of the jaw and are strongly suggestive of a sound production site somewhere in the forehead region. Clicks produced here could be directed forward by the concave front of the skull, then focused by the fatty lens-shaped **melon** (the rounded forehead structure so characteristic of toothed whales, fig. 8.7) to concentrate the clicks into a narrow, directional beam

Fig. 8.7 A bottle-nosed porpoise *(Tursiops)* with a prominent melon. Official photograph U.S. Navy.

A somewhat more complex sound production system has been proposed for the compound click pulses of sperm whales. These whales are noted for their massive and very distinctive foreheads. Inside the forehead is a **spermaceti organ** that may occupy 40% of the whale's total length. This organ is filled with a fine-quality liquid or waxy spermaceti oil (sometimes over a ton of it) once prized by whalers for candlemaking and for burning in lanterns. The spermaceti organ is encased within a wall of extremely tough ligaments, and the entire structure sits in the hollow of the rostrum and amphitheaterlike forehead (fig. 8.8).

At either end of the spermaceti organ are two large air sacs. These sacs are connected to each other and to the remainder of the respiratory system by two unequal **left** and **right nasal passages.** The large left nasal passage penetrates the spermaceti organ and leads directly to the blowhole at the tip of the snout. One branch of the much smaller right nasal passage extends to the **frontal air sac** at the posterior end of the spermaceti organ; the other is directed anteriorly along the base of the spermaceti organ and ends at the ***museau du singe,*** or **monkey's muzzle.** The museau du singe actually consists of a pair of hard, well-matched, and tightly oppressed lips. In front of these lips, the **distal air sac** continues upward to the blowhole. Here it connects with the left nasal passage and completes the loop of air passages associated with the spermaceti organ.

Norris and Harvey propose that these structures are responsible for the production of the multiple-click pulses of sperm whales. They suggest that clicks are produced when air is forced through the right nasal passage and pressure builds up behind the closed lips of the museau du singe. When the air pressure is sufficient to overcome the tension holding the lips closed, they part, then abruptly snap back together to create a sharp report or click. A portion of this sound signal is emitted directly into the water ahead of the whale, and probably represents the first click of each click pulse. Subsequent clicks of declining intensity within a click pulse may be derived from reverberations of that initial signal as it bounces between two sound mirrors, the distal and frontal air sacs, at each end of the spermaceti organ. The spermaceti

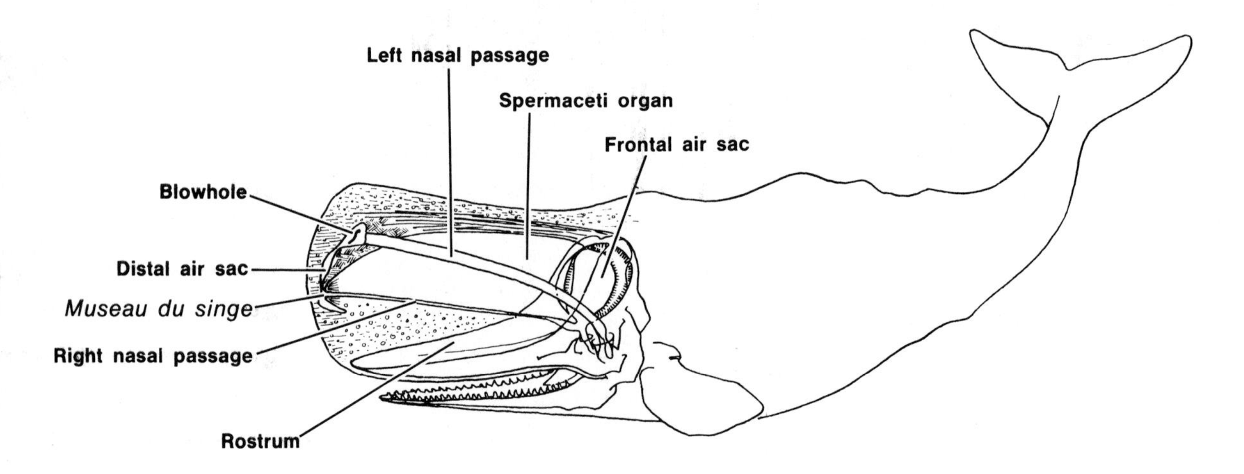

Fig. 8.8 A cutaway view of the complex melon structure of the sperm whale. Adapted from Norris and Harvey 1972.

organ itself may function as an effective sound channel to guide the reflected click between the two air sacs. The air used to activate the lips of the museau du singe can be recycled back through the left nasal passage to be used repeatedly without loss during a dive.

Behavioral studies suggest that all marine mammals have good hearing. Experimental evidence, however, is largely restricted to studies of captive small toothed whales. Humans are sensitive to sound frequencies ranging from 16 to 20,000 vibrations per second (1 vibration/sec. = 1 Hertz [Hz]). The bottle-nosed porpoise, and presumably some other toothed whales, respond to sound frequencies in excess of 150,000 Hz. Their sound-detection systems must be attuned to very weak echoes of their own clicks, but must simultaneously withstand the powerful blast of outgoing clicks generated in adjacent regions of the head. In toothed whales, the sound-processing structures of the middle ear are enclosed in a bony case, the **tympanic bulla.** The bulla is separated from adjacent bones of the skull by air sinuses filled with an insulating emulsion of mucus, oil, and air. The bulla is suspended in this emulsion, supported only by a few wisps of connective tissue. Thus, each middle ear functions as a separate sound receiver to better pinpoint sound sources.

The **external auditory canal** is the usual mammalian sound channel connecting the external and middle ears. The auditory canal of mysticetes is commonly blocked by a plug of earwax; in toothed whales, the canal is reduced to a tiny pore or is completely covered by skin. Mapping of acoustically sensitive areas of porpoises' heads have shown the external auditory canal to be about six times less sensitive to sound than the lower jaw. These results support the hypothesis of a very unique sound reception system in toothed whales. The bones of the lower jaw are flared toward the rear and are extremely thin. On each is a fat body (or, in some cases, liquid oil) that connects directly with the wall of the bulla of the middle ear. The fat or oil bodies, like the oil of the sperm whale's spermaceti organ, may act as a sound channel to transfer sounds from the flared portions of the lower jaw directly to the middle ear. Surprisingly, an area on either side of the forehead is nearly as sensitive as the lower jaw, providing a total of four very sensitive centers for sound reception.

How widespread is echolocation in marine mammals? It is presently uncertain, for it is difficult to establish whether wild populations are indeed using echolocationlike clicks for the purposes of orientation and location. If judgments can be made from the types of sounds produced, then echolocation should be suspected in all toothed whales, some pinnipeds (the Weddell seal, California sea lion, and possibly the walrus), and at least a few baleen whales. Click trains have been recorded in the presence of gray whales in the North Pacific (fig. 8.9) and blue and minke whales in the North Atlantic. It is not unreasonable to assume that these animals use these sounds as well as any other sensory means they possess to find food, locate the bottom, and in other ways evaluate the nonvisible portion of their surroundings.

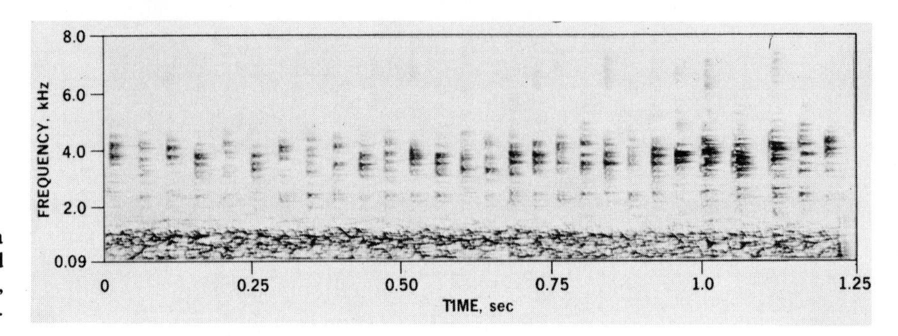

Fig. 8.9 A sonogram of a portion of a click train emitted by a gray whale. From Fish, Sumich, and Lingle 1974.

Respiratory and Circulatory Adjustments to Diving

Aristotle recognized, over twenty centuries ago, that porpoises were air-breathing mammals. Yet is was not until the classic studies conducted by Irving and Scholander nearly halfway into the present century that the physiological basis for deep and prolonged dives by marine mammals was defined. The diving capabilities of marine mammals vary immensely. Some are little better than the Ama pearl divers of Japan who, without the aid of supplementary air supplies, repeatedly dive to 30 m and remain down for 30 to 60 seconds. The maximum free-diving depth for humans is about 60 m; breath-holds lasting as long as 6 minutes have been independently achieved. But even the best efforts of humans pale in comparison to the spectacular dives of some whales and pinnipeds (table 8.1). With dive times often exceeding 30 minutes, these exceptional divers are no longer closely tied to the surface by their need for air.

Several respiratory adjustments are necessary to achieve prolonged dives such as those listed in table 8.1. As the last column of the table suggests, the breathing rates of marine mammals are decidedly less than that of humans and other terrestrial mammals. The pattern of breathing is also quite different. Generally, marine mammals exhale and inhale very rapidly, then hold their

Table 8.1. *Diving and Breath-holding Capabilities of Man and a Few Marine Mammals.*

Animal	Maximum Depth (m)	Maximum Time of Breath-hold (min)	Resting Breathing Rate (breaths/min)
Man *(Homo sapiens)*	66.5	6	15
Porpoise *(Tursiops truncatus)*	305	6	2–3
Sea lion *(Zalophus californianus)*	168	30	6
Weddel seal *(Leptonychotes weddelli)*	600	43	?
Fin whale *(Balaenoptera physalus)*	500	30	1–2
Sperm whale *(Physeter catadon)*	2250	90	?

Adapted from Kooyman and Andersen, in Andersen, 1969, and Norris and Harvey 1972 breaths for a prolonged period before exhaling again. Smaller porpoises, for instance, exhale and inhale in a fraction of a second, then hold for 30–40 seconds before repeating the pattern. Even the larger baleen whales can empty their lungs of 1500 ℓ of air and refill them in as little as two seconds. This **apneustic breathing** pattern is also exhibited by pinnipeds both in and out of the water. In the larger species of whales, dives of several minutes' duration are commonly followed by several "blows" 20–30 seconds apart before another prolonged dive is attempted (fig. 8.10).

Extensive elastic tissue in the lungs and diaphragms of these animals (fig. 8.11) is stretched during inhalation and recoils during exhalation to rapidly and nearly completely empty the lungs. Apneustic breathing provides time for the lungs to extract additional O_2 from the air held in the lungs. Porpoises can remove nearly 90% of the O_2 contained in each breath (humans use only about 20% of the O_2 inhaled). Oxygen uptake within the **alveoli** (air sacs) of the lungs may be enhanced as lung air is moved into contact with the walls of the alveoli by the "kneading" action of small muscles scattered throughout the lungs. In some species, an extra capillary bed surrounds each alveolus and may also contribute to the exceptionally high uptake of O_2.

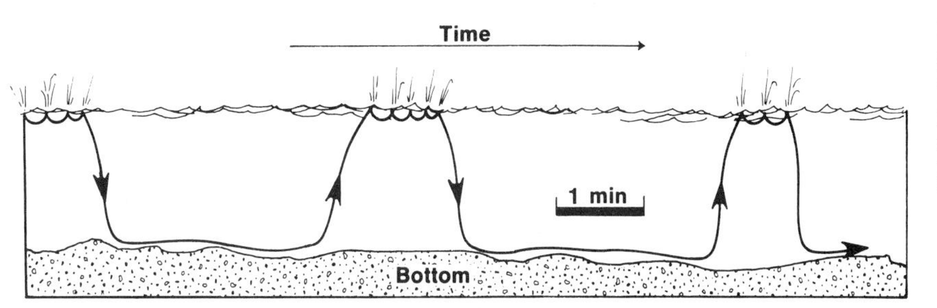

Fig. 8.10 Apneustic breathing pattern of a gray whale, observed while feeding along the west side of Vancouver Island, British Columbia. Blows at the surface represent individual breaths.

Fig. 8.11 Elastic fibers within the diaphragm of a small porpoise, *Stenella*.

Each of these features may seem insignificant by itself, but taken together they represent a style of breathing that permits marine mammals increased freedom to explore and exploit their environment some distance from the sea surface. Still, apneustic breathing alone cannot explain how some seals and whales are capable of achieving the extremely long dive times they do.

Most cetaceans dive with their lungs full of air, yet elephant seals and Weddell seals exhale prior to diving. Sea lions frequently exhale on the way down. These differences suggest that the volume of lung air at the beginning of a dive is adjusted to achieve neutral buoyancy and is of little value in supplying O_2 during a dive. Moreover, the lungs and their protective rib cage are sufficiently resilient to allow the lungs to collapse as the water pressure increases with depth (fig. 8.12). For a dive from the sea surface to 10 m, the external water pressure is doubled, causing the air volume of the lungs to be compressed by half and the air pressure within the lungs to double. Complete lung collapse probably occurs in the upper 100 m; any air remaining in the lungs below that depth is squeezed by increasing water pressure out of the alveoli and into the larger air passages (the **bronchi** and **trachea,** or windpipe). Even the trachea is commonly flexible and undergoes partial collapse during deep dives.

By tolerating complete lung collapse, these animals sidestep the need for respiratory structures capable of resisting extreme water pressures experienced

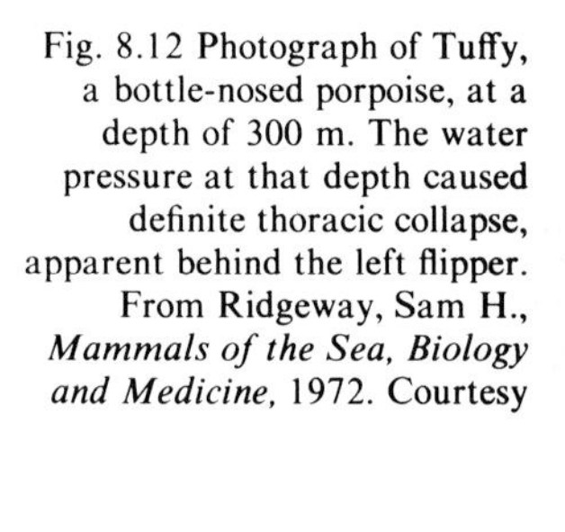

Fig. 8.12 Photograph of Tuffy, a bottle-nosed porpoise, at a depth of 300 m. The water pressure at that depth caused definite thoracic collapse, apparent behind the left flipper. From Ridgeway, Sam H., *Mammals of the Sea, Biology and Medicine,* 1972. Courtesy

during deep dives (over 200 atm for a sperm whale at 2,250 m). And they receive an additional bonus. As the air is forced out of their collapsing alveoli during a dive, the compressed air still within the larger air passages is blocked from contact with the walls of the alveoli. Consequently, little of these compressed gases are absorbed by the blood, and thus, marine mammals avoid the serious diving problems (**decompression sickness** and **nitrogen narcosis**) sometimes experienced by humans when breathing compressed air. After prolonged breathing of air under pressure (with hard hat or scuba gear), large quantities of compressed lung gases (particularly N_2) are absorbed by the blood and distributed to the body. As the external water pressure decreases during rapid ascents to the surface, these excess gases frequently are not discharged quickly enough by the lungs. Instead, they may form bubbles in the body tissues and blood, causing excruciating pain, and occasionally paralysis or even death. Excess N_2 dissolved in the blood also has a narcotic effect on human divers which seriously restricts the time within which they can function effectively at depth. Deep-diving marine mammals avoid both these problems simply because the air within their lungs is forced away from the walls of the alveoli as the lungs collapse during a dive, thereby preventing excess N_2 from diffusing into the blood.

Since the collapsed lungs of deep-diving marine mammals are ineffective as an O_2 reserve, oxygen must be stored elsewhere in the body or its use must be seriously curtailed during a prolonged dive. Actually both options are exercised by diving mammals. Additional stores of O_2 are maintained in chemical combination with hemoglobin of the blood or myoglobin in muscle cells. Red blood cells (which contain the hemoglobin) are about the same size in diving mammals and nondiving mammals; however, there are more of them in divers and each one tends to be somewhat inflated by its extra load of hemoglobin. The blood volume of diving mammals is significantly higher than in nondivers. Much of the additional blood volume is accommodated in numerous *retia mirabilia,* such as the extensive retia found along the dorsal side of the thoracic cavity (fig. 8.13). Other retia are located on either side of the vertebral column, associated with the reproductive organs, in the flukes, flippers, and dorsal fin, and another around the brain, optic nerves to the eyes, and in the air spaces surrounding the middle ear. Some blood is also stored in enlarged blood vessels. The **vena cava** (the major vein returning blood to the heart) is in some species baglike and elastic. In the elephant seal, it alone can accommodate 20% of the animal's total blood volume. These features all contribute to the total reserve of stored O_2 for use during a dive.

The muscles of marine mammals are exceedingly rich in myoglobin, giving them a deep, dark red appearance. About half the total store of O_2 for a dive is bound by the myoglobin of the swimming muscles (O_2 on hemoglobin in the blood accounts for the remainder). These muscles are quite capable of functioning either aerobically or anaerobically. They are also extremely tolerant to accumulations of lactic acid, a metabolic product of anaerobic respiration. These muscles begin dives with a ready supply of O_2. When that is depleted, they switch to anaerobic respiration and continue working for some time before their O_2 reserves need to be replenished.

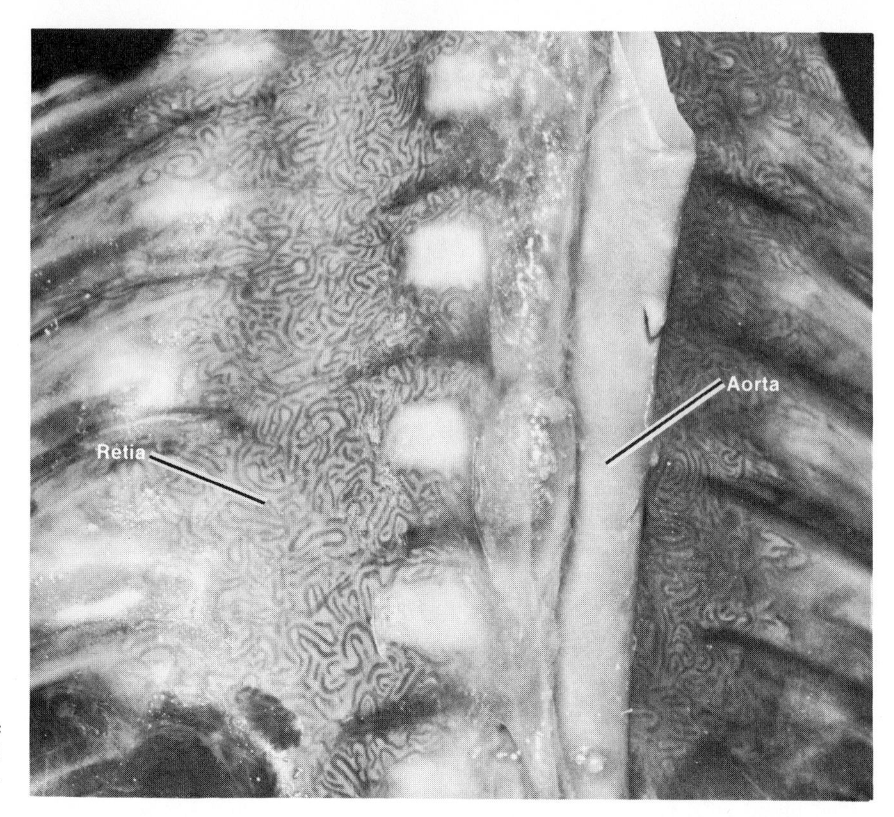

Fig. 8.13 The right thoracic *retia mirabilia* of a small porpoise. *Stenella.*

As the swimming muscles of marine mammals are highly tolerant to anaerobic conditions during a dive, they and other nonessential organs (such as the kidneys and digestive tract) are deprived of the reserve O_2 stored in the blood. The arteries leading to these peripheral muscles and organs constrict, and most of the circulating blood is shunted to a few vital organs, primarily the heart and brain. Simultaneously the heartbeat rate slows dramatically to accommodate pressure changes in a much-reduced circulatory system comprising essentially the heart, brain, and connecting blood vessels. Other circulatory structures also help to smooth out and moderate fluctuations in the pressure of blood going to the brain. An elastic bulbous "natural anurism" in the **aorta** (the large artery leaving the heart) and a rete in the smaller arteries at the base of the brain both help to dampen blood pressure surges each time the heart beats.

Bradycardia (a term referring to the marked slowing of the heartbeat rate that accompanies a dive) probably occurs in all diving vertebrates, including birds, reptiles, and mammals. Even grunion experience bradycardia when they come out of the water to spawn and are deprived of a continuous supply of O_2. The intensity of bradycardia varies widely between marine mammal groups. During a dive, the heartbeat rates of cetaceans are reduced to 20–50% of their predive rates. Many seals drop their resting heartbeat rates of 100–150/min. to 10 beats/min. when diving. The triggering mechanism for bradycardia is not completely understood, but it seems to involve sensors in the face and possibly in the respiratory system.

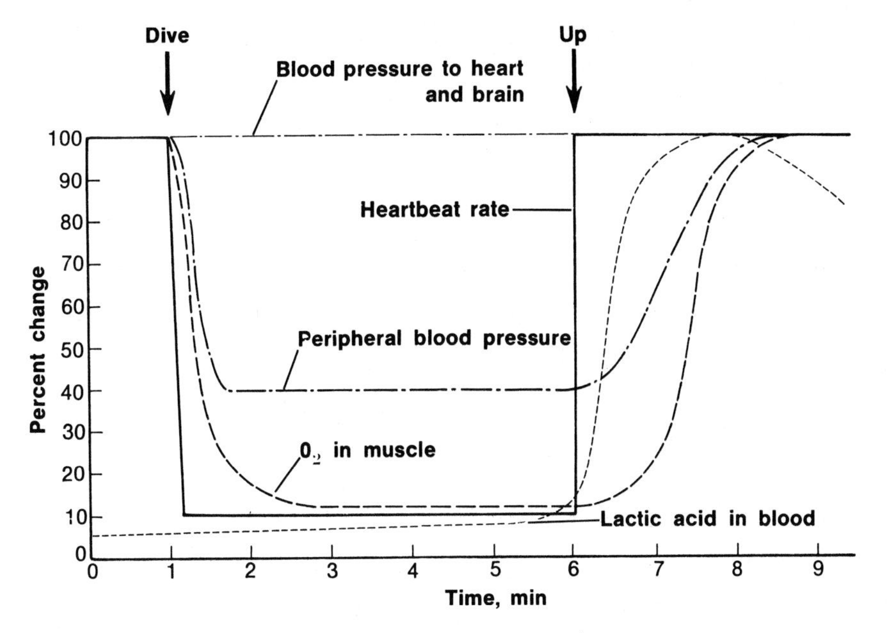

Fig. 8.14 A summary of some physiological adjustments made by a harbor seal during and after a dive.

Immediately after a dive is completed, the peripheral circulation dilates, the heartbeat accelerates, and new supplies of O_2 are rushed to tissues deprived during the dive. The lactic acid isolated in the anaerobic muscles floods into the bloodstream and is soon metabolized. The depleted hemoglobin and myoglobin O_2 reserves are recharged, and soon the animal is prepared for another dive. Several of these crucial physiological adjustments to diving are summarized in figure 8.14.

Temperature Regulation

For most of their lives, marine mammals exist in direct contact with seawater much colder than their body temperatures. Most live in the food-rich waters of the Arctic and Antarctic where water temperatures always hover near the freezing point. But even in more temperate latitudes the high heat capacity of water (about 25 times as high as air of the same temperature) makes serious inroads into the heat budgets of these mammals.

Marine mammals exhibit several adaptations to reduce their body heat losses to tolerable levels. Apneustic breathing lessens heat loss, as warm air is exhaled from the lungs less frequently. The reduction of peripheral circulation that accompanies bradycardia during a dive also limits heat loss by restricting the flow of warm blood from the core of the body to the cooler skin. This feature is especially useful during deep dives when an animal usually experiences water temperatures several degrees cooler than those at the surface.

Marine mammals are large, and for the most part, streamlined. Both of these features tend to reduce the extent of body surface in contact with seawater and ultimately the amount of heat transferred to the water. The major muscles of propulsion (which generate considerable heat) are positioned

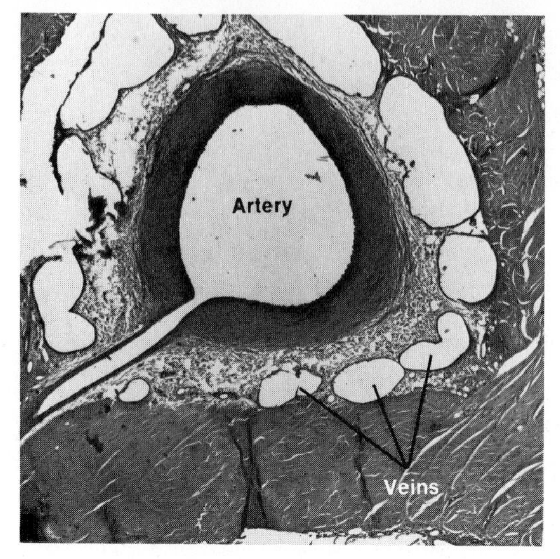

Fig. 8.15 A cross section of a small artery from the tail fluke of a bottle-nosed porpoise. The muscular artery in the center is surrounded by several thin-walled veins carrying blood in the opposite direction. From Ridgeway, Sam H., *Mammals of the Sea, Biology and Medicine*, 1972. Courtesy of Charles C Thomas, Publisher, Springfield, Illinois.

within the animal's trunk rather than on the exposed parts of the much reduced limbs. Finally, the body is wrapped in and further streamlined by an insulating layer of blubber or dense fur.

Internally, the extensive retia described earlier may serve to maintain locally high temperatures as well as to supply oxygenated blood to a few strategic locations, namely the eyes, inner and middle ears, brain, and thoracic cavity. Other heat-conserving mechanisms are associated with the retia of the flippers and for cetaceans, the dorsal fin and flukes (fig. 8.15). These retia are arranged in a countercurrent heat-exchange fashion reminiscent of those found along the flanks of tuna and other warm-bodied fishes. Arteries penetrating these appendages are surrounded by several veins carrying blood in the opposite direction. Heat from the warm blood of the central artery is absorbed by the cooler blood in the surrounding veins and carried back to the warm core of the body before much can be lost to the skin.

These adaptations are not solely to conserve body heat. Actively swimming animals, or those in tropical waters, can become overheated; and it sometimes becomes necessary to dispose of body heat. In these situations, the blood flow to the skin and appendages is increased. The central artery of the countercurrent rete shown in figure 8.15 dilates to transport more blood to the skin and restrict its return through the surrounding veins. The blood then finds alternate return routes through other veins nearer the skin.

Reproduction

Most of our knowledge concerning the reproductive patterns of marine mammals has been gleaned from observations of captive animals in oceanariums, from carcasses on board whaling ships, and from expeditions to pinniped rookeries. Marine mammals, like their terrestrial kin, give birth to live young (fig. 8.16). The young of cetaceans are capable swimmers at birth, and surfacing to breathe is instinctive. Most pinnipeds are unable to swim at birth, and the pups are invariably delivered on land or on ice floes.

Fig. 8.16 A female porpoise *(Tursiops)* in labor, with the fetus partially expelled. Courtesy Marineland of Florida.

The newborn of some marine mammals are relatively large animals. Gray whale calves weigh in at approximately 1.5 tons; blue whales are closer to 3 tons at birth. Still they are necessarily smaller than their parents, and their insulating layers of blubber or fur are usually not well developed. Several factors compensate for the less favorable surface area: volume ratios and the potentially serious problems of body temperature maintenance in newborn marine mammals. Terrestrial pupping in pinnipeds provides some time for growth before the pups must face their first winter at sea. The larger cetaceans, including the gray whale described in the previous chapter (fig. 7.35), spend their summers feeding in cold polar and subpolar waters, then undertake long migrations to their calving grounds in tropical and subtropical seas (fig. 8.17). In these warm waters, their calves have an opportunity to gain considerable weight before migrating back to their frigid feeding grounds.

The growth rates of young marine mammals are truly astounding. Weddell seal pups gain 3 kg each day—and elephant seals as much as 7 kg/day. Pups of both of these species double their weights within two weeks after birth. Nursing blue whales grow from 3 tons at birth to 23 tons when weaned a scant seven months later (an average weight gain of almost 100 kg a day). These prodigious growth rates are supported by an abundant supply of high-fat milk. Cetacean milk is 25–50% fat (cow's milk ranges from 3 to 5% fat). The daily milk yield of a large baleen whale has been estimated at nearly 600 ℓ (over a half ton). In smaller pinnipeds, two to five liters are more typical. Pinniped milk is also generally high in fat; however, it may be as low as 16% in the California sea lion. In both cetaceans and pinnipeds, the species occupying colder waters consistently produce milk with a high fat content.

The energetic demands made on the female to produce a relatively large offspring and then to supply it with large quantities of fatty milk until it is weaned (usually a few weeks to several months) are exceedingly high. Even the water that goes into the milk imposes additional osmotic stresses that are relieved only with further energy expenditures. Marine mammals have a rea-

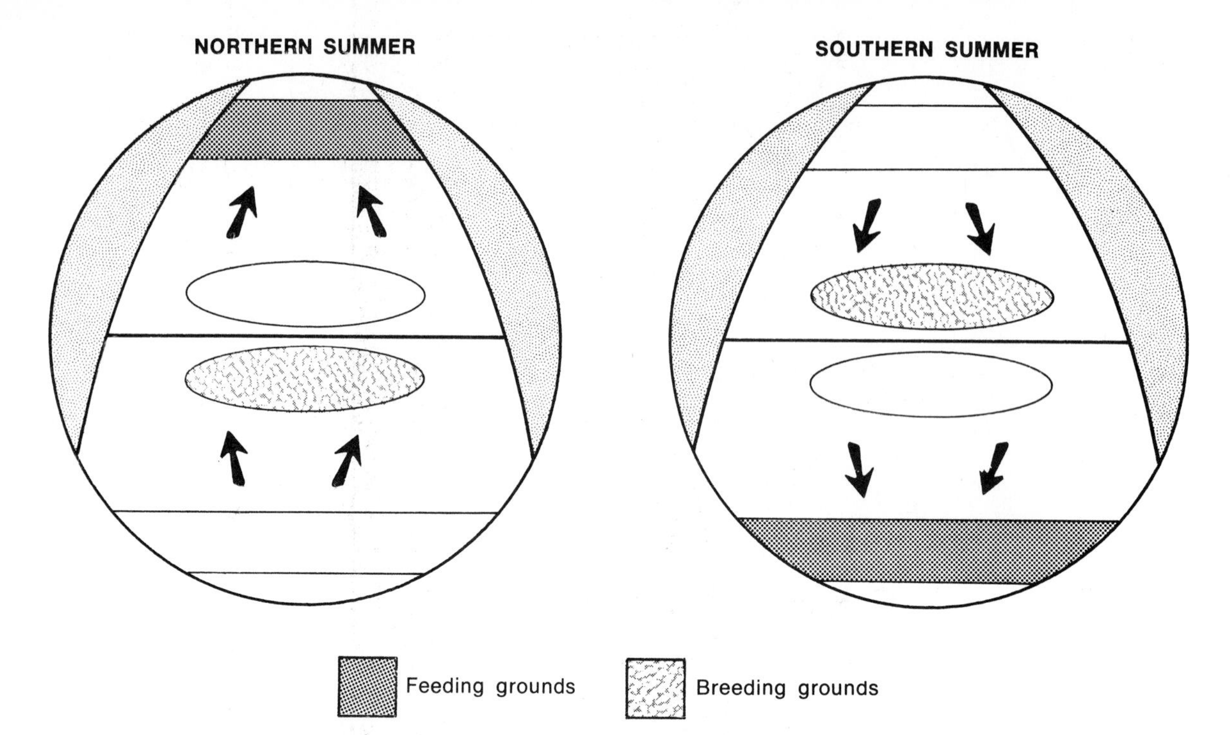

Fig. 8.17 Generalized migratory patterns of large whales between summer feeding and winter breeding grounds. Northern and Southern populations follow the same migratory pattern, but do so six months out of phase with each other. Consequently northern and southern populations of the same whale species remain isolated from each other even though both populations approach equatorial latitudes. Adapted from Mackintosh 1966.

sonably long gestation period (several months to a year) and tend to reproduce not more than once a year. It is not uncommon for the larger whales and at least the walrus among pinnipeds to mate only once every two or even every three years.

The breeding cycle of the larger baleen whales is typified by the fin whale (*Balaenoptera physalus*). The cycle consists of three parts (fig. 8.18). An eleven-month gestation period is culminated by the birth of a 6 m, two-ton calf in subtropical waters. The calf nurses for six months. During that time it and its mother migrate back to their polar feeding grounds. With other food abundant there, the calf is weaned. The female then enters a well-deserved six-month period of rest and recovery. During this feeding period, her fat and blubber reserves are replenished before she again migrates back to the winter breeding grounds to mate and begin the cycle again.

The seasons and areas used for breeding by these migratory cetaceans tend to coincide with those used for calving. The same is true for many pinnipeds. The Pribilof fur seal population, numbering about 1.5 million animals, disperses and forages over much of the North Pacific during the winter. Each summer they congregate in rookeries on the tiny Pribilof Islands in the Bering Sea. Here pupping and breeding occur, for at no other time are these animals aggregated so conveniently for reproduction. A few days after giving birth, female fur seals experience a short but intense period of **estrous** (or "heat") during which they are sexually receptive. This brief estrous is the only time during the year that the female ovulates and can become pregnant.

Here a problem arises, for a fur seal fetus only requires seven months to develop. Yet seven months after estrous and mating, the pregnant female

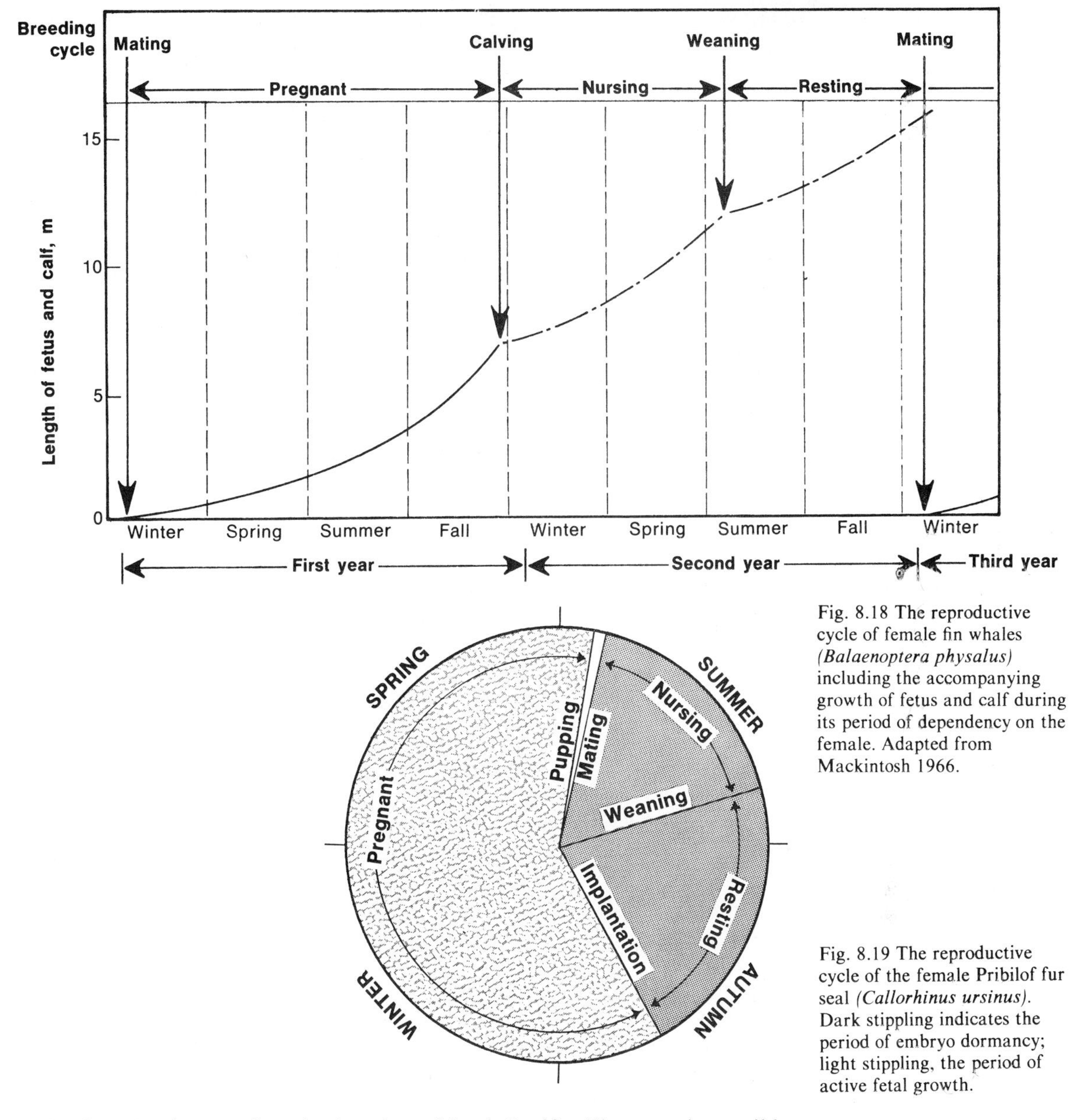

Fig. 8.18 The reproductive cycle of female fin whales *(Balaenoptera physalus)* including the accompanying growth of fetus and calf during its period of dependency on the female. Adapted from Mackintosh 1966.

Fig. 8.19 The reproductive cycle of the female Pribilof fur seal *(Callorhinus ursinus)*. Dark stippling indicates the period of embryo dormancy; light stippling, the period of active fetal growth.

is far from land somewhere in the wintry North Pacific. These are impossible conditions for delivering a pup that cannot swim. This dilemma is neatly solved by a reproductive feature—**delayed implantation**—common to several species of pinnipeds. After mating, the fertilized egg undergoes several cell divisions to form a small ball of cells, the **blastocyst**. Here it departs from the "normal" course of development for mammalian embryos. For the next four months, the blastocyst simply lies dormant in the female's uterus. Following the four-month delay, the blastocyst becomes implanted on the inner wall of the uterus, a placental connection develops between the embryo and the uterine wall, and "normal" embryonic growth and development resume (fig. 8.19).

About seven months later, when the pregnant female has migrated back to the Pribilof Islands, she delivers a full-term fur seal pup one year after mating and conception.

Fig. 8.20

The breeding behavior of fur seals, elephant seals, and sea lions has several notable similarities. In the rookeries, these pinnipeds are extremely gregarious, assembling on the small pupping beaches in unbelievable numbers (fig. 8.20). These animals also exhibit a remarkable degree of sexual dimorph-

ism (fig. 8.21). The adult males are 3 to 6 times larger than adult females; they have large canines, thick blubber and skin around the neck, special structures for physical and vocal threats, and are quite aggressive toward other males. These exaggerated male characteristics serve only one purpose: to secure and hold a harem of females by denying other males the opportunity to mate with them. This behavior of breeding bulls imposes a polygynous social order on the species, with relatively few males monopolizing the breeding activities of the population.

Fig. 8.20 Aerial photograph of a crowded fur seal rockery, St. Paul Island, Pribilof Islands. The clusters of seals near the beach are female harems, each attached to a breeding bull. The isolated individuals inland (upper left) are bulls that have not yet established harems. The elongated structures are elevated catwalks, used for counting and sampling. Photo by V. Scheffer and K. Kenyon, courtesy Marine Mammal Division, National Marine Fisheries Service.

Fig. 8.21 Male (above) and female (below) elephant seals display obvious sexual dimorphism. The females lack the elongated nose, enlarged canines, thickened neck, and large size characteristic of sexually mature males. Top, courtesy Scripps Institution of Oceanography; bottom, courtesy National Marine Fisheries Service.

G. A. Bartholomew has proposed a model to account for the evolutionary development and maintenance of polygyny and sexual dimorphism in some pinnipeds. He suggests that the two significant features of their amphibious life-style, terrestrial pupping and offshore feeding, have been the determinant factors. In the water, these pinnipeds are quite mobile and tend to disperse some distance from the rookery seeking food. Offshore feeding removes the competition for food from the rookery and promotes the fullest use of the few isolated sites that are appropriate as pupping rookeries.

In these congested circumstances, males, even with their very limited mobility on land, can easily contact and mate with several females. As with most mammals, a mature male is physically capable of fertilizing several females. However, the sex ratio of males to females is very nearly 1:1; therefore, any male that mates with more than one female must compete for them by excluding other males from the breeding activites. In fur seals, this competition revolves around the breeding territories. Only the most aggressive and vigorous males that have successfully established and maintained breeding territories throughout the breeding season are successful in breeding a harem of females. The remaining males, although sexually mature, are excluded from the breeding activities and banished to bachelor groups around the fringes of the breeding population. Male aggressiveness toward other males is controlled in part by **testosterone,** a male sex hormone that also controls the male sex drive. The dual effects of testosterone mutually reinforce the fertility of breeding males. Both aggressiveness and sex drive in males are at a peak during the breeding season, when the populations are congested in the rookeries.

Successful territorial defense requires that the male fur seal become a permanent feature of the territory for the duration of the breeding season. If a male leaves to feed in the water, it means giving up its territory to one of the many "bachelor" males. The males most capable of surviving these breeding fasts (which may last as long as two months) are the larger individuals with extensive fat and blubber reserves. The relationship between the large size of males and their reproductive success creates a positive genetic feedback to enhance sexual dimorphism generation after generation. Essentially the only males that contribute genetic information to subsequent generations are the large, aggressive ones with physical and behavioral traits very different from those of the females.

To illustrate the differential genetic contributions of male and female polygynous pinnipeds, consider that a moderately successful fur seal bull maintains a breeding harem of about 40 females for an average of five successive years. When unsuccessful matings are taken into account, this male will sire about 80 male and 80 female offspring. Each female during her reproductive lifetime will produce only about 3 males and 3 females. Thus, the total genetic contribution of a territorial bull to subsequent generations is about 25 times that of each female. This intense selective factor for exaggerated male characteristics in fur seals, elephant seals, and sea lions has led to the most extreme examples of sexual dimorphism of any mammal group.

The gregarious nature and relatively poor terrestrial locomotion of pinnipeds make them easy targets for sealers after skins and oil. In the past two centuries several pinniped species have been severely decimated by commercial slaughters. The Pribilof fur seal population numbered about 2.5 million when discovered by Russian sealers. By 1911, the population was reduced to 100,000 animals. Protective regulations instituted at that time have allowed the Pribilof fur seal herd to recover to a present population of approximately 1.5 million.

In recent years, 60–70 thousand young Pribilof fur seal males (9% of the total male population) have been killed annually for their furs. These 3–4 year-old males had not yet entered the competition for territories and harems, so their furs were undamaged by fighting. Is the impact of harvesting 9% of the males from a population with plenty of excess males really significant? Every year, approximately 500,000 pups are born to the Pribilof fur seal herd; half are female, half are male. About 14% die from starvation, disease, or crushing before they leave the rookery. Another 50% are lost at sea the first winter, leaving about 90,000 males alive at the end of their first year. By the time the young males have reached three years of age, natural causes of mortality have further reduced their numbers to 70–80 thousand. When still another 60–70 thousand are removed for commercial purposes, the number of males remaining for breeding is relatively small.

It is generally assumed that. . ."the killing of these bachelors does not affect the structure or breeding performance of the herd because of the animals' polygamous habits" (King 1964). That assumption completely ignores the significance of male aggressiveness and competitiveness in the evolution and maintenance of polygyny in pinnipeds. Fur seals have excess males because they are polygynous, but those males are not excess until their reproductive worth has been tested against other males. Potential harem masters simply cannot be identified at three or four years of age, and many are slaughtered along with potential nonbreeding males. With competition reduced by the commercial take, the males that do survive have a greatly improved chance of obtaining and keeping a breeding territory regardless of their relative territorial and sexual capabilities. Might the long-term genetic consequences of continued intensive harvesting of the Pribilof fur seal population be too high a price to pay for a fur coat?

The northern elephant seal (*Mirounga angustirostris*) was even more seriously decimated by sealers than was the smaller fur seal. Once distributed from central California to the southern tip of Baja California, this species came under commercial hunting pressure in 1818. A scant half-century later, so few survived that they were not worth hunting. No elephant seals were sighted between 1884 and 1892. In 1892 Townsend discovered 8 animals on Isla de Guadalupe, 240 km off the coast of Baja California. Seven were taken for museum specimens. Early census estimates suggest that in the 1890s as few as 20 individuals survived on a single inaccessible beach on Isla de Guadalupe. Beginning with protection afforded the northern elephant seal by Mexico and the United States around the turn of the century, that remnant population slowly recovered. Since then, the northern elephant seal has again spread throughout its former breeding range. The total population has swelled to more than 40,000 animals, and the future of this species now seems secure.

Or does it? Is the present northern elephant seal population really as viable and hardy as the pre-exploitation population? Comparisons of twenty-one blood proteins from 159 animals of the "recovered" population suggests that they are not. In marked contrast to proteins of other vertebrate species, no structural differences were demonstrated either between individuals or between separate breeding subpopulations of northern elephant seals. The lack of structural differences in these proteins points to a complete absence of variation in the genes controlling the synthesis of these proteins. Bonnell and Selander suggest that the absence of genetic variability in the existing northern elephant seal population is the result of a genetic bottleneck when the population was at its low point in the 1890s. It is quite conceivable that, on that isolated beach on Isla de Guadalupe, a lone elephant seal bull for several years dominated the breeding of all the surviving sexually mature females. If so, half the pool of genetic information possessed by the surviving representatives of the species *Mirounga angustirostris* was funneled through a single animal, and the genetic variability presumably inherent in the predecimation population was lost. The rapid recovery of the protected population indicates that genetic variability may not be essential to the short-term survival of this species, possibly because their existence is cushioned by the relatively uniform and predictable environment of the sea. However, this species may be quite vulnerable to environmental changes occurring in an extended time frame, for it may lack the genetic variability necessary to cope with such changing conditions.

Summary

Marine mammals include two abundant and widespread groups, the cetaceans (whales, porpoises, and dolphins) and the pinnipeds (seals, sea lions, and walruses), and the much less common sea otters, manatees and dugongs. Each has evolved from a terrestrial mammalian ancestor. In some, the evolutionary adaptations to a marine existence have been extreme. The cetaceans, for instance, lack hair, rear legs or flippers, breathe through a dorsal blowhole, and are very streamlined. Even so they are mammals, breathing air, giving birth to live young, and maintaining elevated body temperatures.

To compensate for reduced visibility and their inability to smell underwater, toothed whales (and probably some other groups) have a sophisticated system of echolocation for target detection and orientation.

Air-breathing mammals make several drastic respiratory and circulatory adjustments to prolonged diving, including apneustic breathing, lung collapse, peripheral circulation shutdown, bradycardia, and systemic storage of 0_2.

Large size and reduced surface area: volume ratio is an obvious adaptation to reduced heat loss. Less apparent but also quite significant are insulating layers of blubber or fur, countercurrent heat exchangers, and apneustic breathing patterns.

Marine mammals commonly reproduce annually or at even longer intervals. Frequently, birth and mating occur in breeding areas or rookeries. In some pinnipeds that disperse offshore to feed and congregate on isolated rookeries for reproduction, polygyny and sexual dimorphism are extremely well developed.

Questions for Discussion

1. Discuss and compare the biological significance of the body surface area to volume ratios for a copepod and a whale.
2. Discuss and compare the reproductive cycles and migratory patterns of California gray whales and Pribilof fur seals. What purpose does delayed implantation serve in these cycles?
3. Beginning with the reasonably valid assumption that cetaceans have evolved from herbivorous terrestrial ancestors, discuss the major structural and physiological adaptations that are evident in present-day killer whales.
4. What advantages do cetaceans derive from apneustic breathing patterns besides those directly associated with prolonged breath-holding?

Suggestions for Further Reading

Books

Andersen, H. T., ed. 1969. *The biology of marine mammals.* New York: Academic Press.

Haley, D., ed. 1978. *Marine mammals of Eastern North Pacific and Arctic waters.* Seattle: Pacific Search Press.

Kellogg, W. N. 1961. *Porpoises and sonar.* Chicago: Univ. of Chicago Press.

Leatherwood, S. *et al.* 1976. *Whales, dolphins, and porpoises of the Western North Atlantic.* Washington, D.C.: U.S. Government Printing Office.

Rice, D. W., and Wolman, A. A. 1971. *The life history and ecology of the gray whale (Eschrichtius robustus).* Special Publication No. 3. American Society of Mammalogists.

Small, G. L. 1973. *The blue whale.* New York: Columbia Univ. Press.

Articles

Baker, R. C.; Wilke, R.; and Baltzo, C. H. 1970. The northern fur seals. *U. S. Fish and Wildlife Service, Bureau of Commercial Fisheries,* Circular 336.

Costa, D. 1978. The sea otter: Its interaction with man. *Oceanus* 21(spring): 24–30.

Geraci, J. R. 1978. The enigma of marine mammal strandings. *Oceanus* 21 (spring):38–47.

Kenyon, K. W. 1971. Return of the sea otter. *National Geographic* 140:520–39.

Kooyman, G. L., and Harrison, R. J. 1971. Diving in marine mammals. *Oxford Biology Reader Number 6.*

McVay, S. 1971. Can leviathan long endure so wide a chase? *Natural History* 80:36–72.

Norris, K. S. 1968. Evolution of acoustic mechanisms in odontocete cetaceans. *Evolution and Environment* 297–324.

Payne, R. S., and McVay S. 1971. Songs of humpback whales. *Science* 173:585–97.

Pryor, K. and Norris, K. S. 1978. The tuna/porpoise problem: behavioral aspects. *Oceanus* 21(spring):31–37.

Ray, G. C. *et al.* 1978. Strategies for protecting marine mammal habitats. *Oceanus* 21(spring) :55–67.

Ryan, P. R. 1978. Marine mammals—a guide for readers. *Oceanus* 21(spring):9–16.

Strauss, M. B. 1970. Physiological aspects of mammalian breath-hold diving: A review. *Aerospace Medicine* 41:1 362–81.

Herring catch. Photo by Aaron Klein/
Taurus Photos.

Food From the Sea?

9

Two thousand years ago, the human population of earth was probably between 200 and 300 million people. The many problems of survival kept life expectancies short. High birthrates were balanced by high death rates and the population grew slowly. Not until 1650 did the population double to 500 million. The Industrial Revolution brought advances in medicine and technological improvements in food production systems that sharply reduced human mortality. Yet the birthrate remained high, and the population doubled again to 1 billion people by 1850. Declining death rates continued to accelerate the rate of population growth into the twentieth century. At this writing, the human population of the world has surpassed 4 billion people and is projected to reach 7 billion by the end of this century.

The demands for food made by the present population are enormous and are increasing at an alarming rate. Existing food production systems are presently incapable of satisfying those demands. Uncounted millions starve to death each year, and hundreds of millions more are deprived of health and vigor because of inadequate diets. Many people regard marine sources of food as a critical part of the solution to tomorrow's food problems.

Fishing

Fishing is a multibillion-dollar industry based on the collection and selling of aquatic organisms. Most are sold for human consumption, but a portion is also used for livestock fodder, pet foods, and industrial purposes. The impact of fishing practices on the stability and even the continued existence of some marine populations has been severe, and it is an area of increasing concern as the burgeoning human population demands ever more food. Only a relatively small number of species make up the bulk of the world fish harvest; they have borne the brunt of commercial fishing efforts. Some of these species have been eliminated from traditional fishing grounds. Others face the real possibility of biological extinction.

Commercially Important Marine Food Species

The raw material of the fishing industry actually includes a number of species of bony and cartilaginous finfish, as well as many mollusks and crustaceans ("shellfish"), a variety of other aquatic animals (worms, sea urchins, whales,

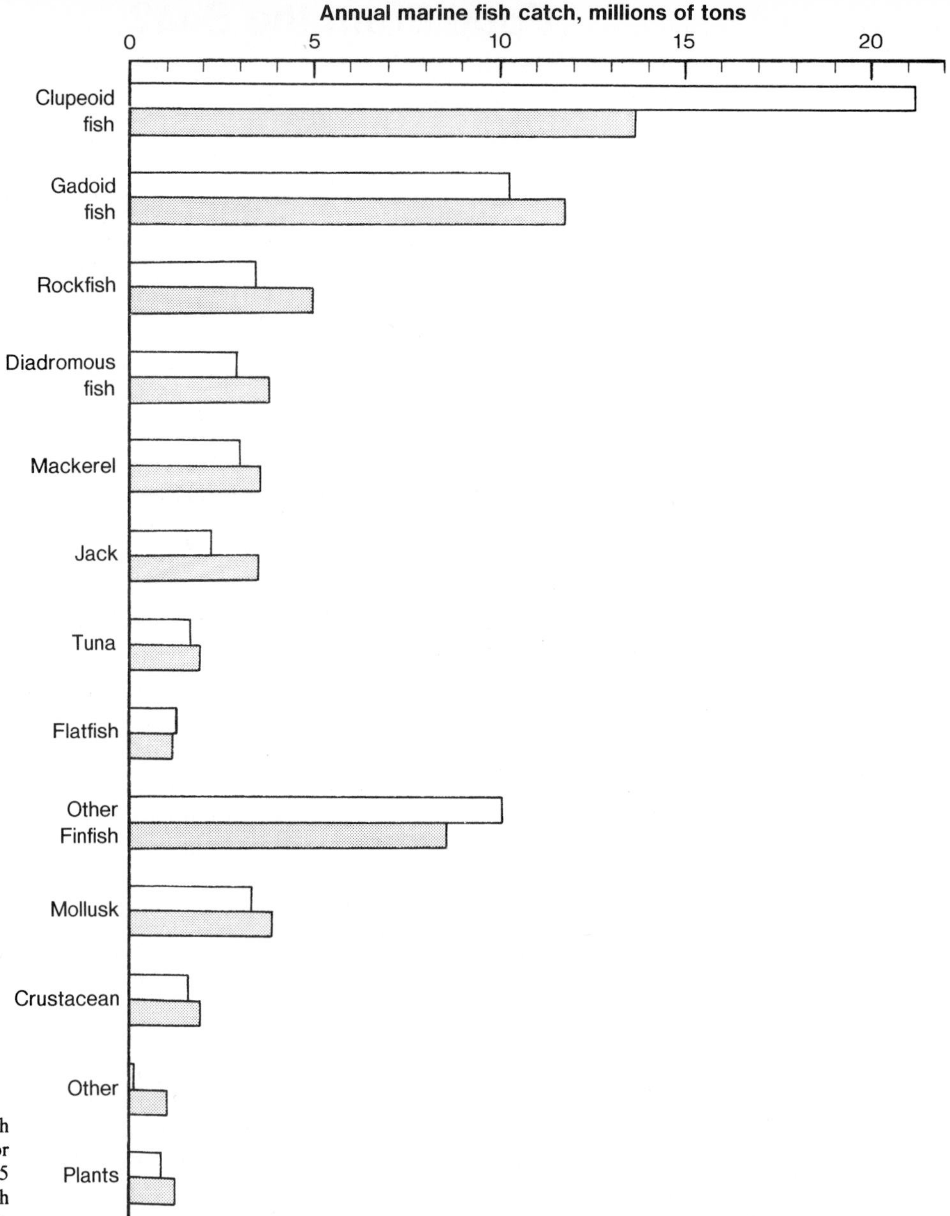

Fig. 9.1 Global marine fish catch by major categories for 1970 (white bars) and 1975 (gray bars). From FAO catch and landing statistics.

etc.), and even small amounts of marine plants. Approximately 10% of the total catch for the past few years has consisted of freshwater mollusks, crustaceans, and finfish. The remaining 90% of the world harvest is taken from the sea.

Each year the Food and Agriculture Organization (FAO) of the United Nations compiles and publishes global fishery catch statistics. The catch results for 1970 and 1975 are presented in figure 9.1. The annual catch size has varied somewhat; however, the ranking of each group in figure 9.1 has remained reasonably consistent from year to year.

The clupeoid fishes, including anchovies (fig. 9.2) and anchovetas, herrings, sardines, pilchards, and menhaden are very abundant and account for about one-third of the total commercial catch. A single species, the Peruvian anchoveta (*Engraulis ringens*), provided nearly 19%, or more than 13 million tons, of the total 1970 catch. But the extensive overfishing nearly caused this fishery to collapse a few years later. The herring catch has long been an important part of the North Atlantic fishing industry. Other herring fisheries in the South Atlantic and North Pacific oceans have been expanding in the last decade. Over a half-million tons of the herringlike kilka (*Clupeonella*) are landed from the Azov, Black, and Caspian seas each year. At its peak in the 1930s, the California sardine (actually a pilchard) industry was landing over 500 thousand tons annually. The menhaden catch annually yields approximately one million tons, largely from the Atlantic Ocean and the Gulf of Mexico.

The huge size of the clupeoid fish catch does not reflect its dollar value as an economic commodity or its significance as a source of protein in human nutrition. Nearly all anchovies, anchovetas, menhaden, and much of the herrings, sardines, and pilchards caught are reduced to fish meal to be used as a protein supplement in livestock and poultry fodder. As fish meal, they make only indirect contributions to the human diet.

Most clupeoid fishes are small, with an average adult length of between 15 and 25 cm. However, their small size is more than compensated for by other characteristics that enhance their economic usefulness. These fish are equipped with fine gill rakers, enabling them to feed on small organisms close to the base of marine food chains. Mature Peruvian anchovetas, for the most part, occupy the second trophic level, feeding directly on chain-forming diatoms and other relatively large phytoplankton aggregations. Herring generally feed at the third trophic level on herbivorous zooplankton, but many variations

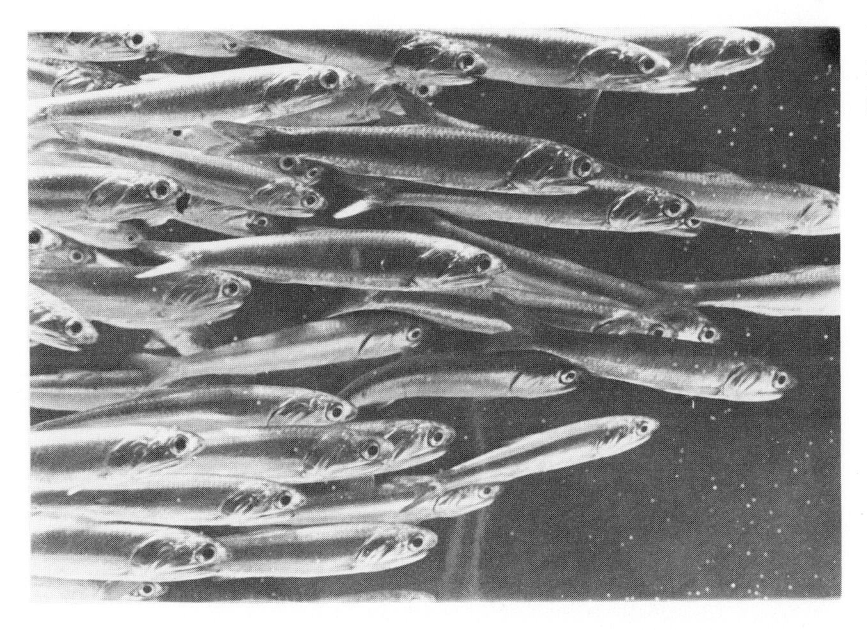

Fig. 9.2 The northern anchovy, *Engraulis mordax*. Courtesy National Marine Fisheries Service.

in diet do occur (see fig. 2.16). Clupeoid fishes are found in shallow waters and upwelling regions in easily accessible coastal waters. Finally, the schooling behavior of these fish (fig. 9.3) simplifies catching techniques and reduces harvesting expenses. Large purse seines (which may be 600 m long and 200 m deep) are used to surround and trap entire schools. Once encircled, the fish are ladled into the ship's hold.

The combined catch of cod, pollack, hake, and other gadoid fishes has remained reasonably constant for the past decade. Gadoid fishes are demersal in habit, living on or near the bottom. They are larger than clupeoid fishes and feed at higher trophic levels. The fishing effort for these fishes is concentrated on continental shelves and other shallow areas. Atlantic cod are taken by fishermen from many coastal nations situated around the North Atlantic. The Alaska walleyed pollack is caught in shallow regions of the Gulf of Alaska and the Bering Sea by Japanese and Russian trawler fleets. Intense fishing efforts by these two nations have increased the catch of walleyed pollack from one million tons in 1965 to over 5 million tons in 1975. Various species of hakes abound on the continental shelves of many oceans. They are prized by Japanese and Russian fishermen, but most taken by United States fishermen are reduced to fish meal.

Redfish, bass, sea perch, and other rockfish are also demersal in habit. No single species of this group dominates the catch statistics, yet combined they accounted for 5 million tons in 1975. Sold fresh or frozen, most of these fish are popular fish-market items.

Diadromous fish (those that migrate between fresh and salt water), especially capelin, salmon, and kilka, contributed more than 4% of the total 1975 catch. Only 34,000 tons of capelin were caught in 1964; a decade later, the catch had increased nearly sixty times to 2 million tons. In contrast, salmon catches have fluctuated little in recent years.

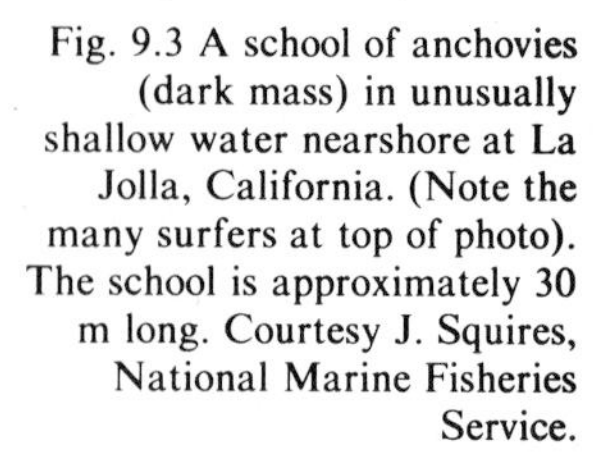

Fig. 9.3 A school of anchovies (dark mass) in unusually shallow water nearshore at La Jolla, California. (Note the many surfers at top of photo). The school is approximately 30 m long. Courtesy J. Squires, National Marine Fisheries Service.

Mackerel of the genus *Scomber* and horse and jack mackerel (*Trachurus*) are primarily pelagic carnivores that generally feed on smaller anchovy-sized fish and invertebrates. Mackerel resemble tuna in form, but seldom exceed 30–40 cm in length. The fisheries for both mackerel groups are scattered in coastal and offshore waters.

Tuna are the largest of the commercial species discussed here. Individuals weighing over 100 kg are not unusual, but most range from 5 to 20 kg. Yellowfin, bigeye, albacore, and skipjack tuna account for the majority of tuna catches. Tuna are often the top carnivores in complex food chains and may be separated from the primary producers by seven or more trophic levels. These fish are active predators on smaller, more abundant animals, especially clupeoid fishes and sauries, and are taken in or near nutrient-rich waters where forage fish abound. United States tuna fishermen rely heavily on fleets of long-range purse seiners to gather schooling species of tuna (fig. 9.4). To exploit the more widely dispersed yellowfin and bigeye tuna, Japanese fishermen use laborious longline fishing methods. The Japanese longline fishery of the equatorial Pacific Ocean has developed rapidly since 1950 into the most valuable oceanic fishery of the Pacific Ocean. The longline gear consists of a floating mainline that typically extends as far as 100 km along the surface. Hanging from the mainline are about 2,000 equally spaced vertical lines terminating with baited hooks. Once a longline set is in place, the fishermen work up the length of the mainline, removing hooked tuna, and rebaiting and replacing the hooks.

Halibut, flounder, sole, and other flatfish are demersal forms that are also conveniently captured in shallow regions. High prices and stable markets for these fish have resulted in extensive fishing of most known stocks. Those in the North Atlantic that have been subject to heavy fishing pressures for decades are seriously overfished. That percentage of the total catch attributable to flatfish has declined steadily to less than 2% in 1975.

The term "shellfish" is used here for those species of mollusks and crustaceans used for food. This group includes a large variety of species, most of which are benthic. Prominent among these are clams, cockles, scallops, oysters, squid, shrimp, prawns, and crabs. Many of these species are expensive delicacies that command very high market prices. As a result many easily accessible near-shore areas have been seriously depleted of abalones, lobsters, crabs, clams, and other prized species.

Marine plants are not widely used for human food. Only in the Orient are a few types commonly used in soups, salads, and other dishes. Irish moss (*Chondrus crispus*) and nori (*Porphyra*) are the most popular types of red algae. Minor amounts of seaweeds are also dried for cattle fodder. Most of the red and brown algae harvest (fig. 9.5) is utilized in industrial processes as a source of **algin** derivatives, **agars,** and **carrageenins**. Algin is extracted from cell walls of large brown kelps such as *Macrocystis*. Various derivatives of algin are incorporated as thickeners and stabilizers in processed foods, in inks and dyes, and even in beer to keep it from losing its "head." Agar and carrageenin are extracted from red algae. They are also employed as thickeners in prepared foods and have limited uses as bulk laxatives. Agar is probably better known as a gelatinlike medium for culturing bacteria.

Fig. 9.4 A tuna seiner with a school of tuna trapped within its purse net. Official photograph U.S. Navy.

Fig. 9.5 A kelp harvester in operation. As the harvester moves backward, the kelp is cut below the sea surface, then pulled up the stern loading ramp. Courtesy Kelco Industries.

Major Fishing Areas of the World Ocean

The global fishing industry is scattered over the world ocean with most of the fishing effort concentrated in relatively small regions. Reasons for the localization of the fishing effort are many, encompassing a broad spectrum of political, cultural, economic, physical, and biological factors. Before the 1950s, most commercial fishing was conducted in waters reasonably close to the fishermen's home port. Expenses of long runs between ports and fishing grounds were kept low, and international competition was not the critical problem it is today. Individual and social choices also played a crucial role. Preferences for fresh fish over canned or frozen products limited the utilization of fish stocks some distance from port. As a result most fishing grounds remained in coastal waters as long as the fish stocks held out.

Today, fish are caught wherever they are concentrated in commercially exploitable quantities. The degree of concentration necessary to sustain a commercial fishing operation depends on the market value of the fish and on the methods necessary to successfully harvest the fish. It is no accident that many of the species that dominate the catch statistics in figure 9.1 are fish that form large schools.

Some migratory fish may congregate at specific locations to feed or spawn. Others, including salmon, follow current patterns in their migratory cycles. Concentrations of fish usually occur near oceanic boundary systems. Sometimes these boundaries are quite obvious, even to humans. Other boundaries, especially those between different water masses, may be too subtle for human detection, yet are easily perceived by the species concerned. It is these areas of fish concentration that are the main focus of the fishing industry.

Three types of oceanic boundaries and their relation to patterns of fish distribution are significant. First, the sea bottom itself is a physical barrier on which many species of demersal flatfish, rockfish, and most shellfish aggregate. Regions of upwelling also establish boundary conditions of varying water temperatures and of food availability. Finally, many species of fish congregate near the boundaries of ocean currents, possibly for food, or because of physiological responses to rapidly changing temperature or salinity conditions.

The shallow water over continental shelves and near-surface banks encourages rapid regeneration of needed plant nutrients to the photic zone. These nutrients are prevented from escaping into deeper water and accumulating below the upper mixed layer where return to the surface requires a much longer time. High levels of production by phytoplankton in neritic waters are even further enhanced because the resulting animal production is "crowded" into a water column usually less than 200 m deep. In contrast, organic material produced over deep-ocean basins must be shared by the many consumers thinly dispersed through several thousands of meters of water.

Bottom fish and benthic invertebrates, which presently constitute nearly 15% of the total catch, are most easily taken in shallow, near-shore waters. It is estimated that about 90% of the marine catch is taken from continental shelves and overlying neritic waters, a region representing less than 8% of the total oceanic area.

Other major fishing areas are centered in regions of upwelling where abundant supplies of essential plant nutrients from deeper waters are returned to the photic zone. Upwelling may, depending on the locality, occur sporadically, on a seasonal basis, or continue throughout the year. (Mechanisms of Antarctic, equatorial, and coastal upwelling were described in chapter 6.)

The nutrient-rich waters surrounding the Antarctic continent sustain a tremendous amount of plant production. Yet, with the exception of the near-defunct pelagic whaling industry, no large fishery has developed in Antarctic waters. Long distances to processing plants and the absence of nearby population centers have surely had a restraining effect on the successful exploitation of this upwelling region.

Development of fish stocks located in equatorial and coastal upwelling regions have been much more successful. A large-scale Japanese longline yellowfin tuna fishery has thrived in the equatorial Pacific since the mid-1950s. The yellowfin aggregate in a narrow zone of relatively high plant productivity, which straddles the equator in the eastern half of the Pacific Ocean (see fig. 6.21). These large predators feed on sardines, myctophids, other small fish, and crustaceans that in turn graze on the smaller zooplankton. Apparently the tuna aggregate near their food source. However, the actual distribution patterns of yellowfin tuna in the equatorial upwelling region are somewhat more complex and cannot be explained solely in terms of feeding associations.

Regions of coastal upwelling are most apparent along the west coasts of Africa and North and South America, but occur to lesser degrees along other coastlines. High yields of commercial species result from increased rates of primary production that are often accentuated because they occur over shallow bottoms. The greatest concentrations of clupeoid fishes, which feed near the bases of their respective food chains, are found in regions of coastal upwelling: Peruvian anchoveta from the Peru Current upwelling area, pilchard from a similar area of upwelling in the Benguela Current off the west coast of South Africa, and, prior to a drastic decline in the 1940s, pilchard from the California Current upwelling system. The Peruvian and Benguelan upwelling systems also support huge flocks of cormorants, pelicans, penguins, and other seabirds.

Behavioral and physiological responses by fish to currents, water temperature fluctuations, and other environmental factors are not well understood. Yet some evidence exists to indicate that such responses play a significant role in spatially concentrating commercially useful species. Relationships between ocean currents and the migratory routes of tuna, salmon, and cod were discussed in chapter 7. The success of those who seek these fishes is in part dependent upon applying what we know of these migratory routes to the practical problems of locating these fish at sea.

In the Barents Sea, the best catches of cod (*Gadus morhua*) are consistently found in areas with bottom water temperatures greater than 2°C, regardless of the water depth. What causes the cod to congregate in waters warmer than 2°C? A combination of factors may be involved. If the temperature barrier is well defined, migrating cod may simply "stack up" when they enter colder water because they swim more slowly at reduced temperatures.

However, such reactions to low water temperature do not explain the almost complete absence of cod in water below 2°C. Cod taken from water colder than 2°C have higher levels of chloride in the blood than do those from warmer waters. Apparently, water temperatures below 2°C cause a partial failure of the chloride-secreting cells in the gills, which normally function to regulate the salt content of body fluids. Consequently, the Barents Sea cod may avert osmotic problems by shunning cold waters. Although the complete mechanism governing cold water avoidance by Atlantic cod is not yet understood, commercial fishermen can still take advantage of existing knowledge to better locate and harvest the species.

The Yield of Food from the Sea

A study of trends in the world fish catch over the past three decades has given cause for some guarded optimism in an otherwise bleak forecast for improving the overall nutrition of the existing human population. In the two decades between 1950 and 1970, the total world population each year increased an average of 2% over the previous year. During that same time the world fish catch was expanding at an annual rate of 6% (fig. 9.6). With fish catches increasing three times as rapidly as the population, some predicted that it was just a matter of time before the gap between food needs and food production was closed. It appeared that the human race might after all avoid the gloomy predictions of Thomas Malthus. In his famous "Essay on the Principle of Population," published in 1798, Malthus recognized that unlimited populations increase geometrically, whereas their needed resources only increase arithmetically. Eventually, he predicted, the human population would outdistance its food supplies, and unlimited expansion would no longer be possible.

Malthus may be correct after all. Even with improving fish-catching technology and wider-ranging fishing fleets, the world fish catch began to decline slightly during the early 1970s. It is presently too early to determine if these fish catches represent a significant and permanent departure from the

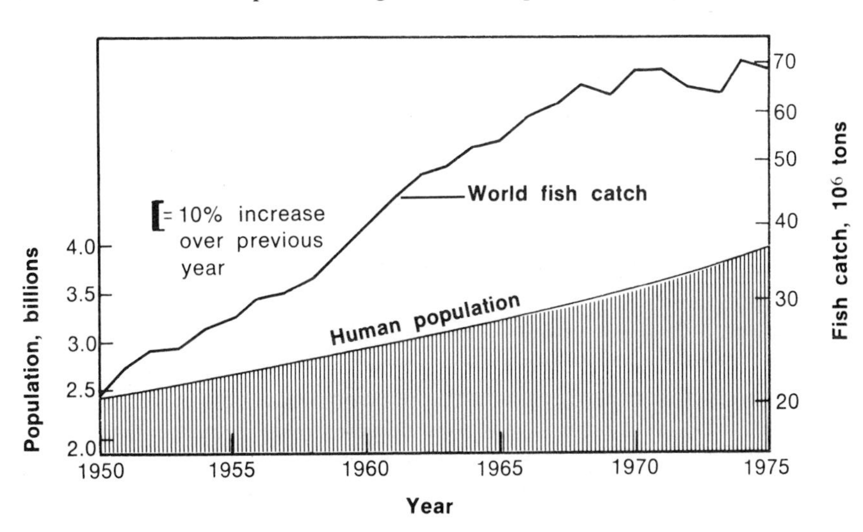

Fig. 9.6 Growth of the world human population and of global fish catches 1950–1975. From FAO catch and landing statistics.

trend of ever-increasing catches established in the previous two decades. But regardless of whether the limits of marine food production occur at 70 million tons each year or at 700 million tons, limits for future yields of food from the sea do exist and they must be examined.

Future Yields

In the past few years, a number of oceanographers and fisheries experts have attempted to estimate the ocean's maximum sustainable yield of fish and other edible organisms. The magnitude of these projections have varied widely (from less than the present harvest to as high as 2 billion tons annually), depending on the information available and the assumptions employed. The problems of predicting potential harvests have been approached in several ways. One method is based on extrapolation from past and present catch results to some future point in time. Predictions have also been based on the total production of organic material by marine phytoplankton, and the efficiency of transfer of this material through various trophic levels to larger, edible animals.

The first method requires detailed information regarding the condition of fish stocks presently being harvested, and reasonably accurate projections of the extent of unused, but potentially useful stocks. Historically, such predictions have generally proved to be quite inaccurate. One of the earliest published estimates (made in 1949) of the maximum potential fish harvest placed the marine portion of the catch at 21.6 million tons or about 20% above the prewar landings of 18 million tons. That estimate was surpassed by the harvest of 1951. Later estimates based on similar extrapolations had been revised upward, but most had been exceeded by the catch of 1970.

An obvious flaw in the predictive value of this method is the lack of reliable information regarding the size and distribution of unexploited stocks of fish. Sufficient investigation necessary to provide basic information on population sizes, recruitment rates of young, migratory patterns, and other essential biological factors is seldom undertaken until stocks are being fully exploited or even overexploited. Recent introduction of new fishing techniques and the redistribution of fishing effort have consistently produced catches that surpassed previous estimates. So subsequent estimates were revised upward, only to be exceeded again.

At the same time, more information dealing with previously little-known fish stocks has been accumulating, thus increasing the accuracy of recent predictions for future fish catches. Using these extrapolation methods, current estimates place the maximum limit on the annual sustainable ocean harvest at approximately 200 million tons, equivalent to a threefold increase over the 1970 catch.

Another approach can be taken. The ultimate limit on marine sources of food is established by the rate of photosynthesis in marine plants. The marine production system begins at the first trophic level with a net production of 200–250 billion ($2–2.5 \times 10^{11}$) tons of plant material annually (refer to table 6.2).

As neither markets nor techniques are presently available for economically "fishing" phytoplankton, the magnitude of the actual fish harvest is determined by: (1) the number of trophic levels in the food chain between that 200 billion tons of plants and the harvestable fish; and (2) the efficiency with which animals at one trophic level utilize food derived from the previous trophic level.

The potential commercial value of a fish or other animal is to a large degree a function of its size. These animals must be larger than a certain minimum size before commercial exploitation is economically feasible. It should be reemphasized that the size of the plants at the base of marine food chains is an essential feature in establishing the number of steps in the food chain. Food chains based on smaller plant cells (nannoplankton) generally consist of a greater number of trophic levels, as do food chains leading to large fish such as tuna.

In general, phytoplankton cells decrease in size from greater than 100 μm in coastal and upwelled waters to less than 25 μm in the open ocean. Moderate-sized zooplankton species such as *Euphausia pacifica,* which function as herbivores in coastal North Pacific waters, must move one step up the food chain and assume a carnivorous mode of feeding in offshore waters where the phytoplankton are too small to be captured. Other forms of oceanic zooplankton that occupy the third trophic level are no more than 1 or 2 mm in length. Virtually all species of herbivorous copepods in the open ocean are preyed upon by chaetognaths that in turn become food for small fish.

Thus, in the open ocean environment, three or four trophic levels are required to produce animals only a few cm in length. In an examination of the relationship between photosynthesis and fish production in the open sea, J. Ryther has estimated that food chains leading to tuna, squid, and other commercially important oceanic species consist of an average of five trophic levels. Ryther also estimated that the average number of trophic levels in the food chains of commercial species in coastal waters is 3, and 1.5 for upwelling areas. The latter number may seem surprisingly low, but many clupeoid fishes taken in large numbers from upwelling areas graze directly on phytoplankton without any intermediate trophic levels.

Accurate estimates of ecological efficiencies in marine food chains are difficult to achieve. Efficiency factors are based on the growth of organisms that is in turn a function of food assimilation minus waste and metabolic costs (such as respiration and locomotion). These factors vary widely between species, between individuals of the same species, and between various stages in the life cycle of a single individual. Young growing individuals often exhibit efficiencies as high as 30% but they decline to nearly 0% at maturity. Senile individuals may even exhibit negative efficiency factors. Thus, efficiency estimates for populations composed of a variety of age groups can be little more than reasonably intelligent guesses. It is even more difficult to approximate the "ecological efficiencies" of entire trophic levels consisting of a diverse group of animal types, each with its own peculiar age structure and growth rate. Basing his estimates on an assumed maximum potential trophic efficiency of 30%, Ryther assigned ecological efficiency factors of 10% to the oceanic province, 15% to coastal regions, and 20% to areas of upwelling. These estimates were provided with the disclaimer that they may be too high.

Armed with the estimates of net phytoplankton production shown in table 6.2 and repeated in part in table 9.1, the number of trophic levels, and the efficiency of exchange between the trophic levels of each marine production province, Ryther was able to estimate the total potential production of fish from the sea. His results are summarized in table 9.1.

How do Ryther's estimates compare with actual production statistics of a well-known fishery? Let's consider the Peruvian anchoveta fishery, which is restricted to an area of coastal upwelling approximately 50 km × 1,200 km. Using the methods developed by Ryther, this area can be expected to produce about 20 million tons of anchoveta each year. The commercial harvest of this species in 1970 was slightly over 13 million tons, near or possibly even over the capacity of this fishery. In addition, predation by tuna, squid, and about 5 million seabirds probably accounts for an annual consumption of another 8–10 million tons of anchoveta. Combined, commercial landings and natural predation of the Peruvian anchoveta reach approximately 22 million tons each year. Ryther's estimate of 20 million tons is sufficiently accurate to justify the use of his predictive methods.

Ryther's prediction of a potential annual production of 240 million tons of animals usable by humans tends to confirm the validity of the 200-million-ton estimate established by extrapolation from past and present harvests. However, the production of 200–240 million tons of catchable fish is not equivalent to an actual harvest of equal magnitude. Losses to birds, larger fish, and other predators are significant in some fisheries. Additionally, human preference for particular species of fish will cause other species to remain greatly underutilized. Finally, to maintain a continuing supply of raw materials, the fishing industry must take care to allow a reasonably large fraction (generally ⅔ to ½) of utilized fish stocks to escape and reproduce so that harvesting can continue on a **sustained yield** basis.

Thus, a somewhat liberal estimate of the maximum future sustainable harvest from the sea is between 150 and 200 million tons annually. Stated another way, the resource potential exists to allow us to double or, at best, triple our present fish catch.

Table 9.1. *Estimates of Fish Production for Each of the Marine Production Provinces Listed in Table 6.2 Based on an Annual Net Plant Production of 20 × 10^{10}* Tons Live Weight.

Province	Primary Production (tons live wt)	Trophic Levels	Efficiency %	Fish Production (tons live wt)
Oceanic	16.3×10^{10}	5	10	0.16×10^{7}
Coastal	3.6×10^{10}	3	15	12×10^{7}
Upwelling	0.1×10^{10}	1.5	20	12×10^{7}
Totals	20.0×10^{10}			24×10^{7}

From Ryther 1969.

A Perspective on Marine Sources of Human Nutrition

Humans are omnivores. We obtain nourishment from a tremendous variety of plants and animals. Yet the staples of the human diet can be narrowed down to three types of plants and four groups of animals. The plants most used are rice, wheat, and corn; followed by other cereal grains, many types of vegetables, fruits, nuts, and berries. Cattle, poultry (plus the egg and milk products of these animals), pork, and fish provide the major share of the food to satisfy the carnivore in us. To obtain a meaningful perspective for the information presented in this chapter, it is important to understand just how significant the present marine contribution of food is to the total human diet and how meaningful it may be in the future.

In a 1967 article, Emery and Iselin made some enlightening comparisons of the significance of food production from ocean and terrestrial sources. The following discussion draws extensively from their work, but is fortified with more recent data.

Categories for plant and animal foods from both terrestrial and oceanic production systems are established, based on the state of technology used in the production of each food category. Plant production is separated into **gathering** (casual usage of untended wild plants) and **farming** (agricultural tending of domesticated plant species). Comparable categories for animals are used: **hunting** of wild, unimproved animals, and **herding** of genetically improved, controlled species of domesticated animals. These terms are also applied to marine food items. Only a very few marine plants such as red algae are presently farmed, while oysters, some clams, and a very few other marine animals can be considered "herded." Table 9.2 lists the 1975 food production statistics for each of the four production categories for land and ocean. Production statistics for wild plants and wild animals grown on land are not well known. The estimates used for these categories may be in error by as much as 25%. The remaining figures used are much more accurately known as they are annually compiled by the FAO.

The information presented in table 9.2 forces some uncomfortable, yet undeniable conclusions. The majority of the seafoods harvested are animals

Table 9.2. *Human Food From Land and Ocean Production Systems, 1975.*

Food Types	Categories of Production	Food Production, in 10^6 tons	
		Land	*Ocean*
Plants	Gathering	100	0.9
	Farming	2828	0.3
Animals	Hunting	45	58.1
	Herding	571	0.6
Total		3544	60.0
	Less That Used for Fish Meal		21.0
	For Human Consumption		39.0

Adapted from Emery and Iselin 1967, and FAO Production Yearbook and Yearbook of Fisheries Statistics, 1975.

three or four trophic levels removed from the primary producers. In terrestrial agricultural systems, the plants themselves are harvested and losses to higher trophic levels are largely avoided. Furthermore, marine animals consist of wild, unimproved stocks that are hunted and captured, rather than controlled and domesticated breeds. Although technologically advanced ships, nets, and fish-finding gear may be used, little of the gains are reinvested to improve the stocks on which the fisheries depend.

Another disturbing trend in the use of living marine resources has developed in the past two decades. In 1950, 90% of the world catch was consumed directly. Only 10% of the catch was reduced to fish meal for use as a protein supplement for domestic livestock. By 1975, the fish meal fraction represented nearly a third of the world catch (fig. 9.7). Assuming the entire 21 million tons of fish reduced to meal in 1975 were fed to pigs and chickens with food conversion efficiencies of 20%, they yielded only 4 million additional tons of edible pork and poultry. So the actual amount of human food derived from the 1975 fish catch was not the 69.7 million tons shown in figure 9.6. Instead, it was nearer 52 million tons (fig. 9.7), 48 million tons of edible fish and 4 million tons of livestock raised on fish meal from 21 million tons of fish.

Long food chains, unsophisticated production systems, and expanding industrial uses of marine organisms all severely limit the capacity of marine food production. The marine environment just does not produce very much food; in 1975, slightly more than 1% of the food consumed by the world human population came from the sea. Even if the marine resources are available to triple our present fish catch in the not-too-distant future, a three-fold increase of 1% is still a very small fraction of human food needs. Continuing population increases will surely diminish any possible future gains in fisheries

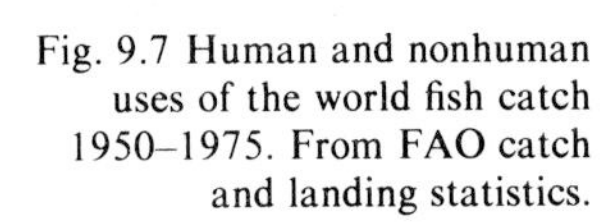

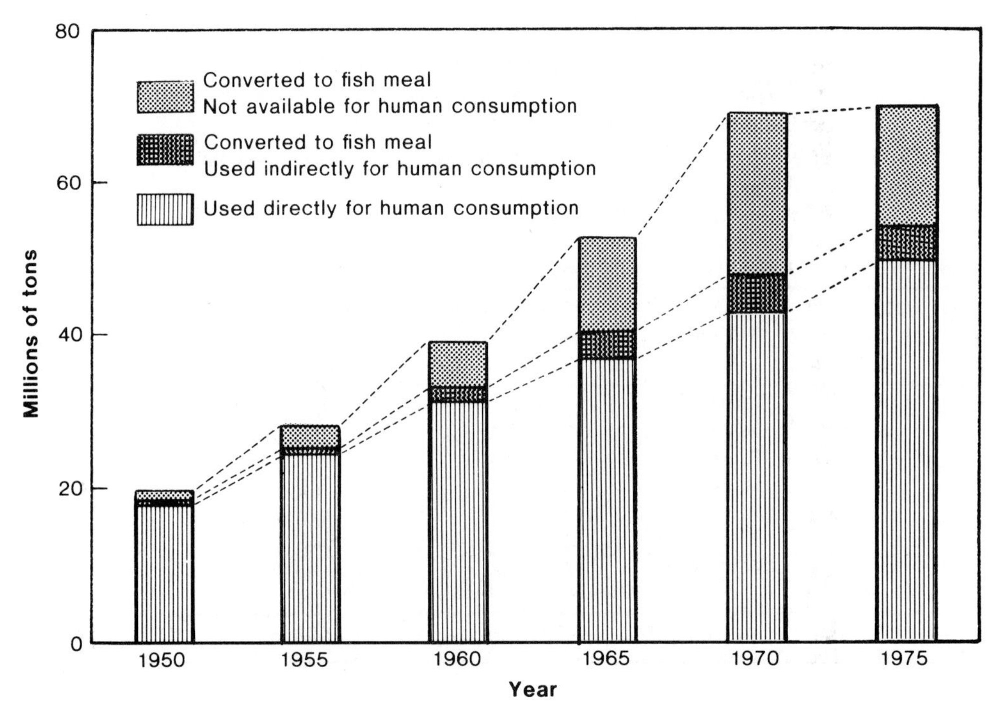

Fig. 9.7 Human and nonhuman uses of the world fish catch 1950–1975. From FAO catch and landing statistics.

production. Thus, despite the hopes and optimism, there is simply little rational basis to expect the ocean to make more than a minor contribution to the problem of feeding new additions to the growing human population.

The Problems of Overexploitation

The increases in the world fish catch shown in figure 9.6 have been accomplished largely with increased fishing effort and improved fish-finding and fish-catching gear. A portion of the gains have been made at the expense of hitherto unexploited or at least underexploited fish stocks. Long-distance fishing fleets (particularly those of Japan and the USSR) employ factory ships and freezer trawlers to process the catch at sea. No ocean is immune to the intense fishing pressure these fleets can bring to bear.

When fishing begins on these new stocks, initial catches are generally large and include a high proportion of large fish. Continued or increased fishing pressure tends to reduce the average size and sometimes the abundance of the stock. If the fishing effort is matched to the growth and reproductive potential of the stock, then a **maximum sustainable yield** of fish can be caught year after year without causing major upsets in the stock abundance. Too often, though, the fishing pressure becomes much greater than the stock can withstand. Losses to fishing and natural predators exceed recruitment of young animals, and catches decline.

Abundant examples of overfished stocks can be found in most segments of the fishing industry. Most of the popular species of halibut, plaice, cod, ocean perch, herring, and salmon of the North Atlantic and Pacific oceans are being or already have been overexploited. So are many of the warm-water tuna stocks and most of the large whales. The two examples discussed here are sufficient to demonstrate some of the problems created by overfishing activities which seem to conflict with the fishermen's own best interests.

The Peruvian Anchoveta

The Peruvian anchoveta *(Engraulis ringens)* is a typical clupeoid fish. It is a small, fast-growing filter-feeder which schools in the upwelling areas of the Peru Current. The first commercial use of the anchoveta was indirect; from the time of the Incas, droppings or **guano deposits** from the nesting colonies of seabirds which fed on anchoveta have been collected and used as a major source of fertilizer. These seabirds, primarily Peruvian boobies, brown pelicans, and guanay cormorants (fig. 9.8), annually converted about four million tons of anchoveta to an inexpensive fertilizer widely used by Peru's subsistence farmers.

Commercial exploitation of the Peruvian anchoveta for reduction to fish meal began in 1950. The next year, 7,000 tons were landed. After 1955, the growth of the fishery was explosive (fig. 9.9); over 2 million tons were landed in 1960. By 1970, the catch of this one species had surpassed 13 million tons, almost one-fifth of the entire world fish harvest for that year. Nearly all the catch was taken by local fishermen and reduced to fish meal and oil for export.

(a)

(b)

Fig. 9.8 (*a*) Guanay cormorants *(Phalocrocorax)* at their nests on an island off the coast of Peru. (*b*) A close-up of the crater-shaped nests of the Guanay cormorant. From Murphy 1925.

Accompanying the meteoric rise in anchoveta catches was a drastic drop in the number of guano birds that depended on the anchoveta for food, also shown in figure 9.9. From 28 million in 1956, the bird population was reduced to 6 million during the El Niño year of 1957 (the causes of El Niño were discussed in chapter 6.). With upwelling blocked by the intrusion of a surface layer of warm tropical water, the plankton disappeared, anchoveta died or

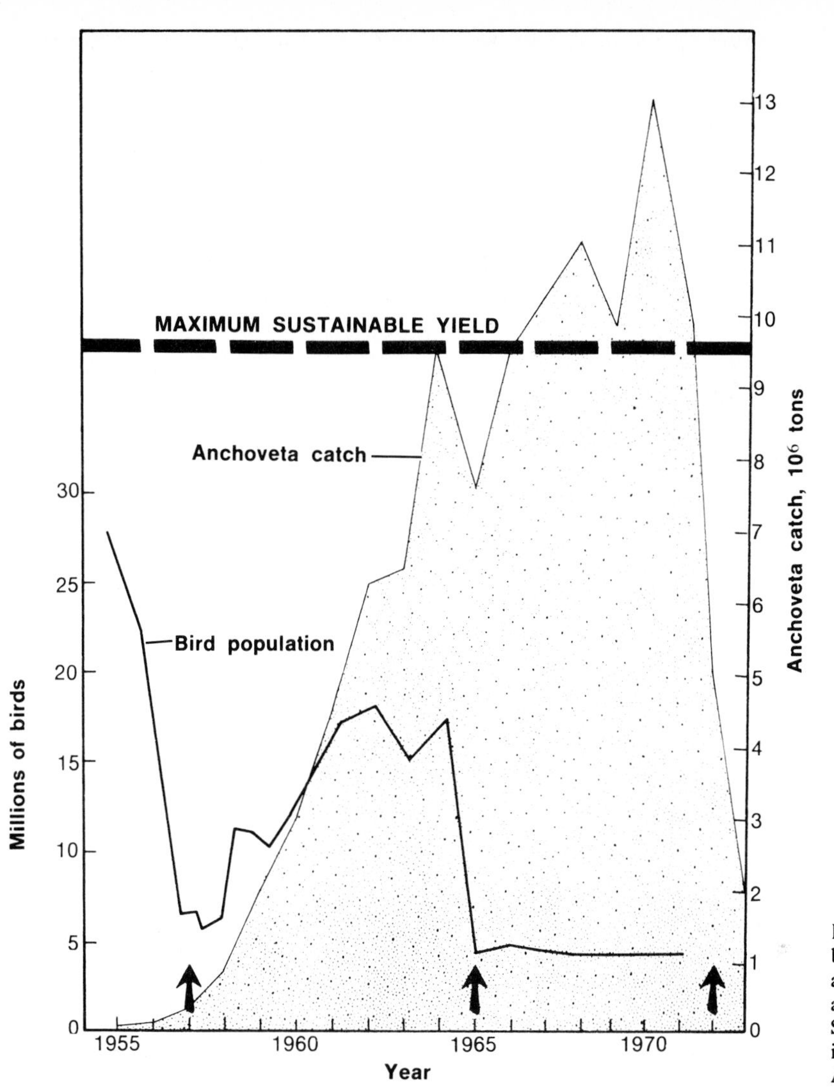

Fig. 9.9 Changes in the guano bird population and the anchoveta fish catch (stippled) along the northwest coast of South America. Arrows indicate El Niño years. Adapted from Schaefer 1970.

moved, and the guano birds quickly starved. Within four years, the bird population had rebounded to 17 million, only to be hit by another El Niño in 1965. That time the bird population plummeted to 4 million and had not recovered by 1971.

A substantial base of biological information was collected during the development and growth of the Peruvian anchoveta fishery. With the advantages this information base provided, proper management procedures were expected to insure a large and continuous harvest from this immense stock. The Instituto del Mar del Peru, an advisory panel of fisheries experts, projected a maximum sustainable yield of approximately 9.5 million tons annually. At the time, the reduced bird populations were taking less than one million tons each year. Tonnage reports alone, however, are inadequate and sometimes misleading. As the fishing pressure increased over the decade of the 1960s, the average size of fish being caught decreased and the number needed to make a ton increased sharply. By 1970, small anchoveta were taken with such efficiency that 95% of the juvenile fish recruited into the population were captured before their first spawning.

A glance at figure 9.9 shows that the catches of anchoveta for 1967 through 1971 exceeded the predicted maximum sustainable yield by at least one million tons each year. The industry and the regulatory agencies responsible for managing the anchoveta stocks had ample warning of what was to come. In 1972, sampling surveys indicated the anchoveta stocks had been severely depleted and recruitment of juvenile fish was very poor. As expected, the 1972 catch dropped to little more than 5 million tons, less than half that of the previous year. Even worse was 1973, with an estimated catch of less than 2 million tons. The next two years showed a slight improvement, but still yielded less than 4 million tons each year. Apparently, the fishing pressures of the previous decade were too much even for this tremendous stock of fish, and it finally collapsed.

The Great Whales

The history of the whaling industry has been a long and tragic one. Aboriginal hunting of coastal whales for food has continued for several thousand years. In the eighteenth and nineteenth centuries, whaling took a new turn. Oceanic whales became major items of commerce as demand for their oil grew; whaling became a very profitable enterprise. Ships from a dozen nations combed the oceans for whales that could be killed with hand harpoons and lances. Right, bowhead, and gray whales were their favorite targets, for they swam slowly and, once killed, they floated accommodatingly at the sea surface. In his famed *Moby Dick,* Herman Melville questioned the future of these great whales, faced, as they were, with

> . . . omniscient look-outs at the mastheads of the whale-ships, now penetrating even through Behring's straits, and into the remotest secret drawers and lockers of the world; and the thousand harpoons and lances darting along all the continental coasts; the moot point is, whether Leviathan can long endure so wide a chase, and so remorseless a havoc.

By the end of the nineteenth century the gray whale, both species of right whales, and the bowhead were on the verge of extinction. Under strict international protection, the gray whale has since recovered, but bowheads and right whales are still a rare sight.

The era of modern whaling was initiated in the late nineteenth century with the cannon-fired harpoon equipped with an explosive head. The explosive harpoon was so devastatingly effective that even the large rorquals, the blue and fin whales, were taken in large numbers. These whales had previously been ignored by whalers with hand harpoons, for they were much too fast to be overtaken in sailboats or oar-powered boats. The subsequent rapid decline of the whale stocks in the North Atlantic and Pacific oceans forced ambitious whalers to seek new and untouched whaling areas. They found the Antarctic, the feeding grounds of the richest populations of whales anywhere. The discovery of the Antarctic whale populations touched off seven decades of slaughter unparalleled in the history of whaling.

Aided by pelagic factory ships fitted with stern ramps to haul the whale carcasses aboard for processing, the kill of large rorquals rose dramatically. From 176 blue whales in 1910, the annual take climbed to almost 30,000 in 1931 (fig. 9.10). After the peak year of 1931, blue whales became increasingly scarce. Blue whale catches declined steadily until they were commercially insignificant by the mid-1950s. In 1966, only 70 blue whales were killed in the entire world ocean. Only then, when substantial numbers could no longer be found to turn a profit, was the hunting of blue whales banned (and then only in the Southern Hemisphere).

The trend of increasing then rapidly declining annual catches shown by the blue whale curve in figure 9.10 is distressingly similar to that of the Peruvian anchoveta fishery. But the ruthless exploitation of the great whales did not halt with the near extinction of the blue whale. As the blue whale populations gave out, whalers switched to the smaller, but more numerous fin whales, catches of which skyrocketed to over 25,000 whales for several successive seasons. But by 1960, the fin whale catch begãn to plummet, and whaling pressure was diverted to even smaller sei whales. The total sei whale population probably never exceeded 60,000. One third of those were killed in 1965 alone. Whaling pressure quickly pushed the catches of this species far beyond a maximum sustainable yield. By the late 1960s sei whales had followed their larger relatives to commercial extinction.

As early as 1940, whaling nations were faced with undeniable evidence that some stocks of pelagic whales were seriously overexploited. In 1948, twenty whaling nations established the International Whaling Commission

Fig. 9.10 Catches of blue, fin, and sei whales in the Antarctic, 1920–1975. From FAO catch and landing statistics.

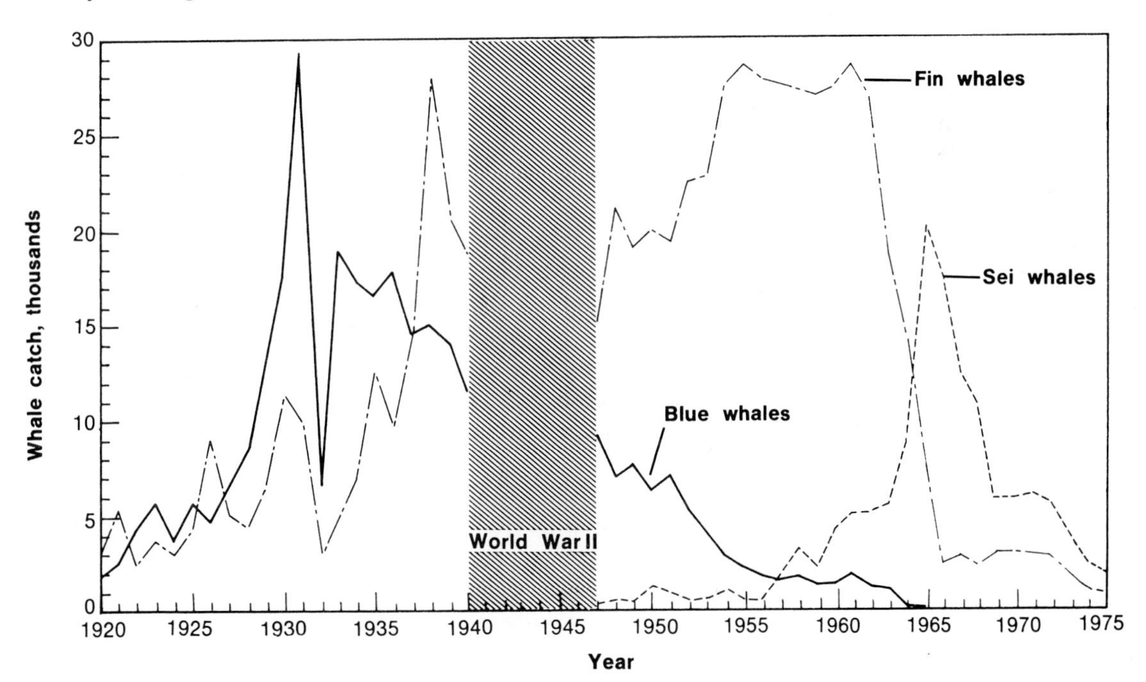

(IWC) to oversee the utilization and conservation of the world's whale resources. Unfortunately, the IWC had neither inspection nor enforcement powers; any nation that did not agree with the regulations of the IWC had 90 days to register an objection. Once registered, the objecting nation was exempt from that regulation.

The IWC lacked authority to limit the numbers of ships or nations pursuing the great whales. It did set quotas for the entire catch, but quotas for individual species were not established until 1972. Prior to 1972, regional quotas were set in **blue whale units** and could be filled with any species of whale available. Other whales were counted according to how their oil yield compared to that of the blue whale.

1 blue whale unit (BWU) = 1 blue whale, or
2 fin whales, or
6 sei whales

The IWC repeatedly recommended unrealistically high quotas. A special committee in 1964 predicted that there were so few whales that the Antarctic whaling fleet could catch no more than 8,500 BWUs. Unconvinced, the IWC set the 1964 quota at 10,000 BWUs. The actual catch was 8,429 BWUs. In 1965, the quota was reduced to 8,000 BWUs, but less than 7,000 were taken. Disregarding their own expert's advice, the IWC continued to place its quotas at unreachable levels. Only once during the decade 1963–73 did the whaling industry manage to achieve the quotas established for it by the IWC. The quotas were, in effect, not quotas at all, as there were no longer enough whales to fill them.

Today, what remains of the pelagic whaling industry faces the specter of complete economic disaster. Blue whales probably number fewer than 2,000 individuals. Fin whales are down from 400,000 to about 50,000, yet they are still hunted. Sei whales also have been reduced to critically small numbers, and they too are still pursued by whalers. Less profitable sperm whales and the smaller Bryde's and minke whales have replaced the blue, fin, and sei whales as primary targets of the pelagic whaling industry.

Several member nations of the IWC in the past few years have proposed a moratorium on all whaling. A moratorium would be a necessary first step to provide man with an opportunity to more accurately assess the impact of a century of intense hunting on the oceanic whale stocks. At the same time, it would give the whales a needed chance to expand their dwindling numbers. If a moratorium is not instituted and the whale populations do not recover, it will be because their destruction provided large short-term profits to overly ambitious whaling companies. And humans, as well as the whales, will be the losers.

It is presently impossible to predict the fate of either the great whales or the Peruvian anchoveta. Of the two, the anchoveta has better possibilities for survival and recovery. They mature very rapidly, often spawning within their first year. Once mature, each female deposits 9–24 thousand eggs each year for two or three years. The road to recovery for a large, slowly-reproducing species like the blue whale is fraught with unanswered questions. Can the few thousand remaining blue whales scattered over the world ocean encounter each other frequently enough to mate, reproduce, and add to their decimated numbers? Will additional blue whales meet stiff competition from other animals for food and other resources appropriated from the whales during their tragic decline? And most importantly, if the population begins to increase, will humans refrain from exploiting it until it can secure a more solid grip on survival? The reproductive resiliency of the great whales is largely unknown. They may bounce back. The gray whale did, but the right and bowhead whales still have not. Mature female fin whales produce a single calf in alternate years (refer to fig. 8.18); female blue whales, every four years. Even with a strictly observed moratorium and the best of luck, a century might pass before definite signs of recovery become apparent.

The Tragedy of Open Access

Why have fishermen and fishing nations repeatedly exploited the fish resources on which they depend to the point that returns on their fishing effort have declined and too often disappeared? Even with the maze of legal and economic considerations that are involved, incentives for these apparently self-defeating actions are not difficult to find. Salmon, tuna, whales, and other oceanic species are unowned resources, belonging to no single nation or individual. They have existed outside the jurisdictional limits of all nations and are therefore open to access by any nation. Historically, the concept of **open access** to the high seas evolved in the sixteenth and seventeenth centuries when the right to navigate freely was more crucial than the freedom to fish. But as coastal fish stocks were depleted, fishermen became increasingly dependent on distant stocks in international waters. They eventually discovered that the freedom to fish on the high seas was fundamentally different than the freedom to navigate. Unlike navigation, fishing activities remove a valuable commodity from a common resource pool at the expense of those who do not fish.

Ideally, it is assumed that oceanic resources are unowned and open to access for all people. But with today's advancing pace of technology, some nations have more quickly than others achieved the ability to exploit these resources. If the fishermen of one nation fail to catch these unowned oceanic species as quickly as possible, someone else soon will. In species after species, such attitudes have led to inevitable and predictable results: increased competition between fishing nations for limited resources, duplication of effort, declining fishing efficiency, and of course, overfishing.

Once in the net, a school of fish is no longer the property of all people, but belongs instead to the fishermen who set the net and haul the fish aboard. All people and all nations share the cost of losing the fish, the great whales, and the other marine animals which have nearly disappeared because of overfishing. Yet the short-term profits derived from overfishing are not similarly shared. The tragedy of this situation is that it best rewards those who most heavily exploit and abuse the unprotected living resources of the open ocean.

International Regulation of Fisheries

Without controls to limit the access of fishermen to fish populations in international waters, concerned nations have created regulatory commissions similar to the IWC. These commissions are charged with the responsibility of governing the management and harvest of regional fish stocks. The International Commission for the Northwest Atlantic Fisheries, for instance, includes Canada, Denmark, France, Germany, Iceland, Italy, Norway, Poland, Spain, USSR, the United States, and the United Kingdom. The regulations established by this commission do not carry the weight of international law, but are binding on member nations. Even so, they have failed to halt serious overfishing of the cod and ocean perch stocks of the northwest Atlantic.

Other commissions, particularly those regulating the halibut and salmon fisheries in the North Pacific, have been much more successful. But their very success is now creating new problems. Too many additional fishing boats from the United States and Canada, as well as Korea, Japan, and the USSR are being attracted to these well-managed fisheries. Under these additional fishing pressures, management problems are magnified, profits of individual fishermen are diminished, and the possibilities for overexploitation are greatly enhanced.

Several nations, either alone or working with international organizations, have taken steps to block overfishing and promote better use of the limited food resources of the sea. Some have advocated United Nations control of all high seas resources: food, minerals, and oil. The drawbacks of this concept are all too obvious. The nations of the world are not yet willing to allow the United Nations or any other international governing body to make the social, political, and legal decisions necessary to regulate fairly and equitably the exploitation of marine resources.

In the absence of effective international controls, some nations have acted on their own to regulate fishing activites within a wide coastal zone adjacent to their shores. By 1974, thirty-five nations had unilaterally extended their territorial limits or created controlled fishing zones beyond the **12 mile** (19.3 km) **limit** recognized by international convention. Several of these nations claim jurisdiction over coastal zones extending 200 miles (323 km) from their shores. Inherent in these actions is the compelling concept that coastal nations have a preferential right to exploit, as well as an obligation to conserve, the fish resources off their shores. Other nations have refused to recognize these extended zones of control, and international disputes over fishing rights have erupted. In the past few years alone, Icelandic gunboats have fired on British cod trawlers; Ecuador and Peru have repeatedly seized United States tuna seiners fishing within 200 miles of their coasts.

In the early 1970s, at the Third United Nations Conference on the Law of the Sea, the prospects for a single international convention to regulate open-ocean fish stocks seemed uncertain. The United States government was under pressure from its own coastal fishermen to extend United States jurisdiction for fisheries out to 200 miles. They could see the distant-water fishing fleets of the USSR, Japan, and West Germany taking huge harvests just off their shores. In 1974, the United States ended its traditional policy of opposition to extended zones of control for coastal nations. In 1976, the United States passed the Fisheries Conservation and Management Act (effective March 1, 1977). Under this act, the United States assumed exclusive jurisdiction over fisheries management in a zone extending 200 miles to sea. Entrance of foreign fishing vessels into this exclusive economic zone is allowed on a permit basis only, and then only to harvest fish stocks with sustained yields that are greater than the harvesting capacity of American fishermen.

Other nations, including Canada and Mexico, were quick to follow the United States in establishing their own 200-mile fishery jurisdiction zones. Extended fishery jurisdiction policies of the United States and other coastal nations will not automatically restore depleted fish stocks or revitalize failing coastal fishing industries at the expense of the distant-water fishing fleets that have developed in the past two decades. Difficulties concerning the rights of land-locked nations and the management of highly migratory species must still be resolved. But in the absence of any clearly identified central authority to enforce regulations, these policies may form an orderly basis to protect, conserve, and exploit the limited living resources of the sea.

Complicating Effects of Pollution

An increasing population and changing lifestyle each year add to an already enormous burden of domestic and industrial wastes. These wastes may be dumped into rivers, sewers, or the atmosphere. Ultimately a large variety of these wastes make their way to the ocean. Although the world ocean has a large and valuable capacity for absorbing and dispersing the effluvia of human civilization, that capacity is not infinite, nor is it the same for all waste materials.

The following discussion is not intended as a catalog of marine pollutants, for the list of potentially damaging materials discharged into the sea is nearly endless. Pesticides, fertilizers, sewage effluents, residues from plastics manufacture, spilled oil, heavy metals, and heat head the list. Most of these substances have serious implications for food production from the sea. All are potentially capable of altering marine fish production, and some already have. It is lamentable that some of the worst offenders, pesticides and fertilizers, are the products of expanding efforts to enhance food production on land.

Pollutants discharged into the sea can adversely affect fish production in several ways. Local changes in water temperature, turbidity, or nutrient concentration may alter phytoplankton production rates. Eventually, these disturbances in phytoplankton production become evident at higher trophic levels occupied by edible fish. Small accumulations of lead, mercury, DDT, or other toxic materials have so poisoned fish from some coastal areas that they are unsafe for human consumption. At higher concentrations, these same compounds may substantially reduce a fish's growth and reproductive rates and even its life span.

Other more visible substances, like oil and silt, can suffocate and choke benthic organisms (fig. 9.11) by clogging their gills and filtering structures. Marine birds and mammals, dependent on clean feathers or fur for insulation and buoyancy, also suffer heavily from oil spills. Oil spills from the wrecked

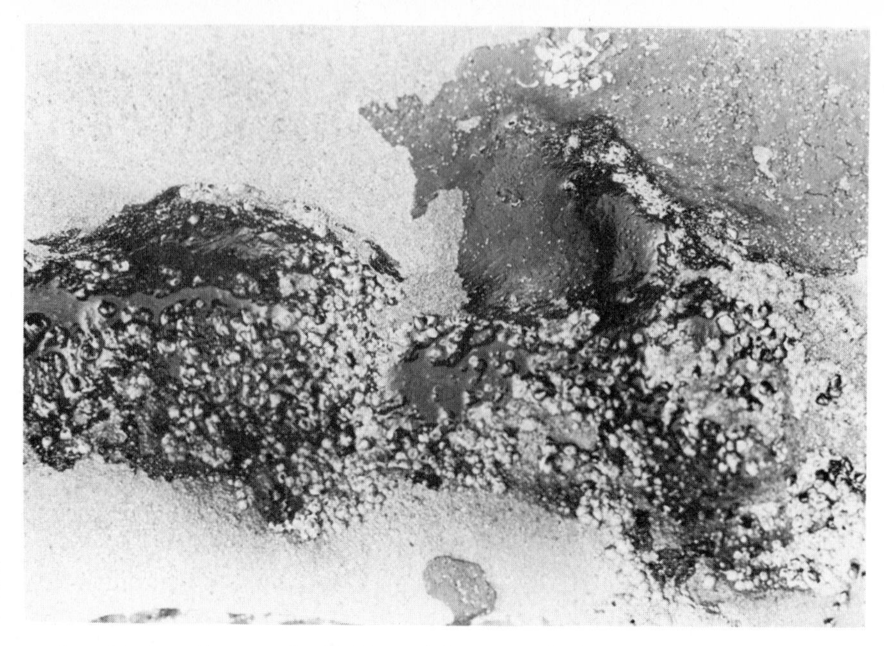

Fig. 9.11 Intertidal barnacles smothered by a thick layer of oil.

tanker *Torrey Canyon*, in 1967, and from the leak near a drilling platform off Santa Barbara, in 1969, each contributed an estimated 100,000 tons of crude oil to the local marine environments. Oil from the *Torrey Canyon* devastated miles of English beaches and intertidal rocks. Less apparent, but no less serious, was the oil's impact on subtidal benthic plants and animals. At Santa Barbara, the oil affected 150 km of coastline and persisted for several months. Disasters such as these are not rare incidents. Twenty-six tanker oil spills, each of 40 tons or more, occurred in 1974 alone. And such spills will probably continue to occur with increasing frequency as our civilization's insatiable appetite for energy demands more oil from offshore drilling sites.

Hot water from power generation plants and nutrients (particularly phosphates and nitrogen compounds) from agricultural runoff and sewage outfalls are serious pollutants of semienclosed bays, estuaries, and lagoons. Increased water temperatures and accelerated algal growth frequently cause drastic changes in the community structure of these coastal marine features. Dredging and construction for boat harbors, ship channels, and roadways further modify and degrade these habitats and reduce their value as spawning and nursery grounds for coastal fish and invertebrates. Very few estuaries along the shores of the United States have survived the industrialization of this nation, and those that have survived are seriously threatened.

Into these same coastal settings, vast quantities of toxic chemicals are dumped each year. By 1965, 8,000 manufacturing firms were formulating more than 60,000 registered pesticides in the United States alone. Through the air, rivers, and sewers, aldrin, chlordane, lindane, heptachlor, DDT, arsenic, and many other common pesticides make their way to the sea. By virtue of its long and widespread use, DDT and its effects on marine life have been well documented; it will serve as a useful model for examining the general behavior of pesticides in marine food chains.

Dichlorodiphenyltrichloroethane (DDT) was the first of a new class of synthetic chlorinated hydrocarbons. It became available for public use in 1945 and quickly gained international acceptance as an effective killer of most serious insect threats: houseflies, lice, mosquitoes, and several crop pests. This inexpensive chemical is credited with saving millions of human lives. In spite of its obvious benefits, the use of DDT has been banned in the United States and some other nations. Several unfortunate characteristics of DDT have transformed it from a benefactor to an ecological nightmare.

DDT is a persistent pesticide; it does not rapidly lose its toxicity. Some degrades to a similar compound, DDE, but it too is very toxic. Decades are sometimes necessary to eliminate the last traces of DDT applied to cropland. And then it is difficult to determine if it has broken down, or has simply been transported elsewhere instead. DDT is only slightly soluble in water, yet it has a peculiar property of evaporating back into the atmosphere in association with water (a process called **codistillation**). When applied to crops or swamps from the air, much of the DDT never reaches the ground and some quickly codistills back into the air. For years, this airborne load of DDT has been dispersed over the globe by surface winds. It is the major source of oceanic DDT contamination (fig. 9.12). Significant amounts of DDT also wash off the land and enter coastal environments via rivers and sewers.

Once in seawater, DDT is rapidly absorbed on suspended particles. As it is nearly insoluble in water, measurable levels of free DDT in seawater are practically nonexistent. Yet DDT contamination from land and air has been so pervasive that it can be found in nearly all parts of the world ocean. Antarctic penguins, Arctic seals, Bermuda petrels, and fish everywhere have accumulations of DDT in their fatty tissues.

Fig. 9.12 Transfer of DDT to and within marine food webs (arrows). DDT is absorbed principally by phytoplankton, then concentrated at each step up the food web. Adapted from Epel and Lee 1970.

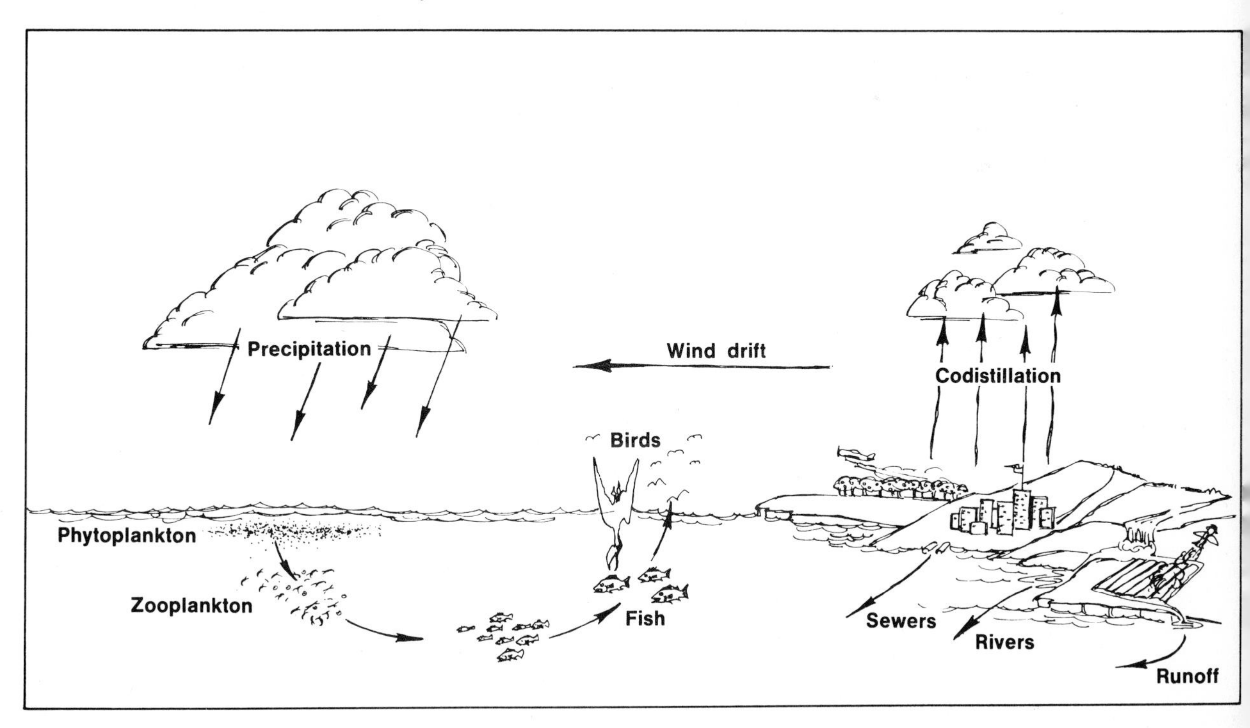

DDT is quite soluble in lipids. Fatty tissues and oil droplets act as chemical "magnets" to attract and concentrate DDT absorbed on suspended particles in seawater. Phytoplankton and, to a much lesser extent, zooplankton are the initial steps in DDT's entry into marine food webs. Fish, birds, and other predators eventually consume this plankton and its load of DDT, concentrating the toxin in their own fatty tissues. At each step in the food web, further concentration or magnification occurs (again, fig. 9.12) until it reaches the top carnivores.

Concentrations of DDT found in marine animals occasionally exceed the permissible limits for human consumption (5 ppm) established by the U.S. Food and Drug Administration. For that matter, even human fat, with an average of 12 ppm of DDT, is beyond the limits considered safe by the FDA. Numerous lots of canned kingfish, jack mackerel, and other species of fish have been seized and removed from distribution.

Marine birds were to suffer the most devastating effects of DDT poisoning from their food. As fish-eating predators, they are sometimes 4 or 5 trophic levels removed from the phytoplankton which initially absorbs the DDT. The **biological magnification** of DDT that occurs at each trophic level assures these predatory birds of high DDT loads in their food. DDT and its residues, DDE and DDD, block normal nerve functions in vertebrates. A few birds have been found dead of extremely high concentrations of DDT. DDT also interferes with calcium deposition during the formation of egg shells in birds. The egg shells of DDT-laden birds are very thin and fragile. They frequently break when layed, or fail to support the adult bird during incubation (fig. 9.13). The broken eggs lie in abandoned nests, mute testimony to the insidious effects of DDT. Our national symbol, the bald eagle, is in very real danger of extinction outside Alaska. The bald eagle is a fish eater, and its DDT load is so magnified by its long food chain that it is losing its ability to successfully reproduce. Bermuda petrels are also threatened by DDT-induced reproductive failures, as are ospreys and many local populations of seabirds.

The brown pelican (*Pelecanus occidentalis*) is a common sight along both coasts of the United States and Mexico. Nesting colonies of these birds exist on islands along the warmer coasts of their range. A decline in the number of brown pelicans along Southern California in the late 1960s was traced to reproductive failures caused by DDT-induced eggshell thinning. In one nesting colony of 300 pelicans on Anacapa Island off the Southern California coast, 12 intact eggs were laid in 1969. Of those 12, only 3 hatched. Some adult birds were sitting on damaged eggs. Others had already vacated nests littered with remnants of thin-shelled and broken eggs.

Late in 1969, the U.S. Bureau of Commercial Fisheries (now the National Marine Fisheries Service) began a survey of DDT and other chlorinated hydrocarbons in coastal fish. Samples of fish livers from the coast of California and Baja California were analyzed for DDT residues (fig. 9.14). DDT and its residues ranged from an average of less than 1 ppm off Baja California to an extremely high average of 370 ppm in Santa Monica Bay adjacent to Los Angeles. Subsequent analyses of the fillets of some of these fish yielded concentrations as high as 57 ppm at Santa Monica Bay. These concentrations exceeded the FDA's acceptable limits by 1,000%.

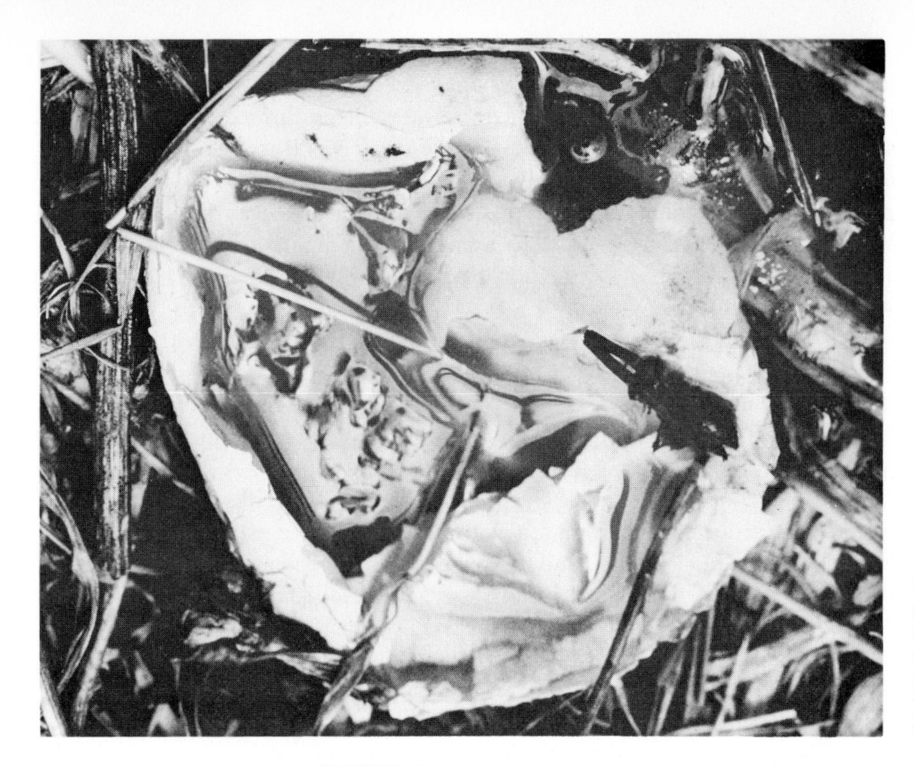

Fig. 9.13 A destroyed pelican egg in its nest off the California coast. The thin shell was not able to support the weight of its parent. Photo by F. Todd, courtesy Sea World, Inc.

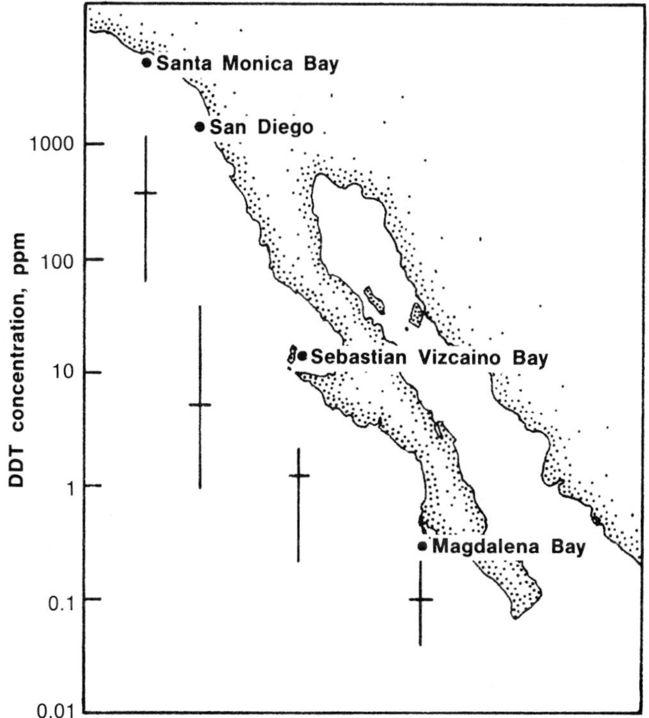

Fig. 9.14 Concentration of DDT and its residues in the livers of fish along the coast of Southern California and Baja California, 1970. The range of values (extent of vertical lines) and averages (horizontal bars) are indicated for each of the four stations shown. Adapted from Mac Gregor 1972.

The heavy DDT contamination in the Los Angeles coastal area was centered around the Los Angeles County sewer outfall at Whites Point. In early 1970, an estimated 360 kg of DDT were being flushed into this sewer system each day! The source of most of the DDT was traced by investigators to a chemical plant that produced most of the world's supply of DDT. Wastes produced in the manufacture of this pesticide were washed into the sewer system at rates exceeding 100 tons a year. For comparison, the entire Mississippi River drainage system each year adds only ten tons of DDT to the waters of the Gulf of Mexico.

DDT from the Los Angeles County sewer outfall was apparently responsible for the local reproductive failure of the brown pelican. It is possible that these high concentrations of DDT adversely affected the reproductive abilities of some coastal fish as well. The losses to fishery production in this instance were not large, but the potential for great damage exists. A greatly underutilized stock of anchovy (*Engraulis mordax*) now thrives in the coastal waters of California and Baja California. Conservative estimates place the annual sustainable yield at 2 million tons. DDT concentrations as high as 2.8 ppm have been detected in these anchovy. If these fish are extensively harvested in the future, most would be processed into fish meal for livestock. That extra trophic level inserted between the anchovy and ourselves is potentially capable of concentrating the moderate levels of DDT found in the fish to dangerously high levels in pork or poultry.

The massive doses of DDT injected into California coastal waters by the Los Angeles sewer system have been reduced. Yet DDT is still being used in other parts of the world, and more is carried to the ocean each year. By itself, DDT is a threat to the continued existence of several species of marine animals. But it is only symptomatic of the greater danger posed by the many other persistent toxins of which we know very little.

Looking Ahead

By now, it should be apparent that, until more workable international agreements governing the use of renewable living resources of the sea are established, fishing nations will continue to compete for diminishing stocks of fish. Even with the best of international cooperation, future increases in traditional types of seafoods are extremely limited. Two approaches hold some promise for evading the limits on fish production discussed earlier.

Moving Down the Food Chain

In theory, if we could harvest what the fish eat, rather than harvesting the fish themselves, a tenfold increase in the harvest could be realized. Rather than contemplating limits of 100 or 200 million tons of fish, we could look forward to harvesting one or two billion tons of marine food each year. Serious problems, however, block this path to greatly increased marine harvests. Almost without exception, animals occupying lower trophic levels are smaller and more dispersed than the animals now harvested.

The technological developments necessary to practically harvest zooplankton and smaller fish that comprise these lower trophic levels are not insurmountable. However, they may not be worthwhile. These smaller, more dispersed animals are more difficult to harvest; the additional energy needed to collect these small food items may exceed the energy gained from the harvest. It may continue to be more efficient energetically to wait until the larger animals have eaten the smaller ones, then to harvest a portion of them.

A century ago, the phytoplankton crop around the Antarctic continent supported a tremendous assemblage of zooplankton, particularly the krill *Euphausia superba.* In turn, krill fed large populations of blue, fin, and humpback whales. With these whale populations now reduced to the verge of extinction, they no longer serve as effective intermediaries, harvesting the krill for us. Fishing authorities in Japan and the USSR are now test harvesting krill with an eye to expanded future production. At least 50 million tons of krill, enough to double the world's present fish catch, could be harvested on a sustained yield basis.

The greatest problem inhibiting the use of krill is this: What do you do with it once it is caught? There is little demand for fresh or frozen krill. It is nutritious, but few people will buy it in its natural form. Most plans for using krill include some sort of processing to disguise it or to convert it to an odorless, powdered protein concentrate. The protein concentrate could then be mixed with flour to make high-protein breads, pastas, rice cakes, tortillas, or almost any other common food item.

The energy costs involved in catching krill, processing it to a palatable form, and transporting it to markets in the Northern Hemisphere will be enormous. Had the Antarctic stocks of great whales been properly managed while they still thrived, humans might now derive more benefit from krill indirectly through a controlled harvest of the whales. The potential for harvesting krill and other exotic organisms low in the food web is presently marginal at best. If any hope exists for massive increases in food production for the immediate future, it lies instead with getting marginal land into production using techniques that are immediately available to grow crops very familiar to us.

Mariculture

Another possible approach to expanding the production of marine food centers is mariculture—using agricultural techniques to grow and manage marine plants and animals. As the data in table 9.2 indicate, the "farming" of marine species is an extremely underdeveloped source of food production.

Fish farming has been practiced for centuries in Southeast Asia and China. Mullets and milkfish are commonly grown in shallow estuarine ponds where they graze on algae, detritus, and small animals. Estuaries, salt marshes, and other productive coastal habitats offer a tremendous potential for cultivating fish in closed pond systems. Yet it is unlikely that "feedlot" production of inexpensive marine organisms will soon be a reality. Intensive mariculture activities necessarily modify the nature of an estuary or salt marsh. For each fish pond installed, a portion of the native fish and shrimp populations will be denied access to these productive coastal waters. Furthermore, these populations may already contribute heavily to previously established local fisheries.

Oysters, mussels, abalones, lobsters, and small amounts of red algae are also "seeded" and grown in controlled environments, supplied with food, and protected from predators. Even genetic selection for improved survival and growth is being employed. But mariculture is a costly business; it is and probably long will be largely restricted to expensive luxury food items which generate large returns on investments. Oysters and lobsters will add little to the diets of most people on earth, certainly virtually nothing to the diets of those who most need it.

Schemes to use the high seas to "graze" herds of genetically improved fish will remain impractical as long as the "farmer" cannot be assured that others will refrain from harvesting his fish after they have been fattened. Excluded from international waters, mariculturists are forced to confine their activities to coastal waters. In special circumstances, polluting nutrients from sewer treatment plants or hot water from coastal power generating stations could be used beneficially. Diverted into fish ponds, nutrients could enhance the growth of plants to feed fish as the warm water accelerates their growth rates. But these are special circumstances. More commonly, mariculture programs are restricted by adverse problems of coastal pollution, habitat destruction, and the general degradation of the near-shore marine environment.

Concluding Thoughts

Humans are the only species on earth capable of understanding the motives and consequences of their actions. Yet the history of our economic involvement with marine populations demonstrates an utter lack of a practical awareness for the confounding, confusing aspects that our intervention introduces into natural systems. In our scramble for food, sport, and profit from the sea, we have repeatedly, and with disastrous results, violated existing ecological relationships and invented new ones. We are positioning ourselves with increasing frequency at the tops of many heavily exploited marine food chains. It would be wise to heed the plight of the pelican as a sensitive indicator of what might be in store for ourselves if we continue our unthinking and uncaring contamination of the world ocean.

Summary

The variety of marine organisms taken for human food is large, including finfish, shellfish, other invertebrates, whales, and some marine plants. Commercial fishing efforts are generally concentrated in shallow waters, upwelling regions, and near ocean current or thermal boundaries.

Presently, slightly more than 1% of the total human diet comes from the sea, and most of that tonnage is wild-caught marine animals. Estimates of future yields suggest that the present harvest of marine food may be doubled or tripled.

One of the problems which is limiting present and future marine food harvests is overexploitation of existing living marine resources. The Peruvian anchoveta and the stocks of great whales are tragic examples of the too common pattern of commercial overexploitation followed by collapse of the stocks. Open access and the absence of realistic, binding regulations to govern the harvest of unowned marine resources continue to promote overexploitation with little regard to its ultimate consequences.

Marine pollutants are also reducing the food production potential of the marine environment. Most of these pollutants are concentrated in coastal waters that also support fisheries. Pollutants may interfere with food production by reducing growth rates of marine organisms, interfering with their reproduction, or simply contaminating them so badly that they are unsafe to eat.

Some optimistic possibilities, including mariculture and the use of zooplankton, still exist. Yet the basic problem remains: the human population continues to increase in size, and the mere existence of that human population will have an increasingly detrimental impact on the yield of food from the sea.

Questions for Discussion

1. Most of the world's important fishing areas are located in relatively shallow waters, especially along western coasts of continents. Discuss some of the reasons for this, including physical, chemical, biological, and economic factors in your discussion.
2. Describe some of the ways in which human efforts to increase food production on land have reduced the potential yields of food from the sea.
3. Discuss the conditions which cause 99.8% of the world's plant mass to be on land, even though the oceans cover over 70% of the earth's surface.
4. Describe the fate of the Peruvian anchoveta fishery from the mid-1950s to the present. What impact has the collapse of that fishery had on the price of pelican eggs in West Germany? On the abundance of pelican eggs in Peru?
5. Discuss the factors which limit the contribution of marine sources of food (for humans) to less than 2% of the total volume of food presently consumed.

Suggestions for Further Reading

Books

Crutchfield, J. A., and Pontecorvo, G. 1969. *The Pacific salmon fisheries: A study of irrational conservation.* Baltimore: Johns Hopkins Press.

Cushing, D. H. 1968. *Fisheries biology. A study of population dynamics.* Madison, Wis.: Univ. of Wisconsin Press.

Gulland, J. A. 1971. *The fish resources of the ocean.* Surrey, England: Fishing News (Books) Ltd.

Idyll, C. P. 1978. *The sea against hunger.* New York: Thomas Y. Crowell.

Johnston, R., ed. 1977. *Marine pollution.* New York: Academic Press.

Mangone, G. J. 1977. *Marine policy in America.* Lexington, Massachusetts: Lexington Books.

Ruivo, M., ed. 1972. *Marine pollution and sea life.* Surrey, England: Fishing News (Books) Ltd.

Articles

Archer, E. J. 1968. Can we prepare for famine? *Bioscience* 18:685–90.

Carter, L. J. 1974. Law of the sea: Fisheries plight poses dilemma for United States. *Science* 185:336–39.

Goldwater, L. J. 1971. Mercury in the environment. *Scientific American*, May: 15–21.

Harlan, J. R. 1976. The plants and animals that nourish man. *Scientific American*, September:89–97.

Holt, S.J. 1969. The food resources of the ocean. *Scientific American*, September:178–94.

Leeper, E. M. 1976. Seaweed: Resource of the 21st century? *Bioscience* 26:357–58.

Peakall, D. B. 1970. Pesticides and the reproduction of birds. *Scientific American*, April: 72–78.

Pinchot, G. B. 1970. Marine farming. *Scientific American*, December:15–21.

Robinson, M. A., and Crispoldi, A. 1975. Trends in world fisheries. *Bioscience* 18:23–29.

Ryther, J. H. 1969. Photosynthesis and fish production in the sea. *Science* 166:72–76.

———. 1975. Mariculture: How much protein and for whom? *Oceanus* 18:10–22.

Schaefer, M. B. 1970. Men, birds, and anchovies in the Peru Current—dynamic interactions. *Transactions of the American Fisheries Society* 99:461–67.

Appendix

Systems of Measure

The Système International d'Unités (SI), commonly known as the metric system, is internationally accepted as the system of measure for reporting scientific and engineering data. This system is widely used because of its simplicity and ease of conversion. Unlike the so-called English system that we commonly use, the three basic SI units for distance, volume, and mass (weight) are closely interrelated. Each basic unit is related to the others by a simple equality, making it relatively easy to convert from one unit to another. Subdivisions and multiples of each basic unit based on a factor of 10 increase their flexibility (table A.1).

The basic unit of distance measure is the **meter (m)**; the meter is slightly longer than a yard. The meter, like all other basic units of the SI, is subdivided into smaller units by factors of 10. The next smaller distance unit is the **decimeter (dm)**, or 0.1 m. Each decimeter is further subdivided into 10 **centimeters (cm)**. Further subdivisions or multiples of the meter provide the distance units listed in table A.2

Two types of SI units are employed to measure area. Some are simply squared distance measures, such as **square meters (m^2)** and **square centimeters (cm^2)**. Other SI units are exclusively for area measure. They are listed in table A.3.

Two separate, but related, systems of units are also used for volume measure. Some are based on the cube of distance measures, others on the **liter** (ℓ) and its subdivisions. Some of the more common volume units are listed in table A.4.

The basis for all SI units of mass is the **gram (g)**. Other mass units derived from multiples or subdivisions of the gram are listed in table A.5.

Some of the more commonly used SI-English unit equivalents are included in table A.6. Until using the SI becomes automatic, it may be helpful to learn a few of these equivalents so that you may quickly develop a mental concept of the magnitude of the units you are considering.

Table A.1. *Common SI Prefixes.*

				Decimal Notation		Exponential Notation
Micro* (μ)	=	one millionth	=	0.000001	=	10^{-6}
Milli (m)	=	one thousandth	=	0.001	=	10^{-3}
Centi (c)	=	one hundredth	=	0.01	=	10^{-2}
Deci (d)	=	one tenth	=	0.1	=	10^{-1}
Basic unit	=	one	=	1	=	1
Deka (dk)	=	ten	=	10	=	10
Hecto (h)	=	one hundred	=	100	=	10^2
Kilo (k)	=	one thousand	=	1,000	=	10^3
Mega*	=	one million	=	1,000,000	=	10^6

*These prefixes have been adopted by general usage and are not part of the original metric system. Mega has no accepted abbreviation.

Table A.2. *Distance.*

Nannometer (nm)	=	0.000000001	meter
Micrometer (μm)	=	0.000001	meter
Millimeter (mm)	=	0.001	meter
Centimeter (cm)	=	0.01	meter
Decimeter (dm)	=	0.1	meter
Meter (m)		1	meter
Kilometer (km)	=	1,000	meters

Table A.3. *Area.*

Square millimeter (mm^2)	=	0.000001	square meter
Square centimeter (cm^2)	=	0.0001	square meter
Are (a)	=	100	square meters
Hectare (ha)	=	10,000	square meters
Square kilometer (km^2)	=	1,000,000	square meters

Table A.4. *Volume.*

Milliliter (ml)	=	0.001	liter	=	1 cm^3
Liter (ℓ)	=	1	cubic decimeter	=	1000 cm^3
Cubic centimeter (cm^3)	=	0.000001	cubic meter	=	1 ml
Cubic decimeter (dm^3)	=	0.001	cubic meter	=	1 ml

Table A.5. *Mass or Weight.*

Milligram (mg)	=	0.001	gram
Gram (g)	=	1	gram
Kilogram (kg)	=	1,000	grams
Metric ton	=	1,000,000	grams

Table A.6. *SI-English Unit Equivalents.*

1 meter	=	39.37	inches
1 inch	=	2.54	centimeters
1 mile	=	1.6	kilometers
1 kilometer	=	0.62	mile
1 pound	=	453.6	grams
1 kilogram	=	2.2	pounds
1 liter	=	1.06	liquid quarts
1 liquid quart	=	0.95	liter

Selected References

General Works

Note: This compilation may also be used as a suggested guide for library acquisitions.

Books

Briggs, J. C. 1974. *Marine zoogeography.* New York: McGraw-Hill.

Cushing, D. H., and Walsh, J. J. 1976. *The ecology of the seas.* Philadelphia: W. B. Saunders.

Gross, M. G. 1976. *Oceanography: A view of the earth.* Englewood Cliffs, N. J.: Prentice-Hall.

Hardy, A. H. 1971. *The open sea: Its natural history. Part I: The world of plankton. Part II: Fish and fisheries.* Boston: Houghton Mifflin.

Hedgpeth, J. W., ed. 1957. *Treatise on marine ecology and paleoecology. Volume 1: Ecology.* Geological Society of America. Memoir 67.

Hersey, J. B., ed. 1967. *Deep-sea photography.* Baltimore: Johns Hopkins Press.

Hill, M. N., ed. 1962–63. *The sea: Ideas and observations on progress in the study of the seas,* 3 vols. New York: Interscience Publishers.

Idyll, C. P. 1976. *Abyss: The deep sea and the creatures that live in it.* New York: Thomas Y. Crowell.

McConnaughey, B. H. 1974. *Introduction to marine biology.* St. Louis: C. V. Mosby.

Nicol, J. A. C. 1967. *The biology of marine animals.* London: Pitman and Sons.

Sieburth, J. M. 1975. *Microbial seascapes: a pictorial essay on marine microorganisms and their environments.* Baltimore: University Park Press.

Steel, J. H., ed. 1970. *Marine food chains.* Berkeley, Calif.: Univ. of California Press.

Sverdrup, H. U.; Johnson, M. W.; and Fleming, R. H. 1942. *The oceans: their physics, chemistry, and general biology.* Englewood Cliffs, N. J.: Prentice-Hall.

Vernberg, W. B., and Vernberg, F. J. 1972. *Environmental physiology of marine animals.* New York: Springer-Verlag.

Zenkevitch, L. 1963. *Biology of the seas of the U.S.S.R.* New York: John Wiley.

Periodicals

Bioscience

Copeia

Deep-sea Research

Fishery Bulletin

Journal of the Marine Biological Association, U.K.

Oceanography and Marine Biology, an Annual Review

Oceans Magazine—mostly pictorial

Oceanus

Scientific American—frequently contains articles pertaining to marine life.

Sea Frontiers

Chapter 1

Barkley, R. A. 1968. *Oceanographic atlas of the Pacific Ocean.* Honolulu: University of Hawaii Press.

Bogdanov, D. V. 1963. Map of the natural zones of the ocean. *Deep-sea Research* 10:520–23.

Dietrich, G. 1963. *General oceanography.* New York: Interscience Publishers.

Munk, W. H. 1950. *Origin and generation of waves.* Proceedings First Conference on Coastal Engineering. Council on Wave Research, Berkeley, Calif.

Reibish, J. 1902. In *Treatise on marine ecology and paleoecology, Volume 1: Ecology,* edited by J. W. Hedgpeth, 1957. Geological Society of America.

Chapter 2

Dietz, R. S., and Holden, J. C. 1970. Reconstruction of Pangaea: Breakup and dispersion of continents, Permian to Present. *Journal of Geophysical Research* 75:4939 –56.

Hardy, A. C. 1924. The herring in relation to its animate environment, pt. 1. The food and feeding habits of the herring. *Fisheries Investigations, London, Series II,* 7:1–53.

Miller, S. L. 1955. Production of some organic compounds under possible primitive earth conditions. *Journal of the American Chemical Society* 77:2351.

Oparin, A. I. 1953. *The origin of life.* New York: Dover Publications.

Rice, D. W., and Wolman, A. A. 1971. *The life history and ecology of the gray whale (Eschrichtius robustus).* Special Publication No. 3, American Society of Mammalogists.

Russell-Hunter, W. D. 1970. *Aquatic productivity.* New York: Macmillan.

Chapter 3

Barnes, R. D. 1963. *Invertebrate zoology.* Philadelphia: W. B. Saunders.

Brady, H. B. 1884. *Report on the Foraminifera dredged by H. M. S. Challenger during the years 1873–1876.* Reports of the Scientific Results of the Voyage of H. M. S. *Challenger,* vol. 9, (Zoology): 1–814.

Meglitsch, P. A. 1967. *Invertebrate zoology.* New York: Oxford Univ. Press.

Muscatine, L., and Lenhoff, H. M., eds. 1974. *Coelenterate biology: Reviews and new perspectives.* New York: Academic Press.

Russell-Hunter, W. D. 1968. *A biology of lower invertebrates.* New York: Macmillan.

Russell-Hunter, W. D. 1969. *A biology of higher invertebrates.* New York: Macmillan.

Chapter 4

Barlow, G. W. 1972. The attitude of fish eye-lines in relation to body shape and to stripes and bars. *Copeia* 1:4–12.

Connell, J. H. 1961. The influence of interspecific competition and other factors on the distribution of the barnacle *Chthamalus stellatus. Ecology* 42:710–23.

Correll, D. L. 1978. Estuarine productivity. *Bioscience* 28:646–50.

Dana, T. F. 1975. Development of contemporary Eastern Pacific coral reefs. *Marine Biology* 33:355–74.

Darwin, C. 1962 (originally published 1842). *The structure and distribution of coral reefs*. Berkeley, Calif.: Univ. of California Press.

Dayton, P. K. 1971. Competition, disturbance, and community organization: The provision and subsequent utilization of space in a rocky intertidal community. *Ecological Monographs* 41:351–89.

Dayton, P. K., and Hessler, R. R. 1972. Role of biological disturbance in maintaining diversity in the deep sea. *Deep-sea Research* 19:199–208.

Fankboner, P. V. 1971. Intracellular digestion of symbiotic zooxanthellae by host amoebocytes in giant clams (Bivalvia: Tridachnidae), with a note on the nutritional role of the hypertrophied siphonal epidermis. *Biological Bulletin* 141:222–34.

Goreau, T. F.; Goreau, N. I.; and Yonge, C. M. 1971. Reef corals: autotrophs or heterotrophs? *Biological Bulletin* 141:247–60.

Harger, J. R. E. 1972. Competitive coexistence among intertidal invertebrates. *American Scientist* 60:600–607.

Hayes, F. R. 1964. The mud-water interface. In *Oceanography and Marine Biology, an Annual Review,* edited by Harold Barnes. Vol. 2:122–45. New York: Hafner Press.

Hessler, R. R.; Isaacs, J. D.; and Mills, E. L. 1972. Giant amphipod from the abyssal Pacific Ocean. *Science* 175:636–37.

Hoar, W. S. 1966. *General and comparative physiology*. Englewood Cliffs, N. J.: Prentice-Hall.

Isaacs, J. D., and Schwartzlose, R. A. 1975. Active animals of the deep-sea floor. *Scientific American,* October: 84–91.

Lewis, J. H. 1964. *The ecology of rocky shores*. London: English Universities Press.

Limbaugh, C. 1961. Cleaning symbiosis. *Scientific American,* August: 42–49.

Losey, G. S. Jr. 1972. The ecological importance of cleaning symbiosis. *Copeia* 4:820–33.

Mariscal, R. N. 1972. Behavior of symbiotic fishes and sea anemones. In *Behavior of Marine Animals,* edited by H. E. Winn and B. L. Olla, Vol. 2:327–60. New York: Plenum Publishing.

Menzies, R. J.; George, R. Y.; and Rowe, G. T. 1973. *Abyssal environment and ecology of the world oceans*. New York: John Wiley.

Odum, H. T., and Odum, E. P. 1955. Trophic structure and productivity of a windward coral reef community on Eniwetok Atoll. *Ecological Monographs* 25:291–320.

Palmer, J. D. 1974. *Biological clocks in marine organisms: The control of physiological and behavioral tidal rhythms*. New York: Interscience Publishers.

Remane, A. 1934. Die brackwasserfauna. *Zoologischer Anzeiger*. Supplementband 7:34–74.

Ricketts, C., and Calvin, J. 1968. *Between Pacific tides,* edited by J. W. Hedgpeth. Stanford, Calif.: Stanford Univ. Press.

Rokop, F. J. 1974. Reproductive patterns in the deep-sea benthos. *Science* 186:743–45.

Sanders, H. L. 1968. Marine benthic diversity: A comparative study. *American Naturalist* 102:243–82.

Sorokin, Yu. I. 1972. Bacteria as food for coral reef fauna. *Oceanology* 12:169–77.

Tait, R. V. 1968. *Elements of marine ecology*. London: Butterworths.

Thorson, G. 1957. Bottom communities. In *Treatise on Marine Ecology and Paleoecology. Vol. 1: Ecology,* edited by J. W. Hedgpeth. Geological Society of America. p. 461–534.

Thorson, G. 1961. Length of pelagic life in marine bottom invertebrates as related to larval transport by ocean currents. In *Oceanography, AAAS*, edited by M. Sears, p. 455–74.

Wells, J. W. 1957. Coral reefs. In *Treatise on Marine Ecology and Paleoecology. Vol. 1: Ecology*, edited by J. W. Hedgpeth. Geological Society of America. pp. 609–31.

Chapter 5

Dawson, E. Y. 1966. *Marine botany, an introduction.* New York: Holt, Rinehart and Winston.

Goering, J. J., and Parker, P. L. 1972. Nitrogen fixation by epiphytes on sea grasses. *Limnology and Oceanography* 17:320–23.

Keegan, H. L., and MacFarlane, W. V., eds. 1963. *Venomous and poisonous animals and noxious plants of the Pacific region.* London: Pergamon Press.

Lipps, J. H. 1970. Plankton evolution. *Evolution* 24:1–22.

Moll, R. A. 1977. Phytoplankton in a temperate-zone salt marsh: Net production and exchanges with coastal waters. *Marine Biology* 42:109–18.

Moore, R. E. 1977. Toxins from blue-green algae. *Bioscience* 27:797–802.

Paasche, E. 1968. Biology and physiology of coccolithophorids. *Annual Review of Microbiology* 22:71–86.

Phleger, C. F. 1971. Effect of salinity on growth of a salt marsh grass. *Ecology* 52:908–11.

Pomeroy, L. W. 1974. The ocean's food web, a changing paradigm. *Bioscience* 24:499–504.

Scagel, R. F., *et al.* 1965. *An evolutionary survey of the plant kingdom.* Belmont, Calif.: Wadsworth.

Schmitz, K., and Lobban, C. S. 1976. A survey of translocation in Laminariales (*Phaeophyceae*). *Marine Biology* 36:207–16.

Walsby, A. E. 1977. The gas vacuoles of blue-green algae. *Scientific American,* August:90–97.

Chapter 6

Bainbridge, R. 1953. Studies on the interrelationships of zooplankton and phytoplankton. *Journal of the Marine Biological Association, U. K.* 32:375–445.

Bainbridge, R. 1957. Size, shape and density of marine phytoplankton concentrations. *Biological Review* 32:91–115.

Boney, A. D. 1975. *Phytoplankton.* London: Edward Arnold.

Fleming, R. H. 1939. The control of diatom populations by grazing. *Journal du Conseil Permanent International pour l'Exploration de la Mer* 14:210–27.

Malone, T. C. 1971. The relative importance of nannoplankton and net plankton as primary producers in tropical oceanic and neritic phytoplankton communities. *Limnology and Oceanography* 16:633–39.

Mann, K. H. 1973. Seaweeds: Their productivity and strategy for growth. *Science* 182:975–81.

Qasim, S. Z.; Bhattuthiri, P. M. A.; and Devassy, V. P. 1972. The effect of intensity and quality of illumination on the photosynthesis of some tropical marine phytoplankton. *Marine Biology* 16:22–27.

Raymont, J. E. G. 1963. *Plankton and productivity in the ocean.* New York: Pergamon Press.

Russell-Hunter, W. D. 1970. *Aquatic productivity*. New York: Macmillan.

Ryther, J. H. 1969. Photosynthesis and fish production in the sea. *Science* 166:72–76.

Ryther, J. H., and Yentsch, C. S. 1957. Estimation of phytoplankton production in the ocean from chlorophyll and light data. *Limnology and Oceanography* 2:281–86.

Steele, J. H., ed. 1973. *Marine food chains*. Edinburgh: Oliver and Boyd.

Steemann Nielsen, E. 1952. Use of radioactive carbon (C^{14}) for measuring organic production in the sea. *Journal du Conseil Permanent International pour l'Exploration de la Mer* 18:117–40.

Venrick, E. L.; McGowan, J. A.; and Mantyla, A. W. 1973. Deep maxima of photosynthetic chlorophyll in the Pacific Ocean. *Fishery Bulletin* 71:41–52.

Whittaker, R. H., and Likens, G. E. 1973. Carbon in the biota. In *Carbon and the biosphere,* edited by G. M. Woodwell and E. V. Pecan. Technical Information Center, U.S. Atomic Energy Commission, Oak Ridge, Tenn.

Chapter 7

Alldredge, A. 1976. Appendicularians. *Scientific American,* July:94–102.

Barham, E. G. 1966. Deep scattering layer migration and composition: Observations from a diving saucer. *Science* 151:1399–1403.

Boden, B. P., and Kampa, E. M. 1967. The influence of natural light on the vertical migrations of an animal community in the sea. *Symposium of the Zoological Society of London* 19:15–26.

Bright, T. *et al.* 1972. Effects of a total solar eclipse on the vertical distribution of certain oceanic zooplankters. *Limnology and Oceanography* 17:296–301.

Brinton, E. 1962. The distribution of Pacific euphausiids. *Bulletin, Scripps Institution of Oceanography* 8:51–270.

Carey, F. G. 1973. Fishes with warm bodies. *Scientific American,* February: 36–44.

Carr, A. 1965. The navigation of the green turtle. *Scientific American,* May: 79–86.

Cushing, D. H. 1968. *Fisheries biology*. Madison, Wis.: Univ. of Wisconsin Press.

Denton, E. J. and Gilpin-Brown, J. B. 1973. Flotation mechanisms in modern and fossil cephalopods. *Advances in Marine Biology* 11:197–268.

Denton, E. J., and Gilpin-Brown, J. B. 1973. Flotation mechanisms in modern and fossil cephalopods. *Advances in Marine Biology* 11:197–268.

Ege, V. 1939. A revision of the genus *Anguilla* Shaw, a systematic, phylogenetic, and geographical study. *Dana Reports* 3:1–256.

Fierstine, H. L., and Walters, V. 1968. Studies in locomotion and anatomy of scombroid fishes. *Southern California Academy of Science, Memoirs* 6:1–34.

Gilmer, R. W. 1972. Free-floating mucus webs: A novel feeding adaptation for the open ocean. *Science* 176:1239–40.

Hardin-Jones, F. R. 1968. *Fish migration.* London: Edward Arnold.

Hasler, A. D. 1966. *Underwater guideposts: Homing of salmon.* Madison, Wis.: Univ. of Wisconsin Press.

Hoar, W. S. 1966. *General and comparative physiology*. Englewood Cliffs, N.J.: Prentice-Hall.

Kalmijn, A. J. 1977. The electric and magnetic sense of sharks, skates, and rays. *Oceanus* 20:45–52.

Kanwisher, J., and Ebeling, A. 1957. Composition of swim bladder gas in bathypelagic fishes. *Deep-sea Research* 4:211–17.

Koehn, R. K. 1972. Genetic variation in the eel, a critique. *Marine Biology, Berlin* 14:179–81.

Lagler, K. F.; Bardach, J. E.; and Miller, R. R. 1962. *Ichthyology.* New York: John Wiley.

McGowan, J. A. 1972. The nature of oceanic ecosystems. In *The biology of the oceanic Pacific,* edited by C. B. Miller. Corvallis: Oregon State Univ. Press.

Marshall, N. B. 1966. *The life of fishes.* New York: Universe Books.

Mauchline, J., and Fisher, L. R. 1969. The biology of euphausiids. *Advances in Marine Biology* 7:1–454.

Pike, G. C. 1962. Migration and feeding of the gray whale *(Eschrichtius gibbosus). Journal of the Fisheries Research Board of Canada* 19:815–38.

Robertson, D. R. 1972. Social control of sex reversal in a coral-reef fish. *Science* 177:1007–9.

Rommel, S. A. Jr., and McCleave, J. D. 1972. Oceanic electric fields: Perception by American eels? *Science* 176:1233–35.

Royce, W.; Smith, L. S.; and Hartt, A. C. 1968. Models of oceanic migrations of Pacific salmon and comments on guidance mechanisms. *Fishery Bulletin* 66:441–62.

Russell, R. S. 1935. On the value of certain planktonic animals as indicators of water movements in the English Channel and North Sea. *Journal of the Marine Biological Association, United Kingdom* 20:309–32.

Russell-Hunter, W. D. 1969. *Biology of higher invertebrates.* New York: Macmillan.

Schmidt, J. 1923. Breeding places and migrations of the eel. *Nature* (London) 111:51–54.

Steele, J. H., ed. 1973. *Marine food chains.* Edinburgh: Oliver and Boyd.

Tucker, D. W. 1959. A new solution to the Atlantic eel problem. *Nature* (London) 183:495–501.

Warner, R. R. 1973. Ecological and evolutionary aspects of hermaphroditism in the California sheephead, *Pimelometopon pulchrum.* Ph.D. dissertation, Univ. of California, San Diego.

Chapter 8

Anderson, H. T., ed. 1969. *The biology of marine mammals.* New York: Academic Press.

Baker, R. C.; Wilke, R.; and Baltzo, C. H. 1970. The northern fur seals. *U.S. Fish and Wildlife Service, Bureau of Commercial Fisheries Circular* 336.

Bartholomew, G. A. 1970. A model for the evolution of pinniped polygyny. *Evolution* 24:546–59.

Bonnell, M. L., and Selander, R. K. 1974. Elephant seals: Genetic variation and near extinction. *Science* 184:908–9.

Brown, D. H.; Caldwell, D. K.; and Caldwell, M. C. 1966. Observations on the behavior of wild and captive false killer whales, with notes on associated behavior of other genera of captive delphinids. *Contributions in Science, Los Angeles County Museum* 95:1–32.

Fish, J. F.; Sumich, J. L.; and Lingle, G. L. 1974. Sounds produced by the gray whale, *Eschrichtius robustus. Marine Fisheries Review* 36:38–45.

Kellogg, W. N. 1961. *Porpoises and sonar.* Chicago: Univ. of Chicago Press.

King, J. E. 1964. *Seals of the world.* London: British Museum of Natural History.

Laws, R. M. 1961. Reproduction, age and growth of southern fin whales. *Discovery Reports* 31:327–486.

Mackintosh, N. A. 1966. The distribution of southern blue and fin whales. In *Whales, dolphins, and porpoises,* edited by K. S. Norris. Berkeley, Calif.: Univ. of California Press.

Nemoto, T. 1959. Food of baleen whales with reference to whale movements. *Scientific Reports of the Whales Research Institute, Tokyo* 14:149–290.

Norris, K. S., ed. 1966. *Whales, dolphins, and porpoises.* Berkeley, Calif.: Univ. of California Press.

Norris, K. S., and Harvey, G. W. 1972. A theory for the function of the spermaceti organ of the sperm whale (*Physeter catodon* L.). In *Animal Orientation and Navigation,* pp. 397–417. Washington, D. C.: National Aeronautics and Space Administration.

Ridgway, S. H., ed. 1972. *Mammals of the sea: biology and medicine.* Springfield, Ill.: Charles C. Thomas.

Slijper, E. J. 1962. *Whales.* New York: Basic Books.

Chapter 9

Archer, E. J. 1968. Can we prepare for famine? *Bioscience* 18:685–90.

Bardach, J. E.; Ryther, J. H.; and McLarney, W. O. 1972. *Aquaculture—the farming and husbandry of freshwater and marine organisms.* New York: Interscience Publishers.

Blus, L. J., *et al.* 1971. Eggshell thinning in the brown pelican: Implications of DDE. *Bioscience* 21:1213–15.

Carter, L. J. 1974. Law of the sea: Fisheries plight poses dilemma for United States. *Science* 185:336–39.

Cox, J. L. 1972. DDT in marine plankton and fish in the California Current. *CalCOFI Reports* 16:103–11.

Cushing, D. H. 1968. *Fisheries biology.* Madison, Wis.: Univ. of Wisconsin Press.

Emery, K. O., and Iselin, C. O. 1967. Human food from ocean and land. *Science* 157:1279–81.

Epel, D., and Lee, W. L. 1970. Persistent chemicals in the marine ecosystem. *The American Biology Teacher* 207–11.

Firth, F. E. 1969. *The encyclopedia of marine resources.* New York: Van Norstrand Reinhold.

Food and Agricultural Organization of the United Nations. 1972. *Atlas of the living resources of the seas.* Rome: Department of Fisheries (FAO).

Food and Agricultural Organization of the United Nations. Rome: *Yearbook of fisheries statistics, catches and landings.*

Holt, J. S. 1969. Food resources of the ocean. *Scientific American,* September: 178–99.

Idyll, C. P. 1968. *The sea against hunger.* New York: Thomas Y. Crowell.

Mangone, G. J. 1977. *Marine policy in America.* Lexington, Massachusetts: Lexington Books.

Murphy, R. C. 1925. *Bird islands of Peru.* New York: G. P. Putnam's Sons.

Risebrough, R. W., *et al.* 1967. DDT residues in Pacific seabirds: A persistent insecticide in marine food chains. *Nature* 216:389–91.

Ryther, J. H. 1969. Photosynthesis and fish production in the sea. *Science* 166:72–76.

Ryther, J. H., *et al.* 1972. Controlled eutrophication—increasing food production from the sea by recycling human wastes. *Bioscience* 22:144–52.

Schaefer, M. B. 1970. Men, birds, and anchovies in the Peru Current—dynamic interactions. *Transactions of the American Fisheries Institute* 99:461–67.

Wurster, C. E. 1968. DDT reduces photosynthesis by marine phytoplankton. *Science* 159:1474.

Appendix

La Maraic, A. 1973. *The complete metric system with the international system of units(SI)*. Somers, New York: Abbey Books.

Glossary

Absorptive feeding—a means of taking up dissolved food material either through specialized organs or across the general body wall.
Abyssal plains—flat, sediment-covered areas in the deep ocean basin, usually at depths between 3,000 and 5,000 m.
Adenosine triphosphate (ATP)—a complex organic compound, composed of adenosine and three phosphates, which serves in short-term energy storage and conversion in all organisms.
Aerobic—in the presence of oxygen.
Alcoholic fermentation—a form of anaerobic respiration in which sugar is degraded to alcohol and CO_2, and energy is released.
Algal ridge—low, jagged coral ridge common on the windward side of coral reefs.
Algin—a complex organic substance found in brown algae.
Alveoli—minute air sacs in the lungs of vertebrates.
Amebocyte—a body cell capable of feeding and locomotion with pseudopodia.
Amino acid—an organic acid used in constructing protein molecules.
Anadromous—an animal (such as a salmon) which spends much of its life at sea, then returns to a freshwater stream or lake to spawn.
Anaerobic—without oxygen.
Androgen—a male sex hormone in vertebrates.
Antherozoid—flagellated gamete produced by a male gametophyte of some seaweeds.
Aorta—large artery carrying blood away from the heart.
Aphotic zone—the portion of the ocean where the absence of sunlight prohibits plant growth.
Apneustic breathing—breathing pattern exhibited by marine mammals in which several rapid breaths alternate with a prolonged cessation of breathing.
Areolus—a structural unit of diatom frustules.
Aspect ratio—index of propulsive efficiency obtained by dividing the square of a fish's fin height by the fin area.
Atoll—a ring-shaped chain of coral reefs from which a few low islands project above the sea surface.
Autosome—a chromosome not designated as a sex chromosome.
Autotroph—an organism (such as a photosynthetic plant) capable of manufacturing its own food from inorganic raw materials and energy.
Auxospore—the naked cell of a diatom after the frustule has been shed.
Baleen—rows of comblike material which project from the outer edges of the upper jaws of filter-feeding whales.
Barrier reef—a coral reef which is separated from the shore by a lagoon.
Benthic—pertaining to the sea bottom and the organisms that inhabit the bottom.
Biological clock—an innate time sense found in most, or probably all, organisms.
Bioluminescence—production of visible light by living organisms.
Blade—the flattened, usually broad, leafy structure of seaweeds.
Blastocyst—a small ball of cells representing an early stage of embryonic development in mammals.
Bloom—a dense concentration of phytoplankton which occurs in response to optimum growth conditions.
Blue whale unit (BWU)—a unit for measuring whale catches in which other whales are counted in terms of their oil yield as compared to that of the blue whale.
Bradycardia—marked slowing of the heartbeat rate during a breath-hold dive.
Buffer—substances dissolved in seawater which resist changes in pH.
Buttress—seaward face of a coral reef, extending from a depth of about 20 m to just below the low-tide line.
Byssal thread—a strong elastic fiber used by mussels to attach themselves to a solid substrate.
Carnivore—an animal which preys on other animals.
Carposporophyte—a generation of plants unique to red algae which produces carpospores.

Catadromous—a species (such as the Atlantic eel) which spawns at sea, then migrates into a freshwater lake or stream where it grows to maturity.
Caudal fin—an enlarged fin at the posterior end of most fishes.
Caudal peduncle—the area where the caudal fin joins the rest of the body.
Cell membrane—the selectively permeable outer membrane of a cell.
Cell wall—a supportive structure which encloses the cells of most plants, bacteria, and fungi.
Centric diatom—a diatom which appears radially symmetrical from an end view.
Cephalization—the evolutionary tendency to concentrate the brain and specialized sense organs in the anterior end of an animal's body.
Cerata—fingerlike projections along the dorsal sides of some nudibranchs.
Chitin—complex organic substance that is the major component of arthropod exoskeletons.
Chloride cell—a specialized gill cell of bony fishes which excretes chloride.
Chlorophyll—the green pigment of plants and bacteria which is necessary for photosynthesis.
Chloroplast—a subcellular structure of eucaryotic plants which contains photosynthetic pigments and enzymes, and serves as the site of photosynthesis.
Chromatophore—surface pigment cell found in many animals, which expands and contracts to produce changes in color and appearance.
Chromosome—a subcellular structure which contains the genetic information of the cell.
Ciguatera—a toxin found in some tropical fish that is thought to be produced by blue-green algae which the fish has eaten.
Circadian rhythm—a cycle of activity or behavior which recurs about once a day.
Cleaning symbiosis—a form of mutualism in which one partner picks external parasites and damaged tissue from the other.
Climax stage—the stable, usually complex, end result of a series of successional stages.
Cnidoblast—a special cell of cnidarians which produces nematocysts.
Coccolith—a small calcareous plate inbedded in the cell wall of coccolithophores.
Colloblast—an adhesive cell found in the tentacles of ctenophores.
Commensalism—a symbiotic relationship in which the symbiont benefits without seriously affecting the host one way or another.
Compensation depth—the depth at which primary production equals plant respiration.
Conduction—the transfer of heat through a medium by molecular exchange.
Continental drift—the gradual movement of continents in response to seafloor spreading processes which are thought to have occurred for hundreds of millions of years.
Continental shelf—the relatively smooth underwater extension of the edge of the continent which slopes gently seaward to a depth of about 200 m.
Continental slope—the relatively steep portion of the sea bottom between the outer edge of the continental shelf and the deep ocean basin.
Convection—the transfer of heat or materials by mixing processes.
Corallite—the calcareous skeletal cup in which a coral polyp sits.
Coriolis effect—the apparent change in direction of a moving object (to the left in the Southern Hemisphere and to the right in the Northern Hemisphere) due to the rotation of the earth.
Countershading—the coloration pattern found in pelagic animals, with the upper surfaces darkly pigmented and the sides and ventral surfaces silvery or only lightly pigmented.
Cropper—a deep-sea animal in which the roles of predator and deposit feeder have merged.
Ctene—an external longitudinal band of cilia found in ctenophores.

Cypris—a larval stage of barnacles which develops from the nauplius and eventually attaches to the bottom.
Cytoplasm—the internal fluid environment of a cell.
Deep scattering layer—one or more layers of mid-water marine animals which reflect and scatter the sound pulses of echo sounders.
Delayed implantation—a pattern in the reproductive cycle of some mammals, causing the blastocyst to remain dormant in the female's uterus for some time before implanting on the uterine wall.
Density—ratio of the mass of a substance to its volume.
Deposit feeder—an animal which engulfs masses of sediments and processes them through its digestive tract.
Detritus—excrement and other waste products of all types of organisms including their remains after death.
Diadromous—an animal which migrates between fresh and salt water; includes both anadromous and catadromous fishes.
Diffusion—the transfer of substances along a gradient from regions of high concentrations to regions of lower concentrations.
Diploid—cells which contain two of each type of chromosome characteristic of its species.
Diurnal tide—a tidal pattern with one high and one low tide each lunar day.
Electromagnetic radiation spectrum (EMR)—the continuum of radiant energy emitted by natural and artificial sources, including X rays, light, heat, radio, and television waves.
Endoplasmic recticulum—a system of folded membranes within the cytoplasm of eucaryotic cells.
Enzyme—a protein which acts as a catalyst for chemical reactions.
Epicone—one end of a dinoflagellate cell wall separated from the hypocone by an equatorial groove containing a flagellum.
Epifauna—benthic animals which crawl about on the sea bottom or sit firmly attached to it.
Epipelagic zone—approximately the upper 200 m of the oceanic province.
Epiphyte—a plant which attaches itself to other plants or animals without parasitizing them.
Epitheca—the larger portion of a diatom frustule.
Estrogen—a female sex hormone in vertebrates.
Estrous—the period of highest sexual receptivity (or "heat") in some female mammals which coincides with the time of egg release by the ovary.
Eucaryotic cell—a cell characterized by an organized nucleus and other membrane-bound subcellular structures.
Euryhaline—an organism capable of withstanding a wide range of salinities.
Exclusive economic zone—the seaward zone bordering coastal nations in which they exercise exclusive control over economic resources. For the U.S., this zone is 200 miles wide.
Exoskeleton—an external skeleton, particularly characteristic of arthropods.
External auditory canal—the sound channel connecting the external and middle ears.
Fecundity—the rate of production of eggs or offspring.
Fetch—the extent of the ocean over which winds blow to create waves.
Finlet—small median fin on the dorsal and ventral sides of the rear parts of tuna and similar fishes.
Flagellum—whiplike structure used by cells for locomotion.
Food chain—a diagrammatic representation of trophic relationships arranged in a linear order.
Food web—a diagrammatic representation of the complete set of trophic relationships of an organism.
Frictional drag—the resistance created by an animals' body surface when moving through a fluid medium.

Fringing reef—a large coral reef formation which closely borders the shoreline.
Frustule—the cell wall of diatoms, composed of pectin and silicate.
Fucoxanthin—a golden or brown pigment characteristic of Phaeophyta, Chrysophyta, and Pyrrophyta.
Gamete—an egg or sperm cell.
Gametophyte—a gamete-producing haploid plant.
Gas gland—a lactic-acid-secreting structure associated with fishes' swim bladders.
Gastrovascular cavity—the central digestive cavity in cnidarians.
Gestation period—the portion of the reproductive cycle in a female mammal extending from fertilization to birth of its offspring.
Gill filament—a flat, bladelike extension of the gill tissue which projects from the gill arch.
Gross primary production—the total amount of organic material produced by photosynthesis.
Guano—the droppings from nesting colonies of sea birds.
Haploid cell—a cell containing only one of each type of chromosome characteristic of its species.
Haptera—short, sturdy rootlike structures that form the holdfast of seaweeds.
Hemoglobin—the red blood pigment which serves to transport oxygen.
Herbivore—an animal adapted to feed on plants.
Hermaphrodite—an animal which has the sex organs of both sexes.
Hermatypic corals—reef-forming corals.
Heterocercal tail—a fish tail, such as that of a shark, which is asymmetric about the long axis of the body.
Heterotroph—an organism which is unable to synthesize its own food from inorganic substances and must utilize other organisms for nourishment.
Holdfast—a structure which attaches seaweeds to the sea bottom or to other substrates.
Holoplankton—species of zooplankton that remain as permanent members of the plankton community.
Homeostasis—tendency of living organisms to maintain a steady state in their internal environmental conditions, including body temperature, blood sugar level, and metabolic rate.
Homeotherm—an animal, such as a bird or mammal, which maintains precisely controlled internal body temperatures using its own heating and cooling mechanisms.
Homocercal tail—a fish tail which is symmetrical about the long axis of the body.
Hydrogen bond—a weak bond formed by the attractive force between the charged ends of water molecules and other charged molecules or ions.
Hydrostatic skeleton—the internal fluid volume of soft-bodied organisms against which body wall muscles contract.
Hypertonic—a water medium with a higher concentration of ions than that of another solution separated from the first by a selectively-permeable membrane.
Hypocone—one end of a dinoflagellate cell wall separated from the epicone by an equatorial groove containing a flagellum.
Hypotheca—the smaller portion of a diatom frustule.
Hypotonic—a water medium with a lower concentration of ions than that of another solution separated from the first by a selectively-permeable membrane.
Infauna—animals which live within the sediment of the sea bottom.
Interstitial animal—an animal which occupies the spaces (interstices) between sediment particles.
Iridocyte—a fish skin cell which contains reflecting crystals of guanine.
Isotonic—a water medium with the same concentration of ions as another solution separated from the first by a selectively-permeable membrane.
Kelp—a group of larger brown seaweeds.

Langmuir cells—parallel pairs of counter-rotating convection cells driven by surface winds.

Latent heat of fusion—the heat which must be extracted from a liquid to freeze it to a solid at the same temperature. For water, it is 80 cal/g.

Latent heat of vaporization—the heat energy required to convert a liquid to a gas at the same temperature. For water, it is 540 cal/g.

Lateral line system—a series of vibration detectors arranged along the sides of most fishes.

Leptocephalus larva—leaf-shaped transparent larva of some eels.

Lipid—a class of organic compounds, including fats, oils, waxes, and steroids.

Littoral—the intertidal zone.

Lophophore—the crown of ciliated feeding tentacles found in the Ectoprocta, Phoronida, and Brachiopoda.

Lorica—a vase-shaped enclosure of tintinnid cells made of cemented particles or secreted material.

Mariculture—the collective techniques applied to growing marine organisms in captive, controlled situations.

Maximum sustainable yield—the maximum level of fishing effort which a fish stock can withstand without causing major upsets in the stock abundance.

Medusa—the free-swimming life stage of a cnidarian (commonly called a jellyfish).

Meiofauna—benthic animals intermediate in size between macrofauna and microfauna.

Meiosis—a process of cellular division which reduces the chromosome number by one-half.

Melon—fatty lens-shaped forehead structure of toothed whales.

Meristematic tissue—specific tissue sites within some seaweeds where most cell division for growth occurs.

Meroplankton—larval forms of benthic and nektonic adults that are temporary members of the plankton community.

Mesoglea—the gelatinous layer between the inner and outer body walls of cnidarians.

Mesopelagic zone—the portion of the pelagic division which extends from the bottom of the epipelagic zone to about 1,000 m.

Metamere—one of several sequential body units characteristic of segmented animals.

Metamorphosis—the change in structure of an organ or organism during maturation.

Mitochondria—a subcellular organelle of eucaryotes which conducts cellular respiration.

Mitosis—a process of cell division resulting in two daughter cells genetically like their parent cell.

Mortality—the rate at which individuals of a population are lost.

***Museau du singe* (monkey's muzzle)**—a pair of hard, well-matched and tightly oppressed lips associated with the spermaceti organ of sperm whales.

Mutation—spontaneous alteration of the genetic information of an organism.

Mutualism—a type of symbiotic relationship in which both the symbiont and the host benefit from the association.

Myoglobin—a red muscle pigment with a strong chemical affinity for oxygen (similar to that of hemoglobin).

Myomere—one of a series of muscle segments along the trunk of vertebrates, especially fishes.

Nannoplankton—phytoplankton which have cell sizes smaller than the 60 μm mesh opening of a fine-mesh silk plankton net.

Nasal plug—a pair of heavily-muscled valves near the blowhole of toothed whales.

Natural selection—the process of genetic change in a population resulting from differential contributions of offspring to subsequent generations.

Nauplius—microscopic free-swimming planktonic stage of barnacles and some other crustaceans.

Neap tides—sets of moderate tides which recur every two weeks and alternate with spring tides.

Nekton—large, actively swimming marine animals.

Nematocyst—a microscopic stinging cell used by cnidarians to capture prey.

Neritic—pertaining to the portion of the marine environment that overlies the continental shelves.

Net primary production—the excess plant production after the plants themselves have utilized whatever photosynthetic products they need for respiration.

Niche—the functional role of an organism as well as the suite of physical and chemical factors which limit its range of existence.

Notochord—a flexible, cartilaginous supportive rod in chordates.

Nucleic acid—a long-chain organic polymer, such as DNA and RNA.

Nucleus—the membrane-bound central structure of eucaryotic cells which contains the chromosomes.

Oceanic—pertaining to the portion of the marine environment which overlies the deep ocean basins.

Olfaction—sense of smell.

Ooze—fine grained oceanic sediment deposit composed chiefly of the skeletal remains of microscopic plankton.

Osculum—a large excurrent pore which allows water to exit from the internal cavity of sponges.

Osmosis—diffusion of material across a selectively-permeable membrane.

Osmotic conformers—organisms which tolerate large variations of internal ionic concentrations without serious damage.

Oviparity—a condition which describes the habit of releasing eggs which later hatch.

Ovoviviparity—an intermediate condition between viviparity and oviparity in which the eggs are essentially incubated inside the mother until hatching.

Oxygen minimum zone—an intermediate depth in the ocean where animal respiration and bacterial decomposition reduce dissolved oxygen to a minimum.

Pangaea—a still somewhat hypothetical supercontinent which consisted of all the present land masses prior to their breakup and subsequent drift to their present positions.

Parapodia—paired paddlelike extensions used for locomotion by marine annelids.

Parasitism—a type of highly evolved symbiotic relationship in which the parasite lives on or in the host and benefits at the expense of the host.

Pelagic—pertaining to the waters of the ocean and the organisms which inhabit the water column.

Pen—a thin, chitinous structure extending the length of the mantle tissue in squids.

Pennate diatom—a diatom which displays bilateral symmetry from an end view.

Pharyngeal slit—one of a series of openings between the pharynx (throat) and the outside found in chordates.

Pheromone—a variety of chemical substances used for communication between organisms of the same species.

Photic zone—the portion of the ocean where light intensity is sufficient to accommodate plant growth.

Photoinhibition—the reduction of photosynthesis by strong light near the sea surface.

Photosynthesis—the biological synthesis of organic material from inorganic substances using light as an energy source.

Phycocyanin—a blue photosynthetic pigment characteristic of blue-green and red algae.

Phycoerythrin—a red photosynthetic pigment characteristic of blue-green and red algae.

Phylogeny—the known or assumed evolutionary history of a group of organisms.
Physoclist swim bladder—a swim bladder lacking an air passage to the esophagus of fish.
Physostomous swim bladder—a swim bladder with an air passage or duct to the esophagus of fish.
Phytoplankton—microscopic plant members of the plankton.
Pinocytosis channel—a channel through which liquids or small particles of food are actively engulfed by cells.
Plankton—free-floating, usually minute, organisms of the sea.
Pleopods—abdominal paired appendages in crustaceans.
Pneumatic duct—the connection between the esophagus and swim bladder in fish.
Pneumatocyst—gas-filled float present in several of the large kelp plants.
Pneumatophore—a gas-filled float used by some siphonophores to maintain buoyancy in the water.
Poikilotherm—an organism whose body temperature varies with and is largely controlled by environmental temperatures.
Polar easterlies—winds which blow from east to west at very high latitudes.
Polygyny—a type of social and breeding organization in which a male is dominant over and mates with several females.
Polyp—the sessile, benthic form of cnidarians.
Primary production—the synthesis of organic material by plants.
Proboscis—an extendable feeding structure associated with the mouths of several types of marine worms.
Procaryotic cell—a simple cell (bacteria and blue-green algae) which lacks the structural complexity and defined nucleus found in eucaryotic cells.
Productivity index (P.I.)—the primary production rate divided by the standing crop size.
Protein—a long-chain polymer of amino acids which functions as enzymes and structural components of cells.
Pseudopodia—strands of cytoplasm which extend from the cells of some protozoans to be used for locomotion and food collecting.
Radula—a rasping tonguelike organ used by mollusks to graze algae and break up food.
Raphe—a groove in the frustules of pennate diatoms through which cytoplasm extends for locomotion.
Red tide—a bloom condition in which some species of dinoflagellates produce toxins which may cause serious mortality to other forms of marine life.
Reef flat—the portion of a coral reef which extends behind the algal ridge to the island.
***Rete mirabile* (wonderful net)**—an extensive network of minute blood vessels which serves a variety of functions in vertebrates.
Rhizome—a horizontal underground stem of sea grasses.
Ribosome—a small, subcellular organelle involved in protein synthesis.
Ridge and rise system—a rugged, linear seafloor feature which forms a continuous underwater mountain chain encircling the earth.
Rookery—isolated breeding or nesting grounds of air-breathing marine vertebrates.
Salinity—a measure of the total amount of dissolved salts in seawater.
Saturation light intensity—the light intensity which maximizes the photosynthetic rate.
Saxitoxin—a paralytic toxin produced by dinoflagellates, then accumulates in the butter clam *(Saxadoma)*.
Scavenger—an animal which feeds on the dead remains of other animals and plants.
School—a well-defined social organization of marine animals consisting of a single species with all members of a similar size.
Seafloor spreading—a global process of oceanic crust moving away from ridge and rise systems where it is formed.
Seamount—an undersea volcano.

Secondary lamella—a small extension of gill filament containing blood capillaries for gas exchange.
Semidiurnal tides—tidal patterns with two high and two low tides each lunar day.
Sequential hermaphrodite—an animal which first functions as one sex, then changes to the opposite sex as it increases in age.
Sexual dimorphism—the structural differences between sexes of a species.
Siphon—tubelike structure of mollusks used to take in and expel water from the mantle cavity.
Siphuncle—a central tubelike tissue connecting the chambers of shelled cephalopods such as *Nautilus.*
Smolt—a young salmon just before it migrates downstream and out to sea.
Species—a group of closely related individuals which can and normally do interbreed to produce fertile offspring.
Spermaceti organ—a large organ in the forehead of sperm whales which is filled with a fine-quality liquid or waxy spermaceti oil.
Spicule—rod of calcium carbonate or silicate which forms the skeleton of sponges.
Spongocoel—the internal cavity of sponges.
Sporangium—a special cell or structure which produces spores.
Sporophyte—a spore-producing diploid plant.
Spring tides—extremely high and low tides which alternate with neap tides and recur every two weeks.
Standing crop—total amount of plant or animal material in an area at any one time.
Stenohaline—an organism which only tolerates exposure to slight variations in salinity.
Stipe—the flexible, stemlike structure found in the large seaweeds.
Surface tension—the mutual attraction of water molecules at the surface of a water mass to create a flexible molecular "skin" over the water surface.
Suspension feeder—an animal which uses a filtering device to obtain plankton or detritus from the water for nutrition.
Swim bladder—a gas-filled organ which enables fish to adjust their buoyancy in the water.
Symbiosis—an intimate and prolonged association between two (or more) organisms in which at least one partner obtains some benefit from the relationship.
Taxonomy—the process of classifying organisms.
Temperature—a relative intensity measure of the condition caused by heat.
Testosterone—a male sex hormone in vertebrates.
Thermocline—an oceanic subsurface zone of very rapid temperature (and density) change with depth.
Tide—a long period wave which is noticeable as a periodic rise and fall of the sea surface along coastlines.
Trace element—an element needed for normal metabolism, but available only in minute amounts from the environment.
Trachea—windpipe.
Trade winds—subtropical winds which blow from northeast to southwest in the Northern Hemisphere and from southeast to northwest in the Southern Hemisphere.
Trench—deep area in the ocean floor, generally deeper than 6,000 m.
Trophic level—the position of an organism or species in a food chain.
Turnover rate—the rate at which members of a population or community replace themselves.
Tympanic bulla—bony case in the middle ear which encloses the sound-processing structures of mammals.
Upwelling—a process which carries nutrient-rich subsurface water upward to the photic zone.

Vacuole—a liquid or food-filled cavity within a cell.
Vena cava—the major vein returning blood to the heart of vertebrates.
Vertebral column—series of supportive bones or cartilage along the dorsal sides of vertebrates.
Vertical migration—the diurnal migration of mesopelagic animals vertically over a few tens or hundreds of meters to feed in near-surface waters.
Viscosity—the resistance of water molecules to external forces which would separate them.
Viviparity—a conditon describing the act of giving birth to live young.
Water-vascular system—the circulatory system of some echinoderms used to transport oxygen, wastes, and to hydraulically operate the tube feet.
Wave period—the time required for two successive waves to pass a reference point.
Westerlies—winds which blow primarily from the west in the mid-latitudes.
Xanthophyll—golden or yellow-brown photosynthetic pigments.
Zooplankton—animal members of the plankton.
Zoospore—a single-celled, flagellated plant spore.
Zooxanthellae—symbiotic unicellular dinoflagellates found in corals, sea anemones, mollusks, and several other types of marine animals.
Zygote—the product of the fusion of two gametes to produce a diploid single cell.

Index to Taxonomic Names

Italicized page numbers indicate figure references.

General Index

Italicized page numbers indicate figure references